GENERALSHIP
ON THE
EASTERN FRONT
1941–45

OSPREY
PUBLISHING

GENERALSHIP ON THE EASTERN FRONT 1941–45

A STUDY IN COMMAND

ROBERT FORCZYK

OSPREY PUBLISHING
Bloomsbury Publishing Plc
Kemp House, Chawley Park, Cumnor Hill, Oxford OX2 9PH, UK
Bloomsbury Publishing Ireland Limited,
29 Earlsfort Terrace, Dublin 2, D02 AY28, Ireland
1385 Broadway, 5th Floor, New York, NY 10018, USA
E-mail: info@ospreypublishing.com
www.ospreypublishing.com

OSPREY is a trademark of Osprey Publishing Ltd

First published in Great Britain in 2026

ISBN: HB 9781472874382; eBook 9781472874399; ePDF 9781472874412; XML 9781472874405;
Audio 9781472874368

26 27 28 29 30   10 9 8 7 6 5 4 3 2 1

Plate section image credits are given in full in the List of Illustrations and Maps (pp. 6–10).

Front cover: top row (left–right): Generaloberst Gotthard Heinrici, Generalfeldmarschall Ewald
von Kleist, Generalfeldmarschall Fedor Von Bock (author's collection), Generaloberst Hermann
Hoth (Photo by Heinrich Hoffmann/ullstein bild via Getty Images); bottom row (left–right):
General-major Fedor I. Tolbukhin, General Nikolai F. Vatutin, Marshal Ivan S. Konev (author's
collection), Marshal Konstantin K. Rokossovsky. (Courtesy of the Central Museum of the
Armed Forces, Moscow via Stavka)

Maps by www.bounford.com

Index by Mark Swift

Typeset by Lumina Datamatics Ltd
Printed and bound in Great Britain by Clays Ltd,
Elcograf S.p.A.

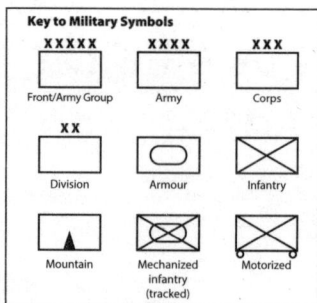

Key to Military Symbols

XXXXX	XXXX	XXX
Front/Army Group	Army	Corps

XX		
Division	Armour	Infantry

Mountain	Mechanized infantry (tracked)	Motorized

Osprey Publishing supports the Woodland Trust, the UK's leading woodland conservation charity.

To find out more about our authors and books visit www.ospreypublishing.com. Here you will
find extracts, author interviews, details of forthcoming events and the option to sign up for our
newsletter.

For product safety related questions contact productsafety@bloomsbury.com

Contents

List of Illustrations and Maps

Plate Section Illustrations

German officers conducting a map exercise in 1936. The officers of the Wehrmacht had been trained to conduct planning in idealized, comfortable pre-war conditions that did not reflect the harsh realities of warfare on the Eastern Front. (Author's collection)

A winter supply train in Russia, 1941–42. Ensconced in their warm bunkers in Zossen, 1,500km from the front line, Halder's General Staff could not comprehend the ferocity of the Russian winter and its impact on front-line troops. (Author's collection)

In September 1935, the Red Army tried out its new military doctrine in the Kiev maneuvers. Maneuver warfare was emphasized, using large armored units supported by tactical aviation. However, enemy antitank defenses and logistic problems were ignored. (Author's collection)

German officers confer in a roadside ditch during Operation *Barbarossa*. The basic German operational scheme at this point was to simply keep conducting pincer attacks with their fast-moving Panzer units until the enemy ran out of troops. (Author's collection)

German doctrine for maneuver warfare stressed high operational tempo, with mixed Kampfgruppen of tanks, motorized infantry and artillery advancing rapidly to envelop enemy formations and seize key objectives. However, the doctrine proved less effective under the unfavorable terrain and weather conditions found in Russia. (Author's collection)

An abandoned Soviet KV-1 heavy tank, summer 1941. While the Germans were astounded that Soviet industry could design and mass-produce powerful tanks, the Red Army lacked the skill or experience at the outset of the war to achieve any notable operational successes with these vehicles. (Author's collection)

From the beginning of the war in Russia, the Germans knew how to use tactical airpower in conjunction with ground forces in order to achieve operational-level success. Even as the war turned against Germany, the Luftwaffe continued to play a major role in shaping Eastern Front operations. (Author's collection)

Hitler studies a map of the Eastern Front, 1942. Hitler strongly influenced German operational outcomes in Russia, but his preferences were usually driven by propaganda or economic considerations, rather than military logic. (Author's collection)

Generalfeldmarschall Fedor Von Bock was the best German operational commander on the Eastern Front in terms of victories gained through the effective use of the principles of war. Despite the defeat at Moscow in 1941, none of the forces under his command were ever encircled and destroyed. (Author's collection)

Generalfeldmarschall Erich von Manstein had a great talent for operational-level warfare and could run rings around his Soviet opponents when conditions were favorable. However, von Manstein had difficulty accepting that the Red Army was improving in 1943, which led him to make serious operational mistakes. (Author's collection)

Generalfeldmarschall Ewald von Kleist was one of Germany's premier operational commanders. As a cavalry officer, von Kleist was comfortable with maneuver warfare and knew how to employ Panzer forces to achieve decisive results. I rank von Kleist as the Ostheer's third best commander. (Author's collection)

Walter Model proved to be one of the Ostheer's best defensive generals, with a good working relationship with Hitler and the OKH, and an understanding of Russian capabilities and tactics. I assess Model to the be the Ostheer's fourth best commander. (Courtesy of Nik Cornish at www.Stavka.photos)

Generaloberst Hermann Hoth was one of the best German senior Panzer leaders during the 1941–43 period, and often used operational maneuvers to inflict stinging defeats upon the Red Army. However, Hoth suffered from command burn-out and was relieved of command in November 1943. (Author's collection)

Generalfeldmarschall Ernst Busch is mostly remembered for his poor performance against Operation *Bagration* in June 1944. Based upon his earlier successes in defensive combat around Leningrad, I have assessed him as the eighth best senior operational commander in the Ostheer. (Author's collection)

Generaloberst Gotthard Heinrici shows the strain of command in early 1945. The war in the East was an endurance contest, with many senior leaders dropping out. Heinrici was one of the few stolid commanders who proved capable of slowing the inexorable Red Army advance into the heartland of the Third Reich. (Author's collection)

General der Kavallerie George Lindemann, commander of the 18. Armee, visits a front-line position in the Leningrad sector, early 1942. Most German officers employed a paternalistic relationship with their troops, which helped to instill confidence in the chain of command and maintain fighting spirit. (Author's collection)

General der Panzertruppe Friedrich Paulus, the ill-fated commander of the 6. Armee at Stalingrad, was an excellent staff officer and capable of conducting professional set-piece operations, but he was ill-suited to deal with sudden crises on the battlefield and passively waited for others to act. (Courtesy of Nik Cornish at www.Stavka.photos)

The Red Army developed a sophisticated doctrine for Deep Operations in the 1930s, but was unprepared to put it into practice due to the decimation of senior leaders in the Purges. In the summer of 1941, the Red Army launched numerous counteroffensives, most of which failed miserably with heavy losses. (Author's collection)

A column of Soviet ZiS-5 medium trucks moves along a dirt road. The Red Army's logistical capabilities were limited in 1941–42 due to the shortage of trucks, remaining inadequate until 1944. Soviet fronts only possessed a few motor transport regiments and keeping the armored spearheads in supply was a significant challenge. (Author's collection)

Soviet engineers prepare to launch pontoons into a river during a pre-war exercise. The N2P pontoon bridge could be used to cross a 170m-wide water obstacle and support up to 60 tons. The Red Army's river-crossing capabilities became a crucial component of its operational methods in 1943–45, catching the Germans by surprise on numerous occasions. (Author's collection)

Soviet soldiers march through a sea of mud near Odessa, 1944. Napoleon once said that mud was the "fifth element of war"; not only did the thick Ukrainian mud slow operational tempo, but it also tended to destroy equipment, particularly vehicle transmissions. (Author's collection)

The Red Army continued to send large armored formations into major urban areas in 1944–45, leading to excessive tank losses. Here, JS-2 heavy tanks move through the bombed-out streets of Berlin. (Author's collection)

Zhukov's relationship with Stalin was critical for the Red Army's ability to conduct successful operational warfare. While Stalin wanted to keep Zhukov and the other senior Red Army commanders on a short leash at first, Zhukov and the General Staff were given greater latitude in planning operations from late 1942. (Author's collection)

By dint of his longevity in front-level commands and number of victories, I have assessed Marshal Ivan S. Konev as the best Soviet operational-level commander of the war. By 1943–44 he had mastered the ability to break through fixed German defensive lines, which enabled the Red Army to keep pushing westward. (Author's collection)

General Nikolai F. Vatutin as commander of the Voronezh Front in 1943–44. Vatutin showed great talent in operational warfare and he was the Red Army's best front-level commander by early 1944; his death was a serious blow. I assess him as the second best operational commander in the Red Army. (Author's collection)

Marshal Konstantin K. Rokossovsky was in senior command billets for the entire war and I rank him as the third best operational-level commander in the Red Army. He had a good sense for maneuver, as opposed to the majority of Red Army commanders who favored brute force methods. (Courtesy of the Central Museum of the Armed Forces, Moscow via Stavka)

General-major Fedor I. Tolbukhin on the Stalingrad Front, late 1942. I assess him as the fourth best Soviet operational-level commander. While he was intelligent and skillful, he was not fully able to demonstrate his command abilities until the last year of the war. (Author's collection)

General Konstantin K. Rokossovsky and General-major Konstantin F. Telegin (NKVD), mid-1943. Telegin was the commissar of the Central Front and part of the military council which approved all orders. Having been beaten and imprisoned during the Purges, Rokossovsky was ever mindful that his actions were scrutinized by the NKVD. (Author's collection)

Andrei Eremenko, another cavalry officer, was the man who laid the groundwork for the decisive victory at Stalingrad and played a major role throughout the war. I assess him as the fifth best operational-level commander in the Red Army. (Author's collection)

Marshal Rodion I. Malinovsky and members of the 2nd Ukrainian Front staff during the Balkan campaign in late 1944. On his left is General-leytenant Ivan Z. Susaikov, the front commissar, who served as "eyes and ears" for Stalin. On his right is General-major Mikhail M. Stakhursky, who served as the front's quartermaster. (Author's collection)

General-leytenant Ivan K. Bagramyan, c. 1942–43. As an ethnic Armenian and non-Communist Party member with limited command experience prior to 1942, Bagramyan was an unusual senior commander in the Red Army. However, he performed well as both an army- and front-level commander in 1943–45. (Author's collection)

General-leytenant Mikhail E. Katukov was one of the Red Army's top armor commanders; he proved more successful than Rotmistrov and ended the war leading the 1st Guards Tank Army. Known to conduct rapid advances, Katukov was capable of going toe-to-toe against some of the most capable German commanders. (Author's collection)

General-polkovnik Ivan K. Bagramyan, commander of the 1st Baltic Front, and his chief of staff, Vladimir V. Kurasov. Bagramyan enjoyed a good working relationship with Kurasov, who was an efficient general staff officer. (Author's collection)

Nikita Khrushchev, senior commissar for the Voronezh Front at the Battle of Kursk in 1943, talks on the phone with Moscow while Vatutin (the front commander) and Rotmistrov (5 GTA) watch. Khrushchev played a major part in the premature commitment of the 5 GTA, then tried to blame Rotmistrov for its failure. (Author's collection)

General-Polkovnik Ivan E. Petrov (left) and Konev (right), April 1945. After fumbling the spring campaign in the Carpathians, Petrov was demoted and assigned as Konev's chief of staff for the final push into Germany. (Courtesy of the Central Museum of the Armed Forces, Moscow via Stavka)

General-leytenant Pavel A. Rotmistrov was one of the most prominent armor commanders in the Red Army in 1941–44. He had a reputation as a good planner but his record on the battlefield was erratic; his superiors continually pushed him into conducting rash attacks and he lacked the morale courage to stand up to them. (Courtesy of the Central Museum of the Armed Forces, Moscow via Stavka)

General Ivan D. Cherniakhovsky with his chief of staff during the Kursk campaign in July 1943. Despite lack of any special accomplishments, Cherniakhovsky managed to attract Stalin's attention and was rapidly promoted to front commander in 1944. I have assessed him as the tenth best Soviet operational commander of the war, which is generous. (Author's collection)

Prior to 1941, the Wehrmacht had not spent any effort to develop a doctrine for conducting joint operations with allied military forces. Consequently, the Ostheer had great difficulty working with its Romanian, Hungarian and Italian allies in Russia. Here, Romanian infantry and a German assault gun operate together during the Stalingrad relief attempt in December 1942. (Author's collection)

Maps

Introduction

"Military science rests upon principles which can never be safely violated in the presence of an active and skillful enemy.... Plans of operations are made as circumstances may demand: to execute these plans, the great principles of war must be observed."

Jomini[1]

"The fundamental truths that govern the art of war remain immutable, just as the principles of mechanics always govern architecture, regardless of whether one is building with wood, stone, iron, or reinforced concrete; just as the principles of harmony govern music whatever the genre might be. It is therefore still necessary to establish the principles of war."

Foch[2]

The War on the Eastern Front between 1941 and 1945 comprised the largest sustained air-ground warfare in military history. Unlike previous wars, active campaigning did not subside in the winter months but continued, irrespective of lethal weather conditions. Except for a few brief operational pauses, continuous campaigning was the norm on the Eastern Front. Altogether, the War on the Eastern Front lasted a total of 46½ months, involving over 10 million combatants at its peak in 1942–43 and resulting in roughly 15 million military deaths. About 20 million civilians also died as a direct result of the conflict. The campaigns in the East involved an unprecedented amount of tanks and other motorized vehicles, which often afforded a very dynamic and fluid nature to battles; both sides were able to achieve spectacular breakthroughs followed by rapid advances of several hundred kilometers. It is important to remember that both sides were fighting an existential conflict, with the end goal being the extermination of the other regime and its adherents. As a result, both sides fought without regard to accepted international norms in warfare and had no qualms about committing atrocities to achieve their objectives. In addition to its sheer scale, dynamism and ferocity, the War on the Eastern Front also played the decisive role in the defeat of the Third Reich, through the destruction of its primary ground forces. More than 50 percent of all German military fatalities in 1941–45 occurred on the Eastern Front, against about 10 percent on the Western and Italian Fronts. By the time that the Western Allies invaded France in June 1944, the Wehrmacht was already decimated and lacked the resources to fight a protracted multifront war.

Who were the generals who led these campaigns on the Eastern Front? The standard historiography of the Second World War tends to focus on a few prominent commanders, such as Zhukov, Guderian, Manstein and Paulus, while ignoring the mass of commanders who actually fought most of the war. Readers accustomed to this approach might be surprised to learn that Zhukov held no field commands during the decisive year of 1943 or that Guderian only commanded on the Eastern Front for six of the 46 months of that conflict. Paulus gets a lot of attention because of the Stalingrad disaster, but also only commanded a single army for just over 12 months; other than being defeated, Paulus is not known for accomplishing much. Of the Soviet commanders, Georgi K. Zhukov is the only one with a significant number of biographies in English, including William J. Spahr's *Zhukov: The Rise and Fall of a Great Captain* (1993), Otto Preston Chaney's *Zhukov* (1996), Geoffrey Roberts' *Stalin's General: The Life of Georgy Zhukov* (2012) and my own *Georgy Zhukov* (2012). In contrast, Konstantin K. Rokossovsky has only a single biography in English – Boris Sokolov's *Marshal K.K. Rokossovsky: The Red Army's Gentleman Commander* (2015) – but prominent Soviet commanders such as Ivan Konev and Andrei Eremenko have none. Both Konev's and Rokossovsky's memoirs have been translated into English, but virtually no other Soviet commanders from the Second World War have a significant footprint in Western military historiography. On the German side, there is a slightly larger number of English language biographies of German senior commanders on the Eastern Front, primarily Erich von Manstein, Walther Model and Heinz Guderian, and plenty of translated post-war memoirs/diaries from the likes of Fedor von Bock, Erhard Raus, Hermann Balck and Hermann Hoth.

There are also a number of English-language compendiums that cast a slightly wider net. *Hitler's Generals* (1989) is an anthology of bibliographical essays on 26 German commanders written by a variety of historians, but of the officers profiled, only 13 served on the Eastern Front.[3] *Stalin's Generals* (1993) is an anthology of bibliographical essays on 26 Soviet commanders written by Eastern Front experts such as David Glantz, Geoffrey Jukes and John Erickson.[4] There are some non-English language studies, such as Johannes Hürter's *Hitlers Heerführer: Die Deutschen Oberbefehlshaber Im Krieg Gegen Die Sowjetunion 1941/42* (2007), but that only details the German senior commanders and is more biographical than analytic in nature.

Another historiographical problem caused by the overemphasis on a few prominent Eastern Front commanders is that the role of operational-level military staffs (as opposed to General Staffs in Moscow and Berlin) has been largely ignored. While a few accounts from front-line staff officers such as Friedrich Wilhelm von Mellenthin's *Panzer Battles* (1956) and Sergei M. Shtemenko's *The Soviet General Staff at War 1941–1945* (1970) have been translated into English, the mass of professional staff officers who planned the campaigns are virtually invisible, even in major accounts of the war. In fact, large-scale modern warfare can only be efficiently conducted through the use of well-trained staffs who are capable of coordinating intelligence, operations and logistics into a coherent mosaic. Other support functions, such as engineering and aviation, medical and rear area operations become increasingly important for staffs to coordinate as operations become more complex and more protracted in length. The role of the commander is to provide guidance to the staff on his operational objectives, but it is the staff that translates these broad-brush strokes into actual plans that can be executed. The relationship between the commander and his staff is critical in assessing operational outcomes – did the commander accept staff recommendations or did he ignore them? Without addressing the role of staffs in operations on the Eastern Front, it is virtually impossible to develop anything beyond a simplistic impression of how crucial decisions were made.

As a result of this skewed historiographical approach, the majority of German and Soviet commanders on the Eastern Front are now virtually unknown and the methods they employed to conduct their operations have slid into obscurity. Questions such as which generals (and their staffs) were the most effective or which had the greatest impact on the overall conflict from 1941 to 1945 are essentially unanswerable based upon the available literature. While battles and campaigns have been addressed in great detail – particularly iconic ones like Stalingrad and Kursk – the nature and ability of the men who planned and conducted these campaigns remains mostly in the shadows. Indeed, no major systematic study has been attempted of senior Eastern Front commanders, which has left a clear void. It is the purpose of this work to begin filling that gap.

This study is not a military biography, nor is it intended to cover every senior commander in the same level of detail. Instead, this study seeks to develop an objective analytic framework for assessing the senior German and Soviet commanders on the Eastern Front through the lens of two interrelated concepts: generalship and battle command. According to the Oxford English Dictionary, the term "generalship" has been around since 1575 but its meaning remains somewhat nebulous. For the purposes of this study, generalship will be defined as the "demonstrated skill in exercising military command, specifically battle command." Whereas the term generalship could encompass peacetime aspects of military leadership, the term "battle command" explicitly ties these skills to mission-focused aspects, particularly the ability to make timely tactical/operational decisions and to motivate subordinates to achieve specific campaign objectives in accordance with an overall plan. History is replete with examples of generals who excelled at organization or training but were failures at battle command, such as Major General George B. McClellan in the American Civil War. Other generals proved skillful in terms of diplomacy (George C. Marshall), developing military theory or managing large defense projects (Leslie Groves), but were unremarkable in terms of generalship and battle command. Thus, this study seeks to assess the relative effectiveness (or ineffectiveness) of generalship/battle command exercised by the two opposing sides on the Eastern Front over the course of 1941–45. In terms of bias, I harbor no favoritism for either army since, in my view, both were responsible for widespread war crimes, conducted at the behest of odious criminal regimes.

My analysis in this study is shaped by my own experiences and training in the US Army, where I served as an intelligence officer at the battalion, brigade and division levels, and as a logistics officer at the battalion level. I learned staff procedures in the US Army's Combined Arms and Services Staff School (CAS3) and then the Command and General Staff Course (CGSC), both of which adopted many procedural methods from the old Prussian General Staff system. Over the course of 12 years as a primary staff officer in maneuver units, I helped draft many operational orders and also worked with staffs in other units and higher headquarters. Although my own military experience is hardly unique, it does provide me with a hands-on perspective for analyzing German and Soviet operational planning procedures and battle command in 1941–45. While Voltaire may have quipped in 1770 that "God is always on the side of the big battalions," my own experience is that fortune in war favors the side that plans the best, employs combined arms methods and makes the fewest mistakes. In this study, I intend to examine that hypothesis using generalship on the Eastern Front as my litmus test.

Scope and Definitions

Military operations occur on three levels: the strategic, the operational and the tactical. The scope of this study is to examine the senior operational-level leadership, primarily at the Army Group/Front and Army level of command, for it was at this level that the main campaigns were planned and directed. Generals at the operational level of command typically directed anywhere from 100,000 to 1 million troops and were tasked with achieving campaign objectives. Some armies were able to fight important campaigns in a semi-independent style, such as the 9. Armee at Rzhev, the 6. Armee at Stalingrad and the 11. Armee in the Crimea. While the overall strategic outcome would be decided by a series of successful operational campaigns, it makes little sense to compare the strategic-level decision-makers (Hitler and the German OKH versus Stalin and the Soviet Stavka) since much of their work encompassed non-military factors such as economic/industrial priorities and political objectives. Deciding which weapons to build and how many was critical for the strategic war effort, but these decisions took many months to implement and could not influence events on the battlefield in real-time. At the other end of the spectrum, tactical level decision-making is very relevant and time-sensitive on the battlefield but tends to only influence localized operations, not entire campaigns. Indeed, the Wehrmacht demonstrated a consistent ability to win tactical victories on the Eastern Front, even though they ended up failing to achieve their operational objectives in almost all of their major campaigns.

This study will examine a total of 54 German officers [*see Appendix 3*] who commanded at the Army Group (*Heeresgruppe*) or Army (*Armee*) level on the Eastern Front in 1941–45. Although a number of Axis satellite generals – Romanian, Hungarian and Italian – commanded individual armies on the Eastern Front, they had limited autonomy and they will only be addressed in terms of their impact on German military operations. German forces operating in Finland will also be excluded, since operations in that sector were atypical compared to the rest of the Eastern Front. On the Soviet side, a total of 140 officers [*see Appendix 4*] commanded at the Front or Army level. Given that a number of officers on both sides only temporarily held these commands (often after a senior leader became a casualty or was relieved of command) or only held them while a formation was in reserve, only officers that held command of a higher-level formation for a minimum of two months at the front will be examined. Analysis of the military staffs within these formations is more difficult, but will primarily focus on the chiefs of staff, operations officers and intelligence officers who planned major operations and served in these roles for at least six months.

At this point, it is important to mention the key functions of the modern military staff. At the army level, a German staff reported to a *Chef des Generalstabes* (chief of staff) and consisted of three basic components: the command group (*Führungsabteilung* or Abteilung I), the administrative group (*Adjutantur* or Abteilung II) and the supply group (*Oberquartiermeisterabteilung*). Three *Generalstabsoffiziere* (General Staff officers) were the primary players on this staff in planning future operations and directing current operations: the 1a (responsible for operations), the 1b (quartermaster) and the 1c (intelligence). In addition to these primary staff officers, the army staff included a number of specialist officers (*waffenoffiziere*) responsible for administration and planning in specific functional areas; these included the senior artillery commander (*Höherer Artilleriekommandeur* or *Harko*), the senior engineer commander (*Armeepionierführer* or *A.Pi.Fü.*) and the senior signal communications officer (*Armeenachrichtenführer* or *A.Nachr.Fü.*). Depending upon attachments to the army, other specialty functions might also have senior officers designated for planning in these areas. At the Heeresgruppe level (Army Group), according to *Kriegsstärkenachweisungen* (KsTN.) 9 (January 1940), the entire staff was authorized 470 personnel, including 67 officers. Of this number, the command group comprised just 35 personnel, including the commander and chief of staff. At the army level, according to KStN. 12 (January 1942), the entire staff was authorized 188 personnel (including 25 officers), with 20 in the command group. By the standards of many other armies, German higher-level staffs were quite lean and the *Generalstabsoffiziere* were expected to be hard-driving workaholics. The German staff system, honed to a fine degree during the First World War, often resulted in an extremely efficient planning process, although the vagaries of personality could induce unnecessary friction.

The Soviet staff at the front and army level was broadly similar to the German staff structure, with a chief of staff responsible for harmonizing all staff functions in order to produce viable operational plans. The four senior staff sections were operations, intelligence, communications and personnel. Rear services (including technical support) was a bit more compartmented than the German system. Soviet senior formation staffs also included officers responsible for specialty functions: artillery, air defense, engineering and aviation. However, unlike the German structure, Soviet headquarters staffs had a strong political component with active involvement by officials from the Main Political Directorate (*Glavnoye politicheskoye upravleniye*) and the Communist Party of the Soviet Union (CPSU). Although the staff was responsible for operational planning, it was the Military Council (*Voyennogo soveta*) which actually decided which plans to adopt. The army or front commander was a member of the council, but the army/front *Kommissar* was a key player in the planning process and at least until October 1942, he wielded considerable authority. The actual strength of Soviet army and front-level staffs varied considerably, particularly at the beginning of the war in 1941, when the Red Army (*Raboche-krest'yanskaya Krasnaya armiya* or RKKA) was desperately short of trained (or even partly-trained) staff officers. In order to coordinate multifront operations, the Stavka sent senior representatives to supervise the planning of key operations. Although the Stavka representatives were able to interject themselves into front-level planning, they actually possessed no staff, which limited their ability to shape outcomes – they could direct modifications to plans, but they really could not create content.

In terms of campaign planning, three staff functions are critical: operations, intelligence and logistics. Based upon accepted practices going back to the First World War and earlier, the senior commander is expected to inform the staff – through the chief of staff – about the mission assigned, his intent (what he hopes to achieve in a given operation), provide some guidance on the "how" and "when" of the operation, and any other useful insight that might assist the planning process. Based upon the commander's initial guidance, the operations officer is expected to develop one or more courses of action to accomplish the stated mission objectives. The intelligence officer assists the development of the operational concept by providing details about the terrain, weather and enemy forces in the expected operational area. The logistic (quartermaster) officer provides input on equipment availability and supplies (ammunition, fuel, rations) on hand and forecasting what additional supplies would be required to accomplish the mission. Ideally, the result is a synthesis assessment between these three key staff functions, which leads to the creation of a viable operational plan. The staff, led by the chief of staff, presents the proposed plan to the commander for review; the commander's responsibility is to approve the plan, direct modifications or reject it. If the basic plan is approved, the other staff functions (artillery, communications, engineers, aviation) start adding in their pieces in order to create the actual operational plan. A well-trained army-level staff can typically develop a basic operational plan in about 48–72 hours, but putting together the finalized plan with coordination between multiple moving parts typically requires at least 2–4 weeks depending upon the complexity of the operation. Planning at the Army Group/Front level typically requires at least two months for a major operation. In both the German and Soviet armies, it was the chief of staff who played the primary role in ensuring that the staff produced a workable plan in the time available.

Although commanders only have a limited role in the campaign planning process after giving their initial guidance, their decision-making becomes an essential function once actual operations begin. Commanders should designate where/when the main effort will be made during the planning process but this can be shifted during the course of operations, based upon enemy reactions, terrain/weather issues or fleeting opportunities. One of the most important decisions that commanders make during the course of operations is when/where to commit their mobile reserves. On the Eastern Front, time and again, the question of when to commit the armored reserves to exploit a breakthrough or to block an enemy breakthrough proved to be one of crucial determinants in operational outcomes. Commanders also play key roles in setting operational tempo (the speed at which operations are conducted) and requesting additional resources from higher headquarters. A trained staff knows how to anticipate the kind of information that their commander will need to make informed decisions, and incorporate these requirements into their planning (known in modern military parlance as Commander's Critical Information Requirements or CCIR).

Analytic Methodology

Given that the primary purpose of this study is to examine the key operational-level leaders (and their staffs) involved in the Eastern Front campaigns of 1941–45, some objective method is necessary to gauge their relative ability to efficiently accomplish assigned missions. In essence, what distinguishes "good generalship" from "bad generalship"? While a general with endless resources can often win battles, such as Marshal Semyon Timoshenko achieved in breaking through the Mannerheim Line in February 1940, the brute-force approach is a wasteful, inefficient approach to generalship. Nor is the outcome of a given battle, in itself, a reliable indicator of efficient generalship, particularly in cases of Pyrrhic victories or close-run defeats. Based upon my training and experiences in military staff planning and professional studies, the objective methodology I choose to employ to evaluate battle command is in terms of the principles of war. This methodology of using the principles of war to evaluate historical campaigns has been employed by the US Army's Command and General Staff School since the 1920s.[5] Historically, generals and their staffs who plan their operations in accordance with the principles of war have done better than those that have not. Indeed, since the emergence of professional armies, ignoring the principles of war has become akin to committing military malpractice. A commander need not employ every principle of war in developing their plan of operations – some simply do not apply under all circumstances – but they should be considered.

While the definition of the principles of war has varied from country to country and over time, the fundamental (immutable) truths of successful war-making are generally considered to be timeless. For example, generals stretching back to the dawn of organized warfare recognized that attaining surprise was good and in contrast, being surprised by an enemy was bad – nothing has changed in that regard in 30 centuries. Yet these fundamental truths of warfare, even though practiced for centuries, were not codified until the modern era. Prior to the campaigns of Napoleon and the American Civil War, the limited body of formal military theory was bifurcated between the tactical level (how best to win battles) and the strategic level (how to win wars). Campaign planning was very short-term in outlook and most generals even in the mid-19th century still thought in terms of seeking decision in a single major battle. Despite hackneyed aphorisms from Sun Tzu and others, the emergence of the scientific study of warfare did not begin until the post-Napoleonic era, with Antoine-Henri Jomini's *Précis de l'art de la guerre* (1838). Jomini was one of the first military theorists to try to codify principles of war and he identified the offensive/initiative, mass and objective/decisive point as fundamental to sound generalship.[6] Although in Jomini's day the terms "principles" and "maxims" were not well-defined and often used interchangeably, his theories sparked an interest in codifying the principles just as formal systems of training officers were being adopted in Europe, Russia and the

United States. Indeed, Jomini had profound influence in Russia, where he helped establish the Imperial Military Academy in St Petersburg in 1832. Carl von Clausewitz's *Vom Kriege* (1832) was also very influential, but adopted a different approach. Whereas Jomini sought to identify and define a systematic approach to warfare, von Clausewitz regarded war as an art form that defied simple codification because he said each situation was unique. While von Clausewitz discussed principles of war in *Vom Krieg*, as well as implying an operational-level of warfare, he steered clear of endorsing any systematic approach to warfare. Likewise, Helmuth von Moltke, chief of the Prussian General Staff from 1858 to 1888, adopted von Clausewitz's prejudice against codifying principles of war because he thought they would inhibit a commander's freedom of action. Formal principles implied an obsequious, checklist approach to battle command, which went against the Prussian ideals of inspired leadership. Consequently, it was not until the 1890s that some German army officers, such as Colmar von der Goltz and Rudolf von Caemmerer, began to write about fundamental principles of war.

By the late 19th century, most European armies had grown to accept the idea that a defined set of principles of war could assist commanders in developing campaign plans. In Russia, Genrikh A. Leer, head of the Nikolaev Academy of the General Staff, outlined 12 principles of war in 1894 that included mass, offensive, concentration at the decisive point, economy of force, security and surprise.[7] French army officers, eager to avenge their humiliation in the Franco-Prussian War, sought new theories to help them regain their former status as Europe's premier military force. Concluding that defeat in 1870 had been due to inadequate morale and initiative, the French theorists focused on the moral-psychological elements of warfare. Ardant du Picq's *Études sur le combat* (*Battle Studies*, 1880) discussed principles of war, but only at the tactical level. Ferdinand Foch expanded upon Ardant du Picq's theories with his own *Des principes de la guerre* (1903), but still focused on the moral elements of battle. Four years later, the concept of "élan vital" appeared, which stressed offensive operations while denigrating the defense. The danger of this approach to principles of war – which placed excessive emphasis on moral factors – was that it tended to discount other fundamentals, such as maneuver and surprise. Consequently, the French Army in 1914 embraced reckless offensive methods, resulting in crippling casualties. Although technological advances should not undermine the fundamental principles of war, the advent of mass conscription and industrial era warfare did undermine the short-campaign model that military leaders had regarded as an ideal.

Once million-man armies with large amounts of equipment were fielded, it became more and more difficult to defeat even badly-led armies in a single battle or campaign.

Thus it was not until the stalemate and fruitless battles of the First World War that military theorists began to question whether tactical victories alone could lead to strategic success. Attritional campaigns like Ypres and Verdun proved counterproductive, grinding both sides' armies into pulp and victory left elusively beyond reach. Even outright battlefield victories like Tannenberg in 1914 and Caporetto in 1917 did not lead to operational success. Consequently, military theorists began to attach more significance to the operational level of warfare, in order to provide a linkage between tactical-level battles and strategic-level campaign objectives. If operational art could form the bridge to harness tactical victories to achieve strategic ends, then the principles of war were the planks that held the bridge together.

After three years of deadlock on the Western Front, there was also increased professional interest in the principles of war as a means of finding a path to victory. In the British Army, Colonel J. F. C. Fuller began writing about principles of war in 1917 and developed a list of nine principles, seven of which were later incorporated into the 1920 *Field Service Regulations* (FSR).[8] Although the new Royal Air Force (RAF) became involved in the debate over the principles of war, leading to some modifications, most of Fuller's theoretical contributions remained part of official British Army doctrine in 1939 (even if the emphasis had declined).[9] Keenly aware of evolving British military theory, the US Army began discussing nine principles of war in 1921 and by 1939 they were officially codified in *FM 100-5, Operations*.[10] Consequently, both the American and British armies entered the Second World War with a fairly similar perspective on the principles of war, particularly in terms of the importance attached to objective, mass (concentration), surprise and the offensive.

Yet in contrast to the Anglo-French-American armies, Soviet military theorists expended little effort in the interwar period on addressing the principles of war. The basic problem was that Tsarist officers like Leer had developed lists of principles in the 1890s which were embraced by the Russian General Staff, but such theories became toxic "bourgeois military thinking" after the outbreak of the 1917 Revolution. The new Bolshevik minister of war, Leon Trotsky, declared that "war cannot have eternal laws." Nevertheless, even Trotsky recognized that the Soviet Union needed a General Staff and he was forced to employ former Tsarist staff officers (referred to as *Voenspets* or "military specialists") in the 1920s. In the aftermath of the Russian Civil War, the most erudite of these specialists were assigned to the Military Academy of the General Staff and tasked with developing a new "scientific" theory of war. It was soon apparent that pre-revolutionary military theory could not simply be discarded and even J. F. C. Fuller's lectures were eventually imported. Ieronim P. Uborevich began lecturing about the principles of waging battle at the academy, even though he focused on just a few, such as surprise and initiative.[11] By 1936, the principles of war had become embedded in Soviet military doctrine and appeared either explicitly or implicitly in the *Provisional Field Regulations for the Red Army* (PU–36). In PU–36, it is clear that Soviet military theorists regarded the principles of mass, offensive, surprise, maneuver, objective and security as essential elements for a successful campaign. Depth and (logistic) sustainability were also regarded as indispensable, even though these were not enduring principles but rather geared toward the specific conditions the Red Army expected to face on the modern battlefield. However, the Red Army explicitly rejected the principle of unity of command due to the Communist Party's (CPSU) insistence on exercising tight control over military leaders through the use of Commissars and political officers. Stalin was paranoid about military leaders amassing too much power or being able to make independent decisions without reference to the party (or him), so he mandated command arrangements at the division to the front level, which shared command. Thus, collective decision-making through party-controlled councils became *de rigeur* – but the Red Army would pay dearly for this deviation from military common sense.

The Principles of War, as understood by major armies in the interwar period, consisted of six core axioms: objective, offensive, mass/concentration, maneuver/mobility, surprise and security. Several other concepts, such as depth and economy of force and unity of command, were widely recognized, but had not been accepted as axiomatic. Table I outlines the Principles of War as recognized by four of the major armies in 1939. Although the core concepts are fully explained in Appendix 1, a brief explanation might be helpful. Objective is the axiom that any given military plan needs a clearly defined goal that it seeks to obtain. Offensive is the necessity to retain momentum in operations to obtain stated objectives, lest the enemy gain the initiative and achieve their objectives. Mass is the concept of concentrating overwhelming combat power to achieve a decisive result, rather than dispersing one's efforts. Maneuver seeks to use mobility to put the enemy at a disadvantage, striking them at a time and place most favorable to one's own army. Likewise, surprise is sought to put the enemy at an additional

Table I: Principles of War, 1920–39

US Army FM 100-5 (1939)	British Army FSR 1920/1924	Soviet Army PU-36 (1936)	German Heer *Truppenführung* (1933/1934)
Objective	Objective	Objective	Objective
Offensive	Offensive	Offensive	Offensive
Mass	Mass (concentration)	Mass	Mass (concentration) (*Schwerpunkt*)
Maneuver	Mobility	Mobility	Maneuver (*Bewegungskrieg*)
Surprise	Surprise	Surprise	Surprise
Security	Security	Security	Security
Economy of force	Economy of force		
Unity of Command		NO	
Simplicity			
	Endurance	Depth	
	Determination	Sustainability	

disadvantage, by doing something that they did not anticipate. Finally, security is the axiom by which commanders seek to prevent an enemy from using maneuver to achieve surprise against their own army.

Although theorists in the Imperial German Army were discussing principles of war prior to the First World War, they were generally averse to embracing the concept. In 1912, Friedrich von Bernhardi published *Vom heutigen Kriege* (*On Today's War*), which outlined fundamental principles of war but then cautioned that they could promote a dogmatic approach to warfare. German officers placed great value on their "freedom of action" and worried that explicit principles could somehow constrain their latitude on decision-making. Furthermore, von Clausewitz's theory that every military situation was unique and required a unique approach to solve worked against acceptance of any kind of checklist-based method. Consequently, the Imperial German Army went into the First World War aware of the principles of war, but unwilling to be guided by them in any serious way. While the traditional German approach of relying upon inspired generalship and quick decision-making provided the basis for German tactical victories in the First World War, they did not produce the desired end-goals. Defeat in the First World War led to exhaustive efforts by the post-war Reichswehr to identify the reasons for failure and then develop solutions. Nevertheless, even the Reichswehr and follow-on Wehrmacht remained averse to codifying any principles of war and continued to rely upon the traditional preference for unique solutions. However, when the *Truppenführung* doctrinal manual was published in 1933–34, it explicitly mentioned the principles of objective, offensive, mass, maneuver, surprise and security as essential elements of battlefield command. Despite this, German senior officers going into the Second World War tended to evince an instinctive mental stubbornness against accepting explicit principles of war as guidelines for decision-making.

The German attitude toward the principles of war bears all the marks of intellectual dissonance. If there were no fundamental principles of war, why did every major German operation in both the First and Second World Wars rely on maneuver to achieve specific operational objectives? Indeed, it is virtually impossible to imagine campaign planning without maneuver or objective being part of the process. The one exception might be a protracted and dispersed insurgency campaign that goes on for decades – but this was never part of the German approach to war-making. Furthermore, German General Staff officers were fully aware of current theory on the principles of war. Major Hans von Greiffenberg, who would head the OKH operations section in 1940 and was one of the planners involved with Operation *Barbarossa*, attended the American Command and General Staff School in Fort Leavenworth in 1932 and 1933 (where the principles were a major part of the curriculum). In my opinion, for what it's worth, the dissonance was caused by Prussian chauvinism embedded in the ethos of the Große Generalstab; they simply could not admit that any of their success could be traced to theories developed by Jomini, J. F. C. Fuller or other outsiders. So in regards to the principles of war, the Große Generalstab adopted a stance of deliberate obtuseness – denying the principles even as they were employing them in their planning process. While this dissonance might seem irrelevant, I intend to demonstrate that it did impair the German campaign planning process.

After this lengthy, but necessary exposition on the principles of war [*see Appendix 1 for definitions of each principle*], I return to my intent to use them as the basis for evaluating generalship on the Eastern Front. It is an imperfect method, since the Red Army and Wehrmacht did not recognize all the same principles and both sides were handicapped by erosion of unity of command from above. Nevertheless, the principles of war are sufficiently enduring and fundamental to provide common reference points, at least among military professionals. Since operational analysis is at the crux of this study, I will break the campaign narratives into one year per chapter, with sub-divisions for the main theaters of operations (north/center/south). Each major operation will be addressed, looking at the planning and the decisions made during the campaign, to assess the opposing leaders (and their staffs). For each principle of war, if applied correctly, the commander receives a "+", "0" if not applied or not applicable and "-" if failed to apply. Scores will then be totaled for each commander/staff. Admittedly, this is a crude method of comparison, but it does possess an objective quality that is lacking in subjective histories.

CHAPTER 1

Overview of German/Soviet Senior Leader Training, Doctrine and Pre-War Plans

"Gentlemen, I notice that there are always three courses open to the enemy, and that he usually takes the fourth."
Helmuth von Moltke, 1880

"Don't worry, they're only killing the smart ones."
Marshal Voroshilov, 1937

Before delving into campaign analysis, it is necessary to examine the opposing leadership training methods, operational doctrine and pre-war planning to provide deeper insight into how the senior commanders on both sides were prepared for these campaigns.

German

Most of the German senior officers who served in high-level command billets on the Eastern Front between 1941 and 1945 entered active service in the period 1900–14. Most – but not all – came from traditional military families and volunteered for service as teenagers. In Germany, the two paths to an officer's career were either to enroll in the Cadet Corps (*Kadettenkorps*) and spend several years in training academies like Groß-Lichterfelde in Berlin, or to apply directly to a regimental commander for admission as a volunteer, after having passed their civilian *Abitur* examination. In either case, cadets or volunteers usually spent their first year in the army as enlisted soldiers, progressing through basic and branch training, then being assigned to a battalion. In the course of their first year of service, volunteers were evaluated for leadership aptitude and if approved, they would become officer candidates (*Fahnenjunker*) and be sent to a *Kriegsschule* for officer training. Prior to the First World War, there were ten Kriegsschulen in Germany and the Bavarian Army had its own in Munich. After the First World War, many of these schools were closed but by the 1930s four Kriegsschulen were back in operation, located in Potsdam (Berlin), Munich, Hanover and Dresden. After the Austrian Anschluss in 1938, the Austrian Kriegsschule at Wiener-Neustadt was also added to the portfolio of training schools.

The peacetime program of instruction at a Kriegsschule lasted eight months and consisted of a mix of classroom and hands-on training. Officer cadets (*Fähnrich*) were taught battalion-level tactics and learned critical skills such as map reading and topographical analysis, basic military engineering (e.g. building tactical bridges, obstacle construction), mastery of infantry weapons, requesting fire support and communications. Cadets also learned battalion-level staff duties and were taught to make tactical decisions quickly and issue clear, concise orders. Critical thinking was an important part of German officer training and "school solutions" to tactical problems (*Aufgaben*) were frowned upon by the school instructors. Military history, including staff rides to battlefields, were used to teach cadets how to translate theory into practice. Siegfried Knappe, who attended the Kriegsschule Potsdam in 1937–38 said about these staff rides that "we learned why things went right and why things went wrong."[1] If successful, officer cadets (*Fähnrich*) would become an *Oberfähnrich* at graduation. Actual commissioning into the officer ranks, as a *Leutnant*, usually occurred within a few months after graduation from the Kriegsschule. The newly minted Leutnant would then return to his battalion/regiment and spend the next several years gaining further hands-on experience in his branch of service. Of the 55 German senior officers surveyed, more than two-thirds (38 of 55) came from the infantry branch, nine from the artillery branch, five from cavalry and just three from other branches (two signal, one Pioniere). Heinz Guderian, as a signal officer, was a real outlier.

After 7–9 years of service in their branch, officers who had demonstrated excellent potential and passed a rigorous entrance examination were sent to the Kriegsakademie in Berlin; the Bavarian Army maintained its own academy in Munich. Only about half the officers who would later hold senior command billets on the Eastern Front between 1941 and 1945 had been selected to attend a Kriegsakademie and the overall selection rate was even lower, just 10–15 percent of all officers. The coursework at the Kriegsakademie consisted of a two-year training program, which was intended to create professional staff officers for service either in the German (or Bavarian) General Staff (Großer Generalstab) or to serve as a primary staff officer at division/corps/army level. Graduates of the Kriegsakademie were authorized to wear the double crimson trouser stripes (*Lampassen*), in order to indicate their elite status. As a result of the Treaty of Versailles, the Reichswehr was forced to abolish the Großer Generalstab and close the Kriegsakademie. However, General Hans von Seeckt, head of the Reichswehr and the last head of the old Großer Generalstab, arranged to conduct General Staff training in secret, beginning in 1920. The Troop Office (*Truppenamt*), specifically through its T4 Training Section, became the means for this artifice. The so-called commander's assistant courses (*Führergehilfe*) replicated the two-year Kriegsakademie training.[2] Although von Seeckt hoped to produce about 70 new General Staff officers per year, his covert system was only capable of training half that number. It was not until October 1935, with the creation of the Wehrmacht, that the Großer Generalstab was re-established and the Kriegsakademie was officially re-opened. Despite efforts to boost enrollment in 1936–39, the Wehrmacht went to war in 1939 with just 811 General Staff officers to fill 824 authorized billets. In order to make up the shortfall, the Wehrmacht was forced to shut down the Kriegsakademie and employ its training cadre in the field army and to recall retired officers.[3]

The first year of study at the Kriegsakademie focused on regimental-level duties, whereas the second year focused on division and larger formations. Prior to the First World War, about one-third of students at the Kriegsakademie were allowed to remain for a third year of training, which had a broader scope than the two previous years. Most of the training focused on tactics, military history, logistics and the various support branches. Military history lessons tended to focus on Napoleonic-era battles and campaigns, as well as the American Civil War, the Austro-Prussian War and the Russo-Japanese War (later updated to include the

First World War). Students were exposed to foreign military theories, including the principles of war. Yet the Kriegsakademie environment was hostile to rote learning methods and students were expected to learn by rapidly solving tactical problems (*Aufgaben*) in writing and then brief them to their instructors. There were no school solutions to these problems, but students were expected to employ sound military principles in devising their responses. German staff training was realistic and hands-on, expecting students to be rational and quick-thinking, thereby enhancing their ability to respond to unexpected opportunities or crises on future battlefields. In addition, the Kriegsakademie used wargames, tactical exercises without troops (TEWT) and staff rides (*Stabsreise*) to enable students to bridge the gap between classroom and field training. The Kriegsakademie was also used to familiarize students with others service branches, since they were mixed in with officers from all the across the army spectrum. Unlike Kriegsakademie training prior to the First World War, the course of instruction in 1935–39 used the *Truppenführung* manual as its primary doctrinal source and covered mechanized operations and new military technology in considerable detail. By the end of their training, a German General Staff officer was expected to be capable of rapidly and efficiently producing orders for formations up to the army level; in this regard, they had no peers.

In 1936, the Kriegsakademie in Berlin began accepting foreign students, including several US Army officers (Captains Albert C. Wedemeyer, Herman F. Kramer and Harlan N. Hartness); Wedemeyer's report to the US Army's G-2 section (intelligence) on the Berlin Kriegsakademie provides great insight into the training at that institution.[4] Although the German Kriegsakademie training system has often been criticized post-1945 for its lack of attention to inculcating strategic thought, leading to an inability to form a viable military strategy for the Third Reich, it is highly unlikely that Hitler would have given the Großer Generalstab any greater input on strategy even if the curriculum had been modified. Furthermore, the notion that contemporary General Staff officers in Western and Soviet armies had some kind of an intrinsic advantage in strategic planning over their Wehrmacht counterparts does not align well with actual results in 1940–43. Just as Hitler permitted the Großer Generalstab only a minimal role in strategic development, Allied strategic priorities were skewed by Winston Churchill's preference to attack "the soft underbelly of Europe" and to devote additional resources to tertiary theaters of operations like Burma. Eisenhower's "grand strategy" in the European Theater of Operations was incredibly simplistic and certainly not beyond the planning abilites of the Großer Generalstab. Likewise, Stalin's hand was on all Soviet strategic direction, which constrained professional military recommendations from the Red Army's General Staff.

It is also important to note that over one-third of the future senior German leaders never attended the Kriegsakademie or received General Staff training. As in other armies, the German military cultivated officers who were good field commanders or demonstrated exceptional battlefield leadership. Busch, von Bock and Schörner had been awarded the prestigious Pour le Mérite in the First World War and Hube had lost an arm at Verdun – all achieved rapid advancement in the post-war Reichswehr and Wehrmacht. In addition, the proportion of General Staff trained senior commanders declined during 1943–45, as more junior leaders rose to fill vacancies; many of these officers had been commissioned in 1914–17 and not been able to attend clandestine General Staff training in the Reichswehr era.

Since the 18th century, German military doctrine had been shaped by the imperative need to fight short, decisive campaigns before numerically-superior enemy coalitions could grind down their field armies. Aggressive maneuver warfare (*Bewegungskrieg*), not positional warfare, offered the best chance of achieving quick, decisive results. From the German perspective, the ideal outcome of a campaign was mobile operations that ended with a battle of annihiliation (*Vernichtungsschlacht*) that destroyed the main enemy armies.[5] The German preference for maneuver was also closely tied to the concept of concentrating combat power at a decisive point on the battlefield, which evolved into the concept of the *Schwerpunkt*, which in practice meant designating where the main effort of maneuver would be applied. These methods had worked at Königgrätz in 1866 and Sedan in 1870, but failed to produce decisive success at Tannenberg or at the Marne in 1914 or Caporetto in 1917. Nonetheless, German military theory did not fault the methods but regarded failure as due to other factors, seemingly beyond their control – which fit in nicely with the traditional German practice of eschewing fundamental principles of war.

In the aftermath of the First World War, General Hans von Seeckt, head of the Reichswehr, put maximum effort into identifying lessons learned from the recent conflict and incorporating the most salient points into a "new" doctrine. Foremost, post-war study groups identified the lack of tanks and adequate air support as two reasons for defeat, which prompted von Seeckt to incorporate both mechanization and airpower in his doctrinal requirements.[6] However, the new doctrinal manuals published in 1921 and 1923 (known as *Das FuG* and the *Grundzüge*) were far from revolutionary. Instead, these manuals stressed the importance of traditional German operation-tactical thinking about *Bewegungskrieg*, particularly in regard to the imperative for rapid action, but tanks and airpower were envisioned as simply combat support elements for the infantry.[7] At any rate, new doctrinal manuals could not change the fact that the Reichswehr was severely constrained by the limits imposed by the Treaty of Versailles, with defensive operations the only practical course of action throughout the 1920s. Despite the Versailles limitations, German military theorists in the interwar period became increasingly interested in operational-level warfare, even though protracted campaigning did not align well with Germany's resource-constrained circumstances.[8] Nevertheless, von Seeckt and his successors actively promoted an offensive-oriented doctrine, particularly Ludwig Beck, which resulted in the publication of *Truppenführung* in two parts in 1933 and 1934. The *Truppenführung* manual was the primary doctrinal source for training German officers in the 1930s, so it becomes an essential element for understanding how leaders were intended to conduct operations.[9] Yet like von Seeckt's earlier regulations, *Truppenführung* was heavily focused on the tactical level of warfare (particularly division to regiment) and tended to see operational-level of warfare as merely a string of tactical-level engagements tied together with a common objective in mind.

Once Hitler came to power and initiated a massive rearmament program in 1933, the doctrinal elements assembled by von Seeckt provided an excellent framework to create an offensive-oriented, combined arms army. Despite economic-industrial constraints, Germany was able to quickly assemble a potent air-ground team in just five years and expand its army seven-fold. Nevertheless, only a small proportion of the Wehrmacht could be motorized – the balance would consist of infantry divisions little changed from 1918. One lingering doctrinal problem concerned the degree of independence to be afforded to the new Panzer divisions and the Luftwaffe. Should the Panzer divisions be unleashed to conduct mobile operations on their own, or should they be used to support the slower-moving infantry armies? Likewise, should the Luftwaffe be used as an independent strike force – like Britain's Bomber Command – or assigned to support ground operations? At the outbreak of the Second

World War in September 1939, the new Wehrmacht doctrine was still a work in progress, but it served well in the Polish, Western and Balkan campaigns. The Panzer divisions were allowed to conduct independent operations but Sturmartillerie units with assault guns were created to give the infantry armies some armor support. During the Battle of Britain, the Luftwaffe was given its head and allowed to conduct independent operations in anticipation of an amphibious landing that never occurred. After the Luftwaffe's failure to achieve its operational goal of establishing air supremacy over southeast England, its leadership accepted the role of providing close air support for the army.

By the time that Operation *Barbarossa* commenced in June 1941, the Wehrmacht had been able to further refine its tactical and operational doctrines. Any pre-war doubts about the ability of mechanized forces to achieve rapid and decisive results had been dispelled in these successful campaigns and even the older officers like von Rundstedt recognized that the use of combined arms with the close integration of Panzers, motorized infantry and artillery, with close air support, was a winning formula. At the tactical level, German commanders had learned that a motorized corps comprising two Panzer divisions and one motorized infantry division was capable of conducting rapid double envelopments that could stun a larger enemy formation into inaction while it was being chopped into pieces. Based upon the experience of Panzergruppe Kleist in France, the Wehrmacht decided to create four Panzer groups for Operation *Barbarossa*. The Panzer groups of June 1941 were not yet full-fledged armies but they typically had two or three motorized corps, which enabled them to conduct independent operational-level missions. The accepted operational model was to use the Panzer groups to conduct simultaneous pincer operations to pin and encircle enemy formations and then the follow-up infantry armies would destroy the trapped enemy in a *Kesselschlacht* (cauldron battle). Campaigns were now conceived as sequential encirclement operations, to continue until the enemy's field armies were broken and routed, eventually leading to a collapse in morale. Seizing territorial objectives was less important than destroying the enemy's combat power and will to resist, in the opening moves, if possible. The shock effect of sudden, powerful blows was expected to paralyze an enemy, preventing them from seriously interfering with German operations. Yet in doctrinal terms, the Wehrmacht had simply "scaled up" its tactical doctrine to fit operational needs without making the necessary adjustments in support services to enable campaigns that lasted for more than a month or so. German leaders expected lengthy refit periods between campaigns, in order to replace casualties and equipment losses; in other words, German generals did not anticipate conducting major operations with formations that had been reduced to just 30–50 percent of their authorized strength.

While this formula worked well in the French and Balkan campaigns, the Oberkommando des Heeres (OKH) failed to appreciate that these successes only occurred during periods of favorable weather conditions and over fairly short distances. During the first three campaigns of 1939–41, the German mechanized forces had conducted short-pulse offensives, lasting no more than two weeks at a time. In France and the Balkans, German Panzer units had been able to advance 300–350km in ten days, but then were able to pause and refit. Mechanized spearheads had outrun their logistic support in France, but only briefly and without serious consequences. At the operational level, the mechanized spearheads were still tied to supply from friendly railheads, but through a variety of field expedients (e.g. aerial resupply, capturing enemy fuel depots) they could operate up to 100km beyond them for short periods. Furthermore, only 18 percent of the Wehrmacht's divisions were motorized in 1941 – the rest still relied on tens of thousands of horses to move their artillery and their supplies, adding an incongruous element to German operational-level warfare. German operational doctrine was geared towards high-intensity mobile warfare intended to keep a larger opponent off-balance, but the majority of their army could only advance at a walking pace. The result was a serious disconnect, exacerbated as distances increased, with the mechanized spearheads leaving the supporting infantry armies far behind and themselves beyond efficient logistic support range. Another serious but unrecognized deficiency in German operational level doctrine was the failure to work out procedures for joint operations incorporating allied formations from Italy, Romania and Hungary. Most German senior leaders tended to have condescending attitudes toward the other Axis armies, while ignoring significant differences in doctrine, planning procedures and equipment. Trying to develop efficient procedures for joint operations during active campaigning proved nearly impossible.

One of the most critical aspects of German operational-level warfare was the close integration of air and ground combat power. In June 1941, each German *Heeresgruppe* (Army Group) was assigned a *Luftflotte* (Air Fleet) to support its operations, which was far ahead of any other contemporary army. Indeed, the German emphasis on maneuver was predicated on the availability of air support, but when that air support was not available, German ground forces quickly tended to lose their edge. In addition to close air support, battlefield interdiction and air supremacy missions, the Luftflotte provided critical aerial resupply for isolated ground units, which could keep an advance rolling. The German concept of combat power was not based upon mass, but upon speed of maneuver – arriving at a time and place that caught the enemy by surprise and put them at a great disadvantage; this was the essence of the *Sichelschnitt* ("Sickle Cut") plan in May 1940 and then the Kiev encirclement operation in September 1941. Yet German operational methods tended to make overly-optimistic assumptions about logistic sustainability which proved dangerously false when campaigns did not end on schedule; this occurred with the advance on Paris in 1914 and then with Operation *Barbarossa* in 1941. Consequently, achieving rapid success before the various frictions of war brought everything to a standstill was a necessity in German military operations.

Soviet

The career path for Soviet senior command cadre in the Second World War was substantially different than that of their Wehrmacht opponents. Unlike the German officer corps, most of the future Soviet senior field commanders came from peasant or worker backgrounds (or so they claimed) and at least one quarter had limited primary school education (providing just basic literacy) prior to entering service. Two-thirds of the senior command cadre were ethnic Russians, but 15 percent were Ukrainians, as well as a few from minority ethnic groups (Armenian, Latvian, Belarusian, Georgian, Ossetian). None of the senior field commanders came from prestigious military families, which meant that soldiering was a profession, not a tradition, for them. With only a few exceptions (such as Kirill Meretskov), the majority of senior Soviet commanders began their military careers by being conscripted or volunteering for service in the Tsarist Imperial Russian Army (*Russkaya imperatorskaya armiya*) during the First World War; about half served as junior officers, the rest as non-commissioned officers. Unlike their German counterparts who served for the duration in the First World War, most of the future Soviet military leaders only saw active service for a year or so before the Tsarist collapse. Although most of these men joined the Red Army in 1918–20, a few actually fought with the White armies during the early period of the Russian Civil War. Whatever their origins, membership in the

Communist Party of the Soviet Union (CPSU) became a *sine qua non* for career progression in the Red Army (unlike the Wehrmacht generals, very few of whom became members of the NSDAP (National Socialist Workers' Party)); of the 140 examined in this survey, 62 percent were party members. Thus unlike the German officers who inherited traditions, doctrinal influences and a wealth of recent combat experience, the future Soviet command cadre had little organizational or doctrinal continuity in their early years of military service. Indeed, the only constant factor in their military careers was the inculcation of Communist political ideology and values.

In contrast, the senior command cadre in the General Staff of the Red Army (*General'nyy shtab RKKA*) came from more eclectic sources. Vladimir Triandafillov was ethnic Greek, Aleksei Antonov was ethnic Tartar and Boris Shaposhnikov came from a Cossack family. Unlike the post-war Reichswehr, which could pick and choose the best 4,000 officers to fill its ranks, the Red Army had to make do with whatever trained officers it could harvest from the defunct Tsarist Imperial Army or defectors from the White armies. Rather than coming from peasant backgrounds with limited education, the *genshtabisty* (general staff officers) typically came from military or bourgeois families who could afford to educate their sons. Aleksandr A. Svechin had been a general-major in the Tsarist Army and Shaposhnikov had been a *polkovnik* (colonel); both were graduates of the pre-war Nikolaev Military Academy. It was these men – the *Voenspets* or "military specialists" – who trained neophyte officers like Zhukov, Konev and Rokossovsky in the early 1920s.

From the beginning of the Red Army in 1918, there was an urgent requirement for thousands of junior officers in the field armies and 26,000 were cranked out in two years. However, training was haphazard and rudimentary. Given the factional nature of the Russian Civil War, the emphasis in training was on political indoctrination – stressing loyalty to the CPSU – not military doctrine or knowledge. In fact, the Red Army had no real doctrine in 1918–21 – it would have to be created from scratch. In order to transform former non-commissioned officers like Zhukov and Konev into junior officers, a number of branch-specific basic officer courses were established to train officer cadets; the courses typically lasted about six months and were frequently interrupted by the ongoing civil war. According to Zhukov, other than hands-on cavalry training, most of the instruction he received in the course consisted of "political and economic subjects taught by half-baked instructors."[10] As the Russian Civil War began to wind down, the Red Army began to enact measures to expand officer training. Advanced officer courses were created, for each branch, to train future battalion and regimental commanders; these courses had a sprinkling of military theory but still devoted excessive time to political training. The *Vystrel* schools were also established for follow-on instruction, with more emphasis on hands-on field training over classroom. Compared to the German Kriegsschulen, the Soviet junior officer training system in the 1920s was incredibly insular and not capable of producing well-rounded or efficient mid-level leaders. Yet the Red Army leadership was satisfied with a system that could produce junior leaders in quantity, which it did.

The Bolshevik leadership established the People's Commissariat for Military and Naval Affairs (*Narodnyy komissariat po voyennym i morskim delam or* NK ViMD), headed by Leon Trotsky, to oversee military affairs.* However, Mikhail Frunze was a senior Bolshevik activist-turned-soldier who played a major role in shaping the Red Army in its early days. For the defense of the Soviet state, Trotsky wanted to create a strong workers' militia, led by members of the CPSU. In contrast, Frunze wanted to create a professional army, but one whose doctrine was shaped by Marxist ideology. The two visions were incompatible and they led to strident debates about the merits of each approach. At the 10th Party Congress in March 1921, Frunze spoke about a "Unified Military Doctrine" (UMD), which would take the best components of existing military doctrines in order to create a "scientific proletarian way of war."[11] Despite Trotsky's objections, the Communist Central Committee approved Frunze's concept of developing a UMD, on the notion that it would strengthen party control over the military. Unlike Trotsky, Frunze wanted the UMD to become an offensive-oriented doctrine, so that the Red Army could not only protect the Soviet state but spread the revolution to capitalist states. Furthermore, Frunze was a Bolshevik fanatic who believed that all military training and doctrine should emphasize Marxist political theories. After a slow start in outlining his UMD, in 1922 Frunze began adding some details of the fundamental military principles to be at the core of the UMD, including maneuver and the offensive. He anticipated a long, drawn-out war against the capitalist states so he rejected "bourgeois" ideas (including von Clausewitz and Jomini) about conducting quick knock-out campaigns.

---

*In 1934, this organization became the People's Commissariat of Defense (*Narodnyy komissariat oborony or* NKO).

Trotsky intended that the Red Army's primary training center for its future senior leaders would reside in the Military Academy of the RKKA (later renamed the Frunze Military Academy), which was headed by Mikhail Tukhachevsky in 1921–22. The academy's cadre of *Voenspets* included some excellent theoreticians such as Triandafillov, Aleksandr Svechin, Ieronim Uborevich and Gregory Isserson, but they were receiving contradictory input from Trotsky, Frunze and Tukhachevsky about how to develop the UMD, which led to a certain incoherence. For students, the program of instruction at the academy varied, from one year in the early 1920s up to two years by the 1930s. Zhukov spent just six months at the academy (Zhukov's memoirs gloss over his time at the Frunze) but Rodion Malinovsky spent two years there.[12] At the academy, student officers were given their first exposure to military theory, combined arms tactics, logistics and operational-level warfare. The course included students from all RKKA service branches, which helped to break down some of the barriers between them.

In 1925, Trotsky was forced to resign and Frunze died in surgery under suspicious circumstances. Tukhachevsky became Red Army chief of staff and Kliment Voroshilov, an old crony of Stalin, took over the defense commissariat.* Since Voroshilov had no head for theory, Tukhachevsky took the reins of directing the development of a new military doctrine. Unlike Frunze, Tukhachevsky was not hostile to foreign military ideas and he brought in thousands of copies of J. F. C. Fuller's lectures on mechanized warfare and distributed them to Red Army officers. Tukhachevsky did not want a Tsarist-style army that was based on infantry and cavalry divisions, since that type of force structure would inevitably place the Red Army at a disadvantage against better-equipped capitalist foes. Instead, he envisioned a Red Army that possessed the latest in military technology, including tanks and aircraft, and he wanted a revolutionary doctrine that was specifically crafted to use these tools on the battlefield. Furthermore, Tukhachevsky wanted the Red Army relieved of the material constraints that had hampered previous Russian armies; he did not want the Red Army handicapped by shortages of basic necessities such as ammunition and boots. Thus, Tukhachevsky sought a new military doctrine for the Red Army that was based on new concepts and supported by a robust

---

*Until 1942, Stalin demonstrated clear favoritism to veterans of the *Konarmia* (1st Cavalry Army) who fought in the Russian Civil War and the Russo-Polish War. Most prominent in this group were Semyon Budyonny, Semyon Timoshenko, Grigory Kulik and Kliment Voroshilov.

military-industrial base that could provide the latest equipment in quantity. It was a tall order for a country that was largely poor and semi-illiterate.

Once armed with clear marching orders, the Soviet military theorists rose to the occasion. Aleksandr A. Svechin, a former member of the Tsarist General Staff who joined the Red Army, had been using the term 'operational art' (*operativnoe iskusstvo*) since the early 1920s, but without attracting much notice. Svechin's seminal work of military theory was *Strategiya* (*Strategy*), published in 1926–27. Nikolai E. Varfolomeev expanded upon Svechin's theories on operational art and began developing the concept of Deep Battle (*glubokiy boy*), involving successive operations to achieve a breakthrough into the depth of an enemy's front line. Essentially, Svechin and his associates were looking for a tactical solution to defeating a First World War-style defense by coordinating artillery, tanks, infantry and airpower, but they realized that a single battle was unlikely to achieve a decisive victory. Instead, Soviet military theory regarded sequential battles in a series of campaigns as necessary to secure a decisive victory. Employing combined arms attacks using successive echelons until a deep breakthrough was achieved seemed the best approach.

Vladimir K. Triandafillov, head of operations in the Red Army's General Staff, wrote another seminal work, *Kharakter operatsiy sovremennykh armiy* (*Characteristics of the Operations of the Modern Armies*) in 1929. Triandafillov sought to convert Svechin's tactical methodology into a true operational approach, known as Deep Operations (*glubokaya operatsiya*). Triandfillov died in 1931 but Georgy S. Isserson, another member of the Frunze Military Academy brain trust, wrote *The Evolution of Operational Art* (1932) and *The Fundamentals of the Deep Operation* (1933). Taken together, the works of Svechin, Triandafillov and Isserson, along with contributions by Nikolay E. Varfolomeev and Ieronim P. Uborevich, created a robust and sophisticated doctrinal model for the Red Army. The Red Army's first provisional field regulations, PU-29 (1929), was a collaborative effort by Tukhachevsky and Triandafillov. It was followed by PU-33 (1933), which emphasized the Svechin/Varfolomeev concept of Deep Battle (*glubokiy boy*). Tukhachevsky tasked Aleksandr I. Sediakin, deputy chief of the General Staff, with transforming Deep Battle into practical training guidelines. By 1934, Sediakin had created a playbook for Soviet commanders, which instructed them on how to employ a combined arms attack using armor, motorized infantry, artillery and airpower.

In conjunction with doctrinal developments, Tukhachevsky (who became deputy commissar for defense in 1931) advocated for extensive investments in armaments production as part of the First Five Year Plan

(1929–33). Foreign military technology was imported from England, Germany and the United States, enabling Soviet industry to examine the latest designs. By 1933, Soviet industry had begun serial production of new tanks, fighters and bombers. The Red Army formed its first mechanized brigade in 1930 and by 1932 it possessed enough tanks and vehicles to form two complete mechanized corps – three years before the first Panzer divisions were formed in Germany. Tukhachevsky added three brigades of paratroopers as well, to enable vertical envelopment. Between September 12 and 17, 1935, Tukhachevsky tested the new mechanized corps in large-scale field maneuvers, involving over 65,000 troops, 1,000 tanks, 600 aircraft and an *ad hoc* division of paratroopers.[13] The results were promising and appeared to validate the potential of Deep Operations, which were now fully integrated into the new *Provisional Field Regulations for the Red Army* (PU-36) in 1936.

Mikhail Tukhachevsky in his role as deputy defense commissar sought to transform the entire Red Army's approach to warfare. He and his Deep Operations disciples urged the rapid mechanization of the Red Army and introduction of new equipment like the BT-7 fast tank, to enable mobile operations. The Soviet cavalry branch, the largest in the world with 32 mounted divisions in 1937, was to be downsized and the remaining units motorized.[14] Tukhachevsky also managed to detach some of the staff of the Frunze Academy to create a new Academy of the General Staff, which would train experts to successfully employ the new doctrine in campaign planning. Supported by a fast-growing armaments industry, the Red Army appeared to be on the cusp of achieving a major leap forward in the theory and practice of operational warfare.

One key difference between German operational-level doctrine and the theories embedded in PU-36 was that the Wehrmacht intended to employ virtually all its available forces from the outset of a campaign, in order to achieve a rapid knock-out blow. Very few forces would be kept in operational or strategic reserve. In contrast, the Red Army had begun to think in terms of echelonment, with successive formations entering the battle in sequential style, to overwhelm the enemy. Strategic reserves would also play a prominent part in every major Soviet offensive campaign. In Deep Operations, Soviet doctrine envisioned first echelon formations, referred to as Shock Armies (*udarnaia armii*), being used to penetrate an enemy defense and then a second echelon, of mechanized formations, exploiting that success. Then, as Isserson wrote, additional echelons would be drawn from strategic reserves to sustain any advance and thereby convert a local success into a decisive victory. However, based upon experience from the First World War, Soviet theorists eschewed the idea that a peer enemy like Germany could be defeated in a single campaign, because they could be expected to commit their strategic reserves to re-establish a new defensive front. Thus the Soviet General Staff regarded a series of offensives, conducted in echelon, as the logical progression to eventual victory in a protracted war. Soviet pre-war doctrine was eminently rational, based upon their understanding of the principles of war and the material requirements of industrial-era warfare.

Although PU-36 represented the acme of Soviet pre-war doctrine, it was virtually dead on arrival due to the beginning of the Stalinist purges in May 1937. Egged on by Lavrenty Beria's NKVD secret police and Voroshilov's disdain for new ideas and technology, Stalin came to regard the new Academy of the General Staff as a hotbed of anti-Soviet agitation. Tukhachevsky's concept of an elite General Staff and independently-operating mechanized forces appeared to threaten Communist Party dominance over the Red Army, which was intolerable for Stalin. Voroshilov resented plans to reduce his beloved cavalry in order to create new mechanized units. As a result, Tukhachevsky and many other senior military leaders were arrested and executed or imprisoned. Most of the military theorists and General Staff officers involved in the creation of the new Deep Operations doctrine, including Svechin, Uborevich and Sediakin, were eliminated. Petro Grigorenko, a student at the Academy of the General Staff in 1937, later wrote that arrests of both faculty and students occurred regularly in this period, creating an atmosphere of doom.[15] Altogether, 60 of the 138 students in Grigorenko's General Staff class were executed. Voroshilov disbanded the mechanized corps and consigned the PU-36 regulations to temporary obscurity. Ideas like Deep Operations were now regarded as toxic and were shunned. Voroshilov rejected the idea of independent large-scale mechanized formations and instead dispersed the tank brigades to support infantry units. Consequently, the Red Army's doctrinal development was arrested due to the purges, leaving it with many new weapons but few senior officers who knew how to use them.

By suppressing PU-36, Voroshilov left the Red Army without a coherent doctrine. Instead, Voroshilov and Stalin emphasized mass – more tanks, more planes, more artillery – at the expense of maneuver. After the purges, the only real doctrinal advantage maintained by the Red Army was that the People's Commissariat of Defense of the Soviet Union (*Narodnyy komissariat oborony Sovetskovo Soyuza* or NKO) was preparing for protracted war and was creating the industrial infrastructure to provide the field armies with massive amounts of equipment. Yet as the purges continued through 1938–41, the NKVD decimated the ranks of the senior field commanders: 14 of 16 army-level commanders were purged, as well as 60 of 67 corps commanders and 136 of 199 division commanders. Altogether, over 54,000 military personnel were purged during 1937–41.[16] The haphazard elimination of so many command cadre forced the Red Army to expand its training schools and to accelerate officer training, in order to fill vacant command billets with somebody, or anybody. Not surprisingly, too many of the new commanders lacked the professional training or experience to lead large formations, which seriously undermined the Red Army's ability to conduct operational-level warfare. During the 1939 Finnish campaign, the Soviet numerical advantage in manpower and tanks counted for little in the initial phase, since commanders could not coordinate multiple units on the battlefield. The purges also damaged the morale of the Soviet officer corps, which left the survivors risk-averse and passive, awaiting higher authority to tell them what to do – the exact antithesis of their German opponents.

Pre-War Planning

Soviet DP-41

Prior to the German invasion, the Red Army's strategic guidance was developed by the Main Military Council (GVS) and the People's Commissariat of Defense (NKO); the key players were Stalin and his military cronies – Budyonny, Kulik and Voroshilov. The Soviet General Staff (*General'nyy shtab Sovetskoy Armii* or GSHKA), led by Marshal Boris M. Shaposhnikov, began preparing strategic plans for a two-front war against Germany and Japan in 1938. The NKO decided that the bulk of the Red Army would be committed in the western Soviet Union, against Germany and its Axis allies. Aleksandr M. Vasilevsky, the 45-year-old head of the operations department in the General Staff, was the key strategic planner.[17] Shaposhnikov was conservative in outlook, so early Soviet planning was primarily defensive in nature, with the intention of absorbing an enemy's initial attacks while Soviet mobilization occurred, then launching a series of counter-offensives once the Red Army was fully mobilized. Due to Tukhachevsky's influence, Soviet planning took on more of an offensive mindset and assumed that most combat would occur in the border regions, not the interior of the Soviet Union. Shaposhnikov also stated that he expected an invader (not directly referred to as Germany) would probably make their main effort in the north, through the Baltic States.[18] Vasilevsky estimated that the Red Army needed about 170 divisions to defend the western borders, but there were only 206 divisions extant in December 1940 (152 rifle, ten motorized, 26 cavalry and 18 tank). Nor were the regular divisions fully manned, even though the Red Army had doubled in size since September 1939. As an expedient measure, the NKO decided to create two peacetime division organizations ("12 and 6", also referred to as Category A/B), that possessed either 80 percent or 40 percent of authorized strength. Most divisions were not really combat capable because they lacked trucks and horses, which would not become available until after mobilization.

Soviet pre-war operational planning placed great emphasis on using the Category A and B covering forces to contest the border regions and to create a defense in depth that prevented the enemy from interfering with mobilization in the interior regions. The defense consisted of three echelons. The first echelon was positioned within 5–50 kilometers of the border and was tasked with absorbing the initial enemy attacks until reinforced. The second echelon, deployed within 50–100 kilometers of the border, was tasked with mounting local counterattacks to prevent any breach of the first echelon. The third echelon was deployed 100–400 kilometers back and constituted the primary operational-level reserves; these units would not be available until at least one week after mobilization. Several key assumptions also governed Soviet pre-war planning: (a) that Germany would require several weeks to mobilize its own forces, which would deprive them of surprise, (b) that Soviet covering forces could hold the border regions in the early stages of a war, (c) rapid Soviet mobilization would allow the Red Army to quickly seize the initiative and (d) Soviet losses would be heavy, requiring continuous force regeneration. Soviet planning was also seriously undermined by inadequate intelligence about enemy operational-level capabilities and likely courses of action.

While preparing strategic plans for war with Germany, the Soviet General Staff also had to develop no-notice operational plans to invade Poland in September 1939 and Finland in November 1939. Shaposhnikov's original assessment that a hastily-improvised campaign against Finland in winter would be difficult was rejected by Stalin – thereby consigning the General Staff's professional input to the wastebasket. Instead, Stalin opted for an operational plan developed by Leningrad Military District Commander Kirill A. Meretskov, who told Stalin what he wanted to hear – that victory could be achieved in just a few weeks. Meretskov's plan simply ignored the terrain, weather and the enemy, which led to catastrophic Soviet casualties in the early stages of the invasion. Eventually, the Red Army was able to mass enough infantry and artillery to smash through the Mannerheim Line in February 1940, forcing Finland to capitulate. However, the Russo-Finnish War proved to be the nadir of Soviet operational-level planning, with the Red Army embarrassed by a third-rate opponent.

After the fall of France in June 1940, the Soviet General Staff was forced to revise its defense plans as conflict with Germany appeared inevitable. Due to the demonstrated capabilities of the Panzer divisions in France, the NKO decided to re-form eight mechanized corps and equip them with the brand-new T-34/76 and KV-1 tanks; this decision meant that the Red Army had to create new units and train personnel on new equipment, but without an experienced cadre to lead that effort. As usual, Stalin acted by *diktat*, ignoring practical difficulties and simply demanding that the project would be resolved on time – or else. Even if the mechanized corps had been in better shape in June 1941, they were dispersed, rather than concentrated into tank armies like the German Panzer groups. Each of the Soviet first-echelon armies deployed to protect the border regions was provided with at least one mechanized corps.

Despite the failure of Meretskov's campaign plan against Finland, Stalin decided to elevate him to chief of the General Staff (GSHKA) in August 1940, while awkwardly shifting Shaposhnikov to the People's Commissariat of Defense under Timoshenko. Meretskov did bring a fresh mindset to GSHKA planning, although he apparently rankled the senior staff; Vasilevsky referred to him as "cunning" although "indecisive" was more appropriate. According to Vasilevsky's memoirs, Meretskov initially stated that he expected an enemy invasion to focus on the southwest axis, in the Ukraine, not in the Baltic States. According to American historian David Glantz, Vasilevsky had developed a separate assessment that an enemy invasion was most likely to make its main effort in the center to seize Minsk, with possible supporting offensives into the Baltic States and western Ukraine.[19] Meretskov told Vasilevsky to plan for two variants – one with the enemy main effort north of the Pripet Marshes and the other one south of the marshes – so that all eventualities would be covered. In order to defend the western border districts, the GSHKA recommended the creation of three fronts (the Northwestern, Western Front and Southwestern) as well as five reserve armies under Stavka control, to be used as a strategic reserve. Apparently, Meretskov and the GSHKA could not really agree where they expected an enemy main effort to occur, but created a safe plan that could be molded to fit all eventualities. In any case, when Meretskov briefed the GSHKA's draft war plan to Stalin on October 5, 1940 he included Vasilevsky's assessment of an enemy focus on the central sector, which Stalin rejected outright. Stalin stated that he expected the Germans to make their main effort in the south, to seize the economic resources in the Ukraine. Unwilling to disagree with Stalin, Meretskov concurred and the revised Soviet strategic war plan that was approved in October 1940 prioritized the defense of the western Ukraine, at the expense of the Northwestern and Western Fronts.[20] Half of the available Soviet armor was deployed in the Kiev Special Military District. Nor could the GSHKA consider the possibility of the enemy conducting a surprise attack, since Stalin said that was impossible, despite numerous warnings.[21]

In January 1941, Marshal Semyon K. Timoshenko (the new Commissar for Defense) and Meretskov supervised two wargames in Moscow to test the October 1940 war plan and Soviet operational-level methods. Oddly, Vasilevsky was not present for the wargames and in his memoirs, he claimed that he was "seriously ill." In the first wargame, held between January 2 and 6, General Georgy Zhukov led the "Blue" team representing the Germans, while General-polkovnik Dmitry G. Pavlov led the "Red" team representing the Red Army. The scenario was set in August and only covered the area of East Prussia, Belarus and the Baltic States. After Zhukov's Blue forces launched an attack from East Prussia, Pavlov dutifully launched a counterattack with his mechanized reserves – which failed miserably. Once the Soviet mobile reserves were gone, Zhukov's forces were able to achieve a breakthrough before Timoshenko ended the game and declared "Red" the winner. The second wargame, held between January 8 and 11, focused on the southern sector of the front, covering southern Poland and western Ukraine. In this wargame, Zhukov controlled the "Red" defending team, while General-leytenant Vasily Kuznetsov led the attacking "Blue" team. Zhukov's efforts to defend the Lvov salient failed and the "Blue" team achieved significant success.[22] Stalin was angered by the Red Army's poor showing in both wargames and decided to relieve Meretskov on January 14 and replace him with Zhukov. In his five months as chief of the GSHKA, Meretskov had been weak and indecisive. Although Zhukov lacked General Staff training he was strong-willed and had a tough, ruthless edge, which Stalin valued more than professional education. In response to the problems that surfaced in the Moscow wargames, Stalin tasked Timoshenko and Zhukov with improving the combat readiness of the Red Army and its ability to conduct successful operations.

As a first step, Timoshenko and Zhukov labored to complete a new mobilization plan, which was approved as MP-41 in February 1941. MP-41 assumed that the Red Army would have several weeks to mobilize its reserve forces, without any real hindrance from the enemy. Zhukov also began working on a new war plan, designated State Defensive Plan 41 (DP-41), which emphasized forward defense and allocated the bulk of the Red Army's combat power to the southern sector. A total of 163 divisions were assigned to the three echelons defending the western border region, with another 57 divisions in operational reserve under Stavka control. On paper, this deployment seemed to offer an adequate deterrent to German aggression, since the border forces comprised 3.3 million troops, equipped with over 10,500 operational tanks and 35,000 artillery pieces, supported by 10,800 VVS aircraft. DP-41 left four armies, with 500,000 troops, to hold the Far East against the Japanese. In reality, the Soviet forces deployed along the border were understrength and unprepared for combat. As a quick fix, Timoshenko and Zhukov convinced Stalin to begin a quiet partial mobilization in April 1941, in order to provide reservists to fill some of the manpower gaps on units stationed near the western borders. Zhukov also organized the transfer of one mechanized corps and four rifle divisions from interior military districts to reinforce the border districts and the creation of four reserve armies.[23] As concerns about border security increased, Zhukov asked for more reservists and 800,000 had been called up before the German invasion – of which the OKH remained ignorant. By mid-June 1941, the Red Army had tripled in size to 4.5 million troops.[24]

Further complicating the Red Army's predicament, Stalin ordered the border military district commanders to avoid provocations. Any kind of active defense measures were discouraged. As a result, units in the first echelon were unprepared to do anything but conduct a positional defense at the start of any conflict. Clearly a prudent war plan would have kept a large reserve, with most of the mechanized corps held back from the border regions until the enemy's main effort was actually identified. However, Stalin was unwilling to risk any loss of territory, so he forced Zhukov to deploy more than two-thirds of the Red Army up front, within easy reach of the German sledgehammer. Under these conditions of dictatorial interference, the GSHKA was only allowed to function as a rubber stamp for Stalin's off-the-cuff judgments.

Soviet pre-war planning further illuminates some of the doctrinal weaknesses lurking just below the surface. The military theorists at the Frunze Academy had placed little doctrinal emphasis on defense after 1925 and none at all on covering force missions, even though these were essential requirements of their strategic war plan. The GSHKA assumed that NKVD border defense units and first-echelon units from the frontier military districts would somehow coalesce into an impregnable defense, even though they did not train together and operated under separate chains of command. Nor was there any serious effort to develop joint operational planning with the Soviet Air Force (*Voenno-Vozdushnye Sily* or VVS) or Red Banner Fleet (*Krasnoznamennyy flot*). While the Frunze Academy had a department covering aviation tactics, theoretical lectures by Aleksandr N. Lapchinsky about ground attack missions, long-range bombing and the use of paratroops had virtually no influence on Soviet pre-war planning. Indeed, both Lapchinsky and his theories ended up being victims of the purges.[25] The Red Army leadership that survived the purges had little time for considering joint operations and integration of VVS capabilities was an afterthought in operational planning. Even though the VVS was the largest air force in the world in 1941, it had no equivalent of the German Luftflotten and would not begin forming its own air armies until May 1942. Consequently, the VVS had great difficulty massing its combat power to support ground operations and the situation would not improve until mid-1943. The consideration of naval forces was even lower in Soviet pre-war planning, despite the publication of Kapitan Boris B. Zherve's *Fundamentals of Naval Strategy* (*Osnovy voyenno-morskoy strategii*) in 1921, and *The Assault Landing Operation* (*Desantnaya operatsiya*) in 1931 provided a wealth of insight on how the Red Banner Fleet could be used to conduct amphibious landings, transfer armies by sea and provide supplies to army forces in coastal regions. Alas, Zherve and his theories did not survive the year 1937 either.

Upon mobilization, the Red Army forces assigned to defend the western borders of the Soviet Union consisted of:

- Northwest Front with the 8th and 11th Armies in first echelon and 27th Army in second echelon. Comprised of 24 divisions, incl. three tank divisions.
- Western Front with the 3rd, 4th and 10th Armies in first echelon and 13th Army in second echelon. Comprised of 43 divisions, incl. 12 tank divisions.
- Southwest Front with the 5th, 6th, 12th and 26th Armies in first echelon. Comprised of 78 divisions, incl. 20 tank divisions.
- 9th Army in the Odessa Special Military District. Comprised of 21 divisions, incl. four tank divisions.
- Stavka Reserves with the 16th, 19th, 20th, 21st, 22nd and 24th Armies, along with the 21st and 26th Mechanized Corps.

The Soviet War Plan, DP-41, was based more upon Stalin's personal biases and inclinations rather than sound military planning. By placing the majority of the Red Army's regular formations within 200 kilometers of the western border – but in a poorly prepared state – DP-41 risked giving the Wehrmacht exactly the conditions necessary to make Operation *Barbarossa* feasible.

After the German invasion began, the Headquarters of the Supreme High Command (SVGK) was formed, comprised of Stalin, Marshal Timoshenko, Marshal Voroshilov, Marshal Budyonny, General Zhukov, Admiral Kuznetsov and foreign minister Molotov.

As initially formed,* the Stavka was not exactly a brain trust. In July 1941, Shaposhnikov, who resumed his position as chief of the Soviet General Staff (GSHKA), was added to the Stavka. The State Defense Committee (GKO) was also created, which included Stalin, Marshal Kliment Voroshilov, Vyacheslav Molotov, Lavrenty Beria (NKVD) and Georgy Malenkov. Compared to Hitler and the OKH/OKW, Stalin packed his supreme decision-making bodies with political cronies and military sycophants, rather than professional military experts – which would cost the Red Army dearly.

German *Unternehmen* Barbarossa

Only five days after Hitler issued Führer Directive 16, which stated his intent to conduct an amphibious invasion (Unternehmen *Seelöwe*) of England if necessary, he met with his three senior service leaders on July 21, 1940 to discuss the strategic situation. After further discussions about *Seelöwe*, Hitler held a sidebar conversation with Generalfeldmarschall Walther von Brauchitsch, commander-in-chief of the German Army (Heer); Hitler told him that "our attention must be turned to tackling the Russian problem and prepare planning."[26] Without providing any specific strategic guidance, Hitler instructed von Brauchitsch to begin planning an invasion of the Soviet Union and casually said that the operation could begin that autumn. The next day, on July 22, von Brauchitsch informed Generaloberst Franz Halder, head of the Oberkommando des Heeres (OKH) to begin planning for an operation against the Soviet Union.[27] Halder's staff had its hands full at the moment – *Seelöwe* was still in its early planning stages and Hitler was demanding staff studies

---

*The Stavka went through several name changes in the first two months of the war. I employ the naming convention adopted on August 8, 1941, which remained in effect to the end of the war.

about other military options, including an invasion of Switzerland and an attack on Gibraltar. Halder duly tasked his operations (Oberst Hans von Greiffenberg), intelligence (Oberstleutnant Eberhard Kinzel) and quartermaster (Generalmajor Eduard Wagner) sections with conducting staff estimates of a potential invasion of the Soviet Union. While Halder's OKH was beginning its estimates, the Oberkommando der Wehrmacht (OKW) – which was nominally superior to the OKH – began its own concurrent planning effort on August 7 for an invasion of the Soviet Union. General der Artillerie Alfred Jodl, head of the OKW operations section, tasked Oberstleutnant Bernhard von Loßberg with conducting a staff study on the problem.

Typically, staff estimates for a major campaign require several weeks to complete and require input from multiple sources for information on terrain, weather and the enemy. However, both Halder and Jodl decided to devote minimal effort to this task. After just five days, the OKH staff presented their initial estimates to Halder.* Kinzel's intelligence estimate by Fremde Heere Ost (FHO) was highly flawed and based mostly on guesswork; he assessed that the Red Army had only 50–70 "good divisions" and their main strength was in Belarus and the Baltic States. Furthermore, Kinzel stressed that the northern sector had better road and rail networks and important objectives like Leningrad were within reach. However in a complete disconnect between intelligence and operations, von Greiffenberg's operations estimate judged that the southern sector offered better terrain for rapid mechanized advances and could lead to the rapid conquest of the Ukraine. From the beginning, Halder favored the northern sector because he regarded Moscow as the primary goal (even though it had not been mentioned by Hitler in his initial guidance) and he rejected von Greiffenberg's estimate. He decided not to waste any more of his own staff's time on this task and on July 29 brought in Generalmajor Erich Marcks to conduct an independent operations estimate. Although Marcks had received General Staff training, he was not a member of the OKH but was instead chief of staff of the 18. Armee stationed in East Prussia. The selection of Marcks – who had very limited experience in campaign planning – to help plan the largest ground operation in military history probably indicates something about Halder's unenthusiastic attitude toward the mission.

---

*As a frame of reference, I have drafted intelligence estimates for division-level peacekeeping operations which required far more time and effort than one week. The time allotted by Halder for initial staff estimates was grossly inadequate.

The key question in the planning process was to identify valid operational objectives and the lines of operation (LOO) necessary to reach them. Hitler held a 90-minute planning conference at the Berghof on July 31, 1940 (with Keitel, Jodl, von Brauchitsch and Halder present) and provided some basic guidance: he stated his overall intent was to quickly destroy the Red Army, remove any threat of air attack upon Germany or Romania, and then acquire economic resources in the Ukraine. He specified advances to seize Kiev, the Baltic States and Moscow (in that order) and set spring 1941 as the start time.[28] Hitler's off-the-cuff guidance was made without any reference to OKH/OKW estimates, which he had not yet seen. The OKH had already identified the Pripet Marshes region as a 'no-go' area for large-scale mechanized operations, which imposed major operational constraints since it effectively bifurcated the Eastern Front into a northern sector and a southern sector. Operations in the southern sector would require greater cooperation with Romania, which Halder found unappealing (the OKH was averse to sharing planning details with allies), and the distances involved were much greater. On August 1, after just three days of effort, Marcks presented his estimate (known as *Operationsentwurf Ost* or Operational Draft East) to Halder. Marcks' concept envisioned a main drive by a reinforced army group in the center to seize Moscow, while a secondary effort by a second army group was made in the south to take Kiev. Based upon Kinzel's flawed estimate of enemy strength, Marcks seemed to think that 50 German divisions could simply bash their way across 1,000 kilometers of hostile territory to seize the Soviet capital, and then the Red Army would duly collapse. He estimated that the entire operation would require up to four months to complete. According to Marcks, only a minor flank guard operation would be made in the Baltic States. The so-called Marcks Plan was a hastily assembled piece of garbage staff work, with minimal input from the OKH intelligence or logistic estimates, which meant that it ignored terrain, weather and the enemy. Nevertheless, Halder decided to accept it on August 5 since it aligned with his operational preferences and he apparently regarded it as a malleable framework that he could bend into his desired shape. Yet after this brief frenzy of planning activity, the OKH virtually shelved planning on Russia and instead focused on *Seelöwe*, Gibraltar and the possibility of sending an expeditionary force to help the Italians in Libya.

Again and again, the lack of hard information about the Red Army came back to haunt the planning process. An estimate from July 18, 1940 assessed that the Red Army had 84 divisions and 20 tank brigades in the border regions and another 14 divisions in reserve – this estimate was about 30 percent below the actual Soviet strength on the border and significantly underestimated Soviet reserves.[29] Despite their prowess in drawing arrows on maps, the OKH was never known for the quality of its intelligence products. It was only after the initial staff estimates had been produced that anyone thought to increase intelligence collection against the Soviet Union, which required authorization by Hitler. On September 21, Hitler authorized Sonderkommando Rowehl to begin clandestine high-altitude photo reconnaissance over the Soviet Union.[30] While Rowehl's missions helped to identify many forward Soviet airfields and some field fortifications, they did little to help the army planners. Instead, the OKH turned to signals intelligence (SIGINT) and increased the number of radio collection units in the East, but this only brought in tactical information. In particular, the skimpy German intelligence collection effort missed the fact that the Red Army had re-formed its mechanized corps. Nor was the German military attaché in Moscow, General Ernst Köstring, much help because the Soviets had excluded him from summer maneuvers since 1938. Furthermore, Köstring had a negative view of the Red Army and downplayed its capabilities in official reports.[31] Consequently, German planning for the invasion of the Soviet Union was conducted in a virtual intelligence vacuum and heavily influenced by subjective opinions about the Red Army's poor showing against Finland. Even maps and reliable terrain information about the western Soviet Union proved grossly inadequate.

On September 19, Oberstleutnant von Loßberg completed the OKW's operational estimate (*Operationsstudie Ost*, Operational Study East). Unlike the hastily assembled OKH estimates, the OKW had taken six weeks and assembled more data, including consulting General Köstring. Köstring bluntly told the OKW that the capture of Moscow would not cause a Soviet collapse, but this was not included in the estimate. Von Loßberg's estimate, dubbed "Fritz," envisioned three army groups advancing to seize Leningrad, Moscow and Kiev. One key discriminator between the OKH planning and the OKW planning was that von Loßberg's estimate addressed the role of seapower in the campaign. Von Loßberg assessed that the rapid capture of Baltic ports and the use of the Kriegsmarine to provide supply by sea could supplement the limited rail network in the Soviet Union and facilitate the drive upon Leningrad. However, this point was moot, since the Kriegsmarine was not brought into the initial planning process – a clear demonstration of the Third Reich's inability to conduct joint operations.

Once it was clear that *Seelöwe* had been postponed, Halder directed his deputy, Generalleutnant Friedrich Paulus, to add more details into the Marcks Plan, particularly in terms of logistics. Thanks to recent intelligence collection, the plan now assumed that the Red Army could deploy about 116 divisions in the western USSR, but the Wehrmacht would be able to match this with about 105 divisions – so rough numerical parity became a key assumption. Three army groups would be employed (Nord, Mitte, Süd), each with at least one Panzer group to be employed as its spearhead force. The plan still rested on three core assumptions: (1) that all objectives could be accomplished in just 3–4 months, (2) terrain and weather would have no major impact on the conduct of the campaign and (3) the Red Army's best forces would be destroyed in the first six weeks. Based upon Paulus' logistic estimates, the OKH concluded that it needed to assemble enough fuel to support an advance of 640 kilometers by three army groups, even though all the primary objectives were beyond that range. Furthermore, Halder inserted into the plan that the advance would continue to a line running from Archangel to Astrakhan (the so-called "A-A Line"), a distance of more than 1,500 kilometers from the original starting positions. The draft plan was dubbed "Otto."

Paulus organized three wargames to validate the updated plan. The first two wargames were conducted on November 29 and December 3 and concluded that German forces would easily win the border battles and reach the line Kiev-Smolensk-Lake Peipus within about six weeks. Satisfied with his adjustments and prospects for rapid success, Halder briefed plan "Otto" to Hitler on December 5 at the Führer conference. Hitler was far from satisfied with the OKH plan and he had already read the OKW estimate. He stated that Moscow was "of no great importance" and wanted the main effort made in the south, not the north.[32] Hitler was also a bit more sanguine about the Red Army's powers of resistance than the OKH and was concerned that it would make an all-out effort to defend Leningrad and Moscow. He rejected the idea of narrow advances and preferred a broad front advance that limited the risk of enemy counterattacks on vulnerable flanks (he had the same concern during *Fall Gelb* in May 1940). Consequently, Hitler wanted options built into the plan whereby Heeresgruppe Mitte could pivot and use its Panzer groups to support the advance of either Heeresgruppe Nord or Heeresgruppe Süd if they encountered heavy resistance. Despite the constant criticism of Hitler's interference in the planning from former OKH officers and later historians, the creation of options in campaign planning is a sound concept and affords some flexibility to dealing with unexpected events.

Two days after the Führer conference, Paulus conducted his third wargame, which covered the exploitation phase with the advance to the A-A Line. Unlike the previous two map exercises, this one indicated that the German supply situation would become more precarious, the deeper their forces advanced into the Soviet Union. Halder did not inform Hitler about these negative conclusions. Instead, Halder combined some elements of Loßberg's Plan "Fritz" with "Otto," along with options to protect the flanks of Heeresgruppe Mitte. At this point, Hitler stated that his preference was not to move against Moscow until Leningrad had fallen and Heeresgruppe Nord could release forces to augment Heeresgruppe Mitte. After these additional refinements, Hitler accepted the hybrid OKH/OKW plan on December 16, 1940 and two days later it was designated as Operation *Barbarossa* in Führer Directive 21. In his strategic intent, Hitler stated that "the bulk of the Russian Army in western Russia will be destroyed by daring operations led by deeply penetrating armored spearheads." As planned, Operation *Barbarossa* consisted of three distinct phases: (1) the initial border battles to annihilate the bulk of Soviet forces, (2) the advance to seize intermediate objectives such as Smolensk and the elimination of Soviet reserves and (3) the exploitation phase, which included capture of the primary territorial objectives and final mop-up operations to the A-A Line.

After the release of Führer Directive 21, the planning process for Operation *Barbarossa* gathered speed, but focused primarily on redeploying forces from Western Europe to Eastern Europe without alerting the Soviets. On January 15, 1941, Kinzel's Foreign Armies East (Fremde Heere Ost, FHO) published a 72-page intelligence summary of the Red Army, entitled "The War Forces of the Soviet Socialist Republics," which provided plenty of erroneous information and little insight. Later, just three weeks before the invasion began, FHO published a report about Soviet tanks, which disclosed the existence of a new heavy tank mistakenly identified as the T-35C. In fact, the Finns had provided some information about the KV-1 heavy tank they encountered, but Kinzel's report falsely stated that existing German antitank weapons could defeat the new tank.[33] The Luftwaffe also seriously underestimated the number and capabilities of the Soviet VVS. The three German army groups began conducting operational-level wargames in March 1941 to examine various courses of action and refine their schemes of maneuver. As a result of adjustments made by army group staffs, planning began to diverge significantly from the original concept in the OKH-produced plans.[34]

The OKH began transferring divisions to East Prussia and Poland in September 1940, but initially only a few at a time. In particular, the Panzer divisions were afforded extra time to rest and refit in Germany before shifting eastward. The transfer of forces to the east accelerated in early 1941 and the bulk of the divisions arrived in the last eight weeks prior to hostilities. Operation *Barbarossa* assigned the following forces and operational objectives:

- Heeresgruppe Nord (GFM von Leeb): comprised of 26 divisions (23 infantry, three Panzer) with 16. Armee, 18. Armee, Panzergruppe 4, supported by Luftflotte 1 (609 aircraft). Total 712,000 troops and 635 tanks. Objective Leningrad (800km from start line).
- Heeresgruppe Mitte (GFM von Bock): comprised of 47 divisions (37 infantry, one cavalry, nine Panzer) with 4. Armee, 9. Armee, Panzergruppe 2, Panzergruppe 3, supported by Luftflotte 2 (1,470 aircraft). Total 1.3 million troops and 2,230 tanks. Objective Moscow (1,000km from start line).
- Heeresgruppe Süd (GFM von Rundstedt): comprised of 40 divisions (35 infantry, five Panzer) with 6. Armee, 11. Armee, Panzergruppe 1, supported by Luftflotte 4 (1,020 aircraft). Total 1 million troops and 822 tanks. Axis allies: Romanian 3rd and 4th Armies (comprised of 14 divisions). Objective Kiev and the Donbas (1,200km from start line).
- OKH Reserves comprised of 2. Armee headquarters and 24 divisions (incl. two Panzer divisions). Total of 408,000 troops.

Thus, ten German army-size formations with a total of 137 divisions (excluding security units and the Finnish front) were initially committed to the invasion of the western Soviet Union. The initial invasion force comprised 3.2 million German troops, 3,100 tanks, 24,435 artillery pieces, 588,000 vehicles and 600,000 horses. Aside from some third-rate divisions left to garrison Western Europe, the only appreciable strategic reserves were about 20 divisions committed to the Yugoslav campaign, which would not be available until later. The German main effort would be made in the center, with more than half the available armor, even though Hitler had stated that Moscow was not the main objective.

Between December 17 and 20, the OKH conducted a four-day wargame of Operation *Barbarossa*, which focused on logistic issues; the exercise identified further problems and concluded that the forces assigned were "barely sufficient" to achieve their primary objectives and that the logistic system would crash after advancing east of the Dnepr River. The OKH quartermaster staff planned that each Heeresgruppe would receive 24 trains per day, carrying roughly 32,000 tons of supplies (ammunition, fuel, fodder and rations), but this turned out to be a very low estimate.[35] As a possible solution, Paulus suggested an operational pause for up to one month after reaching Smolensk, but this went against Hitler's intent not to give the Red Army a chance to regroup. Thus, Halder and the OKH recognized that the *Barbarossa* plan was a conundrum with no simple solutions and that failure was a distinct possibility. Essentially, in *Barbarossa*, the Wehrmacht was trying to accomplish too much with too few resources, but no one in the OKH or OKW possessed the moral courage to tell that to Hitler. Instead, in the proud tradition of the Großer Generalstab, the OKH/OKW staffs hoped that a string of tactical victories – combined with some luck – would precipitate a Soviet collapse before *Barbarossa* culminated with the German spearheads running out of fuel, ammunition and manpower.

CHAPTER 2

C3 and Intelligence Capabilities

Two critical functions that were required for army/front-level commanders and their staffs to conduct operational warfare were command, control and communications (C3) and intelligence collection/analysis (ergo C3I). If commanders could not communicate with their subordinate formations, they could not direct them toward a common objective. In order to make sound decisions, commanders also required accurate and up-to-date intelligence about the terrain and enemy forces in their area of operations. Both the Wehrmacht and the Red Army inherited methods from their predecessor organizations about C3I, as well as from other foreign pre-war sources. Overall, the Germans tended to have an edge in military communications technology throughout the war, since Soviet Five-Year Plans had emphasized the heavy armaments industry (tanks, artillery, aircraft) over the electronics sector. Indeed, the Red Army was habitually short of radios throughout much of the war. In terms of operational-level intelligence, the Germans also tended to have some advantages, but this did not prevent them from suffering numerous operational failures, such as Stalingrad, due to inadequate intelligence.

German and Soviet C3

The Wehrmacht used a wide variety of communications equipment throughout the Second World War and these systems served as a key enabler for its mobile warfare doctrine. By the start of *Barbarossa*, the Wehrmacht had perfected its C3 in two prior major campaigns and was well-practiced in the art of orchestrating a fast-moving operation via radio. At the tactical level (division and below), all German ground units possessed the means to communicate by radio (using voice or morse) with higher headquarters and units on their flanks. When defending in static positions, the Ostheer tended to rely more on wire communications at the tactical level. At the operational level, each army group had a signals regiment which it used to establish long-range radio networks and each army had at least one signal battalion in a similar role. The effective command radius of army/army group level C3 was about 500 kilometers with voice communications and double that with morse. The Wehrmacht relied heavily upon the Enigma enciphering system to protect its long-range communications. Although the Western Allies succeeded in breaking into some of the German Enigma ciphers in 1941, little of the information was relevant to the Eastern Front and the British did not begin passing any intelligence gleaned from this source to the Soviets until mid-1943. One problem area in German C3 was communication between Luftwaffe and army commands, which was not perfected until mid-1942. Yet on the whole, German operational C3 capabilities on the Eastern Front were efficient and fairly secure against Soviet collection efforts.

The Red Army of 1941 was haunted by the memory that the Tsarist Imperial Army was badly defeated in the Tannenberg campaign in 1914, in part due to German intercept of Russian radio messages sent in the clear. Unfortunately, this collective negative experience, combined with the ingrained paranoia about espionage in the Stalinist regime, led to an aversion in the pre-war Red Army to using radios. Armies and military districts had long-range radios (although not enough) but they tended to be under-utilized in pre-war wargames. Instead, the Red Army preferred secure telephone systems and wire communications, although these quickly proved impractical when the German invasion began overrunning one position after another. Consequently, the Red Army of 1941–42 lacked sufficient tactical radios below division level, which made coordination of army and front-level operations that much more difficult. Indeed, only the artillery branch had adequate C3 in the first phase of the war. Given the primitive state of Soviet C3 in 1941–42, the

Red Army's operations had to be highly scripted and could not easily be altered due to suddenly changing battlefield conditions. By 1943–44 the Red Army did acquire more radios (particularly from Allied Lend Lease) and its leaders were more willing to employ radio communications to direct fast-moving operations.

Under the direction of the 8th Directorate of the General Staff (GSHKA), Soviet industry developed several communication encryption systems in the late 1930s, such as the M-1939 "Spectrum," K-37 and M-100. These systems (often referred to generically as "BODO" devices) were capable of sending text-based encrypted messages from the Stavka to front and army level headquarters. The encryption systems were typically used to transmit orders, plans and directives, but were not geared for use in dynamic battlefield environments. So far, there is no indication that the German signals intercept units succeeded in breaking into Soviet enciphered communications networks.

German and Soviet Operational Intelligence Capabilities

In the military intelligence field, collection and analysis is conducted at three levels: strategic (or national level), operational (at army group/front or army level) and tactical (corps and below). Tactical intelligence tends to focus on what the enemy is doing today, against one's own forces in contact, whereas operational intelligence is intended to look at what the enemy intends to do next week or beyond. For operational-level intelligence, the Ostheer relied primarily upon aerial imagery intelligence (IMINT), signals intelligence or communications intercepts (SIGINT/COMINT), prisoner interrogations and captured document exploitation (DOCEX).

The Luftwaffe assigned one long-range reconnaissance squadron (*Fernaufklärungs staffeln*) with seven to nine aircraft to each army group and some field armies. Each army also had short-range reconnaissance squadrons for tactical intelligence collection. In 1941, the primary Luftwaffe long-range reconnaissance aircraft was the Ju-88D, which could conduct IMINT-collection sorties up to several hundred kilometers beyond the forward line of troops (FLOT). The Ju-88D was equipped with two or three Zeiss-made framing cameras (typically either the Rb 75/30 camera or Rb 50/30 camera for high-altitude photography and the Rb 20/30 camera for low-altitude work) and was capable of collecting useful imagery from altitudes up to 27,000 feet.[1] In June 1941, the Luftwaffe had 14 long-range reconnaissance squadrons with 118 aircraft deployed in the East, but losses were heavy during *Barbarossa* and by mid-1942 there were only seven squadrons with 70 aircraft left in the East. The Luftwaffe introduced new reconnaissance aircraft in 1943, including the Do-215B, Ju-188F, as well as converting some Bf-109 and Fw-190 fighters into high-speed reconnaissance platforms. Throughout 1943–44, the Luftwaffe generally had 80–100 long-range reconnaissance aircraft in the East. Luftwaffe aerial imagery collection was best suited for fixed targets, such as airfields, bridges and railyards or trench systems, but it was not well suited to finding Soviet artillery or tank units. Consequently, IMINT was of limited value in answering key questions such as where are the enemy armored reserves located or has the enemy redeployed his army-level artillery units to a new sector?

The Ostheer relied heavily upon SIGINT for operational intelligence. At the start of *Barbarossa*, each German army group had a fixed intercept group (usually located near the headquarters) and mobile intercept companies assigned to each army. In 1941–42, the majority of Soviet tactical radio traffic was not sent using cipher codes and even when it was employed, the German signal troops were able to break the simple ciphers in about one-third of the intercepted messages. Soviet units could be amazingly indiscreet in their radio messages, which enabled German intercept units to identify units and the radio frequencies in use.[2] Even when the Germans could not read intercepted messages, traffic analysis could hint at enemy intentions (e.g. increased message traffic on a given network could indicate an impending offensive). However, the Red Army gradually began to improve its communications procedures in 1943–44, which reduced the amount of intelligence that the German signals units could collect with COMINT.[3] Nevertheless, Erhard Raus, commander of the 4. Panzerarmee, stated that even in 1944, "radio interception provided as much as 70 percent of our best intelligence."[4]

Finally, the Germans proved particularly adept at prisoner of war (POW) interrogations and exploitation of captured documents, such as maps and orders. During 1941–42, the Ostheer captured numerous high and medium-ranking Soviet officers and masses of documents, which were analyzed and used to build fairly accurate assessments of the enemy order of battle. German interrogators were skilled at extracting all sorts of useful qualitative information from prisoners, such as the state of front-line morale or the quality of leadership in a given unit. In addition to prisoners, the Ostheer received large numbers of defectors on a daily basis (typically Ukrainians, Tatars or Kazakhs with no love for the Soviet system) and these men willingly offered up valuable information about their units. Overall, the Ostheer was able to collect useful information about enemy front-line strength and dispositions and some information about enemy intentions. However, the quality of operational intelligence produced by the Ostheer was generally inadequate and could not answer priority intelligence requirements, such as the location of enemy armored reserves. Too much German intelligence was tactical in nature, which gave army commanders an incomplete and often distorted impression of future enemy actions.

Most of the Red Army's intelligence expertise was centralized in the Main Intelligence Directorate (GRU) in Moscow, leaving few trained personnel for the field armies. The intelligence functions conducted at front and army level were relatively primitive in the first half of the war and tended to focus almost exclusively on tactical matters. Unlike the Wehrmacht, the Red Army in the field had limited means to collect operational-level intelligence until late in the war. The VVS had a number of long-range reconnaissance aviation regiments (DRAP), which were equipped with SB and DB-3 light bombers at the start of the war; these aircraft did not prove survivable over the front line. Soon thereafter, the VVS began updating its DRAP units with Pe-2 and Pe-3 high speed reconnaissance bombers, which were equipped with one or two AFA-I cameras. Soviet long-range aerial reconnaissance was directed to identify enemy troop concentrations, road/rail traffic and activity at forward airfields. Even when sorties succeeded in bringing back imagery on such targets, they rarely provided much insight into enemy intentions. During Operation *Uranus* in 1942, the lead Soviet tank units had to ask local peasants about the location of the German bridge in Kalach, since no army-level intelligence on this key objective was available. In the final year of the war, the VVS's long-range reconnaissance capabilities did improve and in April 1944, a Tu-2 bomber from the 2nd DRAP flew over 1,200km from Smolensk to take imagery over Berlin. Nor was Soviet SIGINT/COMINT of much value in determining enemy intentions. Between Enigma and better German communications security methods, Soviet intercept units were not able to do much more than traffic analysis.

Soviet efforts to extract useful information from enemy prisoners and captured documents was of minimal value prior to January 1943 because there were few enemy prisoners before the surrender at Stalingrad (by the end of 1941, the NKVD only held 9,000 enemy POWs). Furthermore, when the war was going poorly, Axis prisoners were often shot immediately after capture, without regard to interrogation; this is apparently what happened during the Reichel incident on June 19, 1942. The Reichel incident also demonstrated the limitations of Soviet document exploitation – Stalin did not believe that the captured notes related to Case *Blau* were genuine. After Stalingrad, the Red Army captured 22 generals as well as thousands of other officers, but the NKVD took charge of the prisoners and the GRU had minimal access to them. The primary objective of the NKVD was political indoctrination of the captured German officers, not extraction of useful military information. In sum, the Red Army's ability to collect, analyze and produce operational intelligence was rather limited throughout most of the war, which often forced Soviet front/army commanders to make imprudent decisions.

CHAPTER 3

Barbarossa: 1941 Operations

"You can't believe everything in intelligence reports."
Stalin, June 14, 1941[1]

Northern Axis, June 22–September 20, 1941

By mid-June 1941, the Germans could no longer fully conceal their attack preparations from Soviet troops stationed near the border. As a result, some commanders who were aware of these ominous developments grew concerned about the lack of guidance from Moscow. Standing orders to avoid provocations – including responding to Luftwaffe reconnaissance overflights – had not been modified. One of the most exposed sectors was the Baltic Military District (PribOVO), commanded by General-polkovnik Fedor I. Kuznetsov, who was responsible for defending the relatively flat Lithuanian countryside. Due to the German occupation of Memel in 1939, Kuznetsov's forces would be essentially outflanked from the start of any conflict. Aside from scattered forests and marshes, the only real natural obstacle of any defensive value was the Dvina River, located further back in Latvia. Unlike other border regions, the PribOVO also had to contend with an occupied local population that was likely to welcome any German invaders as liberators. Kuznetsov was tasked with conducting a "stubborn defense" along the state border, repelling any enemy offensive and ensuring the unhindered mobilization of the district's reserves.

Kuznetsov had two armies to defend the border region: General-major Petr P. Sobennikov's 8th Army and General-leytenant Vasily I. Morozov's 11th Army. Further back, in second echelon, the 5th Airborne Corps was stationed near Daugavpils and General Major Nikolai E. Berzarin's 27th Army was in the vicinity of Lake Peipus/Pskov. Berzarin was focused on coastal defense against potential enemy amphibious attacks around Riga, not support of the two first echelon armies. Although the PribOVO had 325,000 troops on paper, the first echelon rifle divisions along the East Prussian border were at about 60 percent of authorized strength and were required to defend excessively long frontages, between 30 and 80 kilometers in width.[2] By doctrine, a full-strength Soviet rifle division was capable of properly defending a 9km-wide sector, with all three rifle regiments on line. Yet stretched to 30 kilometers or more, an understrength rifle division became little more than a tripwire. The two mechanized corps under Kuznetsov's control had over 1,300 tanks, including about 100 of the new T-34 and KV-1 tanks, but their readiness levels were very low due to inadequate training and limited availability of ammunition and fuel. Here, the danger of the Soviet fetish about operational depth – at least when haphazardly applied to the defense – should be evident. It made little sense to place one-third of the PribOVO's rifle divisions in second echelon, when the first echelon could not even meet basic doctrinal norms. In terms of air support, General-major Aleksei P. Ionov had a total of 1,211 combat aircraft in the region.

Kuznetsov could not expect much immediate help from outside the PribOVO. The Leningrad Military District had the 23rd Army and two mechanized corps over 600 kilometers distant, but they would initially be needed to defend the city until Finnish intentions were clear. The Stavka had a single mechanized corps deployed as an operational reserve for the PribOVO, about 380 kilometers from the border. However, the condition of the 21st Mechanized Corps demonstrates the Potemkin Village-nature of Soviet pre-war measures; on June 22, 1941 the corps had just 42 BT-7 tanks and very few trucks, and most of its troops were untrained reservists.[3]

Both Kuznetsov and Sobennikov had been instructors at the Frunze Academy during the purges and managed to avoid arrest. Likewise, General-leytenant Pyotr S. Klenov (PribOVO chief of staff) had been an instructor at the Frunze and General-major Ivan T. Shlemin, chief of staff of the 11th Army, had been the head of the Academy of the General

Staff between 1937 and 1940. Despite the damage inflicted by Stalin's purges, there were still some talented officers left in the Red Army who possessed the requisite knowledge to conduct operational level warfare. Recognizing the imminent threat to the PribOVO, Kuznetsov on his own authority decided to move the 12th Mechanized Corps forward from its bases near Riga to Siaulia on June 19/20, where it could serve as a mobile reserve for the vulnerable right wing of Sobennikov's 8th Army. He also directed units deployed along the border to begin emplacing defensive minefields and preparing bridges for demolition. However, when word of these unauthorized measures reached Moscow, Zhukov angrily ordered Kuznetsov to rescind the movements and accused him of cowardice. In a rare display of moral courage in Stalin's Russia, Kuznetsov ignored Zhukov and ordered Klenov to set up a tactical command post in the woods south of Daugavpils. Unfortunately, Kuznetsov and his subordinates were set up for failure by the leadership in Moscow. It was not until late on the evening of June 21 that Timoshenko and Zhukov belatedly convinced Stalin to authorize some kind of war warning from Moscow, which went out just after midnight as NKO Directive No. 1. The last-minute directive warned that "a surprise attack was possible" and that all frontier units should be brought to "full combat readiness" – but still cautioned against causing provocations. Military district commanders began receiving NKO Directive No. 1 around 0130 hours on June 22, less than two hours before Operation *Barbarossa* was to commence, but few army commanders were aware of it prior to hostilities.[4]

On the opposite side of the border, in East Prussia and the Memel enclave, Generalfeldmarschall Wilhem Ritter von Leeb's Heeresgruppe Nord was already in its attack positions. Generaloberst Erich Höpner's Panzergruppe 4, with the XLI (Georg-Hans Reinhardt) and LVI (Erich von Manstein) motorized corps, was the main strike force and it was tasked with seizing Leningrad – a distance of about 780 kilometers from its starting position. Höpner had 590 tanks in his three Panzer divisions (1, 6, 8), led by veteran commanders. Generaloberst Georg Wilhelm von Küchler's 18. Armee (AOK 18) was tasked with clearing out the Baltic States and following in the wake of Höpner's Panzers. Generaloberst Ernst Busch's 16. Armee (AOK 16) was assigned to secure the right flank of Heeresgruppe Nord and to maintain contact with Heeresgruppe Mitte's advance to the south. Von Leeb had three infantry divisions in reserve and OKH had earmarked additional reinforcements once the campaign started. Altogether, von Leeb had 712,000 troops in his command, which was the smallest army group participating in Operation *Barbarossa*.

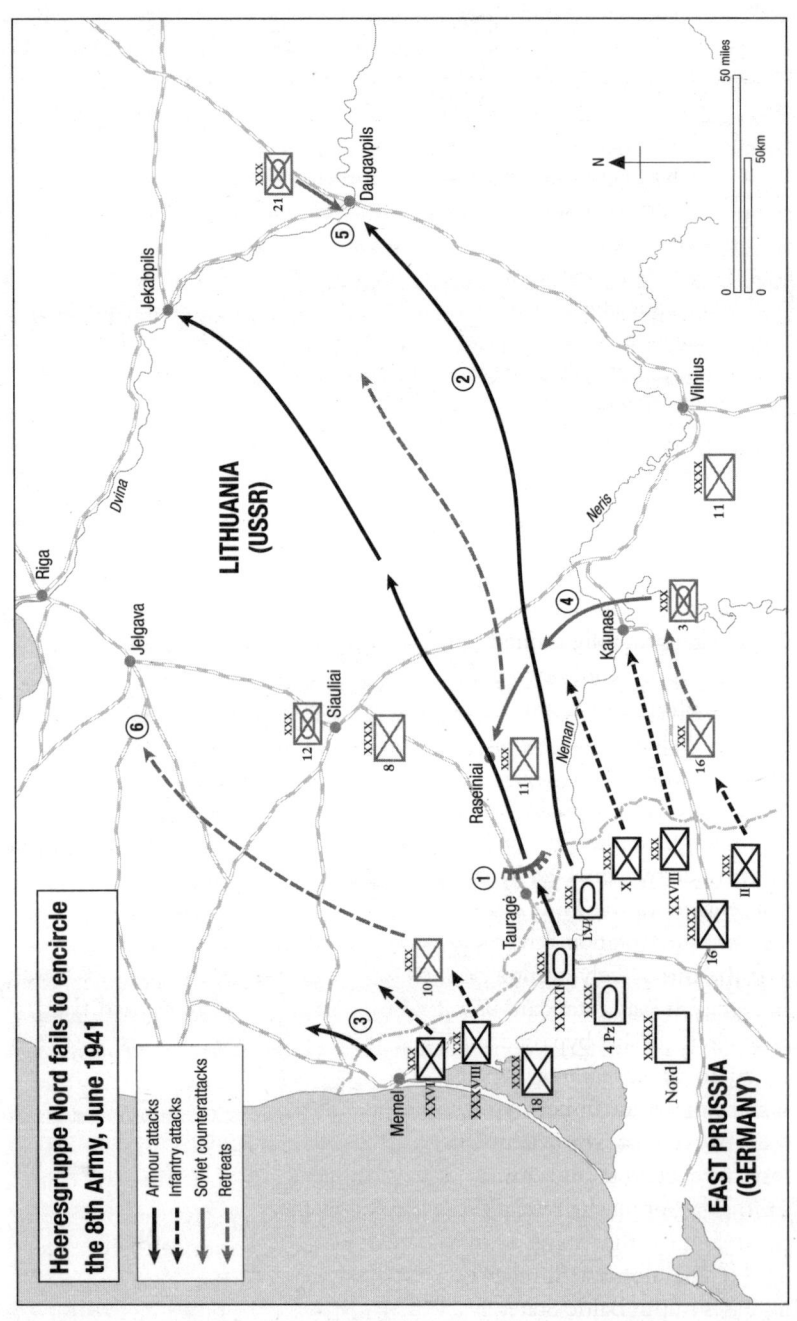

Heeresgruppe Nord fails to encircle
the 8th Army, June 1941

Armour attacks
Infantry attacks
Soviet counterattacks
Retreats

MAP KEY

1. The XXXXI Armeekorps (mot.) wastes a day fighting through the Soviet fortified town of Tauragė.
2. The LVI Armeekorps (mot.) bypasses Soviet resistance and races forward over 300 kilometers to seize the bridges at Daugavpils.
3. The German infantry from 18. Armee advances slowly, failing to encircle any large elements of the Soviet 8th Army.
4. The Soviet 8th Army attempts to use the 3rd and 12th Mechanized Corps to conduct a pincer attack against the XXXXI Armeekorps (mot.) but only manages a piecemeal effort at Raseiniai.
5. The Soviet 21st Mechanized Corps counterattacks but fails to eliminate the German bridgehead at Daugavpils.
6. The Soviet Northwest Front succeeds in withdrawing a large portion of its personnel back to the Stalin Line.

Yet unlike the Red Army units in the PribOVO, von Leeb's units were close to full strength, fully trained and well-stocked with fuel and ammunition. Heeresgruppe Nord's two primary supply bases in Tilsit and Gumbinnen had 27,800 tons of ammunition and 29,485 tons of fuel – a lavish amount by later Wehrmacht standards.[5] Von Leeb's army group was like a coiled spring, concentrated and ready to strike.

At 0305 hours on June 22, Operation *Barbarossa* began with a brief artillery preparation in the pre-dawn darkness, followed by a surge across the border by von Leeb's assault divisions. Von Leeb initially placed his *Schwerpunkt* in the Tilsit sector, with Reinhardt's XLI Armeekorps (mot.) crossing the Niemen River and then pushing on to Tauragė, but this was also the most likely avenue of approach and Kuznetsov had fortified the small city. It was a standard part of German maneuver doctrine that urban areas were to be bypassed and reduced by follow-on forces, as clearly stated in *Truppenführung*.[6] Nevertheless, Höpner committed nearly half his armor to an unnecessary day-long fight for a well-defended urban area. In contrast, von Manstein's LVI Armeekorps (mot.) bypassed Soviet resistance centers and advanced 70 kilometers on the first day of the campaign. Along the rest of the front, the 16. Armee and 18. Armee easily overwhelmed the Soviet border units and began advancing at a marching pace. Generaloberst Alfred Keller's Luftflotte 1 struck most of the Soviet air bases in the Baltic States and inflicted very heavy damage upon Ionov's

VVS formations deployed in this region. By June 30, the VVS units in this region had lost 1,077 aircraft destroyed or damaged, or roughly 94 percent of their starting strength. Nevertheless, VVS reinforcements were quickly rushed to the Baltic sector, partly redressing the balance.[7] The Luftwaffe was less successful in limiting the operations of the Red Banner Baltic Fleet, which was able to continue supporting Red Army formations in the Baltic States until late August.

Once hostilities commenced, the PribOVO was redesignated as the Northwest Front (*Severo-Zapadnyy front*). Kuznetsov's priority decision was where and how to commit his mechanized reserves to block the German advance. He correctly identified Höpner's Panzergruppe 4 as the enemy main effort and intended to use the 3rd and 12th Mechanized Corps to launch pincer attacks against it from the east and the west. However, coordinating two dispersed mechanized corps proved extremely difficult in the face of intense Luftwaffe bombing raids and the front's limited communications capabilities. As a result, Kuznetsov's mobile reserves were committed in piecemeal fashion. Nevertheless, the counterattack by part of the 3rd Mechanized Corps at Raseinini on June 24 caught Reinhardt's corps by surprise and inflicted further delay on Höpner's main body. The appearance of two battalions of KV heavy tanks that defied the capabilities of the standard German 5cm Pak 38 antitank gun came as a great technical shock to Reinhardt's troops. Although Kuznetsov quickly realized that he lacked the strength to hold Lithuania against Heeresgruppe Nord, he hoped to fall back behind the Dvina and use Berzarin's 27th Army to create a steadier line until reinforcements arrived. In fact, the 27th Army did not begin moving forward to the Dvina until June 25 and had not yet established a defensive line when the Germans appeared. Kuznetsov's hopes to stabilize a line on the Dvina were dashed when von Manstein boldly advanced to seize the bridges at Daugavpils on June 26; the LVI Armeekorps (mot.) had advanced 315 kilometers in four days. However, von Manstein's rapid advance consumed all his on-hand fuel, leaving his corps temporarily immobilized. By this point, the Stavka had released the poorly-equipped 21st Mechanized Corps to Kuznetsov, who promptly directed it to attack von Manstein's bridgehead at Daugavpils on June 28. Despite a desperate effort, this counterattack failed to eliminate the German bridgehead and the next day, Reinhardt's XLI Armeekorps (mot.) finally crossed the Dvina at Jekabpils. On the same day, Kuznetsov ordered his troops to fall back to the Stalin Line fortifications around Pskov-Ostrov. Enraged by the rapid loss of Lithuania and the retreat of the Northwest Front, Stalin ordered Kuznetsov and his chief of staff

Klenov relieved of command. Kuznetsov managed to survive, but Klenov, a member of the General Staff, was executed by the NKVD. Sobennikov took over command of the Northwest Front. Ionov, commander of the VVS-Northwest Front, was also arrested and later executed.

The left flank of Kuznetsov's Northwest Front, comprised of Morozov's 11th Army, was quickly defeated by Generaloberst Hermann Hoth's Panzergruppe 3 (from Heeresgruppe Mitte), which succeeded in securing intact bridges over the Nieman River on the first day of Operation *Barbarossa*. During the Battle of Alytus, Hoth's Panzers encountered the new Soviet T-34 medium tank for the first time. Nevertheless, Morozov's army could not stem the German advance. After evacuating both Kaunas and Vilnius on June 24, Morozov's 11th Army retreated eastward into northern Belarus. Given the paranoid nature of the NKVD (which claimed that any setback was the result of conspiracy), the Stavka ordered Kuznetsov to cease communications with Morozov's headquarters – which was not a wise decision in the face of a massive enemy invasion. Consequently, Morozov retreated east to Polotsk, away from the Leningrad axis, before finally being ordered by Sobennikov on July 9 to concentrate his forces near Pskov. Part of the pre-war Stalin Line fortifications were located near Pskov and Sobennikov hoped that these could be used to increase the defensive combat power of Morozov's troops.

On the surface, German Heeresegruppe Nord operations in phase one of Operation *Barbarossa* seemed like an unqualified operational success, because von Leeb was able to seize Lithuania and most of Latvia in ten days and was in a good position to continue toward his ultimate objective. Von Leeb adhered to the principles of mass, offensive and maneuver, which enabled his army group to use its superior combat power to overwhelm a poorly-prepared foe – but it proved to be an ordinary victory, not a decisive one. Hitler's stated intent was for the Wehrmacht to destroy the bulk of the Soviet forces in the border districts, but Leeb and Höpner were far more focused on seizing terrain, particularly bridges over the Dvina. Despite being right on the border, elements of all four rifle divisions (10, 48, 90, 125) from Sobennikov's 8th Army managed to escape and the only one of Kuznetsov's major units that was destroyed was the 2nd Tank Division. German records indicate that Heeresgruppe Nord captured only 6,200 prisoners by the end of June, which was a remarkably small number.[8] Consequently, about 80 percent of Kuznetsov's troops escaped, albeit after losing much of their equipment. Overall, Höpner's performance was sub-par and his Panzer group failed to encircle or destroy any significant portion of Sobennikov's 8th Army. While Küchler's 18. Armee easily rolled over the vulnerable 10th Rifle Corps, Höpner wasted time attacking into a fortified city. He also failed to coordinate Reinhardt's and von Manstein's corps to conduct a double pincer attack to encircle the 8th Army and allowed his two corps to become separated. Höpner was also caught by surprise by the sharpness of the Soviet counterattack at Raseinini and failed to coordinate for Luftwaffe close air support when confronted by KV-1 heavy tanks.

For his part, Kuznetsov and his staff did the best they could with their limited resources. Thanks to excellent security measures (amidst a hostile Lithuanian population which was willing to provide information to the German Abwehr), Kuznetov was able to conceal enough about his dispositions to prevent von Leeb from recognizing where the weakest points in the defense were located. If one of Höpner's corps had been deployed against the vulnerable 10th Rifle Corps on the coast, Sobennikov's 8th Army would likely have been quickly enveloped and crushed. Kuznetsov and Klenov also knew when and where to employ their armored reserves, but the Soviet mechanized corps proved too fragile to accomplish their missions. Furthermore, Kuznetsov had the moral courage to order a withdrawal before his front was overrun and destroyed – without permission from the Stavka – so that many of his troops would survive to participate in the defense of Estonia and the Luga Line. Had Kuznetsov simply obeyed orders and conducted a hopeless die-in-place effort to appease Moscow, von Leeb would have encountered far less resistance in the next stage of his advance toward Leningrad.

Commander	Objective	Offensive	Mass	Maneuver	Surprise	Security	Other*	TALLY
Von Leeb	–	+	+	+	+	o	o	3
Höpner	+	+	+	+	–	o	o	3
Kuznetsov	o	+	–	+	o	+	+	3

Northern Axis, Phase 1 Leadership Assessment

As Sobennikov took over the defeated, retreating Northwest Front, the Stavka sent General-leytenant Nikolai F. Vatutin to serve as his chief of staff. The 39-year-old Vatutin was not only the head of the operations directorate in the General Staff (GSHKA), but he was one of the most talented and capable officers remaining in the Red Army. Zhukov had recognized Vatutin's talent, picking him to be his chief of staff in the Kiev

*One extra point added for moral courage in saving his command from annihilation.

Military District in 1938–40, then brought him to Moscow. Sobennikov desperately needed a blocking force to delay Höpner's Panzers, but he had little more than dispersed battlegroups. Berzarin's 27th Army was disorganized and falling back toward Pskov and its infantry could not stop German mechanized units. On the first day of the war, the Stavka had ordered General-leytenant Markian M. Popov's Northern Front (the Leningrad Military District or LVO) to keep the 1st Mechanized Corps at Pskov, but Popov ignored this order and moved the unit 260 kilometers back to Leningrad, in case the Finns attacked. The 38-year-old Popov was one of those officers who had benefited from the purges, being catapulted from an obscure staff officer position to front commander in just three years. Popov did have some talent and initially impressed Stalin in pre-war exercises, but he was also considered a serious drunkard (in an army not known for sobriety) by Vasilevsky and other senior officers.[9] Furious at being disobeyed, Zhukov simply transferred the 1st Mechanized Corps to Sobennikov, who ordered the formation to move back to Ostrov, 50 kilometers south of Pskov, to set up a blocking position. The Soviet operational intent at this point was to delay the German advance into Estonia until Popov's Leningrad Front could create a strong defensive line along the Luga River. The Soviet commanders knew that the Luga offered an excellent natural defense, with thick forests and marshy terrain that inhibited rapid mechanized movement.

On the German side, Höpner took several days to regroup his Panzer group around Daugavpils, which gave Sobennikov a brief but vital respite. Then, on July 2, von Leeb directed Höpner's Panzergruppe 4 to continue its attack on the axis Daugavpils-Pskov-Luga and even authorized him to swing as far east as Lake Ilmen to envelop Soviet forces in Pskov.[10] Von Leeb made several critical operational mistakes here. First, von Leeb simply ignored the heavily wooded and marshy terrain in the Pskov-Luga sector, which did not favor rapid mechanized operations. Indeed, the kind of rough terrain in this sector favored the defender, not the attacker. Keller's Luftflotte 1 had two squadrons of long-range reconnaissance aircraft which were quite capable of surveying terrain conditions along both axes of advance, but apparently this resource was not utilized to support operational decision-making in Heeresgruppe Nord. Höpner apparently followed this ill-judged order without protest. According to von Manstein's not entirely reliable memoirs, he tried to convince Höpner that the terrain was unsuitable for armor, to no avail.[11] Von Leeb was a General Staff-trained officer and should have been able to recognize the unsuitability of this terrain (along with his veteran primary staff officers, Generalleutnant Kurt Brennecke and Oberstleutnant Paul Hermann) but he also proved to be a relatively weak-willed officer. Throughout the campaign, Halder attempted to influence von Leeb with OKH operational preferences, rather than encouraging a single-minded and ruthless drive on Leningrad. Von Leeb's second major error was allowing the operations of Küchler's 18. Armee and Höpner's Panzergruppe 4 to become increasingly divergent, with the slow-moving infantry divisions no longer within supporting range of the Panzers. Instead of working together toward a common objective, the two German armies were essentially fighting separate campaigns for most of July–August; Höpner's Panzers needed more infantry support and Küchler's infantry needed armor support. For his part, Höpner did not use his two motorized corps to accomplish a single mission, but continually assigned them diverging missions. Consequently, neither von Leeb nor Höpner properly employed the principles of maneuver, mass or objective to gain an advantage over the enemy after the initial border fighting.

In phase two of Operation *Barbarossa*, the key operational decision facing Heeresgruppe Nord was where to place its *Schwerpunkt* and there were only two possible answers: either the direct axis from Pskov to Luga or the Narva-Kingisepp sector. Halder and the OKH pressured von Leeb to weight his main effort on his right, through Luga, because they wanted to maintain close contact between Heeresgruppe Nord and Heeresgruppe Mitte.[12] Von Leeb and his staff made another key error in failing to recognize that an advance toward Narva, either on the west side of Lake Peipus or on the eastern side, offered more favorable terrain and would likely catch the Soviet defenders by surprise. Furthermore, an advance through Estonia would enable better logistic support – the Kriegsmarine was already organizing coastal supply convoys into Riga by early July – and the ability to work with von Küchler's 18. Armee in destroying the Soviet 8th Army remnants (now under General-leytenant Fedor S. Ivanov). Instead, Höpner advanced toward Ostrov, 200 kilometers distant, with just Reinhardt's XXXXI Armeekorps (mot.), while von Manstein's LVI Armeekorps (mot.) served as a flank guard. After crossing the Dvina, von Küchler's 18. Armee advanced slowly northward with just five infantry divisions. Ivanov's 8th Army, though consisting of just six depleted rifle divisions in Estonia, was able to hold its own for the moment against von Küchler's sluggish advance. Generalfeldmarschall Walter von Brauchitsch, commander-in-chief of the Heer, visited von Leeb's headquarters on July 7 and concurred with these flawed dispositions.

Sobennikov and Vatutin could see that the German armored vanguard was massing against the Ostrov-Pskov sector, so they tasked Morozov's 11th Army and the 1st Mechanized Corps to conduct a rearguard action along the Velikaya River. Two fortified regions of the pre-war Stalin Line were also in the Ostrov-Pskov sector, although they had been partly stripped of troops and weapons. Popov's Northern Front (*Severnyy front* or SF) had already begun to create a series of fortified positions along the Luga River, to protect the approaches to Leningrad, but this effort would require time. The result was the Battle of Ostrov on July 4–6, a meeting engagement in which the Soviet 1st Mechanized Corps desperately tried to halt Reinhardt's advance – and failed. By July 9, Reinhardt had taken Pskov and secured crossings over the Velikaya River, enabling a direct advance upon Luga. However, at this point, German tactical success at Ostrov-Pskov failed to produce operational-level results due to the unsuitability of the terrain in this sector and Höpner's inability to mass more than a single corps in his *Schwerpunkt*. Thanks to the lack of any deception effort by von Leeb or Höpner, German operational intentions were now fairly obvious, which helped the Soviets to concentrate their limited forces in the most important sectors. Popov, commander of the Northern Front, recognized that creating a 226-kilometer-long defensive line along the Luga River, from the Gulf of Narva to Laken Ilmen, was the key to holding Leningrad. Three days before Reinhardt crossed the Velikaya River, Popov put General-leytenant Konstantin P. Piadyshev in charge of the Luga Operational Group (*Luzhskaya operativnaya gruppa*), which was assigned four rifle divisions and three militia divisions. Initially, Piadyshev placed his steadiest troops near Luga and at Kingisepp, just in case the Germans broke through in Estonia. CPSU officials in Leningrad assembled over 50,000 Russian civilians as forced labor to dig antitank ditches and build bunkers in the Luga Line. Popov also positioned two armored units behind the line to serve as an operational reserve.[13] By the time that Höpner's vanguard reached Luga, the Soviets were just beginning to create a fairly coherent defense along the river. Reinhardt's vanguard managed to seize the town of Luga, located 10 kilometers south of the river, but halted when they encountered an entrenched Soviet rifle division at the river line. Attempts to get around this obstacle proved fruitless due to the lack of off-road mobility imposed by the swampy terrain. In these situations, when firm enemy resistance was encountered, the German tactical preference was usually to conduct a wide flanking maneuver. Reinhardt decided to shift to the northwest along forest tracks; it took the lead elements of his XXXXI Armeekorps (mot.) two days to move roughly 90 kilometers through the rough terrain. However, Piadyshev had yet to garrison the Porech'e-Sabsk sector in strength and Reinhardt was able to seize two small crossings over the Luga River on July 14, just 100 kilometers from Leningrad. In modern military parlance, this is termed the selection of a "sub-optimal" route.

Even before Reinhardt encountered Soviet defenses on the Luga Line, von Leeb and the OKH had been advocating a wide envelopment to the east, using von Manstein's LVI Armeekorps (mot.). Essentially, the OKH was looking for a cheap victory, hoping that von Manstein could not only envelop the enemy defenses on the direct path to Leningrad, but sever enemy supply lines and precipitate a retreat (a Jomini-based solution rather than a Clausewitz one); this was rather high expectations for a formation that possessed a single Panzer division equipped mostly with Czech-made tanks. Von Manstein was ordered to advance eastward toward Lake Ilmen, which split Höpner's command into two non-supporting pieces. The marshy and wooded terrain proved atrocious and von Manstein found himself advancing in division columns along a single road. In Moscow on July 10, GKO Resolution No. 83ss was issued, which created Main Commands of Directions (*Glavnye komandovaniia napravleni*) to coordinate one or more fronts operating along a single strategic axis, including air and naval forces. Stalin sent Marshal Kliment Voroshilov to Leningrad to coordinate Popov's Northern Front and Sobrennikov's Northwest Front.[14] When the Soviets detected von Manstein's attempted flanking maneuver, Voroshilov and Popov decided to mount a counterattack against this isolated German corps. Vatutin, in his role as front chief of staff, was sent to organize the counterattack; he was able to assemble one tank division and four rifle divisions on both sides of von Manstein's advancing columns. On July 15, Vatutin sprung his trap, catching the 8. Panzer-Division by surprise and succeeded in isolating it for two days – the first time that a German Panzer division had been surrounded by enemy action. Another rude shock for the Germans was the appearance of the VVS to provide air support, while the Luftwaffe was occupied elsewhere. Although von Manstein managed to extricate the 8. Panzer-Division, the division was badly mauled and had to be pulled out of line to refit, leaving him without armor support.[15] Vatutin's tactical success temporarily blocked the German wide envelopment of Leningrad and deprived Höpner of the services of one of his two motorized corps. By July 17, it was clear that Höpner's advance was stymied on the Luga Line and that significant numbers of Soviet reinforcements were starting to arrive on the battlefield. Already, the newly-raised Soviet 34th Army had appeared in the Staraya Russa sector and Popov had enough forces to begin creating an inner defensive line to protect Leningrad.

Although some historical sources like to point fingers at Hitler, Halder or von Leeb for halting Höpner from initiating phase three of Operation *Barbarossa* and pushing on to Leningrad, the real reason for the delay was the lack of infantry, logistic support and air support to sustain Heeresgruppe Nord's *Schwerpunkt*. Largely unheralded is the successful delaying action by Ivanov's 8th Army in Estonia against von Küchler's 18. Armee or the fact that Busch's 16. Armee was dispersed in a flank guard operation; von Leeb was only able to reinforce Höpner's drive with a handful of infantry divisions. Furthermore, Ivanov was able to hold onto the port of Tallinn until August 29, which seriously reduced German theater logistics in the Baltic region and delayed an advance against the Narva-Kingisepp sector. The commitment of von Manstein's corps to support von Küchler would have been the logical course of action to accelerate the clearing of Estonia, but apparently this was not considered. By choosing to establish bridgeheads in the Porech'e-Sabsk sector, Reinhardt could only be supplied along crude dirt tracks through wooded, marshy areas, which essentially ignored the logistic requirements of high-tempo maneuver warfare. For their part, the Soviet command was facing their own problems. Since the Germans had succeeded in gaining toeholds over the Luga River, Stalin and Voroshilov agreed that someone was to blame, so on July 22, General-leytenant Piadyshev was arrested for "anti-Soviet agitation" and died in prison. Although professionally incompetent, Voroshilov had enough common sense to order counterattacks against Reinhardt's bridgeheads, which inflicted some painful casualties and further delayed the drive on Leningrad.

Despite the defeat at Soltsy, Hitler and the OKH were still fixated on an outflanking maneuver near Lake Ilmen, rather than a costly breakthrough attack to Leningrad. On July 30, Hitler issued Führer Directive No. 34, which stated that "the main attack will continue between Lake Ilmen and Narva towards Leningrad, with the aim of encircling Leningrad..." The directive also stressed the need to clear up enemy resistance in Estonia before moving against Leningrad.[16] Hitler's directive was suitably vague, which enabled von Leeb to develop a "please everyone" scheme of maneuver: Reinhardt would break out of his bridgeheads and advance to Leningrad once Estonia was cleared, while von Manstein's corps would mount a secondary drive from the bridgehead in the Luga sector and Busch's 16. Armee would renew the push east toward Lake Ilmen with a single corps (General Christian Hansen's X Armeekorps). Von Leeb's plan for phase three identified no *Schwerpunkt* and employed no mass or surprise. In every sector, the Soviet forces mounted a tenacious defense and only grudgingly yielded ground. Hansen's advance toward Lake Ilmen encountered stiff resistance from Morozov's 11th Army, resulting in a week-long slug-fest. Along the way, von Leeb decided to make Staraya Russa and Novgorod objectives for the 16. Armee, as well as the town of Chudovo, a key town on the Moscow-Leningrad rail line.

In order to stop Busch's 16. Armee's flanking maneuver, the Stavka formed two new formations – the 48th Army (General-leytenant Stepan D. Akimov) at Novgorod and 34th Army (General-major Kuzma M. Kachanov) near Staraya Russa. Voroshilov was ordered to mount counterattacks with these formations as soon as possible. On August 6, Hansen's corps took Staraya Russa and Höpner's two corps began their breakout attacks on August 8. Amazingly, von Leeb decided that most of the Luftwaffe air support would be assigned to assist 16. Armee's flanking maneuver, rather than the direct assaults through the Luga Line.[17] Vatutin organized the counteroffensive at Staraya Russa, using Kachanov's 34th Army as its main assault formation. Kachanov had a wealth of prior combat experience, having served as a military advisor to the Republicans in the Spanish Civil War and against the Japanese in the Far East (he was in China during most of the purges). Under heavy pressure, Hansen was forced to abandon Staraya Russa rather than become isolated. In response to this minor Soviet tactical success, von Leeb ordered Höpner to break off the fighting at Luga and send von Manstein's LVI Armeekorps (mot.) to assist Hansen's X Corps. With plentiful air support, von Manstein was able to inflict a sharp tactical defeat upon Kachanov's 34th Army (12,000 prisoners taken) by mauling five Soviet divisions. By August 20, Heeresgruppe Nord had crushed all resistance along the Luga Line from Kingisepp to Lake Ilmen, as well as encircling several Soviet divisions. As per OKH guidance, Heeresgruppe Mitte transferred General der Panzertruppe Rudolf Schmidt's XXXIX Armeekorps (mot.) to reinforce Busch's 16. Armee's flanking maneuver. Advancing from the south, Schmidt's corps captured Chudovo, thereby severing the Moscow-Leningrad rail line. Once again, a German operational-level victory at Leningrad seemed possible.

German successes near Leningrad incited panic in Moscow and Stalin sent a deputation from the Stavka headed by political commissars Lev Z. Mekhlis and Nikolai A. Bulganin to examine the situation. Mekhlis quickly established a reputation for ruthless and arbitrary punishment of senior commanders. Sobennikov was relieved of command of the Northwest Front and replaced by General-leytenant Pavel A. Kurochkin;

Sobennikov was demoted, then arrested, then sent to prison. Ivanov was relieved of command of the 8th Army and arrested, but later released. Akimov (48th Army) was also relieved of command for the loss of Novgorod. Kachanov and his artillery commander, General-major Vasily S. Goncharov, were both arrested on Mekhlis' orders and executed. In order to "encourage" other officers not to retreat without orders, Mekhlis had Goncharov executed in front of his troops. As a result of these purges, Soviet front-line commanders were acutely aware that the slightest mistake could result in immediate arrest by Mekhlis' NKVD goons, which further discouraged initiative.

Although Heeresgruppe Nord was finally closing in on Leningrad, Soviet resistance around the city was increasing by the day. The garrison still had two battalions of KV heavy tanks which were nearly impervious to most German antitank weapons and intimidated Höpner's Panzer crews. The Soviet VVS was also beginning to play a major role by contesting air superiority over the Leningrad sector and bombing German motorized columns.[18] Nevertheless, the Germans took Mga, severing the final rail line into the city, the 8th Army was pushed back into a hedgehog around Oranienbaum and Höpner's Panzers reached the Pulkovo Heights just outside the city on September 12. The Stavka reacted by relieving Popov of command, shoving Voroshilov aside and sending Zhukov to take command of the Leningrad Front. By the time that Zhukov arrived in the city on September 13, Leningrad was completely isolated and heavy fighting had been ongoing in the outskirts for over a week. Zhukov immediately massed the best militia units and remaining KV heavy tanks and launched a series of hasty counterattacks which helped to halt the German advance, but also squandered his tactical reserves. Soviet naval gunfire support from the Red Banner Baltic Fleet also played a role in stemming further German advances toward the city. In addition, on September 18 Zhukov informed all subordinate commanders via Combat Order No. 0064 that anyone who retreated would be shot.[19]

Unknown to Zhukov, Hitler had already decided that Leningrad would be starved into submission, not taken by storm. Since the beginning of Operation *Barbarossa*, Heeresgruppe Nord had taken over 126,000 casualties (including 30,000 dead or missing) or roughly 17 percent of its starting strength; an assault into a heavily defended city would certainly cost thousands more. Anxious about preserving combat power for other missions, Hitler ordered von Leeb to transfer most of Höpner's Panzers to Heeresgruppe Mitte and reduce Leningrad's garrison by siege. Likewise, the best Luftwaffe units, such as Fliegerkorps VIII, were also shifted southward.

Although Heeresgruppe Nord achieved some measure of tactical success by isolating Leningrad, it had not achieved its primary operational objective. Hitler had tasked Heeresgruppe Nord with destroying most of the Red Army units assigned to the Northwest and Northern Fronts as well as capturing the city. Hitler also expected that once Leningrad was secure, Heeresgruppe Nord and Luftflotte 1 could transfer forces to assist the drive on Moscow. Instead, von Leeb's army group was in desperate need of replacements and could ill afford to transfer Panzergruppe 4.

Another factor to consider is that Heeresgruppe Nord missed a golden opportunity to impact the Red Army's strategic center of gravity (COG) – namely, the Soviet armaments industry.* Leningrad was home to a great deal of the Soviet Union's armaments industry, including Zavod 100 (which made the KV heavy tanks) and Zavod 185 (which made artillery). Without these critical armaments factories, the Red Army would have less ability to replace its material losses or improve its combat capabilities. However, due to the sluggish German advance, the Soviets were able to evacuate Zavod 100 by rail to Chelyabinsk, as well as other armaments factories. Once in the Urals, Soviet armaments industry would be well beyond the reach even of the Luftwaffe.

How did Heeresgruppe Nord come up short? The primary reason for German operational failure on the Leningrad axis was that von Leeb and Höpner envisioned phase two as a pursuit operation, but they moved their forces so slowly that it became an assault on a fortified line and then a siege operation. Von Leeb and Höpner failed to learn or adapt from their operational mistakes and kept trying to push their armored units through slow-go/no-go terrain. The whole region around Lake Ilmen became a veritable magnet for German resources, as Heeresgruppe Nord kept shifting ground units and air support to try to create a stable front line in this quagmire region. Instead of an economy of force effort, the 16. Armee's flank guard mission ended up tying down almost 50 percent of Heeresgruppe Nord's combat power. Von Leeb proved unwilling to accept operational risk to his flanks and failed to understand the requirements of mechanized warfare; to his credit, he did ask to be relieved of command when he recognized he was not up to the task. Höpner's anti-regime attitudes (he was an active member of the anti-Hitler resistance) may have undermined his performance in the

---

*Von Clausewitz first raised the issue of a center of gravity (COG) in his 1832 *Vom Krieg*. A COG provides a critical capability, without which a given military force cannot accomplish its missions – it is an essential factor. COGs exist at both the strategic and operational level and are contingent upon critical requirements and possess critical vulnerabilities.

field. Von Küchler was the only German operational-level commander in Heeresgruppe Nord who remained consistently focused on his objective until it was accomplished and was not caught by surprise by enemy counterattacks. Yet it is noteworthy that von Küchler's 18. Armee required over nine weeks to defeat the relatively weak Soviet forces in the Baltic States (excluding the islands of Saaremaa and Hiumaa), indicating that von Leeb failed to provide this army with the resources required to complete its primary mission in a timely manner. Key operational lessons from Heeresgruppe Nord's campaign were: (a) route reconnaissance/terrain analysis is critical for the proper use of maneuver in operational-level warfare, (b) commanders must maintain the agility to switch to alternative avenues of approach if the primary route proves unsuitable and (c) the main effort has to be properly reinforced to accomplish its mission in the initial advance, not paused to await reinforcements.

Commander	Objective	Offensive	Mass	Maneuver	Surprise	Security	TALLY
Von Leeb	-	o	-	-	-	-	-5
Höpner	+	+	-	-	-	-	-2
Küchler	+	+	o	+	o	o	3
Busch	o	+	-	+	-	-	-1
Kuznetsov	-	+	-	+	o	+	1
Popov	+	o	+	o	o	o	2
Sobennikov	+	o	o	o	o	o	1
Vatutin	+	+	+	+	+	+	6
Voroshilov	+	o	+	o	o	o	2
Ivanov	+	o	o	o	o	o	1

Northern Axis, Phase 2 and 3 Leadership Assessment

Compared to their German opposite numbers, Soviet operational-level commanders made fewer mistakes during the initial phases of the Leningrad campaign. All of the Soviet commanders were focused on the same critical objective – preventing the enemy from reaching Leningrad – without any debate about competing priorities. Indeed, the threat of arrest or execution for failing to achieve this objective ensured that all senior Soviet commanders remained unswervingly focused on this goal. For the most part, Soviet commanders could not use operational-level maneuver or offensive action to try to accomplish this objective, due to lack of sufficient combat power. Instead, tenacious positional defense and local counterattacks was the order of the day, hoping to degrade German combat power sufficiently for their offensive to culminate short of its ultimate objective. The one exception on the Soviet side was Vatutin; although serving in a staff role for Voroshilov, Vatutin acted as a *de facto* field commander in orchestrating two major counterattacks. By massing the best available reserves and employing surprise, Vatutin was able to achieve two tactical successes that delivered operational-level results. Nevertheless, the Soviet defenses around Leningrad began to crack in August 1941 as Heeresgruppe Nord continued to pound on the improvised defenses. Despite post-war hype, Zhukov had no appreciable impact on the final outcome, since he arrived just as Heeresgruppe Nord's offensive was culminating and Hitler's attention was shifting elsewhere. Zhukov's counterattacks were a series of desperate tactical measures, already in progress when he arrived. Of note, at Leningrad Zhukov did begin to demonstrate a personal tendency to be profligate with other people's troops and equipment, then moving on to another front. Between June and September 1941, the Red Army forces in the Northwest and Northern Fronts suffered nearly 400,000 casualties, about half of whom were dead or captured.[20] Material losses were also exceedingly heavy. While Leningrad was surrounded by mid-September, Heeresgruppe Nord had lost its best chance to seize the city and would soon find itself over-extended and vulnerable.

Central Axis, June 22–September 10, 1941

After the occupation of eastern Poland in September 1939, the Red Army was left holding the Bialystok salient, which was vulnerable to attack from two sides. The Soviet Special Western Military District (*Zapadnyy osobyy voyennyy okrug* or ZapOVO) was commanded by General-polkovnik Dmitry G. Pavlov and his chief of staff was General-major Vladimir Y. Klimovskikh, with his two primary staff officers being Polkovnik Semyon V. Blokhin (intelligence) and General-major Ivan I. Semenov (operations). Pavlov was responsible for defending a 470-kilometer-long stretch of border, which stretched from the southwest corner of Lithuania through the fortress of Brest-Litovsk to the northern edge of the Pripet Marshes. In July 1940, the Soviets began building a new series of fortified areas along the western border known as the Molotov Line, but one year later it was far from complete in the ZapOVO.[21] In any case, the wargames in Moscow in January 1941 concluded that border fortifications would probably add little to the Soviet defense of the region. Nor could Pavlov's Western Front (*Zaapadnyy front*) expect any help from the occupied Polish population. Under these conditions, it would have been prudent for the Red Army to only leave a covering force along the border and deploy their main strength further back in Belarus, but Stalin was unwilling to consider such an approach.

Pavlov was an experienced soldier, having seen combat in Spain and Manchuria, yet he had never commanded a formation larger than a tank brigade. He was one of the early Soviet armor officers and was quite knowledgeable about tanks – it was his recommendations from Spain that led to the development of the T-34 tank – but he possessed a tactical mindset, not an operational one. Klimovskikh, a former Tsarist infantry officer and trained in the Soviet General Staff, was to assist Pavlov with the massive amount of work required to bring the units in the ZapOVO up to a high state of readiness. The highly political General-leytenant Ivan V. Boldin was also assigned as deputy front commander. Pavlov was assigned three armies to defend the western border region: the 3rd Army (General-leytenant Vasily I. Kuznetsov) held the north flank of the Bialystok salient, the 10th Army (General-leytenant Konstantin D. Golubev) defended the face of the salient and the 4th Army (General-leytenant Aleksandr A. Korobkov) held the southern flank of the salient. While the senior Soviet commanders in the ZapOVO had a modicum of professional experience and training, they were severely constrained by directives from Moscow to avoid border provocations and a doctrine which stressed rapid counterattacks to deal with any border incursions.

On paper, Pavlov had an adequate force for defending the ZapOVO, with roughly 670,000 troops on hand. In June 1941 his front-line rifle divisions averaged 80 percent of their authorized peacetime strength but were significantly weaker than the German infantry divisions they would be opposing.[22] Likewise, Pavlov had six mechanized corps with 2,220 tanks (including about 100 KV heavy tanks and 150 T-34 medium tanks), although only four of these formations were anywhere near combat readiness. Both the KV and T-34 tanks were far superior to the best German medium tanks, but logistic support (shortages of ammunition and fuel) and training deficiencies significantly undermined the combat potential of these new tanks. General-major Ivan I. Kopets commanded the VVS units in the ZapOVO, which consisted of three mixed, two bomber and one fighter division. Kopets was assigned some of the best pilots and newest aircraft, including the 9th Mixed Aviation Division

(9 SAD) under General-major Sergei A. Chernykh,* which had 233 of the brand-new MiG-3 fighters.[23] The first regiment of Il-2 Sturmovik ground attack aircraft was also scheduled to join Kopet's command. Altogether, the VVS-ZapOVO had over 1,700 aircraft on hand, but training and logistic deficiencies greatly reduced readiness. It is not clear if Pavlov, Boldin or Klimovskikh were aware of the extent of the logistic problems in their command – but they should have been aware of it and doing something to improve this shortfall. Instead, Pavlov deployed his forces by the book, in two echelons, with his three field armies up front and the best mechanized corps held in reserve to mount counterattacks against any border incursions. The second echelon, further to the rear, comprised 11 rifle divisions, three airborne brigades and two cadre-size mechanized corps. Pavlov dutifully followed all orders from Moscow; when told to avoid border provocations, he did not put any of his troops on alert and kept them in or near their peacetime garrisons. Kopet's aircraft, including his brand-new MiG-3 fighters, were deployed in the open on airfields that had been already identified by the Luftwaffe. Pavlov did not even take the basic steps of dispersing his available ammunition and fuel stockpiles prior to hostilities or to test back-up communication procedures with his subordinate armies.

Meanwhile, Heeresgruppe Mitte under Generalfeldmarschall Fedor von Bock had assembled powerful forces to mount a concentric attack against the Bialystok salient. Von Bock was one of the most experienced senior commanders in the Heer, having commanded an army group in the invasion of Poland in 1939 and Belgium in 1940. A classic product of the Prussian military system, von Bock had impeccable military credentials, having received General Staff training in the Kaiser's Army and awarded the Pour le Mérite in the First World War. As his chief of staff, he was provided Generalmajor Hans von Greiffenberg, one of the primary OKH planners involved in the development of Operation *Barbarossa*. Oberstleutnant Henning von Treskow was von Bock's operations officer (1a); von Treskow was also one of the leaders of the covert anti-Nazi resistance in the Heer. Von Bock intended to destroy Pavlov's Western Front in a classic battle of annihilation (*Vernichtungsschlacht*) by means of

---

*The 29-year-old Chernykh was a model Soviet warrior. He was sent to Spain in 1936–37 where he shot down five enemy aircraft, including the first German Bf-109 fighter claimed by the VVS. Returning to Russia, he was awarded the Hero of the Soviet Union (HSU) and enjoyed an extraordinarily rapid rise from leytenant to general-major in just four years. He was also an ardent Communist Party member and elected as a representative to the Supreme Soviet in 1937.

two consecutive pincer attacks, first against the Bialystok salient, then quickly followed by one against Minsk. The OKH had provided von Bock with the bulk of the combat resources allocated for Operation *Barbarossa*: 43 percent of the personnel (1,308,000 troops), 58 percent of the tanks (1,786) and 47 percent of the aircraft (1,020). Von Bock's formations would be operating close to friendly supply lines, in favorable weather conditions, at full strength and with local numerical superiority – a recipe for operational success.

Von Bock intended to conduct a campaign based on aggressive, relentless use of offensive maneuver to accomplish his assigned objectives, beginning with the destruction of Pavlov's Western Front. He deployed his armor on the flanks of Heeresgruppe Mitte, with Generaloberst Hermann Hoth's Panzergruppe 3 forming the northern pincer and Generaloberst Heinz Guderian's Panzergruppe 2 forming the southern pincer. Generalfeldmarschall Albert Kesselring, commander of Luftflotte 2, assigned the VIII Fliegerkorps to provide close air support to Hoth and the II Fliegerkorps to support Guderian. Generaloberst Adolf Strauß's 9. Armee (AOK 9) and Generalfeldmarschall Günther von Kluge's 4. Armee (AOK 4) would attack the center of the Bialystok salient, pushing toward Grodno and Bialystok while the Panzers skirted around the enemy's flanks. The only significant terrain obstacles in von Bock's path were the 90m-wide Bug River in front of Guderian and the 100m-wide Nieman River confronting Hoth's Panzers. Both Panzer groups were assigned additional bridging assets, as well as specialized equipment to expedite assault river crossings. The Soviet-held fortress of Brest-Litovsk was also of some concern, but was expected to be bypassed and reduced by follow-on infantry forces.

Kesselring's Luftflotte 2 began X-Tag at 0305 hours on June 22 with carefully timed air strikes on most of the Soviet forward air bases. Most of Chernykh's MiG-3 fighters were destroyed on the ground in the initial attacks and altogether Kopets' VVS units lost 738 aircraft on the first day (41 percent of its initial strength). Kopets apparently committed suicide within 24 hours of the beginning of the invasion and Chernykh was soon arrested and later executed. General-major Andrei I. Tayursky, another Spanish Civil War fighter ace, moved up to command the shattered remnants of the VVS-Western Front, but Pavlov could expect little or no air support. Follow-on Luftwaffe bomber raids demolished Soviet supply warehouses, fuel storage dumps and damaged communications facilities, inflicting considerable disruption. In the north, Hoth's Panzergruppe 3 surged across the border, easily punching through Morozov's 11th Army, and then seized two intact bridges over the Nieman at Alytus, just 8½ hours after the start of *Barbarossa*. In the south, Guderian spent most of the first day getting his armored spearheads across the Bug River, but with little interference from the enemy. In the center, infantry divisions from the AOK 4 and AOK 9 overran the Soviet border defenses and began steadily advancing toward Bialystok.

In Minsk, Pavlov quickly lost contact with his front-line armies due to enemy air attacks and radio communication problems. He did receive some sporadic messages from the 3rd and 10th Armies, indicating large-scale enemy border crossings and air attacks in their sectors. Initially, Pavlov simply parroted the last orders he had received from Moscow – to avoid provocations – but he gradually realized that he was dealing with an actual invasion.[24] Nevertheless, Pavlov made no major operational decisions until that evening, when NKO Directive No. 3 arrived after 2115 hours. The directive, signed by Timoshenko and Zhukov, ordered the Northwest, Western and Southwestern Fronts to use their mechanized corps to launch immediate counterattacks to destroy enemy forces that had crossed the border.[25] Based upon pre-war planning, Pavlov decided to commit the 6th and 11th Mechanized Corps and the 6th Cavalry Corps to a major counterattack in the 3rd Army sector near Grodno. He sent Boldin by air on the night of June 22/23 to Bialystok to coordinate these formations, which were supposed to attack early on June 23. It is important to note that Pavlov committed his best mobile reserve units based upon fragmentary reporting and without any input from the 4th Army sector, where Guderian's Panzers were getting ready to break out. In fact, all three front-line commanders were already committing elements of their assigned mechanized corps into combat before Pavlov's order was received. Kuznetsov committed the 11th Mechanized Corps at Grodno, where it was pounded by air strikes from VIII Fliegerkorps. Boldin arrived at Golubev's 10th Army headquarters in Bialystok and according to his memoirs, found that Golubev was trying to use the 6th Mechanized Corps simply to plug gaps in his line.[26] Considerable argument ensued between Boldin and Golubev and unity of command was further eroded by the arrival of Marshal Grigory I. Kulik on June 23. Kulik was a deputy commissar of defense and had been sent as a Stavka representative to assess the situation in the Bialystok salient. Instead, with no staff and limited awareness of the situation, Kulik tried to assert his own control over the counteroffensive.

In fact, it took Boldin all of June 23 to try to assemble the 6th and 11th Mechanized Corps, which were badly battered by Luftwaffe interdiction sorties. The lack of reliable radio communications made coordination very difficult and fuel shortages (particularly diesel for the KV and T-34 tanks) forced Boldin to postpone his counterattack for another day. In the meantime, the German infantry from the VIII Armeekorps occupied Grodno and solidified their positions, expecting a Soviet counterattack. Furthermore, the German Panzer groups were on a rampage and gave no respite. In the 4th Army sector, Korobkov committed his 14th Mechanized Corps on the morning of June 23 in a futile effort to stop Guderian's Panzers, but the unsupported Soviet armor was quickly demolished. Meanwhile, Hoth's Panzers were romping across southern Lithuania, barely hindered by Morozov's 11th Army, which was in full retreat. Although Pavlov and his staff were still focused on localized actions around Grodno, he was not completely unaware of the German armored pincers maneuvering to close east of Bialystok. From his front reserves, he dispatched a rifle corps to establish a blocking position at Slonim, 140 kilometers east of Bialystok, and a cadre mechanized corps to reinforce the garrison at Baranovichi. He also shifted the 13th Army from his second echelon to reinforce the defenses of Minsk.[27] Yet he did not order Boldin to break off his counterattack. Instead, Boldin did launch his counterattack on June 24–25, which caused some tense moments for the German infantrymen of the XX Armeekorps, but the uncoordinated armored jabs were eventually repulsed with heavy losses. It was not until after the counterattack had failed, at 1645 hours on June 25, that Pavlov authorized Boldin to withdraw his remaining mechanized forces to Slonim. It was too late. Hoth's Panzers occupied Vilnius on the morning of June 24 and pivoted to the southeast, directly toward Minsk. Meanwhile, Guderian's Panzers occupied Slonim before the Soviets could create a blocking position and then stormed Baranovichi on June 25. All three of Pavlov's first echelon armies were conducting unauthorized and disorderly withdrawals, further opening the floodgates.

Pavlov still hesitated to order a general withdrawal until it became apparent on June 26 that a large portion of his Western Front was being herded into a pocket east of Bialystok. By the end of the day, the German armored pincers had nearly closed around the 3rd and 10th Armies, but a narrow corridor remained open along the Nieman River. Part of Korobkov's 4th Army was also escaping into the Pripet Marshes. Heeresgruppe Mitte was on the cusp of a major operational victory, but German senior leaders could not agree on the next step. The OKH (Von Brauchitsch, Halder) wanted von Bock to close the pincers east of Bialystok as soon as possible, to destroy the maximum number of encircled Soviet forces. Von Bock regarded this as a "premature" measure and was already looking beyond Minsk, since he assumed that Pavlov would extricate most of his forces before the pincers closed. Amazingly, by the second day of the invasion, von Bock was becoming fixated on the Vitebsk-Polotsk sector (almost 500km from the start line), since he felt that seizing crossings over the Dvina River would prevent the Western Front from stabilizing a new defensive line.[28] Adding to this uncertainty, on June 25 Guderian decided to send one of his corps (XXIV AK(m).) toward Bobruisk, 140 kilometers southeast of Minsk, to secure a crossing across the Berezina. Furthermore, Guderian assumed that destroying the Soviet forces in the Bialystok pocket was somebody else's problem – he wanted to push on from Bobruisk to Roslavl and Smolensk.[29] Guderian only assigned one motorized corps (XXXXVII AK(m).) to proceed up the highway toward Minsk and link up with Hoth's Panzers, but this formation was slowed when it encountered strong Soviet blocking forces. The Stavka had committed the 13th Army from its reserves to the Minsk sector, in an effort to slow the German advance on the city. Despite the fact that Guderian's Bobruisk diversion represented a serious diversion from the army group's phase one objectives, von Bock decided to give Guderian freedom of maneuver and thereby scatter his armor.[*] Only Hoth remained focused on reaching Minsk quickly and by June 27 his armored spearhead (the XXXIX AK (m.)) had reached the northern outskirts of the city. After heavy fighting, Hoth captured Minsk on June 28, with no real help from Guderian. A total of three Soviet armies (3, 10, 13) were now isolated in separate pockets around Bialystok, Volkovysk and west of Minsk, while the 4th Army was scattered and retreating toward Bobruisk. Pavlov only had a vague awareness of these events, due to the collapse of his front's command and control. With Minsk lost, he ordered a general withdrawal to the Berezina River, although Guderian's Panzers crossed that obstacle at Bobruisk before the Red Army could form a line.

After a week of intense fighting, von Bock's Heeresgruppe Mitte had succeeded in conducting two sequential double envelopments, more or less, which succeeded in trapping about two-thirds of Pavlov's Western

---

[*]On June 26, the OKH ordered von Bock to make Guderian's Panzergruppe 2 subordinate to von Kluge's 4. Armee, in order to focus more effort on containing the Bialystok-Minsk pockets, which created more confusion. For the most part, Guderian ignored this order.

Front. The Soviet units fought desperately, in an uncoordinated attempt to break out to the east. Over the course of the next week, the infantry of the AOK 4 and AOK 9, reinforced with part of the 2. Armee (AOK 2), crushed the three Soviet pockets with all organized resistance ending by July 6. Due to the German failure to properly seal the pockets, thousands of Soviet soldiers did succeed in escaping eastward, minus their heavy equipment. Boldin managed to lead out one group, which reached Soviet lines near Smolensk after a six-week trek; afterwards he was lionized by Soviet propaganda as an example of undaunted resistance. Generals Kuznetsov (3rd Army) and Golubev (10th Army) escaped with fragments of their commands, while Marshal Kulik, disguised as a peasant, also made good his escape. Altogether, the Germans claimed to have taken 287,000 prisoners and Soviet sources indicate that the Western Front suffered 341,000 dead or missing and another 76,000 wounded, totaling over 417,000 casualties (66 percent of starting strength).[30] Soviet material losses included over 2,000 tanks and 9,000 artillery pieces. The Soviet 4th and 10th Armies were disbanded after the battle but were soon re-formed. Tayursky's VVS-Western Front also suffered crippling losses, amounting to 1,669 aircraft in nine days of combat.[31] Simply put, the Western Front had been demolished. German losses were relatively modest, roughly 18,000 casualties (1.5 percent of starting strength), as well as 5 percent of their armor and 20 percent of their aircraft.

In Moscow, news of the fall of Minsk stunned Stalin and the Stavka. In Stalin's paranoid mind, this kind of military defeat could only be attributed to treason, not incompetence or material deficiencies. On June 30, the axe began to fall. Pavlov, his chief of staff Klimovskikh, Korubkov (4th Army), Tayursky (VVS), most of the senior front-level staff officers (the chiefs of artillery, communications) and one corps commander were recalled to Moscow, arrested and later executed. Some family members were also arrested and imprisoned, such as the wife of former VVS-Western Front commander Kopets. General-major Ivan I. Semenov, Pavlov's chief of operations and a General Staff-trained officer, was one of the lucky ones – he received a ten-year sentence in the gulag, but was released after one year. Polkovnik Semyon V. Blokhin, the head of intelligence in the Western Front, was the only one to escape unscathed (as a career intelligence officer, he was a much scarcer asset in the Red Army than a combat arms officer). There is no doubt that Pavlov and his subordinates failed to ensure that their units were properly alerted, dispersed and prepared to conduct their wartime missions. Once they found themselves under attack, they simply fell back on rigid pre-war planning, which led to the immediate commitment of mobile reserves and bombers before the critical point on the battlefield was identified. By prematurely throwing away his reserves at Grodno, Pavlov lost any chance to prevent the enemy armor from smashing in both his flanks and dismembering the Western Front. In terms of the principles of war, Pavlov and most of his subordinates failed at objective, mass and security, but they remained committed to offensive action even when withdrawal was the only sensible course of action. Nevertheless, a large portion of the blame for the destruction of the Western Front in the Bialystok salient should be directed toward Stalin, who imposed overly-restrictive guidance for border security on his front-line commanders and set unrealistic goals for re-equipping the Red Army. On top of this faulty micromanagement, the purges had intimidated many leaders like Pavlov into becoming obsequious drones, rather than commanders capable of independent judgment.

Von Bock's operational plan for two sequential double envelopments was an excellent one and he had the means at his disposal to accomplish it. Heeresgruppe Mitte's success in the Bialystok-Minsk *Kesselschlacht* (cauldron battle) was one of the Wehrmacht's great operational victories in the early stages of Operation *Barbarossa*. Yet after a brilliant beginning, the German commanders still allowed one-third of Pavlov's forces to escape because they (particularly von Bock, von Kluge and Guderian) could not maintain their focus on a single objective. Instead, German commanders became more fixated on jumping the next river line than they were on completing their assigned link-ups to achieve the intended operational objective. The German conception of *Kesselschlacht* proved more idealized than the actual gritty reality of crushing a cornered foe in a pocket. Previous German pocket battles in Poland and France had been resolved fairly quickly, with most of the defenders choosing to surrender. In Russia, the Germans were dismayed that encircled Soviet troops – under the control of political commissars – often opted for fanatical resistance and violent breakout attempts. German losses, particularly in terms of infantry, were far heavier in these mop-up operations than anticipated. Von Kluge began to demonstrate an indecisive quality – noted by von Bock – in order to minimize casualties to his command; consequently, he was less committed to an offensive mindset than other German commanders.[32] Overall, Hoth proved to be the most aggressive and mission-focused senior commander in Heeresgruppe Mitte, while von Kluge and Guderian were already demonstrating that they were not team players.

Commander	Objective	Offensive	Mass	Maneuver	Surprise	Security	TALLY
Von Bock	–	+	+	+	+	o	3
Von Kluge	o	o	+	o	o	o	I
Strauß	+	+	+	o	o	o	3
Hoth	+	+	+	+	+	o	5
Guderian	–	+	–	+	+	o	I
Pavlov	–	+	–	o	o	–	-2
Boldin	–	+	o	+	o		o
Kuznetsov Golubev	–	+	–	+	o	–	-I

Central Axis, Phase 1 Leadership Assessment

After Pavlov and his most of his subordinates were eliminated, Stalin sent Marshal Semyon K. Timoshenko to take over command of the remnants of the Western Front on July 2, which consisted of about 100,000 troops from the 13th Army and other survivors from the Minsk-Bialystok debacle. On the day the German invasion began, the NKO initiated its wartime mobilization plans and began activating reserve armies at a frantic rate. Initially, Marshal Semyon M. Budyonny was placed in command of the Stavka Reserve Front forming at Bryansk, but after the disaster in the Bialystok-Minsk pockets he was ordered to turn over his four cadre armies (19, 20, 21, 22) to Timoshenko. Within a week, these four armies would add nearly 450,000 troops to replenish the Western Front's depleted ranks.[33] The Stavka ordered Timoshenko to use these forces to re-establish the Western Front and create a new defensive line between the Dvina and the Dnepr, centered on the region between Mogilev and Vitebsk. In order to buy time to create a coherent front line, Timoshenko ordered the 13th Army to concentrate at Mogilev and the 20th Army at Vitebsk; while these two formations had 17 rifle divisions, they had virtually no armor and very little artillery. In order to rectify these deficiencies in this critical sector, the Stavka decided to provide Timoshenko with the 5th and 7th Mechanized Corps from its strategic reserve (RVGK); these two corps had over 1,400 operational tanks, including about 90 of the new KV and T-34 tanks. In addition, four army-level artillery regiments were transferred from the RVGK to the Western Front to provide fire support. Timoshenko himself was a 46-year-old career cavalryman, with limited experience outside that branch, but admired by Stalin because of his success in breaching the Finnish Mannerheim Line in February 1940. By volunteering to take on a tough assignment like the Finnish front, Timoshenko ingratiated himself with Stalin. For his success against the Finns, Stalin made him People's Commissar of Defense in 1940 and then a member of the Stavka (SVGK) in June 1941. Stalin liked tough soldiers, particularly ones with cavalry backgrounds, hence his willingness to surround himself with the likes of Voroshilov, Budyonny and Timoshenko. Yet despite his pointedly macho command style, Timoshenko was handicapped by a limited military education, having attended the V. I. Lenin Military-Political Academy instead of the Frunze, and negligible staff experience. Now with the Soviet defeat at Bialystok-Minsk, Stalin once again turned to a reliable warhorse like Timoshenko to salvage a victory from the wreckage. Recognizing his limitations in operational-level warfare, the Stavka provided him with General-leytenant German K. Malandin as his chief of staff, to assist him in rebuilding the Western Front. Malandin was regarded as a rising star in the General Staff and had worked directly under Vatutin in the operations branch.

Although Heeresgruppe Mitte could not resume a serious offensive eastward until the Bialystok-Minsk pockets were destroyed and a forward supply base could be created in Minsk (the first German train did not reach the city until July 5), von Bock authorized both of his Panzer groups to begin a reconnaissance in force toward the Dvina and Dnepr Rivers. By the morning of July 4, Hoth's XXXIX Armeekorps (mot.) had occupied Lepel, 100 kilometers southwest of Kurochkin's 20th Army in Vitebsk. That evening, just two days after Timoshenko arrived in Smolensk, he received an order from the Stavka:

> While holding off the onslaught of the Third and Second Panzer Groups, organize a firm defense along the Western Dvina and Dnepr River lines and, after concentrating reserves arriving from the depths of the country, deliver a series of counterstrokes along the Lepel, Borisov and Bobruisk axes.[34]

With no time spent on reflection, Timoshenko decided to conduct an immediate counteroffensive, using the two fresh mechanized corps and General-leytenant Pavel A. Kurochkin's 20th Army, to strike at Hoth's advancing armor. At 2315 hours on July 4, Timoshenko informed Kurochkin that both mechanized corps would be subordinated to the 20th Army and that he was to launch his counteroffensive at 0600 hours on July 5.[35] Timoshenko also promised air support, even though the VVS-Western Front could barely scrape up 100 operational aircraft at this point. It is doubtful that Malandin played any significant role in this counteroffensive, which was marked by its total absence of planning. Timoshenko ignored the fact that both mechanized corps were still in the process of unloading from rail transport and would have to move over 120 kilometers during the night of July 5/6 to participate in the operation; this was the kind of *diktat* methods he had seen Stalin employ – snap one's fingers and things were just supposed to fall into place. Staff coordination, intelligence estimates and logistics had no place in this kind of decision-making environment.

The results of the Western Front's counterattack at Lepel on July 6–7 were totally predictable. Kurochkin was a capable, General Staff-trained officer but he could not improvise an attack involving over 100,000 troops in less than seven hours, as Timoshenko ordered. Consequently, the operation began with just the 5th Mechanized Corps attacking on July 6, followed by part of the 7th Mechanized Corps the next day. The Soviet armored units arrived tired, with many of the KV tanks falling out with mechanical defects, and commanders having no clue about enemy dispositions or the terrain. Despite possessing an overall numerical superiority of about 4-1 in manpower and tanks, Kurochkin could not mass units that were arriving piecemeal on the battlefield. Hoth deftly switched to the tactical defense and his Panzerjäger units chewed up the Soviet armor, followed by counter-punches with his Panzer units.[36] The promised VVS air support arrived as a small number of Il-2 Sturmovik sorties, which inflicted some damage on the German Panzer units, but Luftflotte 2 retaliated by bombing the Vitebsk airfield – thereby eliminating about one-quarter of Kurochkin's air support.[37] After three days of heavy fighting, both Soviet mechanized corps were completely smashed and Kurochkin was forced to retreat to Vitebsk. The 13th Army also tried to counterattack Guderian's spearhead corps, but was easily repulsed. Not only had Timoshenko squandered 80 percent of his armored reserve on a half-baked counteroffensive, but now he had insufficient combat power left west of Smolensk to oppose the advance of the two Panzer groups. Emboldened by the relatively easy defeat of the Lepel counteroffensive, both Hoth and Guderian began surging forward to seize small crossings of the Dvina and Dnepr Rivers.

Von Bock had placed von Kluge nominally in command of coordinating the advance of both Panzer groups, but von Kluge was barely on speaking terms with Guderian. On July 9, von Kluge went to Guderian's headquarters and ordered him not to cross the Dnepr River until Heeresgruppe Mitte's infantry armies arrived to support the attack. Guderian did what he always did in such situations, which was to ignore von Kluge's direct order, and stated that Panzergruppe 2's preparations for the river-crossing "had already gone too far to be cancelled."[38] Unable to exert any control over Guderian's course of action, von Kluge left and informed von Bock that he was ill.[39] In doctrinal terms, von Kluge was correct that the conditions for a successful offensive were not yet adequate, in terms of infantry and logistic support, but in terms of the prevailing aggressive *Bewegungskrieg* mindset of the Ostheer, it was overly timid. Von Kluge was the kind of commander who preferred methodical, predictable operations, rather than the kind of free-wheeling, slashing maneuver battles embraced by Guderian and Hoth. Guderian was a risk-taker and Hitler admired him for it – as long as it succeeded.

As Heeresgruppe Mitte pushed further east, its supply situation became more and more difficult, as predicted in the pre-invasion wargames. The German Panzers and Stukas depended upon rail lines to keep them in supply, but all the captured Soviet rail lines had to be converted from broad gauge to standard gauge by German *Eisenbahntruppen*, which was a tedious and resource-intensive exercise. Whenever the Panzer groups advanced rapidly, they left the repaired rail lines and the nearest railheads far behind. Despite the critical nature of their task, upon which German operational success depended, the *Eisenbahntruppen* were given low priority for personnel and vehicles, which hindered their ability to efficiently regauge track and rebuild damaged facilities (rail yards, bridges, etc.). In addition, the German system for rail management on the Eastern Front was hindered by excessive bureaucratic muddle: Julius Dorpmüller, the transport minister (*Reichsverkehrsministerium*), allocated rail transport in Germany, but Generalmajor Rudolf Gercke, OKW Transport Chief, controlled the trains in Russia. Generalmajor Edouard Wagner, OKH *Generalquartiermeister*, was responsible for moving supplies forward from the railheads to the field armies. Local occupation officials in Poland also had a say in when and where trains traversed through their zone. Each army group and army were provided some additional junior staff to assist in planning and supervising rail operations (particularly unloading), but this *ad hoc* effort proved grossly insufficient.[40]

After the debacle at Lepel, Timoshenko continued to try to build a strong front on the line Vitebsk-Orsha-Mogilev. He ordered General-leytenant Ivan S. Konev's newly formed 19th Army to proceed to Vitebsk, while Kurochkin's 20th Army held Orsha and the 13th Army held Mogilev. By July 8, the Soviet front line in this sector was relatively cohesive but lacked mobile reserves. Furthermore, it was evident from his deployments that Timoshenko expected the Germans to make a direct drive toward Smolensk along the Minsk highway and was unprepared to counter any other enemy course of action. Timoshenko also placed most of his available combat power in the front line. General-leytenant Mikhail F. Lukin's 16th Army was deployed in second echelon at Smolensk, but had transferred most of its forces to replenish the 20th Army and was left with just two rifle divisions. The only other major forces at Timoshenko's disposal were the 22nd Army, which anchored the Western Front's right flank in the Polotsk fortified region, and the 21st Army on his left flank near Gomel. Although Timoshenko ordered his front-line armies to mount local counterattacks whenever possible, he was essentially opting for a static defense against the most mobile army in the world. The lack of significant mobile reserves and poor situational awareness only exacerbated his problems. Von Bock utilized the principle of economy of force, using the infantry from the 2. Armee to fix the enemy's attention at Orsha, while his two Panzer groups struck at Timoshenko's flanks.

On July 9, Hoth broke out of his bridgehead across the Dvina River at Ulla and advanced rapidly toward Vitebsk, which was only defended by militia. The Soviet 22nd Army, responsible for the Ulla sector, tried to interfere with Hoth's breakout but was shoved aside. By the time that the lead elements of Konev's 19th Army reached Vitebsk, Hoth's XXXIX Armeekorps (mot.) had already occupied the western portion of the city. Nevertheless, Konev put up a tough fight with his limited forces on hand, which stymied Hoth for two days. On July 10, Guderian conducted a near-perfect crossing operation over the Dnepr River, first by sending one of his motorized corps (XXIV) across south of Mogilev, then two (XXXXVI, XXXXVII) north of Mogilev. The 13th Army had created a strong defense in the immediate environs of Mogilev with General-major Fedor A. Bakunin's 61st Rifle Corps, but only had screening forces along the river. Consequently, Bakunin's corps was quickly encircled by Guderian's Panzers in Mogilev and the rest of the 13th Army retreated eastward. By July 13, both of Timoshenko's flanks had been defeated, although this was not immediately apparent to him. Another Stavka directive, signed by Zhukov, ordered him to counterattack, so he dutifully ordered the 21st Army to mount a counteroffensive against Guderian's right flank near Rogachev; this effort achieved some success, but failed to seriously delay Guderian's advance. With the Western Front's flanks torn open, both Hoth and Guderian maneuvered rapidly for the kill. Hoth's Panzers, with XXXIX Armeekorps (mot.) in the lead, advanced over 150 kilometers to seize Yartsevo on July 15, thereby severing the Smolensk-Moscow highway. Guderian advanced over 100 kilometers from his bridgeheads, with one motorized division from his XXXXVII Armeekorps (mot.) reaching the southern outskirts of Smolensk. Amazingly, Lukin's 16th Army did not hold the city in strength and Guderian's vanguard division was able to capture Smolensk by 2000 hours on July 16.

By the morning of July 17, Timoshenko's Western Front was disintegrating, with four of its armies more or less isolated. The battlefield was extremely fluid, with German and Soviet units intermixed over a 150 × 120km-wide region. From his headquarters in Vyazma, Timoshenko only had sporadic communications with his isolated armies – particularly Kurochkin's 20th Army – but it was obvious that the fall of both Smolensk and Yartsevo was a disaster. Another 60,000 troops from General-major Vasily F. Gerasimenko's 13th Army were encircled in Mogilev and Timoshenko ordered them to hold the city at all costs. On the flanks, Timoshenko ordered Konev's 19th Army to continue attacking to regain Vitebsk and the 21st Army to continue its attacks near Rogachev. The Stavka managed to provide the Western Front with 300 tanks from its limited armor reserves and some additional infantry, instructing Timoshenko to retake Yartsevo and Smolensk as soon as possible. General-major Konstantin K. Rokossovsky, who had just arrived in Vyazma that day, was assigned the mission to retake Yartsevo from Hoth's Panzer group. The Western Front was virtually in convulsions at this point, with various formations trying to launch impromptu attacks or break out of pockets, but with minimal coordination or support.

On the German side, unexpectedly rapid success at Smolensk led to debate, not consensus, about the next step. Hoth's and Guderian's Panzers had not actually linked up or sealed Kurochkin's 20th Army into a tight pocket; there was a 50km-wide gap between Yartsevo and Smolensk and another 30km-wide gap south of the city. Only three German divisions – two from Hoth's XXXIX Armeekorps (mot.) and one from Guderian's XXXXVII Armeekorps (mot.) – formed the loose perimeter that had enveloped the Soviet forces between Orsha and Smolensk. The obvious move at this point, in regard to the stated operational-level objective of destroying the Red Army, was for Hoth and Guderian to complete their link-up and seal off the pocket. However, Guderian did not see the situation that way. His attention was now focused on seizing Yelnya, a town 75km southeast of Smolensk; in his mind, Yelnya would be the springboard for the final assault toward Moscow.* Consequently, Guderian ordered his

---

*The idea that Yelnya was a "springboard" to Moscow was nonsensical, in that it was not even located on or near a main road or rail line that led to the Soviet capital, unlike Yartsevo.

XXXXVI Armeekorps (mot.) to advance to Yelnya, which was seized on the evening of July 19.[41] He used his XXIV Armeekorps (mot.) to fend off attacks against his flank from the 21st Army and used the three divisions of the XXXXVII Armeekorps (mot.) to form the southern side of the Smolensk *Kessel* (cauldron). Hoth appealed to Guderian to cooperate in sealing off the *Kessel* and in his memoirs, Guderian stated that he was "very anxious to help him," but instead sent his spearhead to Yelnya. In his memoirs, Hoth stated that, "Guderian apparently believed that holding the heights of Yelnya was of greater importance to the development of the eastward offensive than closing the pocket in the combat zone of Panzer Group 2."[42] When Guderian jubilantly reported the seizure of Yelnya to von Bock, the latter said that, "that was not what mattered, and that the only thing that did was the hermetic sealing of the Smolensk pocket while screening to the east." Nevertheless, von Bock endorsed Guderian's recommendations about pushing toward Moscow as soon as possible.[43]

As with the Bialystok-Minsk *Kesselschlacht*, Hoth seemed to be the only senior German commander single-mindedly focused on destroying the isolated Soviet forces. On July 13, at the noon conference at the Wolfsschanze (Rastenburg) in East Prussia, Halder briefed Hitler on Heeresgruppe Mitte's situation and specifically mentioned Soviet reinforcements gathering on Hoth's left flank between Nevel and Velikiye Luki and stated that, "it would pay to mount a special operation to destroy it [the Soviet 22nd Army] for good."[44] Halder managed to convince Hitler that Timoshenko would use the Polotsk fortified region as a springboard to launch a major counteroffensive into Hoth's flank. Von Brauchitsch also weighed in on the matter, claiming that Panzergruppe 3 should redirect toward the north, instead of the east in order to clear up the enemy concentrations on the boundary between Heeresgruppe Nord and Heeresgruppe Mitte. Once again, Hitler's fears about unexpected enemy flank attacks influenced the conduct of German operational-level warfare. Hoth was ordered to send his LVII Armeekorps (mot.) to deal with the flank threat, leaving only the overstretched XXXIX Armeekorps (mot.) to hold the northern perimeter around the Smolensk *Kessel*. This diversion resulted in the capture of Polotsk on July 15, then Nevel and Velikiye Luki on July 17. Stalin immediately ordered Timoshenko to retake Velikiye Luki and General-leytenant Filipp A. Ershakov's 22nd Army launched a successful counteroffensive that retook the city on July 21 – one of the first Soviet tactical victories of the campaign. Once Hitler learned of this setback, Hoth was obliged to detach more of his Panzers to deal with this situation, which served to further dilute Heeresgruppe Mitte's forces at the critical point. On July 23, Hitler issued a supplement to Führer Directive No. 33, which temporarily transferred Hoth's Panzergruppe 3 to Heeresgruppe Nord, to clear up the situation at Velikiye Luki and assist von Leeb's offensive toward Leningrad.[45] Von Bock was under heavy stress at this point in the campaign, spending considerable time arguing with troublesome subordinates (von Kluge and Guderian) and dealing with attempts at micromanagement by Hitler and the OKH, which seriously undermined his battle command.

On July 21, Rokossovsky scraped up the equivalent of three divisions and about 100 tanks, which he used to mount a major counteroffensive at Yartsevo. The 19th Army also began strong counterattacks at Yelnya and an assault group from the 28th Army attacked north from Roslavl with 220 tanks. Given the limited German motorized forces holding a loose perimeter between Yartsevo and Yelnya (a distance of over 60km across heavily wooded terrain), the Soviet counterattacks achieved some success. Rokossovsky even managed to briefly retake Yartsevo on July 29. Consequently, over 40,000 Soviet troops (some sources claim up to 100,000) were able to escape eastward from the *Kessel*. Yet Soviet tactical successes came at a high price in casualties and by the end of July, Timoshenko's combat power was much reduced. German infantry from VII Armeekorps (from Generaloberst Maximilian von Weichs' 2. Armee) finally finished off the Mogilev *Kessel* on July 26. Although the Mogilev garrison commander Bakunin had done a superb job tying down four German infantry divisions for over two weeks, he was relieved of command by Stalin – as was 13th Army commander Gerasimenko – for conducting an unauthorized breakout to save some of the remaining troops. On the same day, Guderian's forces finally completed their link-up with Hoth's forces, thereby completing the ring around the rapidly shrinking Smolensk *Kessel*. Yet Guderan remained uninterested in the Smolensk *Kesselschlacht* and instead sent his XXIV Armeekorps (mot.) south to capture Roslavl on August 1 and destroy the assault group from the 28th Army.

On August 5, von Bock announced that the Battle of the Smolensk *Kesselschlact* was over and that Heeresgruppe Mitte had taken 309,000 prisoners.[46] In just 45 days from X-Tag, Heeresgruppe Mitte had accomplished its primary objectives for the first two phases of Operation *Barbarossa*, namely by smashing the Western Front twice and by seizing critical territorial objectives (Minsk, Smolensk) that opened up a corridor to Moscow. There is little doubt that the Western Front had been badly defeated again, with total losses exceeding 500,000 troops and over 1,300 tanks. Based upon the guidance received in Führer Directive No. 34 on July 30, which ordered Heeresgruppe Mitte to temporarily shift to the defensive while its Panzer groups were refitted, von Bock envisioned a reduction in the operational tempo for the next several weeks. Hitler had informed von Bock that the immediate priority was now Leningrad, followed by the Ukraine – an advance upon Moscow could wait. However, the Stavka did not accept defeat so easily at Smolensk and began dispatching more reinforcements to Timoshenko and directives to conduct a front-level counteroffensive as soon as possible. On July 30, Zhukov arrived from Moscow and took command of the new Reserve Front,* which was tasked with reducing the Yelnya salient.[47] Guderian had turned the defense of the salient over to von Kluge's 4. Armee, while the bulk of his Panzer group turned south toward Roslavl. After the capture of Roslavl, Guderian's Panzer group began a period of refitting to restore its combat power. East of Smolensk, Strauß' 9. Armee took over the front line with its infantry divisions, while Hoth's Panzergruppe 2 pivoted to the north to support the drive on Leningrad. The 61-year-old Generaloberst Adolf Strauß proved unequal to the rigors of hard campaigning and when he fell ill in late August, Hoth stepped up to command both 9. Armee and his own Panzergruppe 3 for two weeks.[48] Between August 22 and 26, Gruppe Stumme (a mixed force of infantry and Panzers) crushed the Soviet 22nd Army at Velikiye Luki, in a textbook tactical victory. Yet as German combat power ebbed in the Smolensk sector and shifted to other sectors, Timoshenko became more aggressive and local army-level attacks escalated into front-level operations. The Stavka Directive No. 001254 ordered a multifront attack to begin against Heeresgruppe Mitte on August 25, using several armies from the Western and Reserve Fronts.

On the morning of August 25, the Soviets began two simultaneous front-level offensives – the first real operational-level attacks since the beginning of the campaign. Timoshenko's Western Front attacked the German V Armeekorps (AOK 9) at Dukhovshchina, 50km northeast of Smolensk, with General-major Vasily A. Khomenko's 30th Army and Konev's 19th Army. Khomenko and Konev attacked primarily

---

*This was Zhukov's first field command in the Second World War. He was in command of this front for 40 days.

with partly-trained infantry, assisted only by limited air, artillery and armor support, but were able to stress the German defense by dint of numbers. Nevertheless, these frontal attacks lacked maneuver or mass and ended up becoming pointless brawls that inflicted heavy casualties on both sides. An attempt to slip the Dovator Cavalry Group into the rear of the AOK 9 proved to be little more than a nuisance and the Soviet infantry failed to achieve a breakthrough. By September 3 it was obvious that the Dukhovshchina offensive had failed, but the Stavka forced Timoshenko to continue it for another week. Zhukov's offensive against the Yelnya salient employed General-major Konstantin I. Rakutin's heavily-reinforced 24th Army (11 divisions) to attack three German infantry divisions from the XX Armeekorps (AOK 4). Unlike Timoshenko's unimaginative frontal attacks, Zhukov tried to pull off a double pincer attack to cut off and destroy the German divisions in the Yelnya salient. He was able to get 14 heavy artillery regiments from the Stavka reserves (including a battalion of the new BM-13 multiple rocket launchers) to support his offensive, but only token amounts of armor and close air support. Zhukov's concept was sound but his three assault groups proved only capable of grinding forward, slowly digging into the German defenses. By September 3, von Bock decided that he had suffered enough casualties trying to hold onto a useless position like Yelyna and authorized von Kluge to evacuate the salient; there was no push-back on the withdrawal from either Hitler or the OKH. Zhukov noticed the German withdrawal and tried to accelerate his attacks, but von Kluge managed to extricate all three divisions from the salient and the 24th Army occupied Yelnya on September 6. Afterwards, Zhukov claimed to have destroyed several German divisions in the Yelnya salient, which was a lie, but he had achieved a significant tactical victory. The truth was that Rakutin's 24th Army suffered over 31,000 casualties (over 30 percent of its strength) to push von Kluge's 4. Armee out of a vulnerable salient. Marshal Boris M. Shaposhnikov, chief of the General Staff (GSHKA), stated that Zhukov's offensive "did not provide completely positive results and led only to excessive losses both in personnel and equipment."[49]

By September 10, the Soviet offensives had culminated and the Western Front shifted to the defense. Altogether, the Soviet Western, Reserve and Bryansk Fronts had suffered about 759,000 casualties in the 63-day Smolensk campaign, with only the tactical victory at Yelnya to show for their efforts. At the end of the campaign, Timoshenko's Western Front was seriously weakened and most of its remaining troops were partly-trained recruits. On September 12, the Stavka decided to replace Timoshenko with Konev, who had done relatively well as an army commander during the campaign. Timoshenko was sent to deal with the crisis in the Ukraine, while Zhukov was sent to Leningrad. In contrast, Heeresgruppe Mitte suffered around 100,000 casualties in the Smolensk campaign, but had achieved its objectives and retained the freedom of maneuver to redeploy its two Panzer groups, despite near-continuous Soviet attacks. While it has become common coin for historians such as David Glantz and David Stahel to claim that Heeresgruppe Mitte suffered crippling personnel and material losses in the Smolensk campaign, the fact remains that the Germans had a large numerical and qualitative superiority in armor in the critical sectors for the next three months. German combat power may have been eroded at Smolensk, but after this campaign the Red Army would be desperately short of tanks, artillery and trained infantry until well into 1942.

In terms of battle command, von Bock and Hoth were the most effective leaders on the German side. Von Bock remained focused on the intermediate objective (destroying the encircled forces in the Smolensk *Kessel*) and the longterm objective (Moscow).[50] However, von Bock was unable to mass his combat power due to distractions on both flanks and constantly-shifting priorities imposed by Hitler and the OKH. After the seizure of Smolensk, Heeresgruppe Mitte had no *Schwerpunkt* and its sub-components fragmented in pursuit of diverging tactical objectives. When under pressure, von Bock became irascible and argumentative, which did little to foster a spirit of teamwork and common purpose among his subordinates. Hoth proved not only a very capable field commander and loyal subordinate, but also capable of taking on additional responsibility when Strauß was incapacitated by illness. Guderian's battlefield performance was sufficient to achieve several tactical victories, but he proved a problematic subordinate who flagrantly ignored orders he disagreed with and scattered his Panzer groups in pursuit of multiple objectives. On September 4, von Bock wanted to relieve Guderian of command for insubordination but was dissuaded by von Brauchitsch.[51] Von Kluge was the least effective German senior commander and his behavior bordered on the bizarre at times, probably due to an aversion to risk and his incipient anti-regime attitudes. Operational decision-making in Heeresgruppe Mitte during the Battle of Smolensk was convoluted, which made it difficult for von Bock to complete the mission in linear fashion; instead, operational needs became subordinated to fleeting tactical priorities.

Commander	Objective	Offensive	Mass	Maneuver	Surprise	Security	TALLY
Von Bock	+	+	–	+	+	o	3
Von Kluge	–	–	+	o	o	+	o
Strauß	o	o	o	o	o	+	1
Hoth	+	+	–	+	+	+	4
Guderian	–	+	–	+	+	o	1
Timoshenko	o	+	o	o	o	–	o
Zhukov	+	+	+	+	o	o	4
Kurochkin	+	+	–	+	o	o	2
Konev Rokossovsky	+	+	o	–	–	o	o

Central Axis, Phase 2 Leadership Assessment

Although Heeresgruppe Mitte's scheme of maneuver using the proven double pincer method had proved effective, German logistic planning fell far short of perfection. First, the Panzer groups had begun crossing the Dvina and Dnepr Rivers several days before Heeresgruppe Mitte had created a supply base in Minsk. Consequently, both Hoth and Guderian were soon complaining about their Panzers running out of ammunition and fuel at awkward moments.[52] Second, the Heeresgruppe Mitte quartermasters were told that they would be supporting a pursuit operation, so they emphasized fuel at the expense of ammunition.[53] Once operations shifted to positional combat during the *Kesselschlact*, German front-line units quickly expended their ammunition and could not get immediate resupplies. Third, both Panzer groups were working well beyond the nearest railhead, often by 200–300km, which forced German commanders to reduce their maneuvering and artillery support. Finally, both the troops and vehicles were beginning to suffer from weeks of continuous combat, which reduced their overall operational effectiveness. In contrast, Timoshenko's armies were operating close to friendly rail lines and their supply depots, which increased their ability to conduct protracted fights around places like Yartsevo and Yelnya.

On the Soviet side, Timoshenko ended up being little more than a push-button for the Stavka by executing their orders with little thought or planning on his part or that of his staff. The only principle of war that Timoshenko really adhered to was the offensive, even when this was not a prudent course of action. He prematurely squandered his reserves as they arrived and was content to conduct unimaginative frontal assaults, eschewing maneuver and surprise. His failure to ensure security also allowed Guderian and Hoth to gain a decisive advantage by enveloping both his flanks and capture Smolensk in a single day. Timoshenko's brute force efforts to break through the thin German ring around the Smolensk *Kessel* ended up sacrificing more troops than the number who escaped from the pocket. Zhukov was the only Soviet commander in this campaign to accomplish his operational objective, of eliminating the Yelnya salient, albeit at a high cost. Kurochkin also showed some promise in the campaign, both in the offense and defense, even though he failed to accomplish any of his assigned missions. Konev and Rokossovsky were both essentially bit players in the campaign, although they made the best of unfavorable circumstances. Unlike the German side, there was negligible discussion about mission priorities on the Soviet side at Smolensk, which should have translated to an advantage in decision-making, but it did not. The Soviet tendency to be profligate with men and material also left the Western Front in a vulnerable condition for the next phase of the campaign.

Despite the drubbing suffered at Smolensk, the Red Army leadership did accomplish a positive objective in August 1941, which would provide them with a longterm operational advantage. By means of GKO Secret Order No. 0257 (August 1) the Main Directorate of the Rear Services of the Red Army was established under the command of General-leytenant Andrei V. Khrulev. Unlike the Germans, the Red Army achieved unity of command over its logistic and transport services, including rail operations. Furthermore, Khrulev proved to be an innovator, not a bureaucrat, and he constantly strove to improve the ability of the Red Army's logistic services to support armies at the front. As a result, the Stavka soon gained the ability to rapidly move men, material and supplies to the fronts where they were needed most. Khrulev was given wide authority, being made a deputy People's Commissar of Defense and later People's Commissar of Railways.

Southern Axis, June 22–September 20, 1941

Since Stalin publicly stated his belief that he expected the Germans to make their main effort in the Ukraine – if they attacked – the NKO ensured that the Kiev Special Military District (*Kiyevskogo osobogo voyennogo okrug* or KOVO) was given a significant edge in manpower and equipment. General-polkovnik Mikhail P. Kirponos was commander of the KOVO, which would become the Southwestern Front (*Yugo-Zapadnyy front*) in wartime. Kirponos was provided more manpower and equipment than any other frontier district commander, totaling 58 divisions with 907,000 troops, 4,500 tanks and 7,700 artillery pieces. With these forces, he was responsible for defending more than 800 kilometers of frontier in Galicia and southwestern Ukraine, including the border with Hungary and German-occupied Poland. On Kirponos' left flank, the Odessa Military District (OdVO, which would become the Southern Front) commanded by General-polkvnik Ivan Tyulenev, guarded the 420km-long border with Romania with another 15 divisions. The Soviet frontier in the Ukraine also had some of the best fortifications of the Molotov Line, plus additional fortifications of the Stalin Line on the old pre-1939 border. In terms of air support, the VVS-KOVO under General-leytenant Evgeniy S. Ptukhin and VVS-OdVO under General-major Fedor A. Astakhov had over 2,700 aircraft in the Ukraine, amounting to more than 1,400 operational fighters and 780 bombers, of which more than one-quarter were the latest models.

Kirponos had made his reputation as a competent division commander on the Finnish front in 1940 and been awarded the Hero of the Soviet Union (HSU). However, his military record was otherwise undistinguished and he was under NKVD scrutiny due to his Polish wife and suspect connections. Consequently, Kirponos had to toe the line with Moscow and avoid making any obvious errors, which tended to make him risk-averse. The NKO assigned General-leytenant Maksim A. Purkaev as chief of staff and Polkovnik Grigory I. Bondarev as senior intelligence officer; both Purkaev and Bondarev were career staff officers and fully capable in their assignments. The primary mission of the KOVO and OdVO was to defend the frontier zone and then mount immediate counterattacks against any hostile intrusions. Kirponos deployed four armies in his first echelon along the border, but his defense was weighted on his center-right, between Przemysl and Kovel, since this was the likely invasion area for German forces in southern Poland. General-major Mikhail I. Potapov's 5th Army held a 100km-wide sector on the right flank with five rifle divisions and three mechanized corps, while General-leytenant Ivan N. Muzychenko's 6th Army held a 150km-wide sector around Lvov with six rifle divisions, a cavalry corps and three mechanized corps. Potapov was unusual in that he was a veteran tank officer who had served with Zhukov at Khalkhin Gol in 1939 – most Soviet field army commanders in 1941 were infantry officers. Kirponos deployed two smaller armies (General-leytenant Fedor Kostenko's 26th Army and General-major Pavel

Ponedelin's 12th Army) on his left flank to guard a 500km stretch along the Hungarian and Romanian borders. Kirponos kept more than one-third of his forces (13 rifle divisions, an airborne corps and one mechanized corps) under front-level control in second echelon, further back from the border. The Stavka also had three reserve armies (16, 19, 21) scheduled to form along the Dnepr River, even further back. In doctrinal terms, the KOVO was deployed in depth and with ample mobile reserves and air support, but its front-line rifle divisions were unrealistically expected to defend up to 25–30km-wide sectors. Nevertheless, the terrain in Galicia tended to favor the defense, since the Pripet Marshes in the northeast and the Carpathian Mountains in the south would force the Germans to attack along predictable routes. Kirponos had a war plan, designated as KOVO-41, which followed the NKO-imposed template: hold the border with infantry armies and immediately counterattack any incursions with the first-echelon mechanized corps.

The NKO was less concerned about the Romanian border, even though Soviet intelligence was aware that German combat units had arrived in that country. General-polkvnik Ivan Tyulenev's Odessa Military District (OdVO) only had a single army – General-polkovnik Yakov Cherevichenko's 9th Army – to defend the border from any German-Romanian forces that crossed the Prut River into Moldavia (which the Red Army had seized by force in June 1940). The Romanian Army was not held in high regard and had obsolete tanks and limited airpower, which made it much less of a threat. In essence, the NKO opted for an economy of force role for the OdVO, so that more forces could be deployed to reinforce the KOVO.

By early June 1941, Kirponos and his staff were well aware of hostile reconnaissance activity along the border and the possibility of a no-notice attack. Kirponos tried to quietly raise the alert status of units on the border and take other precautionary steps, but the ever-vigilant NKVD officers in the KOVO reported his actions to Moscow and he was ordered to rescind any such orders at once.[54] Purkaev also tried to improve the combat readiness of some units in second echelon, but was similarly rebuked. Consequently, the lesson was clear – only top-down decisions were permitted and individual initiative was discouraged. General-leytenant Evgeniy S. Ptukhin, the VVS-KOVO commander, was under intense scrutiny by the NKVD and he was about to be arrested for "Anti-Soviet activities" on the day before Operation *Barbarossa* began. Ptukhin, who had commanded a fighter group in Spain in 1937–38, was caught up in a new purge of VVS officers which relied primarily upon innuendo.

On the other side of the border, Heeresgruppe Süd under Generalfeldmarschall Gerd von Rundstedt faced its own set of unique difficulties. Unlike the other two German army groups involved in *Barbarossa*, Heeresgruppe Süd had to work closely with Axis troops from Romania, Hungary, Slovakia and Italy, which was problematic for a number of reasons. First, the Wehrmacht had no doctrine for coalition warfare and was unwilling to adapt its methods in the interest of improving its ability to operate alongside other armies. Second, the other Axis armies participating in Operation *Barbarossa* had doctrines that were geared more toward the defensive positional warfare methods of the First World War, rather than offensive operations. None of the other Axis armies possessed much in the way of tank or motorized units, which made it impossible for them to keep up with fast-paced German *Bewegungskrieg* campaigns. Third, Axis coalition commanders and their staffs were accustomed to a detailed, explicit planning process, rather than the free-wheeling German intuitive orders approach, which often led to confusion and acrimony during joint operations. Finally, none of the Axis coalition partners had been informed of Operation *Barbarossa* until just two days or less prior to the invasion, which meant that their armies started at a much lower state of preparedness than the German armies. Von Rundstedt had to integrate these various heterogenous Axis formations, which constituted about 38 percent of his field forces, into a viable chain of command in order to achieve his army group's objectives. The Romanian contingent was the largest, with two field armies comprised of 15 divisions with a total of 325,000 troops, plus an air group with over 200 aircraft.

Although Gerd von Rundstedt was normally accorded a healthy respect by his wartime adversaries and post-war historians, by 1941 he was already a 65-year-old brought back from retirement and with little zest for war or understanding of modern military technology. Hitler accepted him as a living link to the old-style Prussian commanders, although von Rundstedt had been a career General Staff officer who had not made his reputation on any battlefields. Von Rundstedt's staff, particularly General der Infanterie Georg von Sodenstern (Chief of Staff) and Oberstleutnant August Winter (Ia), were top notch and did all the serious planning. The cutting edge of von Rundstedt's Heeresgruppe Süd was provided by Generaloberst Ewald von Kleist's Panzergruppe 1, which had three motorized corps, totaling five Panzer divisions and four motorized infantry divisions (two of which were Waffen-SS). Although von Kleist only started the campaign with 730 AFV, over 60 percent were PzKpfw III/IV medium tanks. Nor was von Kleist handicapped with any Czech-made tanks, as were the Panzer groups in the other two army groups. Von Kleist was easily the most experienced of the four Panzer group commanders and he was comfortable with commanding large formations, as he already had in France in 1940. Von Kleist also had an experienced chief of staff in Oberst Kurt Zeitzler, who had served with him through both the French and Balkans campaigns.

Altogether, Heeresgruppe Süd had just over 1 million troops in four army-size formations, with a total of 43 German divisions. In addition to von Kleist's Panzer group, Generalfeldmarschall Walther von Reichenau's 6. Armee (AOK 6) and General der Infanterie Carl-Heinrich von Stülpnagel's 17. Armee (AOK 17) were based in southern Poland and Slovakia. Generaloberst Eugen Ritter von Schobert's 11. Armee (AOK 11) was based in Romania with six German infantry divisions and would work with both Italian and Romanian forces. Generaloberst Alexander Lohr's Luftflotte 4, comprised of IV Fliegerkorps and V Fliegerkorps with about 670 combat aircraft, would provide air support for Heeresgruppe Süd. Von Rundstedt's campaign objectives were to (1) destroy the bulk of the Red Army forces west of the Dnepr River, (2) capture Kiev and then (3) advance to seize economic resource areas in the Donbas and complete the conquest of the Ukraine. The scheme of maneuver was to place the *Schwerpunkt* in the sector between Lvov and Kovel, with von Kleist's Panzers punching through the Soviet first echelon defenses along the axis Rovno-Novgorod Volynskiy-Zhitomir. Von Reichenau's 6. Armee would reinforce von Kleist's advance and protect the left flank, while von Stülpnagel's 17. Armee advanced directly on Lvov, then aiming for Vinnitsa. Since the OKH had a low estimate of Romanian combat effectiveness, von Schobert's 11. Armee would not cross the Prut River into Moldavia until the advance of Heeresgruppe Süd's main effort caused the Soviet defenses in southern Ukraine to begin to unravel.

As with the rest of the Eastern Front, Heeresgruppe Süd began operations at 0305 hours on X-Tag, June 22. Luftflotte 4 began with powerful strikes against Soviet air bases in the region, which inflicted considerable losses, but Ptukhin was still able to get large numbers of his VVS-KOVO aircraft into the air. In particular, the presence of significant numbers of modern MiG-3 fighters flown by some of the best VVS pilots resulted in a real fight for air supremacy over southwest Ukraine. Von Reichenau's 6. Armee was able to seize two intact bridges over the Western Bug River on the first day, and then von Kleist began to send his lead Panzer divisions across into the bridgehead. The two Soviet rifle divisions from Potapov's 5th Army in the area of the bridgeheads were too dispersed to offer serious resistance, but two fortified regions of the Molotov Line gave von Reichenau's infantry some trouble.[55] Furthermore, the two German penetration corridors were 40 kilometers apart and due to the narrowness of the attack sectors chosen, von Kleist's Panzers initially had little elbow room. Each of his two motorized corps pushed eastward with a single vanguard Panzer-Division but von Kleist's Panzer group was vulnerable to a sudden riposte. It would require two days to get all of Panzergruppe 1 across the river and deployed on line, which gave Kirponos a brief window of opportunity.

At the start of hostilities, Kirponos and his staff moved from their headquarters in Kiev to their tactical command post (CP) at Tarnopol and established the Southwestern Front. Not having rehearsed deploying to his CP, the staff convoy took many hours to reach its destination and had no real means to communicate during this gap. Although on May 27, 1941 the NKO had ordered each front to establish a tactical CP located away from their normal peacetime garrison, Kirponos was shocked to find that his CP was not completed or even functional. From the beginning, Kirponos was bedeviled by nagging communication problems, which seriously hindered his ability to direct his subordinate formations. Soviet army commanders also relocated to their tactical CPs shortly after the invasion began and suffered similar communication problems. Due to excessive concerns about communications security, the Red Army had not practiced setting up radio networks much in peacetime or coding/encoding procedures – this was a self-inflicted wound that could have been rectified with some command post exercises, but it was not. Consequently, when war came, radio procedures were rusty and even finding the correct code books proved difficult, so Kirponos and his army commanders were forced to rely upon unsecure civilian phone networks for the first several days of the war.[56] Eventually, Kirponos was able to talk to his forces on the quiet Hungarian border and on the Romanian frontier (where only minor action was occurring), but not to his 5th and 6th Armies, which were under heavy pressure. In contrast, the Wehrmacht had honed its radio network procedures to a fine degree after the Polish, French and Balkan campaigns, which gave them a critical advantage in command and control (C2) and situation awareness.

Unfortunately, Kirponos' CP had good communications with Moscow and he received NKO Directive 3 around 2300 hours on June 22, which ordered him to mount a counterattack with five mechanized corps against von Kleist's Panzers within 48 hours.[57] When Kirponos received the directive from Moscow, all he knew about the situation at the front was that both the 5th and 6th Armies were under heavy pressure and that German armor was already across the Western Bug River in the Vladimir-Volynskiy and Sokal sectors. Moscow was now ordering him to commit the bulk of his mobile reserves into an intelligence void, when he could not even effectively communicate with his front-line commanders. General-leytenant Maksim A. Purkaev, his chief of staff, was against trying to organize an immediate large-scale counterattack as per the KOVO-41 pre-war plan under the conditions of poor C2 and inadequate time to assemble dispersed units; he sensibly counseled establishing a firm defensive line first, then prepare to counterattack. However, Nikolai N. Vashugin, the front-level political commissar, would have none of this and accused Purkaev of being a coward.[58] Given the fear of arrest and execution for failing to follow an NKO directive, Kirponos acquiesced and ordered Purkaev and his deputy, Polkovnik Ivan K. Bagramyan, to begin planning the counteroffensive.

With limited time available, on the night of June 22/23 Purkaev and Bagramyan threw together a bare bones plan for the counterattack. Potapov's 5th Army was supposed to hold off the enemy while six mechanized corps (4, 8, 9, 15, 19 and 22) moved to the frontier region and assembled to conduct a pincer attack against von Kleist's spearhead units. On paper, Kirponos did possess a very strong mobile reserve with some decent corps commanders, including Konstantin Rokossovsky and Andrei Vlasov, but the individual divisions were scattered over a large number of peacetime garrisons and massing them into a cohesive strike force would take several days. Indeed, once units moved out of their peacetime garrisons, Purkaev was not even sure where all the units earmarked from the operation were located. Despite having a significant number of modern tanks, most of the mechanized corps were short of ammunition, fuel, motor transport and radios, which hindered a rapid transition to combat readiness. Most of the so-called motorized rifle divisions were in fact forced to walk to the front on foot, for lack of transport. Nor did Purkaev have any time to plan for air support, since Ptukhin and the VVS-KOVO were in an even greater state of command confusion. Later in the war, Soviet front commanders were able to ask for additional time to prepare for offensive operations, but in the circumstances of June 1941 this proved impossible.

With NKVD officers and political commissars supervising his every decision, Kirponos could not afford to argue. Instead, he ordered all five mechanized corps to proceed to the Lutsk-Brody sector and counterattack German forces in that vicinity as soon as possible. He also ordered two rifle corps from his second echelon to move up and support the counterattack, although they would need at least five days to reach the front. At any rate, the bulk of Kirponos' armored reserves would be committed piecemeal into a meeting engagement with von Kleist's Panzergruppe 1. Nor did the deployment of the mechanized reserves progress smoothly, due to excessive vehicle breakdowns (50 percent in some units), Luftwaffe battlefield interdiction sorties and the confusion caused by multiple corps-size units trying to use a few secondary roads at the same time. Adding to Kirponos' problems, Zhukov arrived at the Tarnopol CP on June 24 and stayed for three days, hectoring Kirponos to attack without delay. Since Zhukov had been commander of the KOVO until January 1941, he was familiar with the terrain and the forces in this region.

Nevertheless, Kirponos was able to begin limited counterattacks on the afternoon of June 24, which gradually escalated into the six-day Battle of Dubno. At this point, von Kleist had one Panzer division from the III. Armeekorps (mot.) near Lutsk and one from the XXXXVII Armeekorps (mot.) near Radekhov enroute to Dubno; the advancing German spearheads were spread thinly. Initially, only part of one Soviet mechanized corps was able to attack on the first day, achieving very little, but Kirponos fed more and more armor into the battle as units reached the front. The Germans were certainly shocked by the appearance of significant number of KV and T-34 tanks, which outclassed their own medium tanks, but the lack of coordination among Soviet units allowed von Kleist and his corps commanders to fend off most of these attacks. The Soviet armored counterattacks went in without benefit of prior reconnaissance or artillery support, whereas Von Kleist's two mechanized corps benefitted from effective close air support from the Luftflotte 4. Thanks to poor Soviet operational security (OPSEC), the Germans were able to identify the tactical CPs of the 8th and 15th Mechanized Corps and target them with a powerful air strike, which wounded one corps commander and seriously disrupted the C2 of both mechanized corps.[59] Amid this chaos, the front commissar, Vashugin, showed up and demanded that the 8th Mechanized Corps continue its attacks and threatened to shoot the corps commander, General-leytenant Dmitry I. Ryabyshev, unless he complied at once. Ryabyshev did as ordered and the fragments of his corps were quickly routed with heavy losses.[60] Commissars like Vashugin were political fanatics and were unwilling to listen to military common sense or any kind of objective facts – these were the kind of men who hijacked the Red Army's decision-making process at the beginning of the war, often with catastrophic results.

Amazingly, the Soviet mechanized corps achieved some local tactical success by committing large amounts of armor into the battle, but von Kleist temporarily shifted to the tactical defense and brought up two infantry divisions to steady his line. Von Kleist was able to fight the battle under perfect conditions for the Wehrmacht: good weather, plentiful air support, full-strength ground units and short supply lines. Kirponos' armor dashed itself to pieces against an immovable German defense. By June 27, Zhukov had had enough and returned to Moscow, having accomplished nothing. On June 28, von Kleist – who had managed to keep his third motorized corps in reserve – committed it now to shatter the wobbly Soviet front line. The next day, the German 9. Panzer-Division enveloped the right flank of Muzychenko's 6th Army, which forced the Southwestern Front to order an evacuation of Lvov. When it became clear that the battle on the frontier was lost, Vashugin shot himself in the Southwest Front CP. The Battle of Dubno was a train-wreck in slow motion for the Southwest Front and there was nothing that Kirponos could do to stop it. At the conclusion of the battle, Kirponos was left with an armored reserve that had been reduced by two-thirds and which was too depleted to halt the inexorable advance of von Kleist's Panzers.[61] Withdrawal became the only option and on June 30, the GKO ordered Kirponos to begin pulling back to the pre-war Stalin Line fortifications.

Most historians examining the German invasion of southwest Ukraine have focused on the Battle of Dubno, without paying much attention to the fact that without benefit of armor support, von Stülpnagel's 17. Armee was able to steadily push Muzychenko's 6th Army back toward Lvov and take the city. Furthermore, Muzychenko had General-major Andrei A. Vlasov's 4th Mechanized Corps as a tactical reserve; Vlasov's formation was the strongest mechanized corps in the Red Army and was equipped with nearly 900 tanks (including 313 T-34 and 101 KV). From the beginning, Kirponos and Muzychenko struggled for control over Vlasov's corps, with the result that this powerful formation spent the first four days of the war marching and counter-marching without really engaging the enemy much. The one minor effort Vlasov made to stop von Stülpnagel's infantry failed, with the loss of 35 tanks. Zhukov was flabbergasted when he discovered how the 4th Mechanized Corps was being mismanaged and ordered Kirponos to keep it near Lvov in support of the 6th Army. However, it made no difference.

The 55-year-old von Stülpnagel was a General Staff-trained officer who had helped draft the *Truppenführung* manuals, but he was also one of the most active anti-Hitler resistance conspirators in the Wehrmacht.[62] His infantry divisions overwhelmed Muzychenko's rifle divisions, which had the benefit of border fortifications and armor support. The Soviet 6th Army did put up stiff resistance, but von Stülpnagel's advance proved inexorable and Lvov fell on the morning of June 30. The rapid defeat of Muzychenko's 6th Army left Kirponos no option but to begin withdrawing from the entire border region. Ponedelin's 12th Army began pulling back from the Hungarian border, even though it was not in contact. On the northern flank of von Kleist's penetration, Potapov's 5th Army managed to save about half its forces by retreating into the Pripet Marshes. Von Reichenau, who was in poor health at the start of *Barbarossa*, was not very aggressive in his pursuit and spent most of the Battle of Dubno protecting von Kleist's left flank.[63]

Von Rundstedt's performance during the initial phase of *Barbarossa* was cautious and Kirponos' aggressive armored counterattacks around Dubno-Brody increased his innate caution. His army group was facing a numerically-superior enemy, equipped with better tanks, and despite suffering heavy losses in the Battle of Dubno, the Southwest Front was still largely intact. When the Soviet withdrawal was detected, von Rundstedt was of two minds. First, he saw an opportunity to cut off the retreating Soviet 6th and 12th Armies once Romania fully entered the war and crossed the Prut River into Moldavia (Bessarabia). Von Stülpnagel's 17. Armee was on a roll and with some Panzer support, it could potentially remove quite a few of Kirponos' pieces from the chessboard. Second, a direct advance on Kiev was feasible – which Hitler urged – but which promised hard fighting to get through the Stalin Line. Von Reichenau's 6. Armee would only be able to provide one or two infantry corps to support a rapid advance to Kiev, since most of his units were dispersed and conducting mop-up actions. Von Kleist argued for concentration on a single objective and not to split up Panzergruppe 1, but was overruled. Von Rundstedt ordered von Kleist to send his main spearheads toward Kiev, with von Reichenau's infantry tagging along behind, while sending one motorized corps (XIV) to assist von Stülpnagel's 17. Armee in conducting an envelopment operation in the vicinity Proskurov-Vinnitsa.

On the Soviet side, Kirponos badly fumbled the initial phase of the German invasion and his subordinate army commanders did little better, although much of this was due to the rigid adherence to the KOVO-41 contingency plan. Kirponos knew that he would be expected to conduct an immediate counterattack with his mechanized reserves in the event of an enemy invasion, but as it turned out, rehearsals and C2 procedures had not been done. The reliance on civilian phone networks to command his formations clearly indicates that Kirponos, Purkaev and the rest of the KOVO staff set the conditions for mission failure prior to the first German bomb falling in the Ukraine. Yet having lost the battle on the frontier, Kirponos still had a good chance to hold Kiev and a line on the Dnepr. Given the relatively slow German pursuit, Kirponos was able to build a new line along the Sluch River, anchored on Stalin Line positions at

Novgorod Volynskiy (Zviahel), 200 kilometers west of Kiev. The Southwest Front still had 1,200 tanks and a dozen second-echelon divisions that were intact. The front CP in Tarnopol was evacuated and the 6th, 12th and 26th Armies were ordered to occupy positions along the rest of the Stalin Line, stretching 220 kilometers from Novgorod Volynskiy to Kamenets-Podolski.

After reorganizing, von Kleist began advancing along the main road to Novgorod Volynskiy with just two motorized corps (III, XXXXVIII). Surprisingly, the 13. Panzer-Division was able to gain a bridgehead across the Sluch River on July 5 and began eliminating positions in the Stalin Line. The Stavka immediately ordered Kirponos to commit his remaining armor to eliminate the German bridgehead, but once again, the attacks were uncoordinated and were repulsed with heavy losses. Nevertheless, Zhukov personally ordered Kirponos to keep attacking, which resulted in the decimation of his remaining armored reserves. Again, von Kleist shifted to the tactical defense to fend off the Soviet armor, then once their fury was spent, he committed his own reserves. On July 8, General der Kavallerie Eberhard von Mackensen's III Armeekorps (mot.) achieved a breakthrough and sliced through Kirponos' front line to capture Zhitomir. Von Mackensen pushed his spearhead on during the night, moving another 110 kilometers and by dawn it had reached the western outskirts of Kiev. It was only a very narrow penetration by a single Panzer division, but Kirponos no longer had the mobile reserves to crush this imprudent advance. Having broken through the Stalin Line, von Kleist used Zhitomir as a pivot point for his Panzer group, sending units north and south to widen the breach. Kirponos' line rapidly began to disintegrate. At the same time, von Stülpnagel's 17. Armee continued to advance and was able to overrun portions of the Stalin Line near Proskurov before Ponedelin's 12th Army could react. While there were still plenty of mop-up actions, the Stalin Line had not proved to be a significant obstacle for Heeresgruppe Süd's operations.

Meanwhile, in Moldavia (Bessarabia), Tyulenev was the only Soviet front commander who had ten days to transition his command to a wartime footing before the enemy attacked in force. The German 11. Armee and the Romanian 3rd and 4th Armies were planning an attack across the Prut River into Moldavia, known as Unternehmen *München* (Operation *Munich*). The timing was based on the progress of Heeresgruppe Süd, particularly von Stülpnagel's 17. Armee. The Axis commanders opted for a broad front crossing of the Prut, with no explicit *Schwerpunkt*. Von Schobert's 11. Armee would make two corps-size crossings in the north and center, while Lieutenant General Nicolae G. Ciuperca's Romanian 4th Army sent its III Corps across in the south. The initial crossings of the Prut River on July 2 were not seriously opposed, because Tyulenev was expecting orders from the Stavka to evacuate the province and form a line behind the Dniester River. Instead, the Stavka ordered Tyulenev to hold his ground and counterattack. On July 3, Cherevichenko's 9th Army began counterattacking. Ciuperca took five days to get three divisions from the III Corps across the Prut, which provided Cherevichenko a golden opportunity. On July 6, the Soviets conducted an unusually coordinated attack with a tank division and a rifle corps, which badly mauled a Romanian division and forced Ciuperca onto the defensive for a week. Von Schobert was obliged to divert some of his limited forces to prevent the Romanian 4th Army bridgehead from being overrun. Von Schobert's own two bridgeheads were secure, but he could not defeat Tyulenev's Southern Front with just five German infantry divisions. Unlike anywhere else on the Eastern Front, the Red Army in Moldavia had the ability to achieve some degree of operational success in the opening battles.

At the critical moment, Marshal Semyon Budyonny arrived from Moscow on July 10 to take over as Southwestern Theater commander, charged with directing both Kirponos and Tyulenev. As with the other Stavka representatives, Budyonny arrived without a significant personal staff, which would have made it difficult for him to coordinate complex multifront operations even if he had the skill for operational-level warfare, which he did not. Budyonny made a string of bad decisions, beginning with his order to abandon the westernmost end of the Dniester River line, even though it had not been breached. He also ordered Kirponos and Tyulenev to create a new line anchored on Uman, utilizing elements of the 6th and 12th Armies. The 26th Army would be used to fill in the line between the right flank of the 6th Army and the forces holding Kiev. However, the idea of building a defensive line in open steppe country against a German-style offensive was ill-judged. The only thing that saved the Southwestern Front from immediate disaster was that Heeresgruppe Süd had outrun its supply lines, forcing von Kleist's Panzer group to pause for several days. Kirponos used the respite to build up his forces in front of Kiev.

On July 15, von Kleist shifted his axis of attack from due east toward the southeast, blasting through the 26th Army. Von Kleist then pushed his XIV Armeekorps (mot.) through the gap to exploit and envelop Muzychenko's 6th Army, while von Stülpnagel's 17. Armee accelerated its attacks against the front of the forming salient. For once, the Soviets reacted with alacrity, committing two mechanized corps to stop von Kleist's Panzers and a third to delay the 17. Armee. The battle swung in doubt for a week, with the Soviet 6th and 12th Armies retreating eastward

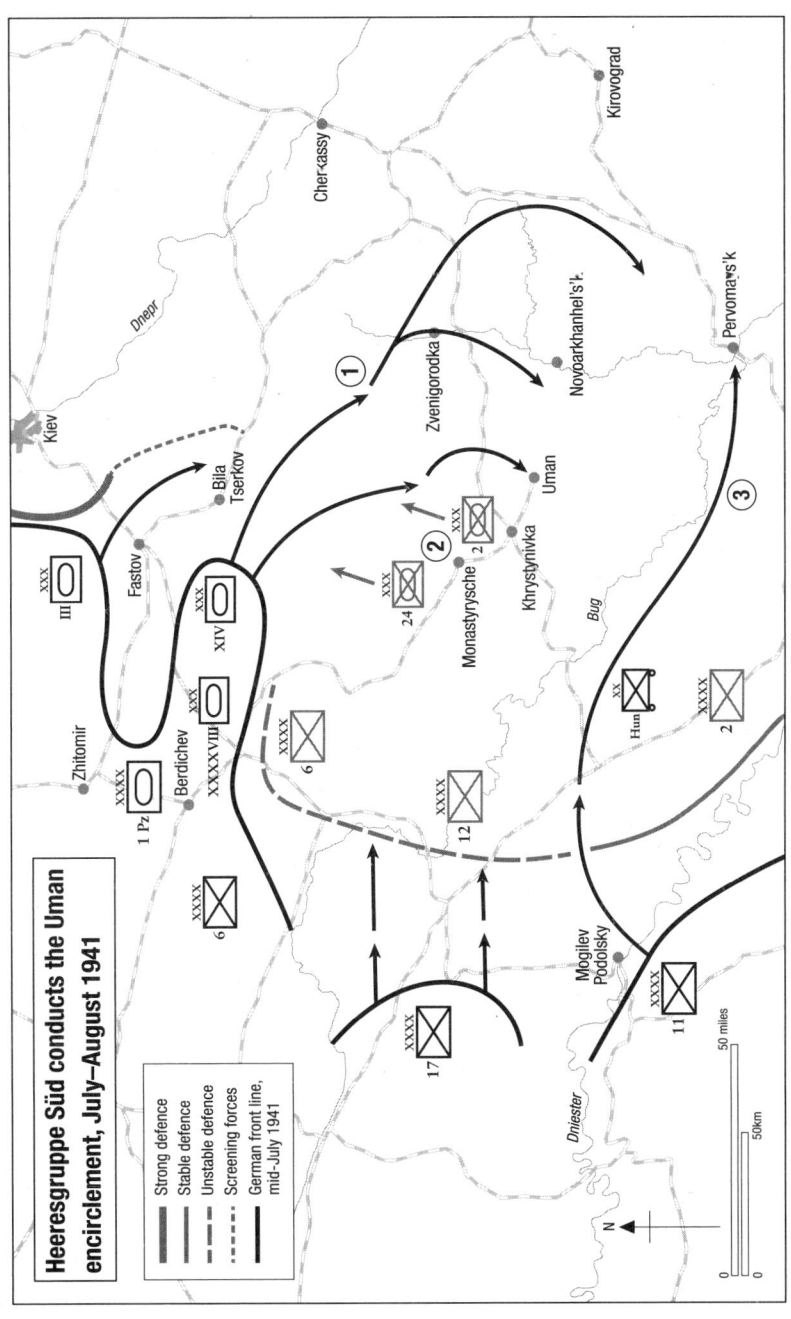

Heeresgruppe Süd conducts the Uman encirclement, July–August 1941

MAP KEY

1. Panzergruppe 1 envelops the right flank of the Soviet 6th Army.
2. Soviet mechanized reserves counterattack German spearheads.
3. Hungarian motorized division advances to Pervomaysk to complete Uman encirclement.

---

to escape the trap. Due to the retreat of the left wing of the Southwest Front, Tyulenev was authorized to abandon Moldavia and retreat behind the Dniester River. The Romanian Army resumed its offensive on July 15 along with 11. Armee and quickly occupied the region, while the Soviet 9th Army successfully retreated across the Dniester. The Romanian Army suffered 22,765 casualties to recover its lost province of Bessarabia, whereas Tyulenev's Southern Front only suffered 17,893 casualties – the one sector where the Red Army achieved a favorable casualty exchange ratio.[64] Meanwhile, von Kleist's Panzers finally fought their way past the Soviet mechanized rearguards and completed the encirclement of the Uman *Kessel* on August 3, trapping over 200,000 troops from the Soviet 6th and 12th Armies. Unlike other pocket battles, the Germans were able to crush the Uman *Kessel* in just four days; both Muzychenko and Ponedelin were captured along with 15 other Soviet generals.

On July 29, just before the Uman *Kessel* was closed, Zhukov had recommended to Stalin that Kirponos and Tyulenev should withdraw all their forces east of the Dnepr River, but Stalin rejected this advice. Instead, he removed Zhukov as chief of the General Staff (GSHKA) and replaced him with Marshal Boris M. Shaposhnikov (who had been chief of the GSHKA in 1937–40). Zhukov was temporarily put in charge of the Reserve Front, engaged in mobilizing new armies for the front.[65] Having crushed the Uman *Kessel*, von Rundstedt now resumed his advance against Kiev with von Reichenau's 6. Armee, while von Kleist's Panzers and 17. Armee pushed rapidly toward the lower Dnepr River. The Romanian Army did not at first want to cross the Dniester River, having accomplished its primary war objective with the liberation of Bessarabia, but was finally persuaded to expand its war aims. On August 3, the Romanians headed toward Odessa, while the 11. Armee headed toward the Crimea. Kirponos was able to mount a very active defense of Kiev, which not only kept von Reichenau's 6. Armee at bay but forced him to shift to the defense. On August 12, Hitler ordered von Rundstedt to discontinue attacks on Kiev for the moment, in order to keep casualties down. So far, the 6. Armee had suffered over 42,000 casualties (including 11,500 dead or missing) since the start of the campaign, which was the highest losses of any of the 12 German armies then engaged on the Eastern Front.

During the first phase of Operation *Barbarossa*, Heeresgruppe Süd inflicted significant losses on the Southwest Front west of the Dnepr River but failed to take Kiev; von Rundstedt's performance was decent but not outstanding and he equivocated on prioritizing objectives. The operational performance of both von Kleist and Stülpnagel was outstanding and von Kleist deserves extra credit for well-timed use of his reserves. Von Reichenau's performance was poor, accomplishing little except taking heavy casualties. On the Soviet side, Kirponos was hamstrung by NKO/GKO directives and interference from Zhukov, but he did manage to hold onto Kiev and his constant attacks did inflict considerable losses on Heeresgruppe Süd. Both Kirponos and Tyulenev performed fairly well in positional battles where they could just pound away, but neither operated well when the battlefield became fluid. Budyonny was poorly suited as a theater commander and his ill-judged decisions only made the Soviet position in the Ukraine worse. Among the Soviet army commanders, Potapov put in a dogged defense with his 5th Army that distracted German attention away from Kiev while Cherevichenko demonstrated some skill in discomfiting the Romanian 4th Army. The other Soviet army commanders failed to accomplish their missions or cause much hindrance to the enemy invasion.

Commander	Objective	Offensive	Mass	Maneuver	Surprise	Security	TALLY
Von Rundstedt	o	+	o	+	+	+	4
Von Kleist	+	+	+	++	+	+	7
Stülpnagel	+	+	+	o	o	+	4
Von Reichenau	o	o	o	o	o	+	1
Kirponos	+	+	o	+	o	-	2
Tyulenev	+	+	o	o	o	o	2
Budyonny	o	+	o	o	o	-	0
Potapov	+	o	o	+	o	o	2
Cherevichenko	+	o	o	o	+	o	2
Ponedelin, Muzychenko	+	o	-	o	o	-	-1

Southern Axis, Phase 1 Leadership Assessment

One of the primary lessons for operational-level warfare offered by the opening moves in the Ukraine in June 1941 is the importance of practicing essential command and control procedures (e.g. establishing effective secure radio networks, army-air coordination), unit deployment to wartime assembly areas and vital logistic tasks (e.g. issuing fuel and ammunition from depots) in peacetime. Senior leaders need to participate in command post exercises and rehearsals in order to ensure that deficiencies are rectified. Had Kirponos and his staff conducted realistic rehearsals of KOVO-41, some of the most serious problems would likely have been addressed prior to the German invasion. Unfortunately, even modern armies tend to pay lip service to rehearsals, with the most recent demonstration provided by the embarrassing Russian C2 and logistic failures in the opening weeks of the Ukraine invasion in 2022.[66]

In the wake of the Uman disaster, von Kleist's Panzergruppe 1 spread eastward and seized bridgeheads over the Dnepr River at Kremenchug and Dnepropetrovsk. The Romanian 4th Army closed in on Odessa, which was defended by about 35,000 Soviet troops from the Southern Front, and initiated siege operations. However, von Reichenau's 6. Armee was not only stymied at Kiev, but its left flank was under frequent attack from Potapov's 5th Army, lurking in the Pripet Marshes near Chornobyl. The Stavka reinforced Potapov's depleted army so it could conduct a larger counteroffensive and created a new Central Front under General-polkovnik Fedor I. Kuznetsov (who had been relieved of command of the Northwest Front) to hold Gomel and prevent Heeresgruppe Mitte from threatening to isolate Potapov's army. Potapov's counteroffensive between August 4 and 8 achieved some tactical success against von Reichenau's overextended left flank but Soviet losses were very heavy. As usual, Soviet flank attacks caused Hitler to become agitated, and suddenly eliminating the 5th Army became a priority; in Führer Directive 34 he specifically stated that "the 5th Red Army, fighting in the marshland northwest of Kiev, must be brought to battle west of the Dnepr and annihilated."[67] Von Reichenau was not capable of putting much pressure on Potapov's army, but Heeresgruppe Mitte was in a better position to achieve rapid results. On August 6, von Weichs' 2. Armee was ordered to begin pushing south toward Gomel with two infantry corps; progress was slow in the face of stiff Soviet resistance by the 21st Army. By 16 August, von Weichs' troops were finally nearing Gomel. The GKO reacted to the German pressure at Gomel by authorizing Potapov to withdraw east across the Dnepr and to create a new Bryansk

Front under General-leytenant Andrei I. Eremenko (another one of Stalin's favorites from the *Konarmia* clique). Kuznetsov was briefly replaced by General-leytenant Mikhail G. Efremov, but the Central Front was soon folded into Eremenko's command. Eremenko was now expected to hold the 250km-wide sector between Gomel and Bryansk with three badly-depleted armies (4, 13, 21). In fact, the Soviet front was very shaky and on August 21 the Soviets were forced to abandon Gomel.

Hitler was always drawn to strike at perceived weakness. Although Halder, von Bock and Guderian were all urging him to authorize a direct advance toward Moscow, he recognized that taking the Soviet capital would require hard fighting and plenty of German casualties – so he shrank from this course of action. Instead, he saw the Gomel-Bryansk sector as highly vulnerable to a sudden armored attack and if successful, this could lead to a major operational victory. So far, the Wehrmacht had enjoyed plentiful tactical successes in *Barbarossa*, but the Minsk-Bialystok and Smolensk encirclements were the only significant operational victories. In order to put a positive spin on *Barbarossa* – which was increasingly unlikely to cause a Soviet collapse in 1941 – Hitler needed another major success. Unable to obtain any more cheap victories in the north or the south, Hitler looked to Kiev and the Ukraine for his next triumph of arms. On August 23, Halder arrived at von Bock's headquarters in Borisov for a meeting to discuss new orders with Guderian. Halder transmitted a direct order from Hitler that the capture of the Ukraine was the priority and to that end, Guderian's Panzergruppe 2 would swing south from the Roslavl area and aim for Chernigov.[68] Guderian was also to coordinate with von Kleist, who would break out from his Kremenchug bridgehead and advance north for a link-up. The operation was expected to achieve the largest double pincer attack in military history. Although Guderian complained both to Hitler and von Bock about the diversion from Moscow and the poor mechanical condition of his Panzers, he and his staff were able to efficiently organize the operation with a bare minimum of planning – a testament to the value of the German staff training methods. On August 25, Guderian began attacking southward toward Konotop with just one of his mechanized corps (XXIV). Guderian's logistic situation did not favor a large-scale advance and his armored spearhead was down to barely 100 operational tanks. Nevertheless, his spearhead was able to seize an intact bridge over the Desna River at Novgorod-Siverskiy on August 26, which was a major coup.[69]

Most accounts of Guderian's enveloping maneuver suggest a rapid *Blitzkrieg*-style operation, but in fact the effort by the XXIV Armeekorps (mot.)

to reach Konotop was a rather sluggish, contested advance; Guderian's spearhead unit (Model's 3. Panzer-Division) only advanced 60 kilometers in 16 days. Eremenko quickly recognized the threat Guderian represented to the Southwest Front and requested reinforcements. The GKO promptly created the new 40th Army under General-major Kuzma P. Podlas, an experienced commander who had been purged in 1938. Podlas was tasked with holding a line on the Desna River and preventing Guderian from reaching Konotop; for two weeks he did exactly that. Guderian experienced considerable difficulty in breaching Podlas' thin line along the Desna, which deprived him of offensive momentum. Not satisfied with mere defensive measures, the Stavka also decided to hit Panzergruppe Guderian with whatever tools were handy. The VVS-Western Front was ordered to conduct mass attacks on Guderian's road-bound columns on August 29–31; although not very successful, this was the first time that the Stavka tried to use airpower in an operational-level effort to interdict the battlefield.[70] The massed air strikes were intended to buy time for Eremenko's Bryansk Front to prepare a major counteroffensive against Guderian's flank, held by the XXXXVII Armeekorps (mot.) near Starodub. On the morning of August 30, Eremenko received his orders in Directive No. 001428 from the Stavka, in which Stalin added that, "Guderian and his entire group must be smashed to smithereens."[71] Although the doctrine espoused by PU-36 was in abeyance, Eremenko attempted to build his offensive as a combined-arms operation using some of its principles. He also hoped to prepare a carefully coordinated operation but instead, Stalin dictated that attacks must begin just 12 hours after receiving the Stavka directive. Consequently, Eremenko's armor was committed prematurely and came to grief, partly surrounded while the rest of the offensive went awry. Nevertheless, Stalin ordered the counteroffensive to continue for a full week. The result was that Eremenko's Bryansk Front was bled white with heavy casualties and most of its armor gone, but Guderian's forces were not seriously harmed. The only positive result of Eremenko's failed counteroffensive was that it prevented Guderian from committing the XXXXVII Armeekorps (mot.) to reinforce the drive on Konotop for a full week. Meanwhile, Podlas' 40th Army, which had few antitank guns or artillery pieces, was fighting a losing battle against the XXIV Armeekorps (mot.). On September 10, Model's 3. Panzer-Division finally achieved a clean breakthrough and vaulted past Konotop to seize Romny, a 70km advance in a single day. Although Model's division was temporarily isolated, Podlas' ruptured line disintegrated and his units began retreating eastward.

While Guderian had been slowly grinding southward with a single motorized corps, von Kleist had been planning a large-scale breakout from the 17. Armee bridgehead at Kremenchug. Kirponos had most of his forces deployed around Kiev, leaving the 26th and 38th Armies to hold the Dnepr line from Cherkassy to Kremenchug. Budyonny ordered General-major Nikolai V. Feklenko's 38th Army to repeatedly attack the German bridgehead at Kremenchug, but it suffered 40,000 casualties and lost 279 tanks in the process. Thus, Kirponos was left with no mobile reserves just as the decisive moment of the campaign approached. Three German armies were now converging on Kiev, with von Weichs' 2. Armee in the north, von Reichenau's 6. Armee in the west and von Stülpnagel's 17. Armee in the south. Potapov's 5th Army in Chernigov was being squeezed and Kirponos repeatedly requested permission from the Stavka to withdraw this army before it was crushed, but this was not approved until September 9, by which point Potapov was trapped. At the Southwest Front headquarters, the chief of staff, General-major Vasily I. Tupikov, urged Kirponos to request permission to evacuate Kiev before the flanks gave way completely. Tupikov was a gifted staff officer, who had served in intelligence roles and been military attaché in Berlin until June; he had tried to warn Stalin about the impending German invasion months before *Barbarossa* and been rebuffed for his efforts. Stalin openly referred to him as a "panic-monger." Kirponos tried raising the issue of withdrawal but Stalin quickly shut him down. Yet after German Panzers reached Romny, even Budyonny could see what was about to happen and he contacted the Stavka hoping to use his personal relationship with Stalin to achieve a more favorable outcome. On September 11, Budyonny stated that it was "perfectly apparent" that the enemy was about to encircle the Southwest Front and unless the Stavka could immediately provide powerful reserves, then a withdrawal should be conducted to avoid heavy losses in men and material. Instead, Stalin was angered by Budyonny's request and relieved him as theater commander the next day, appointing Timoshenko in his stead.[72] The die was cast.

On the morning of September 12, von Kleist's Panzers began breaking out of the Kremenchug bridgehead and quickly overwhelmed Feklenko's decimated 38th Army. Over the next two days, von Kleist moved two of his mechanized corps (III, XXXXVIII) across the Dnepr River and began pushing northward. Soviet efforts to stop this armored juggernaut failed completely. By the evening of September 14, von Kleist's spearhead had established a tentative link with Model's 3. Panzer-Division and by the next day, the two German Panzer groups had established a loose encirclement around the bulk of the Southwest Front, including four armies (5, 21, 26, 37). Three other Soviet armies (6, 38, 40) were shattered and retreating eastward in disorder. Once encircled, Kirponos pleaded with Moscow for orders to attempt a breakout to the east but did not receive a response (and an ambiguous one at that) until nearly midnight on September 17. The Stavka authorized the abandonment of Kiev, but provided no other useful guidance. Kirponos decided to mount a breakout effort anyway, since remaining in place would result in rapid annihilation. Once Kirponos gave the order, the Kiev *Kessel* deflated rapidly as Soviet troops attempted to escape eastward.[73] German troops entered Kiev on September 19, only to find that Soviet sappers had left behind dozens of radio-controlled mines – which caused hundreds of casualties.

Kirponos and his staff spent most of the day on the run, with a small NKVD escort, but the breakout attempt proved costly. Kirponos and Tupikov were killed, along with many of the front staff, while others were captured. Timoshenko, who had not had time to reach the *Kessel*, set up his front headquarters in Poltava, then shifted it back to Kharkov. Potapov, commander of the 5th Army, was captured and spent four years in German captivity; unlike most captured senior Soviet leaders, Potapov was not sent to the Gulag upon his return, but awarded by Stalin for valor and allowed to resume his military career. Altogether, Heeresgruppe Süd captured about 440,000 prisoners in the Kiev *Kessel*, along with a vast amount of equipment. Only about 15,000 Soviet troops managed to escape the *Kessel* on foot, including Bagramyan, Kostenko (26 Army) and Vlasov (37 Army).[74] Altogether, Soviet sources admit that the Southwest Front lost over 531,000 troops during the 82-day operation, or roughly 84 percent of its personnel strength.[75] Von Rundstedt's army group had accomplished a stunning operational-level victory and, temporarily, faced no serious opposition in its path. German losses were significant, but they still had formations that were intact and combat-effective. In contrast, the Red Army had lost about 40 divisions in the defense of Kiev and had nothing but poorly-equipped rifle divisions left in the rest of Ukraine. After the Kiev debacle, the remnants of the Southwest and Southern Fronts could only retreat, pulling back to the Donbas and the Crimea.

Commander	Objective	Offensive	Mass	Maneuver	Surprise	Security	TALLY
Von Rundstedt	+	+	o	+	o	+	4
Von Kleist	+	+	+	+	o	+	5
Stülpnagel	+	+	o	+	+	+	5
Von Reichenau Von Weichs	+	+	o	+	o	+	4
Guderian	+	+	-	+	o	+	3
Kirponos Budyonny	o	+	-	o	o	-	-1
Eremenko	+	+	+	-	o	-	1
Potapov Podlas	+	o	o	o	o	+	2
Feklenko Vlasov Kostenko Kuznetsov	o	+	o	o	o	-	0

Southern Axis, Phase 2 Leadership Assessment

The senior leadership in Heeresgruppe Süd – even von Reichenau – conducted operations with great skill during the Battle of Kiev. With the Romanians and the 11. Armee detached to deal with Odessa and the Crimea, von Rundstedt and his subordinates could focus squarely on Kiev. While von Kleist played the key role in preparing and executing the main attack which created the encirclement, it is important to note that it was von Stülpnagel's aggressive maneuvering to seize bridgeheads over the Dnepr which played an equally critical role in setting up the final victory. Guderian's performance was better in the Kiev encirclement than his two previous failed efforts to close the Minsk-Bialystok or Smolensk pockets because he was not distracted by other objectives. He also did a superb job fending off Eremenko's counteroffensive, but his failure to get a second motorized corps into the main effort delayed his breakthrough for over a week. However, Guderian's recurring insubordinate attitude caused von Bock to ask for him to be relieved of command and even Hitler was irked by Guderian's prima donna behavior.[76]

On the Soviet side, Kirponos was both passive and aggressive, gradually allowing the situation to slip out of control. Even though the Stavka kept ordering him to attack, he should have kept some kind of operational reserves (even just a brigade or two) to counter any breakthroughs on his flanks. Budyonny was dense, ordering Kirponos to keep attacking until the larder was nearly bare, followed by a last-minute realization that withdrawal was the only option. Eremenko showed a glimmer of skill in trying to organize a counteroffensive to relieve some of the enemy pressure on the Southwest Front, but his efforts were undermined by micromanagement from Moscow. With the exception of Potapov and Podlas, who accomplished their missions until they ran out of resources, the Soviet army-level commanders in the Battle of Kiev demonstrated a great deal of mediocrity. In terms of operational art, the German Ostheer was at its apex at Kiev whereas the Red Army was at its nadir.

The Culmination of Operation *Barbarossa*, September 30–December 5, 1941

Even before the conclusion of the Battle of Kiev, Hitler was considering his next move. By this point, Heeresgruppe Nord had not accomplished its mission objectives of either seizing Leningrad or destroying Soviet forces in northern Russia. Heeresgruppe Mitte had taken its intermediate objectives of Minsk and Smolensk and inflicted heavy losses on the Western Front, but the Stavka had quickly managed to rebuild these shattered forces and create a new line from Vyazma to Bryansk. The OKH referred to this new line as "Army Group Timoshenko." Heeresgruppe Süd was the closest to achieving its original *Barbarossa* objectives of taking Kiev and smashing the Southwestern Front. Logically, reinforcing success in the Ukraine could lead to even larger operational successes. Hitler was eager to accomplish more in the south, but proved unwilling to transfer forces to what he now regarded as essentially a mop-up operation. Instead, Hitler looked to settle accounts along the central and northern axes, where Soviet resistance was still firm. In Führer Directive 35, issued on September 6, Hitler directed that Heeresgruppe Mitte would attack at the end of September and crush "Army Group Timoshenko" in a vast pincer operation, then pursue the shattered remnants toward Moscow. The new offensive was designated as Operation *Typhoon* (Unternehmen *Taifun*). However, Hitler did not make the Soviet capital a specific objective and the details of the follow-up pursuit operations were left rather vague. The directive also stated that as soon as Heeresgruppe Nord could scrape up enough forces for an offensive, it should attack east across the Volkhov River to further tighten the screws on besieged Leningrad.[77] In other words, in Führer Directive 35, Hitler's intent was clearly to continue attacking on all three fronts, although the main effort would shift back to the center.

Hitler made the decision to remain on the offensive in early September, even though the Ostheer had been attacking nearly continuously for 11 weeks without respite; the troops were exhausted and the vehicles were in very poor condition. Casualties were well over 450,000 men (including 119,000 dead or missing), yet only half these losses had been replaced. In the four Panzer groups, only about 40 percent of the original tanks and trucks were still operational.[78] In an epic failure of combat sustainment, the Ostheer lost 613 tanks *Totalausfalle* (total losses) in the first three months of *Barbarossa* but received only 74 replacement tanks.[79] Another 1,200 tanks were damaged and awaiting spare parts and/or repair. Likewise, the Luftflotten supporting the Ostheer were worn out from constant flying and heavy losses, reduced to just 30 percent of their starting strength, which limited their ability to support multiple ground operations. Furthermore, the German logistic situation on the Eastern Front was extremely poor by September, particularly in the south; only a trickle of ammunition, fuel and spare parts were reaching the front line and they were immediately consumed. Heeresgruppe Mitte was only receiving about 60 percent of the supplies it needed by rail, which meant that it could not assemble any stockpiles for *Typhoon*.[80] Nor did the OKH possess any significant reserves of troops, equipment or supplies to continue offensive operations at the current tempo. Two fresh Panzer divisions (2, 5) that had been refitting in Germany after the Balkan campaign were sent to join Heeresgruppe Mitte in late September, but there were no other units in the pipeline. Another factor to consider was the weather – the autumn rainy season would begin soon, which would seriously impair the ability of the Ostheer to conduct long-distance operational maneuvers.

Operation *Typhoon* would be one of the largest German offensives of the Second World War, involving six armies with 1.1 million troops attacking across a 500km-wide front.[81] Von Bock was particularly keen on striking before the onset of bad weather but he was forced to wait while forces were transferred to him from the two neighboring army groups. Von Leeb transferred most of Höpner's Panzergruppe 4 to Heeresgruppe Mitte and Guderian's Panzergruppe 2 was expected to rejoin as soon as the Kiev *Kessel* was eliminated, but that continued to push the start date back. By September 20, von Bock was considering beginning *Typhoon* with the forces available, but he ultimately decided this was too risky.[82] Von Bock issued his operations order for *Typhoon* to his subordinate armies on September 26.[83] Once Guderian's Panzer group returned, von Bock would have 14 Panzer divisions with about 1,000 tanks to provide the cutting edge. Although the OKH operations staff led by Generalmajor Adolf Heusinger created a broad-brush operational concept for *Typhoon*, involving double pincer attacks to crush the Soviet forces around Vyazma and Bryansk, it was up to each army to develop their own detailed offensive planning. *Typhoon* developed as rather an improvised operation, with few details settled beyond the initial breakthrough and envelopment phase. The level of coordination between the six armies involved was much less than usual, particularly since the Panzer groups were moving to their assembly areas until just days before the start of the operation. Another serious problem for *Typhoon* was faulty intelligence about the enemy situation. Based upon estimates provided by Fremde Heere Ost (Foreign Armies East or FHO), the German operational-level leadership was led to believe that they enjoyed a numerical superiority over the Red Army by mid-September.[84] The FHO had no way to count Soviet divisions that were not yet at the front, such as newly-created divisions or divisions that might be transferred from Siberia, so these outliers were downplayed or ignored. Consequently, this optimistic intelligence assessment led German commanders to expect that one more big victory on the battlefield would cause a catastrophic Soviet military collapse.

On the Soviet side, each German victory made Stalin and the Stavka more desperate to halt the seemingly inexorable advance of the invaders, but there was also a better understanding that the Red Army still had a vast pool of resources to draw upon. Soviet mobilization was proceeding at a frantic pace, creating new rifle divisions and tank brigades to replace losses, even if the quality and combat effectiveness of these new units was often low. Incredibly, the GKO was able to create 258 new rifle divisions in the six-month period June–December 1941, against the loss of 107 rifle divisions in combat.[85] Thirty new tank brigades were also formed in August and September 1941 to begin providing some armor support to the new rifle units. In an effort to provide some quality, the first Guards units were formed from veteran divisions after the Yelnya counteroffensive and they were given priority for new equipment and replacements. Despite suffering punishing defeats at Bialystok-Minsk, Uman, Smolensk and Kiev, the Red Army was actually larger than it had been in June 1941, albeit less well-equipped.

On the Smolensk-Moscow axis, the Western Front (now under Konev) had six armies (22, 29, 30, 19, 16, 20) with a total of 36 divisions to block the main route to the capital. On Konev's left flank, the Bryansk Front under Eremenko, with three armies (3, 13, 50) comprised of 30 divisions, blocked the southwest approaches to the capital. Wedged in between Konev and Eremenko, Budyonny's Reserve Front controlled six newly-formed armies (24, 31, 32, 33, 43, 49) totaling 31 divisions. Altogether, these fronts possessed a total of 864,000 combat troops, 849 tanks and 364 aircraft. Due to Heeresgruppe Mitte's temporary shift to the defensive, the Western Front had been provided a vital respite, which it used to replenish its depleted divisions and to create field fortifications. However, the Stavka reserves (RVGK) were rather thin in late September 1941 because three new reserve armies had been sent to the Volkhov Front near Leningrad and other divisions were sent south to rebuild the shattered Southwest and Southern Fronts.

After the German evacuation from the Yelnya salient and Guderian's turn to the south, the Stavka assessed that Moscow was relatively safe for the moment. Instead, Stalin expected Hitler to make his next main effort in the south in order to go after the economic resources in the Donbas region, not against Moscow. However, once again, Stalin was wrong about German operational intentions. As a result, the Stavka committed a good portion of its remaining reserves to help rebuild Timoshenko's shattered Southwest Front. Nor did Soviet operational-level intelligence officers notice that Guderian's Panzer group was shifting northward after the destruction of the Kiev pocket.

Guderian kicked off Operation *Typhoon* on the right flank of Heeresgruppe Mitte, beginning his attack against Eremenko's Bryansk Front on the morning of September 30 with two motorized corps (XXIV, XXXXVII). General-major Arkadiy Ermakov commanded an operational grouping of five divisions, which had been involved in the recent failed counteroffensive against Guderian and was tasked with launching additional spoiling attacks in the Sevsk sector. Ermakov's group was immediately hard-pressed by Guderian's attack but the fragmentary reporting he sent to Eremenko did not suggest a major enemy offensive. In the Bryansk Front CP, 180 kilometers to the north in Bryansk, Eremenko assessed Guderian's attack to be merely a diversionary effort and decided not to commit any of his reserves to reinforce Ermakov. Instead, he ordered Ermakov to clear up this local situation with his own resources. Consequently, Guderian's Panzers overwhelmed and routed Group Ermakov on October 1, opening a pathway north. With characteristic energy, Guderian exploited the breakthrough and sent the 4. Panzer-Division from XXIV Armeekorps (mot.) to seize Orel on the morning of October 3. Guderian used his other motorized corps (XXXXVII) to envelop General-major Avksentiy M. Gorodnianskiy's 13th Army, which retreated towards Bryansk. Eremenko's situational awareness at this critical moment was poor, since Soviet subordinate commanders tended not to report unauthorized withdrawals and just went silent.* He was not aware of Guderian's breakthrough until October 2, when Soviet aerial reconnaissance reported German armor advancing north on the road to Orel.

While Eremenko was trying to assess what was going on in the south, von Bock began the main part of Operation *Typhoon* on the morning of October 2. Unlike previous German offensives, *Typhoon* would not have operational-level surprise and relied more on brute force than maneuver. Hoth's Panzergruppe 3 attacked with two motorized corps (XXXXI, LVI), striking the boundary between the Western Front's 19th and 30th Armies. Despite the fact that Hoth only had about 250 operational tanks and the Soviet first echelon divisions were entrenched, Hoth succeeded in achieving a clean breakthrough within 36 hours and pivoted southeast towards his primary objective – Vyazma. Simultaneously, Höpner's Panzergruppe 4 attacked the Soviet 43rd Army south of Vyazma. Höpner had the strongest Panzer group (he had 560 tanks – half of the Panzers committed to *Typhoon*) because he had been assigned both of the fresh Panzer divisions (2, 5), so he was able to attack with two motorized corps (XL, XLVI) abreast and keep one in reserve (LVII) to exploit the expected breakthough. General-leytenant Petr Sobennikov – who had been relieved as commander of the Northwest Front in late August – was now in command of the 43rd Army, assigned to the Reserve Front. Sobennikov was forced to defend an 85km-wide front with just four rifle divisions and two tank brigades in tactical reserve. Höpner's Panzers easily smashed through Sobennikov's thinly-spread army in a day and advanced rapidly to Spas-Demensk. Budyonny's Reserve Front had the 33rd Army deployed in second echelon to delay such an enemy breakthough but this army consisted mostly of militia divisions, which were easily overrun by Höpner's Panzers. By October 5, Höpner was able to commit his reserve motorized corps to exploit the breakthrough. The three German infantry armies assigned to *Typhoon* – Strauß' AOK 9, von Kluge's AOK 4 and von Weichs' AOK 2 – did not begin their attacks until October 4. Von Bock wanted to avoid heavy infantry casualties and waited to commit these formations until the Soviet front

---

*Zhukov would eventually relieve Ermakov and have him placed under arrest for unauthorized withdrawals, but punitive measures like this only tended to exacerbate the problem of subordinates failing to provide accurate situation reports.

was destabilized. Once committed, the primary role of the infantry armies was to conduct fixing attacks to prevent Konev, Eremenko and Budyonny from shifting forces to counter the Panzer breakthroughs. For the first time, von Kluge demonstrated some aggressiveness, conducting a skillful set-piece attack near Yelnya that crushed four rifle divisions and a brigade of T-34 tanks.

The three Soviet front commanders found it difficult to react to the sudden German offensive due to poor situational awareness. While the newly-created armies had plenty of infantry, they had few radios or trained staff officers, so reporting from forward units was often delayed and incomplete. By the time that Eremenko belatedly sent some of his reserves toward Orel, Guderian's Panzers had already taken the city. Konev tried to commit his tactical reserves to halt Hoth's advance. He assigned his deputy General-leytenant Ivan Boldin (who had escaped the Minsk pocket) to lead a mobile group against Hoth, just as Pavlov had ordered him to do three months prior. Once again, Boldin's counterattack failed miserably and Konev's front was soon split wide open.[86] Budyonny's Reserve Front lacked the equipment or training to mount serious counterattacks and his armies simply held their positions, while the situation was deteriorating on both flanks. Even though it was apparent that the German armored pincers were about to close, Stalin refused to consider any retreats until October 5. Marshal Boris M. Shaposhnikov, chief of the General Staff (GSHKA), stated that "stubborn defense of manned defense lines" was the best way to counter the German offensive, which Stalin fully supported. The only place that the Red Army was able to delay *Typhoon* was at Mtensk, northeast of Orel, where General-major Dmitri D. Lelyushenko's 1st Guards Rifle Corps was able to make a stand. The Stavka also committed a brigade of paratroopers from the RVGK to reinforce Lelyushenko and they were flown in – an interesting operational-level deployment by the standards of 1941.[87] For the first time, Guderian had encountered a competent enemy commander who had steady troops and a well-handled brigade of T-34 tanks, enabling Lelyushenko to achieve a small but poignant tactical victory at Mtensk. Lelyushenko was also aided by the fact that Guderian's spearhead had completely run out of fuel in its dash to Orel and was nearly immobilized. Guderian had outrun his supplies, with the nearest railhead 230 kilometers away.

On the morning of October 5, a Soviet Pe-2 reconnaissance bomber spotted a massive German column near Yukhnov, which was the spearhead of Höpner's Panzergruppe 4. The Germans had achieved a major breakthrough and were advancing to envelop Vyzama from the south.

Likewise, Hoth's Panzers had also achieved a major breakthrough and were enveloping Vyazma from the north. Konev begged for permission to pull back his three embattled first-echelon armies (16, 19, 20) to reconcentrate near Vyazma, but Shaposhnikov rejected the request. Polkovnik Nikolai A. Sbytov, VVS commander for the Moscow Military District, brought the aerial reconnaissance report to Shaposhnikov's attention – who rejected it. Sbytov was ordered to fly additional reconnaissance missions to verify whether or not German armor had broken through – two more missions confirmed the breakthrough. Instead of taking this information and using it as the basis for decision-making, Sbytov was handed over to the NKVD for interrogation and accused of "panic-mongering." The GKO also convened an emergency meeting on the evening of October 5 and – finally accepting the VVS reconnaissance reports as valid – agreed that Konev would be allowed to retreat and that a new defensive position would be established at Mozhaisk.[88] Since Zhukov was still in Leningrad, Voroshilov was sent as Stavka representative to begin organizing the Mozhaisk Line. By the time that Konev received permission to pull back, it was too late.

On the afternoon of October 6, one of Guderian's Panzer divisions suddenly appeared at Bryansk, overrunning Yeremenko's comand post and then quickly capturing the city in a *coup de main*. Yeremenko and his staff escaped but were scattered and their decryption machine was lost, which left them unable to decipher encoded messages from the Stavka for over a day.[89] In the north, Hoth's spearheads enveloped Vyazma and cut the Minsk-Moscow highway behind the city. The militia divisions of the 32nd Army were no match for Hoth's Panzers and Vyazma itself was captured on the morning of October 7. Rokossovsky, commander of the 16th Army, was in Vyazma with his staff and was forced to flee.[90] Incredibly, Heeresgruppe Mitte had simultaneously encircled the bulk of six Soviet armies with over 400,000 troops in three large pockets: one just west of Vyazma, one near Bryansk and another near Trubchevsk. The three German infantry armies moved forward quickly to crush these encircled Soviet armies and unlike previous *Kesselschlachten*, the Vyazma pocket was efficiently sealed off. In Moscow, the Stavka was stunned. Soviet C2 in all three fronts virtually collapsed, as headquarters units focused on survival. Budyonny had gone forward to the front to assess the situation and when his command post displaced to the rear, he lost all communications. General-major Andrei F. Anisov, his chief of staff, informed the Stavka that he did not know Budyonny's status. Just before the jaws of the German armored pincers closed, Konev shifted his headquarters all the way back to Mozhaisk (100km west of Moscow). The staff of the Bryansk Front headquarters escaped and joined up with General-major Mikhail P. Petrov's 50th Army, but Eremenko was missing and he was erroneously reported as dead, so the Stavka ordered Petrov to take over as temporary front commander.

In Moscow, Stalin was seething in anger about the sudden German breakthrough and focused his ire entirely on Konev; apparently Budyonny and Eremenko, both being *Konarmia* veterans, were exempted from his ire. Stalin sent Marshal Voroshilov with foreign minister Molotov in tow and Vasilevsky from the GSHKA to Mozhaisk, to assess Konev's handling of the situation. When Zhukov arrived back in Moscow from Leningrad on the evening of October 7, he too was directed to go to Mozhaisk to assess the military situation. When he reached Konev's command post on the morning of October 8, Zhukov was surprised to find that the direct routes to Moscow were virtually unguarded. He then went to find Budyonny, who had somehow misplaced his command post; it was apparent to Zhukov that Budyonny was completely befuddled by the rapid turn of events.[91] Zhukov reported Budyonny's incompetence to the Stavka and he was promptly relieved of command, with Zhukov ordered to take over the Reserve Front. According to Zhukov's account, Stalin wanted to relieve Konev and execute him, as he had done to Pavlov. Instead, Zhukov claimed that he convinced Stalin of Konev's abilities and managed to have him relieved without punitive measures. Once Konev was removed, Zhukov took over command of the Western Front and folded the Reserve Front into the new structure. He was now tasked with holding the Mozhaisk Line.

Von Bock's Heeresgruppe Mitte was on the cusp of another stunning operational victory. The Vyazma-Bryansk *Kesselschlacht* lasted just one week, with organized resistance crushed by October. 14 Eremenko remained inside the pocket until he was seriously wounded and was flown out to Moscow. Of the Soviet army commanders in the *Kessel*, two were killed (Petrov, 50th Army and Rakutin, 24th Army) and three were captured (Lukin, 19th Army, Ershakov, 20th Army and Vishnevsky, 32nd Army). Rokossovsky (16th Army), Yakov G. Kreizer (3rd Army), Sobennikov (43rd Army) and Boldin (deputy commander Western Front) managed to fight their way out of encirclement and reach friendly lines. Although the other commanders were applauded for their fighting withdrawals, Sobennikov was relieved of command, arrested and then convicted of retreating without authorization; he was sentenced to five years in a forced labor camp. The fact that some senior commanders were still being severely punished for trying to save their commands from annihilation gave pause to all the others. Initially, Zhukov was only able to gather up about 90,000 survivors from the Western Front to hold the Mozhaisk Line and he immediately demanded reinforcements from the RVGK. The 50th Army, which was one of the fortunate formations that managed to fight its way out of the Bryansk pocket, was only able to muster 8,105 troops and 29 artillery pieces from its seven rifle divisions – roughly 10 percent of its authorized strength.[92] When the *Kesselschlachten* concluded, von Bock claimed that Heeresgruppe Mitte took 673,098 prisoners in the Vyazma-Bryansk fighting, with other sources suggesting that the Red Army lost roughly an additional 180,000 casualties, dead and wounded.[93] There is little doubt that the Western Front had suffered catastrophic losses in the opening round of *Typhoon*.

Von Bock was eager to press on to Moscow and as early as October 8 he was advocating for a reconnaissance in force in that direction, even though the *Kesselschlachten* were just beginning in earnest. However, the logistic problems facing Heeresgruppe Mitte were becoming acute due to insufficient rail deliveries, which was restricting operational maneuver even before the first snowflake fell. Guderian's Panzer group was stymied near Mtensk in part due to Soviet resistance and in part due to crippling fuel shortages.* The fuel situation was only slightly better for the other two Panzer groups. Nor did it help that the OKH kept pressing other secondary objectives such as Kalinin and Kursk upon von Bock, preventing Heeresgruppe Mitte from directing all its remaining combat power toward one objective. On the night of October 6/7 the first light snow fell, but the onset of winter weather did not become a serious factor for several more days. On October 9, the SS-*Das Reich* Division (from Höpner's 4. Panzerarmee) advanced down the Moscow highway and captured Gzhatsk, just 170 kilometers from the Kremlin. Although many accounts tend to emphasize the impact of winter weather and the mud (*rasputitsa*) upon German mobility, the fact is that not all the roads in such a large area (400 × 30 kilometers) were simultaneously turned into quagmires, nor did the mud have as much impact upon infantry operations. Strauß' 9. Armee was assigned to clear the area north of the Smolensk-Moscow highway and it did an admirable job, seizing Rzhev on October 12 and then Kalinin on October 14. Von Weichs' 2. Armee was able to advance rapidly as well and captured Kaluga on October 14, in spite of rain, mud

---

*On October 5, 1941, all four Panzer groups were officially re-designated as "Panzerarmee," although terms like "Panzergruppe Guderian" were still in common use until the end of the year.

and sleet. In many places, Soviet resistance was feeble, which enabled even weak German probes to achieve success.

Even before Zhukov arrived at Mozhaisk, Polkovnik Semyon I. Bogdanov was sent to coordinate the arrival of three new tank brigades that were arriving from the RVGK. Given the chaotic situation, Bogdanov was also made commander of the Mozhaisk fortified position. Without orders from the Stavka or anyone else, Bogdanov decided to deploy two of these tank brigades to conduct delaying actions along the main avenues of approach to Moscow. Bogdanov, who had been arrested and imprisoned for over a year during the purges, showed great presence of mind and moral courage in making this decision – which proved to be a critical one for the defense of Moscow. Bogdanov's armored delaying actions bought time for Zhukov to take command of the Western Front without worrying about German tanks suddenly appearing outside his command post.

Zhukov offically took charge over the Western Front on October 10. He knew that he could not establish a solid linear defense, so he opted to form fortified regions along the most likely enemy avenues of advance; in this, he showed an appreciation for the principle of concentration, even at the expense of sacrificing some territory. Somehow, he was able to convince Stalin that trying to hold every town with the limited forces at hand would result in total defeat. Zhukov also made clear to the Stavka that he needed the best leaders, troops and equipment left available to stop von Bock from reaching the capital. Based upon his demonstrated competence at Mtensk, Zhukov wanted Lelyushenko transferred to his command to form the bedrock of the defense at Mozhaisk. The Stavka had already ordered the re-creation of the 5th Army (recently destroyed in the Kiev pocket) to anchor the Mozhaisk position and Lelyushenko was appointed its commander on October 11. He was given the first of the fresh divisions brought from Siberia – the 32nd Rifle Division with a full complement of 15,000 troops and division artillery – to hold the key position on the Moscow highway at Borodino. For the rest of his front, Zhukov assigned Rokossovsky's 16th Army to hold Volokolamsk, General-leytenant Mikhail G. Efremov's 33rd Army to hold Naro-Fominsk, General-leytenant Stepan D. Akimov's 43rd Army to hold Maloyaroslavets and General-leytenant Ivan G. Zakharkin's 49th Army to hold Kaluga. Since Kaluga was quickly lost, the 49th Army fell back to Serpukhov. Zhukov's defensive framework was hurriedly improvised and consisted of only a single echelon.

Just three days after assuming command of the Western Front, Zhukov was confronted by the German XL Armeekorps (mot.) attacking

Lelyushenko's positions near Borodino. Lelyushenko conducted a skilled defense, but the Waffens-SS troops finally fought their way into Mozhaisk on October 18. Lelyushenko was wounded during the Battle of Borodino and replaced by General-leytenant Leonid A. Govorov, an artilleryman. Govorov was one of the most erudite officers in the Red Army – having learned German on his own – and had actually served with the Whites during the Russian Civil War. The German victory at Borodino sparked a panic in Moscow, prompting much of the Soviet government to evacuate to Kubyshev. Elsewhere, 3. Panzerarmee, now under General der Panzertruppe Georg-Hans Reinhardt, pressed hard against Rokossovky's 16th Army at Volokolamsk, while one of Höpner's motorized corps pushed the 43rd Army out of Maloyaroslavets on October 18.[*] By that point, the Mozhaisk Line had been breached and von Bock had five Panzer divisions within 100 kilometers of Moscow, but Heeresgruppe Mitte had shot its bolt. Heeresgruppe Mitte was now crippled by ammunition and fuel shortages, with only about one-fifth of necessary supplies reaching front-line units.[94] By October 20 an operational pause had settled over most of the front, which provided Zhukov a welcome respite to strengthen his battered front line. The one exception was near Mtensk, along the Zusha River, where Guderian had spent two weeks accumulating supplies in order to make an unexpected attack on October 23. Zhukov had weakened this sector by transferring Lelyushenko and his best troops, so Guderian saw an opportunity. Amazingly, Guderian's armored spearhead was able to advance 120 kilometers in one week – in spite of muddy roads – and reached the outskirts of Tula on October 29. However once again, Guderian's spearhead ran out of fuel just when success was within reach and Soviet counterattacks against 2. Panzerarmee's long, exposed flanks forced him to redirect forces away from the *Schwerpunkt*.

By late October it was obvious that winter weather was fast approaching and that *Typhoon* had inflicted grievous – but not fatal – damage upon the Red Army. Heeresgruppe Mitte was critically low on essential supplies and the muddy road conditions made it that much more difficult to resupply front-line units. Military common sense suggested that it was time for Heeresgruppe Mitte to shift to the defense and establish a solid front line before winter arrived. Von Kluge, commander of the 4. Armee, apparently made this decision on his own after the conclusion of the Vyzama-Bryansk *Kesselschlacht* and unlike Strauß or von Weichs, he spent an inordinate time reorganizing his army prior to resuming any advance eastward. Von Kluge

---

[*]Hoth had been transferred to take command of the 17. Armee on October 6, 1941.

failed to promptly push his infantry forward to support Höpner's Panzers and lied to von Bock about the level of Soviet resistance in his sector. Von Kluge undoubtedly could see that Heeresgruppe Mitte was burning itself out and he opted to try to conserve his own army with subtle acts of insubordination. Consequently, the 4. Armee was in better shape than the other five armies in Heeresgruppe Mitte, but it came at the cost of failing to press the enemy when there was still a remote chance of breaking Zhukov's forces before winter arrived. In addition to von Kluge's unenthusiastic performance, von Bock also had to contend with a serious diversion of effort due to the volatile situation on his left flank at Kalinin. Although the city had been captured easily on October 14, Stalin was determined to recover it. Three days later, Konev was sent to command the newly-created Kalinin Front and tasked with liberating the city. Konev immediately began counterattacks with his three available armies (22, 29, 31), which forced Strauß and Reinhardt to keep sending additional forces to strengthen the German hold on the city.

Despite these distractions and problems, both von Bock and the OKH stated that it would be foolish to terminate *Typhoon* when Heeresgruppe Mitte was within 90 kilometers of Moscow and the Red Army was on the ropes. Von Bock's position, based upon faulty OKH intelligence assessments about the enemy, was that one more big push would succeed in taking Moscow and inflicting a catastrophic defeat on the Red Army. Of note, von Bock's logistic officers were openly opposed to the resumption of *Typhoon* due to the crippling fuel shortage, but he ignored them.[95] Hitler had never been particularly enthusiastic about going to Moscow and was even more undecided now that supplies and weather were limiting German operational options. Nevertheless, on October 30 Hitler approved an OKH-developed plan to resume *Typhoon* after a pause of two more weeks in order to resupply. Unlike the first part of *Typhoon*, the second phase lacked the resources to attack all along the front and instead opted for a classic double pincer scheme of maneuver, with Reinhardt's 3. Panzerarmee and Höpner's 4. Panzerarmee forming the northern pincer while Guderian's 2. Panzerarmee would form a southern pincer. However, von Bock dissipated his combat power by detaching one of Reinhardt's motorized corps to support the useless tactical actions at Kalinin, leaving just three motorized corps for the northern pincer with a total of about 550 tanks. Guderian was in even worse shape, with just one motorized corps available for the offensive, and he had yet to deal with Tula, which was stoutly defended by the 50th Army under General-leytenant Ivan V. Boldin (who had just escaped the Bryansk pocket). At best, von Bock had only enough ammunition and fuel for a short offensive. Luftwaffe support, which had been crucial in the earlier offensives, was reduced to fewer than 300 operational aircraft. On November 13, Halder and some of his senior OKH staff travelled to Orsha to meet with von Bock and his staff to discuss the resumption of *Typhoon*, but no binding decisions were made.[96]

In contrast, Zhukov and the Stavka had achieved a near miracle in rebuilding the shattered Western Front between October 10 and November 14. Since much of the Soviet armaments industry had been displaced to the Urals, production had temporarily fallen off, leaving the Red Army short of equipment and ammunition. Nevertheless, Zhukov and Konev had received about 150,000 reinforcements and plenty more brigades and divisions were in the process of forming. By mid-November, Zhukov's Western Front had amassed about 500 tanks and the VVS had also regained air superiority over Moscow.[97] Additional reinforcements were en route from the Far East, whereas the OKH had no reinforcements for von Bock. Soviet intelligence was also performing now, providing Zhukov with some insight into German capabilities and intentions. Based upon intelligence assessments, Zhukov weighted his defense in favor of Rokossovsky's 16th Army at Volokolamsk, which he correctly assessed as the likely German *Schwerpunkt*.

The second and final phase of *Typhoon* began with limited attacks by one of Strauß' infantry corps against Lelyushenko's 30th Army southeast of Kalinin.* The *rasputitsa* period had ended and colder temperatures froze the ground, which the Germans hoped would restore some of their operational mobility. On November 17, Reinhardt committed one of his motorized corps against the right flank of Rokossovsky's 16th Army. Over the next three days, Reinhardt and then Höpner fed more divisions into the battle and gradually drove a wedge between the Soviet 30th and 16th Armies. However, Rokossovsky's 16th Army put up ferocious resistance and reduced the German advance to a crawl. Reinhardt's 3. Panzerarmee was finally able to capture Klin on November 23 and exploit to the east, but Höpner's spearhead was held up for three days by a single "Siberian" rifle division holding a blocking position at Istra. Reinhardt was able to reach the Moscow-Volga Canal at Yakhroma (60km north of Moscow) on November 27 and effect a crossing, in an effort to follow the *Typhoon* plan of enveloping Moscow. However, Reinhardt had stumbled into the assembly area for General-leytenant Vasily I. Kuznetsov's 1st Shock Army, part of

---

*Khomenko had been relieved on November 1 and replaced by Lelyushenko, who was still recovering from wounds received at Borodino two weeks earlier.

Zhukov's front reserves, which soon launched vigorous counterattacks that convinced Reinhardt to evacuate his bridgehead. By November 30, the German armored spearheads were stalled in the outskirts of Moscow, about 20–25 kilometers northwest of the Kremlin, with Rokossovsky's army blocking any further advance. No fuel had reached the forward Panzer units since November 17, which did more to halt Typhoon than the weather.[98] Just as the attacks by Reinhardt and Höpner culminated short of their objective, von Kluge – who had not budged for two weeks – finally launched a carefully-planned set-piece attack that pierced the front of General-leytenant Mikhail G. Efremov's 33rd Army and unexpectedly captured Naro-Fominsk. Yet the success was short-lived since Zhukov sent reserves to assist Efremov, who counterattacked on December 2. Faced with strong resistance, von Kluge withdrew without orders and reverted to a defensive stance. Meanwhile, Guderian's southern pincer tried several times to envelop and isolate Boldin's 50th Army in Tula but failed. By early December Heeresgruppe Mitte was stymied on all sectors, and von Bock officially terminated Typhoon on December 5 and shifted to the defense. In addition to the harmful effects upon exposed troops in the open, freezing temperatures led to heavy losses among Heeresgruppe Mitte's horses, which were essential for moving artillery in the non-motorized divisions.

Zhukov had been carefully waiting for the German offensive to grind to a halt in order to conduct his own riposte. Shaposhnikov and the Stavka had been quietly assembling a theater reserve for a counteroffensive, consisting of Kuznetsov's 1st Shock Army (1 SA), General-major Andrei Vlasov's 20th Army and General-leytenant Filipp I. Golikov's 10th Army. None of these formations were particularly impressive – Kuznetsov's 1 SA consisted of about 30,000 infantry, a single regiment of artillery and no tanks – but they were fresh formations and the enemy troops opposing them were overextended and exhausted. Vasilevsky had been working with Zhukov's chief of staff, General-leytenant Vasily D. Sokolovsky, since late November to create a plan for a counteroffensive using these fresh formations.[99] Freezing winter temperatures had just arrived, which seriously impacted morale of the unprepared German front-line troops.[*] Von Bock had made a serious error by taking most of the infantry divisions

---

[*]About 20 percent of the German front-line troops in early December 1941 had received some winter gear, while others had taken winter clothing from Soviet prisoners. However about two-thirds of the German combat troops had no protection against winter temperatures. The initial freezing spell (0°F/-17°C) lasted from December 4–7, then warmed up a bit from December 8–12 and went sub-zero again on December 13–15.

from Reinhardt's 3. Panzerarmee to reinforce Strauß' vulnerable 9. Armee positions around Kalinin – a clear violation of the principles of objective and mass. Reinhardt compounded this error by concentrating the bulk of his remaining tanks and artillery facing the enemy on the Moscow-Volga Canal, but his left flank was guarded only by screening forces and his connection with the 9. Armee was tenuous. Although Konev's Kalinin Front began its own counteroffensive on December 5, Zhukov waited until the next day, then mounted a fairly coordinated attack by the 1 SA, 20th and 30th Armies against Reinhardt's vulnerable 3. Panzerarmee. On December 7, Rokossovsky's 16th Army began attacking Höpner's 4. Panzerarmee near Istra. German commanders seemed rather apathetic during this stage of the Soviet counteroffensive, probably due to a combination of exhaustion and cold-weather-induced illness. Within days, all of the Soviet armies were advancing and by December 11 Heeresgruppe Mitte's entire left wing was near collapse. The Soviet armies came close to isolating Reinhardt's 3. Panzerarmee in the Klin bulge, but lacked the radios and trained staff to execute complex maneuver operations under these conditions. Nevertheless, Kuznetsov's 1 SA liberated Klin on December 15 and Strauß was forced to evacuate Kalinin on December 16. Reinhardt's 3. Panzerarmee managed to escape the impending Soviet encirclement at the cost of abandoning most of its heavy equipment. In the south, Guderian's 2. Panzerarmee was routed by the combined attacks of Golikov's 10th Army and Gorodnianskiy's 13th Army from the Southwest Front. Gorodnianskiy achieved the most success by encircling the German XXXIV Armeekorps near Livny on December 10–13; although the three German infantry divisions managed to escape the pocket, they suffered heavy losses and were forced to abandon most of their artillery. Eventually, both of Guderian's flanks were torn open by enemy attacks, leaving him no alternative but to retreat southward as rapidly as possible. At midday on December 16, Hitler called von Bock directly and said, "there was only one decision and that was not to take a single step back, to plug the holes and hang on."[100] Later that day, Hitler decided to issue a no-retreat order to the other two army groups as well.[101]

Zhukov's counteroffensive quickly ran out of steam after mid-December, but he had succeeded in defeating all three of von Bock's Panzer armies and hurling the Germans back from the outskirts of Moscow. Only von Kluge's 4. Armee, which had begun preparing its defenses earlier, lost no significant ground to Zhukov's counteroffensive. In desperation, German units formed defensive strongpoints (*Stützpunkte*) in villages and towns to fend off Soviet attacks. Upon learning about the success of this tactic,

Hitler issued an order on December 26 that all units should employ it to hold ground – this would become cemented in his mind as the preferred doctrinal solution to repelling enemy offensives.[102]

Heeresgruppe Mitte's material losses in Operation *Typhoon* had been crippling, with almost 500 tanks and 983 artillery pieces lost. All of the Panzer divisions involved were left combat ineffective and would remain so for several months. Hitler was incensed by the failure of *Typhoon*, which coming after the partial success of *Barbarossa* represented the first serious operational failure by the Wehrmacht. The German command performance during *Typhoon* had started out with a dazzling display of maneuver skill then quickly degenerated into a muddled, brute-force approach that had difficulty forming a coherent *Schwerpunkt*. Von Bock was the strongest advocate of pushing on to Moscow but was caught unprepared to exploit success when the bulk of the Western Front was devoured in the first ten days of *Typhoon*; he ended up sending a single Waffen-SS motorized division to tentatively push down the Minsk-Moscow highway and failed to attach any priority to this effort until the Vyazma-Bryansk *Kesselschlacht* was completed. In the final phase of *Typhoon*, von Bock approved an operations plan that essentially ignored terrain, weather, logistics and the enemy. Of the three Panzer army commanders, Guderian was the most aggressive, but as usual he scattered his forces, ignored orders he did not like, failed to properly seal off encircled Soviet forces and failed to anticipate enemy countermoves. Höpner probably put in the best performance, particularly in sealing off the Vyazma pocket, but despite having the strongest armored group in Heeresgruppe Mitte he still failed to achieve his objective. Strauß' performance throughout *Typhoon* was mediocre at best, while von Weichs proved capable in set-piece battles but was little more than a flank guard during *Typhoon*. Twice during *Typhoon*, von Kluge conducted superb set-piece attacks that achieved tactical success, but as an operational commander he was a failure; his protracted inactivity in the center allowed Zhukov to shift forces that helped to stall the German armored breakthrough around Klin and Istra.

While Soviet losses in the defense of Moscow were enormous, the Red Army and its commanders had conducted a courageous goal-line stand in front of their capital and then hurled their enemy back in disarray. Zhukov put in one of the best command performances of his career in stopping *Typhoon*, then pivoting to administer a well-timed counteroffensive that reversed the threat to the Soviet capital. Lelyushenko and Rokossovsky also demonstrated excellent battlefield command skills, although the latter had fewer opportunities for counterattacks and was forced to conduct a die-in-place mission. Konev was unfortunate in being struck by the full force of the Wehrmacht in the opening week of *Typhoon* and the rapid German success left him with few options but to try to salvage something from the wreckage of the Western Front. Likewise, as commander of the Kalinin Front, Konev had the thankless task of tying down von Bock's left flank while Zhukov achieved all the operational success on his front. Eremenko and Budyonny both ended up being hapless victims of *Typhoon* and were quickly removed from command, although Eremenko would soon return to the front. Budyonny would be sent to command in the Caucasus in 1942, but his rank incompetence was now apparent. Among the other Soviet army commanders involved in stopping *Typhoon*, only Boldin and Kuznetsov stand out, although both only held their commands in the last few weeks of the campaign.

Commander	Objective	Offensive	Mass	Maneuver	Surprise	Security	TALLY
Von Bock	-	+	-	+	o	-	-1
Von Kluge	-	-	+	-	+	+	0
Strauß	o	o	o	o	o	o	0
Von Weichs	o	+	o	+	o	-	1
Reinhardt	+	+	-	+	+	-	2
Höpner	+	+	+	+	o	o	4
Guderian	-	+	-	+	+	-	0
Konev	+	+	o	o	o	-	1
Zhukov	+	+	+	+	+	+	6
Rokossovsky	+	o	+	o	o	o	2
Lelyushenko	+	+	+	+	+	+	6

Central Axis, Phase 3/Typhoon Leadership Assessment

While Operation *Typhoon* was occurring, the Ostheer was also involved in three other smaller offensive operations, near Leningrad, in eastern Ukraine and in the Crimea. Technically, each of these operations was a sequel to Operation *Barbarossa*, although they tried to achieve objectives stated in Hitler's subsequent directives (33a, 34a and 35). Leningrad had been encircled on September 8, trapping four Soviet armies (8, 23, 42, 55) with 300,000 troops and 3 million civilians in the city. Initially, the OKH hoped to win a victory through starvation but after just a few weeks of siege, the mood shifted to look for more active solutions. Doctrinally, the Wehrmacht was ill-disposed toward siege warfare and German officers had been trained "to solve problems," not sit and wait. Even though Führer Directive 35 had stated that "the link-up with the Karelian Army on the Svir [River] will only take place when the destruction of the enemy around Leningrad is assured," it appeared to the OKH staff in Zossen that the remaining Red Army forces east of Leningrad were now too weak to prevent a link-up with the Finns.[103] Furthermore, capture of the rail stations at Volkhov and Tikhvin would seriously degrade the Soviet ability to get even a trickle of supplies through to Leningrad over Lake Ladoga. Consequently, the OKH directed von Leeb's Heeresgruppe Nord to mount an attack eastward from the Volkhov River as soon as possible to seize the rail centers and link up with the Finns (who would make no effort to assist). Von Leeb was not entirely sanguine about this operation, since he was desperately short of front-line combat troops after transferring most of Höpner's Panzer group to Heeresgruppe Mitte.[104] Indeed, Heeresgruppe Nord was so short of infantry to fend off constant Soviet counterattacks that OKH was forced to send five elite *Fallschirmjäger* battalions from the 7. Flieger-Division to help hold the siege lines (a complete waste of a scarce resource) and the volunteer Spanish Blue Division (which had been earmarked for von Bock).[105] Furthermore, the swampy terrain east of the Volkhov River was ill-suited for maneuver operations and would become a quagmire during the rainy season.

Nevertheless, von Leeb was able to scrape together an attack group comprising two corps and began his offensive across the Volkhov on October 16. Snow showers prevented Luftwaffe close air support and the German tanks had limited mobility in the marshy terrain. The Soviet Leningrad Front, temporarily under General-major Ivan F. Fediuninskiy, had three armies east of the Volkhov: General-leytenant Mikhail S. Khozin's 54th Army, General-leytenant Vsevolod F. Iakovlev's 4th Army and General-leytenant Nikolai K. Klykov's 52nd Army. Fediuninskiy was extremely junior but he was one of Zhukov's protégés who had served under him at Khalkhin-Gol in 1939. When Zhukov left for Moscow, he ordered Fediuninskiy to mount a major offensive to break the siege of Leningrad, primarily relying upon Khozin's 54th Army. Unfortunately, the so-called First Siniavino Offensive failed to produce results and it left the armies along the Volkhov ill-deployed to meet a German offensive. Consequently, the German shock group, led by a motorized corps, was able to penetrate Iakovlev's 4th Army after four days of fighting and achieve a significant breakthrough. Fediuninskiy (who was also directing the four armies within besieged Leingrad) was unable to effectively coordinate the three armies on the Volkhov and the Germans exploited a large gap between the 4th and 52nd Armies. Iakovlev was provided strong reinforcements, including the 60th Tank Division, but dispersed them in order to launch piecemeal counterattacks. Despite adverse terrain and weather, the German 12. Panzer-Division was able to reach Tikhvin on November 8 and capture the rail center. However, the German offensive ran out of steam and could advance no further.

The Stavka shifted Khozin to take over the Leningrad Front and put Fediuninskiy in charge of the 54th Army. Recognizing that the loss of Tikhvin could lead to the fall of Leningrad, the Stavka immediately took measures to reverse the situation. General Kirill A. Meretskov, who had been arrested, beaten and detained in isolation for three months because he had been friends with the ill-fated Pavlov, was sent to take charge of the 4th Army and organize a counterattack. Meretskov was provided with three full-strength divisions from the Far East. Unlike most of the other Soviet army-level commanders at this point in the war, Meretskov was a skilled professional, even if he was wobbly on his feet (literally). Just three days after assuming command, Meretskov was able to orchestrate a concentric attack against the German forces in Tikhvin, using the 4th, 52nd and 54th Armies. The German position at Tikhvin was extremely fragile and did not even have a reliable line of communications, which made a protracted fight out of the question. By December 6, the Germans were forced to abandon Tikhvin and retreat back to the Volkhov River, giving the Red Army a significant victory. For his success, Meretskov was put in charge of the new Volkhov Front and tasked with breaking the siege of Leningrad. Khozin was fairly ineffective during the Tikhvin operation because he lacked the resources to accomplish much of anything. Meretskov had the good fortune to receive significant reinforcements to conduct a credible counteroffensive and the Germans were overextended.

Of all the setbacks that the Ostheer suffered in Russia in 1941–42, the defeat at Tikhvin was one of the most unnecessary. Not only had von Leeb failed to hold Tikhvin, but the operation deprived Heeresgruppe Nord of any remaining reserves and created a crisis in an area that was supposed to be a quiet sector. It should also be noted that von Leeb did not do a particularly good job at applying direct pressure on besieged Leningrad; while there were air raids and artillery bombardments, these were fairly small scale and achieved little. By going for the indirect approach, von Leeb gave the Soviets invaluable time to improve their defenses in Leningrad, which would make any future German attacks upon the city prohibitively expensive. While von Leeb did raise the possibility of reducing the 8th Army in the Oranienbaum salient – which would have freed up three German divisions – he quickly dropped the idea in favor of Tikhvin. Von Küchler (18. Armee) and Busch (16. Armee) were primarily resources managers during the Tikhvin operation, which was conducted by the two corps commanders involved.

Commander	Objective	Offensive	Mass	Maneuver	Surprise	Security	TALLY
Von Leeb	-	+	o	+	+	-	1
Khozin	+	-	-	-	o	-	-3
Meretskov	+	+	+	+	+	o	5

Northern Axis, Tikhin Leadership Assessment

Although the Finnish Front is somewhat outside the scope of this study, operations (or lack of operations) in that sector did affect the Ostheer's main operations. Finland had only very reluctantly agreed to participate in military operations against the Soviet Union and then only for the sake of recovering lands lost in the previous Russo-Finnish War. Finland's political leadership refused to be publicly identified as an Axis ally – even though they were hosting over 60,000 German troops on their soil – instead using the transparent subterfuge that they were a "co-belligerent" or even a neutral. At the start of Operation *Barbarossa*, the Finns agreed to support an operation (Unternehmen *Silberfuchs* or Operation *Silver Fox*) by the German AOK Norwegen to seize the port of Murmansk. The OKH committed five divisions to the Finnish sector, expecting to seize an important objective and to help the Finns link up with the advance of Heeresgruppe Nord. Initially, the Finns supported the drive to isolate Murmansk with two divisions, while their Army of Karelia recovered all of the territory lost in 1940. However, once they accomplished their own objectives, the Finns decided that they would shift to a passive defense. When the United States demanded on October 25 that Finland cease hostilities against the USSR, Finland complied.[106] Marshal Mannerheim would not attack or even bombard Leningrad and the Army of Karelia ceased advancing after reaching the Svir River, even though Heeresgruppe Nord was still fighting – in vain – to achieve a link-up. Due to the passivity of the Finns, Murmansk was never taken and only nine Soviet divisions were required to block the 14 Finnish and five German divisions in the northern sector – a real deal for the Stavka. Obviously, the five German divisions in Finland would have been of far more value under Heeresgruppe Nord than sitting out the war in a quiet sector. Furthermore, the lack of threat from Finland allowed the Red Army to leave a bare minimum of forces in this sector. Not having prepared for coalition warfare, the OKH was chagrined to learn that the Finns had their own agenda and proved to be unreliable partners.

After the great victory at Kiev, von Rundstedt's Heeresgruppe Süd found itself scattered across most of the Ukraine and confronted with new missions that would require further divergence. The army group's primary combat power lay between Kremenchug and Poltava, with von Kleist's Panzergruppe 1 and von Stülpnagel's 17. Armee. Von Reichenau's 6. Armee was conducting mop-up operations around Kiev and would take time to reorganize before heading east. Generaloberst Eugen Ritter von Schobert's 11. Armee had already crossed the lower Dnepr but was assigned two diverging missions by the OKH: advance east toward Melitopol and advance south to seize the Crimea. Lieutenant General Nicolae G. Ciuperca's Romanian 4th Army was besieging General-leytenant Georgiy P. Sofronov's Separate Coastal Army (*Otdel'naya Primoorskaya armiya*) in Odessa. Based upon Führer Directive 35, dated September 6, von Rundstedt's objectives after Kiev were to seize Kharkov, the Donets basin, Melitopol and the Crimea, but Rostov was not specified as an objective.[107] The 6. Armee and 17. Armee were assigned to push east to Kharkov while von Kleist was sent to take the Donbas – this would require an advance of at least 400 more kilometers eastward.

On the Soviet side, Timoshenko was left in command of the wreckage of the Southwest Front, which consisted of five battered armies (6, 17, 21, 38, 40), with little armor or artillery left. Given his limited resources, Timoshenko focused on defending Kharkov with the 21st and 38th Armies and Sumy with the 40th Army, which meant that his connection to the Southern Front was maintained by the depleted 17th Army and the reconstituting 6th Army. General-leytenant Dmitry I. Ryabyshev's Southern Front had the 9th and 18th Armies holding Melitopol along the Sea of Azov, the newly created 51st Army in the Crimea and the 12th Army reconstituting in second echelon. At this point, the Stavka's main concern in the Ukraine was to establish a cohesive defensive line to protect the Donbas and the Crimea and to reconstitute formations shattered at Uman and Kiev. Since the bulk of Heeresgruppe Mitte would be focused around Kiev until late September, the German advance in southern Ukraine was initially limited to von Schobert's 11. Armee against the Southern Front. By one of the hazards of war, von Schobert was killed on September 12 when his Fiesler Storch aircraft inadvertently landed in a Soviet minefield; the OKH ordered Erich von Manstein to take over AOK 11. However, von Manstein was up in Heeresgruppe Nord and would not arrive to take command for five days. Furthermore, the 11. Armee was split up, with one corps at the Perekop Isthmus facing the Soviet 51st Army in the Crimea and the rest pushing east along the Sea of Azov.

Despite the fact that the Southern Front had established a stable defensive front to protect Melitopol, Ryabyshev was eager to strike back at the enemy. Ryabyshev was of Don Cossack ethnicity and a *Konarmia* veteran, but he had already demonstrated a lack of aptitude as a mechanized corps commander in the Battle of Dubno. Having just received some tank brigades from the RVGK, on his own initiative he developed a plan for a counteroffensive against the 11. Armee west of Melitopol, focusing on the weaker Romanian units. Although Ryabyshev submitted the plan to Shaposhnikov, it was not approved. Nevertheless, on September 26, Ryabyshev began his counteroffensive and General-major Fedor M. Kharitonov's 9th Army was able to achieve some tactical success against two Romanian brigades. Von Manstein immediately committed his reserve – a Waffen-SS motorized infantry division – to contain Ryabyshev's counteroffensive while conferring with von Rundstedt for an offensive solution. Von Kleist's Panzer group was ready to resume its eastward advance and the obvious place for its *Schwerpunkt* was the thinly held boundary between the Southwest and Southern Fronts. On September 30, von Kleist attacked with a single motorized corps and within 24 hours he achieved a major breakthrough, then pivoted southward to roll up Ryabyshev's right flank. Initially, Ryabyshev continued his attacks against the 11. Armee and paid little heed to events on his far right, until October 2, when von Kleist's Panzers enveloped General-leytenant Andrei K. Smirnov's 18th Army at Zaporozhe. Suddenly recognizing the danger, Ryabyshev tried to pull his front back, but it was far too late. By October 6 the Germans had taken Berdyansk on the Sea of Azov and soon von Kleist's Panzers had completed the encirclement of both the 9th and 12th Armies. Within four days, the Melitopol *Kessel* was crushed between the 11. Armee and Kleist's 1. Panzerarmee, removing another 106,000 Soviet troops from the Soviet order of battle. Stalin had Ryabyshev relieved of command for this debacle, but his *Konarmia* connections saved him from worse. With the defeat of the Southern Front, von Manstein was now free to focus his attention solely upon the Crimea and he was able to breach the strong defenses at both Perekop and Ishun by late October. The 51st Army fell back in disorder toward Kerch, leaving Sevastopol protected only by a small garrison.

Throughout September 1941, the Romanian 4th Army had conducted a lackluster siege at Odessa, incurring very heavy casualties for modest gains. In contrast, the Independent Coastal Army – in conjunction with the Black

Sea Fleet – conducted a skillful active defense which forced Heeresgruppe Süd to dispatch artillery, combat engineers and other support troops to keep the Romanian siege going. However, as the situation in the rest of the Southern Front deteriorated, the Stavka finally decided on September 29 to evacuate Odessa and shift the Separate Coastal Army, now under General-major Ivan E. Petrov, to the Crimea. In one of its best operations of the war, the Black Sea Fleet was able to transport Petrov's army to Sevastopol, just in time to prevent von Manstein's 11. Armee from seizing the city in a *coup de main*. By November 17, von Manstein had overrun most of the Crimea and taken Kerch, but Petrov's army still held Sevastopol.

Meanwhile, the rest of Heeresgruppe Süd was slowly advancing toward Kharkov, but without armor support. By late September, von Stülpnagel's 17. Armee had advanced past Poltava but was facing serious resistance from General-major Viktor V. Tsyganov's 38th Army. Von Reichenau's 6. Armee was not in position to support this advance until early October, by which point Podlas' 40th Army had established a firm defense southwest of Sumy. While von Stülpnagel's performance had been excellent up to this point in the campaign, he suddenly asked to be relieved of command on October 4, allegedly for reasons of ill health. Von Stülpnagel was a prominent member of the covert resistance and had disagreed with occupation policies, but his sudden resignation was rather bizarre.[*] The OKH sent Hermann Hoth from Heeresgruppe Mitte – at the height of Operation *Typhoon* – to take over the 17. Armee. By October 10, Hoth and von Reichenau were able to commence a steady broad front advance which pushed the 21st Army out of Sumy and slowly closed in on Kharkov. Tsyganov's 38th Army put up a tough fight for Kharkov and the city did not fall until October 24. At the same time, von Kleist's Panzers swept along the northern shore of the Sea of Azov and were within 22 kilometers of Rostov when their supplies ran out. Although the OKH continued to suggest that Heeresgruppe Süd continue advancing eastward against scattered Soviet resistance, most of the objectives specified in Führer Directive 35 had been taken.

After Ryabyshev was sacked, General-polkovnik Yakov T. Cherevichenko was put in charge of the Southern Front and tasked with holding Rostov. He was provided with replacements to rebuild the 9th Army and fresh troops from the Caucasus military districts to form a new 56th Army.

---

[*] After several months in reserve, he was sent to Paris to take command of German forces in occupied France. Doubtless, von Stülpnagel's "opting out" from the Eastern Front did not sit well with the subordinates he left to suffer through the terrible winter campaign of 1941/42.

Timoshenko was able to stabilize his front east of Kharkov, particularly since both Hoth and von Reichenau were no longer in pursuit. The situation in the Ukraine might have remained that way for some time, had not Hitler pressed von Rundstedt to push on and take Rostov. Von Kleist had little fuel for his remaining 200 worn-out tanks and very little infantry support, which was not auspicious for seizing or holding that objective. Nevertheless, von Kleist attacked on November 5, but Soviet resistance had stiffened and he suffered some annoying tactical setbacks. Renewing the attack on November 17, von Kleist's armored spearhead was able to fight its way into Rostov and capture most of the city by November 20. However, Cherevichenko had been assembling an operational reserve in General-major Anton I. Lopatin's 37th Army, which attacked von Kleist's overextended forces on November 25. After a few days of desperate fighting, it became obvious to von Rundstedt and von Kleist that the city could not be held by a handful of unsupplied German divisions and they requested permission to withdraw. Hitler refused. Yet von Kleist's forces were in danger of encirclement and on his own authority, von Rundstedt ordered the 1. Panzerarmee to withdraw 70 kilometers to the Mius River. Hitler reacted by relieving von Rundstedt of command and replacing him with von Reichenau, but by that point Rostov had already been abandoned. Von Kleist's 1. Panzerarmee was saved, but all of its Panzer divisions were now combat ineffective.

The last German offensive of 1941 occurred in the Crimea, where von Manstein mounted a hastily improvised offensive with just five infantry divisions against Petrov's dug-in Coastal Army. Hitler's Führer Directive 39, issued on December 8, stipulated that "Sevastopol will be captured as soon as possible."[108] However, Hitler sent von Manstein no reinforcements to conduct this offensive and Heeresgruppe Mitte's logistic situation east of the Dnepr River was still extremely poor. Nevertheless, von Manstein's first offensive began on November 11–21, but it proved so weak that it was unable to breach Sevastopol's outer defenses. After gathering up additional forces from the dispersed 11. Armee (which was also tasked with coast defense in the Crimea), von Manstein launched a more substantial offensive on December 17, which managed to breach the outer defensive perimeter. Yet Petrov received three fresh divisions by sea during December, which gave him the strength to win a grinding battle of attrition. Just as von Manstein's offensive was culminating, General-leytenant Dmitri T. Kozlov's Transcaucasus Front decided to mount its own counteroffensive in the Crimea using the Azov Flotilla and Black Sea Fleet. In the Red Army's first major amphibious landing, the Soviet 51st Army landed at Kerch on December 26 and three days later the 44th Army captured the port of Feodosiya in an amphibious *coup de main*.[109] The German defenders were able to crush some of the landings but they were overstretched and obliged to retire to the Parpach Narrows, ceding the Kerch Peninsula to the Red Army.[110] Von Manstein seriously underestimated his opponent at Sevastopol, simply assuming that Soviet resistance would collapse in the face of a German assault, which it did not. He also seriously underestimated the ability of the Black Sea Fleet to support the defense of Sevastopol with naval gunfire support, amphibious landings and bringing in supplies and reinforcements. Nor did von Manstein make good use of his Romanian allies; for the most part, he ignored them. In contrast, Petrov made excellent use of his time and resources, quickly building up three lines of defense while keeping von Manstein at bay until help could arrive from the sea.

In the final phase of Operation *Barbarossa* in the southern axis, the German commanders continued to rely upon the offensive and maneuver principles, but no longer had the mass to achieve rapid results as in the two previous phases. Once across the Dnepr River, German ground and air combat power became increasingly dispersed in the open steppe country. The German commanders still managed to achieve some operational-level surprises, as at Melitopol, but the Soviets were now more alert and beginning to anticipate some moves. Von Rundstedt's battle command was effective, if overly reliant upon delegation, and he did show some moral courage in authorizing the withdrawal from Rostov in spite of Hitler's refusal. Von Kleist and von Manstein demonstrated considerable competence, even though von Reichenau was the only one to take and hold a primary objective in this phase. On the Soviet side, Timoshenko was effective at rebuilding the shattered Southwest Front and slowing – if not stopping – the German drive upon Kharkov. Timoshenko was less impulsive at Kharkov than he was at Smolensk, being more careful with his limited reserves. On the other hand, Ryabyshev's brief tenure as Southern Front commander was a disaster and an unnecessary one at that. Cherevichenko and Petrov demonstrated an ability to adapt to fast-moving battlefields and prevent two of the best German commanders from achieving their operational objectives – which was no small accomplishment. Throughout this phase, during October–December 1941, Soviet commanders in the eastern Ukraine and Crimea were undermined by poor C2 due to the shortage of field radios in their subordinate armies. Trying to direct the movement of forces over sectors that were hundreds of kilometers in width with a handful of radios (often operating in unencrypted mode) was a virtually impossible task. While Heeresgruppe Süd was running out of ammunition, fuel and operational tanks, it still had a major edge in field communications, which enabled its leadership to conduct and coordinate complex operations involving several armies.

Commander	Objective	Offensive	Mass	Maneuver	Surprise	Security	TALLY
Von Rundstedt	+	+	o	+	o	o	3
Von Kleist	+	+	o	+	+	o	4
Von Manstein	+	+	o	+	+	o	4
Von Reichenau	+	+	o	o	o	o	2
Timoshenko	+	o	+	o	o	o	2
Ryabyshev	o	+	o	o	o	-	o
Cherevichenko	+	+	o	+	o	o	3
Petrov	+	o	o	o	o	+	2

Southern Axis, Phase 3 Leadership Assessment

Assessment of Operational Outcomes, 1941

By early December, it was evident that Operation *Barbarossa* had only been partly successful; some major territorial objectives had been taken (Minsk, Smolensk, Riga, Kiev, Orel and Kharkov) and huge losses inflicted upon the Red Army. Since June 1941, the Red Army had suffered over 4.4 million casualties, including over 3.1 million dead or missing. It is also important to note that the Germans had succeeded in severely degrading the Red Army's operational center of gravity (COG) by demolishing every one of its pre-war mechanized corps, a total of 107 rifle divisions and a large portion of its corps/army level heavy artillery.[111] The loss of 20,500 tanks, 10,600 combat aircraft, 24,000 field guns (76mm and above), one-third of its motor vehicles and over 50 percent of its radios left the Red Army with minimal offensive capabilities.[112] Nevertheless, on January 1, 1942 the Red Army on the Eastern Front still had 3.5 million troops in over 300 divisions, equipped with about 2,500 tanks and 1,200 combat aircraft. Even though the Wehrmacht had degraded the Red Army's operational level COG, it had barely scratched the Soviet Union's strategic COG – its armaments industry and oil/mineral production facilities. Consequently, the Soviet Union's ability to generate new forces to continue the war remained intact, with its factories producing over 1,200 tanks per month as well as large amounts of artillery, aircraft and ammunition. A total of 258 rifle divisions had been raised in the last six months of 1941 and plenty of manpower was in the training queue to provide replacements. Soviet strategic fuel reserves – a necessary prerequisite for operational-level maneuver warfare – were also ample.

In contrast, the Ostheer had suffered 830,903 casualties and had difficulty replacing even half of them.[113] In addition, cold-weather injuries, illness and exhaustion were sapping the Ostheer's vitality, with 133,620 frostbite casualties incurred by the end of 1941.[114] The Ostheer had kept attacking until its best units were burnt out and combat ineffective – thereby effectively crippling its own COG. By the end of 1941, the 19 Panzer divisions on the Eastern Front had barely 300 operational tanks.[115] German tank production, averaging 350 tanks and assault guns per month, was unable to replace losses. The Ostheer's operational COG was also degraded by the increasing inability of the captured rail lines to support front-line logistics, which led to critical shortages at the front.[116] In terms of organic transport, at least one-quarter of the Ostheer's motor vehicles were lost during *Barbarossa* and many more were sidelined awaiting repairs. The Ostheer's non-motorized divisions were highly dependent upon horses for mobility, but equine losses mounted rapidly with the onset of cold weather, increasing to 180,000 in December 1941/January 1942.[117] The Luftwaffe had also suffered heavy losses during *Barbarossa*, totaling 2,093 aircraft destroyed and another 1,100 damaged.[118] In terms of Germany's strategic center of gravity, oil reserves were seriously depleted by the unexpectedly protracted war in Russia and ammunition production had actually begun scaling back in anticipation of the *Endsieg*.

The Ostheer had demonstrated great operational-level skill and efficiency during the campaigns of 1941, which enabled it to pull off six major battles of encirclement (*Kesselschlachten*) that demolished 21 Soviet field armies. By any standards, this was a remarkable achievement in operational warfare. For the Ostheer, *Barbarossa* confirmed that fast-moving double-pincer attacks supported by the Luftwaffe were the key to operational success. In contrast, the Red Army nearly encircled large German formations at Klin, Tikhvin and Rostov but on each occasion lacked the skill and C2 capability to efficiently complete this type of operation. Consequently, by the end of 1941, the Ostheer had captured over 1 million Soviet soldiers but the Red Army had taken only 10,600 German prisoners – a ratio of nearly 100-1. The German ability to quickly plan and coordinate operations involving several armies – honed during previous campaigns and years of peacetime training – gave the Ostheer a major advantage in efficiency over the Red Army of 1941. In terms of the OODA loop (Observe-Orient-Decide-Act), the Ostheer of 1941 typically enjoyed a 2–3 day advantage over the Red Army of 1941.* However, the German advantage was fleeting for a number of reasons: (1) the Wehrmacht was not prepared for protracted campaigning in terms of doctrine or resources, (2) Hitler and the OKH were unable to link short-term operational objectives to long-term strategic victory – victories piled up but goals remained elusive, (3) the Ostheer had no doctrinal solution for dealing with well-defended enemy cities such as Leningrad and Sevastopol and (4) increasing opposition to Hitler's regime within the senior ranks of the Ostheer led to constant arguments over missions, objectives and the conduct of operations. Despite the Red Army's problems, Soviet military doctrine and industrial strategy were premised upon the concept of protracted warfare and the Stavka/GKO was adept at harnessing the nation's resources to generate and regenerate combat power. Nor was Stavka planning undermined by anti-regime attitudes or generals who decided to ignore orders – NKVD oversight ensured obedience. Nor had political commissars exerted too negative an influence on Soviet operations in 1941 (with a few exceptions, such as Vashugin) – mostly because military councils were usually reacting to one disaster after another – but this would change in 1942.

Aside from the lack of efficiency in the planning and conduct of operations, the Red Army suffered from an addiction to an offensive doctrine that was applied without regard to battlefield realities. Red Army pre-war doctrine had paid little attention to defensive operations and Stalin enforced a knee-jerk offensive mindset on his commanders. Attack became the one-size solution for all battlefield problems. Consequently, Soviet reserves were often frittered away in hastily improvised attacks instead of husbanding them to respond to German moves. Nowhere was this tendency more destructive than in the Red Army's misuse of its armored units, which meant that the Winter Counteroffensive of 1941/42 would be conducted with minimal tank support. Likewise, Soviet commanders were terrified about trading space

---

*The OODA Loop is a decision-making model developed by the US military in the 1970s; it posits four steps required to assess a given military combat situation: observe, orient, decide, act. Under this model, the side which accomplishes these steps first will likely gain a significant military advantage. Although the Wehrmacht commanders of 1941–45 did not use the term OODA Loop, they certainly understood the decision-making principles which it codified.

for time because unauthorized withdrawals would often lead to arrest and summary punishment. So, in most cases, Soviet defensive operations were undermined by the lack of mobile reserves and the prioritization of obeying orders over force preservation.

Grudgingly accepting that the war in the East was going to continue, Hitler wanted a new command team for the next campaign season and decided to remove those he regarded as responsible for failure or simply not sufficiently aggressive. Von Rundstedt was the first to go, due to his unauthorized retreat from Rostov. Hitler still valued von Rundstedt's dedication but regarded him as now unsuited for high-tempo maneuver warfare and relegated him to the quiet Western Front. Von Bock was not relieved of command but transferred to the Führer Reserve due to ill health and Hitler pointedly told him that he intended to use his services again in the near future (which was true).[119] Illness and mental exhaustion were becoming serious problems for the Ostheer, impairing the efficiency of soldiers from private to general. Höpner, Guderian, Strauß and von Leeb were all relieved of command and would receive no further major field commands. Hitler blamed each one for a variety of shortcomings, including insubordination, tardiness and simply being unenthusiastic about the *Endsieg* (final victory). Guderian's fall was just as sudden as his rise and not unexpected, since von Bock had been trying to get rid of him since the Battle of Smolensk. Von Leeb, as the least successful army group commander, had been asking to be relieved for some time and Hitler obliged. Höpner had his moment of success in *Typhoon*, but his anti-regime attitudes were more evident after the defeat at Moscow and when he retreated without orders he was singled out by Hitler for extra-punitive measures (not only relieved of command but ejected from the Heer). Strauß was simply too undynamic a commander for the Ostheer and 9. Armee under his command had been frequently accused by Hoth of lagging behind. Of note, Hitler promoted both von Reichenau and von Kluge to army group commanders, even though neither one had turned in a particularly impressive performance as army commanders. In any case, Hitler's changes in senior leadership in the Ostheer hardly represented a "purge," and most armies after a defeat engage in house-cleaning (e.g. the British 8th Army, 1941–42). It is also important to note that at the staff level, there were far fewer changes; in the three army groups, five of the six senior staff officers remained in place throughout the winter of 1941/42. In the four Panzer armies, seven of eight senior staff remained. As the situation deteriorated on the Eastern Front, Hitler became increasingly prone to micromanagement but was still willing to allow Halder and his OKH staff to play an active role in operational planning.

Table II: German Command Changes after Failure of *Barbarossa*

Name	Command	Date of Relief	Replacement	Further Command(s)
Von Rundstedt	Heeresgruppe Süd	December 1, 1942	Von Reichenau	Yes
Von Bock	Heeresgruppe Mitte	December 19, 1941	Von Kluge	Yes
Guderian	2. Panzerarmee	December 25, 1941	Schmidt	No
Höpner	4. Panzerarmee	January 8, 1942	Ruoff	No
Strauß	9. Armee	January 15, 1942	Model	No
Von Leeb	Heeresgruppe Nord	January 17, 1942	Von Küchler	No

On the other hand, Stalin used purge tactics throughout the 1941 campaign, arresting senior commanders who suffered major defeats or simply disappointed him; this resulted in the execution of one front commander, two front-level chiefs of staff, three army commanders and a number of other senior staff. Other commanders were held for interrogation by the NKVD, sometimes for months. In addition, the Red Army lost one front commander and seven army commanders killed in action and five army commanders captured.[120] The fear in Soviet senior commanders – even Zhukov – during the 1941 campaign was palpable, with widespread recognition that failure or unauthorized actions could have fatal consequences. Unfortunately, this fear did nothing to improve the battlefield efficiency of Soviet commanders, who were often forced to execute absurd orders without question. For his part, Stalin appeared to have learned nothing during the 1941 campaign and remained committed to his mercurial command-by-*diktat* style, with only a nod to professional recommendations from Shaposhnikov and his General Staff (GSHKA).

CHAPTER 4

Fall Blau: 1942 Operations

"Attack. Regain the initiative. Impose your will upon the enemy."
Generaloberst Walther Model, 1942

*"An error in filling a command post always has unfortunate
consequences for the troops."*
General der Panzertruppe Friedrich Paulus, 1942[1]

Soviet Winter Counteroffensive, January 1–April 11, 1942

Although the Red Army had not seriously degraded the Ostheer's operational center of gravity (COG) in the 1941 campaign, the Germans had done a fairly effective job sabotaging their own rail networks that kept their field armies in supply. The jury-rigged German theater logistic system was already failing by October but the final blow came when freezing winter temperatures arrived and disabled many of the German steam engines, which were not built with Russian winters in mind. By the end of 1941, about 70–80 percent of the German train engines on the Eastern Front were non-operational due to burst pipes in their boilers – which left the Ostheer starved for ammunition, fuel, rations and winter clothing.[2] Motor transport and horses were also badly impaired by shortages of fuel and fodder, as well as freezing temperatures. Indeed, it was the collapse of the German theater logistic system which was the main cause of the winter crisis facing the Ostheer. In contrast, the Soviet logistic system, run by General-leytenant Andrei V. Khrulev, was usually able to deliver just enough supplies and fresh units to the front to sustain operations. Shortages of motor transport did limit Soviet logistic throughput, although this would later be rectified in 1943–44 by Allied Lend Lease aid.

Even as Zhukov's December counteroffensive was fading, the Stavka was already discussing how best to exploit the sudden turn of fortune. Zhukov and most other front-level commanders knew that the Red Army's offensive capabilities were still limited and preferred to delay any further major offensives until units could be re-equipped and better prepared. Recognizing that even a temporary shift to the defense would be unacceptable to Stalin, Zhukov instead advocated attacking along only one axis – his. He argued that by focusing all of the Red Army's capabilities against Heeresgruppe Mitte (using the principles of mass and offensive) it would be more likely to achieve decisive results rather than dispersing resources across multiple fronts. Zhukov's assessment was professionally sound, but Stalin would not consider leaving Leningrad and the Donbas region in the lurch. Stalin was elated about the German retreats from Moscow and Rostov and regarded the Ostheer as a spent force, so he demanded a general offensive by all nine Soviet fronts, from the Baltic to the Black Sea. He also wanted this general offensive to begin as soon as possible, so as to afford the Ostheer no time to recover. Instead of concentrating the RVGK reserves in one sector, he ordered them dispersed to provide some reinforcements to each front, thereby violating the principle of mass. Despite their professional reservations, the Stavka and the front commanders could only obey. Stalin's call for a general offensive was the greatest Soviet strategic mistake made in 1942, which had serious operational-level consequences.

Zhukov could see that the hastily improvised Soviet field armies of December 1941 were not capable of conducting anything like the pre-war Deep Battle doctrine of PU-36 or even any fancy maneuvers. Deep Battle had envisioned conducting encirclement operations with fast-moving, full-strength tank and cavalry units in fair weather, not with slow-moving, understrength infantry units in the middle of winter.

The Stavka ordered the formation of four 'shock armies' (*udarnaya armiya*) in December to lead the counteroffensive: the 1 SA was provided to the Western Front, 2nd Shock Army (2 SA) to the Volkhov Front and 3rd and 4th Shock Armies to the Northwest Front. While these shock armies had more troops than other Soviet field armies (50–70,000 versus 30–40,000), they were primarily built around newly raised rifle brigades and ski battalions. Artillery and armored support in these formations was minimal and engineer support nonexistent. In order to try to mass available combat power and create something like a combined arms approach, Zhukov issued an order directing each front, whether or not they had a designated shock army, to create 'shock groups' to lead their offensives. A typical shock group was based around a rifle brigade, a tank battalion and a ski battalion – perhaps 5,000 troops with 20–30 tanks, but only mortars or light artillery in support. While the ski units provided the Red Army with better tactical mobility than the Ostheer in winter, even the shock groups lacked the firepower needed to capture strongly defended German *Stutzpunkte*.

The general offensive was set to begin on January 6, with simultaneous attacks by Khozin's Leningrad Front, Meretskov's Volkhov Front, Kurochkin's Northwest Front, Konev's Kalinin Front and Zhukov's Western Front. The mission of Khozin's Leningrad Front and Meretskov's Volkhov Front was to conduct a pincer attack against the German-held Kirishi salient, then push on to Lyuban to create a wide breakthrough in Heeresgruppe Nord's front. The Kirishi salient was also located near the boundary between Küchler's 18. Armee and Busch's 16. Armee. Meretskov would make the main effort by attacking across the Volkhov River with three armies in the first echelon (4, 52, 59) and one army (2nd Shock Army) in second echelon. Meretskov received General-major Ivan V. Galanin's 59th Army from the RVGK in mid-December; Galanin was an experienced commander who had led a division at the Battle of Khalkhin-Gol in 1939. On the other hand, the 2nd Shock Army was an improvised formation, commanded by an inexperienced NKVD officer, General-leytenant Grigory G. Sokolov. Khozin's Leningrad Front would conduct its main attack with Fediuninskiy's 54th Army, while the 8th Army conducted fixing attacks near Siniavino. Although the attacking Soviet armies had a substantial advantage in manpower, they had very limited artillery support (mostly light 76mm field guns), or other combat multipliers. The heavily wooded frozen marshland along the Volkhov River, with few roads, also favored the defense. When the Leningrad and Volkhov Fronts attacked on the morning of January 6, they were repulsed at most points and only managed to make minor inroads in the German front line at two places. General Nikolai K. Klykov's 52nd Army had the most success, gaining a small bridgehead across the Volkhov River in the sector held by Busch's 16. Armee. Two German *Stutzpunkte* blocked further advance, but Meretskov decided to commit Sokolov's 2 SA into the "gap" to exploit eastward. Time and again, due to pressure from Moscow for rapid results, Soviet front commanders were forced to prematurely commit their exploitation groups before the German line had actually been breached. Sokolov began squeezing his army through a narrow gap between the two German *Stutzpunkte* until most of 2 SA was behind the German lines by mid-January. It was quickly apparent that Sokolov had no idea how to command an army and Meretskov relieved him of command on January 10 and put Klykov in charge.[3] Nevertheless, the Soviet shock groups could not eliminate the German *Stutzpunkte* because they lacked adequate firepower. Under pressure from the Stavka to get on with the advance to Lyuban, Meretskov committed the 13th Cavalry Corps into the narrow gap, but it could not advance any further. By late January, over 40,000 Soviet troops were semi-isolated behind German lines and Meretskov's counteroffensive had made minimal progress.

On the German side, von Leeb's nerves were frazzled by the constant pounding on his front-line units and asked Hitler for permission to retreat – this request was refused and Hitler decided to replace him with Küchler. Generaloberst Georg Lindemann, the L Armeekorps commander, took over the 18. Armee. Küchler and Lindemann worked well together and they knew how to use interior lines to their advantage by shifting units from quiet sectors to threatened ones. While the infiltration of Klykov's 2 SA caused a temporary crisis, Küchler and Lindemann contained it by moving elements of five divisions to surround Klykov's army. Küchler directed his staff to begin planning an operation, Unternehmen *Raubtier* (Operation *Beast of Prey*), to crush the 2 SA once additional reinforcements were available. Meretskov was temporarily stymied but fed additional units into the battle and in February slowly widened the breach in the 16. Armee front. One of the basic rules of commonsense soldiering is not to reinforce failure, but that is exactly what Meretskov did, sending more divisions into the salient. Fediuninskiy's 54th Army also achieved some success in a new round of attacks, which managed to seriously dent the right flank of Lindemann's 18. Armee. However, this proved to be the high-water mark for Meretskov and Khozin. On March 15, Küchler launched *Raubtier* with two divisions, supported by Stukas from Luftflotte 1, making a pincer attack against the narrow neck of the salient held by Klykov's 2 SA. Five days later, the German pincers closed, trapping 50,000 Soviet troops in the pocket. Meretskov desperately tried to reopen a corridor to the isolated 2 SA, which enabled thousands to escape before the Germans blocked any further rescue attempts. At that point, the spring thaw set in, turning the frozen marshes into wetlands and most of the 2 SA troops soon found themselves virtually underwater. Lindemann was put in charge of crushing the *Kessel*, which he accomplished efficiently with artillery and Luftwaffe bombing.

On April 20 General-leytenant Andrei Vlasov was flown in to take charge of the battered remnants inside the pocket, but he could not reverse the situation. Recognizing that the winter offensive on the Volkhov had failed, Meretskov on his own ordered his front to shift to the defense. Stalin promptly relieved him and told Khozin he was now in charge of both the Leningrad and Volkhov Fronts, although the latter was now referred to as the Volkhov Operational Group. Lindemann spent May crushing Vlasov's trapped army and by June 5, all resistance in the pocket had ended; the Germans eventually counted 33,000 prisoners, including Vlasov. Unlike most Soviet generals captured by the Germans, Vlasov became an open collaborator – which proved highly embarrassing for Stalin.[4] In response, he relieved Khozin, brought Meretskov back to reorganize the Volkhov Front and put an artilleryman, General-leytenant Leonid A. Govorov, in charge of the Leningrad Front. Govorov was one of the few Red Army generals who had fought with the Whites during the Russian Civil War and he was not a member of the Communist Party (CPSU) when he was made a front commander. However, Govorov was a graduate of the General Staff Academy and he would prove to be one of the best front commanders in the Second World War.

The winter counteroffensive and spring fighting cost the Volkhov Front 403,000 casualties (including 150,000 dead or missing), and the Leningrad Front had suffered heavy casualties, as well.[5] In return, Meretskov had made no headway towards breaking the siege of Leningrad (the ultimate objective) and only succeeded in capturing small parcels of worthless marshland. To be fair, Meretskov did as he was ordered (he had just undergone a brutal NKVD imprisonment four months prior) and was hamstrung by Stalin's ridiculous guidance. Likewise, Meretskov's chief of staff, General-major Grigory D. Stelmakh, had spent two years in prison during the purges. Fear of repression, not professional judgment, directed the decisions made during the Volkhov Front's winter counteroffensive, which ended in disaster. On the German side, Küchler and Lindemann won a significant defensive victory and achieved their operational objective of maintaining the siege lines around Leningrad. Altogether, Heeresgruppe

Nord suffered 125,000 casualties in this period (including 30,000 dead or missing), implying a casualty ratio of about 4-1 in their favor. German defensive tactics improved considerably as a result of this campaign and Heeresgruppe Nord would become a much tougher nut to crack in the next Soviet offensive.

General-polkovnik Pavel A. Kurochkin's Northwest Front was ordered by the Stavka on December 18 to begin preparing for the winter counteroffensive, but it was primarily intended to support its neighbors – Meretskov's Volkhov Front on the right and Konev's Kalinin Front on the left. By early January 1942, the Northwest Front had 170,000 troops in four armies: Morozov's 11th Army, General-major Nikolai E. Berzarin's 34th Army, General-leytenant Maksim Purkaev's 3rd Shock Army (3 SA) and the 4th Shock Army (4 SA) under General-polkovnik Andrei Eremenko (who was still recovering from wounds). Kurochkin was now an experienced front commander and he was fortunate in having General-leytenant Nikolai F. Vatutin as his chief of staff and veteran commanders like Morozov, Purkaev and Eremenko. Amazingly, Morozov had remained in command of the same field army since the first day of *Barbarossa* – a feat no other Soviet officer had accomplished. Kurochkin's counteroffensive against Busch's 16. Armee was not expected by the Stavka to achieve major results, simply attract German reserves that might be deployed elsewhere. Of all the Soviet fronts involved in the winter counteroffensive, the Northwest Front was provided the least in terms of artillery, replacements or supplies; even rations for the front-line troops were irregular. Kurochkin was simply told that if he wanted those things, he needed to go capture them from the Germans.

Busch had deployed two of his corps (II, X) to hold a 190km-wide front between Lake Ilmen/Staraya Russa and the town of Peno, which was the inter-front boundary between Heeresgruppe Nord and Heeresgruppe Mitte. One corps from the 9. Armee held the sector between Peno and Rzhev. Busch's front line was paper-thin, with units at 50 percent strength assigned to hold double-width sectors. Nor were any significant reserves available to deal with any unexpected crises. Luftflotte 1 was still capable of providing some assistance, at least when the weather was not too bad, but also had to support the 18. Armee, as well. In December, Busch had requested permission to pull back to the Lovat River to shorten his front, but Hitler forbade it. Instead, Hitler told him to build more *Stutzpunkte*, so he did. Given that the ground was covered with 80cm of snow and temperatures hovered around 17°F (-8°C), Busch did not expect the Soviets to attack his front.

Kurochkin and Vatutin carefully planned a counteroffensive that relied upon stealthy infiltration and surprise, rather than brute force. Beginning on the night of January 7/8, shock groups from Morozov's 11th Army began moving forward to isolate some of the German forward *Stutzpunkte*. The Germans were particularly surprised to discover that Soviet ski battalions and light tanks had moved across the frozen Lake Ilmen to get behind them. On the night of January 8/9, Purkaev's 3 SA used similar tactics, crossing frozen Lake Seliger to infiltrate around German positions. Although the Soviets had difficulty reducing the German strongpoints, the right flank of the 16. Armee rapidly disintegrated in just a few days. Kurochkin then ordered Eremenko's 4 SA to exploit the breakthrough by advancing to seize the German supply base at Toropets. Purkaev was assigned three diverging objectives: Demyansk, Kholm and Velikiye Luki. For a week, Eremenko's 4 SA advanced slowly, but relentlessly, like a 60,000-man battering ram. Shocked by the enemy breakthrough, the OKH provided Busch with the 81. Infanterie-Division, just arrived by rail from France. Busch sent the lead regiment to try to slow Eremenko, but it was surrounded and annihilated on January 12–15. Eremenko kept advancing and took the German supply dumps in Toropets on January 20; for once, his troops enjoyed the stockpile of German rations.[6] Kurochkin's Northwest Front was achieving success across the board: the 11th and 34th Armies had isolated (but not yet fully encircled) most of the German II Armeekorps in Demyansk, while Purkaev's 3 SA had encircled the German garrison in Kholm. Meanwhile, on Kurochkin's left flank, Konev's Kalinin Front had surrounded the German XXIII Armeekorps in Olenino. The boundary between Heeresgruppe Nord and Heeresgruppe Mitte had been ripped apart, thereby creating a 100km-wide gap in the German front line. Although the OKH managed to move in some forces to block Purkaev from reaching Velikiye Luki, it was clear that the Ostheer was facing a real disaster.

Kurochkin recognized that finishing off the encirclement of the German II Armeekorps was his primary task, then pursuing other objectives. He requested additional reinforcements from the RVGK to help expedite the encirclement operation. Instead, Stalin became involved and made some incredible operational decisions. He ordered that the 3rd and 4th Shock Armies – on the verge of achieving a major operational success – be transferred to Konev's command on January 22. Purkaev's army was hung up at Kholm, but Eremenko's was in a good position to seize Velikiye Luki before it was fortified. Yet once transferred to Konev's command, Eremenko was ordered to turn south to seize the town of Velizh. In return,

Kurochkin would receive Kuznetsov's 1st Shock Army from the Western Front, although that would take time. Rather surprisingly, Kurochkin argued over the radio telephone with Stalin about losing the 3 SA, which would seriously weaken his front's offensive at a critical moment. Stalin refused to listen, but it was unusual for one of his generals to show any backbone in dealing with his *diktats.*[7] While the Soviet leadership was arguing about how best to take advantage of this unexpected breakthrough, the Germans were finally reacting. General der Infanterie Kurt von der Chevallerie, commander of the LIX Armeekorps from France, arrived in Velikiye Luki in late January and quickly organized a patchwork defense to try to stop the Soviet steamroller – all he could deploy was a single regiment in Velikiye Luki and another in Velizh. On February 1, the LIX Armeekorps was placed under Reinhardt's 3. Panzerarmee, which had been shifted to Vitebsk.[8] Busch anchored the northern end of the shaky German front by establishing several large *Stutzpunkte* around Staraya Russa, to hold this critical position. At the same time, the Luftwaffe began organizing an airlift to keep the garrisons in Demyansk and Kholm in supply, with little interference from the VVS.

Kurochkin and Busch fought a tenacious battle in February along the Lovat River and east of Staraya Russa. Busch succeeded in holding Staraya Russa, but Kurochkin finally completed the encirclement of the II Armeekorps in Demyansk by February 25. A total of five German divisions were now surrounded in the Demyansk pocket, which Hitler designated as a *Festung* (fortress). In the south, Eremenko was badly wounded on January 20 in a Luftwaffe air raid but remained in command for three more weeks until finally turning 4 SA over to General-leytenant Filipp Golikov. The 4 SA encircled German garrisons in Velizh and Demidovo and its advance guards reached within 40 kilometers of Vitebsk, forcing Reinhardt to commit rear area troops and staff to form blocking detachments.[9] Eremenko came very close to achieving a major victory, but the German defenders mounted a desperate defense at the key points, which halted the 4 SA. Likewise, Purkaev's 3 SA repeatedly pounded on Kholm but could not break its stalwart defense. By early March, it was clear that the Northwest Front counteroffensive had culminated. Busch now began planning for relief operations to rescue his trapped forces and Hitler promised to provide five divisions for the effort (in fact, only two complete divisions and parts of three others were provided). Busch put General der Artillerie Walther von Seydlitz-Kurzbach in charge of the relief operation for the Demyansk pocket, designated Unternehmen *Brückenschlag* (Operation *Bridge Building*). Seydlitz began his operation on

March 21, gradually fighting his way through Morozov's 11th Army. On April 21, Korpsgruppe Seydlitz finally re-established a ground link to the Demyansk pocket, making its commander a national hero (but not for long). Busch expected Hitler to allow 16. Armee to evacuate the still vulnerable Demyansk salient – which was only accessible via the narrow Ramushevo corridor – but instead he was told that he was required to hold this position indefinitely. The garrison in Kholm was relieved on May 5 and this position was also to be retained. Kurochkin's winter counteroffensive had seriously stressed Heeresgruppe Nord and came very close to achieving a major operational success; as it was, the German inter-army group boundary remained a point of great vulnerability. Altogether the Northwest Front suffered 245,000 casualties during the winter counteroffensive, including almost 89,000 dead or missing – Kurochkin's forces were completely spent. For their part, the Germans suffered about 73,000 casualties (including about 20,000 dead or missing), stopping Kurochkin's counteroffensive.[10] While Luftflotte 1 did a magnificent job sustaining the encircled garrisons, it lost 152 Ju-52 transports plus another 100 damaged.[11] Yet the most significant outcome was that Hitler and the OKH were left with the impression that the Luftwaffe could supply encircled formations entirely via air transport until help arrived – this impression would shape German operations during the rest of 1942–43.

Kurochkin's performance as a front commander was very good during the winter counteroffensive and he used offensive maneuver to try to achieve his objectives, as well as surprise in the opening week. While not a complete success, he achieved a partial victory which left the 16. Armee's right flank in great jeopardy. Likewise, the Soviet army commanders on this front made excellent use of their limited resources, but the failure of the Stavka to provide adequate artillery support made it impossible for them to reduce most German *Stutzpunkte*. Stalin's interference also seriously undermined the front's offensive rhythm at the critical moment. On the German side, Busch and his subordinates fought a dogged defensive battle, using interior lines to rush blocking detachments to threatened points just in the nick of time. Busch's right flank was essentially obliterated in the opening week of Kurochkin's offensive, yet he managed to create a patchwork front from bits and pieces that just managed to hold. Very few senior commanders can recover from having a 100km-wide hole blown in their front and one-third of their forces surrounded, but Busch did. Once the Northwest Front was exhausted, Busch conducted a well-timed offensive that successfully rescued his besieged garrisons.

On Kurochkin's left flank, Konev's Kalinin Front was tasked with capturing the city of Rzhev and crushing the German 9. Armee in the process. While he would get some assistance in this effort from the right wing of Zhukov's Western Front, it was primarily up to Konev to accomplish this mission. In January 1942, Konev had five armies (22, 29, 30, 31, 39) with 346,000 troops under his command and unlike Kurochkin, he had been provided with a fair amount of artillery (including nine battalions of BM-13 multiple rocket launchers) and about 100–150 tanks. The Kalinin Front had suffered 92,000 casualties during the December phase of the winter counteroffensive, but it had received some replacements and was still combat effective. Strauß' 9. Armee was holding the Rzhev sector with three corps, totaling 11 infantry divisions. Strauß had a very wide sector to defend with units that were now well understrength and suffering badly from the freezing temperatures and irregular supplies. German front-line morale was shaky at this point and some commanders were inclined to pull back without orders. The only place that 9. Armee had any real strength was around Rzhev and its right flank, but the army's left flank was paper-thin. Konev and his chief of staff General-major Matvei V. Zakharov planned to use a combination of maneuver and brute force to dislodge the 9. Armee, then crush it. The main maneuver/exploitation force would consist of General-major Vladimir I. Vostrukhov's 22nd Army and General-leytenant Ivan I. Maslennikov's 39th Army; these two armies would strike AOK 9's vulnerable left flank. At the same time, the 29th, 30th and 31st Armies would attack Rzhev from the north and east, hopefully overwhelming the defense. After capturing Rzhev, Konev was expected to assist Zhukov's advance to Vyazma.

Konev's counteroffensive began on January 8, with Maslennikov's 39th Army attacking the sector between Olenino and Rzhev; within three days the Soviet shock groups achieved a major breakthrough. At the same time, Vostrukhov's 22nd Army easily pushed through the German screening forces west of Olenino, isolating the German XXIII Armeekorps there. Although the 9. Armee succeeded in repulsing the Soviet attacks against Rzhev, at considerable cost in losses, the army's left flank was broken and all contact with the 16. Armee lost. Konev ordered the 22nd Army to push south to Yartsevo (on the main Minsk-Smolensk highway) to sever the German line of communications, while the 39th Army advanced south and east to envelop the 9. Armee from behind. Six divisions from General-major Vasily I. Shvetsov's 29th Army were sent to reinforce Maslennikov's breakthrough and Konev also committed the 11th Cavalry Corps as a mobile exploitation group into the enemy rear area. As a result of this major breakthrough, the Ostheer faced its greatest crisis in the winter of 1941/42 and defeat would lead to the disintegration of Heeresgruppe Mitte's left flank. The 62-year-old Strauß withered in the crisis, partly from illness and in part from nerves, but he could not deal with this situation and asked to be replaced.

The OKH selected Generaloberst Walther Model, a corps commander in the 3. Panzerarmee, to take over the 9. Armee. Model arrived at the army headquarters in Sychevka on January 18 and found that his new command was a complete shambles. After studying the situation map for a few moments he then turned to his staff and told them that the 9. Armee would conduct a multi-division counterattack within 72 hours to relieve the XXIII Armeekorps and thereby isolate Maslennikov's 39th Army. The staff protested about the impossibility of attacking with understrength units under brutal weather conditions (-40°C at night and one meter of snow on the ground) but Model was adamant that the 9. Armee would attack. Model was able to convince Heeresgruppe Mitte to loan him some units from the 3. Panzerarmee for his counteroffensive, as well as getting the OKH to airlift a fresh infantry regiment in from France to join his command. From the beginning, Model was able to instill fighting spirit (*Kampfgeist*) in his troops and he had a knack for begging/borrowing/stealing units and resources from other commands to make his operations feasible. The 9. Armee attacked on schedule and re-established a ground link to the XXIII Armeekorps on January 22. Despite this success, Maslennikov's 39th Army attacked Sychevka on the same day, nearly overrunning the town and Model's headquarters. Konev's spearheads continued their slow advance southward and on January 27 the 11th Cavalry Corps temporarily occupied the Minsk-Smolensk highway (and the adjoining rail line) west of Vyazma. For a brief moment, Konev was threatening the German operational center of gravity by disrupting Heeresgruppe Mitte's main line of communications, but the moment soon passed.

Using a Panzer division borrowed from 3. Panzerarmee and pieces of other divisions, Model was able to isolate and immobilize Maslennikov's 39th Army and part of the 29th Army, which were ensconced behind his left flank. He also deployed strong blocking detachments between Rzhev and Olenino to keep Maslennikov isolated. Beginning on February 1, Konev made repeated, furious attacks to try to break through to Maslennikov and this continued for two weeks – but Model's improvised defenses held. By early February, the battlefield between Rzhev and Vyazma had become completely non-linear, with German and Soviet forces intermixed, as well as Soviet partisan detachments and airborne landings thrown into the mix. Despite being hard-pressed on all fronts, Model began his so-called "Snail Offensive" to gradually crush the isolated 29th and 39th Armies. Shvetsov's 29th Army crumbled first, with only Shvetsov and 5,200 troops escaping, while the Germans captured 5,000 prisoners; six rifle divisions had been eliminated. Yet Model's forces were not yet strong enough to annihilate Maslennikov's larger 39th Army and the 11th Cavalry Corps, so they were obliged to nibble away at them. Konev's Kalinin Front was ordered to keep pounding the Rzhev sector, but it was apparent by March that the counteroffensive in this sector had failed, with no major objectives taken. By mid-April, the Kalinin Front had suffered 341,000 casualties – nearly 100 percent of its starting strength – for negligible gains. Somehow, Konev survived this disaster, but Stalin's confidence in him must have been at an all-time low. Model was badly wounded by enemy fire on May 23 and was out of action for 11 weeks. Generaloberst Heinrich von Vietinghoff temporarily took over the 9. Armee and executed Unternehmen *Seydlitz* (Operation *Seydlitz*) – Model's plan to destroy the 39th Army – between July 2 and 12. Maslennikov and a few staff officers were flown out of the pocket before the end, but most of his army was killed or captured.

Hitler tried to micromanage the 9. Armee as he did during any crisis, but Model would have none of it. When Hitler tried to direct how reserves would be used, Model took the unusual step of flying to East Prussia and demanding an immediate audience at the *Wolfsschanze*. Aside from a few loose cannons like Guderian and Rommel, Hitler had become accustomed to the obsequious General Staff-type generals like von Brauchitsch and Halder, who were nervous and uncertain in his presence. He was thus caught by surprise when Model openly demanded, "who commands the 9. Armee, mein Führer, you or me?"[12] Hitler was taken aback by this kind of resistance by one of his generals, but not only did he concede Model's authority to use the reinforcements as he deemed appropriate, but he gained respect for the one general who did not kowtow before him. Henceforth, Model would operate on the Eastern Front with far greater autonomy than most other German commanders. However, Model's success was not just based upon chest-thumping, but on sound staff work. Back in Sychevka, he assembled a superb staff, led by Generalmajor Hans Krebs. Krebs had been assigned as a military attaché in Moscow in 1940–41 – he spoke fluent Russian and had a good grasp of Soviet military methods. By mid-April, Model had re-established a coherent front for the 9. Armee, removed the threat to Heeresgruppe

Mitte's line of communications and was in the process of eradicating the remaining enemy forces behind his lines. By any standards, this was a significant operational-level achievement.

As it turned out, Zhukov did little to support Konev's counteroffensive because he was primarily focused on achieving his own objectives. In January 1942, Zhukov's Western Front was the largest command in the Red Army, with nine armies (1 SA, 5, 10, 16, 20, 33, 43, 49, 50) comprised of 713,000 troops. Zhukov was also provided with about one-third of the available artillery (including 34 of the 73 multiple rocket-launcher battalions), nearly half the available tanks and even four airborne brigades with 11,000 paratroops. Zhukov's vision for the counteroffensive was a Deep Battle-style operation utilizing armor, cavalry and airborne forces to attack the enemy in depth, but his actual methods relied primarily upon brute force frontal attacks, devoid of subtlety or surprise. Zhukov also felt that the Western Front was strong enough to simultaneously pursue two operational objectives: the main effort would be made along the Mozhaisk axis to seize Vyazma, while a secondary effort would be made in the south along the Sukhinichi axis. Zhukov's attacks in late December had opened a 15km-wide breach in the German 4. Armee front northwest of Maloyaroslavets, which would become the main axis of advance in the next phase of the winter counteroffensive. General-leytenant Mikhail G. Efremov's 33rd Army would advance into the gap and advance toward Vyazma, while Govorov's 5th Army and Golubev's 43rd Army conducted supporting attacks on his flanks to widen the breach. Meanwhile, General-leytenant Filipp Golikov's 10th Army had just isolated a German *Kampfgruppe* of six battalions (5,000 troops) under Generalmajor Werner Freiherr von und zu Gilsa in Sukhinichi on January 3. The Stavka expected this pocket to be quickly crushed and then for Golikov to use this position as a springboard to tear apart the already loose connection between the German 4. Armee and the 2. Panzerarmee. Heeresgruppe Mitte's situation was grave, with multiple gaps in its front and minimal reserves on hand. Nor was any substantial Luftwaffe air support available.

Despite his apparent advantages, the second phase of Zhukov's winter counteroffensive got off to a slow start and did not really make much progress until mid-January. The initial attacks on his right wing were mostly repulsed and Govorov's 5th Army did not take Mozhaisk until January 20. However, Golikov's 10th Army on the left wing enjoyed unexpected success, creating an 80km-wide gap between the 4. Armee and the 2. Panzerarmee. Unfortunately, Govorov had no armor, cavalry or ski troops assigned to his army, so he could not fully exploit this opportunity. Govorov also had to keep a portion of his army besieging the German garrison in Sukhinichi, which had created a hedgehog- (*Igel*) style defense. Zhukov had heavily weighted his main effort on his right wing but he sent General-major Pavel Belov's 1st Guards Cavalry Corps to pass through the gap created by Govorov and advance north toward Vyazma. Belov argued that the best use of his cavalry was to block the road to Yukhnov, thereby making the German defense in this sector untenable, but Zhukov overruled him.[13] Since the beginning of the war, Stalin and his cavalry cronies had been eager to see Soviet cavalry unleashed in the enemy's rear areas and now Zhukov intended to give them just that, by sending Belov's corps and the 11th Cavalry Corps from the Kalinin Front to converge upon Vyazma. Zhukov had also begun the first of three major airborne landings near Vyazma and the cavalry was directed to link up with the paratroopers and partisan detachments operating in the wooded areas.[14] Von Kluge, at Heeresgruppe Mitte headquarters in Smolensk, kept requesting permission to fall back to avoid having his front-line forces enveloped, but Hitler refused. Nevertheless, Heeresgruppe Mitte was forced to cede ground. By January 20, Efremov's 33rd Army had achieved a breach in the 4. Armee front and began pushing its way through toward Vyazma. By January 27–28, Soviet cavalry had blocked the Moscow-Warsaw highway. Zhukov seemed to be on the cusp of a major victory. On February 1, the Stavka elevated Zhukov to Western Theater commander, giving him command over the Kalinin, Western and Bryansk Fronts.

By late January, Hitler's insistence on *Stutzpunkte* tactics was beginning to disrupt Zhukov's operational tempo. The XIII Armeekorps had created a strong position in Yukhnov as the XX Armeekorps did near Temkino; together, these two groups constricted the Soviet breakthrough corridor to Vyazma. While Zhukov was focused on the Vyazma axis, Generaloberst Rudolf Schmidt's 2. Panzerarmee (PzAOK 2) managed to recover enough of its equilibrium so that it could quietly assemble a corps-size relief operation to save von Gilsa's garrison in Sukhinichi. Led by the 18. Panzer-Division, the Germans managed to attack into the flank of Govorov's 10th Army, advance 50km and reach the garrison by January 24.[15] Hitler was pleased because he regarded this episode as validation of his hold-at-any-cost philosophy and it also demonstrated that the Ostheer was capable of mounting significant operations in winter. Schmidt lacked the strength to hold the town so the position was evacuated on January 29, but the protracted fight for Sukhinichi had robbed Zhukov's left wing of its offensive momentum. Zhukov ordered Boldin's 50th Army to support Govorov and transferred Rokossovsky's 16th Army to Sukhinichi, but the temporary reprieve enabled Schmidt's PzAOK 2 to stabilize its front line. With the 10th Army stymied, Zhukov placed all his effort on reaching Vyazma with Efremov's 33rd Army.

General der Infanterie Gotthard Heinrici had been in command of AOK 4 since January 20. Heinrici was part of the new wave of commanders that began to emerge in the Ostheer during the winter crisis of 1941/42. He was not a General Staff-trained officer but rather a hard-bitten infantry officer with decades of practical experience and was regarded as a superb defensive tactician. Until now, the offensive-minded Wehrmacht had not placed much value on this aspect of the military art, but with the Red Army at the gates of Vyazma, defensive specialists were suddenly in style. Like Model, Heinrici moved quickly to plug holes in his front but sought a solution to his army's long-term problem with Efremov's 33rd Army. Within ten days of taking command, Heinrici organized a pincer counterattack with the XX and XXIII Armeekorps that managed to isolate Efremov's army. Undeterred, on February 4 Zhukov ordered Efremov to launch an all-out assault on Vyazma with help from Belov's cavalry, but Generalleutnant Richard Ruoff, commander of the 4. Panzerarmee, had moved the 5. Panzer-Division to hold the city. Efremov's assault was repulsed. In one last bid to assist Efremov, Zhukov dropped two more airborne brigades south of Vyazma, but they added no real offensive power. Although the area south and northwest of Vyazma was crawling with Soviet troops and partisans, Heeresgruppe Mitte was just able to clear its line of communications and fortify Vyazma. In frustration, Zhukov used three armies (43, 49, 50) to reduce the Yukhnov salient, which Heinrici was finally forced to evacuate in early March, but this did not provide any assistance to Efremov's isolated 33rd Army, the two cavalry corps and the thousands of paratroopers scattered near Vyazma. Once the spring *rasputitsa* season arrived, it was clear that Zhukov's counteroffensive had failed. In April, Heeresgruppe Mitte was finally able to assemble enough ground and air combat power to crush Efremov's 33rd Army and clear the area south of Vyazma. Efremov committed suicide to avoid capture, some of Belov's cavalrymen escaped and some paratroopers became partisans – but most of the army was dead or captured.

Zhukov's Western Front was able to advance about 150 kilometers during the winter counteroffensive, but it failed to capture its primary objective and the fighting between January and April cost it over 435,000 casualties (including 149,000 dead or missing). Efremov's army was annihilated, along with half the cavalry and two-thirds of the paratroopers. In January, Zhukov had a chance to inflict a serious defeat upon Heeresgruppe Mitte but the opportunity gradually slipped away. Zhukov demonstrated a tendency to reinforce failure – continuing to add more paratroopers and cavalry to join Efremov's encircled army – akin to Napoleon committing more and more troops to the diversionary attack upon the Chateau de Hougoumont at Waterloo. Instead of looking for ways to bypass enemy resistance, Zhukov adamantly kept trying his straight-down-the-middle approach to get to Vyazma even though Govorov had already blasted a massive hole in Heeresgruppe Mitte's front line. Govorov's tactical success could easily have been converted into an operational-level victory if he had been provided an adequate exploitation force in a timely manner. Instead, the two Soviet cavalry corps were only used to raid the enemy rear areas, not encircle enemy forces. The use of airborne forces was daring, but dropping four brigades over a period of a month was a piecemeal effort that violated the principles of surprise and mass. Zhukov's mental inflexibility in this campaign fared poorly against the mental agility demonstrated by his primary opponents, Heinrici, Ruoff and Schmidt. On the German side, each of the senior commanders took charge of their formation at a time when the situation was absolutely chaotic – but each managed to pull their forces together and gradually restore order. It is also important to note that while the OKH provided Heeresgruppe Mitte with a handful of infantry divisions from Western Europe, it was nothing on the scale of reinforcements that Zhukov was receiving from the RVGK during the counteroffensive.

Further south, General-polkovnik Yakov T. Cherevichenko's Bryansk Front was also tasked by the Stavka with attacking Schmidt's PzAOK 2 and seizing Bolkhov and Orel. In addition, the Stavka wanted Cherevichenko to encircle and destroy the German corps holding the Bolkhov sector; by accomplishing these objectives, the Bryansk Front would assist the left wing of the Western Front's offensive. Cherevichenko's command consisted of three armies (3, 13, 61) with a total of about 317,000 troops. After suffering heavy losses in December, the front's rifle divisions averaged only 43 percent of authorized strength and Cherevichenko was not provided with much artillery or armor to support his offensive. Even if he managed to achieve a breakthrough, Cherevichenko only had the 3rd Guards Cavalry Corps and a single tank brigade to commit as an exploitation force. Schmidt's army was in somewhat better shape and had been able to fortify the Bolkhov salient. Cherevichenko made General-polkovnik Fedor I. Kuznetsov's 61st Army the main effort and dutifully began his offensive on January 7.* Even by Russian standards, the weather was unfavorable for offensive action, with temperatures down to -25°C (-13°F) and deep snow. The attacks completely failed to break the German front line, even when joined by the 3rd and 13th Armies. After a week of futile pounding, it was evident that the Bryansk Front lacked the offensive power to breach PzAOK 2's defenses. Nevertheless, the Stavka ordered Cherevichenko to keep attacking. When the Bryansk Front failed to achieve any success, the Stavka replaced all three of Cherevichenko's army commanders, but this had no positive effect. The Stavka did not allow Cherevichenko to halt his offensive until March 17, but this was only temporary, and it added a sequel in early April, which also failed. Ultimately, the Bryansk Front suffered over 60,000 casualties in order to inflict 10,000 casualties on Schmidt's PzAOK 2, while failing to liberate Orel or encircle any German formations.[16] The Stavka's direction of the Bryansk Front's winter counteroffensive was one of the most egregious examples of incompetent operational planning, conducted completely without regard to the principles of war or even common sense.

   Timoshenko's command was still recovering from its massive defeat in September 1941 and had only conducted limited operations in December in order to conserve its strength. During that time, Timoshenko resumed his role as theater commander (Southwest Direction) and General-leytenant Fedor I. Kostenko, another *Konarmia* veteran, took over the Southwest Front. Timoshenko was thus responsible for directing the operations of both the Southwest and Southern Fronts. By January, Kostenko's Southwest Front had four armies (6, 21, 38, 40) and Malinovsky's Southern Front had five armies (9, 12, 18, 37, 56). As part of the winter counteroffensive, the Stavka wanted Timoshenko to liberate Kharkov and drive the Germans out of the Donbas region. After that, he was expected to conduct a follow-on operation to advance to seize Dnepropetrovsk and Zaporozhe on the Dnepr. Obviously, this was an overly grand vision of what the Red Army was capable of achieving in southeast Ukraine at this point, but Timoshenko adopted the same kind of optimistic attitude as the Stavka. He planned to take Kharkov by means of a double envelopment: the 21st and 40th Armies would form a northern pincer to advance west over the Northern Donets River to seize Belgorod, then pivot south toward

*This was the same Kuznetsov who had commanded the Northwest Front between June and July 1941.

Kharkov, while the 6th and 38th Armies crossed the Northern Donets near Izyum and then pivoted north.

On the other side, von Reichenau had only recently taken over command of Heeresgruppe Süd, which was tasked with defending a front that stretched from Kursk to the Sea of Azov, a distance of over 500 kilometers. General der Panzertruppe Friedrich Paulus officially took over AOK 6 on January 1; he was tasked with defending the northern end of the line, including Kharkov, with nine infantry divisions. Hoth's AOK 17 defended the center of the line and von Kleist's 1. Panzerarmee (which included the Italian corps) was holding the southern end of the German front. Hoth and von Kleist were veteran commanders but Paulus was an odd choice to take over a critical assignment like the 6. Armee, since he was a career staff officer with negligible prior command experience. Indeed, Paulus had not even been on the Eastern Front in 1941 but rather serving as the senior logistic officer in the OKH.

Timoshenko began his offensive on January 1, with probing attacks which gradually escalated. The northern pincer, spearheaded by General-major Vasily Gordov's 21st Army, managed to reach the outskirts of Oboyan before Paulus committed his reserve – a single infantry division – to stop it with a well-timed counterattack. On January 15, the 57-year-old von Reichenau suffered a cerebral hemorrhage at his headquarters at Poltava and died en route back to Germany. Hitler immediately selected von Bock to take his place and he flew directly to Poltava to take command of Heeresgruppe Süd on the morning of January 20. Timoshenko's southern pincer did not make any progress until January 18, when General-leytenant Akvsentiy Gorodnianskiy's 6th Army succeeded in breaching the boundary between AOK 6 and AOK 17 near Izyum. For the first time, an entrenched German infantry division (the 298. Infanterie-Division) was overwhelmed by Soviet shock groups. By the time that von Bock took command, Timoshenko was already committing Ryabyshev's 57th Army and the 6th Cavalry Corps to exploit the breach at Izyum. Von Bock immediately ordered von Kleist to transfer one of his corps to assist in sealing the breach and even brought up a Romanian division to assist. Nevertheless, the advancing Soviet troops occupied Barvenkovo on January 24 and then the German supply base at Lozovaya on January 27. However, Paulus shifted a large *Kampfgruppe* to block the 6th Cavalry Corps from enveloping Kharkov from the south. Ultimately, Timoshenko's offensive was slowed because the Germans managed to hold the shoulders of the breach with impregnable *Stutzpunkte* – the LI Armeekorps position at Balakleya and the XXXXIV Armeekorps position at Slavyansk. Timoshenko wasted considerable combat power trying to eliminate these positions in a futile effort to widen the breach, rather than following the path of least resistance to the southwest. Malinovsky's Southern Front made repeated but unsuccessful attacks with its 12th and 37th Armies against Hoth's right flank, which did nothing to help the Soviet effort to widen the Barvenkovo salient. The Stavka provided Timoshenko with 315 tanks and four rifle brigades from the RVGK and he decided to transfer General-major Fedor M. Kharitonov's 9th Army from the Southern Front to reinforce his drive in the Barvenkovo salient. Kharitonov was one of the more undistinguished Soviet army commanders in 1941–42, having missed the First World War, not attended the Frunze Military Academy, spent six years as a regimental commander, then catapulted to command of the 9th Army. In any case, Kharitonov was not ordered to attack west but south, to reduce the German strongpoint at Slavyansk. In frustration, Timoshenko had eschewed a battle of maneuver in favor of one of position. Consequently, von Bock was afforded a brief but critical reprieve, which he used to introduce Gruppe Mackensen (a motorized corps from the 1. Panzerarmee) to finally restore a cohesive front on the south and western sides of the Barvenkovo salient.

Fighting continued around the Barvenkovo salient throughout February, but Timoshenko's moment had passed. He did enjoy some brief success on February 20 when he massed four tank brigades against the Romanian 1st Infantry Division and achieved another temporary breakthrough before von Bock sealed it off. The 38th Army also succeeded in gaining a bridgehead across the Northern Donets near Staryi Soltov on March 7/8, which would be useful for future attacks against Kharkov. Nevertheless, by mid-March the spring thaw was arriving, bringing a close to Timoshenko's counteroffensive. Even though he had not taken Kharkov or encircled any large enemy formations, Timoshenko regarded his counteroffensive as a partial victory because the Barvenkovo salient and Staryi Soltov bridgeheads could be used as springboards for a new offensive. Yet Timoshenko failed to learn much about the German ability to retrieve a critical situation and then launch powerful, well-timed counterattacks. Von Bock's ability to fly in and take command during such a dangerous situation and then restore his front in a few weeks was remarkable – probably his best moment as a commander in the Second World War.

In the Crimea, the Soviet winter counteroffensive was essentially a private campaign between von Manstein's 11. Armee and three Soviet armies – Petrov's Independent Coastal Army in Sevastopol and two armies (44, 51) from General-leytenant Dmitri T. Kozlov's Caucasus Front that had landed on the Kerch Peninsula in late December 1941. By early January, von Manstein had one corps holding the 17km-wide Parpach Narrows to keep the Soviet 44th and 51st Armies bottled up in the Kerch Peninsula, while he used the other two corps to besiege Petrov's army in Sevastopol. Recognizing that the Soviet threat would only grow as more troops and equipment were landed at Kerch, von Manstein quietly transferred one corps out of the siege lines at Sevastopol in order to assemble a force to conduct a surprise counterattack against General-major Aleksei N. Pervushin's 44th Army at Feodosiya (which consisted of 23,000 troops). Hitler was annoyed that the transfer required abandoning some of the ground occupied around Sevastopol in December, but von Manstein successfully argued that a counteroffensive capable of achieving operational-level objectives required this kind of tactical sacrifice. He also coordinated with the Luftwaffe to ensure that his operation would receive adequate air support. On the opposing side, Kozlov seemed to feel that he had plenty of time to prepare for his "big push" offensive to break through the Parpach Narrows and that the Germans were too weak to interfere with his plans – both serious miscalculations.

At dawn on January 15, von Manstein struck. Pervushin's army command post – which had been identified – was bombed by the Luftwaffe and the Soviet commander was badly wounded. The leaderless 44th Army proved unable to make a stand. Within two days, von Manstein's troops had recaptured the port of Feodosiya and routed the 44th Army, which left behind 5,300 prisoners.[17] Having misjudged German capabilities, Kozlov now exaggerated them to the Stavka and reported that the 11. Armee was capable of "throwing our forces into the sea."[18] Instead of attempting to halt von Manstein's advance, Kozlov ordered both the defeated 44th Army and General-leytenant Vladimir N. Lvov's 51st Army to retreat further back. After the defeat at Feodosiya, Kozlov's 44th and 51st Armies were so disorganized that they were incapable of offensive action for more than a month. However, Soviet reinforcements began to flow into the Crimea after the Kerch Straits froze over on January 20, enabling 96,000 troops and 6,500 vehicles to cross.[19] On January 28, Kozlov's command was redesignated as the Crimean Front (he also had command over Petrov's army); at the same time, the Stavka directed him to begin planning for a major breakout operation. The 45-year-old Kozlov was poorly suited for front command, particularly one that required coordination between several field armies, the Black Sea Fleet and various air units. Recognizing Kozlov's inexperience, the Stavka provided him with General-major Fedor I. Tolbukhin as his chief of staff, but also saddled him with Commissar Lev Mekhlis. Tolbukhin was a talented staff officer, but Mekhlis routinely interfered with operational planning and argued with Kozlov at every point. Forced to rely upon shipping and over-ice movements, the Crimean Front also found it difficult to conduct operational logistics without rail lines, so the buildup of supplies was unusually slow.

Kozlov was not prepared to launch his "big push" offensive until February 28. Afforded a month to dig in, the 11. Armee created three formidable *Stutzpunkte*, reinforced with mines and antitank guns, which dominated the front line along the Parpach Narrows. Kozlov's initial attacks with the 51st Army managed to capture the northern *Stutzpunkt* but were stopped by German reserves. Kozlov now decided to commit the bulk of his armor to support an attack by the 44th Army against the southern *Stutzpunkt* on March 2, but the Luftwaffe arrived in force and inflicted painful losses on the Soviet shock groups. Kozlov requested additional support from the VVS for the next phase of his offensive, but his effort to create an armored exploitation force was derailed by Mekhlis, who insisted that the 224 available tanks should be split up among the rifle divisions.[20] The Germans used the brief respite to lay another 2,000 antitank mines in the expected enemy attack corridor. Kozlov resumed his offensive on the morning of March 13, amidst snowy conditions over very open ground, and lost 70 percent of his armor in three days of fighting. At great cost, the 51st Army captured the central *Stutzpunkt* but was stopped without achieving a breakthrough. In order to provide AOK 11 with a mobile reserve, the OKH sent von Manstein the 22. Panzer-Division, but he prematurely committed it to an ill-judged counterattack on March 20 that lost 32 tanks for no appreciable results. In late March, Kozlov attacked once more and again on April 11, but without success, which brought the winter campaign in the Crimea to a finish. In the period from January to April 1942, Kozlov's Crimean Front (including Petrov's army in Sevastopol) suffered 352,000 casualties, whereas von Manstein's 11. Armee suffered 24,000 casualties – an extremely unfavorable 14-1 ratio. After making a series of daring amphibious landings, Kozlov's Crimean Front had settled into an unimaginative and predictable method of operations that failed to produce worthwhile results. In contrast, von Manstein's ability to make a stand against long odds at the Parpach Narrows while maintaining the siege of Sevastopol and even mount a powerful counteroffensive was clearly a great feat of generalship.

Commander	Objective	Offensive	Mass	Maneuver	Surprise	Security	TALLY
Küchler Lindemann	+	+	o	+	+	o	4
Busch	+	+	o	+	o	o	3
Model	+	+	o	+	o	o	3
Schmidt Heinrici	+	+	o	+	+	o	4
Von Bock	+	+	o	+	o	+	4
Paulus Hoth	+	+	o	+	o	o	3
Manstein	+	+	o	+	+	+	5
Meretskov Khozin	–	+	+	o	o	–	0
Kurochkin	o	+	o	+	+	o	3
Konev	+	+	+	+	o	–	3
Zhukov	+	+	+	o	–	–	1
Cherevichenko	+	+	o	o	–	o	1
Timoshenko	+	+	+	o	o	–	2
Kozlov	+	+	+	–	–	–	0

Winter Counteroffensive, January–May 1942 Leadership Assessment

On the whole, during the 1941/42 winter counteroffensive Soviet front and army-level commanders were badly handicapped by unrealistic guidance from Stalin and the Stavka, as well as interference from political commissars such as Mekhlis. Kurochkin and Konev achieved the best results under these conditions, followed by Timoshenko. Zhukov came close to achieving success, but his pig-headedness as a commander undermined his ability to adapt to a dynamic battlefield. While Zhukov's use of airborne landings, cavalry raids and partisans showed flair, they actually achieved little and he eventually settled for a battle of attrition, as did Meretskov, Khozin, Cherevichenko and Kozlov. Altogether, the Soviet winter counteroffensive of 1941/42 cost the Red Army roughly 1.8 million casualties – including the loss of four armies – and achieved only partial success in two of six sectors. Except for von Leeb and Strauß, who wilted under pressure, the senior German commanders came through the winter crisis fairly well, in large part due to their ability to adapt to unexpected circumstances. German pre-war wargames had certainly not placed any emphasis on diverse situations such as enemy airborne landings, amphibious landings, partisan raids and over-ice attacks, but the Ostheer's senior leadership had risen to the occasion and countered even novel threats. Excluding the Finnish front, the Ostheer suffered 275,000 casualties (including 77,000 dead or missing) during January to April 1942, suggesting that it inflicted a roughly 6.5-1 casualty ratio on the attacking Red Army.

Table III: Operational Outcomes, Soviet 1941/42 Winter Counteroffensive

Front	Commander	Objective(s)	Result	Soviet Casualties
Leningrad Volkhov	Khozin Meretskov	Lyuban	Failure	308,367
Northwest	Kurochkin	Staraya Russa Toropets Demyansk	Partial victory	245,000
Kalinin	Konev	Rzhev	Failure	341,000
Western	Zhukov	Vyazma Spas-Demensk	Failure	435,000
Bryansk	Cherevichenko	Bolkhov Orel	Failure	60,000+
Southwest Southern	Timoshenko Kostenko	Kharkov liberate Donbas	Partial victory	40,000+
Crimea	Kozlov	Break out of Kerch Peninsula, lift siege of Sevastopol	Failure	352,000
TOTAL				1,781,000+

Although German pre-war doctrine had placed little emphasis on defensive operations, the Ostheer quickly developed the methods needed to stop Soviet offensive pulses. Hitler claimed great credit for the defensive success due to his insistence on hedgehog (*Igel*) tactics. There is no doubt that not only did the Red Army of early 1942 lack the heavy artillery, engineers and specialized tactics to quickly crush these positions even when encircled, but that Soviet pre-war doctrine had not seriously examined the impact of enemy fortified areas on maneuver operations. Essentially none of the larger German *Stutzpunkte* were crushed during the winter counteroffensive, although the defenders were forced to evacuate a few of these positions under pressure. The Red Army of 1941/42 also struggled to break through intact German defensive lines, for much the same reasons. Another factor that influenced operations during the winter of 1941/42 was that of unit reconstitution, in which the Red Army had a pronounced advantage. By late 1941, the Stavka had learned how to cycle decimated units through the RVGK, refit them with new equipment and personnel replacements, then return them to the front in as little as 4–6 weeks. The Moscow Military District offered a superb refuge for unit reconstitution, up to the army level. In contrast, the German system was to send burnt-out divisions back to Germany or occupied Western Europe to refit; typically, these divisions did not return for six months. Due to limited rail capacity, only a few divisions could be sent back home, so most had to try to refit near the front during quiet periods. Although the Ostheer lost no division-size units in the first year of the war, it simply could not compete with the Red Army in this area when large-scale losses did occur. Failure to reconstitute properly served to gradually degrade the quality of Ostheer divisions and the quantity of personnel and equipment within these units.[21]

Conquest of the Crimea, May 8–July 4, 1942

Even before the final culmination of the Soviet winter counteroffensive, both sides were preparing for the next round of campaigning in the spring. In Führer Directive No. 41 (issued April 5, 1942), the OKH stated that the primary effort of the summer campaign would be made in the southern theater and as a necessary prerequisite, mopping-up operations needed to be conducted to eliminate the Soviet position in the Crimea as well as to crush isolated Soviet units behind other parts of the front. Von Manstein was ordered to crush the Soviet armies in the Kerch Peninsula, then turn and mount a set-piece attack against Sevastopol.[22] Von Manstein and Krebs planned a clever offensive operation to drive the Soviet armies out of the Kerch Peninsula, dubbed Unternehmen *Trappenjagd* (Operation *Buzzard Hunt*). Once the first operation concluded, the 11. Armee would conduct Unternehmen *Störfang* (Operation *Sturgeon Haul*) to capture Sevastopol. The OKH provided von Manstein's AOK 11 with a single additional infantry division, as well as a heavy artillery train and some assault engineers to help reduce Sevastopol's defenses. Von Manstein met with Hitler at the Wolfsschanze in mid-April and was promised powerful air support from the VIII Fliegerkorps for his offensive, but only for a relatively short period. He had to win big and he had to win quickly. In planning *Trappenjagd*, von Manstein placed particular emphasis upon surprise and deception, since he was going to attack an enemy force that was more than double the size of AOK 11.

Kozlov had entrenched his forces across the Parpach Narrows, with his main strength assigned to Lvov's 51st Army on his right flank. The Soviet left flank was only defended by a few divisions of Cherniak's 44th Army, since this area was marshy and deemed unsuitable for large-scale offensive action. Both Soviet armies were defending in depth, with two echelons, and had a tactical reserve consisting of four tank brigades. Kozlov also had an unusually strong front reserve: General-major Konstantin S. Kolganov's 47th Army with five divisions deployed back near Kerch. All in all, the Soviet defenses in the Kerch Peninsula appeared quite solid. However, Soviet intelligence failed to detect the deployment of the VIII Fliegerkorps to the Crimea, or that von Manstein was massing the bulk of his forces against the southern end of the Parpach Narrows. Von Manstein intended to feint in the north to attract Kozlov's attention while making his main effort in the south, deliberately choosing to attack through the most unfavorable terrain. Kozlov's chief of staff, General-major Petr P. Vechnyi, tried to warn Kozlov that the Germans might attack at the southern end of the line, but his recommendations to strengthen this sector were ignored. Front-level Commissar Lev Mekhlis also discounted Vechnyi's professional assessment.

Operation *Trappenjagd* began at dawn on May 8 with coordinated artillery and air strikes, followed up by a ground attack supported by three battalions of assault guns. In order to unhinge Cherniak's defense, von Manstein also employed a novel seaborne outflanking maneuver with a single infantry battalion. German tactical breaching operations were exemplary and enabled rapid penetration of the obstacle belt, which included mines, antitank ditches and barbed wire. Within 24 hours, both lines of Cherniak's 44th Army had been breached and von Manstein was able to commit his exploitation force. Kozlov's attention was held by von Manstein's feint against his right flank and did not commit his reserves to stop the breach of his left flank until it was too late. Luftwaffe close-air support decimated Soviet armor caught in the open, throttling Kozlov's last-minute attempts to halt the *Schwerpunkt*. On May 11, the 22. Panzer-Division pivoted north and succeeded in cutting off virtually all of Lvov's 51st Army. Lvov was killed when his command post was bombed. At that point, Soviet C2 collapsed, which precipitated a disorganized stampede to the rear. Abandoned to their fate, the eight divisions in the now leaderless 51st Army soon surrendered, which enabled von Manstein to mount a vigorous pursuit of the remainder of Kozlov's forces, which were fleeing toward Kerch. Vechnyi, the front-level chief of staff, tried to organize a defense of Kerch while the Azov Flotilla evacuated the remaining troops, but only 37,000 managed to flee before all resistance around Kerch was crushed by May 20.

Operation *Trappenjagd* was one of the most astonishing operational-level victories in the Second World War. Von Manstein had crushed three Soviet armies in less than two weeks; Kozlov's Crimean Front suffered 175,000 casualties (including 147,000 captured) and lost all its tanks and artillery, plus 417 aircraft. German losses were light – just 3,397 casualties. Operation *Trappenjagd* was an exquisitely executed set-piece offensive, with near perfect use of a combined-arms *Schwerpunkt* to quickly achieve decisive operational results. Having crushed Soviet forces in the Kerch Peninsula, von Manstein could now devote his entire army toward the reduction of fortress Sevastopol. As a result of Operation *Trappenjagd*, the Stavka disbanded the Crimean Front (the remaining troops were transferred to the North Caucasus Front) and relieved Kozlov of command. Soon thereafter, Kozlov was demoted one rank and his career as a field commander was effectively over – given his contribution to the disaster, he was fortunate. Cherniak (44th Army) and Kolganov (47th Army) were both demoted one rank and re-assigned as corps/division commanders. Stalin was particularly apoplectic about commissar Lev Mekhlis, whom he blamed in part for the disaster, and demoted him two ranks. Vechnyi was the only one of the Crimean Front Military Council who was not demoted.

Von Manstein spent two weeks transferring his assault units back to the siege lines around Sevastopol and preparing for Unternehmen *Störfang*. Altogether, the 11. Armee would employ seven German and two Romanian infantry divisions against Sevastopol, with a total of about 200,000 troops. Petrov's Coastal Army had been built up during the winter and spring to seven rifle divisions and four naval infantry brigades totaling 118,000 troops. In addition, Petrov's troops were heavily entrenched and key positions were often anchored by concrete bunkers – it was a formidable position. In order to crack the fortress, the OKH provided von Manstein with the largest collection of artillery ever assigned to a single German army in the Second World War, including super-heavy weapons such as the 80cm 'Dora' railway gun and two 60cm 'Karl' mortars. Unlike most German operations on the Eastern Front, Unternehmen *Störfang* was based upon firepower, not maneuver. Von Manstein knew that the AOK 11 lacked the infantry reserves to win a battle of attrition, so his planning was based upon suppressing and then overrunning Petrov's defenses, one position at a time. In addition, Hitler imposed strict time constraints upon the completion of the mission, since he wanted to use AOK 11 against Leningrad after the capture of Sevastopol.

Unternehmen *Störfang* began with a five-day air and artillery bombardment, which commenced on June 2. During these five days, the Germans expended over 4,100 tons of artillery rounds and bombs on Sevastopol's defenses, but inflicted comparatively little damage. Von Manstein began his ground assault on June 7 and immediately encountered fierce resistance from Petrov's troops. The Battle of Sevastopol was a series of tactical actions, as von Manstein gradually chewed away at Petrov's outer defenses. By June 21, von Manstein's army had reach Sevastopol's inner defenses, but his infantry divisions were nearly exhausted from two weeks of intense combat and the VIII Fliegerkorps had to depart to assist Heeresgruppe Süd. Two interesting operational aspects of *Störfang* were that von Manstein was obliged to use a Romanian corps in front-line combat to keep his offensive going and that the Soviet Black Sea Fleet was able to keep delivering reinforcements and supplies via sea until nearly the end of the siege. Von Manstein made his final assault into the city at the end of June and all Soviet resistance had ceased by July 4. Von Manstein had succeeded in eliminating virtually the entire Independent Coastal Army and Hitler immediately promoted him to *generalfeldmarschall*. Petrov was able to escape by sea, along with about 5,000 other personnel, but 95,000 troops were captured. Stalin did not impose any punitive measures against Petrov, who would go on to be a front-level commander in 1943–45. Victory had not been cheap for AOK 11, which suffered 27,000 German and 8,400 Romanian casualties. Due to heavy losses in infantry and engineers, the divisions in AOK 11 would require a significant amount of time to rest and reconstitute, which delayed their movement to the Leningrad front. Petrov's defense of Sevastopol was professionally handled and, due to the relative isolation of his command, he had less interference from above. Von Manstein's conduct of the siege and assault required a careful balancing of time and resources in order to avoid a premature culmination.

Commander	Objective	Offensive	Mass	Maneuver	Surprise	Security	TALLY
Von Manstein	+	+	+	+	+	o	5
Kozlov	+	–	o	o	o	–	–1
Petrov	+	o	o	o	o	+	2

Crimea, 1942 Leadership Assessment

Timoshenko's Disaster at Kharkov,
May 12–June 25, 1942

After the culmination of the costly and not very successful Soviet winter counteroffensive, the Stavka was uncertain about the best course of action to adopt for the upcoming spring. Zhukov, Shaposhnikov and Vasilevsky urged caution, since they expected the Germans to make another drive on Moscow. The RVGK reserves were low after the winter counteroffensive, so the General Staff (GSHKA) suggested that reconstitution should be the priority, to rebuild the Red Army's offensive capabilities. However, Stalin – as usual – wanted to attack, not simply sit on the defensive and wait for the Germans to do something. He believed that a preemptive offensive could help to retain the strategic initiative and delay the Ostheer from launching its own offensive against Moscow. Timoshenko, still a favorite of Stalin, advocated a renewed offensive in the Kharkov sector, based upon the recent "partial victory" he had achieved. Stalin concurred and in late March directed the Southwest Front to begin planning an even larger offensive in order to liberate Kharkov. Timoshenko and his chief of staff, General-leytenant Ivan Bagramyan, simply planned a larger double pincer attack against Kharkov, using overwhelming force. Timoshenko requested massive reinforcements from the RVGK, including 250,000 troops, 1,200 tanks and over 1,000 artillery pieces. Even Stalin was nonplussed by Timoshenko's requests, which amounted to the equivalent of five fresh field armies. The RVGK did send Timoshenko over 900 tanks, although one-fifth were British-made Lend Lease tanks and many of the rest were obsolescent models. Nevertheless, on April 10 Stalin approved Timoshenko's draft operational plan, stipulating that all preparations had to be completed by May 6 in order to preempt any German moves. The Stavka had hoped that the Kharkov operation would be the Red Army's first carefully planned deliberate offensive of the war, but it was soon evident that Stalin's impatience was leading to another hastily planned and improvised operation. Once it was obvious that Stalin wanted the operation to proceed forthwith, all objections from the General Staff disappeared.

The basic concept for the Southwest Front operation was to conduct a double pincer attack with Ryabyshev's 28th Army from the Staryi Saltov bridgehead in the north (supported by the 21st and 38th Armies) and Gorodnianskiy's 6th Army from the Barvenkovo salient in the south in order to envelop Paulus' 6. Armee at Kharkov. Gorodnianskiy's 6th Army was designated as the main effort for the entire operation. Timoshenko confidently expected the pincers to close within 4–5 days. Yet from the beginning, Timoshenko's plan violated the principle of unity of command, since he had no real mechanism for coordinating the four armies from the Southwest Front and two from Malinovsky's Southern Front involved in the operation. Vasilevsky was assigned as Stavka representative for the operation, but given his personal misgiving about mission success, he chose to remain passive and failed to fulfill the role of coordinator. Conceptually, Timoshenko's staff used the breach of the Finnish Mannerheim Line two years earlier as a planning model but failed to appreciate that the Finns had lacked mobile reserves or powerful air support. Timoshenko and Bagramyan put their faith in massed artillery – not combined arms operations – to decide the battle, as it had with the Finns. Once the German front line was broken apart by powerful shock groups, Timoshenko would unleash his mobile reserves to encircle the 6. Armee. The RVGK had begun organizing tank corps in April 1942 in order to conduct Deep Operations and Timoshenko was provided two of the new formations as an exploitation force. Intelligence support for the offensive was also poor, providing Timoshenko with little insight into enemy capabilities or intentions. Although aware that von Bock had two Panzer divisions deployed near Kharkov, Timoshenko apparently assumed that they would not seriously interfere with his offensive.

Soviet logistic planning for the Kharkov operation was particularly rushed and the staff work was substandard, significantly underestimating the time needed to move units and supplies forward into assembly areas. Less than half the ammunition and fuel specified in the plan was assembled prior to the offensive.[23] Another problem was that since there were only two intact bridges over the Donets River – which were often under Luftwaffe attack – it was difficult to rapidly build up forces in the Barvenkovo salient, where the main effort was to assemble. Recognizing that the build-up was not going as scheduled, Timoshenko managed to delay the operational start date to May 12. Zhukov and Vasilevsky observed these unfolding developments with foreboding, but said nothing. In essence, Timoshenko's offensive was based on a logistical shoestring, with inadequate C2 and knowledge of the enemy, and simply assumed a static and immobile opponent.

On the German side, von Bock had worked wonders in restoring Heeresgruppe Süd's front-line defenses and ability to conduct limited mobile operations. Hitler's Führer Directive 41, dated April 5, 1942, ordered von Bock to begin planning an offensive, Unternehmen *Fridericus* (Operation *Frederick*), to eliminate all Soviet forces in the Barvenkovo salient. Although the Germans were aware of preparations by the Southwest Front to mount another attempt to liberate Kharkov, von Bock did not expect Timoshenko to launch an offensive until his forces were fully assembled. In the meantime, Paulus' 6. Armee was responsible for defending the Kharkov sector, but was very thinly spread, with just three infantry divisions defending the eastern approaches to the city and three more on the southern approaches. Two Panzer divisions (3, 23) were deployed near Kharkov but they were under the control of the OKH and set aside for use in Unternehmen *Fridericus*. Paulus did not have control over these two Panzer divisions and had only limited army-level reserves. Von Kleist's 1. Panzerarmee was deployed against the southern side of the Barvenkovo salient and was also setting aside one Panzer division and five infantry divisions for *Fridericus*. The strained German logistical situation in Ukraine delayed the build-up for the operation, but unlike Timoshenko, von Bock would not allow himself to be rushed into a premature offensive. Hitler also refrained from trying to micromanage von Bock's planning, as long as Heeresgruppe Süd was able to launch the main summer offensive (*Blau*) by late June. However, von Bock and Paulus failed to anticipate that Timoshenko might attack before *Fridericus* was ready to proceed.

Timoshenko commenced his offensive at dawn on May 12, with a massive 60-minute artillery preparation; in the northern sector, 800 guns fired across a 50km-wide sector, while in the south, 485 guns bombarded a 26km-wide sector. This was the first time that the Red Army conducted such a powerful bombardment against the Ostheer and the front-line 6. Armee units were stunned, but not destroyed. The Red Artillery also fired to a depth of 5 kilometers, even though this served to disperse the effects of the bombardment. After the artillery barrage, the VVS-Southwest Front attacked German front-line positions with Pe-2 bombers and Il-2 Sturmovik ground assault aircraft. Since much of Luftflotte 4 was supporting *Trappenjagd* in the Crimea, the VVS was able to gain air superiority over the Kharkov sector. The Soviets attacked with six division-size shock groups (from the 21st, 28th and 38th Armies) and 300 tanks from the Staryi Saltov bridgehead and overran most of the front-line German positions. In particular, the veteran 13th Guards Rifle Division achieved a breakthrough which threatened to open a pathway to Kharkov. For once, German losses were heavy and Soviet losses were moderate. In the southern sector, Gorodnianskiy's 6th Army managed to advance up to 8 kilometers but failed to achieve a clean breakthrough on the first day of the offensive. While the northern pincer had met expectations thus far, serious mistakes in Soviet planning quickly became apparent. Foremost,

Malinovsky's Southern Front sat idle because it had not been fully brought into the planning process. In addition, Soviet intelligence had failed to identify German tactical reserves, so straight off 6th Army encountered more resistance than expected.

Paulus was caught by surprise by the sudden Soviet offensive and shocked to see an enemy breakthrough occur so quickly. He promptly asked von Bock to request that the OKH release both Panzer divisions – which was granted – and for additional Luftwaffe support. In the meantime, Paulus had to rely upon the proven hedgehog (*Igel*) tactics to slow the Soviet advance until the Panzers and Stukas could intervene. Kampfgruppe Grüner formed a regimental-size *Stützpunkt* in the town of Ternovaya, which proved to be a particularly troublesome obstacle in the path of Ryabyshev's 28th Army. Indeed, Ryabyshev failed to recognize the importance of the Ternovaya position and initially committed insufficient forces to what he considered a "mop up" operation; the result was that the German *Stützpunkt* held. Gordov's 21st Army also encountered stiff resistance from two German *Stützpunkte*. Much the same occurred with Gorodnianskiy's 6th Army in the southern sector, which attacked with four division-size shock groups and 124 tanks. Instead of trying to crush the German *Stützpunkte* in the initial attack, Gorodnianskiy tried to bypass them, which limited his advance to just 6–8 kilometers. Amazingly, the Red Army had not put much thought into how to quickly reduce enemy *Stützpunkte*, even though the German defensive tactics had played a major role in the failure of the winter counteroffensive.

On the left wing of the northern pincer, Moskalenko's 38th Army finally crushed the opposing German infantry division by noon on the second day of the offensive and was poised to advance to Kharkov, just 18 kilometers away. However, before Moskalenko could exploit this advantage, his army was struck by a well-timed counterattack by the 3. and 23. Panzer-Divisions and supported by the Luftwaffe, which knocked the 38th Army back on its heels with heavy casualties. The setback suffered by Moskalenko's 38th Army was the first sign that Timoshenko had miscalculated the German response.[24] When faced with the unexpected, good commanders employ what Napoleon and von Clausewitz called *coup d'oeil* to grasp the essence of the situation and take rapid action to regain the initiative. Unfortunately for the Red Army, Timoshenko lacked *coup d'oeil* and he decided to transfer most of Ryabyshev's second echelon units to reinforce Moskalenko's 38th Army. Incredibly, Timoshenko decided to "reinforce failure" in the 38th Army sector, while depriving his main effort (the 28th Army) of the combat power necessary to sustain its advance toward Kharkov. Although the Soviet northern assault group still had the 3rd Guard Cavalry Corps in reserve, Timoshenko refused to commit it to exploit the breakthrough. Thus, after just two days of attacking, the Soviet northern pincer was already losing the initiative.

Despite overwhelming numerical superiority, the southern assault group struggled to defeat two German divisions and one Hungarian division which stood in their way. Surprisingly, it was the Bobkin Operational Group – a support group formed to protect the left flank of Gorodnianskiy's 6th Army – which made the only substantial breakthrough in the south. General-major Leonid V. Bobkin committed General-major Aleksandr Noskov's 6th Cavalry Corps into a small breach in the German lines and sent it deep toward Krasnograd; however, this unsupported effort ended up becoming little more than another large-scale cavalry raid. Timoshenko refused to commit his two tank corps until Gorodnianskiy had achieved a major breach – this kind of rigid adherence to the original plan stood in stark contrast to the flexible style employed by most German senior commanders.

By the third day of the Soviet offensive, the Luftwaffe regained air superiority over the Kharkov sector. Nevertheless, Ryabyshev nearly succeeded in breaking through the 6. Armee's thin line of infantry battalions east of Kharkov. Unfortunately, Timoshenko failed to provide the 28th Army with the reserves or exploitation force needed to complete the victory. By failing to keep his eye on the objective – Kharkov – Timoshenko deprived the northern assault group of its one chance to achieve a decisive success. German counterattacks on May 15–17, with strong Luftwaffe support, thoroughly disrupted the Soviet northern assault group and relieved the encircled garrison in Ternovaya. Ryabyshev's 28th Army, the main effort, was nearly broken. By May 18 all three Soviet armies in the northern group had been completely halted and continued German counterattacks by the two Panzer divisions forced the 21st and 28th Armies to retreat on May 20. The northern pincer had failed.

In the south, the German VIII Armeekorps had no armor in support and could not launch powerful counterattacks to halt Gorodnianskiy's 6th Army. However, Gorodnianskiy chose to conduct a rather unimaginative set-piece offensive which kept pushing the German VIII Armeekorps back, but without crushing it. General-major Aleksandr Noskov's 6th Cavalry Corps reached the outskirts of Krasnograd on May 15 but could not take the city, even though it was just defended by two battalions of engineers. Nor did Timoshenko commit his main armored reserve – the 21st and 23rd Tank Corps – until May 16. Although the appearance of another 260 Soviet tanks forced the VIII Armeekorps back on its heels, the German line bent, but did not break. After finishing up the battles east of Kharkov, Paulus was able to dispatch a Panzer *Kampfgruppe* to prevent VIII Armeekorps from collapsing. At this point, Soviet operational logistics were beginning to falter, as shortages of ammunition and fuel robbed Gorodnianskiy's attacks of momentum. The Soviet offensive in the south was a near-run thing, with a major operational success within tantalizing reach, but now the accumulation of Soviet operational mistakes began to take their toll.

While focused on the progress of his two assault groups, Timoshenko had been oblivious to the threat developing on the southern side of the Barvenkovo salient. Malinovsky's Southern Front was supposed to defend the southern side of the salient with General-leytenant Kuzma P. Podlas' 57th Army and General-major Fedor M. Kharitonov's 9th Army. Von Bock had deftly played for time on the 6. Armee front while accelerating the timetable for Unternehmen *Fridericus*. Although originally planned as a simultaneous double pincer attack against both sides of the Barvenkovo salient, the offensive was modified to be two corps-size pincers directed against Kharitonov's 9th Army. Von Kleist was in charge of the operation and his forces were modest – two motorized corps, consisting of just two Panzer divisions (14, 16) and five infantry divisions – a far cry from the Panzer group operations of mid-1941. Nevertheless, when von Kleist attacked on the morning of May 17, with powerful Luftwaffe support, he enjoyed rapid success. Kharitonov's command post was bombed, disrupting Soviet C2 in this critical sector at the critical moment. The front-line Soviet rifle divisions proved incapable of stopping German Panzer units and were quickly enveloped, while Kharitonov's limited armor reserves were uncoordinated and easily defeated. On the first day of *Fridericus*, von Kleist recaptured Barvenkovo and shattered the 9th Army defensive line, which consisted of only a single echelon. When Timoshenko learned about this disaster, he decided to pull the 23rd Tank Corps from the 6th Army – just as it was achieving success – and send it to reinforce Kharitonov. Events now moved very rapidly. On May 18, von Kleist completed the destruction of Kharitonov's 9th Army and only 31 hours after the beginning of *Fridericus*, his Panzers reached the Donets and the outskirts of Izyum. Podlas' 57th Army managed to temporarily avoid complete disaster by refusing its left flank, but there was now a huge gap in the Soviet line where the 9th Army had been deployed. Timoshenko sent more reserves east in a futile effort to plug the gap, but then blithely ordered Gorodnianskiy to continue his offensive, even though most of his armor had been taken from him. Without the two tank corps and with supplies running low, Gorodnianskiy's part of the operation ground to a halt.

Von Kleist regrouped and refueled his Panzers on May 19, while his infantry mopped up the remnants of the 9th Army. Timoshenko was finally forced to acknowledge the destruction of his left flank and called the Stavka to update Vasilevsky on the situation. Timoshenko told Vasilevsky that he could clear up the German gains in a couple of days and requested permission to temporarily re-orient the Southwest Front's line of attack from northwest to southeast. Vasilevsky was not sanguine about this outcome but managed to gain Stalin's authorization for Timoshenko to launch a counterattack into von Kleist's left flank. After receiving Stalin's permission, Timoshenko issued new orders to his scattered forces at 1720 hours on May 19. In a fit of sheer idiocy, he decided to scramble Bobkin's command and part of Gorodnianskiy's 6th Army to form an *ad hoc* grouping under his own deputy commander, General-leytenant Fedor I. Kostenko. Yet rather than massing forces to try to prevent von Kleist from closing the encirclement, Timoshenko dispersed them to mount a series of improvised and piecemeal efforts. Inevitably, the poorly planned attempt to mount a counterattack with the two tank corps and the 2nd Cavalry Corps failed. While von Kleist continued to push north to cut off the Barvenkovo salient, von Bock pushed Paulus to use both the 3. and 23. Panzer-Divisions to form a northern pincer, but Paulus dithered and did not commit them until May 22. The next day, von Kleist's Panzers linked up with Paulus' armor, completing the encirclement of the 6th and 57th Armies in the Barvenkovo salient.

Unlike Smolensk in 1941, von Kleist was able to seal the *Kessel* quickly and efficiently, preventing Timoshenko from salvaging much of the encircled forces. The infantry divisions from the 6. Armee, competently supported by the Romanian 6th Corps, helped to close in upon the trapped Soviet divisions, which had already expended most of their ammunition and fuel. Kleist was able to crush the Barvenkovo *Kessel* in just five days, May 24–28. The Luftwaffe played a particularly significant role in this destruction, relentlessly bombing and strafing immobilized Soviet forces caught on the open steppes. The spring weather of May proved to be an ideal season for aerial-delivered slaughter. All Soviet breakout attempts were defeated. Gorodnianskiy, Bobkin, Kostenko and Podlas (57th Army) were all killed in failed breakout attempts. At the end, the best men and equipment available to the Red Army were scattered across the steppes as if they were so much rubbish, with nothing to show for their sacrifice. Altogether, the Southwest Front suffered 277,190 casualties in this catastrophic defeat (36 percent of the engaged forces), including about 239,000 captured. A total of 16 rifle divisions, six cavalry divisions and four tank brigades were annihilated and another dozen divisions were badly mauled. Most of the equipment sent from the RVGK to bolster Timoshenko's offensive – including 64 percent of the tanks and a large portion of the artillery – were lost. German losses in the Second Battle of Kharkov amounted to about 30,000, including 8,700 dead or missing.

After the catastrophe at Kharkov, Stalin was keen to pin the blame on someone. Initially, his ire fell upon General-major Kharitonov, commander of the 9th Army, who was made the scapegoat and court-martialed for the rapid collapse of his army. However, it soon became apparent that the key mistakes were made at front level, so Kharitonov was acquitted – an almost unheard of outcome in the Soviet system of military justice. Stalin recognized that Timoshenko had made a number of bad decisions and he lost confidence in his judgment, but hesitated to remove one of his favorites. For the time being, Timoshenko remained in command of the Southwest Front. The elimination of the Barvenkovo salient enabled von Bock to shorten his front line, allowing him to create reserves for the upcoming main event – Unternehmen *Blau* (Operation *Blue*). With the Southwest Front seriously weakened and new reinforcements arriving from the West, von Bock's Heeresgruppe Mitte was now in a position to regain the strategic initiative by conducting an all-out offensive to reach the Volga and the Caucasus.

Soviet generalship in the Kharkov campaign was not at the level required to defeat the Ostheer. The main advantage that the Red Army possessed in this offensive was surprise, but this dissipated after the first few days. Without adequate logistical planning, the Soviet advantage in combat power also quickly waned. At the top, Timoshenko demonstrated a very limited ability to either plan a complex operation or comprehend a fast-moving, dynamic battlefield. He also lacked the moral courage to request an additional delay in order to increase the odds for a more favorable operational outcome. Instead, Timoshenko went ahead with his flawed plan, assuming that somehow it would turn out right in the end. Other than the fact that Ryabyshev was another *Konarmia* crony, it is difficult to see how this flawed commander – who had played a prominent role in a previous catastrophic defeat in 1941 – was assigned to lead the main effort in the northern group. Ryabyshev allowed a single enemy regimental-size strongpoint to stymie his army, then failed to reach his objective or even crush the strongpoint. Nevertheless, when the dust settled, Stalin attached no blame to Ryabyshev and he kept his command. General-major Kirill S. Moskalenko, commander of the 38th Army, made his share of mistakes in the campaign but also proved able to learn from them; in time he would become a competent field army commander. In terms of lessons learned, the Kharkov disaster taught the Red Army leadership that proper offensives required considerably more logistic preparation and staff coordination than the amateur effort made by Timoshenko and Bagramyan. The Stavka also recognized that operations required better intelligence support to identify enemy reserves and anticipate German response actions, rather than simply ignoring them.

Commander	Objective	Offensive	Mass	Maneuver	Surprise	Security	TALLY
Von Bock	+	+	+	+	+	o	5
Paulus	o	+	o	+	o	-	1
Von Kleist	+	+	+	+	+	+	6
Timoshenko	o	+	o	o	+	-	1
Ryabyshev	o	+	+	o	+	-	2
Moskalenko	+	+	+	o	+	-	3
Gorodnianskiy	+	+	+	o	+	-	3

Kharkov, 1942 Leadership Assessment

On the German side, von Bock conducted a highly competent defensive-offensive campaign, which ensured that adequate forces were committed at the right time and place. Likewise, von Kleist put in a superb performance – one of his best – using just two corps to deal a deathblow to two Soviet armies and cripple the remainder of the Southwest Front. The only sour note on the German side was Paulus, whom von Bock judged to be indecisive in a crisis – an entirely accurate assessment, as it would turn out. The 6. Armee was under intense pressure in the first several days of the Soviet offensive, but it was up to mid-level officers to ensure that front-line morale did not crack. Paulus acted more as a resource manager and conduit for directives from army group, rather than as a dynamic commander guided by *fingerspitzengefühl* (fingertip feel). Once again, German operational doctrine was validated at Kharkov, with pincer operations leading to a successful *Kesselschlacht* and destruction of the enemy's main effort. It was a campaign of which von Clausewitz or von Hindenburg would have been proud. However, one false conclusion reached by senior German leaders was that Axis satellite forces (Hungarian,

Romanian, Italian) could be entrusted to hold lengthy stretches of the front line and they would be assigned greater roles in upcoming operations. In fact, the performance of Hungarian and Romanian units at Kharkov created false impressions that would be proved wrong six months later.

Hitler arrived at von Bock's headquarters in Poltava on June 1 to review the recent victory at Kharkov and to discuss his intentions for the upcoming main summer offensive, *Blau* (Blue). Prior to the main operation, von Bock was tasked with conducting army-level operations to gain jumping-off positions on the east side of the Donets River. Although some sources claim that there was significant friction developing between von Bock and Hitler at this stage, this does not appear likely. Hitler properly recognized von Bock's accomplishments at Kharkov and gave him a relatively free hand in planning the next operations for Heeresgruppe Süd.[25] Von Bock paused to regroup and resupply for two weeks, then conducted Unternehmen *Wilhelm*, a double envelopment by the 6. Armee of Ryabyshev's 28th Army in the Stary Saltov bridgehead on June 10–15. As a result, the 28th Army was decimated and forced to retreat, thereby providing Paulus with a jumping-off position for the main summer offensive. Von Bock was impatient to begin the summer offensive and upset when a week of heavy rains delayed the next preliminary move. On June 22–25, von Bock launched Unternehmen *Fridericus II* with von Kleist's 1. Panzerarmee against the Southern Front's 9th and 38th Armies, which quickly defeated both armies and forced them to retreat up to 40km. The capture of Izyum was particularly important in securing a secure bridgehead east of the Donets for von Kleist's Panzers. Altogether, the Red Army lost another 47,000 prisoners in these two brief German offensives, as well as the loss of 358 tanks and 376 artillery pieces. German losses in these two operations totaled 7,486 casualties and modest material losses. By this point, Stalin was quite annoyed by Timoshenko's repeated defeats and decided to scramble his Southwest Direction command, but left him in charge of the Southwest Front. Timoshenko's Southwest Front and Malinovsky's Southern Front would now report directly to the Stavka and Vasilevsky would coordinate their actions.[26]

The 1942 Kharkov disaster was one of the most embarrassing operational defeats suffered by the Red Army during the Second World War. Unlike the defeats of 1941, Timoshenko had enjoyed numerical superiority, air superiority and operational surprise at Kharkov, yet he failed to achieve his objectives and allowed his best forces to be gutted by the enemy riposte. Over a period of eight weeks, Heeresgruppe Süd inflicted over 612,000 casualties on Timoshenko's forces and eliminated

1,400 Soviet tanks. Von Bock accomplished this at a cost of just 67,000 German casualties and 140 tanks/assault guns, yielding an exchange ratio of 9-1 in personnel and 10-1 in armor. As a result of Timoshenko's defeat, the Southwest and Southern Fronts were badly demoralized and in poor condition to oppose the impending main German summer offensive. Von Bock's victories enabled the Ostheer to regain the strategic initiative in the East, as Hitler had intended.

Fall Blau: Hitler Seeks a Decision in the East, March–June 1942

In late March 1942, there was considerable discussion in the FHQ in East Prussia about what course of action the Ostheer should attempt once warm weather returned. Halder and the OKH were pessimistic, pointing out the heavy losses in men and material to date, and recommended that the Ostheer remain on the defensive until it could fully restore its combat capabilities in order to mount another all-out offensive in 1943. At best, the Ostheer in mid-1942 would only be capable of mounting a large-scale offensive along a single line of operations (LOO). Hitler accepted the data about the Ostheer's losses but rejected outright the OKH's recommendation of a defensive strategy.[27] Hitler was by nature a risk-taker and he recognized that he needed to achieve decisive victory in the Soviet Union before the Anglo-Americans could mount a serious effort in the West. Anything less than an all-out effort in 1942 would likely cause Germany to permanently lose the strategic initiative. Yet the key question was – where could the Ostheer employ its reduced-scale capabilities with the best chance of achieving a decisive victory? Furthermore, should the next major offensive focus on destroying the main Soviet field armies – which had proved elusive in 1941 – or seizing key territorial objectives?

By this point, the OKH recognized that the Soviet Union's strategic COG was its armaments industry, which produced the tanks, artillery, ammunition and aircraft that fed the field armies. In 1941, the Germans managed to overrun or disrupt a significant part of the Soviet industrial base, including iron/steel production, but the GKO was able to evacuate the most important industries to the Urals prior to their loss. In particular, German advances forced the evacuation of KV-1 heavy tank production from Leningrad and T-34 medium tank production from Kharkov, causing short-term drops in Soviet tank production in the last part of 1941. However, by spring 1942, the armaments industry was re-established far beyond the reach of Luftwaffe bombers and turning out weapons in large-scale quantities. The German operational victories that produced the greatest impact on the Soviet strategic COG were in the south, depriving the Red Army of Ukrainian agricultural production and the coal/iron resources in the Donbas region. In terms of the Red Army's operational center of gravity – the RVGK reserves – the Wehrmacht could only target these through large-scale destruction of field armies. However, the Ostheer destroyed no fewer than eight field armies between April and the start of the main summer offensive without draining the RVGK (although rosy intelligence estimates from the OKH/FHO suggested that Russian reserves were depleted); at the very least, a battle of attrition was unlikely to lead to a decisive knock-out conclusion.

Hitler was confronted with a variety of opinions about where the next summer offensive should be conducted. Generalfeldmarschall Georg Wilhelm von Küchler, commander of Heeresgruppe Nord, argued that the capture of Leningrad was the logical objective. Although the Soviets would mount a fanatical effort to defend the encircled city, they could not easily reinforce the defenders and German logistics would not be overly strained by an offensive in this sector. Von Küchler and his staff began developing a plan for an army-size assault on the city, designated Unternehmen *Nordlicht* (Operation *Northern Lights*). In addition, von Küchler proposed a corps-size offensive, Unternehmen *Bettelstab* (Operation *Beggar's Staff*), to eliminate the Soviet Oranienbaum salient. Von Kluge, commander of Heeresgruppe Mitte, argued in favor of limited offensives to crush Soviet forces in the Toropets salient (Unternehmen/Operation *Derfflinger*), another to remove enemy threats to Model's 9. Armee in the Rzhev salient (Unternehmen/ Operation *Seydlitz*) and a third to eliminate the Soviet Sukhinichi salient (Unternehmen *Wirbelwind*/Operation *Whirlwind*). Hitler listened to these proposals but believed that, at best, they could only deliver ordinary victories without significantly enhancing Germany's strategic situation. Nevertheless, he did not actually reject any of these ideas out of hand.

Generalfeldmarschall Hermann Göring, head of the Luftwaffe, was instrumental in making the case to Hitler that oil was the key to strategic success. Göring argued that Germany needed access to oil to guarantee victory in a mechanized war and 70 percent of the Soviet Union's oil reserves were located in the Caucasus; ergo, a German offensive to seize the Caucasus would both gain oil for the Wehrmacht and deny it to the enemy.[28] Deprived of the majority of its oil reserves, the Red Army would be permanently weakened. Even if the Soviet armaments industry remained inviolate in the Urals and continued to produce masses of aircraft and tanks, the lack of oil would prevent the Red Army from conducting high-intensity mechanized warfare like the Wehrmacht.[29] Furthermore, the decimated Soviet armies protecting the Caucasus were assessed to be far less capable than those protecting Leningrad or Moscow. Hitler liked this rationale because it meant that it might be possible to achieve a quick operational victory with strategic implications, and at low cost. Consequently, on April 5, 1942, Hitler released Führer Directive 41, which stated that the overall objective of the main summer offensive was to "destroy the enemy before the Don, in order to secure the Caucasus oilfields." The primary operational objectives were specifically identified as the Maikop and Grozny oil fields. In addition, the directive also specified the capture of Voronezh and Stalingrad, in order to neutralize important Soviet armaments industries in both cities.[30]

The offensive, originally referred to as *Siegfried* but then changed to *Blau* (Blue), was conceived as a multi-phased operation, consisting of consecutive offensive pulses, each synchronized to bring the maximum force to bear at the key place and time.* The main effort would be made by Heeresgruppe Süd, while the other two army groups remained on the defensive. However, rather than choose between prioritizing the destruction of enemy forces or seizing terrain objectives, Hitler ensured that *Blau* was designed to simultaneously accomplish both tasks. The bulk of Soviet field armies west of the Don were to be encircled and destroyed in a series of hard-hitting mobile battles reminiscent of the early days of *Barbarossa.* Subsequently, Hitler specified that the city of Voronezh must be taken, along with crossings over the Don, before the army group moved into the Caucasus to seize the oil fields. However, Hitler regarded the advance toward Stalingrad as merely a flank-guard for the main effort into the Caucasus and Führer Directive 41 was vague about the importance of capturing the city. Instead, Hitler stated that it would be sufficient if "the city was brought under fire from heavy artillery so that it may no longer be of any use as an industrial or communications center."

Phase I of *Blau* would begin on the left wing of Heeresgruppe Süd, with Generaloberst Hermann Hoth's 4. Panzerarmee (PzAOK 4) tearing a hole in the boundary between the Bryansk and Southwest Fronts. Then Paulus' AOK 6 would join in and expand this gap, enabling a strike east

---

*On June 30, 1942, the operation was re-designated as *Braunschweig* since the name *Blau* had been compromised via the Reichel incident. However, I will continue to use the term *Blau* to avoid confusion.

to seize Voronezh. Once Voronezh was taken, the second phase of *Blau* would begin with the left wing of Heeresgruppe Süd wheeling to the southeast, intended to envelop Soviet forces deployed between the Donets and the Don with a great pincer movement to link up with von Kleist's 1. Panzerarmee (PzAOK 1). Following the elimination of the main Soviet field armies west of the Don, the third phase of *Blau* would consist of Heeresgruppe Süd advancing across the Don, the left wing advancing toward Stalingrad while the right wing pushed into the Caucasus. The Italian and Hungarian armies were merely expected to hold the line on the Don, while the German mechanized spearheads raced forward to seize their objectives. The OKH believed that the primary objectives of *Blau* could be achieved in about six weeks, although it was recognized that mop-up operations in the Caucasus might continue for some time. Once *Blau* was completed, Hitler wanted the strike force refitted and made fully operational again as soon as possible. Amazingly, he intended to conduct at least some of the limited objective offensives that von Küchler and von Kluge had recommended.

In order to be able to conduct an offensive on the scale of *Blau*, the Wehrmacht had to concentrate its resources in Heeresgruppe Süd, while taking resources from the other two army groups. During spring 1942, the lion's share of German replacement personnel and equipment went to von Bock's Heeresgruppe Süd, which left the other two army groups in a threadbare state. Von Bock was provided with 70 percent of the Ostheer's armor, amounting to 1,582 tanks. Hitler also turned to Mussolini to gain a greater Italian troop commitment on the Eastern Front, as well as the Hungarians and the Romanians. Mussolini felt that Italy was already making a strong commitment in North Africa and the Balkans but agreed to provide the 8th Army for *Blau*. Altogether, over 600,000 Axis troops in four army-size formations would participate in *Blau*, making up for the shortage of German units. Neither Mussolini nor the other Axis heads of state were brought into the planning of *Blau* due to concerns that they could not be fully trusted to safeguard the details.

Blau, as written by Generalmajor Heusinger's staff at the OKH, was based upon a number of assumptions. First, the OKH's intelligence branch assessed that the Red Army's RVGK reserves were significantly smaller than their actual strength and located around Moscow. In fact, the Stavka had created ten reserve armies, with a total of 63 rifle divisions (three of which were Guards divisions), plus the 3rd Tank Army, to have ready in the RVGK for the anticipated German summer offensive.[31] While the Red Army's main strength was indeed positioned in the center, the

OKH believed that Stalin would not be able to replace heavy losses in the south in a timely manner. The OKH's Abwehr erroneously assessed Soviet armor production as 600–700 tanks per month, but the actual figure was over 2,200. Second, the OKH expected the Soviet forces in the southern theater to stand and fight in the open as they had in 1941, enabling the Wehrmacht's mechanized pincers to surround them and take large hauls of prisoners. Third, while recognizing the lower combat effectiveness of the Axis satellite troops, the OKH assumed that they would at least be capable of holding ground gained by von Bock's mechanized spearheads and protecting the flanks of the German vanguard. Finally, the OKH assumed that Heeresgruppe Süd could attain all its objectives with the forces available in a short campaign that ended well before winter. Many of these planning assumptions for *Blau* were quite dangerous, but they were not recognized as such at the time. In order to deceive the Soviets about *Blau's* true objectives, the OKH developed a deception plan known as Unternehmen *Kreml* (Operation *Kremlin*). Von Klüge's Heeresgruppe Mitte was ordered to conduct activities which suggested that the main German summer offensive would be aimed at Moscow. Von Kluge used preparations for an attack on the Sukhinichi salient to simulate a much larger operation, with 2. Panzerarmee spearheading an attack from the Bolkhov region. The Luftwaffe also increased reconnaissance activity over the Moscow region, to suggest an impending offensive.

In order to make *Blau* feasible, the Germans needed to make substantial improvements to Heeresgruppe Süd's theater logistics capabilities. After the winter crisis, Organization Todt was put in charge of repairing the railroads and bridges in the Ukraine. The first railroad bridge over the Dnepr River, at Zaporozhe, was opened just before the start of *Blau*, greatly improving the delivery of bulk ammunition and fuel to the front. Logistic depots were established at Kharkov and Kursk to support *Blau*, although they only contained enough supplies to support a full-scale offensive for about two weeks. The OKH also promised to provide enough *Grosstransportraum* motor transport to give Heeresgruppe Süd 11,000 tons of logistic lift capability, although this was only 55 percent of the amount allocated to each army group for *Barbarossa*.[32] The Luftwaffe was also expected to support theater logistic shortfalls as necessary, although the 156 Ju-52 transports possessed by Luftflotte 4 could only deliver about 200–250 tons of supplies on a good day. While the logistic support for *Blau* may have seemed adequate to the OKH staff in Zossen, it would quickly become tenuous as Heeresgruppe Süd advanced further eastward.

Blau has been much criticized by historians but the original plan did make good use of the principles of war, particularly surprise, mass and maneuver. The Ostheer did have the resources to reach Voronezh, Stalingrad and at least some of the oil fields in the Caucasus, although it was unclear if achieving these goals would actually cripple the Soviet Union's military-industrial base. *Blau* was a high-risk plan, but it could work if everything went well and there were no unexpected surprises. However, Hitler's predilection for micromanagement was at its worst during the execution of *Blau*, with the Führer constantly shifting operational priorities and subunit missions. Instead of focusing on one goal and ruthlessly carrying it through to successful completion, Hitler wanted to pursue a variety of near-simultaneous objectives, which tended to stretch German resources to the breaking point. Heeresgruppe Süd embarked upon *Blau* with no appreciable operational-level reserves. The successful conclusion of the campaign in the Crimea released von Manstein's 11. Armee for duty elsewhere, but instead of using it to reinforce the main effort in the south, Hitler decided that this formation would go north to participate in an offensive at Leningrad. Later, he would have second thoughts and consider using it to cross the Kerch Straits, into the Caucasus.

Further complicating matters for the Germans, during *Fridericus II*, an incident occurred which threatened to reveal the German operational intentions for the initial phase of *Blau* to the Soviets. On the afternoon of June 19, Major Joachim Reichel, operations officer of the 23. Panzer-Division, was shot down behind enemy lines while flying in a Fieseler Storch liaison aircraft. Imprudently, Reichel was carrying notes that specified the initial objectives assigned to the XXXX Panzerkorps in the impending summer offensive, as well as other operational details. Soon afterwards, the captured documents were brought to the Bryansk Front command post and then forwarded to Vasilevsky.[33] The Stavka assessed the documents as probably genuine but Stalin was personally invested in the view that the Germans intended to attack Moscow again and regarded this as an attempt to draw RVGK reserves away from Moscow. From the German point of the view, the OKH could not be certain whether or not the plans had fallen into enemy hands and they had to assume the worst. Von Bock urged that *Blau* begin immediately, before the Red Army could react, but heavy rains interfered with this and the start date for the operation had to be delayed until June 28.[34]

Although Timoshenko requested additional armored reinforcements – just in case – Stalin decided to concentrate nearly half the available armor in the Western and Bryansk Fronts. In mid-June, the Stavka had formed two tank armies in the RVGK, the 3rd and 5th Tank Armies – these were the first large armored formations created by the Red Army in the Second World War. The 5th Tank Army (5TA) was placed under an experienced armor officer – General-major Aleksandr I. Lizyukov – and deployed to General-leytenant Filipp I. Golikov's Bryansk Front sector as a mobile reserve. The 5TA consisted of two tank corps (2, 11) and a tank brigade, amounting to a total of 439 tanks. The 3TA remained in the RVGK. Unlike the Ostheer, the Red Army began the summer campaign season with a significant amount of operational and strategic reserves in hand or nearly ready. In May 1942, the VVS had also begun to form air armies (*vozdushnaya armiya* or VA) to provide improved air support to ground forces; typically, each Soviet front was assigned at least one air army, occasionally two. Akin to the German *Luftflotten*, the Soviet air armies were comprised of air divisions consisting of fighters, bombers, ground attack and reconnaissance aircraft.

The German Summer Offensive,
June 28–September 30, 1942

While Stalin might not have put any credibility into the captured Reichel documents, General-leytenant Filipp I. Golikov, commander of the Bryansk Front, apparently did. On June 26–27, Golikov ordered surprise artillery strikes and bomber attacks by the 2nd Air Army (2VA) against forward German troop concentrations, in an effort to disrupt the start of *Blau*. Likewise, von Bock ordered the IV Fliegerkorps to conduct battlefield interdiction strikes in an effort to disrupt Soviet rail lines and transport hubs prior to the offensive. In any event, *Blau* was not intended to begin as a simultaneous attack by all of Heeresgruppe Süd. Instead, only Generaloberst Hermann Hoth's 4. Panzerarmee would attack on the morning of June 28, with just eight of von Bock's 48 divisions. Hoth attacked the left flank of Golikov's Bryansk Front – specifically, the *Schwerpunkt* was aimed at the boundary between General-major Nikolai P. Pukhov's 13th Army and General-major Mikhail A. Parsegov's 40th Army. Hoth used his infantry to breach the Soviet line, then committed two Panzerkorps (XXIV, XXXXVIII) to exploit the gap, supported by the VIII Fliegerkorps. Despite fierce Soviet resistance on the ground and in the air, Hoth's Panzers blasted their way through and advanced 30 kilometers by nightfall. Golikov's left flank crumpled under the onslaught. As Hoth advanced, von Weichs' 2. Armee moved to protect his exposed left flank with a single infantry corps (LV).

Stalin ordered Golikov to mount an immediate counteroffensive with all his available armor. On paper, Golikov had a 2.5-1 numerical superiority in armor against Hoth (1,640 tanks vs 633), including Liziukov's 5TA and five other tank corps under front control. Yet in reality, the Germans enjoyed a large advantage in communications, which enabled them to quickly shift their armor to deal with enemy maneuvers. In contrast, Soviet operational art – in terms of planning and execution – was often still rudimentary. On the night of June 28/29, Golikov ordered five of his tank corps (1, 4, 16, 17, 24) to assemble between Stary Oskol and Kastornoye in order to conduct a concentrated strike against Hoth's oncoming armor. The Stavka had sent two representatives to Golikov's headquarters – General-polkovnik Aleksandr M. Vasilevsky (now chief of the General Staff) and General-leytenant Yakov N. Federorenko (commander of the Red Army's tank forces) – and tried to micromanage every move. Golikov asked both representatives to coordinate the armored counteroffensive, but the Bryansk Front actually did most of the planning. At first glance, Golikov's basic plan appeared to employ the principles of offensive, mass and maneuver. However, neither Vasilevsky nor Federorenko were able to coordinate the mass of Soviet armor moving to oppose Hoth's spearheads.[35] One of the weaknesses of the Stavka representative system was that senior officers would show up at a front-level headquarters with only a few aides, not a full staff, so their ability to effect coordination was minimal. Furthermore, most of the Soviet tank corps had been formed recently and were inexperienced, whereas the German Panzer units were veteran formations. The result was a classic, army-size meeting engagement which favored skill over numbers. As soon as Hoth's Panzers encountered Soviet armor, they shifted to the tactical defense and let their 8.8cm Flak and antitank guns conduct much of the fighting. The Soviet tank corps came on piecemeal, often with only a single brigade at a time, and were decimated by the German antitank screens. Federorenko was unable to coordinate air or artillery support, so his tank units went in pure against veteran German combined arms *Kampfgruppen*. The result was a series of costly repulses for the Soviet armor.

On June 30, Paulus' 6. Armee joined the offensive by attacking General-major Aleksei I. Danilov's 21st Army, on the right flank of Timoshenko's Southwest Front. Unlike Hoth, Paulus attacked with only a single Panzerkorps (XXXX), so he did not immediately achieve a breakthrough. Heavy rains also interfered with the German advance. Although new to army command, Danilov was a General Staff-trained officer who was able to conduct a tenacious defense with the resources at hand. Amazingly, the XXXX Panzerkorps had difficulty breaching Danilov's front and Paulus was forced to commit an infantry corps to create a gap. Timoshenko was quick to move up a tank corps (13 TC) to try to seal the breach, but as with Golikov's armored counterstroke, this effort came to naught. The aircraft of the Soviet 2 VA and 8 VA were flung with reckless abandon against the German spearheads in a futile effort to halt the advance. Nevertheless, by July 3 the rainy weather had ceased and Hoth and Paulus managed to create a significant breach between the Bryansk and Southwest Fronts, while threatening to envelop the 21st and 40th Armies, as well as Ryabyshev's 28th Army. Reluctantly, the Stavka authorized these armies to withdraw from the Oskol River in order to avoid being encircled. Hoth immediately shifted to pursuit operations. The retreat toward Voronezh turned into a disorderly mess because the Germans were moving too quickly and Soviet command and control was breaking down. Both Parsegov's 40th Army and Danilov's 21st Army were isolated and forced to fight their way out of encirclement, losing most of their troops and equipment in the process. Ryabyshev's 28th Army was more fortunate, but still lost 50 percent of its personnel in the retreat. Stalin relieved Parsegov but Danilov retained command of the remnants of his army, since he demonstrated panache in organizing a successful breakout.

While it is true that the German pincers failed to take any large haul of prisoners west of the Don, it is also true that two Soviet armies had been shattered and a third decimated. A very large hole had been blown in the Soviet front line and their operational reserves had proved unable to plug the gap due to the breakdown of command and control at the front level. Golikov transferred his headquarters to Voronezh to try to restore order, but this proved too late. Hoth took full advantage of the Soviet confusion and disorder. Despite the fact that his armored spearhead was badly outnumbered and well in front of its supporting infantry, Hoth gambled and sent the XXXXVIII Panzerkorps directly toward Voronezh. At dusk on July 4, Panzergrenadiers from the *Großdeutschland* Division managed to capture an intact bridge over the Don River and the next morning Hoth sent the entire 24. Panzer-Division across to occupy the city of Voronezh. Golikov was caught by surprise and had failed to properly garrison Voronezh, aside from some rear area units. After a day of urban combat, the beaten Soviet rearguards withdrew to the eastern suburbs, leaving Hoth's spearhead in control of most of Voronezh. By July 6, Hoth had achieved one of the major objectives of the first phase of *Blau*.

Astonished by the inability of Golikov's forces to seriously delay Hoth's advance, the Stavka immediately began sending two reserve armies from the RVGK to repair the gap between the Bryansk and Southwest Fronts. Stalin decided to play his potential trump card – General-major Aleksandr I. Liziukov's 5th Tank Army (5 TA) – to conduct a slashing attack into the left flank of Hoth's PzAOK 4 and advance nearly 60 kilometers to sever its lines of communications. Liziukov was one of the most experienced armor officers in the Red Army, but he had only been in command of the 5 TA for three weeks and one of his three tank corps was transferring from the Kalinin Front.* Likewise, his chief of staff, Polkovnik Pavel I. Drugov, was an experienced armor officer and trained at the General Staff Academy, but he too had just joined the command. Liziukov's command was reinforced to three tank corps (2, 7, 11 TC), amounting to over 641 tanks. In addition, the VVS committed over 200 of its fighter reserves from the Moscow region to create a new formation known as the 1st Fighter Aviation Army (1 IA), which was intended to gain air superiority over the Voronezh sector. While impressive on paper, Stalin forced Liziukov into premature action, with virtually no planning conducted prior to battle. Despite the fact that only two of six tank brigades reached the assembly areas in time, Liziukov duly began his counteroffensive at dawn on July 6. Although surprised by the scale of the Soviet armored attacks (German intelligence was unaware of the presence of the 5TA in the Bryansk Front), Hoth conducted a mobile delay operation, while requesting the VIII Fliegerkorps to conduct battlefield interdiction strikes against the 5 TA. By the time that Liziukov finally managed to get all three of his tank corps into the fight – on July 8 – Hoth had all of the XXIV Panzerkorps engaged and this was sufficient to repulse 5 TA's attacks. Golikov also ordered General-leytenant Maksim A. Antoniuk's 60th Army, just transferred from the RVGK, to attack the XXXXVIII Panzerkorps at Voronezh; these impromptu attacks also failed. In addition, the Luftwaffe *Jagdgruppen* shot the 1st Fighter Army to pieces, thereby assuring air superiority over the Voronezh sector.

The fighting around Voronezh led to senior leadership on both sides making changes in their operational commanders. On July 7, the Stavka decided to split the Bryansk Front, with the left wing becoming the new Voronezh Front under Golikov. General-major Nikandr E. Chibisov

---

*Liziukov had been arrested in 1936, tortured and held in solitary confinement by the NKVD for nearly two years. He was awarded the HSU for his role in the Battle of Smolensk and performed well during the Battle of Moscow, but Stalin personally disliked him.

assumed command over the restructured Bryansk Front. Golikov's counteroffensive failed, but it did succeed in tying down Hoth's PzAOK 4 for over a week. At his *Wolfsschanze* headquarters in Rastenburg, Hitler did not appreciate the scale of the Soviet counterstrike and was angry that von Bock had sent a Panzerkorps into Voronezh. As a result of this decision and Hoth's need to fend off Liziukov's 5 TA, von Bock had to delay turning his Panzers to the southeast to assist the impending attack by von Kleist's PzAOK 1. As per the plan for *Blau*, on July 7 von Bock's command was split up with four armies (AOK 2, PzAOK 4, AOK 6, Hungarian 2nd Army) falling under Heeresgruppe B, while Generalfeldmarschall Wilhelm List took command of Heeresgruppe A (PzAOK 1, AOK 17). As far as Hitler was concerned, von Bock's Heeresgruppe B had accomplished its mission and the main effort was shifting to List's Heeresgruppe A; there was no time for dawdling around Voronezh, which Hitler now said was unimportant. In his diary, Halder wielded his poison pen, writing that, "von Bock tolerated Hoth's senseless rush for Voronezh, and even encouraged it."[36] Amazingly, the OKH did not recognize that Hoth was busy fending off a Soviet tank army and instead regarded the situation as akin to a leisurely mop-up operation. Indeed, Hitler was so insistent on rigid adherence to the schedule that he failed to appreciate that von Bock was achieving an amazing operational-level victory around Voronezh. Instead, Hitler kept pressuring him to transfer Hoth's PzAOK 4 to List's Heeresgruppe A at once. When von Bock protested, this only increased Hitler's annoyance with him.

Despite this interference, Hoth's 4. Panzerarmee had not yet concluded its business at Voronezh. Not only did Hoth fend off the Bryansk Front's counteroffensive, but he even managed to conduct a relief-in-place, bringing the 57. Infanterie-Division to hold Voronezh while pulling out the XXIV Panzerkorps. The VII Armeekorps and Hungarian III Corps were also brought forward to hold the flanks on either side of Voronezh. Once it became clear that Liziukov's counteroffensive was faltering, Hoth decided to switch back to the offensive. On July 12, he attacked with the XXIV Panzerkorps, supported by numerous Stuka sorties. In two days of heavy fighting, Liziukov's 5 TA was broken and thrown back in disorder. Altogether, the 5 TA lost about 300 tanks and was no longer combat effective, whereas German armor losses totaled about 50 tanks. In just over two weeks, von Bock's forces had advanced over 160 kilometers, shattered several Soviet armies, routed the Stavka's best armored reserves and captured a major Soviet urban center. The Soviet Bryansk, Voronezh and Southwest Fronts had suffered over 300,000 casualties, whereas von Bock's command had suffered only 24,000 casualties, a 12–1 exchange ratio. It was a significant operational achievement but it was also von Bock's last victory.

List's Heeresgruppe A had begun its part of the summer offensive on July 9, striking the rest of Timoshenko's Southwest Front and Malinovsky's Southern Front. Von Kleist attacked with 330 tanks massed in two Panzerkorps, easily routing Kozlov's 37th Army. With the Southwest Front about to have its right flank enveloped, the Stavka managed to convince Stalin to allow Timoshenko to conduct a withdrawal before the Germans pulled off another one of their clever outflanking maneuvers. Consequently, Hitler's hopes for encircling large Soviet forces between the Donets and Don Rivers came up short, since the main Soviet armies quickly retreated eastward toward the Don. Von Kleist's armored spearheads only managed to scoop up some of Timoshenko's rearguards. In recognition that the campaign was shifting eastward, the Stavka redesignated Timoshenko's command as the Stalingrad Front on July 12 and sent him three more reserve armies (which became the 62, 63 and 64 Armies) to help establish a new front line west of the Don. However, Stalin was enraged by the defeat at Voronezh and he ordered the 5 TA disbanded and Liziukov demoted. Stalin replaced Chibisov as commander of the Bryansk Front with General-leytenant Konstantin K. Rokossovsky. After Golikov's efforts to recapture Voronezh failed, Stalin replaced him with General-leytenant Nikolai F. Vatutin from the General Staff. Antoniuk, in command of the 60th Army for only one week, was also relieved. While Rokossovsky and Vatutin were both skilled commanders, Stalin's spontaneous purge of unsuccessful front-line commanders only served to undermine Soviet operational-level command and control at a critical moment.

At the *Wolfsschanze*, Hitler became convinced that the failure to encircle Timoshenko's armies was due to von Bock's procrastination at Voronezh. Halder influenced Hitler against von Bock, via the kind of whispering campaigns that the OKH staff thrived on (many of whom were also whispering against Hitler). At this point, with the campaign going well, Hitler decided that he did not need independent-minded commanders who might meddle with his unfolding plans, so he decided to relieve von Bock of command on July 13; von Bock was curtly informed of his dismissal via a phone call from Generalfeldmarschall Wilhelm Keitel (OKW). Von Bock never received another command during the war. According to Keitel, the alleged reason for the dismissal was due to the "delay in the departure of the 24. Panzer-Division and the *Großdeutschland* Division from Voronezh to the south," although this made no sense to anyone involved.[37] Two days later, von Weichs arrived to take command of Heeresgruppe B, while General der Infanterie Hans von Salmuth took over AOK 2.[38] Hitler also wanted to relieve von Bock's chief of staff, General der Infanterie Georg von Sodenstern, but agreed to a reprieve. Von Bock had been one of the best German operational-level commanders on the Eastern Front and was peremptorily relieved despite having won two major victories (Kharkov and Voronezh) in the past three months, plus three major victories in the 1941 campaign. Von Weichs was competent but lacked the energy and ruthlessness to lead a major offensive. By splitting up Heeresgruppe Süd, Hitler violated the principle of unity of command and by assigning two mediocrities to command its diverging wings, he significantly reduced the chances for operational success.

Commander	Objective	Offensive	Mass	Maneuver	Surprise	Security	TALLY
Von Bock	+	+	+	+	+	o	5
Hoth	+	+	+	+	+	o	5
Paulus	o	+	o	+	o	o	2
Golikov	+	+	-	+	+	-	2
Timoshenko	o	o	o	+	o	-	0
Liziukov	+	+	-	+	+	-	2

Voronezh, 1942 Leadership Assessment

Von Bock and Hoth clearly demonstrated great operational skill at Voronezh by quickly achieving their objectives and countering all enemy responses; it was a bravura performance. For his part, von Bock was upset by the mediocre performance of Paulus' AOK 6, which appeared capable of making only slow advances against weak enemy resistance. In particular, von Bock noted in his diary that Paulus had difficulty establishing priorities and did not get the best results from his troops. On the Soviet side, Golikov had the basic concepts down, but just could not make them actually work on the battlefield. Likewise, the Red Army could not have picked a better armor officer to lead its first tank army into battle, but Liziukov was pushed into conducting a complex offensive operation with almost no planning or coordination. An officer with moral courage would likely have asked for more time to prepare such an important operation, but any fortitude Liziukov possessed was likely beaten out of him by the NKVD torturers who held him for two years in the Lefortovo Prison; this is not meant to excuse his failure, but to point out that he was likely no longer disposed to argue with authority figures. Timoshenko's performance in the opening stage of *Blau* was simply reactive and his confidence as a commander was probably shaky after the Kharkov debacle. Instead, Timoshenko would simply follow and implement Stavka directives, while hoping to avoid any further disasters.

Hitler and the OKH had not anticipated that the Red Army might conduct a major withdrawal back to the Don instead of standing their ground. Fuel shortages and heavy rains slowed the advance of von Kleist's PzAOK 1, enabling the Southern Front to reach Rostov. On July 21, Stalin finally decided that he could no longer tolerate Timoshenko's cheerful incompetence and replaced him with General-leytenant Vasily N. Gordov. Stalin immediately ordered Gordov to halt the German advance toward Stalingrad by creating a line in the great bend of the Don River; once again, the Soviets blithely opted not to use nearby river lines to bolster their defenses. By constraining Gordov to deploy the three reserve armies sent from the RVGK on the open steppe west of the Don, rather than behind the river, Stalin set the conditions for operational failure. Nor was Gordov, who was given the position through the favor of Politburo member Georgy Malenkov, well suited for command of a critical position. The Luftwaffe also played havoc with the deployment of the three reserve armies by bombing rail centers along the Don. Although Gordov managed to create a line with two of the new armies, the AOK 6 was already close at hand by July 22. In the south, von Kleist's Panzers reached the Don River on the same day and gained two bridgeheads, which caught Malinovsky by surprise. On the next day, von Kleist captured most of Rostov after heavy fighting. Back at the *Wolfsschanze*, Hitler seemed to be on an emotional roller coaster, swinging back and forth between despair and ecstasy. Although disappointed about the failure to bag large numbers of prisoners, he now regarded the first phase of *Blau* as a success and issued Führer Directive 45. Rather than sequential operations, Hitler now mandated simultaneous operations: List's Heeresgruppe A would advance into the Caucasus to seize the oil fields, while von Weichs' Heeresgruppe B would advance toward Stalingrad in order to establish a strong defensive position forward of the Don. As a result, German air and logistic support would be split between two diverging axes of advance.

Paulus tried to mount a double pincer attack against the two Soviet armies defending the Don River bend but fuel shortages deprived his Panzer spearheads of the initiative at a critical moment. The Soviet 62nd and 64th Armies were nearly surrounded but not quite, while the German XIV Panzerkorps was immobilized without fuel – in both Zossen and Moscow, senior staff officers were nearly hysterical over the reports from the battlefront. The Stavka had just formed the 1st Tank Army (1 TA) under General-major Kirill S. Moskalenko near Stalingrad; this was a powerful force with over 500 tanks, which was now the primary mobile theater reserve. Alarmed by the sudden German threat to encircle the two armies in the Don bend, the Stavka hastily authorized Gordov to commit part of it to prevent the destruction of the 62nd and 64th Armies. Gordov flung his armor into the battle piecemeal, thereby negating the principle of mass. Although on the ropes, the now isolated XIV Panzerkorps was kept alive by timely Luftwaffe aerial resupply drops while Stukas from the VIII Fliegerkorps pounded the Soviet tank columns crossing the Don bridges. Gordon even prevailed upon the Stavka to give him part of the 4th Tank Army, which was still forming; it too was fed into battle, one brigade at a time. While Gordov's counteroffensive temporarily forced Paulus' 6. Armee onto the defensive and prevented the annihilation of the 62nd Army, he had committed much of the Stavka's precious armor reserves into a chaotic battle of attrition. In a week of heavy combat from July 24 to 31, 1942, Gordov lost over 600 tanks in the Don Bend, leaving both the 1 TA and 4 TA as gutted formations; Moskalenko's 1 TA was soon disbanded. Yet the OKH was unaware of the extent of Soviet armor losses and Halder bemoaned that "Sixth Army's striking power is paralyzed by ammunition and fuel supply difficulties."[39] A temporary stalemate settled over the Don bend sector.

While most German attention was focused on the Don bend and the Caucasus, the Stavka continued to exert pressure in the Voronezh sector in order to threaten the vulnerable left flank of von Weichs' Heeresgruppe B. The Stavka ordered Rokossovsky, now in charge of the Bryansk Front, to prepare a new offensive against the thinly spread German 2. Armee (under General der Infanterie Hans von Salmuth). Rokossovsky formed Operational Group Chibisov (under General-major Nikandr E. Chibisov), consisting of two tanks corps, five rifle divisions and some artillery units from the RVGK. Chibisov mounted a powerful combined arms offensive on the morning of July 21 against the German VII Armeekorps and succeeded in achieving a breakthrough.[40] Liziukov, having been relieved as commander of the defeated 5 TA, played a major role leading the 2nd Tank Corps. However, von Weichs and von Salmuth were quick to respond and used the 9. Panzer-Division to conduct an improvised counterattack which smashed in the right flank of Operational Group Chibisov on July 23; Liziukov was encircled with his armored spearhead and died trying to lead a breakout attempt. Rokossovsky's counteroffensive continued for a week but ultimately failed and cost the Bryansk Front 30,000 casualties and 171 tanks; the German defenders achieved a 12-1 casualty ratio in their favor.[41] The Stavka did not yet realize that single-echelon offensives, no matter how strong at the start, were unlikely to achieve a decisive breakthrough in any sector where the Germans had adequate mobile reserves. Amazingly, the Stavka failed to launch any major attacks against the poorly equipped Hungarian 2nd Army, which enabled von Weichs to transfer two Panzer divisions to Heeresgruppe Mitte in August. Indeed, von Weichs achieved a remarkable economy of force effort on the Don front, with only three German divisions supporting the Hungarian and Italian armies. In contrast, the Stavka left a mass of forces around Voronezh which could have been better employed elsewhere.

The Soviet forces defending the vital Caucasus region were in a muddled state as List's Heeresgruppe A began crossing the Don in force on July 25. Malinovsky's Southern Front had retreated across the Don in some disorder after losing Rostov and was ill-deployed to defend the river line; the 12th Army (Grechko) and 18th Army (Kamkov) held the front's left flank, while the 37th (Kozlov) and 56th (Ryzhov) Armies were loosely spread to protect the center and right flank. Altogether, Malinovsky had 112,000 troops spread across a 300km-wide front. In fact, Malinovsky's forces were neither retreating nor defending, but merely milling around without coordination. Furthermore, Malinovsky's front had retreated into the region assigned to Marshal Budyonny's North Caucasus Front (*Severo-kavkazskiy front*), which had the 51st Army (Kolomiets) defending a sector of the Don on Malinovsky's right flank. After his incompetent performance at Kiev in 1941, Budyonny had been sent to a backwater command in the Caucasus, but now he found himself once again expected to stop a major German offensive. Before Budyonny and Malinovsky could organize any kind of coordinated defense, the Germans acted first. On July 20–23, von Kleist succeeded in crossing the Don in the sector assigned to Kolomiets' 51st Army and rapidly pushed the XXXX Panzerkorps across. Von Kleist was soon able to seize a second crossing over the Don, with no interference from the Red Army. On July 24–26, Generaloberst Richard Ruoff's AOK 17 seized an intact road bridge over the Don at Bataysk, on the south side of Rostov. On July 27, von Kleist's III Panzerkorps was across the Manych River – all major water barriers barring entrance to the Caucasus had now been overcome, with surprisingly little resistance. Budyonny was only dimly aware of what was developing and waited too long to find out. The OKH redesignated Heeresgruppe A's forthcoming offensive as Unternehmen (Operation) *Edelweiss*. On July 28, List unleashed a coordinated assault with Ruoff's AOK 17 on the right and von Kleist's PzAOK 1 on the left. Budyonny attempted one improvised armored counterattack to try to stop von Kleist's Panzers, which failed abysmally. Malinovsky's armies wilted under the German onslaught and fell back to avoid annihilation. Both Budyonny and Malinovsky lost all control over their shattered forces.

Dismayed by the evident disintegration in the Caucasus, the Stavka ordered the immediate subordination of Malinovsky's Southern Front under Budyonny's North Caucasus Front (which should have been done at least a week prior). Stalin also issued his infamous NKO Order No. 227 (*Ni shagu nazad!* or "Not a step back!"), which signaled that the days of large-scale withdrawals were over and it was now time to fight the enemy to a standstill; it also signaled the adoption of draconian punishments for anyone who retreated without orders.[42] The Stavka also ordered General Ivan V. Tyulenev's Transcaucasus Front to begin forming a fall-back line on the Terek River, based on the 44th Army and four airborne brigades sent from the RVGK. Unlike the Germans, the Soviets were more flexible about planning for defeat, which worked in their favor during the Caucasus campaign. Nevertheless, Budyonny proved a liability in command. Since he could not determine enemy objectives in the region, he fragmented his newly unified command to cover all possibilities: Malinovsky was given the 12th and 37th Armies in the Don Operational Group, while Cherevichenko was assigned the Coastal Operational Group. While Budyonny was still cogitating, von Kleist continued to advance and his Panzers captured Salsk on July 31, tearing a huge gap in the thin Soviet front. Despite Order No. 227, Budyonny's armies now fell back in full retreat, pursued by von Kleist's Panzers. In three days, von Kleist advanced another 100 kilometers and captured Armavir. It is important to note that Heeresgruppe A's advance was also assisted by the use of special forces, particularly the battalion-size Brandenburg z.b.V. 800 infiltration unit. In the Caucasus, the Brandenbergers were tasked with a wide variety of missions, including long-range reconnaissance, capture of key bridges and behind-the-lines raids in enemy uniforms.[43] Although the Brandenbergers suffered heavy losses in the Caucasus, their daring and imaginative tactics set a new standard for the integration of special forces within a conventional campaign.

The critical operational-level question for the Germans after overcoming the Don was what to do with Hoth's PzAOK 4, which was the best-equipped maneuver force in the Ostheer at this moment. According to the original *Blau* planning, PzAOK 4 was supposed to shift to Heeresgruppe A after Heeresgruppe B cleared the Donbas in order to reinforce the main effort in the Caucasus. Indeed, von Bock's relief was premised on Hitler's belief that he had delayed this transfer. However, Heeresgruppe A's logistics across the Don were extremely limited, since the rail bridge at Bataysk was down, making it unfeasible to supply two Panzer armies entirely by motor transport units. Furthermore, the rapid disintegration and retreat of Budyonny's forces made it appear that an additional Panzer army in the Caucasus would be superfluous. Hoth had been transferred to List's command but could not be gainfully employed. Instead, the real trouble spot was in the Heeresgruppe B sector, where Paulus' 6.Armee had been stopped by Soviet resistance at the Don bend. When Paulus and von Weichs reported that they could not immediately resume the offensive due to shortage of fuel, Hitler became apoplectic. Generaloberst Alfred Jodl, the OKW's operation chief, was an expert at mollifying Hiter's outbursts and he suggested transferring Hoth's PzAOK 4 back to von Weichs' Heeresgruppe B in order to help Paulus overcome Gordov's roadblock in the Don bend. Surprisingly, Hitler agreed.[44] On July 31, Hoth's PzAOK 4 reverted to von Weichs' command and used its bridgehead across the Don to attempt an outflanking maneuver against Gordov's left flank. By August 3, Hoth succeeded in capturing the rail station at Kotelnikovo and only chronic fuel shortages prevented him from rolling up Gordov's Stalingrad Front. Gordov quickly dispatched General-leytenant Vasily I. Chuikov with three rifle divisions by rail to block Hoth's advance, which was only partly successful. Chuikov's command post was bombed both by the Luftwaffe and the VVS (by mistake) on the same day – possibly a unique distinction.

Paulus was finally able to resume his offensive in the Don bend on August 7 and the XIV Panzerkorps, refueled and refitted, was able to encircle General-leytenant Anton I. Lopatin's 62nd Army. A total of 12 rifle divisions and ten tank brigades were trapped in the *Kessel*, which was crushed in just three days; the Germans claimed to have taken 52,000 prisoners. Gordov had no reserves left to help Lopatin and immediately ordered all the bridges over the Don destroyed. As a result of this new disaster, Gordov was relieved of command on August 12 and Eremenko arrived to take over the Stalingrad Front. Eremenko was an excellent choice for this important front, but he was still recovering from previous wounds and not at his best. The Stavka assigned Nikita S. Khrushchev as front commissar and General-leytenant Dmitri N. Nikishev as Eremenko's chief of staff; Nikishev was a General Staff-trained officer but had run afoul of Zhukov at Khalkhin Gol in 1939. As an added complication, Stalin decided to create a Southeastern Front from the staff of the defunct Southern Front to oppose Hoth's PzAOK 4, although Eremenko retained control over this formation as well.

After his victory in the Don bend, Paulus moved methodically to tidy up the battlefield before moving on to his primary operational objective – Stalingrad. He eliminated most of the remaining Soviet forces still on the western bank of the Don, except for a heavily defended bridgehead at Kremenskaya. For military leaders raised on a philosophy of battlefield expediency, it was accepted that any non-critical task that proved too difficult to quickly accomplish could be deferred until a later date. Yet again and again, this predilection came back to haunt the Ostheer, as allowing the Soviets to retain the Kremenskaya bridgehead would prove to be a key operational mistake. Next, von Weichs directed a coordinated offensive by Paulus' AOK 6 and Hoth's PzAOK 4 on August 20–21 against Eremenko's Stalingrad Front. Hoth struck first but encountered fierce resistance from General-major Mikhail S. Shumilov's 64th Army south of Stalingrad. Hoth then opted to try to outflank the main enemy defenses, but Shumilov proved to be a steady commander and did not panic. Instead, he forced Hoth into a grinding battle of attrition around Tinguta rail station for over a week. Paulus lurched forward with his 6. Armee and seized a crossing over the Don at Vertyachii with two infantry divisions. Eremenko had expected Paulus to try to cross the Don at Kalach and had left the Vertyachii sector lightly defended. Lopatin's 62nd Army, reduced to a low ebb after its defeat in the Don bend, put up fierce and ineffectual resistance at the German bridgehead. The most important factor in German success at this point was Luftflotte 4's complete air superiority over Stalingrad, which smothered any attempts by the Soviets to reinforce this critical sector of the front. On the morning of August 23, Paulus launched a breakout attack from the Vertyachii bridgehead, spearheaded by the XIV Panzerkorps. Once again, Eremenko was caught by surprise and had not expected an enemy threat to Stalingrad to develop so rapidly. Supported by a maximum-effort from Luftflotte 4, Paulus' spearhead advanced nearly 60 kilometers in 14 hours, reaching the Volga and the northern suburbs of Stalingrad. Despite many delays along the way, Paulus had managed to achieve his primary campaign objective after eight weeks. Adding to Soviet problems, Hoth finally achieved a breakthrough on August 28 and rapidly advanced toward Stalingrad's southern suburbs. Facing converging German pincers, Eremenko scrambled to organize militia and naval infantry units to hold Stalingrad until reinforcements could arrive.

In an effort to divert German forces away from Stalingrad, Eremenko also decided to launch a major attack against the left flank of the 6. Armee and part of the Italian 8th Army. On the morning of August 20, General-leytenant Vasily I. Kuznetsov's 63rd Army attacked across the Don River against the Italian XXXV Corps and managed to gain a bridgehead near Yelanskaya. Amazingly, von Weichs refused to provide any ground or air support to the Italian 8th Army and told its commander, General Italo Garibaldi, to clear up the situation with his own resources. Instead, Kuznetsov managed to expand his bridgehead and nearly broke the Italian front line. In the same period, the 1st Guards Army managed to expand its bridgehead across the Don at Kremenskaya. Consequently, the Soviets now held major bridgeheads across the Don, which could be used as springboards for new counteroffensives.

While Paulus was slowly marching toward Stalingrad, von Kleist was continuing to spearhead the German advance into the central Caucasus. Rather than a single main *Schwerpunkt*, List's Heeresgruppe A split into five dispersed, corps-sized groups, which quickly became very spread out. Here and there, Budyonny's armies tried to make a stand, but they simply lacked the armor and artillery to hold off sustained attacks in open steppe country. In spite of Stalin's Order No. 277, the 12th, 18th, 37th and 56th Armies kept retreating. The fog of war was quite thick in the Caucasus, with neither side quite sure where their opponents' main forces were operating; List knew that he had achieved a major breakthrough, but did not know where the Soviets might try to form another line. Even though the primary objective was the oil fields in the Caucasus, the OKH kept adding tasks for List's army group to accomplish, including clearing the Kuban and the Black Sea coast. List dutifully complied, sending one German and one Romanian corps to the Kuban, and two German corps to take the Maikop oilfield and the port of Tuapse. Consequently, Heeresgruppe A was able to capture Krasnodar in the Kuban and the Maikop oil fields (which had been sabotaged) by August 10.[45] List seemed to be on the cusp of a major victory, but Soviet resistance began to stiffen as they retreated into the mountainous terrain of the central Caucasus. Furthermore, Heeresgruppe A's supply situation rapidly declined as von Kleist's Panzers outran their fuel supplies and the spearpoint was reduced to just two divisions in the XXXX Panzerkorps.

List assigned Ruoff's AOK 17 to clear the Kuban, including capturing the port of Novorossiysk. Ruoff was a "by-the-book" infantry officer with extensive command and staff experience in both world wars, but he was not an imaginative commander. General-major Grigori P. Kotov, a skilled staff officer and veteran of Khalkhin Gol, was assigned to command the 47th Army and ordered to hold Novorossiysk. Kotov was badly outnumbered, with limited air support and his back to the sea, but he managed to draw Ruoff into a costly battle of attrition around the city. After six weeks, Ruoff succeeded in capturing Novorossiysk on September 7, but valuable time had been wasted on a secondary objective. Stalin relieved Kotov of command after the fall of the city but allowed him to play a role as a deputy army commander for the rest of the campaign in the Caucasus.*

It was in mid-August that List demonstrated his inability to properly align available forces with realistic mission objectives. Heeresgruppe A's supposed main effort, von Kleist's PzAOK 1, advanced down the rail line toward Mozdok on the Terek River with only two divisions in the XXXX Panzerkorps. Since this avenue of approach was obvious, Budyonny (North Caucasus Front) and Tyulenev (Transcaucasus Front) were amassing two armies in this critical sector. Meanwhile, List diverted one-third of his army group to capture the port of Tuapse. Ignoring the restrictive nature of the mountainous terrain, he ordered the LVII Panzerkorps to advance toward the coast, along with the rest of AOK 17. Cherevichenko's Black Sea Group (12th and 18th Armies) held all the important mountain passes and easily blocked the German advance to Tuapse. By August 18, it was pretty clear that there would be no rapid advance to the coast, but List kept trying to grind his way through. Doubling down on this mistake, List detached the XXXXIX Gebirgskorps (which had elite mountain troops) to go after the port of Sukhumi but General-leytenant Konstantin N. Leselidze's 46th Army stopped them cold. Leselidze was one of the few ethnic Georgian officers in a senior Red Army command billet, which boosted him in Stalin's opinion. Meanwhile, List sent the LII Armeekorps to advance across the arid Kalmyk Steppe, which was a mission better suited to the motorized troops in the LVII Panzerkorps, which were now stuck in mountainous terrain. All these diversions reduced the resources that could be used to sustain von Kleist's spearhead, particularly fuel and infantry support. Heeresgruppe A's logistic backbone relied upon a single rail line running from Rostov to Pyatigorsk, which meant that von Kleist only received 100–200 tons of supplies every other day, not the 500 tons per day required to sustain high-tempo offensive operations. Furthermore, the IV Fliegerkorps, assigned to support Heeresgruppe A, was spread across

---

*Kotov had the distinction of being the only Soviet general killed by American military forces in the Second World War. He died as result of a fratricide incident in Yugoslavia on November 7, 1944, when US fighter-bombers mistakenly strafed a Soviet convoy.

so many sectors that it could no longer provide adequate air support. By the time that the XXXX Panzerkorps finally reached the Terek River at the end of August, the newly-formed Soviet 9th Army had established a firm defense. The Stavka had wisely shifted six airborne brigades by air to the Caucasus, which were used to form two new guards rifle corps. Von Kleist's fuel-starved Panzers were stymied.

It took List two weeks to move up German and Romanian infantry to the Terek River line, during which time the Soviets further reinforced this sector. Von Kleist only had a narrow window of opportunity to cross the Terek and reach the oil fields at Grozny, before weather and enemy resistance made this impossible. On September 2, von Kleist was able to seize a bridgehead across the Terek near Mozdok with infantry from the LII Armeekorps. Budyonny immediately launched counterattacks on the ground and for the first time in the Caucasus, Soviet airpower appeared in force. General-major Konstantin A. Vershinin's 4th Air Army (4 VA) conducted over 400 sorties against the bridgehead and succeeded in bombing a German pontoon bridge across the Terek.[46] The VVS in the Caucasus was now receiving American-built aircraft like the P-39 fighter-bomber and B-25 bomber via Iran, which greatly enhanced their capabilities. Stalin took a personal interest in the Caucasus campaign, which threatened his native Georgia, but he was not confident in the ability of Budyonny or Tyulenev to stop von Kleist. On Lavrenty Beria's suggestion, Stalin sent General-leytenant Ivan I. Maslennikov on September 8 to take command of the forces defending on the Terek River. As an NKVD officer, Maslennikov was not a bad choice for a defensive operation in a key sector, since he could enforce discipline and motivate subordinates with threats of sending them to the gulag, but his ability to coordinate the operations of four armies was negligible.

In Rastenburg, Hitler was beginning to recognize that the Caucasus operation was not going according to plan and that List's performance was sub-par. On September 7, General Alfred Jodl, the OKW chief of staff, visited List's headquarters in Stalino (Donetsk) to discuss Hitler's displeasure with the slow pace of operations. In particular, Jodl conveyed Hitler's recognition that List was misusing his available troops (which was true) and all his operations were prematurely running out of steam. List made the mistake of complaining that Hitler had promised additional forces for Heeresgruppe A (such as the Italian Alpine Corps) but then failed to deliver. Three days later, Hitler relieved List of command and like von Bock, never employed his services again. Hitler also declared that he was taking over direct command of Heeresgruppe A, although in reality, the chief of staff – Generalleutnant Hans von Greiffenberg – served as interim commander for the next two months. Hitler had also had enough of Halder's complaining and on September 24 he was replaced as chief of the OKH by General der Infanterie Kurt Zeitzler; Halder's military career in the Wehrmacht was over but after the war, he would work for the US Army's Historical Division.

With the offensive nearly stalled, von Kleist opted to take considerable risk and committed one of his Panzer divisions into the bridgehead on September 12. Since PzAOK 1's flanks were exposed, von Kleist was committing his only mobile reserve, thereby presenting the enemy with opportunities to threaten his vulnerable line of communications. Instead, both sides became totally focused on the bridgehead battle. Over the course of three weeks, von Kleist was gradually able to expand the Mozdok bridgehead, but it came at the cost of heavy fighting which exhausted his best units. Although von Kleist gained a larger bridgehead across the Terek, the Soviet 9th Army (which changed commanders three times in just over a month) managed to seal it off with a solid front. By October 3, it was clear that Heeresgruppe A's offensive had culminated and that the oilfields in Grozny could not be reached in 1942.

The Caucasus was the kind of campaign the Panzer divisions were designed to win, using bold maneuvers across flat steppes against a disorganized foe that lacked proper air, artillery or armor support. However, Hitler and the OKH failed to provide their main effort with the logistic resources and air support it needed to succeed. If Heeresgruppe A had received priority for fuel in August, including delivery by air, von Kleist probably would have been able to cross the Terek River before the Soviets were able to cobble together a defense. Yet Heeresgruppe A's poor performance in the Caucasus indicates some of the endemic problems in the Wehrmacht's style of operational planning that go well beyond the mistakes of a few generals. It is not only questionable whether a better-resourced Heeresgruppe A could have achieved its operational objectives, but whether the capture of these objectives would have made that much difference to the Red Army's capabilities.

At Stalingrad, Paulus and Hoth began advancing into the city outskirts on September 3–4, opposed primarily by General-leytenant Anton I. Lopatin's decimated 62nd Army. At first, the Germans made good progress, which led to considerable alarm in the Stavka. On the night of September 3, Zhukov sent Stavka Order No. 170599 to Eremenko, demanding that Moskalenko's 1st Guards Army (1GA) immediately attack from the north to relieve pressure on Stalingrad. Zhukov added in the order that "procrastination now is equivalent to a crime," which was a thinly-veiled threat that heads would roll if Stalingrad was lost. Moskalenko's 1GA duly attacked Paulus' left flank in the First Kotluban Offensive and was repulsed with heavy losses. Overall, the First Kotluban Offensive cost Eremenko's Stalingrad Front 80,000 casualties and 300 tanks at a time when it could ill afford such exorbitant losses. Although Paulus was distracted by the Soviet counteroffensive, the 6. Armee was still able to advance fairly quickly into Stalingrad. Once Chuikov took over the 62nd Army on September 9, Soviet resistance became more fanatical. The 6. Armee reached the Volga on September 14, but further progress slowed to a glacial pace. Thereafter, both at Stalingrad and in the Mozdok bridgehead, operational focus shifted to a strictly tactical level as the German offensives coughed and stumbled along, unable to achieve resolution. By the first week of October, it was clear that the great German summer offensive had conquered territory but failed to achieve its intended purpose of breaking the Soviet Union's military-industrial capabilities. Although not yet recognized, the Ostheer had achieved its high-water mark in the Soviet Union. Soon, the over-extended German armies would have to pay a fearsome price for this operational miscalculation.

In retrospect, *Blau* was a historic gamble, made with desperately thin margins for error. Hitler's ambition to achieve a decisive operational-level success in southern Russia was frustrated more by logistic problems at the front than any other factor. Time and again, German mechanized spearheads were brought to a halt by fuel shortages, just as opportunities for decisive success presented themselves. German operational-level command was generally adequate during the early stages of the summer offensive, although List's inability to prioritize missions or conduct basic METT-T analysis (mission-enemy-terrain-troops available-time) seriously undermined Heeresgruppe A's ability to achieve its objectives. Paulus, as the key German commander, was at his best in planning set-piece battles, particularly when the enemy was badly deployed. Hoth and von Kleist excelled as operational-level maneuver commanders, but the fragmentation of their commands and logistical constraints made it difficult for them to conduct the kind of maneuver warfare they had practiced in 1940–41. Although *Blau* relied heavily upon Hungarian, Italian and Romanian participation, these armies were poorly supported and often ignored. While Hitler's interference was significant during *Blau*, it was never the proximate cause of German operational failures. Had either von Kleist's or Hoth's armies received adequate fuel supplies, at least one of the two German army groups would probably have accomplished its assigned objectives prior to the end of the campaigning season. If that had occurred, the Germans would then have possessed more substantial armored reserves to deal with enemy counteroffensives.

Commander	Objective	Offensive	Mass	Maneuver	Surprise	Security	TALLY
Weichs	+	+	o	+	o	o	3
Hoth	+	+	o	+	+	o	4
Paulus	+	+	+	+	+	-	4
List	-	+	-	-	o	o	-2
Von Kleist	+	+	o	+	+	o	4
Ruoff	+	+	o	+	o	o	3
Budyonny	o	o	o	o	o	o	o
Gordov	+	+	-	-	o	-	-1
Shumilov Kotov	+	o	o	o	o	+	2
Eremenko	+	+	o	o	+	-	2

Don-Caucasus, 1942 Leadership Assessment

The Soviet operational-level performance during the initial stages of *Blau* was uninspiring. Despite the availability of very strong armored reserves, the Bryansk Front managed to lose Voronezh to a *coup de main*, then bungled one counterattack after another against Heeresgruppe B. Timoshenko's Southwest Front avoided total destruction, saving some remnants to fight another day, but it could do little but retreat in front of the enemy juggernaut. Much of the Red Army's problems during the opening weeks of the campaign were caused by direct interference from Stalin and the Stavka, trying to micromanage operations and relieving commanders who failed to achieve unrealistic objectives. Stalin's insistence upon committing entire armies to offensive operations with minimal planning or preparation was a recipe for disaster, but it was symptomatic of a regime that demanded results without regard to costs. Soviet personnel losses in trying to stop Heeresgruppe B in July and August were over 400,000 and nearly 2,000 tanks were lost or disabled. In the Caucasus, Budyonny's command performance was awful, but he was saved from further embarrassment by the tyranny of distance – the further Heeresgruppe A advanced into the region, the more its combat power became dissipated. Gordov's performance on the Stalingrad axis was even worse, but one must have some sympathy for a commander that was forced to operate under the thumb of the Stavka. By the time that Eremenko took over, the Stalingrad Front's armored reserves had been spent and he had little on hand to stop the initial German push into the city. Eremenko was caught by surprise by the German assault and forced to mount an ill-advised offensive with the 1GA at Kotluban, but his strike against the Italian XXXV Corps indicates that he recognized the inherent weakness in the enemy's dispositions.

Other Soviet Summer Offensives, June–September 1942

When the expected German strike against Moscow did not occur, the Stavka decided to authorize offensives on other parts of the Eastern Front in order to achieve their own operational objectives. Even though the Ostheer's resources were stretched thin supporting the main campaign in the south, Hitler was also keen to conduct limited offensives on other parts of the front. Consequently, during the summer of 1942 significant campaigns were fought near Orel, Rzhev, Demyansk and Leningrad, which were essentially sideshows to the main event in the south.

Zhukov, as commander of the Western Front, was chagrined to see that the main action was not occurring in his sector. Rather than offering to transfer forces from his command, which included nearly 60 divisions and six full-strength tanks corps, Zhukov instead pushed to mount offensive operations on his front in order to force the OKH to divert forces away from southern Russia. On July 2, the Stavka authorized Zhukov to mount an offensive against Generaloberst Rudolf Schmidt's PzAOK 2 in the Orel-Bryansk sector, ostensibly to assist the Bryansk Front's offensive into the flank of Heeresgruppe B. Schmidt's army had established a defense in depth, replete with field works and obstacles.[47] Oddly, Zhukov opted to attack in two sectors that were 90 kilometers apart, with General-leytenant Pavel A. Belov's 61st Army assigned to attack in the Zhizdra sector and Rokossovsky's 16th Army in the Bolkhov sector. Belov, one of the Red Army's favorite cavalry commanders, was given just four days to plan the offensive. Belov tried to plan a combined-arms offensive, integrating artillery, air strikes, infantry and armor, but a variety of factors conspired to sabotage his intent. Aside from insufficient time allotted for planning, the NKO had issued an absurd directive – intended to enhance operational security – which forbade the preparation of written orders and instead mandated that all orders had to be delivered orally by liaison officers. Furthermore, artillery units could only be told specific targets three hours prior to the offensive; obviously, such restrictions made complex artillery planning almost impossible. Belov was allotted 250 artillery pieces and over 1,000 tactical air support sorties, but the attempt by the NKO to micromanage army-level planning greatly hindered employment of these resources. Belov began his part of the attack on July 5, employing two echelons. Despite achieving tactical surprise, Belov's attack failed to achieve a breakthrough and when he tried to commit his tank corps (which should have remained in reserve to exploit any success) it was decimated by German Flak and antitank guns.

Rokossovsky was allotted one extra day to prepare his part of the offensive and like Belov, tried to employ combined-arms principles. He was allotted over 400 artillery pieces and 680 tactical aviation sorties to support his offensive. The 16th Army attacked on July 6 and quickly discovered that the heavily wooded and marshy terrain was ill-suited for a fast-paced operation. Attacks quickly bogged down. Furthermore, Schmidt's PzAOK 2 had two Panzer divisions as operational reserves and ample Luftwaffe support. Rokossovsky's first echelon attacks made only slight gains and when he tried to commit his armor, it was ruthlessly pounded by Luftwaffe interdiction strikes. Even though it was soon obvious that the offensive could not succeed, Zhukov ordered it continued for another week. Rather than admit that the operation was futile, Zhukov requested that he be provided the fresh 3rd Tank Army (3 TA) from the RVGK reserves so he could try again. For his part, Rokossovsky downplayed the operation in his memoirs.[48]

Von Kluge had previously recommended an offensive to eliminate the troublesome Sukhinichi salient and in the wake of Zhukov's fumbled operation, he again raised this issue with the OKH. Surprisingly, Hitler agreed to provide resources for a limited counterstroke, designated as *Wirbelwind* (Whirlwind). Schmidt's PzAOK 2 would be temporarily reinforced to a total of six Panzer divisions (none of which were full strength) to spearhead the operation. The basic concept was a pincer attack, with PzAOK 2 attacking from the south while the 4. Armee attacked from the north; ideally this would cut off the Sukhinichi salient and isolate the Soviet 10th and 16th Armies. Schmidt attacked on August 11 and succeeded in gradually isolating three Soviet rifle divisions from the 61st Army, which were later crushed. The 4. Armee part of the operation was canceled, reducing the offensive to a single pincer. Furthermore, Soviet resistance quickly stiffened and the terrain was unfavorable, so the OKH called off the operation after ten days.[49] While *Wirbelwind* succeeded in inflicting some damage on Belov's 61st Army, it did not seize any significant terrain or serve as a useful spoiling attack. At a time when the Ostheer needed every tank battalion, Stuka sortie and liter of petrol available to support the main effort in the south, it could ill afford to divert precious resources to a secondary sector.

Zhukov was still not done with the Sukhinichi sector and in response to *Wirbelwind*, the RVGK finally agreed to provide him with General-leytenant Prokify L. Romanenko's 3 TA, which was a full-strength formation with 700 tanks. He claimed that he would use the 3 TA in conjunction with the 16th Army to cut off the German forces used to spearhead *Wirbelwind*. Zhukov was able to bring the 3 TA up quietly by rail and assemble it near the front, without the Germans noticing it. On August 22, Zhukov launched the second round of his offensive, initially attacking with infantry, which did not achieve a breakthrough. Nevertheless, Zhukov committed Romanenko's entire 3 TA in the hope of using it as a battering ram to smash through Schmidt's front. Romanenko's attack was a fiasco, plagued by fuel shortages, poor C2 and constant Luftwaffe attacks. Again Zhukov allowed the offensive to continue – even after it was obvious that it had failed – until Romanenko's 3 TA was reduced to an immobilized wreck. Altogether, Zhukov's Western Front lost over 1,000 tanks and 35,000 casualties in the two failed offensives and in neither case were the Soviet shock groups able to achieve a significant breakthrough. The RVGK's best operational reserve – the 3 TA – was broken in a futile effort, without accomplishing anything of value. The American historian David Glantz has referred to the Western Front's Bolkhov-Zhizdra offensives as "a case study in how not to conduct a major operation." Zhukov later used his influence to ensure that this campaign was ignored in Soviet official histories of the war in order to avoid negative assessments of his generalship skills.

Nor was Zhukov's attention limited just to the Orel sector. He had been keenly interested in cutting off the German 9. Armee in the Rzhev salient since the failed winter counteroffensive. General-leytenant Ivan Maslennikov's 39th Army was still deeply embedded in the western flank of the Rzhev salient, although Model had managed to partly isolate it with limited tactical actions during the spring. Model was badly wounded on May 23 and the command of the 9. Armee temporarily passed to Generaloberst Heinrich von Vietinghoff.[50] Von Kluge then lobbied – successfully – for additional reinforcements to finally crush the 39th Army and thereby reduce the threat to the Rzhev salient. The OKH agreed to provide the 9. Armee with two more Panzer divisions, which would be used to lead Unternehmen (Operation) *Seydlitz*. Nevertheless, German resources were slim and it was necessary to act before Zhukov could mount his own offensive against the Rzhev salient. The German offensive began on July 2, using the classic double pincer formula. Amazingly, Soviet resistance was so fierce that the Germans could not close the *Kessel* and intense combat occurred in the so-called Belyy corridor. Konev's Kalinin Front directed the operations around the corridor and used the 41st Army to try to maintain a link to the 39th Army. Finally, the Germans managed to find a weak spot and succeeded in encircling the 39th Army. In a week of heavy fighting, the Germans crushed the *Kessel* and claimed to have taken about 37,000 prisoners, while perhaps 18,000 escaped through the forests.[51] Maslennikov and a few other senior officers were flown out of the pocket before the final collapse. *Seydlitz* proved to be a nice tactical victory which eliminated seven Soviet divisions and most of the 11th Cavalry Corps, plus stabilizing the western flank of the Rzhev salient.

Zhukov had been focused on the Orel sector while the 39th Army was being demolished but in the aftermath of that defeat, he began planning a major summer offensive against the Rzhev salient. He told the Stavka that by attacking the salient, the Western Front could draw German reserves away from the Stalingrad sector (in fact, the Germans were doing a good job on their own sending their limited reserves hither and yon, without any help from Zhukov) and possibly achieve a decisive defeat of the vulnerable 9. Armee. The Stavka approved Zhukov's concept for a joint offensive by the Kalinin and Western Fronts against the Rzhev sector on July 16 and allocated two weeks to prepare. Konev's Kalinin Front would attack the northern portion of the salient with the 29th and 30th Armies (supported by the 3 VA) while Zhukov's Western Front attacked the eastern side of the salient with the 20th and 31st Armies (supported by the 1 VA). The 9. Armee held strong defensive positions in the sectors that would be attacked and had significant mobile reserves close at hand, but Zhukov and Konev had an edge in terms of numbers and firepower.

Konev attacked first on July 30, but his infantry assaults could not make any real progress against the German defenses. Unable to achieve a breakthrough, Konev withheld most of his armor. Zhukov waited until August 4, hoping that Konev's attacks would attract German reserves, then committed his own two armies. Zhukov had a flair for pouring overwhelming resources into a battle and he buried the two opposing German front-line divisions under an avalanche of firepower. Within 24 hours, Zhukov's forces had created a 30km-wide hole in the 9. Armee's front and achieved penetrations 12–20km deep. Thus, Zhukov was the first Soviet commander to break through a strongly fortified German line. Yet the fog of war prevented Zhukov from seeing the extent of his success and he momentarily paused before committing his second echelon exploitation forces. Von Vietinghoff took advantage of this brief delay and quickly committed his own reserves – two Panzer divisions – which arrived just in time to establish blocking positions. Suddenly the Red avalanche was slowed to a crawl by the Panzers, although Zhukov ordered his armies to bull their way through. On August 7, Model returned from convalescence and resumed command of the 9. Armee, which was holding on by its fingernails. Frustrated that neither the 20th nor 31st Armies could push through the Panzer divisions in their way or even widen the breach, Zhukov decided to commit his front-level mobile reserves on August 11; these consisted of two tank corps and a guards cavalry corps. The result was an extremely crowded battle zone, with little room for maneuver. Adding to Zhukov's problems, the 9. Armee received some of the new 7.5cm antitank guns, which inflicted crippling losses on some of his best tank units.

Zhukov did what he always did when a battle did not go his way - he added more forces. He ordered the 5th Army to attack the neighboring 3. Panzerarmee at the base of the Rzhev salient, followed by the 33rd Army. With his army stretched almost to the breaking point, Model was forced to grudgingly give some ground, which led to the 31st Army capturing Zubtsov on August 23. By the end of August, Zhukov's offensive had culminated, although he let it continue into early September. Overall, at a cost of 291,000 casualties, Zhukov had managed to advance 32 kilometers in a month but had failed to cut off the Rzhev salient or crush the 9. Armee. The 9. Armee suffered heavy losses, amounting to over 35,000 casualties (about 10 percent of its starting strength), but retained most of its combat effectiveness. In the aftermath of the offensive, Zhukov moved up to become deputy commander of the Red Army and Konev took over the Western Front, while General-leytenant Maksim A. Purkaev took over the Kalinin Front. In terms of generalship, Zhukov's plan and initial execution was essentially sound, but he had not anticipated enemy reactions and ended up settling for a battle of attrition that was unlikely to achieve decisive results. Model recognized that the 9. Armee had only held on by a thin margin and recommended to the OKH that the Rzhev Salient should be evacuated to conserve manpower, but Hitler rejected the idea of any large-scale withdrawals.

The operations at Orel and Rzhev did not do much to bolster Zhukov's reputation and Konev's role was rather passive. It should be noted that operational-level surprise did not play a role in these Soviet offensives, which enabled the Germans to anticipate and position their limited mobile reserves to block likely axes of advance. Later, the Stavka would realize the importance of *maskirovka* (deception) in providing a useful edge in offensive operations, but at this point the imperative for expedient action outweighed a more deliberate approach. Von Kluge served essentially as a resource manager during both campaigns, leaving the actual conduct of operations up to the army commanders, but he ensured that his warfighters had just enough reserves to survive the storm. Yet as a criticism, von Kluge flip-flopped on objectives, one moment wanting attacks to straighten out his front, next to revert entirely to the defense (but keeping his mobile reserves). Von Vietinghoff demonstrated some flair in accomplishing *Seydlitz*, as Schmidt did to some extent with *Wirbelwind*, but for much of these campaigns the German army-level leaders were fighting a battle for survival against numerically superior opponents. Rokossovsky and Belov, like the other Soviet army commanders involved at Rzhev, tried to use combined-arms methods but ended up fighting very unsatisfactory battles of attrition. Another noteworthy factor is that the Luftwaffe could still shape events on the battlefield, even though most of its strength was deployed in the south. As yet, the VVS still had difficulty employing its growing numerical strength at the right time and place to make a difference.

Commander	Objective	Offensive	Mass	Maneuver	Surprise	Security	TALLY
Von Kluge	o	o	o	o	o	+	1
Schmidt	o	+	o	+	+	+	4
Von Vietinghoff	+	+	o	+	o	o	3
Model	+	o	o	o	o	o	1
Zhukov	+	+	+	–	–	o	1
Konev	+	o	+	–	–	o	o
Rokossovsky	+	+	+	–	o	o	2
Belov	+	+	+	–	+	–	2

Orel and Rzhev, 1942 Leadership Assessment

Further north, the Stavka had been embarrassed by the German operations to relieve both the Kholm and Demyansk pockets and immediately demanded that General-polkovnik Pavel A. Kurochkin's Northwest Front take corrective action. Kurochkin received artillery and tanks from the RVGK reserves and was given the month of June to rebuild his battered divisions. Kurochkin and his GSHKA-trained chief of staff, General-major Mikhail N. Sharokhin, developed a relatively simple plan to cut off the narrow neck of the German-held Ramushevo corridor, thereby isolating the German forces at Demyansk again. General Leytenant Vasily I. Morozov's 11th Army would attack the corridor from the north, while General Leytenant Vladimir Z. Romanovskiy's 1 SA attacked from the south. The corridor was only 6 kilometers wide at its narrowest point and Kurochkin and Sharokhin were certain that two reinforced armies should be able to cover this short distance. The plan relied upon brute force and firepower, not maneuver or subtlety. Morozov was a veteran commander, having the unique distinction of being the only Soviet army commander to retain his position since the beginning of *Barbarossa*, a year prior. On the other hand, Romanovskiy had negligible command experience (he had sat out 1941 in remote postings) and was probably picked for his political reliability. Of course, the Germans were well aware that the Soviets wanted to attack the Ramushevo corridor and planned accordingly. Busch's AOK 16 assigned Korpsgruppe Knobelsdorff to defend the corridor with eight divisions, which created a formidable defense in depth with thousands of mines, antitank guns and field works.

Kurochkin launched his offensive on July 17, beginning with a 90-minute artillery preparation. However, the German troops were dug in too deeply to be much affected by a bombardment and when the Soviet tank-infantry shock groups advanced into the carefully prepared engagement areas they were shot to pieces. After a week of futile attacks, the offensive collapsed after gaining less than one mile of terrain. Stalin was infuriated that the Northwest Front had accomplished so little and sent Marshal Timoshenko (who had just been relieved of command of the Stalingrad Front one week prior) to supervise Kurochkin's next offensive. Shlemin was relieved as chief of staff and replaced by General-major Sharokhin, an experienced GSHKA officer. Kurochkin's main problem was that he could not achieve any kind of surprise, since the Stavka condemned him to keep attacking the Ramushevo corridor. In fact, Busch had stripped other sectors of troops and artillery in order to stiffen the defense in the corridor and Soviet attacks elsewhere might have caught the 16. Armee off-balance. Instead, Busch knew exactly where Kurochkin would attack, which gave a huge advantage to the defense.

Kurochkin began his second offensive against the Ramushevo corridor on August 10, this time with less artillery ammunition and fewer tanks, since the Stavka had not replaced his losses from the last attempt. The second offensive went even worse than the first, barely advancing a few hundred meters before the shock groups were annihilated in the German obstacle belt. Nevertheless, Kurochkin was obliged by Timoshenko to continue the futile offensive for another ten days. The August offensive had been a disaster for the Northwest Front and the only thing worse would be to repeat the mistake, which was exactly what the Stavka ordered Kurochkin to do. On September 15, Kurochkin conducted a third attempt to sever the corridor with similar results – the German defenses proved impregnable and the attacking shock groups were decimated. By this point, the Northwest Front's two best armies were totally spent and demoralized by heavy losses without any appreciable gains. Busch had been waiting for this moment and received permission to conduct a corps-size counterattack against Romanovskiy's 1st Shock Army. Busch was able to assemble two divisions and some armor and artillery for the effort, designated Unternehmen (Operation) *Michael*. The Germans attacked on the morning of September 27, supported by Luftwaffe ground attack aircraft. By this point, VVS support in this sector had evaporated and Kurochkin's forces now had to operate under conditions of enemy air superiority. Although Busch lacked the strength to completely defeat the 1 SA, he was able to mutilate it over the course of a one-week battle and force it to withdraw or risk destruction. Consequently, the only side that gained any significant amount of territory during the Battle of the Ramushevo corridor was the German 16. Armee. Altogether, Kurochkin's Northwest Front suffered 300,000 casualties over the course of these operations (including 90,000 dead), against 72,000 German casualties (16,000 dead). As a result of these failures, Kurochkin was temporarily demoted to army commander (he would return to command the Northwest Front in June 1943) and Timoshenko took over as front commander.

Kurochkin was forced by the Stavka to conduct the campaign against the German-held Demyansk salient in an unprofessional manner, which greatly reduced the probability of success. Although Kurochkin and his two assault army commanders were able to mass significant combat power against a clear objective, the lack of surprise or maneuver enabled the German defenders to anticipate their every move and defeat them. Busch's conduct of the battle was professional and a model of how to conduct a defensive battle on a budget, against an enemy with superior resources. Furthermore, Busch's ability to correctly time the *Michael* counteroffensive demonstrated his ability to appreciate the enemy situation and exploit a perceived weakness in a timely fashion. Nevertheless, Busch recognized that the cost of defeating repeated Soviet offensives was excessive and recommended the evacuation of the Demyansk salient in order to conserve his army – which was rejected.

Commander	Objective	Offensive	Mass	Maneuver	Surprise	Security	TALLY
Busch	+	+	+	+	+	+	6
Kurochkin	+	+	+	–	–	0	1
Romanovskiy	+	+	+	–	–	–	0
Morozov	+	+	+	–	–	0	1

Demyansk, 1942 Leadership Assessment

At Leningrad, the Germans were growing impatient at the inability of the siege to cause the city's defense to collapse and annoyed by the constant Soviet attacks on their outer siege lines on the Neva and Volkhov Rivers. In April 1942, Hitler issued Führer Directive 41, which reversed his previous decision to besiege Leningrad and now authorized von Küchler's Heeresgruppe Nord to capture the city when feasible. In July, Hitler further clarified with Führer Directive 45 that Leningrad should be taken by early September. In order to accomplish this task, he stated that von Manstein's 11. Armee would be transferred from the Crimea to lead the offensive. In conjunction with the Heeresgruppe Nord staff and Generaloberst Georg Lindemann's AOK 18, von Kuchler began planning for the offensive against Leningrad in July. The staff produced three operational plans, the most important of which were a major army-size assault against Leningrad (Unternehmen *Nordlicht* or Operation *Northern Lights*) and a smaller, corps-size attack against the Oranienbaum bridgehead (Unternehmen *Bettelstab* or Operation *Beggar's Staff*). However, von Manstein's army only began trickling into the Leningrad sector in late August and would not be ready to conduct either operation until mid-September. In fact, only four divisions from the 11. Armee arrived, with the remainder going to other fronts; the splintering of this veteran army was a major mistake. After examining the *Nordlicht* plan, von Manstein was in no hurry to embark upon such a difficult mission with the limited forces available and von Küchler recognized that mounting an offensive would require him to strip all other sectors of reserves.

Soviet intelligence detected von Manstein's arrival at Leningrad and deduced that a German offensive was imminent. The Stavka had been advocating another attempt to break the siege of Leningrad and decided to expedite matters before von Manstein could strike. Meretskov's Volkhov Front was ordered to conduct a major assault from outside the siege perimeter with General-major Filipp N. Starikov's 8th Army, while Govorov's Leningrad Front mounted a breakout attack across the Neva

River. Lindemann's AOK 18 had just two divisions holding a 15km-wide sector in the Siniavino corridor and they appeared highly vulnerable to a pincer attack from east and west. Meretskov was adept at planning a set-piece attack and he ensured that Starikov's 8th Army had plenty of artillery, tanks and infantry to blast through the German front. Starikov opted for a relatively narrow, 5km penetration corridor, which enabled him to achieve a 4-1 manpower advantage and over 100 guns/mortars per kilometer at the chosen point. However, Meretskov did not fully appreciate the restrictive nature of the swampy terrain and the fact that the Germans had liberally seeded the area with mines and other obstacles. When Starikov attacked on August 27, he was only able to achieve a very narrow penetration in the German line, but he decided to start squeezing units through in the hope of achieving a breakthrough. Nor did Meretskov expect Lindemann to commit his reserves so quickly, but they deployed in time to prevent Starikov from achieving a real breakthrough. Instead, the same thing that had occurred earlier with the 2nd Shock Army on the Volkhov now occurred with the 8th Army on the Siniavino sector – the compacted Soviet units were soon virtually immobilized and running out of ammunition. Furthermore, Govorov's initial efforts to cross the Neva River failed, allowing Lindemann to shift more forces to stop Starikov. Meretskov repeated his earlier mistake and decided to feed his second echelon force, the rebuilt 2nd Shock Army (under General-leytenant Nikolai K. Klykov), into battle to assist Starikov. It is an old military maxim that one should never reinforce failure, but that is exactly what Meretskov did and the result was that the Volkhov Front offensive was halted after just five days. Although Govorov finally managed to get a small force across the Neva River, the two Soviet pincers could not close the 5km gap between the two fronts.

As usual, the German defense weathered the Soviet storm, awaiting the moment to strike an enemy that was exhausted and off-balance. By mid-September von Manstein had enough of his 11. Armee in hand to prepare a proper counteroffensive, which he kicked off on September 21. Using the tried-and-true double pincer method, von Manstein was able to encircle the bulk of Starikov's 8th Army and part of the 2 SA within four days. For good measure, von Manstein also used the 12. Panzer-Division to crush Govorov's bridgeheads across the Neva, then he turned to deal with the *Kessel*. Von Manstein lacked the superiority in numbers of firepower to quickly crush the encircled Soviet forces, so the mop-up operation required a month to complete. Starikov managed to escape the *Kessel*, but von Manstein claimed over 12,000 prisoners were taken. Although von Manstein had won a nice tactical victory, it was now too late in the season to contemplate launching *Nordlicht* and his front-line infantry units needed refitting. Thus, at the exorbitant cost of over 113,000 casualties, the Leningrad and Volkhov Fronts had spoiled German plans to try to capture Leningrad in 1942, although the probability of success for such an operation was far from certain. Amazingly, there were no repercussions for this defeat: Meretskov, Govorov, Starikov and Klykov all kept their commands.

Commander	Objective	Offensive	Mass	Maneuver	Surprise	Security	TALLY
Von Kuchler	+	o	o	o	o	+	2
Lindemann	+	o	o	o	o	+	2
Von Manstein	+	+	o	+	+	o	4
Govorov	+	+	-	+	-	-	0
Meretskov	+	+	+	-	-	-	0
Starikov	+	+	+	-	-	-	0

Leningrad, 1942 Leadership Assessment

The Soviet offensives around Orel, Rzhev, Demyansk and Leningrad reveal certain inadequacies in the practice of operational art. Foremost, the Stavka and front commanders planned attacks with very little regard for terrain and enemy dispositions – they simply assumed that the Red Army would always get through no matter what conditions were extant. Wishful thinking is not a good way to plan military operations. In particular, the Soviets repeatedly sent armies down mobility corridors in restrictive terrain that were best suited to battalions, then were dumbfounded that their spearheads became bottled up and immobilized by enemy reserves, which they failed to anticipate. Another conclusion that seems inescapable is that despite spending years in the interwar period studying how to conduct breakthrough attacks as a prerequisite for Deep Battle, the Red Army of 1941–42 struggled to actually conduct such operations. Commanders employed their artillery poorly and barely considered the use of combat multipliers such as engineer support. Nor had pre-war theories been fully validated in field exercises, which glossed over critical issues such as communications, intelligence and logistics. Instead, the Red Army of 1942 was still trying to conduct operations without adequate intelligence or logistic support and with C2 that was rudimentary and unnecessarily constrained by paranoid security rules. From the German point of view, they were well satisfied by mid-1942 that they knew how to defeat even large-scale Soviet attacks, which typically consisted of two tactical echelons but only a single operational echelon. The Germans already knew that cramming more forces into an already crowded battlefield was counterproductive, but the Red Army never really learned this lesson and would be repeating it on the Seelow Heights in 1945. However, the OKH and its intelligence department, the FHO, accepted these Soviet offensives of mid-1942 as a template for likely enemy course of action and failed to appreciate that the Red Army might be capable of changing its operational methods.

In general terms, the 1942 operations help to demonstrate several important points about the conduct of operational-level warfare. First, deception planning is critical in gaining surprise and forcing errors on the enemy commander – striking the enemy in a time and place they did not expect is a virtual prerequisite for decisive successes. Second, breakthrough battles need to be amply resourced in case a decision is not quickly reached, which is usually the case in anything but the most lopsided situations. Throughout both the First and Second World Wars, most armies planned to achieve breakthroughs quickly and then began to run short on ammunition and manpower when they did not. A third point is raised by the need to have a basic understanding of the enemy, particularly how they are likely to use their reserves to counter friendly moves. Ignoring likely enemy responses usually ends up in disasters like Kharkov in 1942.

Deadlock on the Eastern Front, October–November 1942

On October 14, Hitler ordered all offensive operations on the Eastern Front suspended, except for Stalingrad and the Caucasus. Hitler recognized that *Fall Blau* had not gone as anticipated but kept hoping that Paulus could finish Soviet resistance in Stalingrad with just one more push. He was less sanguine about the Caucasus, which had clearly become a stalemate. Removing List from command of Heeresgruppe A had not changed the unfavorable equation and any success at Stalingrad would not balance the failure to accomplish the main goal of *Blau* – seizing the primary oil fields in the Caucasus. Consequently, Hitler's relations with his primary military advisors deteriorated sharply during the autumn of 1942, with Halder dismissed and Jodl ignored. As a result of growing dysfunction in the FHQ, the field commanders were not getting adequate guidance, so they simply continued to try to achieve their assigned missions, which were no longer achievable.

Paulus kept pounding away at Stalingrad, choosing to fight a tactical battle of attrition which exhausted the 6. Armee but failed to achieve a decisive success. Paulus and Hoth suffered over 50,000 casualties in the fighting in Stalingrad but Hitler and the OKH failed to provide them with any significant reinforcements. By mid-November 1942, the 6. Armee was overextended, poorly supplied and its flanks were protected by inadequately-equipped Romanian troops – it was a recipe for disaster. The protracted defense of Stalingrad by Chuikov's 62nd Army set the stage for the Red Army's eventual victory in the campaign. The only really positive result the Germans achieved at Stalingrad was that the VIII Fliegerkorps inflicted crippling 8-1 losses on the VVS in the air battles over the city, which prevented the Red Army from regaining the initiative as long as the weather was fair. Eremenko was forced by the Stavka to mount repeated counteroffensives around Kotluban, each of which was defeated in turn. At the operational level, the Soviet conduct of the defensive phase at Stalingrad was noteworthy for injecting reinforcements at critical moments but should be faulted for its utter lack of imagination. Soviet intelligence failed to appreciate the 6. Armee's serious logistic problems, which proved to be Paulus' Achilles heel. Indeed, the biggest problem facing the 6. Armee was the delay in rebuilding the railroad bridge over the Don at Rychkovskaya, 28km south of Kalach; until this bridge was repaired in the spring, the 6. Armee's logistic situation would remain unfavorable.[52] Had Eremenko made greater efforts to attack the long, vulnerable lines of communication to Stalingrad, including bridge repair units at the Don, the 6. Armee would have suffered greater harm than it did from mindless frontal attacks at Kotluban.

In the Caucasus, Ruoff continued to slowly push toward Tuapse with the bulk of AOK 17, before finally being halted by Soviet resistance and winter weather by October 23. It also looked like von Kleist's offensive had run its course, but it became briefly re-energized in late October when German intelligence discovered a weakness in the Soviet defenses on the Terek front. Maslennikov had put most of his effort into strengthening General-major Konstantin A. Koroteev's 9th Army to block the direct route to Grozny, but General-major Petr M. Kozlov's 37th Army was exposed. On October 25, von Kleist launched a surprise attack against the 37th Army, beginning with a Luftwaffe air strike on Kozlov's headquarters, which disrupted Soviet C2. Then von Kleist launched a clever pincer attack with two Panzer divisions and a Romanian mountain division which isolated three of Kozlov's divisions. After crushing these encircled units, von Kleist's Panzers pivoted south and struck for the city of Ordzhonikidze; von Kleist knew that he could not reach Grozny, but if he could take the road net around this city it would make it much more difficult for Maslennikov to mount a winter offensive. Initially, the German attack went well, aided by fair weather and Luftwaffe support, enabling the 13. Panzer-Division to reach the outskirts of Ordzhonikidze. However, the onset of rainy weather and increased Soviet resistance halted the German advance. Then Maslennikov organized a counterattack on November 6 which succeeded in encircling the 13. Panzer-Division. For five days Maslennikov's forces pounded the hapless division until its survivors managed to conduct a successful breakout, albeit after leaving most of their vehicles behind. Thus, the final German offensive spasm in the Caucasus resulted in a disaster which substantially weakened von Kleist's PzAOK 1.

As the German offensives waned, the Stavka began to consider its options for the upcoming winter season. During the period September 12–28, 1942, the Stavka and GKO deliberated on where to make the Red Army's main effort in the next round of offensives. Initially, the key players in this debate were Zhukov, Vasilevsky and Vatutin. Zhukov, whom Stalin had recently made deputy commander in chief of the Red Army, favored a pincer offensive by the Kalinin and Western Fronts against the 9. Armee in the Rzhev salient. He claimed that the Rzhev offensive in August had nearly succeeded and that a second attempt with larger forces would lead to the collapse of Heeresgruppe Mitte. As for Stalingrad, Zhukov recommended more offensives to pound away at 6. Armee's flanks, but not anything radically different from previous operations. However, Eremenko arrived in Moscow on October 6 for planning meetings and suggested a new approach. Instead of repeating the same unsuccessful methods used in the previous three Kotluban offensives, he recommended a broad envelopment, with powerful strike groups to break through the Romanian armies on the flanks, then converging on Kalach to isolate the 6. Armee. Eremenko argued that Rokossovsky's Don Front could use its bridgehead over the Don in the Kremenskaya sector to attack the Romanian 3rd Army, while the Stalingrad Front's 51st and 57th Armies could attack the mixed German-Romanian force south of the city. He pointed out that the enemy was less likely to expect a major attack in these relatively quiet sectors and that consequently, fewer mobile reserves were likely to be nearby. Furthermore, the idea of attacking less-capable Romanian units was also appealing.[53] Stalin took an interest in Eremenko's concept, so the Stavka began refining the concept into an operational plan.

Zhukov was less impressed by the concept and simply ordered Eremenko to keep pounding on the 6. Armee in the Kotluban sector; on October 15 he issued a directive for another attack in the same area as before. Rokossovsky's Don Front was provided several fresh rifle divisions and was ordered to attack again in the Kotluban sector. Not surprisingly, the Fourth Kotluban offensive was another failure, which squandered Soviet lives and equipment, for negligible gain.

Sensing that Stalin favored Eremenko's concept, Zhukov and the rest of the Stavka decided to endorse the idea that the Red Army was now powerful enough to launch two near-simultaneous major winter counteroffensives, one at Rzhev and one at Stalingrad. The Rzhev offensive was designated as Operation *Mars*, while the Stalingrad offensive was designated as Operation *Uranus*. Zhukov and General-polkovnik Aleksandr M. Vasilevsky, chief of the Soviet General Staff, personally oversaw the planning for both *Mars* and *Uranus*. As the Stavka transformed Operation *Uranus* from a concept into a plan, measures were taken to prepare for the offensive. In late October, a new Southwestern Front was created in order to spearhead the offensive and General-leytenant Nikolai F. Vatutin was brought in to lead this formation. Vatutin was provided with the 1st Guards Army (1 GA) and the rebuilt 5 TA, both led by veteran commanders (Lelyushenko and Romanenko). Furthermore, the Stavka began planning two follow-on operations, named *Jupiter* and *Saturn*, intended to exploit any success achieved by *Mars* and *Uranus*. Initially, *Mars* and *Uranus* were expected to begin by late October but were twice delayed due to logistic problems and slipped to late November.

Operation *Uranus* was planned as a double envelopment, with formations attacking in a single echelon. Although Soviet doctrine preferred to conduct a major offensive with at least two operational echelons of assault forces to ensure success, the Red Army in November 1942 lacked the resources to execute *Uranus* in this fashion. Vatutin's Southwestern Front was designated as the main effort in Operation *Uranus*, forming the western pincer with its 1 GA, 5 TA and 21st Army, which were expected to break through the Romanian 3rd Army, advance 120–140 kilometers and reach Kalach on the Don within three days. Vatutin's forces were mainly drawn from the Stavka reserve (RVGK) and were in good condition. He was also assigned some of the better staff officers available, including General-major Grigory D. Stelmakh, a veteran of the fighting on the Volkhov Front. The Stavka expected Vatutin's forces to maintain a high operations tempo, advancing about 40–45 kilometers per day – a feat no previous Red Army offensive had achieved. Rokossovsky's Don Front would mount a supporting attack, using three armies (24, 65, 66) to pin down the 6. Armee's left flank and preventing Paulus from shifting forces to block Vatutin's pincer. Eremenko's Stalingrad Front would form the eastern pincer with shock groups from three armies (51, 57, 64), which had to advance 100 kilometers to link up with Vatutin's pincers near Kalach. Since the eastern pincer had less distance to cover, it would launch its attack one day later than the Southwestern Front. Eremenko also had to maintain the 62nd Army's defensive front in Stalingrad, which was under continuous attack until just a few days before Uranus began. Thanks to careful concentration of forces, the Red Army achieved a numerical superiority of 3-1 or better in terms of troops, tanks and artillery in the chosen attack sectors, thereby setting the stage for successful breakthrough battles. Unlike most other Soviet offensives of 1942, Vatutin, Eremenko and Rokossovsky put great emphasis upon the use of *maskirovka* (deception), which helped to deceive the Germans about the timing and location of the offensive, in order to achieve operational-level surprise. By mid-November enough fuel and ammunition had been moved forward to provide sufficient reserves to begin the offensive, but Uranus would commence with just 3–6 days of ammunition and ten days of diesel fuel on hand. The Southwestern Front's shock armies were the best supplied, whereas the Stalingrad Front's strike forces had to make do with barely enough supplies to reach Kalach.

On the Axis side, the Germans knew that the Red Army was likely to launch one or more winter counteroffensives to try to retake ground lost during the summer months, but they misjudged where this might occur. Oberst Reinhard Gehlen's Fremde Heere Ost (FHO or Foreign Armies East), the intelligence department within the OKH, was responsible for assessing likely enemy courses of action. Gehlen concluded that the Soviets were most likely to launch their main winter counteroffensive against Heeresgruppe Mitte, targeting either the 9. Armee in the Rzhev salient or 2. Panzerarmee in the Orel sector. While Gehlen's intelligence estimate of November 18 noted that aerial reconnaissance and signals intercepts had detected Soviet reinforcements moving more forces into the bridgeheads opposite the Romanian 3rd Army, he did not assess this as a major threat. In fact, German reconnaissance completely failed to detect the presence of the 5th Tank Army near the Don bridgeheads. Consequently, Gehlen's anodyne assessment issued only a vague warning that the Soviets might make a limited-scale offensive either west or south of Stalingrad, but not in both places. Gehlen assumed that since earlier Soviet counteroffensives against 6. Armee had been contained, any future enemy offensive could also be dealt with in similar fashion.[54]

As a result of Gehlen's erroneous intelligence estimate, the OKH positioned nine of its 19 Panzer divisions with over half the operational armor in the Heeresgruppe Mitte sector. Heeresgruppe B was left with only one-quarter of available German armor, virtually all of it in close proximity to Stalingrad.

Despite Gehlen's overconfident intelligence assessment, Hitler was not blind to the possibility that the Soviets might attempt to attack the Romanian-held sectors. At one of his daily conferences at *Werwolf* in Vinnitsa on October 26, Hitler directed that three divisions in France, including the rebuilt 6. Panzer-Division, should be sent to reinforce the Romanian sector. However, the OKH staff did not make this a priority and the divisions did not arrive until after Operation *Uranus* had already begun. At von Weichs' Heeresgruppe B headquarters near Starobelsk, there was growing apprehension about the Don Front, but little energy expended to alter the situation. General Petre Dumitrescu, commander of the Romanian 3rd Army, was particularly nervous about the ability of his command to withstand a major Soviet attack. He requested additional antitank guns and antitank mines, so Heeresgruppe B provided him token amounts and assigned Generalleutnant Ferdinand Heim's XXXXVIII Panzerkorps from 4. Panzerarmee to serve as a mobile reserve behind the Romanian 3rd Army.* In the event of an enemy breakthrough in the Romanian sector, Heim was expected to counterattack with his corps, even though von Weichs knew that this formation had very limited combat value. Just prior to the start of *Uranus*, von Weichs also advised Paulus to form a mobile reserve with his three Panzer divisions, but he ended up keeping most of his armor close to the city. Nor did Paulus develop robust contingency plans to respond to any major enemy offensives on his extended flanks.

Zhukov's attention was split between his duties as deputy supreme commander, the ongoing Stalingrad situation and planning for Operation *Mars* against the Rzhev Salient. His basic operational concept was to conduct a double pincer attack to cut off the 9. Armee, with Purkaev's Kalinin Front attacking the western side of the salient with two armies (22, 41) while Konev's Western Front attacked the eastern side with one heavily reinforced army (20). Zhukov would essentially serve as a front-level coordinator and he ensured Operation *Mars* received the best

---

*In mid-November, the Panzerkorps consisted of the incomplete 22. Panzer-Division, the Romanian 1st Armored Division, a Romanian cavalry division and a German motorized *Kampfgruppe*.

available reserves from the RVGK, including the first of the new artillery divisions. He was very confident of victory but he put minimal effort into *maskirovka* or assessing the enemy defenses and terrain in this sector of the front. Like most of the Stavka, Zhukov approached warfare with a mathematical mindset, assuming that with enough artillery, infantry and tanks, enemy resistance would simply collapse. Prevailing Soviet military theory, influenced by Marxist-Leninist principles, attached very little importance to the moral dimension of combat, which led to unrealistic operational assumptions.

As it was, the German 9. Armee detected the preparations for Operation *Mars*. Four weeks before the operation began, Model's intelligence officer (Ic) accurately assessed that the Soviet Kalinin and Western Fronts were preparing to mount a major pincer attack against the Rzhev salient and was even able to specify in which sectors the enemy would make their main effort. For once, German intelligence not only got it right but served a commander who heeded their warning. In contrast to the evident inertia in Heeresgruppe B, Model acted quickly to reinforce the threatened sectors by building a double line of bunkers, laying more mines and repositioning three Panzer divisions as operational reserves. Model strongly believed in *Anschauen* (personal inspection) to verify that subunit commanders perfected their sector defenses and had sufficient resources to ensure mission success. He took the time to meet each of his front-line battalion commanders and to study the key terrain in their sectors. Model also believed in *Vorhalten* (prior planning) and he coordinated with von Kluge to develop contingency plans to receive additional Panzer divisions from army group reserves, if necessary. He also worked with his army-level artillery commander, Generalmajor Max Lindig (HArko 307), to refine fire support plans so that front-line commanders would receive timely final protective fires. Model was a very energetic, hands-on commander who spared no effort to provide his command with every possible combat advantage.

In the Kremlin, the Stavka boldly envisioned the hammer blows of *Uranus* and *Saturn* leading to the collapse of the German front in southern Russia and setting the conditions for the Red Army to advance to liberate Rostov. If *Mars* and *Jupiter* succeeded in the north as well, the Ostheer would be unable to repair two major ruptures in its front, leading to a strategic defeat. One week before Operation *Uranus* began, Hitler decided to leave dreary Vinnitsa and return to Berchtesgaden for a brief holiday, assuming that the Soviets would not launch any offensives until December.

Decision in Southern Russia,
November–December 1942

The Stavka had concentrated 1 million troops in ten armies to participate in Operation *Uranus* – one-sixth of the Red Army's total field strength. Vatutin, Rokossovsky and Eremenko, with Vasilevsky serving as Stavka coordinator, organized their assault armies to conduct a Deep Battle style of operation, in order to shatter the enemy front then advance far into their rear areas – a type of operation the Red Army had not yet successfully accomplished.[55] The three fronts had plenty of armor – over 1,500 tanks – but only half of it was comprised of T-34 medium tanks; Soviet industry was still struggling to replace combat losses and large numbers of light tanks were used to fill out the tank corps. Operation *Uranus* would also enjoy considerably more artillery support than previous Red Army offensives, including two of the new artillery divisions.[56] The Red Army was also learning to use its artillery differently. General-polkovnik Nikolai N. Voronov, commander-in-chief of the Red Army's artillery and a Stavka representative, closely supervised the development of the artillery fire support plans for Operation *Uranus*. The Red Army's artillery arm of late 1942 was capable of massive – although not particularly accurate or responsive – fire support.

In the forward positions of the Romanian 3rd Army, the troops knew several days prior that an enemy offensive was imminent, due to aggressive Soviet probing activity. Heeresgruppe B was informed, but simply agreed to move a few more small German battlegroups closer to the threatened sector. On the morning of November 19, the weather was vile, with freezing cold, heavy ground fog and snow showers, which reduced visibility to just 200 meters. Nevertheless, at 0730 hours the Southwestern Front and Don Front began an 80-minute artillery preparation against the enemy positions. Obscuration rendered the bombardment largely ineffective, but Romanenko's 5 TA surged forward anyway against the center of the Romanian line while General-major Ivan M. Chistiakov's 21st Army attacked the Romanian right flank. Simultaneously, Rokossovsky's Don Front attacked the boundary between the Romanians and the left flank of 6. Armee with General-leytenant Pavel I. Batov's 65th Army. Surprisingly, the Romanian front bent, but did not immediately break under the Soviet onslaught. General Dumitrescu immediately requested assistance, but Heeresgruppe B was unusually slow to react, waiting three hours before finally sending Heim's small Panzerkorps forward. It was soon apparent that Heeresgruppe B had been negligent in coordinating its contingency plans with the Romanians, since Heim's mixed German-Romanian XXXXVIII Panzerkorps was short of fuel and could not even reach the battlefield as a unified formation. While the Axis were fumbling to react, Vatutin ordered Romanenko to commit the rest of his armor in the afternoon and achieved a major breakthrough, but only advanced 10 kilometers before nightfall. Chistiakov's 21st Army achieved more success in its sector, breaking out of the Kletskaya bridgehead and sending the 4th Tank Corps to advance over 20 kilometers. The Don Front's supporting attack by Batov's 65th Army was unsuccessful, since it was blocked by strong German units from the XI Armeekorps in its sector. Late in the day, the weather cleared up a bit and the VIII Fliegerkorps was able to destroy 11 pontoon bridges over the Don, but this did little to stop the Soviet armor from crashing through the Romanian front lines. Instead of striking the Soviet spearheads with a concentrated force, Heim's mixed Panzerkorps stumbled into action, with vehicles short of fuel and the German and Romanian subunits unable to coordinate with each other. Consequently, by the end of the first day of *Uranus*, the Romanian 3rd Army's front was broken in two sectors and the Axis tactical reserves were unable to reverse the situation. Nor were any significant Axis operational reserves nearby. Yet Vatutin's gains were still well short of what the Stavka had expected for the first day of the offensive and the Romanian 3rd Army was still resisting fiercely in some areas.

At the 6. Armee headquarters north of Kalach, Paulus was not unduly alarmed by initial reports about the Soviet offensive and he expected Heim's Panzerkorps to seal any breach in the Romanian front. Nevertheless, he eventually decided to transfer part of Generalleutnant Hans-Valentin Hube's XIV Panzerkorps to protect his line of communications. His chief of staff, Generalleutnant Arthur Schmidt, was upbeat about the situation and expected that the Panzers would soon defeat the enemy breakthrough.[57] However, due to fuel shortages and the difficulty of pulling Panzer units out of the fight in Stalingrad, this transfer would take two days to accomplish – which proved far too long on a fluid battlefield. As the reports grew increasingly alarming, Paulus slipped into a passive, indecisive mood, leaving Schmidt to run operations.

While the Axis leaders struggled to mitigate the attacks by the Southwest and Don Fronts, Eremenko began his part of the offensive on the morning of November 20. Hoth was responsible for protecting the Axis flank southeast of Stalingrad, but his PzAOK 4 had been reduced to just two German infantry divisions and seven Romanian divisions. The full-strength 29. Infanterie-Division (mot.) was also in Hoth's sector but it was under control of the army group, not PzAOK 4. The Stalingrad Front attacked with three armies on-line in staggered fashion, with General-major Nikolai I. Trufanov's 51st Army attacking first. Trufanov's shock groups quickly shattered the Romanian division in his sector, but he was slow to commit his exploitation force, the 4th Mechanized Corps. On Trufanov's right, Tolbukhin's 57th Army achieved a clean breakthrough and forced most of the Romanian 2nd Infantry Division to surrender, then committed its 13th Tank Corps (13 TC) into the gap.[58] Shumilov's 64th Army failed to achieve a breakthrough against Hoth's German divisions, but his efforts served to pin down those units. Unlike Paulus, Hoth acted with great alacrity. Without asking permission from higher headquarters, he took control of the 29. Infanterie-Division (mot.) and ordered it to launch an immediate counterattack to stop the enemy breakthrough. On the face of it, a veteran, full-strength division should have made mincemeat of Tolbukhin's spearhead, the 13 TC, but instead this counterattack proved remarkably ineffectual because it had difficulty identifying the enemy in conditions of low visibility. Instead of landing a solid blow, the Panzers simply skirmished with Tolbukhin's flank guards and missed the main exploitation force, which glided past to the west.[59]

In Berchtesgaden, Hitler was belatedly informed by Gehlen's FHO that the previously undetected 5th Tank Army was leading the Soviet offensive out of the Don River bridgeheads.[60] Hitler recognized the threat to Heeresgruppe B but doubted that von Weichs could handle a real crisis. Consequently, on the evening of November 20 he ordered Generalfeldmarschall Erich von Manstein (who was currently in Vitebsk with his 11. Armee staff) to proceed south to Rostov and once there to form Heeresgruppe Don. Hitler directed that the 6. Armee, Hoth's forces and the remaining Romanian units would all fall under von Manstein's command.[61] Other divisions, *en route* from Western Europe and elsewhere, would be provided to von Manstein as they arrived. Hitler had great faith in von Manstein's ability to complete difficult tasks, although the herculean scale of this current mission was not yet apparent. Meanwhile, Paulus struggled to shift Hube's XIV Panzerkorps west of the Don, but suddenly the 6. Armee found itself with insufficient fuel reserves to conduct large-scale operational maneuvers. During the long months of static urban combat in Stalingrad, German quartermasters had prioritized ammunition deliveries to the 6. Armee, at the expense of fuel.[62] Apparently the 6. Armee's chief of staff, Schmidt, and the operations officer (Oberst Hans-Heinrich Elchlepp) were not fully aware of these logistic constraints – a key failure in staff planning. It was the job of

General Staff officers to know logistic details and Paulus himself had been Oberquartiermeister in the OKH – there really was no excuse for this kind of oversight or failure to anticipate. Although one *Kampfgruppe* from the 24. Panzer-Division crossed the Don to support the vulnerable left flank of the 6. Armee, the rest of Hube's forces were still east of the river. At Heeresgruppe B, General der Infanterie Georg von Sodenstern, chief of staff, told Schmidt that "we have nothing to stop them with. You've got to help yourselves."[63] In the Romanian 3rd Army sector, four divisions (including the Romanian 1st Armored Division) in Group Lascar had been isolated by Vatutin's armored spearheads, but the rest of the broken army was falling back towards the Chir River. Heim's XXXXVIII Panzerkorps could not stop the avalanche with half of a Panzer division and it too fell back. Enraged by the failure to stop Vatutin's breakthrough, Hitler ordered Heim's arrest on November 26.[64]

Paulus made two mistakes that helped shape the outcome of the campaign. First, he ordered the formations on his left and right flanks to "refuse their flanks" (i.e. bending their lines back at an angle), which is a standard military response to an attempted enemy envelopment. However, by giving up terrain without a fight, the 6. Armee was unwittingly helping the enemy to expand their breaches. Second, Paulus decided to relocate his headquarters further south on the afternoon of November 21, which made it seem to Hitler that he was leaving his army in the lurch. When he learned of this move, Hitler angrily ordered Paulus and staff to fly back to Stalingrad and set up a headquarters near Gumrak Airfield.[65] Stung by accusations of cowardice and abandoning his army in a crisis, Paulus resolved to rigidly follow orders thereafter, which effectively scuttled any hopes for him exercising independent command. The weak officer, in a crisis, becomes an automaton – the same thing that happened to so many Soviet commanders in 1941. On the Soviet side, events moved very rapidly as Vatutin, Rokossovsky and Eremenko rushed to exploit the collapse of the Axis flanks. On the morning of November 22, the 26th Tank Corps from 5 TA captured Kalach on the Don with a coup de main, thereby severing the 6. Armee's ground line of communications. The next afternoon, the armored spearheads from the Southwestern and Stalingrad Fronts linked up near Kalach, thereby completing the encirclement of the 6. Armee and part of 4. Panzerarmee in Stalingrad. In order to stop further Soviet expansion south, von Weichs put General der Infanterie Karl-Adolf Hollidt in charge of organizing a new Axis front along the Chir, which was asking nothing short of a miracle; the result was the creation of Gruppe Hollidt, which eventually became Armee-Abteilung Hollidt.[66]

Although the Red Army had achieved a great victory with Operation *Uranus*, its leaders made some poor operational choices in the immediate aftermath of the encirclement; these poor choices were influenced by the lack of hard intelligence about enemy reserves. Instead of focusing on trying to prevent the Axis from forming a new line on the Chir River, the Southwestern, Don and Stalingrad Fronts committed their best units to try to reduce the 6. Armee's perimeter. Vasilevsky and the Stavka were concerned that 6. Armee might either break out of the pocket or the Germans might mount a successful relief effort, so reduction of the Stalingrad pocket became the priority. Vasilevsky quickly developed a plan to crush the encircled Axis forces, which were estimated to comprise about 85,000–90,000 troops.[67] Vatutin was ordered to transfer Chistiakov's 21st Army to Rokossovsky's Don Front, which seriously reduced the forces heading toward the Chir River. Instead, the primary mobile units (4 Mechanized Corps, 4 Tank Corps, 26 Tank Corps, 3 Guards Cavalry Corps) were committed against the west side of the pocket, but without adequate artillery or infantry support. In fact, Soviet intelligence estimates seriously underestimated the 6. Armee, which was three times stronger than expected and still was well-armed. Furthermore, Paulus deployed some of his best units in the Marinovka sector and had sufficient time to lay mines and create obstacles. Consequently, when Rokossovsky's forces began attacking the outer edge of the pocket on November 24, they attacked with less than a 2-1 numerical advantage and suffered heavy losses. Vasilevsky also directed the Southwest Front to continuing spreading out southward, to complicate any German plans for a relief operation. Yet Romanenko's 5 Tank Army, which was assigned to bounce the Chir River, had already lost or transferred most of its armor to support the attack on the Stalingrad pocket. By the time that Romanenko's army reached the Chir River on November 30, he had only one brigade of tanks and had to rely primarily upon infantry units to try to break the thin Axis line.[68] It was not enough.

Once it was clear the Axis forces in Stalingrad were encircled, everyone assumed that Hitler would order the 6. Armee to conduct a breakout operation. The Soviet Stavka and front commanders expected it and began to redeploy their forces to contain a breakout. Paulus and von Weichs expected it and directed their staffs to begin planning for a breakout operation on November 24.[69] At this point, there was only a thin cordon of Soviet forces blocking the escape route. For a brief moment, after the land telephone lines were cut by the Soviets, Paulus had the opportunity to act independently of Hitler and the OKH, but he proved indecisive in the hour of crisis. As it turned out, Hitler had no intention of retreating from Stalingrad because he felt the enemy breakthrough was a temporary setback but a chaotic retreat would be regarded as a major defeat. From the start of the Stalingrad crisis, Hitler grasped for any straw, any miracle, which might avoid a humiliating defeat. While still at Berchtesgaden, Hitler asked Generaloberst Hans Jeschonnek, Luftwaffe chief of staff, if the Luftwaffe could supply the 6. Armee by air. Without putting any real thought into the matter, Jeschonnek thought an airlift was feasible. Two days later, Reichsmarschall Hermann Göring arrived at Berchtesgaden and confirmed that his Luftwaffe could supply the 6. Armee by air; indeed, he promised the delivery of 500 tons per day.[70] The 6. Armee quartermaster claimed that 500 tons per day (including 200 tons of ammunition and 221 tons of fuel) would suffice, which translated to about 250 transport sorties per day.[71] Buoyed by these optimistic assurances, Hitler convinced himself that an airlift would enable 6. Armee to survive until von Manstein's relief effort began. Generalleutnant Martin Fiebig, commander of the VIII Fliegerkorps, had already told Paulus on November 21 that the Luftwaffe did not have enough aircraft to supply 6. Armee by air. Unaware of Hitler's reasoning, at 2345 hours on November 23, Paulus sent a radio signal to the OKW, requesting "freedom of action," which meant permission to conduct a breakout.[72] Early the next morning, Hitler sent a signal to Paulus, informing him that 6. Armee was to hold its position and would be supplied by air until von Manstein restored ground communications.[73] On November 24, the Luftwaffe airlift to Stalingrad began, but only delivered 86 tons of supplies.

After a rather leisurely train ride, Von Manstein and his staff finally arrived in Rostov on November 26, so planning for a relief operation did not even begin until then. Von Manstein's staff was a veteran lot, including Generalmajor Friedrich Schulz as his chief of staff and Oberst Theodore Busse as his operations officer (Ia) and they had already served together through the successful Crimean and Leningrad campaigns. Von Manstein's staff was able to quickly devise a relief plan, designated *Wintergewitter* (Operation *Winter Storm*), but no forces were immediately available to conduct it. The basic concept was to launch a double pincer attack, using the XXXXVIII Panzerkorps from the Chir River and the LVII Panzerkorps from Kotelnikovo rail station in the south. Hitler promised to provide up to nine divisions for *Wintergewitter*, but transport delays wasted two precious weeks.[74] Although assessed as very high risk, the plan appeared feasible in early December, but success was dependent on two key assumptions: first, that the requisite Panzer divisions could be assembled quickly and second, that the Red Army would not pull any more major operational surprises. Both planning assumptions proved false.

In the interim, Romanenko tried to smash through Hollidt's improvised defenses on the Chir, which greatly stressed Heeresgruppe Don. It was fortunate for Hollidt that Romanenko's vanguard units were low on fuel reserves, which deprived them of mobility at a key moment. Grabbing any personnel that were handy, Hollidt did a masterful job organizing *ad hoc Kampfgruppen* to hold key positions, which slowed down Romanenko's 5 TA until more substantial German reinforcements could arrive. The arrival of the fresh 11. Panzer-Division from Heeresgruppe Mitte gave the anemic XXXXVIII Panzerkorps the means to stabilize the situation on the Chir River, which forced the Stavka to commit General-leytenant Markian M. Popov's 5th Shock Army (5 SA) to reinforce Romanenko on December 12.[75] However, Vatutin was preparing to begin his follow-on offensive, *Saturn*, so he could not afford to sustain a protracted fight on the Chir River. The Battle of the Chir River ended up frustrating both sides. Since the XXXXVIII Panzerkorps was literally fighting for its survival it could not participate in *Wintergewitter*, which meant that von Manstein was forced to modify the relief operation into a single thrust by Hoth's forces.[76] For the Soviets, Vasilevsky was forced to divert resources from Operation *Saturn* to reinforce partial success on the Chir front and keep the pressure on Heeresgruppe Don.

Armeegruppe Hoth, now the only formation assigned to *Wintergewitter*, consisted of the LVII Panzerkorps (6. and 23. Panzer-Divisions), and two Romanian corps. The 17. Panzer-Division was supposed to join the operation, but von Weichs proved reluctant to transfer it and tried to keep the division as an operational reserve around Millerovo. Even then, it took until December 10 before Hoth could assemble even two combat-ready Panzer divisions. Hoth preferred to delay the attack until more reinforcements arrived, but von Manstein realized that the situation was slipping past the point of no return and ordered Hoth to commence the operation on December 12 with the forces in hand. Von Manstein was not only concerned about Soviet attacks along the Chir River, but the evident failure of the Luftwaffe airlift to provide adequate supplies to the 6. Armee. Despite Göring's promises, the Luftwaffe was unable to meet the 6. Armee's logistic requirements, which meant that the German forces in the pocket were rapidly losing their combat effectiveness. In order for *Wintergewitter* to have any chance of success, the 6. Armee still had to possess the capability to conduct a breakout attack to meet the relief force.

At dawn on December 12, Hoth commenced *Wintergewitter*. The weather was cold, but skies were clear and visibility excellent. The 6. Panzer-Division, with 141 tanks, was the *Schwerpunkt*, pushing up the rail line, striking the center of Trufanov's 51st Army. Thanks to clear skies, the Luftwaffe was able to provide Hoth with close air support sorties. The VVS, fully committed to reducing the Stalingrad pocket, provided no sorties to Trufanov's 51st Army. Under these favorable conditions, Hoth was able to advance about 20 kilometers on the first day of *Wintergewitter* and inflict serious losses on Trufanov's 51st Army. Eremenko reacted to *Wintergewitter* by moving the 4 MC and 13 TC to establish blocking positions along the most likely enemy avenues of approach.[77] On December 13, Hoth's Panzer spearhead unexpectedly encountered the Soviet 4 MC at Verkhne Kumski; the meeting engagement escalated into a five-day tank battle as Eremenko fed more reserves into the fight. Both sides suffered heavy casualties at Verkhne Kumski. Concerned by Hoth's advance, Stalin made several decisions which had a profound effect on the campaign. First, he ordered General-leytenant Rodion I. Malinovsky's 2nd Guards Army (2 GA), which had been held back for use in the upcoming Operation *Saturn*, transferred to backstop Trufanov's 51st Army.[78] As a result, Operation *Saturn* was reduced in scale to Operation *Little Saturn*. Second, Stalin ordered the 7th Tank Corps transferred from Popov's 5 SA to reinforce Trufanov, which deprived Popov of his best strike unit just as he was winning on the Chir. Finally, Stalin ordered Eremenko to postpone the reduction of 6. Armee and focus on defeating Hoth's forces. Anxiety that somehow the Germans might deprive him of his triumph at Stalingrad caused Stalin to interfere with operations that were all on the verge of achieving decisive success. On the other side, Heeresgruppe B finally released the 17. Panzer-Division, but it would take four days before it could join Hoth's forces.

As a result of the Soviet delaying action at Verkhne Kumski, any prospects for success in *Wintergewitter* rapidly evaporated.[79] Nevertheless, Hoth attacked again on December 19 and gained a crossing over the Myshkova River – only 50 kilometers from the Stalingrad pocket – only to find that Malinovsky's 2 GA had already arrived to block any further advance. Indeed, the Soviets were quickly able to mass a force that was three times larger than Hoth's relief effort, which reduced *Wintergewitter* to a futile gesture. At this point, von Manstein realized that Hoth was unlikely to reach Stalingrad with his depleted forces and his long vulnerable flanks protected by weak Romanian screening forces. On the evening of December 19, von Manstein sent an order via radio to Paulus, directing the 6. Armee to begin a breakout attack, dubbed *Donnerschlag* (Thunderclap), as soon as possible.[80] However, Paulus demurred, making no decision at all, primarily because Hitler had not authorized a breakout operation. Nor did Paulus believe that 6. Armee had sufficient remaining combat power to conduct a successful breakout; he expected it to be a disaster. Paulus thought some troops might escape, but all of the 6. Armee's equipment and most of its personnel would be lost and he would be blamed for an unauthorized withdrawal that resulted in catastrophe. The lack of moral courage demonstrated by Paulus at Stalingrad – in complete contrast to other encircled German commanders – is appalling. Von Manstein continued to press Paulus for the next four days to mount a breakout, but nothing happened. All the while, the Soviet 51st Army and 2 GA mounted attacks against Hoth's small bridgehead over the Myshkova, inflicting losses and threatening to smash in the thinly held flanks, but Hitler would not allow Hoth to withdraw from this exposed position.[81] By December 23, it was clear that 6. Armee was beyond saving and after one last fruitless appeal to Paulus, von Manstein quietly called off *Wintergewitter*.

The next morning, Eremenko's Stalingrad Front launched its own Kotelnikovo offensive, with two rifle corps from Malinovsky's 2 GA attacking across the Myshkova River. Outnumbered more than 8-1 in tanks and manpower, the LVII Panzerkorps was quickly forced back. Once across the Myshkova, Malinovsky began committing his armor (7 TC, 2 GMC), which together possessed over 300 tanks. The 51st Army attacked Hoth's right flank with infantry and the 3 GMC. Under heavy pressure, Hoth conducted a fighting withdrawal to the Aksay River, suffering heavy losses along the way. On Christmas Day, the Soviets continued their offensive, striking both the Romanian corps protecting Hoth's flanks, which quickly crumbled. Eremenko then committed General-mayor Semyon I. Bogdanov's fresh 6th Mechanized Corps with 200 tanks to strike the center of the LVII Panzerkorps. After heavy fighting, the LVII Panzerkorps abandoned its positions on the Aksay River on the night of December 26/27 and fell back south along the rail line. Hoth's forces were too depleted to hold Kotelnikovo, which was captured by Soviet tanks on the evening of December 29. Although Hoth's forces escaped encirclement, both his Panzer divisions had been decimated and were no longer really combat effective. Altogether, Hoth's forces suffered about 15,000 casualties in *Wintergewitter* and lost over 200 tanks. Furthermore, the inability of Hoth's weakened forces to stop the Stalingrad Front's push down the rail line meant that Heeresgruppe A in the Caucasus was now at serious risk of being outflanked and isolated. Reluctantly, Hitler acknowledged that the failure of *Wintergewitter* meant not only the loss of 6. Armee, but that Heeresgruppe A must withdraw from the Caucasus at once.[82] Eremenko's offensive had achieved both an operational and a strategic-level victory.

Meanwhile, since early November, Vasilevsky and his staff had been planning Operation *Saturn* as a follow-on offensive, which would commence after Operation *Uranus* encircled the 6. Armee. *Saturn* was designed as a two-phase operation. In the first phase, two guards armies from Vatutin's Southwestern Front were tasked with demolishing the Italian 8th Army along the Don while the 5th Tank Army completed the destruction of the 3rd Romanian Army and Armee-Abteilung Hollidt. In phase two, Vatutin would commit the fresh 2 GA to exploit the rupture in the Axis front by advancing up to 250 kilometers and thereby set the stage for the liberation of Rostov. Vatutin was provided plentiful resources to conduct *Saturn*, which was intended to demolish the Axis position in southern Russia. On December 8, Lelyushenko's 1 GA was re-designated as the 3rd Guards Army (3 GA) and General-leytenant Vasily I. Kuznetsov took command of the new 1st Guards Army. Kuznetsov's 1 GA was formed as a powerful strike force, comprising four tank corps (17, 18, 24, 25) and nine rifle divisions. Lelyushenko's 3 GA comprised the 1 GMC and seven rifle divisions. Romanenko's 5 TA would also participate in a supporting role for *Saturn*, along with the 6th Army from the Voronezh Front. Altogether, Vatutin would command over 370,000 troops and 1,170 tanks, providing him with a large numerical superiority over the opposing Axis forces.[83]

However, enemy actions began to affect the forces available for *Saturn*. Romanenko's 5 TA suffered heavier-than-expected casualties in the protracted fighting on the Chir and it would not be able to play a major role in *Saturn*. Furthermore, Stalin's decision to transfer Malinovsky's 2nd Guards Army to block Hoth's advance essentially deprived *Saturn* of the second-echelon forces needed to reach Rostov. Consequently, Vasilevsky was forced to reduce the scope of the operation, hence altering its designation to *Little Saturn* (*Malyy Saturn*). Now, instead of Rostov, the final objective for *Little Saturn* was the German airfields at Morozovskaya and Tatsinskaya, as well as the supply base at Tormosin. Vasilevsky rather optimistically expected the Southwestern Front to achieve all its objectives within six days. The primary target of *Little Saturn* was General Italo Gariboldi's 8th Italian Army, which was defending a 125km-wide sector along the Don. Gariboldi's army consisted of ten Italian infantry divisions and one German infantry division. Heeresgruppe B cobbled together an *ad hoc* armored unit designated as the 27. Panzer-Division, to serve as a mobile reserve for the Italians, but this was really just a battlegroup equipped with obsolescent tanks. Soviet pre-battle reconnaissance efforts alerted the Germans that an enemy offensive was imminent in this sector, so they began moving two more of their infantry divisions to further reinforce the Italians. A number of *ad hoc* battlegroups were also created to defend key points behind the lines – a lesson already learned from *Uranus*.

Vatutin began the operation at 0800 hours on December 16 with a 90-minute artillery preparation, which was ineffective due to heavy fog. The adverse weather also forced the VVS to cancel its planned air strikes. As a result, the Soviet infantry began their assaults around 0930 hours against enemy defenses that were not suppressed. General-mayor Fedor M. Kharitonov's 6th Army, attacking from the Samodurovka bridgehead over the Don with four rifle divisions, achieved only a 2km-deep penetration. Vatutin's main effort, delivered by Kuznetsov's 1 GA from the Osetrovka bridgehead, massed three rifle divisions against one Italian division and one German infantry regiment. Despite a massive imbalance in numbers and fire support, Kuznetsov's infantry experienced great difficulty penetrating the enemy's defenses. The 27. Panzer-Division even managed an afternoon counterattack, which further disrupted the Soviet offensive tempo and limited Kuznetsov's army to only minor gains on the first day of *Little Saturn*. Likewise, Lelyushenko's 3 GA attacked but failed to dent the German defense on the upper Chir. The 22. Panzer-Division, with about a dozen tanks, launched a counterattack which pushed back Lelyushenko's infantry. It was not an auspicious start to *Little Saturn*.

Chagrined by the initial lack of progress, Vatutin ordered 1 GA and 3 GA to begin committing their armor on the second day of *Little Saturn*, in order to create a breakthrough. The fighting raged all day, but despite the efforts of the 27. Panzer-Division and a regiment of German infantry, the Soviets finally breached the main Axis defensive line. Kuznetsov immediately moved General-major Petr R. Pavlov's 25th Tank Corps (25 TC) into the breach, followed soon thereafter by General-major Vasily M. Badanov's 24th Tank Corps (24 TC). Once the Italian front was broken, Vatutin ordered the boldest phase of *Little Saturn* – deep armored raids to capture the airfields involved in the Stalingrad airlift. While the rest of 6th Army and 1 GA focused on widening the breach in Italian lines, Pavlov's 25 TC pushed south toward Morozovskaya airfield, while Badanov's 24 TC headed for Tatsinskaya airfield; both of these objectives lay about 240 kilometers from the operational start line. Vatutin had hoped that these two tanks corps could advance over 50 kilometers per day, but this proved impossible in deep snow and with limited fuel supplies. Meanwhile, Vatutin kept up the pressure on December 18, with Kuznetsov's 1 GA gradually widening the breach in the Italian front, while Lelyushenko's 3 GA finally achieved success against the Romanian corps protecting Armee-Abteilung Hollidt's left flank. After strong attacks by infantry and tanks, two Romanian divisions collapsed, enabling the 1 GMC to boldly advance and isolate the Italian XXXV Army Corps and one German division. By the end of December 19, the Italian 8th Army was disintegrating, with most of its units falling back in disorder. Only the Italian Alpini Corps remained solid.[84] During the day, the 17 TC fought its way into Kantemirovka, a major Italian logistics base. Kuznetsov's army pursued the retreating Italian units, taking several thousand prisoners.

Heeresgruppe B tried to form resistance centers in key positions in order to delay Vatutin's advance, while transferring reinforcements from other sectors. One *Kampfgruppe* formed a solid hedgehog at Chertkovo, which effectively tied up one of Kuznetsov's rifle corps and prevented Soviet exploitation to the southwest. The Italian Alpini Corps and the German Gruppe Fegelein managed to block the Soviet 6th Army from rolling up the open right Axis flank north of Kantemirovka. As German reinforcements trickled into the sector, von Weichs dispatched them to threatened areas. The most important blocking force was Kampfgruppe Kreysing (from 3. Gebirg-Division) which defended the vital air base and supply depot at Millerovo. The Soviet 18 TC surrounded the air base but could not take it without infantry support, which further disrupted Kuznetsov's operational tempo. Kampfgruppe Kreysing's stand in Millerovo bought time for Generalleutnant Maximilian Fretter-Pico to form Armee-Abteilung Fretter-Pico in Kamensk on the Donets.

However, the battlefield was extremely fluid as a result of the Soviet breakthrough and as a result, Heeresgruppe B received two unexpected intelligence windfalls. On the afternoon of December 22, General-major Pyotr F. Privalov, commander of the 15th Rifle Corps in Kharitonov's 6th Army, and his chief of artillery were driving in a lone vehicle near Kantemirovka when they were captured by SS troops from Gruppe Fegelein. Privalov was carrying operational documents and under interrogation at XXIV Panzerkorps headquarters, he revealed further details about Soviet operations in his sector. Later that night, General-major Grigory D. Stelmakh (chief of staff of the Southwestern Front), General-major Ivan P. Krupennikov (chief of staff, 3 GA) and Polkovnik Ivan F. Frolov (chief of artillery, 1 GMC) were travelling in a small convoy to visit the command post of the 1st Guard Mechanized Corps (1 GMC) when they unexpectedly bumped into a German Flak unit south of the town of Bokovskaya. In the ensuing skirmish, Stelmakh was killed and Kruppenikov was captured. Even worse, the Germans captured situation maps and orders that revealed a great deal about the Southwest Front's dispositions.[85] Unlike the earlier Reichel incident, the Germans had no doubt that the maps and documents recovered in these two incidents were valid and they immediately used this information to adjust their own plans. Interestingly, neither Soviet official histories of the campaign nor David Glantz's magisterial four-volume study mention either of these incidents. However, both Privalov and Krupennikov survived German captivity and after the war, they were arrested, convicted of collaboration with the enemy and executed.

The Soviet deep tank raids had mixed results. Pavlov's 25 TC was halted short of its objective by a combination of German resistance on the ground and relentless Stuka attacks. However, Badanov's 24 TC attacked and overran Tatsinskaya airfield on the morning of December 24. Over 50 Luftwaffe transports were destroyed and large stockpiles of supplies were lost. Badanov informed Vatutin that he had captured Tatsinskaya, but he was now immobilized for want of fuel and no relief was nearby.[86] The loss of Tatsinskaya airfield provoked a crisis in Heeresgruppe Don because it seriously disrupted the airlift to Stalingrad and threatened to sever the army group's lines of communication. Von Manstein had already decided to transfer one Panzer division from Hoth's command to deal with *Little Saturn* and now Hollidt was forced to commit his only mobile reserve, the 11. Panzer-Division. Using a combination of air strikes and armor, the Germans gradually blasted Badanov's raiding force into pieces. Without authorization, Badanov conducted a breakout on the night of December 27/28 and succeeded in reaching Soviet lines with nine tanks and about 900 of his men. Two Soviet tank corps were essentially destroyed in these raids, but they did seriously degrade the Luftwaffe's airlift operations to 6. Armee.

Vatutin called off *Little Saturn* on December 30. He had succeeded in shattering the Italian 8th Army, forced Armee-Abteilung Hollidt to abandon the Chir River line and disrupted the Stalingrad airlift – all major operational accomplishments. However, Vatutin's forces failed to cause a complete Axis collapse in southern Russia. Somehow, under the worst possible conditions, von Manstein, Hollidt and a number of other Axis mid-level commanders managed to use every bit of their organizational skill to pull off a miracle and stitch together a new front from assorted bits and pieces. It was not an elegant solution like they taught at the Kriegsakademie, but it sufficed. Furthermore, all of the Soviet armored units involved in the operation were in poor condition due to heavy losses, with no more than 10–20 percent of tanks still operational after two weeks of Deep Battle.[87] Heeresgruppe Don survived, just barely, and mostly due to inadequate Red Army logistics.

As for the Axis forces encircled in Stalingrad, the Stavka initially thought that they had surrounded about 85–90,000 troops, whereas the actual number was about 284,000.[88] Rokossovsky's Don Front was given the main responsibility for crushing the pocket, using Chistiakov's 21st Army and Batov's 65th Army to smash in the western side, known as the Marinovka salient. Eremenko's Stalingrad Front would attack the eastern side of the pocket, using Chuikov's 62nd Army, Shumilov's 64th Army and Tolbukhin's 57th Army. By this point, Paulus had managed to establish a fairly strong outer perimeter, supported by his remaining armor and artillery. Consequently, when the Soviet attacks began on December 2, they encountered unexpectedly fierce resistance and suffered heavy casualties. The attacks continued for a week, but the lack of progress was frustrating for Eremenko and Rokossovsky. Paulus and his subordinates used their limited armor and artillery to smash Soviet attacks, but rapidly consumed their stockpiles of ammunition and fuel. It was already apparent that the Luftwaffe airlift was failing to meet the 6. Armee's logistical needs, gradually weakening the defensive effort. General-major Timofei T. Khriukhin's 8th Air Army (8VA) was able to establish an effective air blockade around Stalingrad, which made it increasingly costly for the Luftwaffe to attempt daylight resupply flights into the pocket; in two days the VIII Fliegerkorps delivered 571 tons of supplies but lost 35 transports to enemy action. The 6. Armee gained a brief respite in mid-December, when the Soviets turned to deal with *Wintergewitter*. Thereafter, the Soviets resumed their attacks all around the perimeter, but only made minor gains. By the end of December 1942, the 6. Armee had fended off multiple attacks without losing much ground, but the airlift was failing and the troops were exhausted. Once it was clear that no relief effort was coming, morale within the pocket also began to deteriorate.

While Hitler and Stalin both made their share of negative interference during the Stalingrad campaign, this does not absolve their field commanders of their own mistakes in generalship. Von Weichs, as commander of Heeresgruppe B, seemed uncertain about his operational objectives – whether to prioritize his flank guard mission or to focus on taking Stalingrad – and ended up not performing well at either task. He starved both Paulus and the Romanians of critical resources they needed to accomplish their missions and failed to expend the effort necessary to convince the OKH to provide him reinforcements (which were, in fact, available). Von Weichs, the aging aristocrat, lacked the stomach for extended arguments with Hitler and Halder over resources and instead was satisfied with feeble whining, which was ignored. In contrast, von Kluge won the argument over resource allocation in the autumn of 1942, thereby gaining additional reserves for Heeresgruppe Mitte. Paulus' command performance is extremely controversial. On the offensive, he knew the proper methods, but he conducted them without the flair or imagination of other German Panzer generals. On the defense, he failed to anticipate or deploy his reserves accordingly and he showed remarkably little concern for his starving, freezing soldiers. In particular, his lack of moral courage, demonstrated by his unwillingness to disobey Hitler, doomed his army from the moment it was encircled. Hoth proved as solid in adversity as usual, although he lacked the resources to successfully conduct *Wintergewitter*. Hollidt put in a remarkable performance on the Chir River, conducting a model delaying action against a vastly superior enemy force. While Hitler's interference in the campaign was substantial, among his worst decisions were assigning critical missions to men like von Weichs, List, Paulus and Ruoff, all of whom struggled to lead large formations under less than perfect circumstances. As commander of Heeresgruppe Don, von Manstein did an admirable job juggling resources but ultimately failed to accomplish any of his assigned missions. Although he was a consummate professional, von Manstein did not relish the role of disaster response and was not at his best in situations where the enemy had the initiative.

On the Soviet side, Stalin seriously hampered the Red Army's operations in the early weeks of the campaign, but as the setbacks mounted and the situation hung in the balance, he began to listen to the professionals. With NKO Order No. 307, issued on October 9, 1942, Stalin got rid of unit commissars and restored unity of command – this one action had a huge impact upon the ability of Soviet commanders to make sound and timely operational decisions.[89] Unfortunately, it took Stalin over 15 months of battlefield disasters before he came to this recognition. On a more favorable note, Stalin made excellent choices in senior command cadre to lead the counterstroke at Stalingrad. Vatutin, at age 41, may have lacked the experience of some of his peers, but he was intelligent, aggressive and had a head for operational-level warfare. Vatutin's performance during both *Uranus* and *Little Saturn*, particularly in terms of maneuver warfare, was excellent and achieved unprecedented results against the Ostheer. Rokossovsky's performance was also quite good, although he was given the difficult and thankless task of fighting a battle of attrition to reduce the Stalingrad pocket. Rokossovsky was forced to rely more upon firepower rather than maneuver, leading to siege warfare in the battle of the pocket. Eremenko's performance was also excellent and his recommendation of a double envelopment of the 6. Armee's extended flanks was a critical requirement for Soviet victory. Operating with fewer resources than

Vatutin, Eremenko was forced to fight a defensive campaign, then switch gears and mount a powerful counteroffensive, then switch back to defense against *Wintergewitter*, then back to counteroffensive, all in the space of one month. Eremenko conducted all these missions with great professional competence and succeeded in each one, a remarkable accomplishment. Virtually all of the Soviet army commanders who played major roles in the counteroffensive – Romanenko, Lelyushenko, Chistiakov, Batov, Trufanov, Tolbukhin and Chuikov – did quite well. Without commissars second-guessing their every move, they were able to focus on their mission objectives and usually make sound decisions. The only real problem areas for Soviet command in this campaign were logistics and intelligence. The Red Army had very limited ability to support actual Deep Operations over any great distance from its railheads and logistic planning was a consistent weakness. Likewise, the Soviet commanders in the Stalingrad campaign usually lacked accurate information about enemy strength and dispositions, which hindered their ability to mass superior combat power at the right time and place. It often goes unmentioned that Vatutin and Eremenko did not know whether or not the Germans had strong armored reserves behind the Romanian armies – they simply assumed they did not, gambled and won.

Commander	Objective	Offensive	Mass	Maneuver	Surprise	Security	TALLY
Von Weichs	-	-	-	-	o	-	-5
Von Manstein	+	+	o	+	o	-	2
Paulus*	+	+	+	-	+	-	1
Hoth	+	+	+	+	o	o	4
Hollidt	+	+	o	+	o	-	2
Vatutin Eremenko	+	+	+	+	+	o	5
Rokossovsky	+	+	o	+	+	o	4
Romanenko	+	+	+	+	+	-	4
Chistiakov Trufanov	+	+	+	+	+	o	5
Tolbukhin Shumilov Batov	+	+	o	o	+	o	3

Stalingrad, 1942 Leadership Assessment

*Minus one in addition for lack of moral courage.

The Stalingrad campaign was one of the most important operational-level campaigns of the Second World War and it offers lessons that are still relevant for US military 21st-century campaigns in Iraq and Afghanistan. By late September 1942, the 6. Armee had accomplished its mission in Stalingrad, which was the neutralization of Soviet armament industries in that city. All the main industrial plants had been reduced to bombed-out wrecks and would not be rebuilt until after the war, but Hitler became personally invested in taking the entire city and would not allow Paulus to pull back to more defensible positions. Similarly, the US military had eliminated the bellicose regime of Saddam Hussein in Iraq and al-Qaeda terrorist training camps in Afghanistan by 2002, but successive administrations in Washington would not countenance withdrawals, even to cut losses in troops and expenditures. Just as Heeresgruppe B put too much faith in Romanian armies to protect their flanks, the US military placed too much faith in Iraqi and Afghan troops to hold back the groundswell of anti-Coalition resistance in the hinterlands. The final US evacuation of Kabul in 2021 was eerily similar to Gumrak airfield in the Stalingrad pocket, replete with a desperate aerial evacuation and enemy forces closing in on the last airfield. As the historian George Santayana said, "those who cannot remember the past are condemned to repeat it."

Operation *Mars*, November–December 1942

While Vasilevsky was occupied orchestrating operations *Uranus* and *Little Saturn* in the south, Zhukov was focused on coordinating Operation *Mars* against the Rzhev salient. He deliberately chose to hold off his own offensive for nearly a week, hoping that the OKH would transfer units from Heeresgruppe Mitte to deal with Operation *Uranus*; a few German units (e.g. the 17. Panzer-Division) were sent south to reinforce Heeresgruppe B, but not many. Zhukov massed great combat power against Model's 9. Armee, including 800,000 troops and 2,000 tanks, providing his forces with a numerical superiority of more than 3-1 in manpower and 5-1 in tanks. However, since Model knew approximately where and when the enemy was going to attack, Operation *Mars* lacked the element of surprise that Operation *Uranus* enjoyed.

Operation *Mars* began on the morning of November 25 with four simultaneous assaults around the periphery of the Rzhev salient. Zhukov's main effort was made by Konev's Western Front, which attacked the eastern side of the salient with General-major Nikolai I. Kiriukhin's heavily reinforced 20th Army. Despite massing 53 regiments of artillery (including the 3rd Artillery Division) on a narrow sector, snow and fog severely degraded Konev's 90-minute artillery preparation. When Kiriukhin sent three division-size shock groups forward, they were pulverized by the intact defenses of the XXXIX Panzerkorps. Nevertheless, Zhukov told Konev to keep committing more troops, so he did, until finally a small penetration was made. Again pressed by Zhukov, Konev prematurely committed his mobile groups — the 6th Tank Corps (6 TC) and 2nd Guards Cavalry Corps (2 GCC) to try to expand the breach. The result was a chaotic traffic jam which created a target-rich environment for Model's centrally directed artillery.[90] When the Luftwaffe provided some Stuka sorties to support AOK 9, Model used them against Konev's immobilized armor, wreaking great havoc. At great cost, Konev pushed his armor and cavalry forward, advancing to create a 12km-long but very thin salient, just as had occurred earlier on the Volkhov Front. After four days of fighting, the Germans had blocked any further advance by Kiriukhin's 20th Army and they mounted a counterattack on November 29 with two Panzer divisions. In a classic *Kesselschlacht*, the German Panzers encircled then crushed the 6 TC and 2 GCC. On December, 4 Zhukov relieved Kiriukhin of command.

Purkaev's Kalinin Front attacked the Rzhev salient at three places: two major attacks on the western side by the 22nd and 41st Armies against the XXXXI Panzerkorps and a supporting attack in the north by the 39th Army against the XXIII Armeekorps. General-major German F. Tarasov's 41st Army achieved a major breakthrough south of Belyy by blasting a hole through an inexperienced *Luftwaffe-Feld-Division*, then pushed the 1st Mechanized Corps (1 MC) and 6th Rifle Corps (6 RC) through to advance 35 kilometers to the Nacha River. Model quickly shifted a Panzer division to block any further advance by Tarasov, but the damage was done. At the same time, General-major Vasily A. Iushkevich's 22nd Army tore a substantial gap in the German front northeast of Belyy and exploited with the 3rd Mechanized Corps (3 MC). Due to these two penetrations, the XXXXI Panzerkorps was on the verge of collapse – this was the crisis of the battle. Adding to Model's problems, General-major Aleksei I. Zygin's 39th Army attacked and gained some ground in the north, which also required attention.

Model was faced with four simultaneous enemy offensives against the perimeter of his army, but he was able to quickly assess which threats were the most dangerous and send just enough forces to reinforce the local defenses while assembling his armored reserves for powerful counterattacks. Although the situation on the eastern side of the salient was quickly stabilized, the situation on the western side grew steadily worse as the Soviet 2 MC and 3 MC continued to push eastward. Model now requested von Kluge to release three Panzer divisions from Heeresgruppe Mitte's operational reserve (12, 19, 20); none of these units were close to full strength and altogether they only possessed 188 tanks, of which 33 were the latest versions of the PzKpfw IV medium tank.[91] Von Kluge agreed, but it would take several days for them to arrive, so Model was forced to conduct a desperate delaying action in the Belyy sector. General der Panzertruppe Josef Harpe, commander of the XXXXI Panzerkorps, fought an incredible defense around Belyy, which prevented the two attacking Soviet armies from joining up and which left both their mechanized spearheads at the end of long, exposed salients.

By early December, the Soviet offensive had stalled due to fierce German resistance, heavy losses and Soviet logistic problems. On December 6, Zhukov went to Moscow to meet with the Stavka and rather absurdly stated that Operation *Mars* could still accomplish its objectives.[92] The next day, Model unleashed two of the reserve Panzer divisions to strike the vulnerable flank of Tarasov's 41st Army and they were able to cut off the enemy spearhead, the 1 MC and 6 RC. Zhukov went to Tarasov's command post and angrily demanded that the 41st Army re-establish a ground link to the isolated formations; when these efforts failed, Zhukov relieved Tarasov of command and took over personal control of the 41st Army.[93] It did not make any difference, since the Germans succeeded in crushing these two isolated corps in a week-long battle of annihilation, with only a few thousand troops escaping. Model sent his other reserves to block Iushkevich's 22nd Army from making any further progress, which effectively ended the Kalinin Front's offensive. Surprisingly, only Zygin's 39th Army, designated as just a supporting attack, managed to retain any of its territorial gains. By December 20, even Zhukov had to admit that Operation *Mars* had failed and he called off the offensive. Soviet losses were catastrophic, with approximately 40 percent of the forces committed becoming casualties, later assessed as 100,000 dead and 235,000 wounded. Soviet armor losses were even worse, with the Germans claiming 1,852 tanks destroyed – about 85 percent of the armor committed. Six elite Red Army corps (1 MC, 3 MC, 5 TC, 6 TC, 2 GCC and 6 RC) were either destroyed or crippled. While Model's AOK 9 suffered significant losses, all of its divisions remained combat effective.

Indeed, Model's successful defense of the Rzhev salient against such overwhelming odds was one of the most impressive defensive victories of the Second World War.

Operation *Mars* provides an excellent demonstration in how the use or failure to employ the principles of war can shape the outcome of a major campaign. The quality of generalship exhibited by senior German commanders during the Battle of the Rzhev salient was uniformly excellent, in large part due to rapid decision-making and effective prior planning. Unlike Heeresgruppe B's efforts to contain Operations *Uranus* and *Saturn*, Heeresgruppe B did not need to improvise much. While von Kluge served as resource manager, Model was able to focus on the operational-level fighting all around the Rzhev salient, countering threats and preparing his own well-timed jabs when circumstances permitted. Model and a few other German commanders had come to realize that the Soviet tendency to create long, vulnerable salients during their protracted breakthrough attacks was a fatal mistake which offered the defenders an opportunity to use maneuver to cut off and destroy the best Soviet formations. However, Model also recognized that the defense of the Rzhev salient required an enormous amount of German resources, which was a luxury that the Ostheer could not afford after the Stalingrad disaster. With his reputation boosted by the successful defense, Model again recommended that the 9. Armee should evacuate the Rzhev salient in order to shorten the front line and free up eight divisions for use elsewhere.

While Zhukov was not technically in command of any formations during Operation *Mars*, he essentially acted as a *de facto* theater commander by giving direct orders to Konev and Purkaev. Zhukov focused on mass, offensive and objective, but placed no emphasis on surprise or security. The Soviet offensive really only possessed the principle of maneuver in the commander's intent, but at the line of contact, each army simply launched frontal attacks against alert enemy defenses. Zhukov's insistence on mass, shoving more troops and equipment into narrow penetration corridors, did not produce an advantage but rather a liability. It should be noted that Konev had been a front commander for over a year and had not yet accomplished any of his assigned missions, but his relationship with Zhukov allowed him to avoid any serious consequences for failure. However, Purkaev's reputation was damaged and he would soon be packed off to the Far East. The Soviet army-level commanders performed fairly well at launching set-piece attacks, but they proved at a loss to deal with a dynamic battlefield produced by unexpected German counterattacks. Although the Soviet style of warfare did not attach any importance to human factors, it is also noticeable that the commanders and staff involved in planning and conducting *Uranus* and *Saturn* were considerably more experienced than the ones involved with *Mars*. Vasilevsky was a trained General Staff officer who could focus solely on Stalingrad, while Zhukov had no General Staff training and had multiple distractions. Furthermore, Zhukov's explosive, bullying temper tantrums also created a toxic environment for the front- and army-level commanders involved with *Mars*, with any serious mistakes leading to relief. Of course, Zhukov ignored his own mistakes and made a point of excluding any reference to Operation *Mars* in his memoirs; indeed, the whole sorry fiasco was later completely erased from the Great Patriotic War mythology.

Commander	Objective	Offensive	Mass	Maneuver	Surprise	Security	TALLY
Von Kluge	+	o	+	+	o	+	4
Model	+	+	+	+	+	+	6
Zhukov	+	+	+	+	–	–	2
Konev Purkaev	+	+	+	o	–	–	1
Iushkevich Kiriukhin Tarasov Zygin	+	+	+	o	–	–	1

Operation Mars, *1942 Leadership Assessment*

As a postscript to Operation *Mars*, the Stavka decided that the Northwest Front should have another go against the Demyansk salient. Stalin was disgusted by Kurochkin's inability to sever the Ramushevo corridor and he decided to replace him with Timoshenko on November 17. Kurochkin was demoted and assigned to command the 11th Army, while Morozov was shifted to command the 1 SA. Timoshenko was given barely a week to plan a new offensive, but he at least had the sagacity to move his intended point of attack further east, hoping the German defenses would be less formidable. Nor did the Stavka provide the Northwest Front with significant reinforcements or logistic support, since it was a secondary theater. Even worse, Timoshenko conducted a preliminary attack on November 23 which alerted Busch's AOK 16 to the fact that a new enemy offensive was about to begin and in a new sector. Consequently, when

Timoshenko launched his main offensive on November 28 – with 11th Army attacking the north side of the salient and 1 SA the south side – it was repulsed with heavy casualties. The Stavka ordered Timoshenko to keep attacking.

Recognizing the opportunity to inflict a serious defeat on the Northwest Front, von Küchler, commander of Heeresgruppe Nord, shifted three divisions from the unengaged AOK 18 to reinforce Busch's AOK 16. Timoshenko kept attacking throughout December, but each attack was repulsed in turn. Even worse, the exhausted Soviet armies lapsed into predictable habits, often attacking at the same time each day. When Morozov's 1 SA was spotted massing for another attack on December 27, Busch massed the fires of ten artillery battalions and fired 14,000 rounds at the assembly areas, which rendered the 1 SA combat-ineffective. Timoshenko kept requesting permission to end the offensive but the Stavka did not relent until early January 1943. By that point, the Northwest Front's best units had been thoroughly decimated. Busch had won a major defensive victory over Timoshenko but, as with the Rzhev salient, the Germans recognized that holding onto the Demyansk salient was no longer worth the resources invested. Von Küchler and Busch both recommended evacuating Demyansk before the inevitable next round of Soviet offensives began.

Over the course of 1942, the Red Army conducted 18 major operations (lumping some together, such as the various summer attacks against the Demyansk salient), of which only two were victories (*Uranus* and Eremenko's seizure of bridgeheads over the Don), four were partial victories (the Toropets-Staraya Russa operation, Barvenkovo salient, *Little Saturn*, Don Bend counteroffensive) and the rest were failures. In the same period, the Germans conducted 16 major operations, of which 11 were successful (*Brückenschlag, Störfang, Trappenjagd, Fridericus, Blau I*/Voronezh and *Blau II*/Don Bend, Siniavino Heights, *Raubtier, Seydlitz, Wilhelm, Fridericus II*), three were partial successes (*Edelweiss*, Stalingrad, *Michael*/Demyansk) and two were failures (*Wirbelwind* and *Wintergewitter*). As a result of these operations, the Germans destroyed 12 Soviet armies in 1942 and crippled a similar number, while capturing five important territorial objectives (Voronezh, Sevastopol, Rostov, Krasnodar and Maikop) and reducing another to rubble (Stalingrad). In their operations, the Red Army destroyed one German, one Italian and two Romanian armies. In strategic terms, the Ostheer suffered 1.1 million casualties (including 274,000 dead or missing) in 1942 and lost 2,480 tanks, whereas the Red Army suffered 7.35 million casualties (including 3.25 million dead or missing) and lost

15,000 tanks. While the Soviet victories against Heeresgruppe B enabled the Red Army to temporarily gain the strategic initiative, the Red Army's advantage was not yet overwhelming and the Ostheer was still full of fight (and mostly undefeated in the central and northern parts of the Eastern Front).

CHAPTER 5

Zitadelle: 1943 Operations

"Breaking off action now would be throwing away victory!"
Generalfeldmarschall Erich von Manstein, July 13, 1943[1]

Heeresgruppe A's Retreat from the Caucasus,
January 1–February 25, 1943

After the defeat at Ordzhonikidze in November 1942, von Kleist moved up to take over the command of Heeresgruppe A (which had essentially been vacant since List's removal two months earlier) and General der Kavallerie Eberhard von Mackensen took command of PzAOK 1. Von Mackensen was son of the famous Generalfeldmarschall August von Mackensen, but he had modest command experience prior to *Barbarossa* and remained with the cavalry instead of transitioning into the Panzertruppen in the 1930s. In order to support the *Wintergewitter* relief effort, von Kleist was obliged to transfer two of his best mechanized divisions to Hoth's PzAOK 4, which left his already overextended army group in a precarious state and under constant enemy pressure. Von Mackensen was forced to hold the line on the Terek with both flanks more or less exposed to envelopment. Once *Wintergewitter* failed in mid-December, von Kleist requested permission to withdraw from the Caucasus, but Hitler was adamantly opposed to giving up any territory. By Christmas, Heeresgruppe A was being attacked in multiple sectors and Eremenko's Stalingrad Front was advancing inexorably down the rail line to Tikhoretsk, threatening von Kleist's line of communications to Rostov. On December 28, Hitler issued Operations Order No. 2, which finally authorized von Kleist to pull back, but only 100 kilometers to the Kuma River, thereby retaining the Maikop oil fields, which had just been repaired. The new order also subordinated Heeresgruppe A to Heeresgruppe Don.[2]

Soviet forces in the Caucasus were dispersed, with General-polkovnik Ivan I. Maslennikov's Northern Group of Forces (with the 9, 37, 44, 58 Armies) in the Terek River sector and General Ivan E. Petrov's Black Sea Group (with the 18, 46, 47, 56 Armies) in the Tuapse sector. General Ivan Tyulenev, commander of the North Caucasus Front, was nominally the theater commander, but he was primarily a resource manager. Two air armies, 4 VA and 5 VA, were operating over the Caucasus and had gained local air superiority. Tyulenev had submitted a plan for a limited offensive with the ultimate objective of recovering Maikop, but on December 29 the Stavka instead ordered a much larger offensive, with the intent of either encircling Heeresgruppe A or driving it entirely out of the Caucasus.[3]

Yet the Stavka provided no large armor or mechanized formations to support a major offensive in the Caucasus, so Maslennikov formed two tank groups from his six available tank brigades. For the most part, Maslennikov was forced to rely heavily upon his six cavalry divisions for pursuit operations. Planning time for the entire operation was less than three days. Nor had the Stavka even bothered to provide a high-level representative to coordinate the two dispersed groups of forces, which were separated by over 300 kilometers. Consequently, the Soviet winter counteroffensive in the Caucasus was a very atypical operation for the Red Army.

Just before von Kleist began pulling back from the Terek River, Maslennikov began his offensive on the morning of January 1, with General-major Vasily A. Khomenko's 44th Army (with eight rifle divisions) as his main effort, reinforced by the Lobanov tank group and a cavalry corps, against the left flank of von Mackensen's PzAOK 1. Unlike other parts of the Eastern Front, PzAOK 1 had few infantry strongpoints and its left flank was open on the Nogai Steppe, so Mackensen was forced to conduct a mobile delay operation from the start. On January 3, Maslennikov committed General-major Kontantin

A. Koroteev's 9th Army and General-leytenant Kondrat S. Melnikov's 58th Army against the rest of PzAOK 1's front. Mackensen fought a delaying action back to the Kuma River, although shortages of fuel meant that a considerable number of vehicles and equipment had to be abandoned. Once at the Kuma, the Germans were able to catch their breath for a few days, since Khomenko – another NKVD general bungled the pursuit and failed to maintain contact with the retreating foe. Maslennikov's forces were neither trained nor equipped for the pursuit mission and Stalin was soon enraged by their inability to catch up with the retreating Germans. Mackensen made a brief stand on the Kuma River, but by January 10 Soviet cavalry and tanks were across and PzAOK 1 was forced to fall back. Once again, Maslennikov's pursuit lost contact with the enemy. Petrov's Black Sea Group finally began its own offensive on January 12, divided into two sub-operations: Operations *More* (Sea) and *Gory* (Mountains) to break through Ruoff's AOK 17. General-leytenant Fedor V. Kamkov's 47th Army was tasked with a drive along the coast to liberate the port of Novorossiysk while General-leytenant Andrei A. Grechko's 56th Army advanced through the mountains into the Kuban.[4] Operation *More* was completely repulsed and Kamkov was relieved, but Grechko achieved some minor success in Operation *Gory*. The terrain and winter weather along the coast heavily favored the defense and these operations were infantry-heavy, which limited any advances to a crawl.

Instead of Maslennikov, the real threat proved to be Eremenko's Southern Front (re-designated from Stalingrad Front), which was making rapid progress toward Heeresgruppe A's vulnerable lines of communication. Malinovsky's 2 GA was heavily reinforced, with two tank, two mechanized and one cavalry corps leading the advance toward Proletarskaya on the Manych River. Trufanov's 51st Army was following in support. Hoth had the only force in a position to contest Eremenko's advance, but his PzAOK 4 had been reduced to just the LVII Panzerkorps and a few other fragments, which lacked the strength to form a defensive line. Von Manstein was beginning to receive more reinforcements from the West, but he was also facing simultaneous crises on the Chir and Manych Rivers, forcing him to violate the principle of mass and divide his resources between Armee-Abteilung Hollidt and Hoth. Von Manstein sent Hoth two companies of the new Tiger heavy tanks, which did enable the LVII Panzerkorps to conduct a fierce delaying action along the Manych River for a week, but Eremenko's forces were too strong and too well-led. The Red Army's newly-organized mechanized corps – well-equipped and led by veteran commanders – proved their worth against Hoth's Panzers. By January 15, Hoth was forced to cross the Manych and pull back into a hedgehog defense of the key town of Proletarskaya, in order to protect von Kleist's retreat. The evacuation of Heeresgruppe A was now in serious jeopardy, with Maslennikov closing in from the south and Eremenko from the northeast. Hitler finally gave permission to evacuate the Caucasus. Mackensen's PzAOK 1 was directed to retreat to Rostov, but Hitler required Ruoff's AOK 17 to retreat into the Kuban, where it would hold a bridgehead for future offensives.[5] Even before the 6. Armee had surrendered at Stalingrad, Hitler was consigning another German army to isolation, with the Kuban becoming a cul-de-sac that could only be supplied by sea and air. Hitler grandiloquently referred to the Kuban as the *Goten-Brückenkopfes* or *Gotenkopf* (Goth's Head), but symbolic names did not suffice for the lack of prepared positions.

Eremenko crossed the Manych on January 21 and showed great skill and cunning in trying to cut off the German escape. However, the Germans also displayed their usual tactical flexibility and tenacity in using small *Kampfgruppen* to delay the advance of Malinovsky's 2 GA. By the end of January, PzAOK 1 and Hoth's rearguards had reached Rostov just ahead of the Soviet vanguard, while Ruoff began to consolidate a defense in the Kuban. The retreat of AOK 17 in mountainous terrain in winter was difficult and cost Ruoff about half of his artillery and most of his ammunition, due to shortages of transport and fuel. Stalin was angry that Heeresgruppe A had escaped, but most of the Caucasus had been liberated and the exhausted German formations were no longer very combat-effective. Between July 25, 1942 and January 30, 1943, Heeresgruppe A had suffered over 72,000 German and 45,000 Romanian casualties in the Caucasus (including 34,000 dead or missing). When combined with the losses of Heeresgruppe B from *Uranus* and *Little Saturn*, the losses of Heeresgruppe A further drained German strength in southern Russia to nearly the breaking point. As for the oil – the main objective of Operation *Edelweiss* – the Germans managed to extract barely 1,000 tons of crude oil from Maikop before they were forced to abandon it in January 1943. During the same period, the Red Army suffered 511,000 casualties in the Caucasus, including 247,000 dead or missing, but it had succeeded in denying the Caucasus oil to the German war effort. Ruoff's situation in the Kuban was dire from the outset. The AOK 17, with 325,000 troops (including 64,000 Romanians) and 100,000 horses, required about 2,000 tons of supplies per day. However, the Luftwaffe could only deliver 100–200 tons per day and the Kriegsmarine about another 800 tons by sea, when the Kerch Strait was not frozen over (which it was in January–February), which meant that AOK 17 was receiving less than half of its logistical requirements. Furthermore, AOK 17 had not been configured for independent operations and had relatively few support units – it was much less well-equipped than AOK 6 had been in November 1942. Von Manstein urged Hitler to evacuate the AOK 17 from the Kuban as soon as possible – it would have provided a significant boost to Heeresgruppe Don – but he refused.[6] The Stavka had not expected the Germans to try to hold a bridgehead in the Kuban and initially regarded it as something of a mop-up operation. Maslennikov's command, now designated the North Caucasus Front, assigned three armies (9, 37, 58) to liberate the Kuban while Petrov's Black Sea Group assigned four armies (18, 46, 47, 56) to the task. Thus, by early February Ruoff had seven enemy armies converging on his one isolated, poorly supplied army. Initially, the Soviet armies were slowed more by the weather and terrain, but the 46th Army succeeded in liberating Krasnodar on February 12. Meanwhile, the 47th Army conducted an amphibious landing at Stanichka, just south of Novorossiysk. Maslennikov and Petrov appeared to be on the cusp of destroying another German army.

By February 25, Ruoff pulled back to a shorter, more defensible line (dubbed "the Poseidon Line"), anchored on the town of Krymskaya. The Soviets attacked the line with the 56th and 58th Armies, achieving some success, but suffering heavy casualties. Ruoff then pulled back his vulnerable left flank, with the new position known as the "Blue line" – AOK 17 would hold this position for the next six months. Due to supply problems and miserable rainy weather, the Stavka ordered Maslennikov and Petrov to shift to the defensive on March 16, but to begin preparations for a major assault to break the Blue Line. The Black Sea Group was incorporated into the North Caucasus Front and Petrov became Maslennikov's deputy. The North Caucasus Front's chaotic force structure was rationalized and reduced to four field armies (9, 18, 37, 56), with some formations sent back to the RVGK to rebuild. Using the Soviet naval superiority, Maslennikov was able to steadily reinforce the Stanichka (Malaya Zemlya) bridgehead and shifted the 18th Army headquarters to control the forces there. Maslennikov submitted his offensive plan to destroy AOK 17 to the Stavka on March 22 and it was approved.[7] The Stavka stipulated that the offensive would begin on April 4, giving Maslennikov and his staff less than two weeks to prepare.

In terms of generalship, there is no doubt that von Kleist conducted a masterful withdrawal from the Caucasus under very difficult winter conditions, which saved Heeresgruppe A from encirclement. Hitler recognized this accomplishment by promoting him to Generalfeldmarschall on February 1. Yet von Kleist's Heeresgruppe A was defeated in the Caucasus, which renders his accomplishment into the "not-as-bad-as-it-could-have-been" category. Von Mackensen and Hoth both fought very skillful mobile delaying actions which contributed in no small part to the salvation of Heeresgruppe A, but which only served to slow the pace of the relentless Soviet advance. Ruoff's retreat was noteworthy in that he kept his army from falling apart and brought it back to an unprepared position, where he was able to quickly reassemble it and conduct a successful hasty defense against greatly superior enemy forces. Indeed, Ruoff's talent was clearly in defensive operations, where he could plan and execute a set-piece battle. On the Soviet side, Eremenko was the most effective front commander and his offensive came very close to cutting off Heeresgruppe A. It is evident that Eremenko had learned a great deal about fighting the Ostheer during the Stalingrad campaign and he was able to conduct more professional operations, with limited interference from the Stavka or Stalin. Maslennikov was somewhat less effective due to his limited ability to conduct mobile operations; his tanks and cavalry did not perform particularly well in pursuit and when they encountered even small German rearguards they tended to become stymied. Petrov turned in a mediocre performance, which Stalin recognized, but he did achieve operational surprise by conducting an amphibious operation near Novorossiysk – which the enemy had not expected. The other Soviet commanders who played a key role in these operations were generally competent and often capable of accomplishing their objectives, although months of inactivity on the Caucasus front had conditioned them toward positional warfare.

Commander	Objective	Offensive	Mass	Maneuver	Surprise	Security	TALLY
Von Kleist	+	o	o	+	o	o	2
Hoth Mackensen	+	+	o	+	o	o	3
Ruoff	+	o	o	+	o	o	2
Maslennikov	+	+	o	o	o	o	2
Petrov	o	o	o	+	+	o	2
Eremenko	+	+	+	+	o	o	4
Malinovsky Khomenko	+	+	+	–	+	–	2
Grechko	+	+	o	o	o	o	2

Caucasus/Kuban, 1942–1943 Leadership Assessment

Operation *Ring* and the End of the 6. Armee,
January 10–February 2, 1943

While the Stalingrad Front was temporarily distracted by *Wintergewitter*, the Stavka had not forgotten about the encircled 6. Armee and vowed to complete its destruction as quickly as possible. Since Vasilevsky was focused on *Little Saturn*, the Stavka assigned General-polkovnik Nikolai N. Voronov, head of the Red Army's artillery, to coordinate the final operations at Stalingrad. Noting that standard tank-infantry attacks had not gained much ground in the December fighting, Voronov intended to crush the 6. Armee under an avalanche of Soviet firepower. He requested a large number of heavy artillery units from the RVGK, which would enable him to mass a greater concentration of firepower than had been heretofore used in any single attack on the Eastern Front. Initially, the expectation was that the Don and Stalingrad Fronts would cooperate in reducing the pocket, so both Rokossovsky and Eremenko were involved with the planning. Yet when the plan was submitted to the Stavka on December 27, it was evident that using two fronts violated the principle of command, so it was decided that Rokossovsky's Don Front would be solely responsible for the reduction of the Stalingrad pocket. Eremenko was directed to transfer three of his armies (57, 62, 64) to Rokossovsky's command, so he could focus all his attention on pursuing Hoth's forces to the Manych River. The final plan, designated as Operation *Kol'tso* (*Ring*), was approved on December 30. Rokossovsky would have a total of seven Soviet armies, totaling about 281,000 troops, which he would use to launch concentric attacks against the pocket.[8] General-major Ilia V. Vinogradov, head of intelligence for the Don Front, estimated that Paulus only had about ten divisions with 80,000 troops left, so Rokossovsky thought that he had a 3-1 numerical superiority in manpower. The Stavka expected the operation to last one week.[9]

In fact, Paulus still had 22 divisions with roughly 200,000 troops and 124 operational AFVs, which meant that the Don Front's numerical advantage was illusory.[10] The 6. Armee also still had sufficient artillery and antitank weaponry to fight one last battle, if ammunition was economically used. Nor did the Soviet commanders appreciate that the troops in the 6. Armee saw themselves as being in a no-quarter situation, so they would conduct a fanatical defense. Aside from dwindling supplies, the main problem for Paulus was that he was forced to maintain too large a perimeter (35 × 53km) and Hitler would not allow him to withdraw to a more defensible line. Hitler informed Paulus that the SS-Panzerkorps was en route to the Eastern Front and would spearhead a stronger relief operation in the spring. Initially, Paulus made a professional effort to deploy his forces and strengthen the defenses in the most threatened sectors, but he became increasingly despondent as hope for rescue began to fade.

On the morning of January 10, Operation *Ring* began with a 55-minute artillery preparation against the western side of the pocket. Voronov massed 500 guns/howitzers and 450 multiple rocket launchers on a 12km-wide front, which were supplemented by Il-2 Sturmovik ground attack sorties from the 16 VA. Altogether, Voronov had 202 guns, mortars and rocket launchers per kilometer of front and for the first time, the Red Army began to use mission-focused groupings to direct its artillery to accomplish specific missions, such as artillery destruction groups (*razrusheniia*), long-range artillery groups (*dal'nye deisviia*) and infantry support groups (*podderzhka pekhoty*).[11] Thanks to favorable weather on the morning of the attack, Soviet forward observers were able to properly direct the bombardment, resulting in heavy damage to the German defenders. After the bombardment and air strikes, the Soviet ground forces surged forward. Batov's 65th Army enjoyed the most success and Chistiakov's 21st Army also gained ground. Although Rokossovsky was confident, German resistance toughened up considerably by the second day of the operation and Soviet losses in infantry and tanks were heavy. Some German commanders also decided to disobey Hitler and Paulus by conducting unauthorized withdrawals at night to shorten their lines. After three days of heavy fighting, the German defense had bent, but not broken.

For the next several days, Hube's XIV Panzerkorps fought a delaying action against the 21st and 65th Armies, gradually pulling back from the western perimeter toward the city. On January 16, Chistiakov's 21st Army captured Pitomnik airfield, while Tolbukhin's 57th Army pressed from the south. The next day, Rokossovsky decided to pause Operation *Ring*, since the Don Front had suffered 26,000 casualties and lost half its armor in a week yet failed to crush the German defense. Voronov used the pause to restock the ammunition for his artillery and bring up a second artillery division. On the German side, the 6. Armee reorganized for its final stand. Hitler ordered some key leaders, like Hube, flown out of the pocket. Although the Luftwaffe airlift was a failure, it had managed to fly out nearly 30,000 personnel, many of whom would be used to form a cadre for a rebuilt 6. Armee.

The second phase of Operation *Ring* began on January 21, with Batov's 65th Army attacking from the west, while the 24th and 66th Armies hit the northeast corner of the pocket. On the next day, Rokossovsky launched an all-out assault from multiple directions, preceded by a massive barrage from Voronov's guns. Batov's 65th Army finally achieved a breakthrough, which led to the capture of Gumrak airfield on January 23. Thereafter, the 6. Armee could only receive a trickle of supplies via parachute drop. Having fired their last ammunition, the German artillery was now silent. By January 26, the Soviets managed to split the Stalingrad pocket into two fragments and the 6. Armee's resistance began to quickly fade. Paulus fell into an apathetic state and let his chief of staff Schmidt conduct the final operations as everything fell apart. It is evident from post-war accounts that Paulus was no longer concerned with the fate of 6. Armee, but only his own fate. Nevertheless, Rokossovsky found himself running out of infantry in the final costly battles in the ruined city and was forced to slow down the operational tempo in order to conserve his remaining combat power. Without supplies, the 6. Armee began to fall apart; Paulus and the bulk of the troops surrendered on January 31. The last resistance, in the northern pocket, was crushed under another one of Voronov's barrages and ended on February 2.

The final battle of the 6. Armee (and attached elements) resulted in the death or capture of more than 215,000 Axis troops; the actual number of prisoners is slippery since many of the wounded died within 2–3 weeks of the capitulation and the NKVD killed thousands of would-be evaders. As a result of this catastrophic defeat, a total of 22 divisions were removed from the Ostheer order of battle, including three of the strongest Panzer divisions; these losses permanently changed the military balance on the Eastern Front. Furthermore, the loss of one-third of the Luftwaffe's Ju-52 transport force would also have major implications for future campaigns. Victory did not come cheaply for the Red Army, with Rokossovsky's Don Front suffering 48,000 casualties in the final three weeks of combat.[12] Although the military balance had now shifted in the Soviets' favor, Soviet industry (and Western Lend Lease) could not provide enough material to give the Red Army an overwhelming advantage until mid-1943. The Red Army enjoyed a huge boost in morale due to the victory at Stalingrad, but in the short term, its operations were still hindered by material and logistic shortages. It is evident that the Red Army won at Stalingrad because it had begun to learn from its previous operational mistakes. The Soviet use of massed artillery to smash enemy fortified positions and the use of tactical aviation to disrupt the Luftwaffe airlift were major improvements over past performance. Yet the main game-changer for the Red Army was that Stalin and his political commissars finally accepted the need for greater operational flexibility and less micromanagement, which enabled Soviet commanders to fight campaigns in a more professional manner.

However, two areas that still required improvement were intelligence and logistics. Even a fairly straightforward operation like *Ring* had to be broken up into pieces because the enemy was underestimated and not enough ammunition had been stockpiled for a protracted battle.

In terms of generalship, Paulus' performance in the last six weeks at Stalingrad was extremely poor and indecisive; he appears to have mentally "checked out" under the stress and left decision-making authority to his chief of staff. Von Bock regarded Paulus as a weak, indecisive commander, which proved to be accurate based upon his performance in the final two months at Stalingrad. The unwillingness to attempt a breakout condemned the majority of the 6. Armee to a long, slow death in the snow. Paulus' performance in captivity was even worse, where he showed more interest in his own personal conditions than in the fate of his troops, most of whom quickly died in captivity. His open collaboration with his Soviet captors – in return for creature comforts - only further tarnished his reputation as a commander.* Nor does Paulus' behavior stack up well against other captured army commanders, such as Lieutenant General Arthur Percival (the British commander at Singapore) or Lieutenant General Jonathan Wainwright (the American commander at Bataan/Corregidor). While both Percival and Wainwright made mistakes, they cared about their troops and shared their misfortunes in captivity. The one lesson that Paulus' example instilled in other German commanders was that when surrounded, a formation needed to attempt a breakout as soon as possible, whether it was authorized or not. Avoiding encirclement, even when it meant disobeying direct orders from Hitler, also seemed a better alternative than certain annihilation.

Although Rokossovsky was a veteran front commander, Operation *Ring* was his first victory. After suffering excessive casualties in the first week of the operation, he was astute enough to revise his tactics in order to accomplish the mission. Unlike Zhukov, he did not crowd the battlefield or keep pushing troops into the enemy buzzsaw, like so much cannon fodder. Soviet army-level commanders like Batov and Chistiakov also demonstrated proficiency in high-tempo offensive operations, particularly in the ability to break through prepared defenses and react to enemy

*According to Wilhem Adam's memoirs (*With Paulus at Stalingrad*, p. 222), Paulus and other captured senior officers received three meals per day and a number of special privileges, which was intended to seduce them into active collaboration. Other unverified sources claim that Paulus was allowed to contact the German embassy in Turkey in order to procure Generalfeldmarschall insignia.

redispositions on the battlefield. Tolbukhin fought more of a positional battle, like Shumilov, which was adequate but unremarkable. Operation *Ring* was the first *Kesselschlacht* battle that the Red Army fought in the Second World War, so there was a painful learning curve, but one which would reap benefits in future campaigns.

Commander	Objective	Offensive	Mass	Maneuver	Surprise	Security	TALLY
Paulus	o	o	o	o	o	o	o
Rokossovsky	+	+	+	+	o	o	4
Batov Chistiakov	+	+	+	+	o	o	4
Tolbukhin	+	+	+	o	o	o	3

Stalingrad, 1943 Leadership Assessment

Operation *Iskra* (*Spark*), January 12–18, 1943

Even before operations *Uranus* and *Mars* were launched, the Stavka directed Govorov's Leningrad Front and Meretskov's Volkhov Front to begin planning another offensive to break the German siege of Leningrad. However this time, Govorov and Meretskov were given over one month to plan the offensive and to assemble adequate resources to sustain it. Although still plagued by the presence of Lev Mekhlis as front commissar, Meretskov had a very capable staff led by General-leytenant Mikhail N. Sharokhin. The basic concept was to launch a simultaneous offensive from both east and west against the German-held Siniavino sector, as had been attempted in August 1942. The Leningrad Front would attack across the frozen Neva River with General-major Mikhail P. Dukhanov's 67th Army, while the Volkhov Front would conduct its main effort from the east with General-leytenant Vladimir Z. Romanovskiy's rebuilt 2 SA. The 8th Army, under General-leytenant Filipp N. Starikov, would conduct a supporting attack on Romanovskiy's left flank. Although the scheme of maneuver was essentially the same as the previous failed offensive, the level of support was much greater and there was an increased emphasis upon combined-arms methods; specialized sapper units would be used to breach enemy obstacle belts and increased use of tactical aviation. Dukhanov's 67th Army was actually given time to rehearse assault crossing tactics to get over the Neva – virtually the first time in the war so far that the Red Army employed preoperational rehearsals. Marshal Voroshilov was assigned as Stavka representative, but by this point in the war his military credibility had virtually evaporated, leaving him as little more than a figurehead. Consequently, Govorov, Meretskov and their field commanders had a relatively free hand during the planning process. The Stavka even permitted an operational delay of several days due to adverse weather conditions.[13] However, the command situation became more tense when Zhukov arrived at Meretskov's headquarters two days before the operation was scheduled to begin.

Lindemann's AOK 18 was thinly stretched on the Leningrad Front, particularly after being ordered in October and November 1942 to transfer six of its veteran divisions to other sectors of the Eastern Front.[14] By January 1943, each of the divisions remaining in Lindemann's army were forced to defend an average of 17 kilometers of front line. Only four divisions from the XXVI Armeekorps were assigned to hold the vital Siniavino sector. Heeresgruppe Nord's operational reserves were minimal and instead von Küchler had to rely upon borrowing individual battalions and regiments from quiet sectors to counter any enemy breakthrough. The quantity of Luftflotte 1's air support had also dwindled by late 1942, but the quality of the remaining units was still sufficient to prevent the VVS from gaining air superiority over the Leningrad sector.

On the morning of January 12, Operation *Spark* began with massive 140-minute-long artillery bombardments on both sides of the Siniavino corridor. Govorov's Leningrad Front was able to mass 1,873 guns/ mortars/MRLs (144/km) to support Dukhanov's 67th Army's attack across the Neva, while Meretskov massed 2,885 guns/mortars/MRLs (180/km) to support the attacks of the 2 SA and 8th Army.[15] The 13 VA and 14 VA also committed over 800 aircraft to the offensive, including swarms of Il-2 Sturmoviks that went after the German artillery. Dukhanov attacked across the Neva River in three places along a 12km-wide front but only one of the attempts succeeded. After gaining a bridgehead, Soviet engineers quickly built a pontoon bridge and by nightfall Dukhanov had managed to get a tank brigade and two rifle divisions across the river. Romanovskiy attacked with four division-size shock groups from 2 SA along a 10km-wide front, but failed to gain much ground and some of the German *Stützpunkte* proved nearly impregnable. The German XXVI Corps committed its tactical reserves to contain Dukhanov's bridgehead, while Lindemann scraped up several regimental-size *Kampfgruppen* and sent them to the Siniavino sector. AOK 18 assessed Dukhanov's 67th Army as the main threat and committed virtually all of the reserves to crush the bridgehead before it could be enlarged.

On the second day of *Spark*, the 2 SA and 8th Army made negligible progress, which infuriated Zhukov. He pressured Meretskov into committing his reserves in order to effect a breakthrough – the same mistake Zhukov had made in Operation *Mars*. Romanovskiy sent his reserves into the fight, but his army was stymied by a single German battalion-size strongpoint for two days. The waterlogged terrain in this sector, consisting of wooded areas and peat bogs, was extremely unfavorable for large-scale operations. A sudden onset of adverse weather reduced the amount of Soviet air and artillery support, causing more friction. On January 13, the XXVI Armeekorps was able to counterattack Dukhanov's forces across the Neva, inflicting significant losses. During the next four days, January 14–17, Dukhanov's 67th Army steadily expanded its bridgeheads across the Neva in spite of tenacious German resistance. However, Romanovsky's 2 SA was limited to a painfully slow advance and even when German positions were encircled, the defenders were able to break out and shift to alternate positions. Finally, General-major Nikolai P. Simoniak's 136th Rifle Division from the 67th Army was able to establish a tenuous link-up with the 2 SA on the morning of January 18. Nevertheless, Lindemann was able to quickly establish a new defensive line anchored on the Siniavino Heights. Zhukov pressured Meretskov and Govorov to continue attacking the Siniavino Heights, even though the operational objective (opening a land corridor to Leningrad) had been achieved and the 67th Army and 2 SA were nearly spent. In a ridiculous display of micromanagement, Zhukov tried to issue a direct order by radio to Simoniak – bypassing Govorov and Dukhanov – to continue attacking the Siniavino Heights. Although Zhukov was accustomed to bullying subordinates, he met his match in Simoniak, who had the moral courage to reject his insults and tell him that he only took orders from Govorov.[16] In this case, Zhukov's threats proved empty and Simoniak was awarded the Hero of the Soviet Union (HSU) for his battlefield accomplishments and soon given command of a guards rifle corps. Soviet attacks on the Siniavino Heights did continue until the end of January, but the new German line held firm.

Operation *Spark* was a success, but a very costly one. Altogether, the 67th Army and 2 SA suffered 115,082 casualties (including 33,940 dead), whereas the AOK 18 suffered 8,905 casualties (including 3,176 dead or missing).[17] In large part, the 10-1 casualty ratio in the German favor was due to Zhukov's insistence on throwing more troops into hopeless attacks against impregnable positions. Nevertheless, Meretskov and Govorov succeeded in opening an 8km-wide land corridor to Leningrad and Soviet engineers were able to build a new rail line across the swampy terrain in just two weeks. On February 6, 1943, the first Soviet train used the rail line to reach Leningrad. Although German artillery was often able to interdict the rail line, it still had great symbolic value. Leningrad remained under loose siege, but the blockade had been weakened and the next objective would be to widen the corridor.

German generalship during Operation *Spark* was effective but hampered by limited resources. Von Küchler, as commander of Heeresgruppe Nord, essentially served as a resource manager and he excelled at rapidly shifting reinforcements to threatened sectors while avoiding compromising the security of the rest of his front line. Despite being surprised by the 67th Army crossing the Neva River, Lindemann was able to quickly commit his reserves to the most critical sector and prevent a rapid breakthrough. After the Soviet fronts achieved their link-up, Lindemann was still able to hold the critical terrain in the sector and create a solid front line, while inflicting more than 10-1 losses on the enemy. It should be noted that German tactical execution at the XXVI Armeekorps level was superb, particularly in preventing any of its units from being destroyed. Soviet operational leadership in Operation *Spark* was mixed. Govorov did an excellent job as a field commander, employing almost all the major principles of war in his planning and conduct of *Spark*. Meretskov's performance was somewhat less impressive, since he was forced by Zhukov to conduct a number of costly frontal attacks, which lacked the elements of maneuver or surprise. The two army-level commanders, Dukhanov and Romanovskiy, were good, but fought very differently. Dukhanov eschewed mass and probed across a wide front until he found a weak spot, then he surprised XXVI Armeekorps by quickly pushing armor across the Neva. Romanovskiy relied upon mass and tried to blast his way through a line of German regimental strongpoints, which proved far more difficult than anticipated. Both Dukhanov and Romanovskiy failed to prevent encircled German units from escaping, which should have been anticipated.

Commander	Objective	Offensive	Mass	Maneuver	Surprise	Security	TALLY
Von Küchler	+	o	o	o	o	+	2
Lindemann	+	+	o	o	+	o	3
Govorov	+	+	+	+	+	o	5
Meretskov	+	+	+	o	o	o	3
Dukhanov	+	+	o	+	+	-	3
Romanovskiy	+	+	+	o	-	o	2

Leningrad, 1943 Leadership Assessment

Although Zhukov was not an actual operational commander during *Spark*, his continuous interference with ongoing operations was counterproductive. Later in his memoirs, Zhukov tried to claim a greater role for himself in *Spark* (as he did with *Uranus*), even to the point of making the unlikely assertion that he personally witnessed the link-up of the troops on January 18.[18] In fact, Zhukov rarely went forward of army-level command posts and the idea that the deputy commander of the Red Army was with a shock group of mud-covered *frontoviki* in a peat bog under enemy fire is absurd.[*] Zhukov was promoted to Marshal of the Soviet Union on the day that the Leningrad and Volkhov Fronts linked up, and there is no doubt he tried to add the luster of this operational success to his record. Yet even that success was not enough and Zhukov would soon be promoting a new grand offensive, dubbed "Polar Star," which he claimed would lead to the complete destruction of Heeresgruppe Nord.

The Destruction of the Hungarian 2nd Army, January 12–29, 1943

Even before the culmination of Operation *Little Saturn* in late December 1942, the Stavka was pushing for a follow-on offensive to finish off Heeresgruppe B. The relatively easy elimination of the Romanian and Italian armies suggested that the Hungarian 2nd Army, defending positions along the Don River south of Voronezh, was ripe for the plucking. By eliminating the Hungarian 2nd Army, another huge hole could be torn in Heeresgruppe B's thin front, enabling an advance toward Kharkov and the Donbas region. Golikov's Voronezh Front was assigned the mission and he received General-major Pavel S. Rybalko's 3 TA to lead the offensive. Rybalko, a Ukrainian, was a very unusual field commander in the Red Army of 1943. He had virtually no command experience prior to mid-1942 and had spent the 1930s in a variety of diverse assignments, including military advisor in China, military attaché in Warsaw and intelligence work for the GRU. However, Rybalko was a quick learner, having taught himself how to drive a T-34 tank, and he had assimilated a great deal of knowledge at the Frunze Academy and the Kazan Tank School.[19] Rybalko was also a

---

[*]Although there are photos of Zhukov with troops in the field during the 1939 Khalkin Gol campaign and in the 1940 Kiev maneuvers, I have yet to find any photos of Zhukov with front-line troops in 1941–45.

hands-on, up-front kind of officer, who spent considerable time around the common soldiers (*frontoviki*).

By Christmas, Golikov and his staff had developed the basic plan, which envisioned a three-pronged attack across a 90km-wide front. In the north, General-major Kirill S. Moskalenko's reinforced 40th Army would break out of its Uryv bridgehead across the Don and hit the Hungarian center. There had been nearly continuous fighting around Uryv since August 1942, so Soviet activity in this sector did not attract undue attention. Further south, an independent rifle corps under General-major Petr M. Zykov would hit the Hungarian right flank. Rybalko's 3 TA would attack the Axis group of forces northwest of Kantemirovka (Italian Alpine Corps and German XXIV Panzerkorps) and then exploit west to the Oskol River. Essentially, Golikov wanted to achieve a double envelopment of the Axis forces, with Moskalenko's 40th Army comprising the northern pincer and Rybalko's 3 TA forming the southern pincer, while Zykov's force conducted fixing attacks in the center. Golikov put special emphasis upon operational security (*maskirovka*) to prevent the Axis from learning about the arrival of Rybalko's 3 TA in this sector or Moskalenko's preparations to break out of the Uryv bridgehead. Golikov's plans were well advanced when Zhukov and Vasilevsky arrived at his headquarters on January 3, to "supervise" planning.[20] Zhukov left just prior to the beginning of the offensive, but Vasilevsky remained with Golikov for the duration of the operation.

General Gustav Jány's Hungarian 2nd Army consisted of eight infantry divisions deployed along a 186km-wide sector of front. Although most of the Hungarian units were protected to some extent by the Don River, the Soviet bridgehead at Uryv represented a serious vulnerability in the integrity of their front. The Hungarian units were lightly equipped, particularly in terms of artillery and antitank weapons. Even worse, lack of organic transport (mostly horse-drawn) left the front-line divisions in a very poor state of supply. Jány's tactical reserve consisted of the Hungarian 1st Armored Division - a rather fragile unit, equipped with obsolescent tanks. Like the Romanians, Jány appealed to von Weichs for assistance, but Heeresgruppe B had very limited resources. Von Weichs assigned a corps-size unit (Gruppe Cramer) with two German infantry divisions and some assault guns to serve as an operational reserve in the Hungarian sector, but this formation remained under German command. He also provided the Hungarians with a few 8.8cm Flak batteries for antitank defense, but this was a drop in the bucket. Axis intelligence failed spectacularly – in large part due to Golikov's *maskirovka* – by failing to detect the arrival of

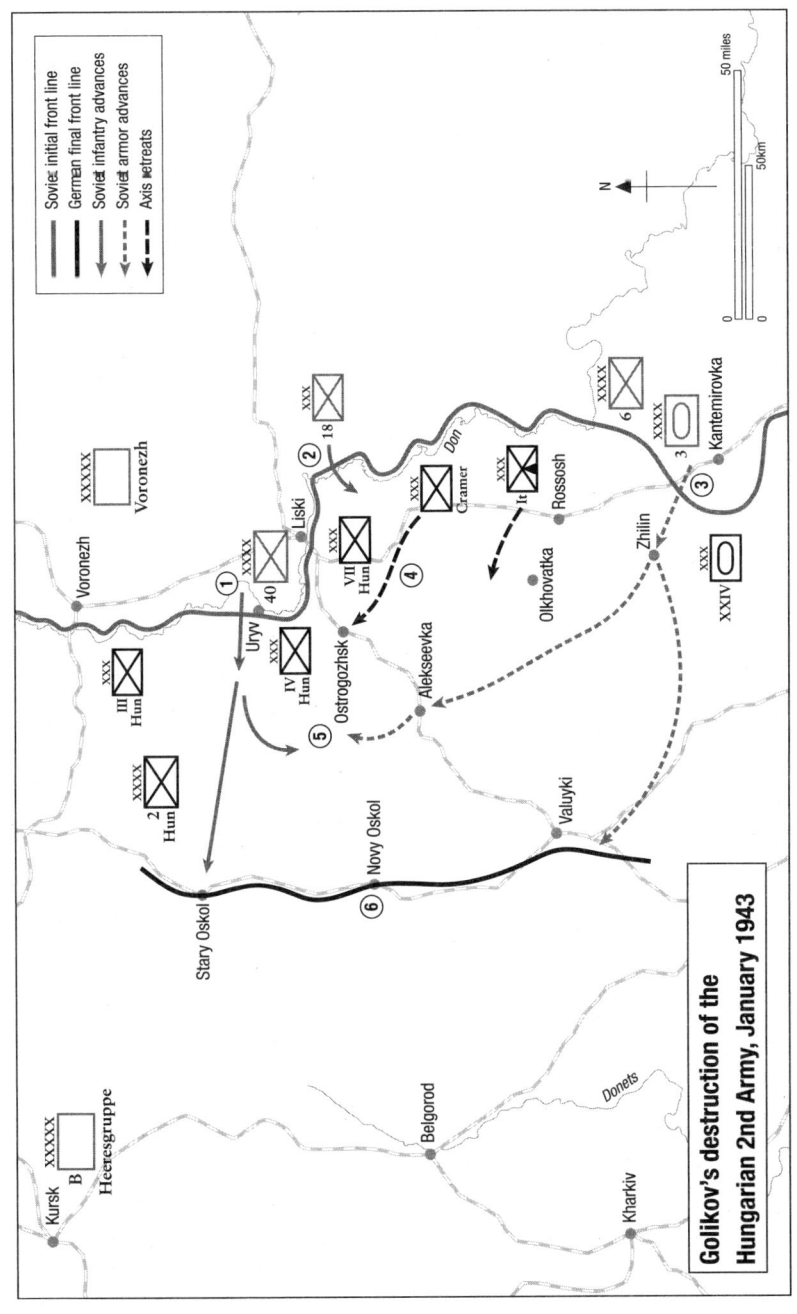

Golikov's destruction of the
Hungarian 2nd Army, January 1943

MAP KEY

1. Moskalenko's 40th Army breaks out of Uryv bridgehead.
2. Soviet 18th Rifle Corps attack disrupts Hungarian right flank.
3. Rybalko's 3rd Tank Army smashes through the XXIV Panzerkorps.
4. Group Cramer and the Italian Mountain Corps retreat westward.
5. Rybalko and Moskalenko's pincers close west of Ostrogozhsk.
6. Heeresgruppe B establishes a new screen line along the Oskol River.

Rybalko's 3 TA. Consequently, Heeresgruppe B remained ignorant of the impending enemy offensive.

Moskalenko started the operation with a shaping attack to expand the 40th Army's Uryv bridgehead.* On January 12, Moskalenko attacked with two rifle divisions and a tank brigade, which mauled a Hungarian regiment and advanced 5km. The next morning, Moskalenko launched his main breakout attack with a large artillery bombardment followed by four division-size shock groups, which quickly overwhelmed the lone Hungarian division in the Uryv sector. Belatedly, the Germans tried to shift a small Panzer unit to contain the breakout, but Moskalenko's T-34 tanks easily defeated the enemy light tanks. Moskalenko then committed his second-echelon forces, including the 4th Tank Corps (4 TC), which pushed west toward the Oskol River. The ruptured Hungarian front recoiled to the north, toward the neighboring German 2. Armee, but this widened the gap in the Axis front. By the end of January 14, Moskalenko's 40th Army had achieved a significant breakthrough and disrupted the center of the Hungarian 2nd Army's front. Further south, Zykov's 18th Rifle Corps defeated one Hungarian division but was blocked when Gruppe Cramer moved up to prevent a complete collapse.

Rybalko's 3 TA attacked on the morning of January 14, supported by the 8th Artillery Division. Generalleutnant Martin Wandel's XXIV Panzerkorps was defending in this area with one German infantry division and several small motorized *Kampfgruppen*, but they were caught completely by surprise when Soviet massed armor appeared out of

---

*A shaping operation is a preliminary action undertaken to facilitate a larger, impending operation. Typically, shaping operations are conducted to seize key terrain or "jump-off" positions for a big-push offensive.

the morning fog. Wandel was killed, his *Kampfgruppen* routed and the XXIV Panzerkorps command post overrun (many of the corps staff were also eliminated). On the first day, Rybalko's tanks advanced 20 kilometers and began to roll up Heeresgruppe B's right flank. Von Weichs was slow to react to this new onslaught and failed to appreciate the threat posed by the rapid advance of Rybalko's 3 TA. Instead, von Weichs and Jány focused on Zykov's 18th Rifle Corps and committed the Hungarian 1st Armored Division into action on January 15. However, the Hungarian light armor suffered heavy losses and failed to make any real difference.[21] On January 16, Rybalko crushed the remnants of the XXIV Panzerkorps and continued to roll up von Weichs' right flank, with little interference from Axis troops. Jány seems to have been unaware that his army was dissolving around him and did not order a retreat until January 17, by which time it was too late. On January 18, the jaws of Golikov's Voronezh Front closed, with 40th Army and 3 TA linking up behind the Hungarians, the Italian Alpine Corps and Gruppe Cramer. Hitler ordered von Weichs to stand fast, but Heeresgruppe B was already in full retreat toward the Oskol River. Golikov had succeeded in blasting a 190km-wide gap in Heeresgruppe B's front, then advancing 140 kilometers in just over one week – a major operational accomplishment. In a fit of arrant stupidity, Jány issued a bulletin from his headquarters, accusing his own troops of "cowardice" and having "lost their honor."

Moskalenko, Rybalko and Zykov all shifted to pursuit, although deep snow and the usual fuel shortages hindered their advance. Amazingly, both Gruppe Cramer and part of the Italian Alpine Corps fought their way out of encirclement, although both these formations were left gutted and combat-ineffective.[22] The Soviet pursuit halted at the Oskol River, as von Weichs' used reinforcements transferred from Heeresgruppe Mitte to form a short-lived blocking force known as Armee-Abteilung Lanz. Rybalko's 3 TA had virtually run out of fuel and many of its tanks were no longer operational, which took the impetus away from Golikov's offensive. Nevertheless, the Hungarian 2nd Army had been virtually obliterated, having lost more than 100,000 casualties, and could only muster 17,000 troops on the Oskol River. The Italians suffered about 30,000 casualties and were left with only 22,000 survivors, who were quickly sent home. Oddly, Hitler did not relieve von Weichs, but simply transferred his remaining units to either Heeresgruppe Mitte or Heeresgruppe Don. On February 9, Heeresgruppe B was effectively dissolved, with von Weichs sent back to Germany, although he would later serve in the Balkan theater in 1943–44. Jány was relieved of command and sent back home; after the war, he was executed by the new regime in Budapest. Soviet losses were extremely light for an operation on this scale, amounting to about 4,500 dead or missing. Although the Ostrogozhsk-Rossosh operation is not well known in the historiography of the Second World War, it was a major victory for the Red Army and demonstrated the increasing sophistication of Soviet operational art.

While the Ostrogozhsk-Rossosh operation was still going on, the Stavka told Golikov on January 20 to prepare a joint offensive with General-polkovnik Maks A. Reiter's Bryansk Front against the German 2. Armee (Generaloberst Hans von Salmuth) in the Voronezh sector. Vasilevsky, who recommended the next operation, expected that the destruction of most of the AOK 2 at this point, following upon the elimination of the Hungarian 2nd Army and Italian 8th Army, would create an irreparable gap in the enemy front. Von Salmuth's AOK 2 had a solid core of German infantry divisions from the VII Armeekorps holding Voronezh, but his right flank was protected only by the Hungarian III Corps. Furthermore, the Stavka had identified the rail junction at Kastornoye, 75km west of Voronezh, as the key node supplying the AOK 2 forces in Voronezh. The basic plan was for Golikov to attack the Hungarian III Corps with Moskalenko's 40th Army and roll up von Salmuth's left flank, while the Bryansk Front attacked the enemy at Voronezh with the 60th Army (Cherniakhovsky) and 38th Army (Chibisov). General-major Nikolai P. Pukhov's 13th Army would attack from the north and aim for Kastornoye.

Moskalenko began his attack on January 24, led by the 4th Tank Corps, in spite of a horrific winter blizzard.[23] The Hungarian corps put up little resistance and began falling back. Seeing his right flank folding, von Salmuth ordered the German VII Armeekorps and XIII Armeekorps to begin evacuating the Voronezh sector.[24] On January 25, General-major Ivan D. Cherniakhovsky's 60th Army attacked and managed to push the German rearguards out of most of Voronezh, which was fully liberated the next day. Not wanting to end up like the 6. Armee at Stalingrad, von Salmuth ordered a fighting withdrawal west to the Kastornoye rail junction, but Pukhov's 13th Army reached there first. On January 29, the Soviet pincers closed, isolating eight German and two Hungarian divisions, which was the bulk of AOK 2. At this point, the Soviets made a classic operational mistake that they would repeat again and again; the Stavka ordered Reiter to leave only Chibisov's 38th Army to contain the encircled German units, while sending his other armies west to seize Kursk and Belgorod. Golikov was told to prepare a follow-on operation (*Star*) to go for Kharkov.[25]

Unlike the 6. Armee, the encircled German forces chose not to sit still but instead to break out to the west, which was only possible because the Soviets misjudged the path they would take. Chibisov seemed to think that the breakout would head due west along the direct rail line to Kursk, which is where he placed most of his forces. Instead, the encircled German forces conducted the breakout in three groups (Gollwitzer, Beukemann and Siebert), heading west/southwest across open country. Chibisov had only two rifle divisions, thinly spread, in their path. From his headquarters in Kursk, von Salmuth sent a battalion-size *Kampfgruppe* from the 4. Panzer-Division to Tim to try to assist the breakout. Apparently Hitler felt that von Salmuth had lost control of the situation and on February 3, von Salmuth was replaced by General der Infanterie Walter Weiß, who was regarded as a tougher customer.

The German breakout through the snow was agonizingly slow, requiring about six days to move 50 kilometers, mostly on foot. However, the Stavka was focused on taking Kursk and Kharkov, not destroying the escaping elements of AOK 2. On February 6, the Soviets took Tim, requiring the German breakout to shift toward the direction of Oboyan. Two days later, Cherniakhovsky's 60th Army took Kursk and on February 9, Moskalenko's 40th Army took Belgorod. Yet by February 12 the three German groups had begun to reach AOK 2's new line southwest of Kursk after a retreat of about 150km. The German line was exceedingly thin – really just a few blocking positions – but the return of the encircled corps prevented the collapse of AOK 2. Soviet post-war accounts are unusually quiet about the Voronezh-Kastornoye operation, even though it was a major operational victory. The Soviets claimed that only "pitiful remnants" (some sources citing the figure 25,000 out of 125,000 Axis troops) escaped the Kastornoye pocket, although these claims are clearly false.[26] Moskalenko even claimed that only 6,000–7,000 Germans escaped. Of the eight German divisions involved, only two (323, 377) were disbanded after the operation and the rest took their place in the line and remained there throughout 1943. Although it is difficult to pin down German losses in the retreat, they were likely in the 20 percent range, not 80 percent. Equipment losses for these divisions were extremely heavy. The fact is that both the Stavka and the relevant field commanders (Reiter, Chibisov, Moskalenko) failed to properly anticipate enemy actions and allowed a large enemy force to elude them. It was still a victory, even if somewhat tarnished by this failure.

Axis generalship in these two operations was mediocre-poor at the operational level, but managed to avoid total catastrophe due to competent tactical leaders. Von Weichs was overwhelmed by the crisis and Hitler essentially dissolved his command and handed the broken pieces over to von Manstein and von Kluge. Von Salmuth deserves credit for belatedly ordering a retreat which ended up saving most of his army, although it soured his relationship with Hitler (a common occurrence in the last two years of the war). Govorov put in his best performance as a field commander in these two tandem operations and his use of *maskirovka*, maneuver and mass gave his armies a major advantage. Reiter's battle command was competent, without quite the level of sophistication of Govorov's methods. At the army level, Rybalko, Moskalenko and Cherniakhovsky were all successful because they conducted very professionally-based operations. The only outlier for the Soviets in this campaign was Chibisov, who failed in his mission to destroy the encircled German AOK 2 elements; his failure was mostly due to poor situational awareness and underestimation of enemy capabilities. Overall, the Red Army demonstrated vastly improved operational art in these two operations, while the Axis performance was decidedly subpar.

Commander	Objective	Offensive	Mass	Maneuver	Surprise	Security	TALLY
Von Weichs	+	o	o	o	o	–	o
Von Salmuth	+	o	o	+	+	o	3
Golikov	+	+	+	+	+	o	5
Reiter	+	+	+	+	o	o	4
Rybalko	+	+	+	+	+	o	5
Moskalenko	+	+	+	+	o	o	4
Chibisov	+	+	–	o	o	–	o
Cherniakhovsky	+	+	+	+	o	o	4

Ostrogozhsk-Rossosh Operation, 1943 Leadership Assessment

Operations *Gallop* and *Star*,
January 30–February 16, 1943

In mid-January 1943, Vatutin was eager to resume offensive operations after the success of *Little Saturn,* but his armies had been temporarily checked on the Donets River by fierce resistance from Armee-Abteilung Hollidt and Armee-Abteilung Fretter-Pico. Indeed, Hollidt played a critical role in stabilizing Heeresgruppe Don's front in the wake of the Stalingrad catastrophe. Yet Vatutin was quick to appreciate that Fretter-Pico's left flank west of Voroshilovgrad (modern Luhansk) was virtually dangling in the wind. In particular, the Starobelsk sector appeared to be nearly denuded of enemy troops; Vatutin regarded this as a golden opportunity not to be missed. Soviet intelligence about the enemy situation was vague, but optimistic assessments by the Stavka suggested that von Manstein intended to evacuate the Donbas and fall back behind the Dnepr River to re-consolidate his remaining forces. Driven by the large void in the enemy front and the possibility that a strategic withdrawal was imminent, Vatutin approached the Stavka on January 19 about authorizing a new offensive.[27]

After receiving encouragement, Vatutin submitted a plan to the Stavka, which proposed using Kuznetsov's 1 GA to smash the left flank of Armee-Abteilung Fretter-Pico, cross the Donets River, then push Mobile Group Popov through Starobelsk to Slavyansk, then exploit south to Mariupol on the Sea of Azov.* Kharitonov's 6th Army would assist the effort by pushing west toward Kupyansk, then Kharkov. Lelyushenko's 3 GA would attack in the Voroshilovgrad sector to pin down Armee-Abteilung Fretter-Pico and hopefully distract German attention away from the envelopment of their left flank. It was a bold plan – heavily influenced by the pre-war concept of Deep Operations – and which promised to sever Heeresgruppe Don's line of communications. Vatutin claimed that the Mobile Group Popov could advance 270km in one week and inflict a decisive defeat on Heeresgruppe Don. At one stroke, Vatutin was promising to liberate the Donbas region and even suggested a follow-on operation to push toward the Dnepr River.[28]

Stalin liked the boldness of Vatutin's concept and immediately approved it, with the plan being designated as Operation *Skachok* (*Gallop*). Yet in the euphoric mood after the success of *Uranus* and *Little Saturn*, inadequate attention was paid to mundane factors like logistics, the weather and the enemy response. Despite an operational pause after *Little Saturn*, Vatutin's own supply situation was poor due to the shortage of trucks and most of his units were at about 50 percent authorized strength.[29] Mobile Group Popov, led by General-leytenant Markian M. Popov, only possessed 212 operational tanks in late January 1943, against an authorized strength of 477 tanks.† Nor were any special provisions made to resupply Mobile Group Popov's dash to Mariupol – it was simply assumed that they would reach their objective before they exhausted their ammunition and fuel.

---

*Armee-Abteilung Fretter-Pico was an *ad hoc* formation created by Heeresgruppe Don to hold Voroshilovgrad and consisted of a mix of German and Italian battlegroups. The strongest unit was the 7. Panzer-Division. On February 3, 1943, the formation was absorbed by PzAOK 1.
†Popov was a drunk and incompetent officer who was tolerated for far too long, unlike other Soviet officers who were relieved after a single failure.

While the Red Army had demonstrated a remarkable ability to operate under severe winter conditions, there was little doubt that 1-meter-deep snow and poor visibility would impact operational tempo. Vatutin appears to have completely discounted any significant enemy response, even though von Manstein had already demonstrated an astounding ability to cobble together effective blocking detachments from whatever elements were handy. Nor was Soviet intelligence helpful in assisting operational planning for the upcoming campaign, since it failed to detect or advise the Stavka on significant German reinforcements that were already en route to Heeresgruppe Don. In fact, the lead elements of the SS-Panzerkorps (under General der Waffen-SS Paul Hausser), equipped with over 400 modern AFVs, had just begun to arrive by rail in the Kharkov sector before Operation *Gallop* even began.[30]

Just before the start of Operation *Gallop*, Stalin and the Stavka had a rethink and decided that it might be prudent for Vatutin's Southwest Front to get some assistance from its neighbors. Vatutin was going to attack in a single echelon with limited reserves and poor logistics, which might disrupt the operational tempo.[31] Furthermore, available intelligence estimates suggested that the Southwest Front had a 2-1 numerical advantage in manpower and 5-1 in armor in its sector, but this advantage might disappear if von Manstein transferred forces from PzAOK 1 or from AOK 17 in the Kuban to reinforce his left flank.[32] Consequently, Eremenko was directed to accelerate his own push toward Rostov to tie down PzAOK 1 and PzAOK 4 in that area. Likewise, Golikov's Voronezh Front was directed to prepare a new offensive toward Kharkov, designated Operation *Zvezda* (*Star*), to begin several days after *Gallop* began. The Stavka decided that hitting Heeresgruppe Don at multiple points, more or less simultaneously, would increase the chances for Vatutin to accomplish a major victory. The Stavka cannot be faulted for its broad concept, which incorporated objective, offensive, maneuver and surprise (von Manstein was expecting the Soviets to pause after reaching the Donets, not continue attacking everywhere), although mass had been undermined by heavy losses in the previous operations and little emphasis was placed on security. However, the wisdom of conducting back-to-back major operations, with the resulting impact upon troops and machines, was not appreciated. Once again, the Red Army's predilection for looking at war as a numbers game led to ignoring the human factors that determine unit efficiency.

Meanwhile, at Heeresgruppe Don's headquarters in Taganrog, von Manstein had to determine how best to deploy his available resources and what course of action to take next. Hoth's PzAOK 4 (one corps) was holding the line east of Rostov while von Mackensen's PzAOK 1 (with three corps) withdrew through the city. Armee-Abteilung Hollidt (with three corps) was holding a line on the Donets from Kamensk south against Vatutin's left wing (the 3 GA and 5 TA). Armee-Abteilung Fretter-Pico was holding Voroshilovgrad with one corps, against Kuznetsov's 1 GA. All three of these sectors had more or less stabilized by late January 1943, as the pursuing Soviet armies outran their supply lines. For von Manstein, the real problem lay in the 250km-wide gap between Voroshilovgrad and Kharkov, which was held by just three German divisions. Heeresgruppe B had formed Armee-Abteilung Lanz, with 30,000 troops, to defend Kharkov and established a strongpoint at Kupyansk, but there was no continuous line from and virtually no connection between Heeresgruppe Don and Heeresgruppe B. Von Manstein had his eye on Hausser's SS-Panzerkorps as a potential solution, but Hitler was adamant that this elite formation would remain under OKH control until it was fully assembled near Kharkov in mid-February and would not be committed piecemeal.[33] Consequently, von Manstein's only real hope lay in transferring at least part of von Mackensen's PzAOK 1 or Ruoff's AOK 17 in the Kuban to reinforce his left flank.

Vatutin began Operation *Gallop* on the morning of January 30 by advancing into the void just west of Starobelsk. Kharitonov's 6th Army attacked with four rifle divisions on Vatutin's right flank, while Kuznetsov's 1 GA attacked with three rifle divisions on the left flank. Heeresgruppe B only had the weak 19. Panzer-Division and two infantry divisions screening this 100km-wide area and they were forced to conduct a fighting withdrawal. Kharitonov pursued slowly but, amazingly, the German rearguards were able to outrun the pursuit and occupy new blocking positions along the Donets northwest of Slavyansk. Kharitonov did not capture Izyum until February 5 and then a single German infantry division managed to delay his advance for six more days.[34] Furthermore, Kharitonov's army became spread out once across the Donets, depriving his advance of mass. Meanwhile, Kuznetsov was able to cross the Donets with the 4th Guards Rifle Corps on February 1 without too much difficulty. The river was partly frozen, but could not support the weight of tanks, so Soviet engineers set up two pontoon bridges in order to establish a crossing site for Popov's armor. On February 2, Vatutin committed Mobile Group Popov across the Donets. Von Manstein quickly appreciated the potential threat to his lines of communications and began shifting Generalleutnant Hermann Breith's III Panzerkorps from the Rostov sector to reinforce Fretter-Pico.[35] By the time that Popov began crossing the Donets, the 7. Panzer-Division was already arriving to block him and two more Panzer divisions (3, 11) were en route. It was soon apparent that the key position was the town of Slavyansk; the Germans got there just ahead of Popov and fortified the position.

On Vatutin's left flank, Lelyushenko's 3 GA was able to cross the Donets east of Voroshilovgrad with a guards rifle division and a tank corps – in a sector held by the Italian "Ravenna" Division. By January 31, Lelyushenko pushed cavalry and more infantry across, enabling his army to carve out a large bridgehead. However, Fretter-Pico sealed off Lelyushenko's bridgehead and the 3 GA spent the next ten days attempting a fruitless breakout toward Voroshilovgrad, but the German defenses had been hardened around the city.

Vatutin was surprised to find that German reinforcements from PzAOK 1 had already arrived in Slavyansk, but rather than bypassing this point of resistance, he ordered Kuznetsov's 1 GA to mount a deliberate assault to take it. However, Kuznetsov's understrength, exhausted rifle divisions were not up to the task and could not budge the Germans from Slavyansk. Vatutin then made a serious operational error – he decided to commit part of Mobile Group Popov to reducing the enemy strongpoint, instead of simply going around the open enemy flank. Although Popov managed to encircle the 7. Panzer-Division, this protracted battle of position diverted him from his true operational objectives. Furthermore, von Manstein rushed additional reinforcements from the PzAOK 1, which strengthened the German defense in the Slavyansk sector. It was not until February 11 that Vatutin came to his senses and decided to pull Popov's armor out of the indecisive fight at Slavyansk and send it to envelop the enemy's open left flank. Amazingly, the 4th Guards Tank Corps (4 GTC) was able to advance over 50km through deep snow and surprised the Germans occupying Krasnoarmeskoye, thereby disrupting (but not quite severing) Heeresgruppe Don's main line of communications back to Dnepropetrovsk. When Vatutin realized that there were virtually no Germans defending a 100km-wide sector on PzAOK 1's left flank, he ordered Kharitonov's 6th Army and the rest of Popov's armor to advance forthwith toward Pavlograd and the Dnepr River. Rather surprisingly, the biggest Soviet success in Operation *Gallop* was achieved by infantry, not tanks. Part of the 4th Guards Rifle Corps managed to occupy the rail junction at Lozovaya, which completely severed Heeresgruppe Don's rail communications to the west. The way to the Dnepr River was now open, with no German forces in the way – Vatutin was on the cusp of a decisive operational victory. On top of this, Golikov's Voronezh Front was now threatening Kharkov.

In late January, the Stavka directed Golikov's Voronezh Front to prepare for a follow-on offensive toward Kharkov as soon as his forces were across the Oskol River. As mentioned previously, Golikov's 40th Army was directed to attack in conjunction with the Bryansk Front against AOK 2, which meant that the Stavka expected the Voronezh Front to run two concurrent offensives. Although Rybalko's 3 TA was still in fighting shape (with 165 operational tanks), most of Golikov's forces were exhausted and worn down after 3–4 weeks of continuous fighting. Supplies were particularly low. Nevertheless, the Stavka assessed that Heeresgruppe B was no longer really capable of offering effective resistance after recent defeats and that even depleted Soviet armies should be able to advance and seize important objectives. Zhukov decided to inject himself into the planning process and unilaterally decided that Golikov's front should also capture Belgorod and Kursk.[36] Consequently, Golikov was forced by the Stavka to sacrifice the principles of objective and mass, by dispersing his armies against multiple objectives on diverging axes. In addition, Rybalko's 3 TA and General-leytenant Mikhail I. Kazakov's 69th Army were expected to advance up to 250 kilometers and encircle Kharkov within just five days. Nor did the Stavka provide Golikov with any additional forces, reinforcements or supplies.

Golikov did as ordered and commenced Operation *Star* on February 1. Rybalko's 3 TA crossed the Oskol River but initially used infantry and cavalry to feel out the enemy to his front. The Germans had established a large blocking position at the rail junction of Kupyansk, but Rybalko wisely decided to bypass it. Once the Germans realized they had been bypassed, they evacuated Kupyansk and retreated – demonstrating the value of bypassing enemy strongpoints rather than hitting them head-on. Rybalko then unleashed his armor on February 3, which hounded the retreated German units and forced them to abandon much of their artillery. Kazakov's 69th Army advanced on Rybalko's left flank, while the 6th Army from Southwest Front protected the inter-front boundary. Operation *Star* appeared to be developing as expected until Rybalko's vanguard reported encountering elements of Hausser's SS-Panzerkorps in their path. Despite Hitler's injunction against premature or piecemeal commitment of the SS-Panzerkorps, von Manstein successfully argued that Armee-Abteilung Lanz was too weak to hold Kharkov on its own without help from Hausser's Panzers. Reluctantly, Hitler consented to using *Kampfgruppen* from the first two SS divisions to arrive (*Das Reich* and *Leibstandarte Adolf Hitler* or *LSSAH*). Rybalko's 3 TA was temporarily stymied by a Waffen-SS regimental-size blocking position in the town of Velikiy Burluk, while Kazakov's army was delayed for several critical days by the *Großdeutschland* Division. On February 4, Rybalko was shocked to discover that most of the *LSSAH* Division was blocking the crossing site over the Northern Donets, on the direct path to Kharkov. Rybalko made three separate attempts to cross the river on February 4–6, each of which was repulsed. Nor were Hausser's troops content with establishing a passive defense but instead launched local spoiling attacks to disrupt Rybalko's 3 TA. Not only had Rybalko failed to take Kharkov on schedule, but his army was no longer capable of making forward progress on its own.

Despite his ability to shuffle forces around, von Manstein simply lacked the resources to counter a seemingly unending series of enemy blows. The weakest point was the area north of Belgorod. Moskalenko's 40th Army bore down relentlessly on this city and took it on the night of February 7/8, which unhinged the German defense north of Kharkov. Von Manstein was obliged to shift the *Großdeutschland* Division to block Moskalenko, which enabled Kazakov's 69th Army to resume its advance toward the city from the northeast. Hausser still only had two of his three divisions in the SS-Panzerkorps to hold Kharkov, which was not quite enough. On February 11, Golikov decided to send a reinforced cavalry corps (6 Guards Cavalry Corps) to envelop Kharkov from the south, while Rybalko's 3 TA mounted a direct assault from the east and Moskalenko advanced from the north. Ignoring Generalleutnant Hubert Lanz, Hausser was in tactical control at Kharkov and he opted for an offensive solution rather than simply wait for the Soviet hammer to fall. While employing half his force to hold off Rybalko, he decided to use the other half to crush the isolated cavalry corps and thereby prevent an envelopment of the city. However, the Waffen-SS counterattacks on February 12–14 failed for a number of reasons and incurred significant losses. The Soviet cavalry managed to slip away and avoid destruction, but Rybalko's 3 TA broke through Hausser's reduced defenses on February 12 and Moskalenko reached the northern suburbs of Kharkov the next day. Suddenly, the SS-Panzerkorps was in serious danger of being cut off and destroyed if it remained in Kharkov. On the evening of February 14, Hausser requested permission to evacuate Kharkov – but Hitler ordered the city held. Von Manstein also ordered Hausser to stand fast. Hausser decided to ignore these suicidal orders and began to evacuate both the SS-Panzerkorps and the *Großdeutschland* Division and by February 15, his units had escaped the closing Soviet pincers. On February 16, Rybalko's tankers liberated Kharkov – Operation *Star* had achieved its objectives. Although Hitler and von Manstein were angry about Hausser's noncompliance, there was no punitive response except against Generalleutnant Hubert Lanz, who was relieved.* Hausser had saved one of the Wehrmacht's most powerful ground combat formations to fight another day, which was grudgingly acknowledged as a positive outcome.

While Golikov was closing in on Kharkov, Vatutin and Eremenko continued to place heavy pressure on the rest of Heeresgruppe Don.† Von Manstein was able to organize some local counterattacks to partly contain Mobile Group Popov by using more of PzAOK 1, but the forces used were drawn from his right flank at Rostov. Once the German forces were reduced at Rostov, Malinovsky's 2nd Guards Army was able to close in on the city and its fall was imminent. During a meeting with von Manstein on February 6, Hitler had already agreed to abandon Rostov and allow von Manstein to pull his right flank back to the Mius River.[37] On February 14, Armee-Abteilung Hollidt began to withdraw westward, evacuating Rostov, Voroshilovgrad and Slavyansk. By February 16, it was evident that both Operations *Gallop* and *Star* had culminated and that the Soviet fronts required at least a brief pause to reorganize for the next phase – an advance to the Dnepr River. Taken together, Operations *Gallop* and *Star* produced amazing victories, with the liberation of Rostov, Kharkov, Kursk, Belgorod and Voroshilovgrad. Yet despite the seizure of vast amounts of territory, no major German formations had been destroyed by either operation; uncharacteristically, German units had withdrawn rather than become isolated. Heeresgruppe Don's defensive operations had also been phenomenal – most other armies would have simply fallen apart under such consecutive attacks and routed from the field. Had the Soviet operations succeeded in destroying a significant portion of Heeresgruppe Don's mobile forces, it is likely that von Manstein would have been unable to reverse any of the Red Army's gains. Instead, by being relieved of the burden of defending cities, von Manstein was now in a better position to mount a counteroffensive of his own.

Due to a variety of constraints, few of the senior commanders involved with the Kharkov and Voroshilovgrad campaigns were able to conduct their operations in a manner consistent with the principles of war. Von Manstein was obliged to create order in a burning house and without adequate resources, serving a national leader who frequently rejected conventional military thinking. During Operations *Gallop* and *Star*, von Manstein was only able to mount local counterattacks, which failed to stop the enemy

*In 1947, Lanz was convicted at Nuremburg for his involvement in the Kefalonia massacre, but he served only four years of a 12-year sentence. Afterwards, he was active in West German politics.
†Heeresgruppe Don was renamed Heeresgruppe Süd on February 13. Heeresgruppe A remained as a separate command in the Kuban.

from reaching all of their objectives except Mariupol. Von Manstein's failure to anticipate an outflanking maneuver at Slavyansk violated the principle of security and allowed Vatutin to threaten Heeresgruppe Don's lines of communications. Hollidt's performance was similarly constrained, but he did a better job with security, which prevented Lelyushenko's 3 GA from fighting its way into Voroshilovgrad. Vatutin's concept of operations was brilliant but undermined by overconfidence and failure to anticipate potential problems. He essentially was gambling that von Manstein had no appreciable operational reserves and was caught by surprise when this assumption proved false. It is also noteworthy that the VVS played no real role in either *Gallop* or *Star*. Vatutin could have requested aerial resupply of fuel to Popov's armor – as the Ostheer often did – but he did not. Likewise, Vatutin could have requested that the VVS conduct battlefield interdiction strikes to hinder PzAOK 1 from moving Panzers west, but this did not occur. Whereas German operational warfare rested on a synchronization of ground and air combat power to achieve a specified objective, Soviet operational methods were still very much ground-focused, with air support remaining something of an afterthought. Golikov was obliged to simultaneously conduct multiple operations without pause and pursue multiple objectives – he did rather well, in spite of lack of reinforcements or supplies. As for the army-level commanders, Rybalko and Moskalenko both accomplished their missions in a professional manner. Kharitonov (6 A), Kuznetsov (1 GA) and Lelyushenko (3 GA) performed adequately, if unspectacularly. Kazakov's performance did little to support the front's main effort and accomplished little.

Commander	Objective	Offensive	Mass	Maneuver	Surprise	Security	TALLY
Von Manstein	+	o	o	+	+	–	2
Hollidt	+	o	o	o	o	+	2
Vatutin	–	+	o	+	+	o	2
Eremenko	+	o	o	+	o	o	2
Golikov	o	+	o	+	+	–	2
Rybalko	+	+	o	+	+	o	4
Moskalenko	+	+	+	+	+	o	5
Kharitonov Kuznetsov Lelyushenko	+	+	o	o	o	o	2
Kazakov	+	o	o	o	o	o	1

Operations Gallop *and* Star, *1943 Leadership Assessment*

Von Manstein's Counteroffensive,
February 19–March 18, 1943

One day after Kharkov fell, Hitler flew to von Manstein's headquarters at Zaporozhe to discuss the situation; they remained in conference for three days (February 17–19).[38] Although angry about the loss of the city and looking for someone to blame, Hitler realized that the escape of the SS-Panzerkorps created an opportunity to launch a powerful counteroffensive – but where? Hitler wanted to make the recapture of Kharkov the primary objective for a counteroffensive, but von Manstein successfully pointed out the more serious danger posed by Vatutin's advance towards the Dnepr. Reinforcing von Manstein's case, tanks from Mobile Group Popov approached to within 32km of the Dnepr. When Hitler examined the situation maps and saw that no German units were blocking any further advance by Popov, he finally understood the gravity of the situation. Hitler agreed that von Manstein could use the SS-Panzerkorps first to stop Vatutin, then to recover Kharkov. He also agreed that von Manstein's command would be redesignated as Heeresgruppe Süd and was solely responsible for dealing with the crisis in the south.[39]

Manstein had begun planning for a counteroffensive even before the loss of Kharkov, but in order to mass sufficient combat power for a decisive operation, he had to accept risk in some areas. Once Armee-Abteilung Hollidt withdrew behind the Mius, von Manstein's right flank was more secure and he began transferring virtually all the available armor to deal with the Soviet advance toward the Dnepr River. Kharitonov's 6th Army (which included three tank corps) occupied a large salient that was over 150km in width and 150km in length, stretching back to the Donets River. Mobile Group Popov held the eastern side of the salient, just southwest of Slavyansk. Manstein's operational concept was the classic *Bewegungskrieg* solution – a pincer attack from two sides to cut off the bulk of Kharitonov's vanguard and Group Popov, then crush it in a *Kesselschlacht*. In order to accomplish this task, von Manstein brought up three Panzerkorps (III, XXXX, XXXXVIII) to form the eastern pincer, while redeploying the now complete SS-Panzerkorps to form the western pincer. Rather than entrusting Hausser with such a critical assignment, von Manstein assigned Hoth to control the main effort, consisting of the SS-Panzerkorps and XXXXVIII Panzerkorps. Von Mackensen would direct his other two corps, which were tasked with eliminating Group Popov.

While von Manstein was preparing to strike, Vatutin was pushing his own forces to the breaking point, under the false assumption that the Germans were withdrawing to the Dnepr. Although the spearhead of Kharitonov's 6th Army was within 32km of the Dnepr, it was virtually immobilized for lack of fuel. Group Popov was in much the same condition, dispersed and nearly combat ineffective. Golikov was doing much the same, by continuing to push the 40th and 69th Armies further west from Belgorod and Kharkov. Victory seemed at hand. Von Manstein assigned the remnants of Armee-Abteilung Lanz to General der Panzertruppe Werner Kempf and gave him the mission to delay the 69th Army. He told Kempf that he could expect no further help until the German counteroffensive had achieved its objectives. Thus, von Manstein took the calculated risk that his own counteroffensive would succeed before Golikov could destroy Armee-Abteilung Kempf.

Von Mackensen began attacking the Popov Group on the morning of February 19; Popov's three tank corps were in poor condition, each reduced to just 30–40 operational tanks, which were almost immobilized by lack of fuel. German intelligence was aware of Popov's problems via radio intercepts, which greatly assisted the German planning.[40] The next morning, Hoth began attacking the right flank of Kharitonov's 6th Army with just two SS divisions, but Kharitonov's army was not deployed for defense and had only weak flank guards. On February 21, the XXXXVIII Panzerkorps joined the operation, attacking from the south; Kharitonov was now being attacked from three directions. Generalfeldmarschall Wolfram Freiherr von Richthofen, commander of Luftflotte 4, ensured that Hoth and von Mackensen both received ample tactical air support. During the first two days of the counteroffensive, von Richthofen's Luftflotte 4 flew 2,631 sorties in support of the advancing German armored groups. In particular, the Hs-129B ground attack aircraft proved highly effective in the battlefield interdiction role.[41] General-major Konstantin N. Smirnov's 2 VA, which was supposed to be supporting Vatutin's ground forces, was ineffectual.

At first, the frozen ground and clear skies enabled the German Panzers to advance over 100km in the first three days of the counteroffensive. Although the regular-army (Heer) Panzer divisions were operating with just 30–40 tanks themselves, they were all veteran formations and well-coordinated by radio. In contrast, Soviet C2 seems to have rapidly fallen apart, since Vatutin was not aware of the extent of the enemy counterattacks for a few days. It was not until the SS-Panzerkorps recaptured Pavlograd on February 22 and moved to isolate Kharitonov's 6th Army that Vatutin recognized the threat. He immediately requested that the Stavka order Golikov to halt the Voronezh Front's westward advance and send reserves to reinforce his own overextended front. However, by the time that Vatutin began to react, it was already too late. Von Manstein's counteroffensive gathered momentum on February 24 and Luftwaffe close air support proved decisive. Now the Ostheer had its winning formula in hand once again – veteran mechanized units supported by Luftwaffe tactical aviation sorties. Popov's isolated tank corps were destroyed piecemeal by von Mackensen's armor and many Soviet units were caught by surprise and fell apart.

Although Kharitonov's 6th Army managed to put up a hard fight at the town of Lozovaya, his army was eventually routed. Amazingly, the pursuing XXXXVIII Panzerkorps had just eight operational tanks – but Vatutin did not know that. Vatutin had virtually no operational reserves in hand to support his hard-pressed front-line armies. Consequently both Kharitonov's 6th Army and Kuznetsov's 1 GA were forced to retreat across the Donets by March 1. The Stavka decided to order Rybalko's 3 TA to head south to support Vatutin, unaware that the 6th Army and 1 GA were already in full retreat. Rybalko's 3 TA had not yet been refitted after taking Kharkov and only had 30 operational tanks on March 1. Nevertheless, Rybalko moved south from Kharkov on March 3 and ran straight into the SS-Panzerkorps (now with all three divisions), which Hoth had begun to reorient northward. The bulk of Rybalko's 3 TA was encircled by March 2 and destroyed the next day.[42] By March 4, Rybalko was forced to shift to the defense south of Kharkov. Despite promises from the Stavka that it was sending reinforcements to Kharkov, the initiative had clearly shifted to the Germans. Vatutin's Southwest Front had been decisively defeated and no longer threatened Heeresgruppe Don's lines of communications. With Vatutin out of the way, von Manstein now turned to deal with Golikov.

Von Manstein's plan for the next counteroffensive was to encircle and destroy the bulk of Golikov's Voronezh Front in and around Kharkov. Golikov had the battered remains of Rybalko's 3 TA defending the southern approaches to Kharkov (with one cavalry corps, four rifle divisions and two tank brigades) while Kazakov's 69th Army had three rifle divisions on Rybalko's right flank. Moskalenko's 40th Army was spread out over a wide area around Sumy and not within supporting range of the other two armies.[43] Hoth was again put in charge of the strike force (now under PzAOK 4), which consisted of the SS-Panzerkorps and the XXXXVIII Panzerkorps. Hoth had learned the hard way during *Wintergewitter* that a minimum of two Panzerkorps was needed to maintain operational momentum. Meanwhile, von Mackensen's PzAOK 1 was left to guard the new line on the Donets and begin refitting.

After repositioning his armor, Hoth began his attack on March 6 and made rapid progress against the infantry of Kazakov's 69th Army. The next day, Armee-Abteilung Kempf joined the operation by launching a corps-size attack against Moskalenko's 40th Army. Kazakov's army began falling back, which obliged Moskalenko to withdraw as well. By March 9, the SS-Panzerkorps had reached the southwest outskirts of Kharkov and Hoth hoped to conduct a double envelopment of the city. However, the XXXXVIII Panzerkorps lacked the strength to form an effective pincer, which left a Soviet line of retreat open to the northeast. Von Manstein preferred to avoid costly urban combat, but Hitler intervened and ordered Hausser to mount an immediate attack into the city. After several days of heavy fighting, Kharkov was recaptured by March 14.

Once Kharkov was secured, von Manstein quickly shifted into the third phase of his counteroffensive, with an advance north toward Belgorod. The spring thaw was just beginning, turning the roads into deep mud and reducing German mobility. Von Manstein wanted to secure as many follow-on objectives as possible before the weather and Soviet reinforcements halted his advance. Surprisingly, it was the *Großdeutschland* Division (under Armee-Abteilung Kempf) which made the most progress, smashing into Kazakov's battered 69th Army and rolling it up with a one-division mini-*Blitzkrieg*. Over the course of five days, the *Großdeutschland* Division defeated elements of three Soviet tank corps, destroying 128 tanks, and enabling the SS-Panzerkorps to advance north and seize Belgorod on March 18. However, Katukov's 1 TA and the 21st Army began to appear north of Belgorod, blocking further progress.[44] Furthermore, Hoth's armor strength was down to barely 140 operational tanks and assault guns spread across six divisions. Although victorious, Hoth's PzAOK 4 desperately needed a pause to refit. Consequently, von Manstein decided to quit while he was ahead, although he hoped to resume the offensive as soon as possible and gain help from von Kluge's Heeresgruppe Mitte.

In one month, von Manstein's counteroffensive had defeated both Vatutin's Southwest Front and Golikov's Voronezh Front, recovered Kharkov and created a new, fairly stable front line for Heeresgruppe Süd. Although the counteroffensive only inflicted about 115,000 casualties on both Soviet fronts (with just over 12,000 taken prisoner), it had succeeded in mauling eight of the 20 Soviet tank corps on the Eastern Front. While none of these tank corps were completely destroyed, they would all require 3–4 months to rebuild, which gave the Ostheer vital breathing space; this respite amounted to a strategic victory. The only substantial gain that the Soviets managed to retain from either *Gallop* or *Star* was the Kursk salient, which jutted into the boundary between Heeresgruppe Süd and Heeresgruppe Mitte. Von Manstein's counteroffensive brought the string of Soviet victories to a sudden, ignominious end and restored some hope to the Ostheer. Despite the debacle at Stalingrad, von Manstein's victory demonstrated that the Ostheer could still conduct successful *Bewegungskrieg* – albeit on a limited scale and under favorable conditions.

It is also important to recognize that von Manstein's success was in no small part due to Armee-Abteilung Hollidt's ability to hold the Mius River front and to prevent the Soviets from taking advantage of the transfer of most of the German armor. Not only did Hollidt prevent Kuznetsov's 3rd Guards Army and Malinovsky's 2nd Guards Army from breaking his thin front, but he even managed to inflict painful losses on the enemy. After the liberation of Voroshilovgrad, Kuznetsov pushed his 7th Guards Cavalry Corps (7 GCC) into a small gap in Hollidt's front, but the Germans quickly encircled this formation and destroyed it on February 22. The Southern Front's offensive efforts after the liberation of Rostov on February 14 were somewhat muddled since Eremenko went on sick leave and was not immediately replaced, so his chief of staff, General-major Ivan S. Varrenikov, seems to have been temporarily directing operations. When Hollidt retreated to the Mius River, Malinovsky's 2 GA was ordered by the Stavka to pursue and bounce the river before the Germans could establish a coherent defense. Malinovsky sent his mobile group, the veteran 4th Guards Mechanized Corps (4 GCM), ahead to spearhead the effort. The 4 GCM succeeded in getting across the river on the morning of February 17 by attacking a sector held by a Luftwaffe *Feld-Division* and then quickly advanced 25km to the west.[45] However, Hollidt repaired the hole in his front and used small, improvised formations to surround the 4 GCM. Despite the limited armor support available in his sector, Hollidt used it well. A pair of Tiger tanks played an outsize role in reducing the 4 GCM, knocking out 23 T-34 tanks in three days of fighting.[46] All efforts by Malinovsky's 2 GA to reach the 4 GCM were repulsed. By February 23, the 4 GCM had been crushed and only 400 troops escaped the pocket.[47] Hollidt's success not only stabilized a critical sector of the front but removed two elite mobile formations from the enemy order of battle. Malinovsky's subsequent efforts to breach the Mius River line failed, with heavy losses.

Von Manstein's counteroffensive (often dubbed "The Backhand Blow" or *Schlagen aus der Nachhand*) is rightly regarded as an operational masterpiece.[48] Furthermore, it was the first time in the Second World

War that the Wehrmacht launched a major offensive in winter.* The only principle of war that von Manstein could not incorporate in this operation was mass, since aside from the SS-Panzerkorps, he was forced to utilize formations that had been reduced to approximately 20–30 percent of their combat power. Unlike previous offensives, the German *Schwerpunkte* in the winter counteroffensive were often just regimental- or even battalion-size *Kampfgruppen*. Hoth was able to use mass in the advance to outflank Kharkov when he finally had all three divisions from the SS-Panzerkorps on line. Although somewhat slighted in most histories, von Mackensen also demonstrated great operational skill in the destruction of Mobile Group Popov.

Soviet generalship during von Manstein's counteroffensive is difficult to evaluate because their C2 broke down quickly, which deprived Vatutin and Golikov of situational awareness. General Sergei Shtemenko, from the General Staff, later stated that "we were badly let down by intelligence and made disastrous mistakes in predicting the enemy's intentions."[49] While it is common for defeated armies to pin blame on "intelligence failures," both Soviet front commanders already knew about the presence of the SS-Panzerkorps prior to von Manstein's counteroffensive but seem to have made no real effort to take defensive measures against a potential German riposte. Likewise, Vatutin and Golikov could have gone forward to get a better picture of the situation at the front – as German senior commanders often did – but they did not. Nor was the unpreparedness of their commands to meet a German counteroffensive due in any large measure to strictures imposed by the Stavka. Ultimately, the blame for the Soviet defeat in the Donbas in February–March 1943 lies squarely upon Vatutin and Golikov, who performed at a much lower level of efficiency than heretofore. The Soviet army-level commanders also performed poorly during the German counteroffensive, particularly in terms of the principle of security.

Zhukov and Vasilevsky arrived at Golikov's headquarters on March 19 to evaluate the situation. As usual, Zhukov's account claims credit for ordering the Stavka to send reserves to the Belgorod sector, but they in fact were already en route (21st Army had begun transferring from the Central Front on March 11).[50] Golikov was soon relieved of command and never given another leadership position; upon Zhukov's

---

*In the 1970 American film *Patton*, which had General Omar Bradley as technical advisor, it was claimed that, "the German army had not launched a winter offensive since Frederick the Great." Apparently, Bradley forgot von Manstein's winter counteroffensives in March and November 1943.

German officers conducting a map exercise in 1936. The officers of the Wehrmacht had been trained to conduct planning in idealized, comfortable pre-war conditions that did not reflect the harsh realities of warfare on the Eastern Front.

A winter supply train in Russia, 1941–42. Ensconced in their warm bunkers in Zossen, 1,500km from the front line, Halder's General Staff could not comprehend the ferocity of the Russian winter and its impact on front-line troops.

In September 1935, the Red Army tried out its new military doctrine in the Kiev maneuvers. Maneuver warfare was emphasized, using large armored units supported by tactical aviation. However, enemy antitank defenses and logistic problems were ignored.

German officers confer in a roadside ditch during Operation *Barbarossa*. The basic German operational scheme at this point was to simply keep conducting pincer attacks with their fast-moving Panzer units until the enemy ran out of troops.

German doctrine for maneuver warfare stressed high operational tempo, with mixed *Kampfgruppen* of tanks, motorized infantry and artillery advancing rapidly to envelop enemy formations and seize key objectives. However, the doctrine proved less effective under the unfavorable terrain and weather conditions found in Russia.

An abandoned Soviet KV-1 heavy tank, summer 1941. While the Germans were astounded that Soviet industry could design and mass-produce powerful tanks, the Red Army lacked the skill or experience at the outset of the war to achieve any notable operational successes with these vehicles.

From the beginning of the war in Russia, the Germans knew how to use tactical airpower in conjunction with ground forces in order to achieve operational-level success. Even as the war turned against Germany, the Luftwaffe continued to play a major role in shaping Eastern Front operations.

Hitler studies a map of the Eastern Front, 1942. Hitler strongly influenced German operational outcomes in Russia, but his preferences were usually driven by propaganda or economic considerations, rather than military logic.

Generalfeldmarschall Fedor von Bock was the best German operational commander on the Eastern Front in terms of victories gained through the effective use of the principles of war.

Generalfeldmarschall Erich von Manstein had a talent for operational-level warfare and could run rings around his Soviet opponents when conditions were favorable.

Generalfeldmarschall Ewald von Kleist was one of Germany's premier operational commanders.

Walter Model proved to be one of the Ostheer's best defensive generals, with a good working relationship with Hitler and the OKH, and an understanding of Russian capabilities and tactics.

Generaloberst Hermann Hoth was one of the best German senior Panzer leaders during the 1941–43 period, and often used operational maneuver to inflict stinging defeats upon the Red Army.

Generalfeldmarschall Ernst Busch is mostly remembered for his poor performance against Operation *Bagration* in June 1944.

Generaloberst Gotthard Heinrici shows the strain of command in early 1945.

General der Kavallerie Georg Lindemann, commander of the 18. Armee, visits a front-line position in the Leningrad sector, early 1942. Most German officers employed a paternalistic relationship with their troops, which helped to instill confidence in the chain of command and maintain fighting spirit.

General der Panzertruppe Friedrich Paulus, the ill-fated commander of the 6. Armee at Stalingrad, was an excellent staff officer and capable of conducting professional set-piece operations, but he was ill-suited to deal with sudden crises on the battlefield and passively waited for others to act.

The Red Army developed a sophisticated doctrine for Deep Operations in the 1930s, but was unprepared to put it into practice due to the decimation of senior leaders in the Purges. In the summer of 1941, the Red Army launched numerous counteroffensives, most of which failed miserably with heavy losses.

A column of Soviet ZiS-5 medium trucks moves along a dirt road. The Red Army's logistical capabilities were limited in 1941–42 due to the shortage of trucks, remaining inadequate until 1944. Soviet fronts only possessed a few motor transport regiments and keeping the armored spearheads in supply was a significant challenge.

Soviet engineers prepare to launch pontoons into a river during a pre-war exercise. The N2P pontoon bridge could be used to cross a 170m-wide water obstacle and support up to 60 tons. The Red Army's river-crossing capabilities became a crucial component of its operational methods in 1943–45, catching the Germans by surprise on numerous occasions.

Soviet soldiers march through a sea of mud near Odessa, 1944. Napoleon once said that mud was the "fifth element of war"; not only did the thick Ukrainian mud slow operational tempo, but it also tended to destroy equipment, particularly vehicle transmissions.

The Red Army continued to send large armored formations into major urban areas in 1944–45, leading to excessive tank losses. Here, JS-2 heavy tanks move through the bombed-out streets of Berlin.

Zhukov's relationship with Stalin was critical for the Red Army's ability to conduct successful operational warfare. While Stalin wanted to keep Zhukov and the other senior Red Army commanders on a short leash at first, Zhukov and the General Staff were given greater latitude in planning operations from late 1942.

By dint of his longevity in front-level commands and number of victories, I have assessed Marshal Ivan S. Konev as the best Soviet operational-level commander of the war.

General Nikolai F. Vatutin as commander of the Voronezh Front in 1943–44.

Marshal Konstantin K. Rokossovsky was in senior command billets for the entire war and I rank him as the third best operational-level commander in the Red Army.

General-major Fedor I. Tolbukhin on the Stalingrad Front, late 1942.

General Konstantin K. Rokossovsky and General-major Konstantin F. Telegin (NKVD), mid-1943. Telegin was the commissar of the Central Front and part of the military council which approved all orders. Having been beaten and imprisoned during the Purges, Rokossovsky was ever mindful that his actions were scrutinized by the NKVD.

Andrei Eremenko, a cavalry officer, was the man who laid the groundwork for the decisive victory at Stalingrad and played a major role throughout the war. I assess him as the fifth best operational-level commander in the Red Army.

Marshal Rodion I. Malinovsky and members of the 2nd Ukrainian Front staff during the Balkan campaign in late 1944. On his left is General-leytenant Ivan Z. Susaikov, the front commissar, who served as "eyes and ears" for Stalin. On his right is General-major Mikhail M. Stakhursky, who served as the front's quartermaster.

General-leytenant Ivan K. Bagramyan, c. 1942–43.

General-leytenant Mikhail E. Katukov was one of the Red Army's top armor commanders; he proved more successful than Rotmistrov and ended the war leading the 1st Guards Tank Army.

General-polkovnik Ivan K. Bagramyan, commander of the 1st Baltic Front, and his chief of staff, Vladimir V. Kurasov. Bagramyan enjoyed a good working relationship with Kurasov, who was an efficient General Staff officer.

Nikita Khrushchev, senior commissar for the Voronezh Front at the Battle of Kursk in 1943, talks on the phone with Moscow while Vatutin (the front commander) and Rotmistrov (5 GTA) watch. Khrushchev played a major part in the premature commitment of the 5 GTA, then tried to blame Rotmistrov for its failure.

General-polkovnik Ivan E. Petrov (left) and Konev (right), April 1945. After fumbling the spring campaign in the Carpathians, Petrov was demoted and assigned as Konev's chief of staff for the final push into Germany.

General-leytenant Pavel A. Rotmistrov was one of the most prominent armor commanders in the Red Army in 1941–44. He had a reputation as a good planner but his record on the battlefield was erratic; his superiors continually pushed him into conducting rash attacks, and he lacked the morale courage to stand up to them.

General Ivan D. Cherniakhovsky with his chief of staff during the Kursk campaign in July 1943. Despite the lack of any special accomplishments, Cherniakhovsky managed to attract Stalin's attention and was rapidly promoted to front commander in 1944. I have assessed him as the tenth best Soviet operational commander of the war, which is generous.

Prior to 1941, the Wehrmacht had not spent any effort to develop a doctrine for conducting joint operations with allied military forces. Consequently, the Ostheer had great difficulty working with its Romanian, Hungarian and Italian allies in Russia. Here, Romanian infantry and a German assault gun operate together during the Stalingrad relief attempt in December 1942.

recommendation, Vatutin was assigned to take over the Voronezh Front. Kazakov was relieved of command of the 69th Army but after spending the rest of 1943 in Stalin's doghouse, he was given command of a guards army in 1944–45. Kharitonov, age 44, died of "a serious illness" two months after his army was routed and Smirnov was relieved of command of 2VA, since Zhukov thought that the VVS should also take some of the blame.[51] Surprisingly, Popov was soon promoted to front commander, even though he had demonstrated very little competence as an army commander. Rybalko and Moskalenko also both survived and remained as field commanders for the duration. The fact that only Golikov really paid a career price for the Kharkov disaster indicates that Stalin was becoming less eager to sacrifice proven field commanders simply because they made mistakes. Stalin certainly liked bold, aggressive commanders like Vatutin and seemed to recognize that not all gambles could succeed. While Stalin still liked to openly threaten commanders with relief, he actually became somewhat more tolerant about failure, at least by his favorite commanders.

Commander	Objective	Offensive	Mass	Maneuver	Surprise	Security	TALLY
Von Manstein	+	+	o	+	+	+	5
Hoth	+	+	+	+	+	+	6
Von Mackensen	+	+	o	+	+	+	5
Hollidt	+	+	o	+	o	o	3
Vatutin	o	+	–	+	o	–	0
Golikov	o	+	–	o	o	–	-1
Rybalko	o	o	o	o	o	–	-1
Moskalenko	o	+	o	o	o	o	1
Kharitonov	o	+	o	o	o	–	0
Kazakov	o	o	o	o	o	o	0
Malinovsky	+	+	o	–	+	–	1

German Winter Counteroffensive, 1943 Leadership Assessment

Rokossovsky's offensive, February 25–March 27, 1943

After the surrender of the 6. Armee at Stalingrad on February 2, the Stavka began transferring Rokossovsky's Don Front headquarters group and three armies (21, 65, 70) to form a new Central Front between Reiter's Bryansk Front and Golikov's Voronezh Front. The Stavka's intent was to use the Central Front, in conjunction with the Bryansk Front, to disrupt Heeresgruppe Mitte's right flank – the PzAOK 2 (Schmidt) and AOK 2 (Weiß) – in order to assist the westward advance of Golikov's Voronezh Front. The boundary between the two German armies, near the town of Sevsk (140km southwest of Orel), was only lightly defended and offered a tempting target. The Stavka's basic concept for the operation was for the Bryansk Front to attack the face of the German-held Orel salient, while the Central Front enveloped the salient from the south, through Sevsk. Rokossovsky was provided with General-leytenant Aleksei G. Rodin's 2nd Tank Army (2 TA) from the RVGK to serve as an exploitation force. Initially, Stalin wanted Rokossovsky's Central Front to begin its offensive on February 15, but transporting such a large force 700 kilometers by rail proved to be a much more difficult task than the Stavka anticipated. As a result, the start date slipped to February 25. Nevertheless, the idea of mounting a hasty front-level assault bordered on the absurd and demonstrated the level of over-optimistic hubris in the Stavka following the victory at Stalingrad.

Reiter's Bryansk Front began its offensive on February 12 and Pukhov's 13th Army succeeded in creating a 60km-wide gap between Schmidt's PzAOK 2 and Weiß' AOK 2. Once Rokossovsky had enough of his forces assembled (but not all) near Livny he began his own offensive on February 25, aiming for the gap between the two German armies. Rokossovsky attacked with Batov's 65th Army on his right, Rodin's 2 TA in the center and Cherniakhovsky's 60th Army on his left. Tarasov's 70th Army was still arriving but would follow when ready. Despite the rushed nature of the operation, Rokossovsky's offensive started well, in large part because he only faced two German divisions. His mission was to aim for the town of Sevsk, 50km to the west, then envelop PzAOK 2's right flank. Surprisingly, a single German security division in Dimitreyev–L'govskiy managed to delay Rokossovsky's advance for five days.[52] At this point, based upon conflicting guidance from the Stavka, Rokossovsky made a serious error – he decided to split Rodin's 2 TA to pursue different objectives. He sent one tank corps from 2 TA and General-major Vladimir V. Kryukov's 2 GCC to bypass Dimitreyev in order to exploit westward, while Rodin's other tank corps was ordered to turn north to outflank PzAOK 2's right flank. Rather than mass his armor, Rokossovsky dispersed it on diverging axes.

Once Tarasov's 70th Army arrived to support Batov's 65th Army, these two formations were able to grind forward and push back PzAOK 2's right flank. Despite bending, the German front south of Orel did not break.

Soon afterwards, the neighboring Bryansk Front operation prematurely culminated due to stiffening enemy resistance. The Stavka's attempt to put additional pressure on the north side of the Orel salient with attacks by the Western Front quickly fizzled out. By March 1, Rokossovsky's offensive was only making significant progress in the exploitation due west. On that day, Rodin's 2 TA captured the initial objective of Sevsk. At this point, there were virtually no enemy forces between 2 TA/2 GCC and the Desna River, aside from some lightly equipped Hungarian units. However, rainy weather, mud and fuel shortages hindered Rodin's advance more than enemy resistance. Nevertheless, Kryukov's 2 GCC reached the Desna River. Just as Rokossovsky was on the verge of achieving a major success, the Stavka intervened on the evening of March 7. The success of von Manstein's counteroffensive led to a re-evaluation of the Sevsk operation. The 21st Army, which was just arriving and which could be used to reinforce the push westward, was transferred posthaste to the Voronezh Front to protect Belgorod. The Stavka also diverted supplies and replacements from Rokossovsky to Golikov. Furthermore, the Stavka directed Rokossovsky to change Rodin's axis of advance from west to north, pivoting 90°.[53] Rather than going for a Deep Battle outcome, the Stavka decided to have Rokossovsky simply chip away at the south side of the Orel salient.

Kryukov's 2 GCC mission was converted from offense to screening along the Desna. The 2 GCC consisted of about 20,000 troops, including 15,000 cavalry and 5,000 ski troops, which were optimized as a winter pursuit force, but ill-prepared for combat against conventional units. Once 2 TA turned north, Kryukov had no tank support and his corps was extremely dispersed. Weiß' AOK 2 was quick to notice that Rokossovsky's forces had ceased pushing west and were redeploying. The only mobile reserve Weiß had available was the extremely weak 4. Panzer-Division, which had about 30 AFVs, but very little infantry. On March 8, the 4. Panzer-Division began rolling up Kryukov's dispersed detachments and eventually Weiß was able to add two infantry divisions to the counteroffensive. Gradually, the German counterattacks isolated Kryukov's 2 GCC, but this formation was not crushed until Sevsk was retaken on March 19; fewer than 3,000 survivors reached Soviet lines.[54] On March 21, the Stavka ordered the Central Front to shift to the defensive once it became apparent that the Germans were mounting a serious counteroffensive. Rokossovsky's inability to break the German defenses south of Orel or fend off the counterattack of a single depleted Panzer division were embarrassing failures. The poor performance of Rodin's 2 TA was also glaringly evident.

In three weeks of fighting, the 2 TA lost two-thirds of its armor but never advanced more than 45km or destroyed any Axis units. Given that the opposition in front of Rodin was often just Hungarian and third-string German units with limited antitank capability, the abject failure of Rodin's 2 TA is remarkable.

Rokossovsky's offensive, sometimes referred to as the Dmitriev-Sevskaya offensive operation or just the Sevsk operation, was an expensive failure. In just a month, the Central Front suffered over 70,000 casualties (roughly 27 percent of its starting strength) and accomplished nothing. The Stavka poisoned the operation from the start by refusing to settle on a single practical objective or to properly synchronize the operations of the Bryansk and Central Fronts. The implied operational objective was to destroy the PzAOK 2 forces in the Orel salient, but the open void to the west proved irresistible and visions of reaching the Dnepr River clouded sober judgment. Once von Manstein's winter counteroffensive defeated the Voronezh Front, the Stavka became distracted and began stripping forces from Rokossovsky's Central Front just when he needed them most. Due to the haphazard nature of the deployment, limited planning and spring *rasputitsa*, Rokossovsky's offensive displayed very little impetus and was easily delayed by almost token enemy resistance. It is also important to remember that most of Rokossovsky's troops had no rest or recovery period following their exhausting combat experience at Stalingrad and were simply trundled off to the next battle; from the soldier point of view, this must have seemed like a cruel joke. The Red Army leadership consistently ignored human factors in warfare, which is why they committed exhausted troops and commanders into back-to-back campaigns; sooner or later the well runs dry, and it ran dry for Rokossovsky at Sevsk.

Despite his talents, Rokossovsky functioned almost as an automaton during the Sevsk operation and he made serious mistakes in regard to the principles of objective, mass and security. Reiter was a rather mediocre commander, but his Bryansk Front committed no serious operational objectives in its attacks against the Orel salient – he simply lacked the resources to complete his assigned mission. Rodin's command performance was extremely poor and it is a wonder that he was not replaced for another six months. The other Soviet army commanders, such as Batov and Pukhov, proved able to lead set-piece operations. On the German side, Schmidt succeeded in fending off multiple attacks against the Orel salient from four separate Soviet armies and yielded very little ground. While Schmidt lacked the forces necessary to mount large-scale counterattacks, his obstinate resistance frustrated the Stavka's plans. Weiß was new to command of

AOK 2 and he took over in the midst of a serious crisis, but managed to calmly delay the enemy, then roll them back, then stitch together a new connection with PzAOK 2 – a considerable accomplishment. Tough, resilient field commanders who could think clearly in a crisis – unlike someone like Paulus – were a precious commodity in the Ostheer.

Commander	Objective	Offensive	Mass	Maneuver	Surprise	Security	TALLY
Schmidt	+	o	o	o	o	o	1
Weiß	+	+	–	+	+	o	3
Reiter	+	+	o	o	o	o	2
Rokossovsky	–	+	–	+	o	–	–1
Rodin	–	o	–	–	o	o	–3
Batov Pukhov	+	+	o	o	o	o	2

Sevsk Operation, 1943 Leadership Assessment

Operation *Polar Star*, February 15–April 2, 1943

On January 14, 1943, Marshal Timoshenko, commander of the Northwest Front, submitted a plan to the Stavka to mount another large-scale offensive to sever the Ramushevo corridor and thereby isolate the German forces in the Demyansk salient. Three days later, Stalin approved Timoshenko's recommendation. Zhukov became interested in the project and took an active role in planning and decided to dramatically expand the concept from a single front attack against the Demyansk salient to a multifront, coordinated offensive with the grand intent of destroying Heeresgruppe Nord *in toto*. Zhukov's concept was based on Deep Operations theory; Timoshenko's Northwest Front would mount a powerful attack to not only sever the Ramushevo corridor but create a major breakthrough in AOK 16's front, through which Zhukov would push a large mobile group with the objective of reaching Lake Ilmen and the Gulf of Finland. The mobile group would be of unprecedented size – a complete tank army and a combined-arms army – and led by veteran commanders. According to Zhukov's concept, Govorov's Leningrad Front and Meretskov's Volkhov Front would also launch supporting attacks to pin down AOK 18 and isolate German forces in the Mga salient. Zhukov's vision of Deep Operations was bold, but it also ignored terrain, weather, enemy resistance and the logistics needed to prepare three fronts for large-scale offensive operations. Zhukov's grand plan was designated Operation *Polar Star* and it was expected to begin in early February.

Up to this point, the Northwest Front had not received major reinforcements for some time, but Zhukov ensured that Timoshenko's forces were greatly strengthened with three new armies, two artillery divisions, 24,000 personnel replacements and hundreds of tanks.[55] A special exploitation force known as Special Group Khozin was formed, consisting of Katukov's 1 TA and Tolbukhin's 68th Army. As usual, Zhukov gave far more weight to quantitative factors than principles of war in planning *Polar Star* and simply assumed that the enemy could be overwhelmed with massed firepower. In fact, the enemy was getting ready to evacuate the Demyansk salient – which Soviet intelligence had failed to detect. Once the Stalingrad airlift began in November 1942, the Luftwaffe was forced to transfer much of its transport units to the south, which reduced the number available to support the units in the Demyansk salient. As the crisis in the south worsened in December, it became evident that the Ostheer could no longer afford to tie down so many divisions holding vulnerable positions like Demyansk. By January 1943, the OKH staff began to broach the subject of evacuating both the Demyansk and Rzhev salients with Hitler. After much argument, on January 31 Hitler finally authorized the evacuation of the Demyansk salient. The next day, he authorized the evacuation of the Rzhev salient.

Soviet logistics in the Northwest Front area were a mess, which greatly hindered the assembly of so many new units. Zhukov granted Timoshenko a delay but directed Govorov and Meretskov to begin their operations (known as the Fourth Siniavino Offensive) on February 10. Initially, the two fronts each committed one army – General-major Vladimir P. Sviridov's 55th Army from the Leningrad Front and General-leytenant Aleksandr V. Sukhomlin's 54th Army from the Volkhov Front. Sviridov's 55th Army inflicted considerable damage on the Spanish "Blue" Division at Krasny Bor but failed to achieve a breakthrough. Sukhomlin's 54th Army made only minor advances and at great cost. Lindemann, commanding AOK 18, was able to shift his tactical reserves and prevented either Soviet front from making any significant gains. After a few days of attacking, the Soviet offensive culminated without even coming close to achieving a breakthrough.

While the indecisive, positional combat was occurring in the Leningrad/ Volkhov sector, Soviet intelligence had finally begun to detect some signs that the Germans might be preparing to evacuate the Demyansk salient. Zhukov immediately ordered Timoshenko to launch his offensive with the forces available. On February 15, the Northwest Front attacked the eastern and northern sides of the Demyansk salient with three armies (11, 34, 53). The hastily-organized and piecemeal attacks were easily repulsed, with heavy losses. Two days later, Busch began the well-planned evacuation of the Demyansk salient, starting from east to west, like a collapsing bag. A period of drenching rain helped to conceal the German evacuation and further hindered Timoshenko's efforts to strike at the retreating enemy. By the time that the 1 SA began to attack the Ramushevo corridor, the Germans had actually shifted two divisions to this critical sector, which held firm. Unable to achieve a breakthrough against an enemy that was slipping away, Group Khozin remained on the sidelines.

Once the Germans completed the evacuation of the salient on February 28 they formed a new fortified line on the Lovat River. Furthermore, the evacuation significantly shortened AOK 16's front, enabling Heeresgruppe Nord to transfer three divisions to reinforce the Volkhov sector. Having invested so much in *Polar Star*, Zhukov tried to salvage the operation by simply shifting the start line west to the Lovat River. He submitted a revised plan to the Stavka, which called for a massive breakthrough attack to take Staraya Russa, then releasing Group Khozin to exploit to the northwest. Stalin approved the revised plan, but the success of von Manstein's counteroffensive began to cloud the future of *Polar Star*. On March 9, the Stavka took Katukov's 1 TA away from Zhukov and sent it south to reinforce Golikov's crumbling Voronezh Front. Despite the loss of his primary exploitation force, Zhukov ordered a smaller version of *Polar Star* to commence on March 14. Timoshenko's Northwest Front attacked first, followed by the Leningrad and Volkhov Fronts on March 19. None of these attacks made any significant gains, but the exhausted Soviet troops suffered very heavy casualties. Even after Zhukov left to go to the Voronezh Front, the truncated *Polar Star* continued out of inertia for two more weeks until the Stavka finally called a halt on April 2.

Operation *Polar Star* was an expensive fantasy which achieved nothing except heavy casualties. In a single month (February 15–March 19), Timoshenko's Northwest Front suffered 136,000 casualties, including 41,800 dead or missing. During the same period, the Leningrad and Volkhov Fronts suffered a combined total of 150,000 casualties, including 35,000 dead or missing. Altogether, *Polar Star* cost the Red Army 286,000 casualties (including nearly 77,000 dead or missing) in a one-month operation that achieved none of its intended objectives. In contrast, Heeresgruppe Nord suffered about 30,000 casualties during the same period, including 7,200 dead or missing – a nearly 10-1 casualty ratio in favor of the defense. Noticeably, Zhukov's memoirs do not mention this disaster or his role in it.[56]

While Busch's AOK 16 was conducting its withdrawal from the Demyansk salient, Model's AOK 9 was planning its evacuation of the Rzhev salient. Model was able to convince Hitler that evacuating the Rzhev salient would release eight divisions for use elsewhere, which was quite appealing after the heavy losses suffered in southern Russia in early 1943. Once authorized, Model's staff planned Unternehmen *Büffel* (Operation *Buffalo*) to conduct the evacuation in a series of phased withdrawals. Unlike Zhukov's haphazard security with *Polar Star*, Model placed a tight veil of security over the evacuation preparations, so the Soviets were unaware until it actually began on March 1. Belatedly, on the evening of March 2 the Stavka ordered Sokolovsky's Western Front and Purkaev's Kalinin Front to start a pursuit operation.[57] In fact, the unplanned Soviet pursuit was sluggish and initially only involved troops from General-leytenant Vitaly S. Polenov's 5th Army. Gradually, Sokolovsky began prodding the 31st and 33rd Armies into the fight as well. Purkaev's Kalinin Front played only a minor role in the pursuit operation. AOK 9 evacuated Rzhev on March 3 and continued pulling back to subsequent phase lines, where the German rearguards would fight for a few days before pulling back to the next phase line. Soviet losses during these meeting engagements were heavy. Sokolovsky did not commit his armor reserves (1st and 5th Tank Corps) until the 12th day after the German withdrawal began.

Unternehmen *Büffel* concluded when Model's AOK 9 reached prepared positions by March 31, where the withdrawal stopped. By means of the evacuation, von Kluge had shortened Heeresgruppe Mitte's front line by over 330 kilometers, which enabled Model to transfer three of his divisions to reinforce PzAOK 2's defense of the Orel salient against Rokossovsky. Not only did the Western Front fail to inflict any significant damage upon the retreating German forces, but the Kalinin and Western Fronts suffered a total of 138,577 casualties (including 38,862 dead or missing) in the month-long pursuit operation. In contrast, AOK 9 suffered just 5,150 casualties in March 1943 (including 1,528 dead or missing). By any standard, this was an exorbitant price to pay to liberate Rzhev and Vyazma. As a result of evacuating both the Rzhev and Demyansk salients, the OKH had offloaded two vulnerable sectors that were under constant enemy attack and released a dozen divisions for use elsewhere on the Eastern Front. Most of Model's AOK 9 was sent to the Orel sector to contain Rokossovsky's offensive. Consequently, the twin withdrawals should be regarded as German operational successes, if not quite victories. While retreats do not win wars, the Ostheer demonstrated considerable precision and efficiency in these two retrograde operations.

German generalship in these operations in February and March 1943 was professional and planning was conducted in accordance with the principles of war, resources permitting. Noticeably, none of the German commanders involved allowed their adversaries to gain a significant advantage over them and inflicted disproportionate losses upon their pursuers. Zhukov's campaign management – he was not a commander in these operations but nevertheless often acted as a *de facto* commander – was one of his worst performances of the war. He refused to use sound military principles as the basis for planning and instead continued to impose unrealistic objectives upon the front commanders. Govorov and Meretskov were improving as field commanders but their armies were still worn out after Operation *Iskra* and not capable of achieving major breakthroughs yet against strong German defenses. Timoshenko served as little more than a cat's paw for Zhukov during *Polar Star* and he took the blame for its failures. Zhukov had Timoshenko removed from command and replaced by Konev. Afterwards, Timoshenko served as a senior Stavka representative for the rest of the war but never held another field command. Purkaev was also relieved of command of the Kalinin Front and replaced by Eremenko; Purkaev was sent to the Far East for the rest of the war.

Commander	Objective	Offensive	Mass	Maneuver	Surprise	Security	TALLY
Lindemann	+	o	o	o	o	+	2
Busch Model	+	o	o	+	+	+	4
Zhukov	+	+	+	o	o	–	2
Meretskov Govorov	+	+	+	o	o	o	3
Timoshenko	+	+	o	o	o	o	2
Sokolovsky	o	+	o	o	o	o	1

Polar Star *and* Rzhev Operations, 1943 *Leadership Assessment*

Results of the Soviet 1942/43 Winter Counteroffensive

The Red Army conducted a total of 12 major operations during the winter of 1942/43: seven were major victories, one was a partial victory and four were failures. As a result of these operations, the cities of

Stalingrad, Voronezh, Rzhev, Vyazma, Rostov and Voroshilovgrad were liberated, five enemy armies were destroyed and two more armies were badly mauled and another was isolated. Furthermore, the Soviet winter counteroffensive erased almost all enemy territorial gains from the Axis 1942 summer offensive. In particular, in the decisive portion of the Eastern Front, Heeresgruppe Süd (including Heeresgruppe A, B) was pushed back between 150 and 450 kilometers. The Red Army paid a very high price for these victories, amounting to 2.83 million casualties (including 967,000 dead or missing) between November 19, 1942 and March 31, 1943.[58] Soviet material losses were also very heavy, including the loss of 5,203 tanks just in the first three months of 1943.[59]

Axis forces conducted four major operations during the winter of 1942/43: three were victories and one (*Wintergewitter*) was a defeat. Only one of the three victories inflicted significant damage on the Red Army and regained any significant amount of territory. Two of the victories were successful withdrawals. Four of the Soviet defeats could be classified as Axis defensive victories. The Ostheer suffered at least 602,000 casualties in this period (including 325,000+ dead or missing), while in addition, Axis forces (Romanian, Italian, Hungarian) suffered about 350,000+ casualties. During January–March 1943, the Ostheer lost 2,152 tanks and assault guns and by the conclusion of von Manstein's counteroffensive, fewer than 800 were still operational.

The relentless winter fighting left the armies of both sides utterly exhausted and in need of rest and refit. Sickness was a subtle but endemic reality of high-intensity protracted warfare that impacted the senior command cadre and mid-level leaders on both sides. Maladies such as typhus and hepatitis did not respect rank and could impair leadership at key moments in campaigns. Commanders such as Model and Eremenko had been seriously wounded in 1942, but still soldiered on at the front. The situation with front-line troops was far worse, with many of the *Landsers* and *frontoviki* impaired by illness during the winter fighting. Nevertheless, both sides were assiduously mobilizing new replacements and producing new equipment to reinvigorate their armies at the front as soon as possible.

Spring Offensives in the Kuban, April 4–May 10, 1943

Once the spring thaw arrived, a strange three-month-long lull settled over most of the Eastern Front – except for the Kuban. Maslennikov's North Caucasus Front was tasked by the Stavka with liberating the Kuban and destroying Ruoff's AOK 17 in the process. While Maslennikov had over 250,000 troops in four field armies (9, 18, 37, 56), Ruoff's AOK 17 had fallen back into a very strong defensive position known as the Blue Line (*Blau Stellung*). The town of Krymskaya, heavily fortified, served as the lynchpin of the German defense and was shielded by marshes on one flank and mountains on the other. The defending XXXXIV Armeekorps (Gruppe Angelis) had time to construct deep bunkers and lay extensive minefields, which meant that only a deliberate offensive had any chance of budging them out of this position. Ruoff also had a small but effective mobile reserve, consisting of the 13. Panzer-Division (19 tanks) and two assault gun battalions. The main problem plaguing AOK 17 was shortages of artillery ammunition due to the inadequacy of supply by sea across the Kerch Strait.

Maslennikov opted to mount a simple 1916-style frontal offensive against the Blue Line, with General-major Andrei Grechko's 56th Army as the main effort and General-major Petr Kozlov's 37th Army making a supporting attack. It is no surprise that Grechko was given a prominent role in the offensive, since he was one of the "fair haired boys" of the RKKA who benefitted from the patronage system and was being groomed for higher rank. The Stavka approved Maslennikov's plan on March 28, apparently without demur.[60] Maslennikov's spring offensive began on the morning of April 4 with a large, noisy 60-minute artillery bombardment. However, Soviet pre-battle reconnaissance had failed to identify the German positions in the main line of defense (the HKL), so most of the artillery rounds landed in the lightly manned outpost zone. Grechko's 56th Army then hurled one rifle corps and five rifle divisions against one German division dug in around Krymskaya. Although badly outnumbered, the German defense remained solid after the ineffectual bombardment and Grechko's shock groups were repulsed. The supporting attack by Kozlov's 37th Army was also repulsed. Nonplussed by this failure, Maslennikov was unable to resume his offensive the next day, which allowed Ruoff to reinforce the Krymskaya sector with some of his tactical reserves. When Grechko resumed his offensive on April 6, his attacks quickly fizzled out in the face of strong enemy defensive fire. The rapid failure of Maslennikov's spring offensive astounded the Stavka and it directed him to regroup and try again in a week; this oft-demonstrated "rinse and repeat" mentality of the Stavka obviated the need to analyze failures in order to find solutions to problems.

Rather than massing his combat power in the Krymskaya sector or figuring out how to better use his combat multipliers (tanks, engineers, air support) to crack the German defense, Maslennikov decided to use all four armies to mount simultaneous attacks across the entire front of AOK 17. The Russians call this method "probing with bayonets," which seeks to identify weak spots in an enemy line. Yet this method also serves to disperse combat power across a broad front, which greatly reduces the chance of achieving decisive results. Grechko attacked on April 15 and managed to reach the outskirts of Krymskaya, but then Ruoff committed his mobile reserve. The Luftwaffe also appeared in force over the battlefield, flying over 1,500 sorties. The ensuing German counterattacks pushed Grechko's 56th Army back to its starting positions and thereby restored the original front. On April 16, the Stavka ordered the offensive halted and a high-level delegation led by Zhukov arrived three days later to assess the situation in the Kuban. Other members of the delegation included Marshal Aleksandr A. Novikov (commander of the VVS) and General-leytenant Sergei M. Shtemenko (head of operations in the GSHKA).[61]

Zhukov was scathing in his subsequent report to Stalin and described Maslennikov's forces as "carelessly and casually organized," which was not far from the truth. Marshal Novikov reorganized the 4 VA and convinced the Stavka to send massive air reinforcements to the Kuban, amounting to nearly 800 aircraft (460 fighters, 165 bombers and 170 Il-2 Sturmoviks).[62] Likewise, Zhukov requested reinforcements for Grechko's 56th Army from the RVGK, including two regiments of the new self-propelled guns and four battalions of the new M-30 (300mm) multiple rocket launchers. Zhukov took an active role in planning the next offensive. Although Grechko's heavily reinforced 56th Army would still be the main effort, Zhukov insisted that both the 9th and 37th Armies would make large-scale supporting attacks in order to put maximum pressure on AOK 17.

Ruoff could see that the North Caucasus Front was reorganizing after its first failed offensive and decided to use the brief reprieve to try to crush the troublesome Myskhako bridgehead near Novorossiysk. Ruoff's staff developed a plan for a hasty counteroffensive, dubbed Unternehmen *Neptun* (Operation *Neptune*), using two German and two Romanian divisions. General-leytenant Konstantin N. Leselidze's 18th Army, operating in the bridgehead, had already been increased to over 20,000 troops and reinforced with tanks and artillery. *Neptune* would be a high-risk plan, relying upon tactical air support and assault guns to make up for the lack of mass on the ground. Another unusual aspect of *Neptune* was the heavy reliance upon Kriegsmarine and Italian light naval forces to disrupt enemy sea supplies to the bridgehead. Thus, *Neptune* was a rare Axis offensive that involved the coordination of ground, air and sea power.

Operation *Neptune* began on April 17 and immediately encountered difficulty due to adverse weather, which limited the effectiveness of artillery and tactical air support. Both attacking German divisions made very limited gains and suffered heavy losses. After a brief pause, the Germans attacked again on April 20 with just a single division, heavily supported by the I Fliegerkorps, three heavy artillery battalions and a battalion of assault guns – but it was not enough. Leselidze committed two reserve brigades which blocked any further advance. The 4 VA also appeared in force over the beachhead and began a major struggle for air control. The 4 VA enjoyed a 5-1 numerical superiority and Novikov ensured that some of the best VVS pilots were sent to this critical sector. Both sides suffered heavy losses, marking this battle as some of the most intense aerial combat over the Eastern Front. Without clear air superiority and only modest ground forces, *Neptune* degenerated into a simple slugging match and fizzled out completely by April 25. Operation *Neptune* failed miserably because the Soviet Myskhako bridgehead had become too strong to eliminate with the limited forces available to AOK 17. Since the bridgehead could not be eliminated, AOK 17's coastal flank would be a constant source of anxiety for Ruoff.

On the morning of April 29, the North Caucasus Front began its second attempt to break through the Blue Line. Zhukov directed Grechko to mass 15 artillery regiments on a 10km-wide front and these units fired a 100-minute preparation against the German defenders. Then the 4 VA flew hundreds of ground attack sorties, further intended to soften up the enemy. After this expenditure of firepower, Grechko then attacked with two large shock groups; one was repulsed outright and the other stalled after a 1km advance. Soon thereafter, German reserves counterattacked and retook most of the lost ground. The supporting attacks by Kozlov's 37th Army also failed. Undeterred by failure, Zhukov ordered Grechko to feed more troops into the battle. Gradually, one of Grechko's shock group managed to make some progress in an area south of Krymskaya that was defended by Romanian troops. The relentless Soviet air attacks – although challenged by the I Fliegerkorps – also began to disrupt the Axis defense. Once it was clear that Krymskaya was slowly being outflanked, the Germans quietly evacuated the town on the night of May 4/5 and fell back to a new line called the D-Stellung. Zhukov ordered Grechko to pursue and keep attacking, but the 56th Army was exhausted and the offensive was halted on May 10.

Zhukov had also pushed the 9th and 37th Armies to escalate their own attacks. Kozlov's under-resourced 37th Army managed to inflict considerable casualties on the German defenders in their sector but lacked the strength to achieve a breakthrough. Koroteev's 9th Army was encouraged to conduct a high-risk coastal infiltration attack along the Azov Sea flank, with the cooperation of Rear-Admiral Sergei Gorshkov's Azov Flotilla. Initially, this infiltration attack achieved some success and threatened the port of Temryuk. However, the German XXXXIX Gebirgskorps quickly adapted to the new enemy tactics, isolating Soviet infiltration units, then using precision Stuka attacks to slaughter enemy coastal traffic. Since 4 VA was entirely focused on the Krymskaya sector, Koroteev received minimal air support, which enabled the Germans to gradually mop up his infiltration attacks. The only value of these coastal attacks was that Ruoff was forced to worry about both his littoral flanks, on both the Black Sea and the Sea of Azov.

Zhukov touted the capture of Krymskaya as a great success, but the North Caucasus Front had expended enormous effort just to get three Axis divisions to retreat 10km. After Zhukov made his report in Moscow, Stalin relieved Maslennikov of command and Petrov was assigned to lead the North Caucasus Front.* Although Grechko suffered no punitive measures for two major consecutive failures, in a rather bizarre twist Koroteev and Kozlov were ordered to swap commands. Zhukov provided Petrov with detailed instructions for the next offensive, which would look much like the two previous attempts, just with more resources added into the mix. Petrov's offensive began on May 26, once again trying to use Grechko's 56th Army as its battering ram. Despite extensive air support from 4 VA, Grechko's attack went poorly and he lost 116 of 145 tanks on the first day. After achieving some limited success, Grechko allowed his army's momentum to become dissipated by accepting a two-day slugging match for the town of Moldavanskoye. Ultimately, Grechko's troops failed to hold onto even this minor objective. By June 2, the offensive had culminated after achieving minimal gains. Nevertheless, the relentless battle of attrition in the Kuban would continue for another four months.

None of the commanders on either side in the Kuban in 1943 demonstrated any great operational talent, for this was essentially positional warfare. The Red Army enjoyed numerical superiority, but not enough to entirely off-set restrictive terrain which favored the defender.

---

*Maslennikov had a "soft landing" and returned to command the 3rd Baltic Front in April 1944.

Furthermore, Maslennikov and his subordinates put little or no effort into *maskirovka*, so the enemy was usually aware of impending offensives. Ruoff's operational control of the defense was professional, but he really could not employ mass or maneuver. Instead, he left it up to his corps-level commanders to aggressively mount local counterattacks and restore any lost ground. Ruoff kept his sight on the bigger picture – preventing the enemy from gaining further lodgments on his coastal flanks and maintaining his line of communications to the Crimea. Although last on the list for replacements, Ruoff's AOK 17 conducted a very effective defense of the Kuban with its available resources. Maslennikov's leadership was pedestrian at best. Zhukov provided him with massive resources, which were poorly managed and employed. Indeed, the utter lack of imagination and rigid adherence to plans prevented Soviet commanders from taking advantage of fleeting opportunities even when their troops achieved some local success. Instead, Maslennikov, Petrov and Grechko all relied upon firepower to unlock the German defense, which it could not accomplish on its own. Grechko's command performance in three separate offensives was extremely poor but was glossed over by senior commanders and he would go on to great glory in the Red Army. The other three Soviet army commanders in the Kuban generally did better than Grechko with less, but received little except scathing criticism from Zhukov.

It is also important to note how useless the Kuban campaign was in the larger context of the Eastern Front of early 1943. Hitler committed Ruoff's AOK 17 (with 13 German and six Romanian divisions) to hold the Kuban, even though there was no realistic chance of resuming an advance to the Caucasus oil fields. Von Manstein was correct – had these forces been evacuated as soon as possible to reinforce Heeresgruppe Don, the overall situation for the Ostheer would have been much improved. Similarly, Stalin committed nearly 400,000 troops (the equivalent of 50 divisions) to crush an enemy force that was better left isolated in a backwater sector of the Eastern Front. In the Pacific theater, the US military was already learning the value of bypassing certain enemy garrisons, but Stalin refused to consider such tactics – he was bent on annihilating every enemy concentration as soon as possible. The problem with Stalin's approach to war was that it removed strategic/operational priorities from the equation and reduced some operational objectives to simply killing or capturing as many enemy personnel as possible. While gratifying for those who don't have to do actual fighting, this is a very illogical and inefficient approach to warfare.

Commander	Objective	Offensive	Mass	Maneuver	Surprise	Security	TALLY
Ruoff	+	+	o	o	o	+	3
Maslennikov Petrov	+	+	+	o	–	o	2
Grechko	+	+	+	–	–	–	o
Koroteev Kozlov	+	+	o	+	o	o	3
Leselidze	+	o	+	o	o	+	3

Kuban, 1943 Leadership Assessment

Preparing for the Showdown, April–June 1943

Hitler had been shocked by the catastrophic defeat at Stalingrad but ultimately regarded it as an aberration. Once von Manstein stabilized the situation in southern Russia, Hitler quickly bounced back to his optimistic mindset and began to think in terms of new offensives to regain the initiative. He reasoned that a quick, substantial operational-level victory would restore the Wehrmacht's prestige and assure the German home front that the *Endsieg* (final victory) was still inevitable. While there were some discussions in the OKH about mounting another offensive in the Leningrad sector, particularly against the annoying Oranienbaum salient, attention quickly focused on Heeresgruppe Süd's area of responsibility. Von Manstein recommended the obvious target – the protruding Kursk salient – which he thought would make a fine capstone to his "Backhand Blow."[63] After his success in holding together the collapsing southern front, von Manstein enjoyed enormous prestige and his views carried great weight.

In early March 1943, Hitler directed General der Infanterie Kurt Zeitzler, chief of the OKH, to begin planning for a new summer offensive to take Kursk, Zeitzler's basic operational concept, which was designated Unternehmen *Zitadelle* (Operation *Citadel*), was a double pincer attack with Heeresgruppe Mitte attacking south from the Orel salient with Model's AOK 9 (recently transferred from the Rzhev sector) and Heeresgruppe Süd attacking north from Belgorod with Hoth's PzAOK 4 and Armee-Abteilung Kempf. According to Zeitzler's plan, the two converging pincers would meet near Kursk and trap five Soviet armies – just like the great *Kesselschlacht* operations of 1941. Zeitzler knew that the Ostheer no longer had the ability to conduct extended, large-scale offensives, but he assessed that a local success under the right conditions was feasible. On March 13,

1943, the OKH issued Operations Order No. 5, which served as a warning order for *Zitadelle*. Once von Manstein's counteroffensive succeeded in recovering Kharkov and Belgorod, the OKH issued Operations Order No. 6 on April 15, which provided additional operational guidance on *Zitadelle*, including specific objectives. The order specified that Hitler wanted the offensive to begin "as soon as the weather permits," which was anticipated in early May. Von Manstein wanted to hit the Soviet forces in the Kursk salient before they fully recovered from his "Backhand Blow," but the weather was not cooperative; heavy spring rains continued until the end of May. There was also concern that the German Panzer units required to conduct a large-scale operation were worn out and would require extensive refitting. Even the SS-Panzerkorps had lost 20 percent of its personnel and 65 percent of its tanks in February and March. Hitler had stipulated that he wanted the "best units, the best weapons, the best leaders and great quantities of munitions ... to be focused at the *Schwerpunkt*," but this set of preconditions caused one delay after another.

On May 3, a major planning conference for *Zitadelle* was held in Munich, with Hitler, von Manstein, von Kluge, Model and Hoth in attendance. Generaloberst Heinz Guderian in his new role as Inspector of *Panzertruppen* also attended the planning conference. One of the key factors that influenced planning was that German intelligence had detected indications that the Soviets were already reinforcing the Kursk salient and creating extensive defensive fieldworks. It was an implicit component of the Wehrmacht's *Bewegungskrieg* doctrine that success was most likely when superior combat power was massed in a *Schwerpunkt* against weak points in the enemy front, preferably at a time and place they least expected. Yet in the Kursk salient, it quickly became evident that the enemy anticipated a German pincer attack and was creating a strong defense. Every week afforded to the Soviets to improve their defenses would only increase the probability of heavy German losses, which needed to be avoided. Consequently, both Guderian and Model argued against conducting *Zitadelle*, which they thought would be a Pyrrhic victory at best. Model regarded the offensive as wasteful of Germany's limited resources and actually wrote a detailed memorandum outlining his objections. Instead of *Zitadelle*, Guderian and Model recommended creating a strong Panzer reserve to deal with future Soviet offensives. However, von Manstein and von Kluge favored the offensive – each for different reasons – and Hitler was opposed to defensive warfare. Von Manstein was convinced that he could break through to Kursk, regardless of enemy defenses. Needless to say, a frank debate among senior leaders and Hitler about operational planning was a highly unusual event. As a concession of sorts, Hitler agreed to postpone *Zitadelle* until June 12, so both army groups would have time to receive additional reinforcements.

In Moscow, the onset of the spring rainy season (*rasputitsa*) gave the Stavka time to evaluate lessons from their winter counteroffensives and discuss future plans. One of the main lessons learned was that carefully prepared operations like *Uranus* and *Little Saturn* had better chances of success than hastily improvised operations like *Star* and *Gallop*. Both Zhukov and Vasilevsky advocated a more deliberate approach in operational warfare methods, which made the best use of the Red Army's growing strength and capabilities. On the evening of April 12, Zhukov and Vasilevsky provided Stalin with their estimate of the situation, which concluded that the Germans would conduct another summer offensive, with Kursk as the likely objective.[64] Von Manstein's counteroffensive had made both Zhukov and Vasilevsky suddenly wary about enemy capabilities and they urged caution; they argued that the best course of action would be to create a multilayered defense around the Kursk salient and wait for the enemy to attack first. Zhukov claimed that German units would be "impaled" on the tough Soviet defenses, wrecking their best divisions, then the Red Army could use its operational reserves to launch a series of powerful counteroffensives that would liberate Kharkov and Orel. Afterwards, the Red Army could pursue the defeated German armies back to the Dnepr. Stalin was impressed by their estimate and, for once, accepted the advice of his military professionals – he ordered the Soviet forces in the Kursk salient to shift to the defense and dig in. He also agreed to provide massive reinforcements to Rokossovsky's Central Front and Vatutin's Voronezh Front.[65] Upon Zhukov's recommendation, Konev was put in charge of assembling the operational reserves behind the Kursk salient, which would eventually become the Steppe Front.[66]

Both sides spent the period April–June steadily reinforcing their armies in the Orel, Kursk and Belgorod sectors. Guderian played a major role in rebuilding the Panzer divisions, which were partly restored to their former level of combat effectiveness. In addition to expediting the shipment of 900 new tanks and 400 assault guns to the Ostheer, Guderian increased the flow of spare parts, which enabled many damaged vehicles to return to service.[67] By July 1, the Ostheer had 2,398 operational tanks and 1,086 assault guns, along with significant amounts of other new equipment. However, Hitler's insistence on using the "best" weapons in *Zitadelle* led to an overemphasis on committing the maximum number of Tiger heavy tanks and the new Panther tank. Despite the three-month delay, only 117 Tiger tanks would be committed to *Zitadelle*, with 90 going to von Manstein and 27 to von Kluge. The situation with the Panther tank was infinitely worse. Although 250 Panther Ausf D tanks had been built by May 1943, the model had serious mechanical reliability issues and on June 16 Guderian informed Hitler that the Panther was not ready for combat. Hitler ignored Guderian's technical analysis and ordered the two existing *Panther-Abteilungen* (battalions) sent to the Eastern Front immediately. Assembled into the Panzer-Regiment 39, the Panthers would only arrive at the front the evening prior to the start of *Zitadelle*. Aside from tanks, the rest of the Ostheer's combined-arms force was also in decline, particularly its infantry divisions. Unable to fully replace its losses, the OKH reduced many of its front-line infantry divisions from nine infantry battalions to six (i.e. two battalions per regiment) and even at the start of *Zitadelle*, most infantry units only had about half their authorized combat troops. Of course, a few elite divisions were maintained at close to full strength, but this came at the expense of other units, which were reduced to little more than "line holders." The German artillery arm was also in decline due to heavy losses and was increasingly reliant on short-range rocket artillery (*Nebelwerfer*) rather than long-range tube artillery. The one bright spot for the Ostheer was that the Luftwaffe was still capable of making maximum efforts, at least for short operations. Luftflotte 6 (supporting AOK 9) and the VIII Fliegerkorps (supporting Heeresgruppe Süd) had a major qualitative edge in the offensive counter-air and close-air support missions, which made up for some of the deficiencies in ground combat power.

While the Germans were trying to mass their armor for *Zitadelle*, the Red Army was busy preparing a warm welcome for them in the Kursk salient. After two years of war, the Soviet General Staff (GSHKA) had a very good understanding of German operational methods and had developed an effective counter – defense in depth, combined with large-scale use of antitank guns and mines. Each of the Soviet fronts tasked with defending the Kursk salient – Rokossovsky's Central Front in the north and Vatutin's Voronezh Front in the south – were ordered to build three lines of defense. In the two previous summer campaigns, German Panzer units had routinely penetrated Soviet linear defenses, which typically consisted of just a single echelon of hastily trained infantry units, equipped with few antitank guns. However, the quality of Soviet infantry units had improved greatly by mid-1943 and the Stavka ensured that Vatutin and Rokossovsky were provided with plenty of veteran guards rifle divisions and antitank guns. The Soviet defense at Kursk was built upon interlocking rifle battalion and antitank strongpoints (*protivotankovyje rajony*), manned by veteran troops and prepared for all-around resistance. In the sector held by Pukhov's 13th Army, there were 138 antitank strongpoints equipped with a total of 700 antitank guns, spread across three lines of defense. In April 1943, the Red Army issued a new mine warfare doctrine which emphasized laying mines in deep belts to stop enemy armor. Although the Red Army had employed mines in defensive combat in 1941 and 1942, their effect had been purely tactical and provided no great impediment to German armored operations. Under the new doctrine, there were no gaps in the minefields and the obstacles would be covered by direct and indirect fire. During April–June, the two Soviet fronts laid a total of 943,000 mines around the Kursk salient, resulting in densities of 2,000–2,400 mines per kilometer.[68] Consequently, the 1943-style integrated Soviet defense would prove to be a very tough nut to crack and the Germans would have to defeat each strongpoint in turn. Hitler hoped to pull off another operational-level victory at Kursk by using the methods validated in 1941–42, but he and some of his generals failed to recognize that those methods could not work against the new Soviet defensive tactics. Even though the Red Army's leadership had not placed any doctrinal emphasis on defensive operations prior to June 1941, a great deal of progress had been made since then – albeit at great cost.

Nevertheless, the Stavka did expect the Germans to gain some ground, so they ensured that adequate tactical and operational reserves would be available to prevent any enemy breakthroughs. At front level, Vatutin had Katukov's 1st Tank Army (600 tanks), two guards tank corps (400 tanks total), a guards rifle corps and two antitank brigades, while Rokossovsky had Rodin's 2nd Tank Army (456 tanks), two guards tank corps and three antitank brigades. The Stavka reckoned that a motorized antitank brigade, with proper support, could stop a Panzer division. Rokossovsky had another trump card up his sleeve, which was the 4th Artillery Corps (it possessed a total of 900 guns, mortars and MRLs); when used in the defense, Soviet massed artillery fire was expected to smother German breakthrough attempts. Finally, the Stavka provided three air armies (2, 16, 17 VA) to defend the Kursk salient, which had a slight numerical edge over the Luftwaffe of 1.3-1. The theater reserves being assembled under Konev east of Kursk consisted of General-leytenant Pavel A. Rotmistrov's 5th Guards Tank Army (5 GTA, with 680 tanks) and General-leytenant Aleksei S. Zhadov's 5th Guards Army (two guards rifle corps and one tank corps). In no previous operation had the Red Army enjoyed this level of ready reserves. On top of the numerical factors, the Stavka also benefited from an intelligence windfall. A subunit of the British Ultra program, known as "Tunny," had compromised the OKH encrypted cypher system used to transmit orders to Heeresgruppe Süd. The British duly passed this information to the Soviets (without revealing their source), thereby apprising the Stavka of the enemy order of battle and objectives. On July 2, the Stavka was informed that *Zitadelle* would start in the next few days; for the first time in the war, the Soviet leadership was forewarned about a major enemy offensive and accepted the veracity of the intelligence.

For the lead-up to *Zitadelle*, the Red Army was afforded an unusually long amount of time to plan a deliberate defense. Zhukov was assigned as Stavka representative to Rokossovsky's Central Front, while Vasilevsky was assigned to supervise Vatutin's Voronezh Front.[69] Rokossovsky had assembled a competent staff, several of whom had been with him for the past two years: General-leytenant Mikhail S. Malinin as chief of staff, General-major Ivan I. Boikov as chief of operations, General-major Nikolai A. Antipenko (an NKVD officer) as chief of logistics and Polkovnik Nikolai P. Savchenko as chief of intelligence. Although the system of dual command had been abolished in late 1942, Soviet front-level commanders still had to operate under the omnipresent surveillance of numerous NKVD (General-major Aleksandr A. Vadis, SMERSH) and Communist Party officials. The Military Council of the Central Front – which still controlled operational decision-making – included General-major Konstantin F. Telegin (an NKVD officer and political ally of Zhukov) and General-major Mikhail M. Stekhurskiy (a communist apparatchik with a background in agriculture). Given that Rokossovsky had been imprisoned and tortured by the NKVD in 1937, it must have been unnerving to have their personnel in his headquarters, observing his every decision. Indeed, the inward-looking paranoia, intimidation and blatant politicization embedded within the Red Army's staff system was unlike anything employed by the armies of the other major combatants. Exercising senior command under such a system added unnecessary distractions and tensions, which required cautious judgment.

Vatutin also had a competent staff, but since he had spent so much of his career as a senior staff officer, he had difficulty delegating tasks and tried to do too much himself. General-leytenant Semen P. Ivanov, his chief of staff, was a veteran staff officer who had been with Vatutin for some time but this did not stop Vatutin from trying to conduct his own planning. Despite the advance warning about *Zitadelle*, Vatutin was unsure whether von Manstein would attack toward Oboyan or toward Prokhorovka, so he planned for both options. Rokossovsky faced similar uncertainty and had to plan for multiple options on where and when to commit his frontal reserves. Zhukov and Vasilevsky allowed the front commanders a certain leeway with defensive planning and instead put their main emphasis upon preparing for the anticipated follow-on counteroffensives. Zhukov's main concern was preparing for Operation *Kutusov*, the counteroffensive to eliminate the Orel salient once Model's attack had been repulsed. In order to crush Model's AOK 9, Zhukov wanted to coordinate a simultaneous counteroffensive by Rokossovsky's Central Front, Popov's Bryansk Front and Sokolovsky's Western Front. Yet faced with the practical difficulties of coordinating three fronts, Zhukov opted to keep the best operational reserves under direct Stavka (and thus his personal) control; this included Rybalko's 3rd Guards Tank Army, Badanov's 4th Guards Tank Army and Fediuninskiy's 11th Army. Zhukov's decision to direct such a large operational reserve force ensured that Soviet mass could be employed at the decisive point, but it also deprived the front commanders of the flexibility to use these reserves in a timely manner and as they saw fit. Thus, Soviet planning for the Kursk campaign was deliberate, but key aspects were still micromanaged by Zhukov and interference from NKVD and Communist Party officials was still an issue.

Model and von Manstein approached operational planning for *Zitadelle* from very different perspectives. Model was unwilling to commit everything he had to this high-risk venture and he also recognized that the Soviets were preparing to mount a major offensive to seize the Orel salient. Furthermore, Model's AOK 9 had significantly fewer tanks and infantry than von Manstein's forces, so he could not afford to suffer heavy losses. Consequently, Model resolved to conserve his Panzers as much as possible and rely primarily upon infantry and artillery to grind their way through the Soviet defensive belts. Model's offensive planning for *Zitadelle* appears premised on the concept of inflicting maximum damage upon Rokossovsky's Central Front, rather than seizing a great deal of terrain. Indeed, it does not appear that Model was serious about trying to reach Kursk, since he knew that he lacked the infantry to hold so much captured terrain. Model also decided to keep two of his Panzer divisions out of *Zitadelle* so he would have an intact operational reserve to deal with any unexpected contingencies. Above all else, Model was cautious and wanted to keep his options open. Although German intelligence was aware of Rodin's 2 TA in Rokossovsky's sector, it was unaware that the 3 GTA and 4 GTA were also nearby – Model did not know that he would eventually have to face three Soviet tank armies. Without authorization from the OKH or Hitler, Model ordered his engineers to begin work on the Hagen Stellung at the base of the Orel salient, so that his army would have a fortified position to retreat to in case of a successful Soviet counteroffensive.

In contrast, von Manstein was unwilling to make any defensive preparations in case *Zitadelle* failed and he decided to commit his entire armored force to the initial attacks, with nothing held back. According to the *Zitadelle* plan, von Manstein was expected to smash through the Voronezh Front with Hoth's PzAOK 4, advance north about 115km and link up with Model's AOK 9 near Kursk in five days. Hoth's intermediate objective was the small city of Oboyan, 60km north of the start line. On May 10–11, Hoth and von Manstein held a planning conference on *Zitadelle*; Hoth argued that PzAOK 4 should not be fixated on one specific route to get to Kursk, but rather should focus on finding and engaging the Soviet armor reserves first. Hoth preferred to advance northeast to Prokhorovka, then north to Kursk, and managed to get von Manstein to concur.[70] Von Manstein's operational concept for *Zitadelle* was to mass three corps-size Panzer wedges, supported by the Luftwaffe, and simply blast through Vatutin's defenses, then push on to Kursk. No effort was made to incorporate deception into the plan and von Manstein did not appreciate the scale of enemy defenses in his path. In particular, von Manstein failed to request any special engineering resources to assist in breaching the enemy minefields (e.g. Goliath and BIV demolition vehicles), as Model did. Furthermore, von Manstein violated the principle of unity of command by dividing the attacking force between two different army-level commands, instead of assigning all three Panzerkorps to Hoth's PzAOK 4. As a result of this mistake, coordination between Hoth's forces and the III Panzerkorps (under Kempf) was poor from the start and grew worse as the operation progressed. Adding to the problem, von Manstein underestimated the terrain problem posed by the Donets River near Belgorod, which greatly inhibited Kempf's ability to synchronize his attack with Hoth's advance. For a general who made his reputation through clever and skillful battlefield maneuvers, *Zitadelle* represented the nadir of von Manstein's operational talent.

The OKH Operations Order No. 6 effectively locked Model and von Manstein into a rigid operational concept (frontal attacks) that left little room for flexibility or initiative. In fact, the Soviet forces holding the Kursk salient were not strong everywhere, but the German field commanders did not have the latitude to look at sectors with fewer mines and antitank guns. Von Manstein accepted this rigid mindset and planned his part of the operation emphasizing objective, offensive and mass, but neglecting maneuver, surprise and security. He committed all his best forces up front and assumed that the Soviets would not interrupt his operation by doing something unexpected, like launching another offensive on the Mius River or near Izyum. In contrast, Model rejected the impractical aspects of *Zitadelle* and opted to fight a limited-objective campaign that inflicted the maximum damage on the enemy at the least cost to his own forces. He emphasized the principle of security above all else. During the defensive phase of the campaign, the Soviet commanders placed their main emphasis on objective (prevent the enemy from reaching Kursk), mass and security, but were prepared to transition to offensive and maneuver as soon as circumstances permitted.

Despite the three-month-long lull, both sides conducted extensive air operations in the run up to *Zitadelle* in an effort to slow their rivals' assembly efforts. In May and June 1943, the Luftwaffe succeeded in inflicting some damage upon the rail network around Kursk, but not enough to seriously disrupt the Soviet build-up. In contrast, Soviet long-range aviation (*Aviatsiya Dal'nego Deystviya* or ADD), which was subordinate to the Stavka, conducted a much more successful battlefield interdiction campaign against the German rail centers supporting preparations for *Zitadelle*. In May, bombers from the ADD conducted several large night raids on the German rail centers at Orsha, Bryansk and Orel, which succeeded in destroying 1,200 tons of ammunition and more than 1 million rations, as well as damaging storage dumps. However, Soviet efforts to attack Luftwaffe forward airfields failed and suffered heavy losses.[71] The Soviets also had some success in directing partisan operations to harass German rail traffic and other rear area logistic targets. While none of these air or partisan attacks proved decisive, they added a significant amount of friction to German operational preparations – which the Ostheer had not previously experienced.

The German logistic build-up for *Zitadelle* was a major failure and this would have a profound impact upon subsequent operations. The OKH plan for *Zitadelle* stipulated that von Kluge and von Manstein needed to stockpile enough ammunition and fuel to support 18 days of sustained high-tempo combat. In fact, by July 1 Model's AOK 9 had only stockpiled 20 percent of the required fuel and 40 percent of the required ammunition. Von Manstein's forces, which had higher priority, assembled a bit more, but only enough to sustain seven days of high-tempo combat. The German logistical weakness meant that *Zitadelle* had to win quickly and that there were no reserves to fight an extended battle. In particular, the fuel shortages would limit the amount of air support that the Luftwaffe could provide.

For once, the Red Army had the advantage in logistics, since their two fronts were sitting astride major rail lines and would not need to expend much fuel in the defensive phase. Under these disadvantageous conditions, it is amazing that Hitler decided to proceed with *Zitadelle* in July 1943.

Zitadelle, July 4–16, 1943

Von Manstein decided to conduct a preliminary counter-reconnaissance operation to strip away Chistiakov's 6th Guards Army (6 GA) forward combat outposts the day prior to the start of *Zitadelle*. At 1700 hours on July 4, the XXXXVIII Panzerkorps attacked with infantry, supported by an artillery bombardment and air strikes. Hausser's II SS-Panzerkorps waited until 2300 hours to attack under cover of nightfall. Immediately, the German troops were shocked by the extent of the enemy minefields and casualties were heavy. The counter-reconnaissance battle succeeded in gaining a few kilometers of terrain but it alerted Vatutin that the German offensive was about to begin.[72] Armee-Abteilung Kempf, which might have benefited from expanding its one small bridgehead across the Donets, made no preliminary attacks. Nor did Model's AOK 9. By the night of July 4/5 it was obvious that *Zitadelle* was about to begin and a nervous impatience took hold of Soviet decision-making. Nikita Khruschev, the Voronezh Front commissar, ordered Vatutin to fire a preplanned counterbarrage against suspected German assembly areas. Likewise, Zhukov ordered Rokossovsky to fire his counterbarrage against Model's forward positions. The problem was that it was night and the fire was not observed. Despite Soviet claims that these counterbarrages disrupted the German offensive, this blind fire did not cause any significant damage and the German assault units moved forward to their jump-off positions on schedule.

Just before dawn on July 5, the VVS was ordered to mount preemptive attacks upon the forward Luftwaffe airfields; the attacks were a disaster that resulted in the loss of 30 Il-2 Sturmoviks. At 0415 hours, Hoth's PzAOK 4 began a 45-minute artillery preparation, immediately followed with ground attacks at 0500 hours. On von Manstein's left, the XXXXVIII Panzerkorps attack was greatly hindered by the 80m-wide Berezovyi Ravine, which was filled with water and infested with mines. Although German aerial reconnaissance had noted this feature prior to *Zitadelle*, no special effort had been planned to breach it. It is also noteworthy that Friedrich von Mellenthin (author of *Panzer Battles*) was chief of staff of the XXXXVIII Panzerkorps and his terrain evaluation failed to note the ravine as a possible obstacle.[73] The new Panther battalions ran into particular trouble at the ravine and their combat debut was a disaster. Nevertheless, at considerable cost, the XXXXVIII Panzerkorps succeeded in pushing through the 6 GA's outer defenses and achieving its initial objectives. In the center, Hausser's II SS-Panzerkorps attacked with the full weight of the VIII Fliegerkorps in support. After heavy fighting, Hausser was able to pierce Chistiakov's first echelon of defense in a few places – which shocked the Soviet leadership – and was able to advance 6–9 kilometers. According to Katukov, Chistiakov was badly shaken by the end of the first day and told him, "I've never seen anything like this before! And what kind of soldiers we have! What soldiers! Guardsmen! Real guardsmen! And they couldn't stand it! They retreated."[74]

On von Manstein's right flank, Kempf attempted to conduct a breakout operation from his preexisting Mikhailova bridgehead near Belgorod, but Shumilov's 7th Guards Army (7 GA) had constructed a formidable defense in this sector. The III Panzerkorps under General der Panzertruppe Hermann Breith failed to gain any ground and suffered heavy losses, including 13 Tiger tanks. Kempf's excessive reliance upon a single 24-ton tactical bridge to support a corps-level attack proved inconvenient when Soviet artillery fire knocked out the bridge.[75] Kempf's fumbled opening assault was an embarrassment to German arms. Even worse, Kempf tried to use two divisions from the XI Armeekorps to gain another crossing over the Donets, but Shumilov's 7 GA defeated this attempt with a well-timed counterattack and inflicted 10 percent losses on both divisions.

Vatutin was immediately under heavy pressure from Khrushchev to "do something" about the German penetration of Chistiakov's first line of defense. Rather than sticking to the plan of letting the Germans wear themselves out before striking, at 1640 hours Vatutin ordered Katukov's entire 1 TA and the two independent tank corps to launch a counterattack against the XXXXVIII Panzerkorps the next morning. Vatutin's decision was premature and excessive, committing the Voronezh Front's entire mobile reserve before the enemy armor had been seriously depleted and when the front-line situation was unclear. In addition, Vatutin ordered Kriuchenkin's 69th Army to transfer two rifle divisions to reinforce Shumilov's 7 GA.

Model conducted his offensive in a very different style than von Manstein. After a preliminary bombardment, he began his attacks in staggered fashion, with three infantry divisions from the XXIII Armeekorps on his left, then his main effort in the center (the XXXXI and XXXXVII Panzerkorps), then two infantry divisions from the XXXXVI Panzerkorps on his right. Although the supporting attacks on both flanks failed, the *Schwerpunkt* in the center managed to grind its way into the first line of defense of Pukhov's 13th Army. Pukhov had failed to pay sufficient attention to the defensive preparations of his subordinates, which led to the near collapse of his left flank on the first day of *Zitadelle*. Model's forces were better prepared to breach obstacles, but still suffered heavy casualties from mines and concentrated enemy artillery fire. By the end of the day, Model's main effort had gained 8–9km at a cost of over 7,200 casualties. During the evening, he moved two Panzer divisions to lead the advance the next morning. In the air, Luftflotte 6 inflicted heavy damage upon the 16 VA, knocking down 100 aircraft for the loss of 25 of their own. Despite the fact that Pukhov's defense was still fairly solid, Rokossovsky was also pushed to "do something," so he ordered Rodin's 2 TA and one independent tank corps to mount a counterattack the next day to restore the original front line. As with Vatutin, the front commanders were being goaded into prematurely committing their mobile reserves while the enemy forces had not yet been seriously reduced. Zhukov and Vasilevsky should have put a break on these actions since it contradicted their battle plan, but they lacked the moral courage to do so.

On the second day of *Zitadelle*, von Manstein continued his efforts to overwhelm Chistiakov's first line of defense. On the left, the XXXXVIII Panzerkorps altered its axis of advance toward the northeast, gradually tearing a wide gap across Chistiakov's front line. Katukov had been ordered to mount a frontal assault against the XXXXVIII Panzerkorps but he had the moral courage to protest this order and instead recommend that his 1 TA would be better employed remaining in defensive positions behind the Pena River. Normally this kind of push-back was not tolerated in the Red Army, but Katukov had a distinguished record and Stalin personally told Vatutin to hold off on the counterattack.[76] Due to this restraint, the 1 TA remained intact and was able to prevent the German armor from pushing northward across the Pena. As a result, the XXXXVIII Panzerkorps had been chagrined to find strong enemy armored units defending behind the river line. Furthermore, Hoth was surprised to discover that the banks of the Pena River were quite steep and marshy, which would make an opposed crossing very difficult.[77] Von Mellenthin's faulty staff work in properly assessing this water obstacle forced XXXXVIII Panzerkorps to shift its axis of advance while heavily engaged. Meanwhile, Hausser's II SS-Panzerkorps continued to attack as Hoth's main effort, fully supported by the VIII Fliegerkorps. At this point, the Germans were able to create their old-style synergy of ground and airpower, enabling them to smash through Chistiakov's defenses and advance 13km to the northeast.[78] In response, Vatutin promptly ordered Katukov to detach his 31st Tank Corps to block Hausser's advance, but in the ensuing meeting engagement the Soviet formation lost 110 of its 160 tanks. Hausser succeeded in breaching Chistiakov's second line of defense on the Prokhorovka axis, but at considerable cost in casualties and his spearhead was now in a narrow salient. Kempf was supposed to be protecting Hausser's right flank, but he was still trying to get his assault units across the Donets. By the end of the second day of *Zitadelle*, Kempf succeeded in gaining some elbow room across the river and denting Shumilov's first line of defense but had fallen well behind schedule and was in no position to help Hausser.

In the north, Model waited until noon on July 6 to resume his offensive, which allowed him to easily repulse the counterattack of Rodin's 2 TA. Rodin only managed to get one of his tank corps into action and it suffered heavy losses from a battalion of German Tiger tanks (which were excellent on the defense). Luftflotte 6 managed to gain air superiority over the northern battlefield, so Model attacked toward the town of Ponyri, hoping to pierce Pukhov's second line of defense. However, Rokossovsky was able to rush fresh reinforcements to this sector, which limited the German advance to just 2–4km for the day. Soviet resistance at Ponyri was intense and the garrison was supported by an entire artillery division. Mines and Soviet artillery fire were rapidly wearing down Model's assault formations, so he began to feed his own mobile reserves into the battle in the hope of achieving some tactical success before his offensive reached its culmination point. The pattern of the Battle of Kursk was already set – Zhukov's strategy was working, since the combination of mines and antitank guns was quickly eroding German armor strength. Neither von Manstein nor Model could sustain heavy losses for long and Soviet losses were still comparatively light, except in the air. Yet Khruschev and Vatutin fretted about each German tactical success and began pressuring the Stavka to release Konev's operational reserves sooner rather than later. Stalin agreed to release one independent tank corps, but not the 5 GTA or 5 GA.

By the third day of *Zitadelle*, the focus of combat in both the northern and southern sectors had shifted to tactical operations. Model focused his attacks on just taking the minor towns of Ponyri and Ol'khovatka. The XXXXI Panzerkorps spent three days trying to take Ponyri, but Soviet resistance could not be overcome and efforts to outflank its defenses failed. Nor was the XXXXVII Panzerkorps able to capture Ol'khovatka. Massive Soviet artillery barrages broke up German armored assaults and the extensive minefields inhibited maneuver. A last desperate roll of the dice on July 10 failed to breach Pukhov's second line of defense, so Model could see that it was no longer possible to gain any significant terrain objectives.

In one week, Model's AOK 9 had suffered 22,200 casualties but advanced less than 15km; this was the highest loss rate suffered by any German army in a similar period of time since June 1941. Three of the attacking German infantry divisions suffered crippling losses. However, Model had kept his armor losses down and ended *Zitadelle* with about 500 AFVs still operational. The OKH was disappointed to hear that Model had terminated his part of the offensive when von Manstein was still attacking and suggested changing the axis of advance, but Model ignored them. There were no repercussions. Rokossovsky had fought a cautious battle, but Pukhov's 13th Army had suffered heavy losses in stopping Model's attacks.

In the south, Hoth fought a conservative battle, focusing most of his effort on July 7–9 on closing the gap between the XXXXVIII Panzerkorps and Hausser's II SS-Panzerkorps. Vatutin conducted a poorly coordinated counterattack with four tank corps (500 tanks) against Hausser's vulnerable right flank on July 8, but lost 20 percent of his armor for no appreciable gain. On the right flank, Kempf's III Panzerkorps fought a virtually separate battle against Shumilov's 7 GA and gradually gained some ground. Vatutin made a crucial operational mistake when he decided to commit the 35th Guards Rifle Corps (from front reserves) and part of General-major Vasily D. Kriuchenkin's 69th Army to reinforce Shumilov's 7 GA – which was holding its own – instead of Chistiakov's 6 GA, which was running out of infantry. Furthermore, the 69th Army was supposed to hold the third line of defense at Prokhorovka but Vatutin gutted it to reinforce a non-critical sector. In large part, this error was caused by the fog of war, which descended heavily over the complex battlefield, distorting perceptions. However, prudent commanders should anticipate communication problems and plan accordingly, but Vatutin did not. Von Manstein was still attacking in three distinct sectors on July 9 and Vatutin was unable to properly assess where the most dangerous threat was located. After linking up with the XXXXVIII Panzerkorps, Hoth resumed his advance northeast along the Prokhorovka axis on July 10. Hausser's SS-Panzerkorps finally broke through Chistiakov's 6 GA and advanced inexorably toward Prokhorovka.

On July 7, the Stavka finally decided to commit Konev's reserve formations, which were designated as the Steppe Front. Beginning at 1330 hours on July 7, Rotmistrov's 5 GTA began a 400km-long road march to the front and by late on July 9 it was assembling north of Prokhorovka.[79] Rotmistrov's road march was an impressive operational feat; although 31 percent of his tanks fell out with mechanical issues, repair units were quickly able to restore most to operational status.[80] Zhadov's 5 GA was also approaching, with seven guards divisions. Even though this massive movement occurred in daylight, Luftwaffe aerial reconnaissance failed to detect it and Soviet operational security measures (e.g. no use of radios) prevented von Manstein from learning about this influx of Soviet reinforcements. Thus, Vatutin was receiving 100,000 fresh troops and 700 tanks to stop Hausser's advance, whereas von Manstein received no reinforcements during *Zitadelle* and his losses were mounting. On the night of July 10/11, the Voronezh Front military council decided to use the 5 GTA and 5 GA to mount a counteroffensive against Hausser's armored spearhead to shut down *Zitadelle's* remaining momentum.

On the morning of July 11, Hausser massed his remaining armor and tried to punch through to Prokhorovka, but was stopped 3km short of that objective. A clumsy flanking movement across the Psel River (which was little more than a water-filled ditch) wasted a great deal of time and effort. Already, guards airborne troops from Zhadov's 5 GA were digging in around Prokhorovka. Just as Hausser's offensive was running out of steam, Brieth's III Panzerkorps finally demonstrated a surge of activity that surprised everyone. Vatutin compounded his earlier error of sending excessive reinforcements to Shumilov by now stripping 7 GA of most of its armor support, which enabled the III Panzerkorps to smash through the Soviet infantry and move toward a link-up with Hausser.[81] The XXXXVIII Panzerkorps, which had been stymied by Katukov's 1 TA for five days, also managed to achieve a small tactical victory on the Pena River and appeared poised to strike north toward Oboyan. Vatutin and Khrushchev were shocked that von Manstein's forces were still advancing and induced a crisis atmosphere that extended all the way back to the Kremlin. Emotion triumphed over reason, since Stalin was now worried that the Germans might actually make it to Kursk. This was not the way that the battle was supposed to develop according to Zhukov; the enemy's armor should have been shattered by this point, but now it was the defense that appeared to be shattered. Committing Rotmistrov's 5 GTA now appeared the only way to prevent a decisive German breakthrough.

Vatutin had intended to use the Steppe Front reserves in a carefully prepared combined-arms attack with air and artillery support, but his plans fell victim to expediency. Khruschev played a major role in pushing for immediate commitment of Rotmistrov's 5 GTA to stop Hausser's advance. During the night of July 10/11, Rotmistrov was informed that he was to attack Hausser's spearhead at first light on July 12. Vatutin promised that 5 GTA would be reinforced with a rifle corps from Zhadov's 5 GA. Katukov was also ordered to use his 1 TA to counterattack the XXXXVIII Panzerkorps. That evening, the planning process at Vatutin's headquarters was chaotic. Although there was plenty of artillery available, the fire support plan fell apart due to communications problems. Likewise, the request for close-air support from 2 VA to accompany the 5 GTA counterattack went astray. Nor were any intelligence updates passed to Rotmistrov's staff, so 5 GTA would attack without any idea about the enemy or terrain in its attack sector. All staff effort was focused on the sole task of getting Rotmistrov's armor to their jump-off positions during the night. Rotmistrov issued his hastily written attack order at 1800 hours and five hours later, the 5 GTA began moving into its positions under cover of darkness.[82] According to Rotmistrov's unreliable memoirs, his subordinate units had time to hold Communist Party and Komsomol meetings prior to moving forward; if true, this was a poor substitute for tactical rehearsals.[83] During the night, Vatutin learned that Breith's III Panzerkorps was advancing toward Prokhorovka from the south so he ordered Rotmistrov to detach a large force to counter this maneuver. Rotmistrov sent a large portion of his 5th Guards Mechanized Corps (5 GMC) off on this side mission, leaving the 5 GTA with just 339 operational tanks to stop Hausser. In compensation, Vatutin gave Rotmistrov two of his battle-worn tank corps (2 GTC, 2 TC) with a total of 190 tanks. Yet rather than massing his armor, Rotmistrov split it up, with two tank corps assigned to attack Hausser's spearhead near Prokhorovka while the two "loaned" tank corps made a flank attack further south.

Without any attempt at deception, Rotmistrov began his counterattacks at 0830 hours, but the Germans were alerted before the first Soviet tank units made contact.[84] The Germans were surprised to see six Soviet tank brigades attack simultaneously, but the great armored counterstroke was a complete disaster. Both of Rotmistrov's tank corps (18, 29 TC) at Prokhorovka were shattered in less than four hours of combat, losing 299 of 339 tanks.[85] The lead tank brigades had been halted by an unexpected antitank ditch and Rotmistrov did not have any engineer support to breach it. Due to poor coordination, the other two tank corps did not attack until noon, lost 69 more tanks, achieved nothing and halted. Rotmistrov's 5 GTA had been thrown away in a hastily planned operation which failed to inflict much damage on the enemy. In his post-war memoirs, Rotmistrov created a fantasy from whole cloth about the action, claiming to have destroyed 350 enemy tanks, including Panther tanks, which were not even in the Prokhorovka sector.[86] Katukov's 1 TA counterattack against the XXXXVIII Panzerkorps on Hoth's left flank was more successful, inflicting significant losses and gaining some ground. Although Vatutin's counteroffensive resulted in heavy and unnecessary losses, it did serve to knock the German leadership off-balance, since they had not been aware of the arrival of such massive Soviet reinforcements. It was evident that the OKH/FHO had underestimated Soviet operational reserves.

By July 13, most of von Manstein's forces were on the defensive and few offensive operations remained. The stockpiles of ammunition and fuel were now nearly exhausted and German operations were increasingly constrained by logistic shortages and casualties. Hitler ordered von Manstein to the *Wolfsschanze* in East Prussia, where he informed him of his intent to terminate *Zitadelle*. He was disappointed by the lack of progress and Model's inability to continue his part of the offensive. Hitler was also concerned about the Anglo-American amphibious landings in Sicily and wanted to transfer some of von Manstein's forces to Italy to deal with that situation. Von Manstein managed to convince Hitler that he needed a few days for mop-up operations, but Hitler would not provide him with any additional forces. In fact, von Manstein was disingenuous with Hitler and sought to implement an unauthorized sequel to *Zitadelle*, which intended to shift forces to Hoth's left flank to push north toward Oboyan. Von Manstein also tried to transfer the mobile reserve for von Mackensen's PzAOK 1, the XXIV Panzerkorps, to reinforce the push toward Oboyan. Hitler soon became aware of von Manstein's subterfuge and he simply began taking units away from him and transferring them to other commands. On July 15, after *Zitadelle* had ended, Breith's III Panzerkorps finally linked up with Hausser's II SS-Panzerkorps, although this success no longer had any meaning.

Von Manstein's forces had achieved nothing of lasting operational value during the 12 days of *Zitadelle* but suffered 33,700 casualties. The failed offensive had cost von Manstein 60 percent of his armored strength, leaving him with just 607 operational AFVs at the end.[87] German planning for *Zitadelle* was seriously flawed at both the operational and tactical levels, particularly in the failure to anticipate the effect of water obstacles and the frequent dispersion of combat power on diverging axes of advance. The German failure to understand that the battlefield of 1943, dominated by mines, artillery and antitank weapons, was different than the battlefields of 1941–42 was a major factor that prevented *Zitadelle* from succeeding. The entire mission of Armee-Abteilung Kempf was poorly framed from the start and the III Panzerkorps failed to contribute to the larger operational goal until *Zitadelle* had failed. After the war, von Manstein claimed that Kursk was a "lost victory" and tried to suggest that Hitler snatched defeat from the jaws of victory. This self-serving assessment ignores the fact that Heeresgruppe Süd lacked sufficient infantry to hold the ground captured or reserves to exploit a deep breakthrough or logistics to sustain a longer battle. The only really positive aspect of *Zitadelle* for the Germans was that the Luftwaffe had won a clear victory over the VVS, maintaining air superiority over critical sectors and inflicting 6-1 losses.[88] Yet success in the air did not make up for failure on the ground.

On the Soviet side, the performance of the Voronezh Front during the defensive phase produced mixed results. Soviet defensive tactics were much improved and the extensive minefields deprived the Panzer divisions of their usual mobility advantage. Vatutin also prevented Hoth and Kempf from seizing any significant objectives or destroying any of his formations, although Chistiakov's 6 GA and Rotmistrov's 5 GTA both suffered crippling losses. On the other hand, Vatutin committed his reserves far too quickly and often head-on at the German spearheads. Vatutin's forces suffered 116,971 casualties (about 13 percent of those committed) and lost 76 percent of their armor. Stalin was angry about the disastrous counterattack by the 5 GTA and wanted to put Rotmistrov on trial, but Vasilevsky interceded on his behalf. Rotmistrov remained in command of the 5 GTA, for now. Later, Rotmistrov had the gall to criticize Katukov's battle command, even though the 1 TA's role at Kursk was far more successful.[89] Khrushchev's role in instigating the disaster was ignored. Zhukov's defensive strategy at Kursk had succeeded in inflicting heavy but not crippling losses on the two German army groups. After *Zitadelle*, the Ostheer's ability to conduct large-scale operations became more and more constrained, while the Red Army's capabilities began to increase at an alarming rate.

In terms of battle command, *Zitadelle* was easily the nadir of von Manstein's generalship, beginning with his allowing a minor preliminary operation on July 4 to sacrifice the principle of surprise. Nor is it clear whether von Manstein regarded Oboyan or Prokhorovka as his primary intermediate objective, since he and Hoth kept switching back and forth on this issue. The poor coordination between Hoth and Kempf was entirely due to von Manstein's violation of the principle of unity of command; Hoth should have been in command of all three mechanized corps. Model did not fight a particularly good battle either, since he had made the conscious decision to emphasize force protection over objective, offensive and mass. Hoth displayed his usual aggressive confidence, particularly in massing in selected sectors to smash Chistiakov's linear defenses. Kempf's performance was the worst of the German army commanders and this was noticed by the OKH. On the Soviet side, Rokossovsky's command performance was solid, if a bit cautious – he made no serious mistakes during the Battle of Kursk. Vatutin's performance was sub-par, in large part due to his mishandling of his reserves and poor situational awareness of actual conditions on the battlefield. Whereas Rokossovsky had considerable experience in conducting defensive battles, Vatutin did not, since he had been primarily selected to lead counterattacks since Soltsy in 1941. Likewise, Chistiakov had not previously experienced the full fury of a German combined-arms offensive and was caught off-balance when his defensive lines began crumbling. Shumilov did somewhat better against Kempf, particularly his early knock-out blow against the XI Armeekorps. Both Pukhov's and Rodin's performances were adequate for an unimaginative battle of attrition, but other than preventing Model from taking Ponyri, they accomplished little else. Katukov put in a good performance as commander of the 1 TA and his display of moral courage in protesting against ill-judged orders enabled him to influence the battle right up to the end of *Zitadelle*. One could make the case that Rotmistrov was herded to the slaughter by Vatutin and Khrushchev, but he appears to have made no protest about the hasty commitment of the 5 GTA or being directed to detach nearly one-third of his army just prior to the attack. Although Rotmistrov was nominally in command of nearly 600 tanks, he was never able to mass them on the battlefield and the temporary advantage of surprise was squandered when his armor was stopped by unexpected obstacles.

Commander	Objective	Offensive	Mass	Maneuver	Surprise	Security	TALLY
Von Manstein	o	+	o	+	–	o	o*
Model	o	+	o	o	o	+	2
Hoth	o	+	+	+	o	o	3
Kempf	o	+	o	+	–	o	1
Vatutin	o	+	o	o	o	o	1
Rokossovsky	+	o	+	o	o	+	3
Chistiakov	+	o	o	o	o	o	1
Shumilov	+	+	o	o	o	o	2
Pukhov Rodin	+	o	o	o	o	–	o
Katukov	+	+	o	o	o	o	3†
Rotmistrov	o	o	o	o	+	–	o

Kursk, 1943 Leadership Assessment

*Minus one for unity of command.
†Plus one for moral courage.

Compared to other campaigns on the Eastern Front, the generalship displayed by both sides during the Battle of Kursk was remarkably mediocre. In large part, these sub-par performances were due to the restrictions imposed by higher authorities upon the field commanders, who were obliged to fight a battle of attrition, not unlike Verdun. Furthermore, the mission of taking Kursk was well beyond the capability of the available German forces, although only Model seemed to have the intellectual honesty to admit this fact. It is no wonder that post-war Soviet sources claimed to have inflicted so much damage upon the German forces, since that was the only real measure of success for them during *Zitadelle*. Technically, all the Soviet commanders achieved their objectives, while none of the German commanders achieved their objectives. However, both sides' best forces had been decimated yet achieved virtually no worthwhile operational advantage. Rather, the true importance of Kursk lies in what each side chose to do in the aftermath of the battle. Hitler thought he would have a brief respite in which to shift forces west to deal with the Anglo-Americans, an assumption which proved false. Stalin, although dissatisfied with the heavy loss of armor and aircraft, saw the German failure at Kursk as the opportune time for the Red Army to gain the strategic initiative through a series of powerful counteroffensives. Yet had Hitler not weakened Heeresgruppe Süd or Stalin not immediately pressed his front commanders to mount their own counteroffensives, *Zitadelle* would likely have gone down in history as a rather sterile battle with few immediate consequences.

Operation *Kutusov*, July 12–August 18, 1943

As soon as Zhukov recognized that Model had suspended AOK 9's role in *Zitadelle*, he began pushing to start Operation *Kutusov*, the Soviet counteroffensive to capture the Orel salient, as soon as possible. The Stavka wanted General-polkovnik Markian M. Popov's Bryansk Front to provide the main effort for the operation, using General-leytenant Aleksandr V. Gorbatov's 3rd Army and General-leytenant Vladimir I. Kolpakchi's 63rd Army to smash in the eastern face of the salient. General Vasily D. Sokolovsky's Western Front would mount a large-scale supporting effort against the northern flank of the salient with General-polkovnik Ivan K. Bagramyan's 11th Guards Army, which would push south in order to seize Karachev on the Orel-Bryansk rail line.[90] Rokossovsky's Central Front would also join in the counteroffensive, once it had recovered from its losses suffered during *Zitadelle*. Zhukov hoped to coordinate three fronts in order to strike the salient and cause it to collapse from concentric hammer blows. As usual with his operations, the basic concept for *Kutusov* was premised on numerical superiority in the ground and air, supported by massive amounts of firepower. Indeed, the amount of artillery provided for *Kutusov* from RVGK reserves was unprecedented: three breakthrough artillery corps and two separate artillery divisions. In addition, three air armies (1 VA, 15 VA, 16 VA) would support the counteroffensive. Although the Western Front made some effort to conceal its attack preparations with *maskirovka*, the Bryansk Front did not. German signals intelligence and aerial reconnaissance were able to identify the Bryansk Front's likely attack sector one week prior to the beginning of Operation *Kutusov*.[91] However, the Germans failed to appreciate the build-up of Bagramyan's 11 GA on the northern flank of the Orel salient.[92]

Furthermore, Zhukov and the Stavka had ignored human factors. Placing a commander like Markian Popov, who had repeatedly failed in 1941–42, in charge of the main effort for such a large operation was a major mistake. Popov's excessive drinking (even by Soviet standards) and indecisiveness were well-known in the upper ranks of the Red Army, noted by both Vasilevsky and Konev in their post-war memoirs.[93] Yet Popov was continually given new commands due to the implicit patronage system that was embedded in the upper ranks of the Red Army. Zhukov met with army-level commanders and was taken aback when Gorbatov expressed doubt about the ability of his 3rd Army to break the German defense and wanted to change his attack sector. In particular, Gorbatov pointed out that his army was expected to cross the 40m-wide Zusha River on the first day of the operation but lacked heavy artillery support. This kind of push-back was amazing, since Gorbatov had been imprisoned and roughly treated during the purges, but he still had the integrity to try to do what was best for his troops. Zhukov exhibited his usual inflexibility, claiming that the *Kutusov* plan could not be changed, but agreed to provide Gorbatov's 3rd Army with an artillery division in support.[94]

On the German side, the eastern and northern sectors of the Orel salient were defended by General der Infanterie Erich-Heinrich Clößner's PzAOK 2. The PzAOK 2 had been denuded of troops and equipment in order to reinforce Model's AOK 9 for *Zitadelle*, so by July 12 it consisted of three army corps (XXXV, LIII, LV) with a total of 15 infantry divisions, along with the 5. Panzer-Division in tactical reserve. On the plus side, PzAOK 2 had well-prepared defenses which included minefields and Generaloberst Robert Ritter von Greim's Luftflotte 6 was still capable of providing powerful air support. Model's AOK 9 defended the southern side of the salient and had a significant mobile reserve. One of the greatest liabilities of PzAOK 2 turned out to be its commander, Clößner, who was indiscreet enough to make some anti-regime remarks which invited the attention of the Gestapo. Just as the Red Army was about to begin Operation *Kutusov*, Clößner was relieved of command and his chief of staff, Oberst August Winter, was too junior to be running an army.[95] Consequently, PzAOK 2 had been virtually decapitated at a critical moment and the three subordinate corps commanders were left without proper direction from higher command. At this moment, the German ability to hold the Orel salient against a massive assault by three Soviet fronts appeared doubtful, but the Ostheer still had a few wild cards in its hands. With Clößner out of the picture, General der Infanterie Lothar Rendulic, commander of the XXXV Armeekorps assigned to defend the eastern face of the Orel salient, was the key man on the spot. Rendulic was a former Austrian Army General Staff-trained officer who joined the Wehrmacht in 1938; as Popov would soon discover, Rendulic was a tough, smart, highly capable and fanatical opponent.

On the morning of July 12, Popov's Bryansk Front commenced Operation *Kutusov* with a massive artillery bombardment, followed by a ground assault by six rifle divisions from the 3rd and 63rd Armies attacking two of Rendulic's infantry divisions. Not only did the artillery bombardment fail to suppress the German defenses, but Popov failed to coordinate the attacks of his two armies. Rendulic was aware of the impending Soviet offensive and had reinforced the sector that was under attack. Furthermore, von Greim quickly committed Luftflotte 6 fighters to support Rendulic and the Luftwaffe achieved air superiority over the battlefield. Despite being heavily outnumbered, Rendulic repulsed Popov's initial attacks and inflicted heavy losses.[96] Although Rendulic achieved a temporary defensive victory against Popov's Bryansk Front, Sokolovsky's Western Front had more success against the German LIII Armeekorps. Bagramyan's 11th Guards Army (11 GA) employed six veteran rifle divisions and an artillery corps against two German infantry divisions. Bagramyan massed over 200 artillery pieces per kilometer of front and unleashed a two-hour barrage which stunned the German defenders. Unhindered by the Luftwaffe, the 1 VA struck the German positions with 70 bombers and Il-2 Sturmoviks.[97] Hit by a well-directed combined arms attack, the German infantry were overrun and Bagramyan achieved a deep penetration in the Ulyanovo sector. Whoever was in charge of PzAOK 2 at this moment – and it is not clear who it was – correctly decided to commit the 5. Panzer-Division to support the LIII Armeekorps. However, no one ensured that this tactical reserve was used properly and 5. Panzer-Division's movement to the Ulyanovo sector proved too slow. Consequently, Bagramyan's 11 GA vanguard advanced 10 kilometers on the first day of *Kutusov*.

Another less noticeable factor in Bagramyan's success was the improvement in Soviet C2. The Stavka had provided Bagramyan's 11 GA with 500 new field radios, possibly including American-made SCR-300 radios; as a result, the 11 GA was able to issue radios down to battalion-level commanders.[98] Heretofore, the Red Army rarely had used tactical radios below the regiment level. The influx of American Lend Lease communications equipment played a major role in enhancing the ability of the Red Army to conduct fast-moving operations, instead of being tied to just field telephone networks. Thus, Bagramyan was afforded significantly better situational awareness than previous Soviet field army commanders.

Despite Bagramyan's success, the OKH was more concerned about the Bryansk Front's attacks. It was expected that the 5. Panzer-Division (which had 100 tanks) would be sufficient to halt the 11 GA, but more would be required to halt Popov. The OKH directed von Kluge to transfer another Panzer division to reinforce PzAOK 2 while the Luftwaffe began stripping fighters and ground attack units from other parts of the Eastern Front to reinforce von Greim's Luftflotte 6. Von Greim believed that the best way to shut down *Kutusov* quickly was to deprive the Red Army of its air support. At dawn on July 13, von Greim committed eight *Jagdgruppen* to gain air superiority over the eastern part of the Orel salient; the Luftwaffe *experten* massacred Popov's close-air support, shooting down 50 Il-2 Sturmoviks.[99] Altogether, the Soviet 15 VA lost 94 aircraft and was rendered combat-ineffective, against Luftflotte 6's loss of 20 aircraft. In addition, Rendulic was provided with strong antitank assets, including two battalions of Ferdinand tank destroyers and some of the new Hornisse self-propelled 8.8cm guns and 7.5cm Pak 41 towed antitank guns.[100] When Popov's two armies resumed their ground assaults on July 13, supported by over 200 tanks, they suffered crippling losses. Three regiments of KV-1 heavy tanks attacked across open terrain and were slaughtered by the new German antitank weapons; Operation *Kutusov* would prove to be the swan song of the KV-1. Despite these casualties, Popov committed part of his mobile reserve, the 1 GTC, to reinforce Gorbatov's 3rd Army. By nightfall, the Soviets had chewed through part of Rendulic's defense and advanced 9 kilometers.

While the Germans were focused on stopping the advance of the Bryansk Front, Bagramyan's 11 GA proceeded to roll up the LIII Armeekorps in the Ulyanovo sector. The ineptly led 5. Panzer-Division proved unable to stop Bagramyan, and Sokolovsky committed two tank corps (1 TC, 5 TC) to exploit the breach. By the end of July 13, Sokolovsky had achieved a major breakthrough on the northern side of the Orel salient, across a 23km-wide front. The only thing slowing Bagramyan's armor was the rough terrain and poor-quality roads in this remote sector. Sensing real trouble, Model transferred three of his Panzer divisions (12, 18, 20) to PzAOK 2 to help counter Bagramyan's breakthrough. Von Greim also shifted Luftflotte 6's focus toward interdicting Bagramyan's advance but suffered heavy losses from the 1 VA.[101] Hitler finally recognized the importance of unity of command and authorized Model to take command of PzAOK 2 as well as his own AOK 9.

On July 15, Rokossovsky's Central Front joined Operation *Kutusov* by committing two tank corps against Model's forces in the Teploye sector. By shifting several Panzer divisions, Model was able to inflict heavy losses on Popov and nearly halt the Bryansk Front. However, Model now had to contend with simultaneous enemy attacks from the north, east and south. Furthermore, the high-operations tempo was beginning to wear down Luftflotte 6, which had nearly exhausted its fuel reserves. On July 16, Model decided to evacuate all the territory AOK 9 had seized during *Zitadelle* and pull his army back to shorten its frontage; by this measure, he could transfer the 9. Panzer-Division to protect the Orel-Bryansk rail line from Bagramyan's advance. Rokossovsky was caught by surprise by Model's sudden withdrawal and Central Front's pursuit was slow. Stymied by the armor sent to reinforce Rendulic's XXXV Armeekorps, Popov committed General-leytenant Pavel A. Belov's 61st Army to conduct an attack toward Bolkhov, which surprisingly gained some ground before being halted. Popov also convinced Zhukov to release Rybalko's 3 GTA to the Bryansk Front, but it would take several days to reach the front. At the same time, Model decided to shift his attention to dealing with Bagramyan's 11 GA and moved more Panzers and air support in order to make a firm stand at Bolkhov. Rokossovsky reinforced Bagramyan with another tank corps, but the Western Front struggled to transform its tactical successes into a true operational-level breakthrough. Sokolovsky was in part to blame, since he was focused on taking tactical objectives, rather than shifting his vanguard toward areas where the German cordon was thinnest. He also seems to have forgotten that his primary objective was severing the Orel-Bryansk rail line. Zhukov was not particularly helpful in the Western Front's breakthrough phase, since he delayed commitment of Stavka reserves, which he kept under his personal control.

By July 17, Model realized that the German situation in the Orel salient was rapidly deteriorating and that he had to do something before the converging Soviet armies achieved a real breakthrough. He used two Panzer divisions to launch spoiling attacks against the Bryansk Front to keep Popov off balance, while shifting another division to counter Bagramyan's 11 GA. He also created a strong defensive position at the town of Bolkhov under one of his most capable and trusted subordinates, General der Panzertruppe Josef Harpe (Gruppe Harpe). In order to take these measures, Model had to denude his front facing Rokossovsky. When Rokossovsky recognized how weak the German forces were in front of him, he decided to launch a hasty attack with Rodin's 2 TA. However, Model had left his one battalion of Tiger tanks to cover this contingency, and these heavy tanks – which were superb on the defense – knocked out 32 of Rodin's T-34 tanks and induced further caution on Rokossovsky's part. For their part, Sokolovsky and Bagramyan became too fixated on taking the town of Bolkhov (which was heavily defended), rather than tearing apart Model's makeshift screening forces and pushing due south or southwest. Although Sokolovsky was winning, he was essentially just fighting with Bagramyan's 11 GA and missed an opportunity to strike a decisive blow against the German forces in the Orel salient. Indeed, the Stavka failed to note that the Germans were stripping other sectors in order to reinforce their defense of the Orel salient and that this presented other operational opportunities. Throughout *Kutusov*, the Stavka proved too conservative, opting to simply push Model's forces backward rather than striking where they were vulnerable to envelopment. Similarly, Zhukov was responsible for coordinating the efforts of the Bryansk, Central and Western Fronts but he proved unable to properly synchronize their attacks. He also failed to transfer Fediuninskiy's 11th Army to reinforce Sokolovsky until July 20; had this powerful formation been provided earlier, Model's screening forces would probably have been overwhelmed.

Thanks to the caution of his opponents, Model was able to fight a battle using interior lines to shift his limited reserves around the salient from one crisis point to the next. He also used tactical withdrawals to shorten his lines and free up forces for judicious counterattacks, whether Hitler and the OKH approved or not. There were no repercussions. By the time that Rybalko's 3 GTA finally entered the battle on July 19, Rendulic's XXXV Armeekorps had already pulled back, so the Soviet blow fell upon empty positions. Nevertheless, by July 20 the 3 GTA was able to push Rendulic out of his new positions and advance up to 20km in a single day. Yet rather than demolish Rendulic's battered corps, Popov decided to split Rybalko's 3 GTA into two diverging columns, one pushing west to Orel and the other toward the south.[102] By eschewing the principle of mass, Popov prevented Rybalko from achieving a decisive breakthrough to Orel and gave Model time to shift the 12. Panzer-Division to block the 3 GTA. Unable to mount a successful frontal assault upon Orel, Popov decided to shift his axis of advance to the southwest to link up with Rokossovsky's front, which also violated his operational objectives. By July 21, all three Soviet fronts were hampered by supply shortages and heavy losses, which led to a respite for several days. It was not until July 26 that the Soviets were able to make another major move, which was a joint attack by the Bryansk and Central Fronts against the boundary between PzAOK 2 and AOK 9. Ryabalko's 3 GTA struck Rendulic's XXXV Armeekorps but suffered heavy losses and failed to achieve a breakthrough. Rokossovsky had more success, coordinating his 13th, 48th and 70th Armies to push back the overextended XXXXVI Panzerkorps. On the northern side of the salient, Zhukov finally released Badanov's 4 GTA (with 496 tanks) to reinforce Sokolovsky's offensive, which convinced Model that it was time to evacuate the Bolkhov position.

After two weeks of heavy fighting, the three Soviet fronts were slowly converging upon Orel. Model created a ring of steel around the city and launched spoiling attacks to keep Popov off balance. Rybalko's 3 GTA had lost 669 of its 731 tanks in a week of fighting and had to be pulled back to reconstitute. Model also created a strong defensive front to prevent Sokolovsky from severing his line of communications to Bryansk; too late, the Stavka had recognized the importance of severing the Orel-Bryansk rail line instead of its fixation on taking Bolkhov. From this point on, the Germans regained a continuous front all around Orel. Model was able to inflict heavy losses on the Soviet armies pressing in from three sides, but even though he now had eight of the 16 Panzer divisions on the Eastern Front, he could not stop them. Nor could he stop the endless barrage of artillery and air strikes that hammered his retreating forces. Model's priorities now shifted to saving as much as possible, particularly the 20,000 German wounded in Orel's hospitals and the 53,000 tons of supplies in its depots.[103] On July 31, Model was also able to persuade Hitler to allow him to evacuate the Orel salient and withdraw to the Hagen Stellung. On August 1, the evacuation, designated Unternehmen *Herbstreise* (Operation *Autumn Journey*), began. Despite heavy rains, the Soviets were quick to detect the German evacuation and accelerated their attacks. Model remained in Orel with a small staff and personally supervised the rearguard action. On the night of August 4, the Germans pulled out of Orel (much of which was on fire) and the next morning, Kolpakchi's 63rd Army liberated the smoldering city. The Soviets continued to pursue Model's forces as they retreated to the Hagen Stellung and for once, the Soviet steamroller became a reality. Nevertheless, German rearguards were able to prevent any units from becoming cut off and Model's forces were able to settle into new defensive positions on a significantly shortened front. All three Soviet fronts were exhausted after weeks of fighting and in no condition to continue the offensive without reconstitution. Finally, on August 18, the Stavka terminated Operation *Kutusov*.

In contrast to the short-lived *Zitadelle*, the 38-day Operation *Kutusov* achieved significant operational results by forcing the Germans to evacuate the Orel salient. Model's forces suffered four times the casualties during *Kutusov*, amounting to 88,000 (including 27,000 dead or missing) as well as the loss of 229 tanks and assault guns. All eight Panzer divisions used to try to stop *Kutusov* had suffered heavy losses in men and material. Altogether, Heeresgruppe Mitte lost one-third of its available armor in July 1943. The Red Army achieved a major operational victory in Operation *Kutusov*, but it paid an exorbitant price to recover Orel. Altogether, the three Soviet fronts involved in the operation suffered 429,890 casualties (including 112,529 dead or missing) and lost a total of 2,586 tanks. Popov's Bryansk Front was particularly hard hit, suffering nearly 40 percent casualties.[104] The three Soviet air armies involved lost 1,104 aircraft, equivalent to more than one-third of their starting strength.[105]

In terms of battle command, Model conducted a skillful defense of the Orel salient which held off vastly superior enemy forces for a month and managed to preserve the bulk of his combat power to fight another day. Model switched back and forth between attack and defense to keep the enemy off balance and used unexpected withdrawals (i.e. maneuvers to the rear) to avoid the worst enemy blows. He also integrated airpower into his operations in order to reduce the enemy's ability to maneuver and mass against critical sectors. Model was fortunate in having some exceptional subordinate commanders, such as Rendulic and Harpe. The three Soviet front commanders accomplished their mission, but they did so in an inelegant manner which gave little regard to the principles of war. Popov turned in the worst performance, which simply relied upon brute force, repeatedly applied. Both Rokossovsky and Sokolovsky were overly cautious and failed to mass overwhelming combat power until the operation was in its final stages. Some of Sokolovsky's caution was due to Zhukov's insistence on keeping personal control over the plentiful operational reserves, which prevented the Western Front from taking full advantage of the near collapse of PzAOK 2's left flank. Nor was the performance of the three Soviet tank army commanders particularly good. Most of Rybalko's attacks failed and he burned through his armor in a week without achieving much. Rodin's mediocre performance during *Kutusov* was consistent with that in previous operations and his 2 TA had negligible impact on the campaign. Badanov's 4 GTA showed up late in the campaign but performed fairly well in the pursuit phase. Among the Soviet field army commanders – Bagramyan, Kolpakchi, Gorbatov and Pukhov – only Bagramyan put in an exceptional performance. Bagramyan was ethnic Armenian and had served primarily as a staff officer until 1942, but he proved to be a competent field commander. The other three army commanders were adequate for set-piece battles, but they made negligible use of maneuver or surprise and tended to just keep attacking in the same sectors, which partly explains excessive Soviet casualties.

Overall, Operation *Kutusov* demonstrated a new style of campaigning for both sides. The Ostheer was increasingly on the defensive and commanders like Model were learning how to shift mobile reserves around to delay enemy breakthroughs until reinforcements could arrive from elsewhere. As long as there were external reinforcements and effective Luftwaffe support, the Ostheer had a chance to achieve tactical success in these kinds of campaigns. However, German resources were becoming increasingly finite and it was taking much larger reinforcements to stop Soviet multifront offensives. For the Soviets, Operation *Kutusov* was the largest offensive organized to date, involving over 1.2 million troops, three tank armies and three air armies. Coordinating this massive operation had proven very difficult, with chronic lapses in C2 at key moments – but the Red Army was learning. The main operational problem the Red Army experienced during *Kutusov* was in synchronizing mass and maneuver to achieve operational-level breakthroughs. Too much Soviet mass, in terms of ground troops and firepower, was directed against tactical objectives such as the town of Bolkhov. Unlike *Uranus*, where the operational scheme of maneuver was designed to envelop the enemy army, *Kutusov* was premised on frontal attacks that simply pushed the enemy backwards. However, *Kutusov* did benefit from a two-echelon approach, which allowed the offensive to continue despite heavy losses. Model had defeated Operation *Mars* against the Rzhev salient in 1942 because he only had to contend with a single echelon, but at Orel Model was continually faced with fresh Soviet armies entering the battle. German defensive methods were not designed to withstand an enemy offensive that employed a second echelon – which inevitably led to a battle of attrition the Ostheer could ill afford.

Commander	Objective	Offensive	Mass	Maneuver	Surprise	Security	TALLY
Model	+	+	o	+	+	+	5
Popov	o	+	o	o	-	o	o
Sokolovsky	-	+	+	o	o	o	1
Rokossovsky	o	o	+	o	o	o	1
Bagramyan	o	+	+	+	+	o	4
Rybalko Rodin	o	+	o	o	o	o	1
Badanov	o	+	o	+	o	o	2
Gorbatov Kolpakchi Pukhov	+	+	+	o	-	o	2

Operation Kutusov, *1943 Leadership Assessment*

Mius River, July 17–August 2, 1943

As soon as it was clear that von Manstein had terminated *Zitadelle*, the Stavka ordered General-polkovnik Fedor I. Tolbukhin's Southern Front and General Rodion Malinovsky's Southwest Front to attack Heeresgruppe Mitte's right flank. Unlike the overstretched and under-resourced Ostheer, the Stavka was able to provide three mechanized corps and one tank corps, totaling 1,300 tanks, to support these two secondary fronts. Vasilevsky was assigned to coordinate the operations of both fronts and the Stavka's basic scheme of maneuver was to conduct a double-pincer attack, with Malinovsky striking from the north and Tolbukhin from the east. Ideally, the two pincers would link up near Stalino (Donetsk) and encircle most of General der Infanterie Karl Adolf Hollidt's rebuilt AOK 6.[106] During the spring, Hollidt's command had been gradually upgraded and reinforced, enabling it to construct a triple line of defense behind the Mius River. On Hollidt's left flank, Generaloberst Eberhard von Mackensen's PzAOK 1 held a line along the Donets. Von Manstein gambled that he could achieve operational success against the Kursk salient, which would provide "a breathing space" on this part of the Eastern Front.[107] He did not appreciate that the Red Army was now capable of conducting concurrent offensives on different parts of the front. Consequently, he left only General der

Panzertruppe Walther Nehring's XXIV Panzerkorps as a mobile reserve to support his right wing. Nehring was one of the most experienced Panzer commanders in the Ostheer, but the XXIV Panzerkorps had only three understrength divisions (17. and 23. Panzer divisions and SS-*Wiking*) with a total of 181 operational tanks and assault guns.[108]

Tolbukhin planned to conduct a two-echelon deliberate offensive against the strongly defended Mius River line, with General-leytenant Viacheslav D. Tsvetaev's 5th Shock Army and General-leytenant Vasily F. Gerasimenko's 28th Army in the first echelon. Once these two armies gained a sizeable bridgehead across the river, Tolbukhin would commit his second echelon: General-leytenant Yakov G. Kreizer's 2 GA and two mechanized corps (2 GMC, 4 GMC) to enlarge and break out of the bridgehead. While Tolbukhin's plan emphasized offensive, objective and mass, it relied upon a heavily-reinforced frontal assault rather than maneuver. Furthermore, Tolbukhin did not enforce good operational security measures – particularly in terms of radio discipline – during his preparation for the operation, so Hollidt was soon aware that a major offensive was imminent.[109] Hollidt responded by reinforcing the XVII Armeekorps sector – where he expected the enemy to attack – and moving up his tactical reserves closer to the front. He also used his artillery and air strikes to harass likely enemy assembly areas. Malinovsky's planning was even more basic and optimistically hoped to slash rapidly across the Donbas region.

Both Soviet fronts began their offensives on the morning of July 17. Gerasimenko's 28th Army attacked with seven rifle divisions and one tank brigade on a 10km-wide front in the Kuibyshevo sector, striking the German XVII Armeekorps. Gerasimenko's attack was supported by plentiful artillery and nonstop bombing by the 8 VA. Nevertheless, Hollidt's countermeasures proved successful and the German defenses proved robust enough to limit Gerasimenko's 28th Army to only minor gains. Tolbukhin's main effort was in the Dmitrievka sector, 13km north of Kuibyshevo, where he massed eight rifle divisions and 2 GMC from the 5th Shock Army and 28th Army, along with 300 tanks, against the XVII Armeekorps. Command and control of the Southern Front's main effort was bizarre, with three army commanders (Gerasimenko, Tsvetaev and Krezier) involved in directing the first day's attacks – a clear violation of unity of command. The main Soviet attacks fell on the weakest sector of the XVII Armeekorps front and hammered the front-line battalions under a huge weight of artillery fire. Although the German defense was tenacious, the attacks gained a 4km-deep penetration across the Mius and inflicted over 2,000 casualties on the XVII Armeekorps in this sector. By evening, Tolbukhin decided to commit Kreizer's 2 GA into the bridgehead.

Malinovsky made his main attack with General-polkovnik Vasily I. Kuznetsov's 1 GA east of Izyum, but barely dented the front line of the German XXXX Panzerkorps. Even after committing a tank corps to reinforce 1 GA, the Soviet shock groups only advanced 2 kilometers. Chuikov's 8 GA, further east, achieved no success at all and he later admitted in his memoirs that "our attacks collapsed everywhere by mid-day." Chuikov attributed the failure to the lack of surprise and the depth of the enemy defenses. In spite of Malinovsky's failure to achieve a breakthrough anywhere along the Donets, von Manstein regarded the Southwest Front's offensive as the more serious threat and immediately committed Nehring's XXIV Panzerkorps to support von Mackensen's PzAOK 1. As a result, Malinovsky's offensive was decisively checked by the end of the first day of the operation, although the Stavka ordered him to continue attacking. Afterwards, Soviet historians tried to depict the Southwest Front's Izyum offensive as merely a fixing attack, although as Chuikov stated the intent clearly was to achieve an operational breakthrough to Stalino. Hitler took a different view than von Manstein and regarded the Soviet breakthrough as more significant – and for once, the Führer's assessment of the situation was correct. Hitler ordered von Manstein to transfer three mechanized divisions as quickly as possible to support Hollidt. Von Manstein sent part of Hausser's II SS-Panzerkorps (SS-*Das Reich* and SS-*Totenkopf* Divisions) and the 3. Panzer-Division south from the Belgorod sector, but they would take almost a week to arrive.

Until reinforcements arrived, Hollidt's AOK 6 was under heavy pressure from Tolbukhin. On July 18, he committed his tactical reserve, one Panzergrenadier division (with 36 tanks), but this unit failed to stop Tolbukhin from expanding his bridgehead. The XVII Armeekorps' front was shattered and the 2 GMC advanced to seize the town of Stepanovka. Despite this setback, Hollidt tried another counterattack on July 19, when part of the 23. Panzer-Division from the XXIV Panzerkorps arrived; this effort was even less successful and suffered heavy losses.[110] Tolbukhin had reinforced his bridgehead with the 4 GMC and had roughly a 5-1 numerical superiority over the defenders (two mechanized corps and 16 rifle divisions with 300 tanks versus four German divisions with 36 tanks), but he proved cautious and gave Hollidt just enough time to cobble together a new front line with *ad hoc Kampfgruppen*. When Tolbukhin first tried to break out of his bridgehead on July 20, his attacks were repulsed by German antitank guns and assault guns. Another attempt on July 21 also failed. Meanwhile, the failure of Malinovsky to achieve a breakthrough across the Donets allowed von Manstein to transfer the rest of Nehring's XXIV Panzerkorps to support Hollidt. By the time that Tolbukhin finally massed enough forces to punch through Hollidt's thin perimeter on July 22, Nehring's Panzers had arrived to stiffen the defense. The Luftwaffe also was able to provide air support from the IV Fliegerkorps and additional 8.8cm Flak batteries for use in the antitank role.[111] The 4 GMC led the Soviet breakout effort and managed to gain some ground, but suffered crippling losses, including 130 tanks.[112] Thereafter, Tolbukhin repeatedly tried to break out of the thin German perimeter between July 23 and 27, but all attacks were repulsed. Hollidt's front-line infantry units were in terrible condition, but he managed to scrape up replacements by culling from his rear-echelon troops and thinning out on other parts of his front. When Tolbukhin learned that the II SS-Panzerkorps was arriving by rail, he shifted to the defense on July 28.

On July 27, Malinovsky was finally allowed by the Stavka to terminate his offensive, which had failed to break through the PzAOK 1 front. Nor had Malinovsky tied down German reserves in his sector, since most of Nehring's XXIV Panzerkorps had already shifted to support AOK 6. Altogether, Malinovsky's Southwest Front suffered 64,390 casualties (including 16,434 dead or missing) and lost 363 tanks, yet achieved no significant objectives. Von Mackensen's PzAOK 1 had accomplished its mission of holding the Donets line at a cost of 12,000 casualties (including about 3,500 dead or missing). Due to Malinovsky's aborted offensive, von Manstein was able to focus his attention almost entirely on Hollidt's front. His intent was to launch a major counteroffensive against Tolbukhin's bridgehead, designated Operation *Roland*, using Nehring's XXIV Panzerkorps and Hausser's II SS-Panzerkorps. Hollidt was tasked with coordinating the counteroffensive. Operation *Roland* was not subtle; Hausser would attack the Soviet salient from the northwest while Nehring attacked from the southwest. Although the distances to be covered were short, the terrain was not particularly suitable for armored operations. Hollidt was provided with about 300 tanks and assault guns, with decent artillery support but negligible infantry. Even Luftwaffe air support and supplies of ammunition and fuel were modest, compared to the scale provided during *Zitadelle*.

Operation *Roland* commenced on the morning of July 30, after an artillery bombardment. The weather was conducive to a German-style offensive, with sunny, clear skies. Soviet resistance proved unexpectedly fierce and it was evident that the Red Army had learned useful lessons from *Zitadelle*, since Kreizer's 2 GA had fortified its bridgehead with mines and antitank guns. Hausser's II SS-Panzerkorps suffered very heavy losses, including 73 of its 119 tanks, and was stopped. Nehring's XXIV Panzerkorps managed to achieve some success and even captured 3,000 prisoners. Kreizer mounted a creditable defense of his bridgehead, using his remaining armor to launch local counterattacks which inflicted painful losses on the II SS-Panzerkorps. Even so, Kreizer was made the scapegoat for Tolbukhin's failure to break out out of the Mius River bridgehead and he was relieved of command and replaced by Georgy F. Zakharov. On July 31, the Germans attacked again, but Hausser's II SS-Panzerkorps suffered further heavy losses and still failed to gain ground while fending off strong Soviet counterattacks. It was Nehring's XXIV Panzerkorps, which never had more than 47 tanks, which smashed the left flank of Kreizer's bridgehead and decided the battle. Sensing victory, Hollidt ordered an all-out assault on August 1. After heavy fighting, the Soviet defense crumbled and Soviet units begin retreating across the Mius. On August 2, the Germans crushed the last resistance in the bridgehead, taking thousands of prisoners, although no major Soviet formations were completely destroyed.

Although Operation *Roland* succeeded in eliminating Tolbukhin's Mius River bridgehead, during the Battle of the Mius River AOK 6 had suffered over 21,000 casualties (including 5,500 dead and wounded) in 17 days and Hausser's II SS-Panzerkorps was reduced to just 45 operational tanks.[113] The Battle of the Mius caused von Manstein to disperse his armor away from the Kharkov-Belgorod sector and crippled his strongest formation, the II SS-Panzerkorps. Furthermore, AOK 6 had consumed about 20,000 tons of ammunition and 7,000 tons of fuel in its 17-day fight on the Mius front, which severely depleted Heeresgruppe Süd's limited logistic reserves.[114] In material terms, the two Soviet offensives had been costly failures. During the Battle of the Mius, Tolbukhin's Southern Front suffered at least 61,000 casualties and over 500 tanks. When combined with Malinovsky's losses, the two failed Soviet offensives resulted in 125,000 personnel casualties and nearly 900 tanks. Nevertheless, the Red Army now had the industrial might (and Lend Lease) to quickly replace these material losses, while the Ostheer did not.

In terms of generalship, the senior commanders on both sides showed little employment of the principles of maneuver, surprise or security. Instead, the battles of the Donets and Mius River fronts became pushing and shoving matches, with plenty of artillery firepower added in. The Stavka's concept for a joint offensive against von Manstein's right flank, following the culmination of *Zitadelle*, was sound, just poorly executed. Malinovsky relied simply upon brute force to force his way across the Donets River and failed to develop a sound operational plan. Tolbukhin did develop a sound plan, except for confused C2 responsibilities on the first day of his offensive. Given the success of the first two days on the Mius front, the 2nd Guards Army and its attached mechanized corps should have achieved a decisive breakthrough before the XXIV Panzerkorps arrived. Thus, slow tactical execution by the Soviet field army commanders was a factor in the failure to break out of the Mius bridgehead. The VVS also failed to interdict the rail lines along which von Manstein shifted his armored reserves, which could have slowed down the German counterstroke. Von Manstein's performance was mediocre, probably due to the frustration of Zitadelle's failure and his continual arguments with Hitler about objectives and priorities. Hollidt's performance was particularly noteworthy, particularly his success in holding off an enemy that started with a 6-1 numerical superiority. As the war in the East increasingly turned against the Third Reich, the Ostheer's ability to stave off defeat depended upon tough-minded commanders like Hollidt, all but unnoticed during the earlier days of victory in 1941–42, but who now rose to prominence in crisis.

Commander	Objective	Offensive	Mass	Maneuver	Surprise	Security	TALLY
Malinovsky	o	o	+	o	–	o	o
Tolbukhin	+	+	+	o	–	o	2
Kreizer Kuznetsov Chuikov Gerasimenko Tsvetaev	o	o	+	o	o	o	I
Von Manstein	o	+	o	+	o	o	2
Hollidt Von Mackensen	+	+	o	o	o	+	3

Mius River/Donets River, 1943 Leadership Assessment

Operation *Rumyantsev*, August 3–23, 1943

After the failure of Zitadelle, von Manstein – not Hitler or the OKH – made the fatal error of underestimating the Red Army's recuperative capabilities. Believing that Vatutin's battered armies were no longer an immediate threat, von Manstein took the risk of transferring the bulk of his armor (including Breith's III Panzerkorps) 300km to reinforce his right wing. Apparently, von Manstein was hoping for a quick, easy tactical victory on the Mius front, but when this did not occur the transfer left the critical Belgorod-Kharkov sector vulnerable. By early August, Hoth's PzAOK 4 was defending the area northwest of Belgorod with the LII Armeekorps and XXXXVIII Panzerkorps, amounting to just four infantry and two decimated Panzer divisions (11, 19); Hoth's tactical reserves amounted to barely 100 operational tanks (including 27 Panthers).[115] Armee-Abteilung Kempf held the front between Belgorod and Kharkov with the XI and XXXXII Armeekorps with five divisions; Kempf's tactical reserve was even weaker, amounting to roughly 50 operational tanks and assault guns. Von Manstein had no operational reserves ready to back up either Hoth or Kempf and it would take at least a week to transfer armor back from the Mius front. Nor was it likely that Hoth's infantry could hold the front for very long against a determined attack, since the divisions in the LII Armeekorps were understrength and holding up to 16km of frontage each. It was a recipe for disaster.

On July 24, the Stavka ordered Vatutin to begin detailed planning for Operation *Rumyantsev*, a joint counteroffensive by the Voronezh and Steppe Fronts to liberate Belgorod and Kharkov. Zhukov was assigned as Stavka representative to coordinate the preparations. This time around, Zhukov wanted no hastily-planned operation that would be vulnerable to one of von Manstein's well-timed ripostes. Instead, he was able to convince Stalin to give Vatutin and his staff ten days to plan *Rumyantsev*, as well as ensuring that overwhelming force would be massed at the weakest point in the enemy front.[116] Both Katukov's 1 TA (6 TC, 31 TC, 3 MC) and Rotmistrov's 5 GTA (18 TC, 29 TC, 5 GMC) were restored to near full strength, with over 500 tanks each. Zhukov organized the transfer of three artillery divisions and an MRL division to Vatutin's command to provide overwhelming firepower. Zhukov also ensured that Soviet C2 would be up to the task of conducting a high-intensity maneuver operation by emphasizing radio communications and more flexible orders processes. Soviet intelligence was able to provide fairly accurate information about Hoth's front-line positions, which greatly assisted the planning process for *Rumyantsev.*

The basic concept for *Rumyantsev* was fairly simple. Vatutin would use Chistiakov's 6 GA and Zhadov's 5 GA to blast through two infantry divisions from the German LII Armeekorps, then commit the two tank armies (1 TA, 5 GTA) to exploit southwest toward Bogodukhov (where Hoth's headquarters was located). From that point, with the German front ripped apart, the two tank armies would pivot to envelop Kharkov from the west. Konev's Steppe Front was the supporting effort and would attack Belgorod from the northeast/east with General-leytenant Ivan M. Managarov's

53rd Army and Kryuchenkin's 69th Army. Vatutin used *maskirovka* to hide his offensive preparations while also creating the false impression that he might attack the boundary between PzAOK 4 and AOK 2 near Sumy; von Manstein was deceived and transferred the 7. Panzer-Division to the Sumy sector.[117] Compared to previous Soviet offensives, *Rumyantsev* was carefully planned and used everything that the Red Army had learned about combined-arms warfare to date. Each field army was provided with a sapper brigade to remove enemy obstacles and a tank corps to use as a mobile group. The VVS would provide over 1,300 aircraft to support the operation. The four Soviet army commanders who would compromise the main effort – Zhadov, Chistiakov, Katukov and Rotmistrov – were afforded adequate time to plan their roles in the upcoming offensive. Amazingly, officers down to platoon level were briefed about the operation a full 24 hours before it began; heretofore, even division commanders had gone into battle with little or no prior guidance.[118]

At 0500 hours on August 3, both the Voronezh Front and the Steppe Front began a 170-minute artillery preparation in their designated attack sectors. The power of the bombardment was unlike anything the Ostheer had experienced previously and the German front-line units were badly hit. While the barrage was still in progress, Soviet sappers moved forward and began clearing lanes through the enemy mine belts. At 0750 hours, Vatutin and Konev began their ground assaults. Both 5 GA and 6 GA attacked in a single echelon, with two corps-size shock groups (each consisting of three rifle divisions, one tank brigade, a regiment of self-propelled guns and two sapper battalions), which was the first time that the Red Army had created truly effective combined-arms teams. Each one of these shock groups was aligned against a single German infantry regiment, resulting in an over-match situation. Zhadov's 5 GA, in the center, rapidly overwhelmed the German first line of defense and achieved a 3km-deep penetration in Hoth's front in less than three hours. By 1100 hours, Vatutin committed both Katukov's 1 TA and Rotmistrov's 5 GTA and they conducted a forward passage through Zhadov's army (a tricky operation under fire), through a narrow 6km-wide corridor. Then the two tank armies spread out abreast, totaling over 1,000 tanks, and began advancing to the south. Rotmistrov had the most success, achieving a 14km-deep penetration by nightfall. However, Chistiakov's 6 GA, on Vatutin's right, ran into pockets of fierce German resistance and advanced only a few kilometers. Zhukov bullied Chistiakov into prematurely committing his mobile group, but this gambit failed to produce success. In Konev's sector, Managarov's

53rd Army, supported by one rifle corps from the 69th Army, managed to advance 8 kilometers, but achieved no breakthrough.

Initially, there was little that Hoth could do to contain the two onrushing Soviet tank armies with the forces he had available. Two of his infantry divisions had been virtually destroyed by the initial attacks. He immediately committed his tactical reserves (19. Panzer-Division and the limited number of Tiger and Panther tanks) to create a *Stützpunkt* in the town of Tomarovka; this had the benefit of blocking Chistiakov's advance and threatening the right flank of Katukov's 1 TA. Rather than throwing his limited reserves into the path of two Soviet tank armies – where they would likely be overrun – Hoth cunningly opted to exploit the Soviet fear of sudden flank counterattacks. Katukov did turn part of his 1 TA west toward Tomarovka, but most of his army bypassed the town. Kempf tried to use his 6. Panzer-Division and some assault guns to close the breach on his left flank but this proved impossible. Instead, Kempf was forced to fight a mobile delay operation against Rotmistrov's armor on his left while pulling his battered infantry divisions back toward Belgorod. By the end of the first day, it was evident that Vatutin had achieved a major breakthrough in Hoth's front line and that Soviet forces were pouring through in great strength. For his part, von Manstein immediately requested permission to transfer the II SS-Panzerkorps and Breith's III Panzerkorps back to Kharkov, but this movement would take days to accomplish.*

On the second day of *Rumyantsev*, Vatutin's right wing became fixated on the fight for Tomarovka; although nearly surrounded, the German garrison managed to disrupt the advance of both the 5 GA and 6 GA. Chistiakov even committed his mobile group (5 GTC) to reinforce the attack on the town, without success. Katukov's 1 TA blew past Tomarovka and advanced another 15km across open terrain, against light resistance. Yet very little infantry followed Katukov's tanks due to the cluster around Tomarovka. Rotmistrov's 5 GTA found itself delayed by a single German Panzer division and only advanced 4km on the second day of the operation. Vatutin should have intervened to prevent so much of his combat power and forward momentum being sapped by a single German strongpoint, but seemed satisfied as long as Katukov's armor was still advancing southward. Vatutin's decision to attack in a single echelon now proved costly, since

---

*Hausser's II SS-Panzerkorps headquarters was sent to Italy with the SS-LSSAH Division in late July. The two remaining divisions of II SS-Panzerkorps, SS-*Das Reich* and SS-*Totenkopf*, were briefly placed under Breith's III Panzerkorps in August.

he lacked the follow-on forces to deal with bypassed enemy strongpoints like Tomarovka and instead had to divert forces away from the main effort. Nevertheless, Hoth's situation remained desperate and he could only play for time until the armored units returned from the Mius sector. Kempf fell back upon Belgorod's inner defenses, pursued by Managarov's 53rd Army.

On August 5, Chistiakov made a deliberate attack to capture Tomarovka – which was nearly surrounded – but could not break the defense. Most of Zhadov's 5 GA was hung up near the town, instead of following Katukov. Amazingly, a German garrison that consisted of just the weak 19. Panzer-Division and remnants of the LII Armeekorps was absorbing the attention of two Soviet armies. The Stavka now ordered General-leytenant Sergei G. Trofimenko's 27th Army and General-leytenant Kirill S. Moskalenko's 40th Army to join the offensive, against Hoth's thin left flank. Vatutin appears to have temporarily lost focus on his operational objective at this point, when he decided that crushing the German forces at Tomarovka was more important than reinforcing the drive toward Bogodukhov. Under heavy pressure from all sides, Hoth was forced to order the evacuation of Tomarovka on the night of August 5/6; the garrison escaped but suffered heavy losses in the retreat, which left 19. Panzer-Division combat ineffective. In the center, Katukov continued to advance but Rotmistrov's 5 GTA was delayed by a German strongpoint at Orlovka. Only part of Zhadov's 5 GA followed the two tank armies, leaving the spearhead units with inadequate infantry support. Konev mounted a deliberate attack against Belgorod, using the 53rd and 69th Armies, as well as part of Shumilov's 7 GA. By 1800 hours, the Red Army had driven Kempf's forces out and liberated the city. Thus by the end of the third day of *Rumyantsev*, both Vatutin and Konev could be relatively satisfied with the course of the operation. However, the first elements of Breith's III Panzerkorps were just beginning to arrive in Kharkov by rail. Hoth put Breith in charge of all the Panzer units assembling near Kharkov and intended to use this formation to mount a counterattack once the Soviet tank armies were overextended. Recognizing that he was facing a disaster, von Manstein also appealed to Heeresgruppe Mitte to transfer two additional mobile divisions as well.

On August 6, Katukov's vanguard liberated Bogodukhov, its initial objective. Katukov's tankers also captured an intact supply depot in Bogodukhov, which held 700 tons of fuel. Further east, Rotmistrov's 5 GTA captured Zolochev but then bumped into the lead elements of the 3. Panzer-Division. One of Katukov's corps had a similar experience, unexpectedly encountering the SS-*Das Reich* Division. The Soviet armor did not do well in these initial meeting engagements, which forced both tank armies to halt and regroup. Breith had sent his Panzers straight into action after detraining on the west side of Kharkov, without pause. Since Hoth had virtually no infantry in the gap west of Kharkov, he was forced to employ Panzer *Kampfgruppen* as blocking detachments, which was in violation of German doctrine. On August 7–8, Katukov and Rotmistrov attacked Breith's Panzer blocking detachments, pushing them back but suffering significant losses in the process.[119] On the night of August 8/9, Katukov boldly pushed a tank brigade across the Merefa River, 60km west of Kharkov, intending to sever the main east-west rail line into Kharkov. However, Breith's III Panzerkorps moved part of the SS-*Totenkopf* Division just in time to protect the German line of communications. For a moment, the Soviet advance to the south of Bogodukhov was briefly stymied.

Meanwhile, Vatutin had allowed a large portion of his infantry and supporting armor to get drawn into reducing German garrisons at Borisovka and Grayvoron, then pursuing the broken LII Armeekorps to the west. Despite the odds, Hoth was still able to form a thin line between Sumy and Akhtyrka with XXXXVIII Panzerkorps and LII Armeekorps, which totaled just five divisions (including 7. and 11. Panzer Divisions and *Großdeutschland*). Vatutin swung his entire right wing to the west, including all of Chistiakov's 6 GA, Trofimenko's 27th Army and Moskalenko's 40th Army in an effort to overwhelm this thin line. While Vatutin's decision helped to widen the breach in Hoth's front, it ended up diverting three armies away from the primary objective of Kharkov. Furthermore, the Germans mounted a spirited defense of Akhtyrka, which slowed the Soviet advance. While Vatutin was trying to direct two separate large-scale battles, Konev singlemindedly focused on just getting to Kharkov. Kempf proved unable to stop the steady advance of the 53rd and 69th Armies from the north, which were closing in on the city by August 9.

Between August 10 and 12, the main action occurred in the Merefa River sector, where Katukov and Rotmistrov tried to reach the east-west rail line and Breith's III Panzerkorps tried to prevent this. By August 12, Hoth had managed to assemble 150 tanks and assault guns in the Merefa sector and he gambled upon a hasty counterattack. Von Manstein was hoping for another "Backhand Blow" to save the day, but this did not occur. While Hoth's counterattack succeeded in inflicting heavy losses on Katukov's 1 TA, German losses were also heavy. Furthermore, the commitment of virtually all of the German armor to stop Katukov and Rotmistrov left Kempf without the means to stop Konev's inexorable advance. By August 14, Konev had four armies pressing against the city's defenses from the north and east. Kempf was unwilling to sacrifice his army in Kharkov and made the mistake of openly complaining about Hitler's do-or-die orders to hold the city. Von Manstein promptly relieved Kempf of command and replaced him with General der Infanterie Otto Wöhler.[120] Soon afterwards, Armee-Abteilung Kempf was redesignated as the 8. Armee. Heavy fighting continued west of Kharkov for days, with no real advantage gained by either side. By August 18, both Soviet tank armies were exhausted, as was Breith's opposing III Panzerkorps.

The final act of *Rumyantsev* occurred near Lyubotin, on the western road leading out of Kharkov. On Zhukov's orders, Vatutin transferred Rotmistrov's decimated 5 GTA to Konev's command on August 20 for the final assault on Kharkov. Amazingly, the Steppe Front was able to partly re-equip two of Rotmistrov's corps in just one day and the formation was soon declared ready for combat. Konev was tasked with supporting an attack by Managarov's 53rd Army against the left flank of the German XI Armeekorps. At dawn on August 22, the 53rd Army fired a large artillery preparation, then sent Rotmistrov's armor forward. The Germans had reinforced this sector with tanks, antitank guns and 8.8cm Flak guns, which proceeded to shoot Rotmistrov's armor to pieces.[121] The 5 GTA attack was another conspicuous failure, but it did succeed in convincing von Manstein that it was time to evacuate Kharkov before the city was isolated. On the morning of August 23, Konev's forces fought their way into Kharkov and liberated the city. Operation *Rumyantsev* had achieved its operational objectives by liberating Belgorod and Kharkov and inflicting a serious defeat upon Hoth's PzAOK 4. However, the cost had been very high. In three weeks, the Voronezh and Steppe Fronts suffered over 255,000 casualties (including 71,000 dead or missing) and lost 1,860 tanks.[122] Hoth and Kempf had suffered a total of 32,000 casualties (including 8,000 dead and 4,000 captured) and lost about 300 tanks and assault guns. In addition, hundreds of tanks damaged during *Zitadelle* had to be abandoned as the Germans retreated. Three of von Manstein's four armies were badly depleted by late August and in no condition to recover any of the lost ground. Nor did von Manstein have any significant operational reserves left.

At the tactical level, Operation *Rumyantsev* was mostly marked by a series of punishing, indecisive battles. While the Ostheer still maintained an edge in battlefield leadership and C2, the Red Army was noticeably closing the gap. Von Manstein was caught by surprise when the Red Army smashed Hoth's fortified line and advanced 50km in a matter of a few days – that had not happened before. Indeed, the Red Army finally had the means and the experience to conduct the kind of Deep Operations envisioned by PU–36. However, the Soviet tendency to try to reduce every German strongpoint in their way instead of bypassing them proved problematic and nearly derailed Vatutin's main effort. The ability of the Red Army to regenerate combat power was also astonishing, driven in part by a new emphasis upon battlefield recovery of damaged vehicles and equipment. After two years of all-out war, the Stavka had become expert at cycling burnt-out formations through the RVGK in order to send a steady stream of replacements to the front. In contrast, the OKH rarely could pull units out to refit and thus had far fewer reinforcements to send to critical sectors. Nor was the Luftwaffe able to stem the Soviet tide, as it had in the past. Worn down by heavy losses during *Zitadelle* and short of fuel, the Luftwaffe was able to periodically appear over the battlefield but it no longer was a dominant force. Without effective close air support, German maneuver warfare doctrine was severely handicapped.

Although Vatutin made a serious error in allowing himself to be distracted by stubborn German strongpoints, Operation *Rumyantsev* demonstrated his ability to employ the principles of war to accomplish significant operational objectives. His ability to combine mass, maneuver and surprise – already demonstrated during *Uranus* and *Little Saturn* – represented a deadly threat to the Ostheer's existence. Konev's performance was far more conservative, relying simply upon mass, repeatedly applied until the enemy line broke – but it worked. In effect, Vatutin's maneuver served as the hammer to Konev's anvil, with Armee-Abteilung Kempf on the receiving end. Katukov's performance was also quite good; he was aggressive and despite suffering a tactical defeat, he demonstrated considerable courage in remaining in the fight. Katukov's inability to fully envelop Kharkov was due to Vatutin's failure to properly support his main effort at the critical moment. Rotmistrov's handling of the 5 GTA was poor from the start and, coming soon after his defeat at Prokhorovka, his days as a front-line commander were numbered. All of the Soviet field army commanders performed well and accomplished their missions, except for Chistiakov, who impaled his 6 GA upon the German strongpoint in Tomarovka. The tendency in operational warfare for some commanders to lose focus on the true objective due to tactical over-commitment is not uncommon in military history, as occurred with Napoleon and the Chateau de Hougoumont at the Battle of Waterloo in 1815. Overall, the Soviet commanders demonstrated that they had learned from previous defeats and could now conduct large-scale, synchronized operations that could overwhelm even a prepared German defense.

Von Manstein bears the primary responsibility for the defeat Heeresgruppe Süd suffered as a result of Operation *Rumyantsev*. Due to his severe underestimation of enemy capabilities, he dispersed his armor after *Zitadelle* (thereby eschewing mass) and failed to take measures to protect Hoth's weakened PzAOK 4 against a major Soviet offensive. Unlike previous battles, von Manstein was unable to mass sufficient force to launch a decisive counterstroke of his own; the Soviet tank armies were no longer sheep being led to the slaughter. Hoth put in another sterling command performance but he was severely handicapped by the limited forces at his disposal. He was only capable of conducting tactical-level counterattacks and mobile delays, which inflicted heavy losses on the enemy, but which ultimately proved insufficient. Kempf's performance was even more hindered by limited resources, but he fought a rather passive battle which could only lead to the loss of Kharkov. At the tactical level, most German commanders still had a significant edge, but at the operational level, they were nonplussed by the new Soviet methods. In particular, the Soviet ability to mass such massive quantities of artillery and air firepower to pulverize German defenses in a given sector was a real shock. Indeed, something like despair was beginning to appear in senior German military leaders, who began to surmise that the war might be lost. In order to survive, the Ostheer had to modify its own methods and toughen up its troops and commanders.

Commander	Objective	Offensive	Mass	Maneuver	Surprise	Security	TALLY
Vatutin	o	+	+	+	+	+	5
Konev	+	+	+	o	o	o	3
Katukov	+	+	+	+	o	o	4
Rotmistrov	+	+	+	o	o	-	2
Zhadov Managarov Kryuchenkin Trofimenko Moskalenko	+	+	+	o	o	o	3
Chistiakov	-	o	+	o	o	o	o
Von Manstein	+	+	-	o	o	-	o
Hoth	+	+	o	o	o	-	1
Kempf	+	o	o	o	o	o	1

Operation Rumyantsev, *1943 Leadership Assessment*

Operation *Suvorov*, August 7–October 2, 1943

Since mid-April, the Stavka had been planning to conduct multiple offensives on other parts of the Eastern Front, as soon as the German summer offensive was defeated. Yet the Red Army did not have the logistic resources to conduct all these operations simultaneously, so they would be conducted in staggered fashion. The Stavka's main priority was focused on Operations *Kutusov* and *Rumyantsev*, to liberate Orel and Kharkov. Following the completion of these objectives, the next priority was for the Western and Kalinin Fronts to liberate Bryansk and Smolensk; this joint offensive was designated Operation *Suvorov*. General Vasily D. Sokolovsky's Western Front would comprise the main effort, while General-polkovnik Andrei I. Eremenko's Kalinin Front would provide a supporting effort. Ideally, the right flank of Heeresgruppe Mitte would be destabilized by the loss of the Orel salient, which would assist Sokolovsky's offensive. Marshal of Artillery Nikolai N. Voronov was assigned as Stavka representative to coordinate the two fronts.[123]

Although the Stavka had developed the broad objectives for Operation *Suvorov* by June 1943, Sokolovsky and his staff were responsible for detailed planning. General-leytenant Aleksandr P. Pokrovsky, Sokolovsky's chief of staff, was one of the most experienced General Staff-trained officers in the Red Army, but he did not have a large organic staff to assist him. Since the Western Front was also involved in planning its role in Operation *Kutusov*, Sokolovsky's staff was burdened with simultaneously preparing two major operations. As a result, coordination with the VVS and *maskirovka* were not given proper attention. In addition, the Western Front did not have a very accurate intelligence picture concerning the enemy defenses they would have to breach. The Stavka established the main axes of advance for *Suvorov*: Sokolovsky would attack the German 4. Armee from the east along the Spas-Demensk-Roslavl axis, while Eremenko would attack from the north toward Smolensk. The initial objective for *Suvorov* was to drive a deep wedge into the center of Heeresgruppe Mitte by capturing Roslavl, then pivot north to crush the Germans in Smolensk between the pincers of the two Soviet fronts. The Stavka transferred three armies (11, 21, 68) and a breakthrough artillery corps from the RVGK to reinforce the Western Front and Marshal Voronov was highly competent in developing fire-support plans, but logistic support was another matter. From the beginning, *Suvorov* was planned on a logistical shoestring, with a bare minimum of ammunition, fuel and rations allocated to the assault armies. In addition, Sokolovsky was obliged to provide all four of his tank corps to support Operation *Kutusov*, leaving him with much less armor to spearhead Operation *Suvorov*.

Although Sokolovsky's Western Front comprised 824,000 troops in 61 divisions, he simply lacked the logistic support to employ more than one-quarter of his forces at any one time. Sokolovsky had plenty of artillery and could mass 165 pieces per kilometer in the chosen breakthrough sector, but the Stavka provided just four days' worth of ammunition. Likewise, the 1st Air Army (1 VA), assigned to support Suvorov, had over 1,000 operational aircraft but was constrained by insufficient fuel stockpiles. Unlike other Soviet offensives in 1943, Sokolovsky had only a single large armored formation (the 5th Mechanized Corps, which was mostly equipped with Anglo-American tanks) and would have to rely heavily upon cavalry units for operational-level maneuvers. Eremenko's Kalinin Front was provided even fewer resources for *Suvorov* and due to food shortages, many of the Soviet troops in his command were malnourished. While Eremenko was one of the most experienced and competent front-level commanders in the Red Army, his health was still fragile due to previous wounds and he was dragged into political squabbles between Stalin and Nikita Khruschev about the Stalingrad campaign. Stalin apparently now regarded Eremenko with some suspicion, while Eremenko saw his assignment to the backwater Kalinin Front as a demotion.[124]

By the summer of 1943, Generalfeldmarschall Günther von Kluge's Heeresgruppe Mitte had been holding the Smolensk-Roslavl sector for 1½ years and had created a robust defense in depth, known as the Büffel-Stellung. Von Kluge granted a great deal of autonomy to Generaloberst Gotthard Heinrici, whose 4. Armee defended this part of the front. Von Kluge was a talented but capricious field commander; by mid-1943 he was infected with defeatism and already talking with members of the anti-Hitler resistance movement within the army. Heinrici was a veteran commander who had gained a reputation as a superb defensive tactician. The 4. Armee had about 250,000 troops in six subordinate corps, comprised of 18 divisions. Heinrici's defense rested upon the quality of his infantry and artillery, but both were in a state of decline due to the Third Reich's inability to fully replace its combat losses. By July 1943, Heinrici's infantry divisions averaged about 68 percent of their authorized strength (*Iststärke*) but their actual combat strength (*Gefechtstärke*) was typically around 45 percent. Nevertheless, these half-strength divisions were required to hold the frontage of a full-strength division. Similarly, Heeresgruppe Mitte only had 77 percent of its authorized artillery and lacked the ammunition reserves to fight a protracted battle. Nor did Heinrici have any appreciable tactical reserves – just one depleted Panzergrenadier division and three assault gun battalions. Heinrici also had a serious rear-area threat from Soviet partisans, which forced him to deploy a large number of troops to protect his road and rail lines of communications.[125] Probably the only bright spot from the German point of view was that Generaloberst Robert Ritter von Greim's Luftflotte 6 was still capable of providing effective air support to the 4. Armee, thanks to its cadre of veteran aircrew and modern fighters.

Sokolovsky and Pokrovsky recognized that Heinrici's front was not going to be easy to penetrate, so they decided to conduct an offensive in two echelons: four armies (5, 31, 33 Armies and 10 GA) would attack in the first echelon and two more armies (21, 68) would attack in the second echelon. The 5th Mechanized Corps (5 MC) would serve as the front's primary mobile reserve, with the remaining armored units serving in the direct infantry-support role. Sokolovsky opted to begin preliminary operations on August 1 to "soften up" the enemy with partisan attacks and deep bomber raids by the 1 VA against the German lines of communications. However, these operations accomplished little and alerted von Kluge to the impending enemy offensive. Probing operations against the 4. Armee on August 6 failed to penetrate the German security zone and discarded any chance to achieve tactical surprise. Thus, before *Suvorov* even began Heinrici had deduced where the Red Army was about to attack and von Kluge was already beginning to transfer some of his limited operational reserves to reinforce the 4. Armee.

On the morning of August 7, the Western Front began a lengthy artillery preparation, focused on the boundary between the German IX Armeekorps and XII Armeekorps in the Yelnya/Spas-Demensk sector. The weather was hot and muggy, underneath cloudless skies. Due to inadequate reconnaissance and the heavily wooded terrain, the Soviets had not identified several important positions in the German HKL (main line of resistance), so the bombardment – which expended 50 percent of the available ammunition – was not particularly effective. Sokolovsky initially attacked with four armies (from left to right): General-leytenant Vasily N. Gordov's 33rd Army, General-leytenant Kuzma P. Trubnikov's 10th Guards Army, General-leytenant Vitaly S. Polenov's 5th Army and General-major Vladimir A. Gluzdovsky's 31st Army. The Western Front's main effort was the armies of Trubnikov and Gordov. Despite attacking with a 3-1 numerical advantage, neither the 5th Army nor the 10 GA were able to advance more than a kilometer due to intense German resistance. Frustrated by the inability of his main effort to gain ground, Sokolovsky decided to commit part of his second echelon, General-leytenant Evgeny P. Zhuralev's 68th Army, to reinforce Trubnikov's 10 GA. This premature and foolish decision ended up crowding an already stalled front with even more troops and vehicles, which did not lead to any immediate success. By the end of the first day of *Suvorov*, Sokolovsky's main effort had cleared out the German security zone but not yet reached the main positions of the Büffel-Stellung. Surprisingly, the only real Soviet success on the first day was achieved by Gluzdovsky's 31st Army, which was intended as a supporting attack against the right flank of the German XXXIX Panzerkorps. Gluzdovsky had the good fortune to strike an inexperienced German infantry division which had just recently arrived at the front; this unit briefly crumbled under the onslaught and Gluzdovsky quickly committed his small mobile reserve (a tank brigade) to exploit. Only prompt action by the XXXIX Panzerkorps prevented Gluzdovsky from achieving a breakthrough.

Heinrici had very limited tactical reserves, but he was able to use them to parry the Soviet thrusts because the Western Front offensive was essentially a series of localized and uncoordinated attacks. Thanks to the limited nature of *Suvorov*'s opening moves, Heinrici was able to shuffle his small reserves around to deal with one local crisis at a time. The Soviet air support for *Suvorov* also proved to be a major disappointment, despite excellent flying weather. The 1st Air Army (1 VA) flew over 1,000 sorties on the first day, but this was less than half of what had been planned. Furthermore, the 1 VA split up its sorties among the four attacking Soviet armies, instead of massing its combat power in one critical sector. In contrast, von Greim's Luftflotte 6 flew almost as many sorties with one-third the aircraft and managed to prevent the 1 VA from achieving air superiority over the battlefield. Von Greim also massed his sorties to prevent Gluzdovsky's 31st Army from achieving a breakthrough. By the end of the first day, it was apparent that the Western Front's offensive was not proceeding well.

Sokolovsky continued his offensive on August 8, but progress was minimal. Most of Trubnikov's 10 GA was stymied by the fierce resistance of a single German battalion-size strongpoint. Sokolovsky continued pounding on the Büffel-Stellung, taking heavy losses, but the hard-pressed XII Armeekorps was under heavy pressure and running out of infantrymen. On August 10, Sokolovsky added another of his armies into the fray – General-leytenant Vasily S. Popov's 10th Army – which attacked Heinrici's right flank from the Kirov salient. Heinrici had accepted greater risk in this sector in order to reinforce his center, which enabled Popov to achieve a small breakthrough and advance 5km. Another Soviet army, General-major Ivan T. Grishin's 49th Army, also soon joined the attack on Heinrici's right. However, Sokolovsky had not provided Popov with any mobile reserves, so the breakthrough could not be immediately exploited. Instead, Sokolovsky began transferring the 5 MC and a cavalry corps to Popov, but it would take two days to move these formations 70km. Just as his right flank was bending, Heinrici realized that he needed to withdraw his center before the XII Armeekorps was crushed. Consequently, with his main effort finally about to achieve success, Sokolovsky found that his primary mobile reserve was in transit and not immediately available. Furthermore, the lengthy positional battle had exhausted most of the Western Front's artillery ammunition reserves. Trubnikov's 10 GA lurched forward, but with limited artillery and tank support. Heinrici opted to abandon the town of Spas-Demensk in order to conserve his forces. On the morning of August 13, elements of Grishin's 49th Army entered the town.

Von Kluge was able to transfer the 9. Panzer-Division from Model's AOK 9, which was used to shore up his right flank, but it was the Luftwaffe that prevented Sokolovsky from effectively employing his operational reserve. Just as the 5th Mechanized Corps reached Spas-Demensk and was poised to demolish the tottering XII Armeekorps, von Greim committed everything that could fly in this one sector. Over the course of three days, von Greim conducted six major attacks on this one hapless Soviet formation and bombed it into combat ineffectiveness before it could strike a blow. By this point in the war, the Germans knew how to use airpower to achieve operational-level results. Without this mechanized corps, Sokolovsky's offensive could not convert its tactical success into operational success. Eremenko's Kalinin Front joined Operation *Suvorov* on August 13, attacking Heinrici's left flank with General-leytenant Aleksei I. Zygin's 39th Army and General-leytenant Konstantin D. Golubev's 43rd Army. The German XXVII Armeekorps managed to limit Eremenko's forces to minor gains and Eremenko lacked the ammunition and logistic support to conduct a protracted battle. Once again, von Greim's Luftflotte 6 played a major role in smashing Zygin's assault groups.

After just a week, Operation *Suvorov* was beginning to ebb by August 14 and Trubnikov's 10 GA was burnt out. Nevertheless, Sokolovsky proceeded to commit another second-echelon army, General-leytenant Nikolai I. Krylov's 21st Army and use it in conjunction with the 33rd and 49th Armies to make one last big-push effort. Yet the attack on August 14–15 failed to budge the XII Armeekorps, which, in one of those stunning demonstrations of the Ostheer's formidable skill at battlefield improvisation, had somehow managed to stitch together a new front. After that, several days of rainy weather put a further damper on operations and Sokolovsky's forward units were virtually out of ammunition. Although the Stavka was reluctant to suspend *Suvorov*, on August 21 Sokolovsky was authorized to halt operations for one week in order to resupply and reconstitute his armies. In two weeks, the Western Front had suffered about 75,000 casualties just to push Heinrici's center back 30–40km. Heinrici's AOK 4 had managed to hold off no fewer than 11 Soviet armies, but at a cost of 28,000 casualties (including 7,200 dead or missing). Three German infantry divisions had been gutted and the other remaining divisions were reduced to less than one-third of their authorized strength. Von Kluge had no significant operational reserves left, which did not bode well for holding off the next phase of the Soviet offensive. The only bright spot for the Germans was that von Greim's Luftflotte 6 had put in a bravura performance, inflicting 6-1 losses on the 1 VA and preventing the VVS from providing effective air support to Sokolovsky's ground troops.

During the operational pause, the Stavka reinforced Sokolovsky's Western Front with additional armor (including the 2 GTC) and artillery, but only enough ammunition for another short offensive pulse. Heinrici could see that the Soviets were about to hit his center again and transferred one division from his left to reinforce the Yelnya sector, but the German front line, held by the IX and XII Armeekorps, was paper thin. Hitler informed von Kluge that he needed to hold his current positions for at least another 4–6 weeks until a new fortified line, dubbed the Panther-Stellung, could be constructed. On August 28, Sokolovsky resumed his offensive, hitting Heinrici's right flank with four armies (21, 33, 68, 10 GA) while two other armies (5, 31) conducted a supporting attack in the Yartsevo sector. Heinrici simply lacked the infantry to hold a solid front line or the reserves to contain any major breakthroughs, so the German situation rapidly deteriorated. By the second day, the German front was beginning to disintegrate under hammer blows and by August 30, the IX Armeekorps was in serious trouble. Having learned something from his earlier mistakes, Sokolovsky now committed his mobile reserve, the 200 tanks of the 2 GTC, which quickly achieved a breakthrough and advanced 20km. Heinrici was forced to abandon the supply depot at Yelnya and by September 1, he was facing a full-blown catastrophe. One more violent push by the mass of Soviet armor could easily cause the reeling 4. Armee to rout, but the Soviet armored spearhead now ran out of fuel just as it was on the cusp of achieving a decisive operational success.

Heinrici was afforded a brief respite, which enabled him to reorganize his battered forces. He ruthlessly culled personnel from support units to reconstitute his front-line infantry, although these replacements were not of the same caliber as veteran combat troops. Von Kluge also transferred a few units from Model's command (including some Tiger tanks), which were just enough to create a new front line. Oddly, the Stavka also chose this moment to pressure Sokolovsky into transferring some of his forces to support the Bryansk Front, which was trying to develop an offensive against the PzAOK 2. By the time that Sokolovsky could refuel his spearheads and resume his attacks, he had lost the moment. Amazingly, the German improvised line repulsed the weak Soviet attacks and logistic shortages soon caused the offensive to prematurely culminate. Trubnikov was made the scapegoat for failure and relieved of command; General-leytenant Aleksandr V. Sukhomlin took over the 10 GA. On September 7, the Stavka authorized another week-long suspension of *Suvorov*. Four days earlier, von Kluge had flown to East Prussia to discuss the situation with Hitler and request additional reinforcements. Von Manstein attended the same meeting, also to solicit reinforcements. Hitler refused both army group commanders, citing the need for Panzer units to crush the Anglo-American landings in Italy. Consequently, neither von Kluge nor von Manstein could expect any major reinforcements before the next round of Soviet offensives began. Hitler expected Heinrici's AOK 4 to hold a 164km-wide front around Smolensk with barely 21,000 front-line combat troops. Model was now responsible for holding Roslavl with Gruppe Harpe. Even worse, a large portion of von Greim's Luftflotte 6 was transferred to other sectors, leaving Heinrici with insufficient air support.

While Sokolovsky was preparing for his next offensive pulse, Eremenko reorganized his forces; he relieved Zygin from command of the 39th Army and replaced him with General-leytenant Nikolai E. Berzarin. Eremenko also created a division-size mobile group. On September 13, Eremenko used Golubev's 43rd Army to attack the German XXVII Armeekorps due north of Smolensk and managed to gain some ground. Heinrici's forces in this sector were defending the Barbarossa-Stellung, which was deemed adequate to hold off the Kalinin Front. Yet when Eremenko launched his main attack on September 14 with Berzarin's 39th Army, the Germans were stunned when the Soviet shock groups achieved a rapid breakthrough which Eremenko exploited by committing his mobile group. Within 24 hours, the XXVII Armeekorps was broken and retreating in some disorder. Sokolovsky resumed his own offensive on September 15, with the 5th and 31st Armies striking the German XXXIX Panzerkorps near Yartsevo, while the 10 GA and 21st Army attacked the IX Armeekorps. Heinrici's entire front line was under attack and inevitably some of the Soviet shock groups achieved success. By September 16, Heinrici's left and right flanks were broken and his center was withdrawing. Sokolovsky had learned from his earlier mistakes and now he deftly committed his operational reserve (the 2 GTC and 5 MC) to advance rapidly up the Yelnya–Smolensk rail line. Heinrici was left with no option than to conduct a rearguard action, using the still-effective XXXIX Panzerkorps. The Soviet pursuit was not particularly aggressive, slowed in part by German scorched-earth tactics. Nevertheless, Gluzdovsky's 31st Army entered Smolensk on September 25 to find that German rearguards had reduced the city to burning wreckage.

Heinrici's broken AOK 4 retreated to the Panther-Stellung, which was anchored on the fortified cities of Vitebsk, Orsha and Mogilev. Heinrici had only five decimated divisions to hold a 133km-wide front, but the Soviet pursuit rapidly ran out of steam after liberating Smolensk. Belatedly, the OKH finally sent enough replacements to Heinrici to enable him to rebuild a thin front line. Soviet probing attacks were repulsed and by a miracle, Heinrici's army was able to stabilize its front. By October 3, Sokolovsky recognized that his offensive had culminated and Operation *Suvorov* was terminated, although the Stavka kept urging him to try to penetrate the Panther-Stellung before the onset of winter. Eremenko briefly tried to continue the offensive with just his Kalinin Front but was repulsed at Vitebsk. Operation *Suvorov* was a Soviet success, having advanced westward about 200 kilometers, seized its primary objective (Smolensk) and inflicted heavy losses on the defending AOK 4. However, due to chronic shortages of ammunition and fuel, the offensive had sputtered along for 57 days in an inefficient stop-go fashion. During the first phase of the operation, the Western Front's tactics were crude and amateurish, resulting in heavy losses and poor results. By the third phase, the Western Front's tactics had significantly improved and Heinrici's dwindling forces were gradually pounded into pulp. Soviet losses in *Suvorov* were excessive, amounting to over 450,000 casualties (including 107,000 dead or missing), 860 tanks and 300 aircraft.[126] Overall, Sokolovsky lost 40 percent of his starting strength and his emaciated armies had lost all combat effectiveness. Heinrici's AOK 4 suffered 54,000 casualties (including 14,000 dead or missing), which left it crippled at the end of the Soviet offensive. As with the other major Soviet summer offensives, the Ostheer now had great difficulty stopping the Red Army, although it could inflict painful losses.

Both von Kluge and Heinrici had very limited options throughout the campaign, but they did fairly well with their limited resources. Aside from focusing on the objective (holding specific defensive lines) and avoiding unpleasant surprises, the German leaders could not even afford to conduct an active defense due to the lack of mobile reserves. Instead, AOK 4 relied on von Greim's Luftflotte 6 to blunt the Soviet offensive edge. Had the OKH provided even one or two fresh Panzer divisions, Heinrici might have been able to do more than just conduct a fighting withdrawal. Von Kluge kept transferring resources between Heinrici's AOK 4 and Model's AOK 9, both of which ended up being defeated (Bryansk was lost on September 17). Sokolovsky's performance was initially poor and he experienced great difficulty massing adequate combat power at the correct time and place on the battlefield. However, Sokolovsky gradually learned from his mistakes and was a more effective commander in the final phase of the operation. Eremenko lacked the resources to mount a full-scale offensive but cunningly chose his moments to strike where the probability of success was best. A total of 11 Soviet army-level commanders participated in Operation *Suvorov* and most performed reasonably well, even if several (Trubnikov, Gordov and Zygin) were relieved of command. Noticeably, the Soviet commanders did not rely upon maneuver, mass or surprise to any great extent, but rather simply kept attacking until German lines gave way. The Stavka was not satisfied with the overall performance of the Western Front during *Suvorov* and afterwards quietly purged a number of staff officers, including the artillery and intelligence chiefs. However, the crux of Sokolovsky's problems lay with the Stavka's insistence on conducting nearly simultaneous multifront offensives without the logistic resources to sustain them. Von Kluge and Heinrici were undermined by the OKH's refusal to release reinforcements to them, just as Sokolovsky and Eremenko were undermined by the Stavka's refusal to provide adequate logistic priority to support their operations.

Commander	Objective	Offensive	Mass	Maneuver	Surprise	Security	TALLY
Von Kluge	+	o	o	o	o	+	2
Heinrici	+	o	o	o	o	+	2
Sokolovsky	+	+	o	o	o	o	2
Eremenko	+	+	o	o	+	o	3
Trubnikov et al.	+	+	o	o	o	o	2

Operation Suvorov, *1943 Leadership Assessment*

Dnepr Campaign, September 15–December 30, 1943

Despite the fact that German forces in the southeast Ukraine had been badly defeated in July and August 1943, Hitler initially refused to consider any large-scale withdrawals. He did grudgingly agree to the creation of the Panther-Stellung as a fallback position behind the Dnepr River, but optimistically assumed that von Manstein would halt the Red Army east of the river. However, the Soviets continued to pound on von Manstein's weakened front line throughout late August and early September. Tolbukhin's Southern Front achieved considerable success against Hollidt's AOK 6 in the south, while Rokossovsky's Central Front continued to push back Hoth's battered PzAOK 4. Rokossovsky also defeated AOK 2, which created a large breach between Heeresgruppe Mitte and Heeresgruppe Süd, which could not be sealed due to the lack of operational reserves. By early September 1943, it was obvious that the German situation was desperate and growing increasingly precarious, but Hitler delayed making a decision for two more critical weeks. Finally, with von Manstein's right flank crumbling and his left flank being outflanked, Hitler finally authorized a withdrawal to the Dnepr River on September 15.[127] He assumed that von Manstein would be able to regroup in relative safety behind the Dnepr. In Moscow, the Stavka had been waiting for the moment when the Germans would bolt for the Dnepr and now unleashed five fronts with a total of 2 million troops in pursuit.

Despite its fancy designation on OKH maps in Zossen, the Panther-Stellung was little more than a concept when von Manstein's forces began retreating toward the Dnepr. No actual field works or obstacles had been constructed as yet. While Hitler finally agreed to evacuate the AOK 17 from the Kuban, he wanted this army transferred to hold the Crimea, instead of reinforcing the southern end of the Panther-Stellung. Consequently, von Kleist's Heeresgruppe A would be obliged to deploy Hollidt's AOK 6 forward of the Dnepr River in order to defend the rail line of communications to AOK 17 in the Crimea. During the Dnepr campaign, the disconnect between von Manstein's desire for force preservation and Hitler's obsession with holding onto territorial and economic objectives introduced a great deal of dissonance into German operations. On paper, von Manstein had three armies (PzAOK 1, PzAOK 4, AOK 8) with 32 divisions and von Kleist had two armies (AOK 6, AOK 17) with 18 divisions, but almost all of these formations were in poor condition. By mid-September 1943, von Manstein's six Panzer divisions averaged only 10–30 tanks each and his infantry divisions averaged

30–50 percent of authorized strength. Luftflotte 4 had been badly reduced by losses and nonstop operations, which left it unable to provide effective air support to von Manstein's ground forces. Under these conditions, von Manstein could not conduct the kind of operational-level warfare in which the Ostheer excelled. Instead, his forces would be forced to conduct a 100km-long fighting retreat to positions with modest defensive value and with a superior enemy in hot pursuit.

Although the Stavka had been planning to cross the Dnepr River since February 1943, this objective did not become feasible until after the liberation of Kharkov and the Donbas. Unlike Operations *Kutusov*, *Rumyantsev* and *Suvorov*, the Stavka's concept for breaching the Dnepr River was rather rudimentary and simply directed that all five fronts (Central, Voronezh, Steppe, Southwest and Southern) would make a rapid and broad advance toward the river. Zhukov would coordinate the Voronezh and Steppe Fronts, while Vasilevsky coordinated the Southwest and Southern Fronts. No main effort was designated but the primary operational objectives were to secure multiple crossing sites and then liberate Kiev. Zhukov claimed that Stalin's pressure to get to the Dnepr necessitated this approach, although that sounds like an *ex post facto* justification; certainly Zhukov had the authority to designate either Vatutin or Konev as the main effort.[128] Furthermore, the Stavka did not make any special effort to allocate additional engineer bridging units or logistic support for an opposed river crossing; Vatutin had only a single pontoon brigade and Konev had no bridging units at all. Due to lack of prior detailed planning, the Soviet fronts were given unusual latitude in their operations, which would be driven by opportunistic factors. While this approach enabled a rapid pursuit to the Dnepr, it also made it more difficult to exploit any crossings that were achieved.

In order to cover his withdrawal, von Manstein positioned most of his remaining armor in the center, around Poltava. The Panzer divisions were expected to hold off Vatutin's Voronezh Front and Konev's Steppe Front while the slow-moving infantry and support units retreated to the Dnepr crossings. However, Rokossovsky quickly ruined this plan by enlarging the gap between AOK 2 and Hoth's left flank, then inserting Bogdanov's 2 TA and Pukhov's 13th Army into the void. In just a few days, Rokossovsky created a direct pathway to the Dnepr which was virtually devoid of German defenses. The OKH responded by quickly shifting an infantry division from Heeresgruppe Nord to create a blocking position at Neshin northeast of Kiev, but Bogdanov and Pukhov easily bypassed this obstacle and reached the Dnepr River by September 20. The next day, Pukhov's troops were able to cross the Dnepr with improvised means and establish a bridgehead north of Kiev, near Chernobyl. Although Pukhov lacked the bridging units to get tanks or artillery across, he quickly reinforced his bridgehead with elements of five rifle divisions. Simultaneously, Vatutin committed Rybalko's refitted 3 GTA, which advanced 165 kilometers in a single day and reached the Dnepr on the evening of September 21. During the night of September 21/22, Rybalko was able to get some of his infantry across the Dnepr to create a bridgehead at Bukrin, southeast of Kiev. Thus, due to the boldness of Rokossovsky and Vatutin, the Red Army had gained two bridgeheads across the Dnepr while the bulk of von Manstein's Heeresgruppe Süd was still east of the river.

Once von Manstein and the OKH recognized that the Red Army had already "bounced" the Dnepr, the Germans had to abandon all efforts to fight a delaying action east of the river and instead conduct a chaotic retreat back to the crossing sites at Kiev, Cherkassy and Kremenchug. The only significant German unit on the west side of the Dnepr was the 19. Panzer-Division, which was little more than a regimental-size *Kampfgruppe* and a few security units. Von Manstein promptly ordered these units to contain the Soviet bridgeheads at Bukrin and near Chernobyl, while ordering Hoth to disengage his armor from Poltava and retreat to the Dnepr crossing sites. Due to the hasty nature of the German withdrawal, Heeresgruppe Süd was forced to abandon a great deal of material and supplies, which exacerbated its already debilitated condition. The crowded crossing sites made excellent targets for Soviet aerial attack, but the front commanders had little appreciation for distant battlefield air interdiction missions, which reduced the amount of VVS sorties for close-air support missions. Meanwhile, Hoth sent General der Panzertruppe Walter Nehring's XXIV Panzerkorps staff to take charge of creating a cordon around the Bukrin bridgehead. As German troops reached the west bank of the Dnepr they were greatly disappointed to find that there were no prepared positions waiting for them and that the Red Army had already crossed in two places. German front-line morale, already lowered by the pell-mell retreat, became worse as the troops began to recognize that the war might be lost. The situation along the lower Dnepr was not quite as chaotic. Wöhler's AOK 8 retreated to Kremenchug pursued by Konev's Steppe Front while von Mackensen's PzAOK 1 retreated to Dnepropetrovsk and Zaporozhe, pursued by Malinovsky's Southwest Front; neither Konev nor Malinovsky were able to "bounce" the river. Von Mackensen had to deploy the XXXX Panzerkorps to hold the Zaporozhe bridgehead on the eastern bank of the Dnepr. Hollidt's AOK 6 occupied positions in the flat Nogai Steppe, anchored on Melitopol, which was temporarily able to halt Tolbukhin's Southern Front.

Von Manstein was unaware that the Stavka had another potential ace up its sleeve – a major airborne operation. While the Red Army had developed doctrine for airborne operations in the 1930s and conducted some small-scale airborne landings in 1941–42, its paratrooper units had mostly been used as elite ground infantry. However, the Stavka had assembled three airborne brigades with nearly 10,000 paratroopers in reserve and Zhukov recognized that a vertical envelopment could play a major role in expanding the bridgeheads over the Dnepr. Consequently, the Stavka assigned all three brigades to Vatutin's command and authorized him to conduct an airborne operation at his discretion. However, the VVS had extremely limited transport capability – barely enough to move one or two battalions at a time – and very limited experience in conducting airborne operations. Furthermore, the Stavka allowed Vatutin and his staff to plan the airborne operation, even though they had no real experience in this area and were focused on current operations. As a result, the plan for the airborne operation was hastily thrown together and chaotic. Instead of massing the airborne units to seize one key piece of terrain, Vatutin and his staff chose landing zones that were widely dispersed and too far from the Bukrin bridgehead.[129] When the Kanev airborne operation commenced on the evening of September 24, it rapidly turned into a disaster due to rainy weather, poor navigation by the transport pilots and the unexpected appearance of a German Panzergrenadier unit on one of the drop zones. The two airborne brigades were badly scattered and lost 20 percent of their troops on the first day; thereafter, they faded into the woods, hoping to link up with partisans or reach the Bukrin bridgehead. The Kanev operation squandered two airborne brigades for no gain and permanently soured the Stavka on attempting any further such operations.

Despite the Soviet airborne failure at Kanev, the German situation along the Dnepr continued to deteriorate. Amazingly, Konev's vanguard was able to bypass Hoth's retreating Panzer units and reach the Dnepr first, and Shumilov's 7 GA managed to gain a small bridgehead across the river on the night of September 25/26. Wöhler's AOK 8 was barely able to contain Konev's bridgehead. Tolbukhin attacked Hollidt on September 26 and nearly broke through but was stopped by German tactical reserves. All along the Dnepr front, von Manstein's armies were under attack and he lacked the operational reserves to destroy the Soviet bridgeheads. The only factor in the Germans' favor at this point was the lack of bridging capability in the forward Soviet armies, which delayed the movement of tanks and heavy artillery across the Dnepr. Hoth desperately wanted to counterattack Vatutin's Bukrin bridgehead as soon as possible, but was unable to assemble a sizeable force until September 29. By the time that Hoth attacked, Rybalko had managed to get tanks across the river and the bridgehead was now too well defended to crush. Not only did Hoth's counterattack at Bukrin fail, but Vatutin was able to gain another bridgehead across the Dnepr with Chibisov's 38th Army at Lyutezh, 25 kilometers north of Kiev. Given the swampy nature of the terrain around Lyutezh, Hoth was not unduly concerned about this development and remained focused on containing the Bukrin bridgehead.[130] By the end of September 1943 – just two weeks after von Manstein began his withdrawal to the Dnepr – three different Soviet fronts had already gained bridgeheads across the river and the Panther-Stellung had been exposed as a fantasy.

Operations in October 1943 focused on Soviet efforts to expand their bridgeheads across the Dnepr and German efforts to contain them. The Stavka ordered Rokossovsky, Vatutin and Konev to break out of their bridgeheads as soon as possible, while Malinovsky and Tolbukhin were ordered to crush the German bridgehead at Zaporozhe. Pukhov's 13th Army and Cherniakhovsky's 60th Army managed to expand their bridgehead around Chernobyl but were stopped by a sudden German armored counterattack on October 4. By using elements from four Panzer divisions, Hoth was able to crush one Soviet rifle corps. Vatutin tried to attack out of his Lyutezh bridgehead after getting 90 tanks from the 5 GTC across, but Chibisov's 38th Army suffered crippling losses for modest gains. Vatutin poured most of his resources into the Bukrin sector, which actually had three unconnected Soviet-held bridgeheads; by mid-October, he had 680 tanks and 14 rifle divisions across the river. However, Hoth and Wöhler placed their best forces around the Bukrin bridgeheads and created a firm defensive line with minefields. Vatutin attacked on October 12 and again on October 21, but failed to link up his bridgeheads or achieve a breakout. Against improbable odds, Wöhler's defense at Bukrin had held. Rybalko's 3 GTA lost 65 percent of its armor and overall, Vatutin's forces suffered over 27,000 casualties in the breakout attempt.[131] As a result, Vatutin was left with a large percentage of his forces crammed into three small, unconnected bridgeheads which were almost useless.

In contrast to Vatutin's difficulties, Konev's Steppe Front conducted a more methodical approach and was able to construct a pontoon bridge over the Dnepr by October 2, which enabled tanks to cross. Once resupplied and supported by armor, Shumilov's 7 GA was able to strike from its small bridgehead and capture Myshurin Rog. Recognizing the potential of this sector, the Stavka transferred Rotmistrov's 5 GTA to Konev's command. Using great stealth, Rotmistrov moved his tank army 200km to the Dnepr, using night marches. Luftwaffe aerial reconnaissance failed to detect the movement of Rotmistrov's 5 GTA. Konev's Myshurin Rog lodgment was near the boundary of Wöhler's AOK 8 and von Mackensen's PzAOK 1. Von Mackensen scraped up enough tanks to attempt a spoiling attack against Konev's bridgehead on October 8, but this effort failed. Konev patiently assembled an overwhelming force on the west bank, consisting of Shumilov's 7 GA and General-leytenant Mikhail N. Sharokhin's 37th Army. Sharokhin was an extremely unusual Soviet field army commander, having served previously in the VVS and on the General Staff (GSHKA) and without prior ground command experience. He had only been in command of the 37th Army for six weeks. On the morning of October 15, Konev began his breakout from the Myshurin Rog bridgehead. Once a breakthrough was achieved, Konev committed Rotmistrov's 5 GTA, which advanced rapidly, overrunning puny German rearguards in its path. Konev had driven a huge wedge between AOK 8 and PzAOK 1 and was presented with a golden opportunity to unhinge the entire German defense along the Dnepr. He was faced with the kind of choice that can decide a campaign: advance west to Kirovograd to roll up AOK 8's right flank or advance south to Krivoi Rog to outflank PzAOK 1. Yet rather than choose one course of action and commit his main effort to achieving it, Konev decided to split his forces and attempt to capture both objectives. In sum, Konev violated the principles of (single) objective and mass by opting to advance on two diverging axes. Rotmistrov's armored thrust also forced von Mackensen to choose: retain his reserves to hold Dnepropetrovsk or send them back to Krivoi Rog to protect his line of communications; he chose to send them to Krivoi Rog. As a result, Malinovsky was able to secure Dnepropetrovsk and a crossing over the Dnepr.

Just as Konev was on the cusp of a major operational level victory, entropy set in and Rotmistrov's armor outran their fuel supplies. As usual, the Red Army had afforded no priority to logistics and the vanguard units could not easily be resupplied. Furthermore, the OKH finally decided to send reinforcements to von Manstein and he received two fresh Panzer divisions (14, 24), which were assigned to Wöhler's AOK 8 near Kirovograd. Von Manstein also transferred two mobile divisions from other sectors; his intent was to use these four divisions to conduct a "backhand blow"-type counteroffensive to smash Rotmistrov's overextended 5 GTA. However, Hitler decided to interfere in the planning for the counteroffensive by insisting that one of his favorites – General der Gebirgstruppe Ferdinand Schörner – be put in charge of the operation. Schörner was in Finland and completely unfamiliar with the situation in Ukraine, but he was an ardent Nazi Party member and Hitler was beginning to value loyalty over expertise. After being hastily flown to the Ukraine, Schörner wasted no time studying the situation and imprudently ordered the attack schedule accelerated, even though part of the two fresh Panzer divisions were still en route. Von Manstein lacked the moral courage or strength of character to stand up to Hitler or Schörner and simply acquiesced without complaint. Schörner's counteroffensive began on October 28 and caught Rotmistrov by surprise, particularly since his right flank was wide open. Yet rather than encircling any Soviet armored units, Schörner was content to push the enemy away from Krivoi Rog and seal the gap between AOK 8 and PzAOK 1. Rotmistrov was obliged to retreat, but his 5 GTA remained intact and still dangerous. Schörner had squandered a rare opportunity to destroy one of the Soviet tank armies and settled for an ordinary victory.

Meanwhile, Malinovsky committed his main effort (Lelyushenko's 3 GA and Chuikov's 8 GA) to crush the German XXXX Panzerkorps in the Zaporozhe bridgehead. Malinovsky massed two artillery divisions to methodically smash the German defenses and after two weeks of heavy fighting, von Mackensen was obliged to evacuate Zaporozhe on October 14. Tolbukhin was able to penetrate Hollidt's thin line near Melitopol on October 10, but a German counterattack with a single Panzer division prevented a breakthrough. Nevertheless, after weeks of hard pounding by Tolbukhin's forces, Hollidt was forced to evacuate Melitopol on October 23 and fell back toward Kherson. Yet Hitler stipulated that AOK 6 had to keep two full corps east of the Dnepr to defend the Nikopol bridgehead, which condemned Hollidt to eventual defeat. Consequently, the bulk of von Kleist's Heeresgruppe A was tied down defending Nikopol and the Crimea, leaving few forces to defend the lower Dnepr. On October 20, the Stavka re-designated all the fronts involved in the Dnepr operation; the Voronezh Front became the 1st Ukrainian Front, the Steppe Front became 2nd Ukrainian Front, Southwest Front became 3rd Ukrainian Front and Southern Front became 4th Ukrainian Front.

Despite many tense moments, Heeresgruppe Süd had somehow managed to prevent any of the Soviet fronts from achieving a complete breakthrough along the Dnepr. All of the Soviet bridgeheads were still more or less contained, particularly the Bukrin bridgehead. Zhukov, who was assigned to coordinate the 1st and 2nd Ukrainian Fronts, urged another breakout attempt from the Bukrin bridgehead, but the Stavka recognized that the probability of success in this sector was not favorable.[132] Even Stalin regarded the Bukrin bridgehead as a dead end, so Zhukov, for once, was overruled. Instead, the Stavka recommended that Vatutin should shift his main effort to the Lyutezh bridgehead, which was closer to Kiev and where German defenses were not as strong. On October 25, Stalin concurred and Vatutin was ordered to shift Rybalko's 3 GTA 150 kilometers from Bukrin to Lyutezh. Vatutin instituted an elaborate *maskirovka* operation which prevented the Germans from learning about the transfer, which helped ensure operational surprise. Vatutin also moved an artillery corps into the Lyutezh bridgehead and reinforced the 38th Army (now under Moskalenko). Hoth only had four battered infantry divisions from the XIII Armeekorps deployed around the Lyutezh bridgehead, with a single depleted Panzer division in tactical reserve. Neither Hoth nor von Manstein expected a major Soviet offensive from Lyutezh.

Moskalenko's 38th Army commenced its breakout from the Lyutezh bridgehead on the morning of November 3, preceded by a massive 40-minute artillery barrage that disrupted the German defense. The 7th Breakthrough Artillery Corps concentrated 380 guns and mortars per kilometer of the chosen attack sector.[133] Vatutin was able to employ two corps-size combined-arms shock groups that gradually punched a hole in the enemy defense. Then Vatutin committed Rybalko's 3 GTA as dusk was falling; a large-scale tank attack at night over broken terrain was a highly unorthodox approach, but von Manstein certainly did not expect it. Indeed, von Manstein remained focused on the Bukrin sector and thought that Hoth could handle the situation at Lyutezh. Instead, the Red Army moved with astonishing alacrity and Rybalko put in his best performance of the war, overrunning German rearguards and routing the XIII Armeekorps. For once, the Red Army moved faster than the Germans could react and Rybalko's armor was on the outskirts of Kiev by the night of November 4/5. Rather than reinforce the small garrison in Kiev, Hoth opted to assemble his reserves around Fastov, where a fresh Panzer division was due to arrive. Consequently, Rybalko's armor was able to pour into Kiev on November 5 and the city was fully liberated by the next day. Even worse, Rybalko continued to advance southward and captured the rail station at Fastov on November 7, discomfiting Hoth's plans for a riposte. The sudden loss of Kiev – almost without a fight – was a bitter humiliation for von Manstein and Hoth.

Yet von Manstein had one last card to play. Hitler and the OKH had finally consented to release more reinforcements from the west and they were just beginning to arrive when Kiev fell. These reinforcements included three fresh Panzer divisions (1, 25 and SS-*LSSAH*) and a battalion of Tiger tanks, amounting altogether to 558 tanks (including 172 Panthers and 72 Tigers). For the first time since Kursk, von Manstein had a powerful armored operational reserve at his disposal and he intended to use it to encircle and demolish Rybalko's 3 GTA.[134] However, it took time for the German reinforcements to arrive by rail, unload and assemble and Vatutin went after their disembarkation points. Rybalko's 3 GTA continued pushing southeast from Fastov and threatened the rail station at Bila Tserkov, which was one of the main assembly points for General der Panzertruppe Hermann Balck's XXXXVIII Panzerkorps. Hoth was obliged to commit armor as it arrived to defend the assembly point; the effort was successful but costly. Meanwhile, Moskalenko's 38th Army daringly sent a mixed cavalry-tank mobile group to capture the vital rail junction at Zhitomir on November 13. The loss of Zhitomir was a disaster, since it disrupted von Manstein's rail line of communications and forced him to choose between concentrating on Rybalko or Moskalenko. On November 15, von Manstein began his counteroffensive, using five Panzer divisions (1, 7, 25, *LSSAH*, *Das Reich*) under control of Balck's XXXXVIII Panzerkorps, with the main effort initially directed against Moskalenko's vanguard. Due to heavy rain and limited air support, the German counteroffensive moved in slow motion but succeeded in retaking Zhitomir on November 20.[135] Von Manstein then turned to deal with Rybalko, who was gradually pushed back with the loss of about 150 tanks, but 3 GTA survived. By November 24, von Manstein's counteroffensive had culminated. The results were unsatisfying – the Soviet spearheads had been pushed back, but Rybalko's 3 GTA was still combat-effective and a threat. Hitler had also been under the impression that von Manstein might retake Kiev, although that was clearly beyond the capability of the small forces involved. Hitler had already decided to relieve Hoth of command of PzAOK 4 for losing Kiev and he was replaced by General der Panzertruppe Erhard Raus. Hoth was one of the finest commanders in the Ostheer, having performed well since *Barbarossa* in 1941, but now he was cast aside and received no further command assignments.

On the lower Dnepr, Konev decided to make another push for Krivoi Rog using Sharokhin's 37th Army, with Rotmistrov's 5 GTA poised to exploit any success. General der Panzertruppe Hans-Valentin Hube had replaced von Mackensen in command of PzAOK 1, which had built a strong defense around Krivoi Rog. Konev attacked on November 14 but Hube's defenses held and after a week of heavy fighting, Sharokhin was only able to advance 6–8km. Konev decided to shift his axis of advance toward the right flank of Wöhler's AOK 8, using Zhadov's 5 GA. When Zhadov attacked on November 20, he quickly shattered the front of the German XI Armeekorps.[136] Two days later, Konev committed Rotmistrov's 5 GTA, which smashed Wöhler's right flank. Hube hastily transferred two Panzer divisions to Wöhler to help repair the breach, but the Germans were only partially successful. It was only the onset of winter weather and fuel shortages which prevented Konev from completing the destruction of Wöhler's right flank. During this period, Konev also quietly gained another bridgehead across the Dnepr with General-leytenant Konstantin A. Koroteev's 52nd Army, near Cherkassy. Malinovsky's 3rd Ukrainian Front tried to support Konev's offensive against Krivoi Rog by attacking Hube's right flank, but suffered heavy losses for no gains. By mid-November it was clear that the Ostheer had recovered some of its balance and its prompt use of tactical reserves was usually able to fend off the sporadic Soviet offensive jabs. The most impressive German defensive performance occurred in the Nikopol bridgehead, where Hollidt's AOK 6 successfully repulsed repeated attacks by Tolbukhin's 4th Ukrainian Front. Despite a massive numerical superiority, Tolbukhin not only failed to dislodge the German position but also suffered embarrassing losses from enemy counterattacks.[137] By the end of November 1943, an operational pause settled over the lower Dnepr. Both Malinovsky and Tolbukhin continued attacking in December, without any success, but the Stavka did not allow them to pause their operations until nearly the end of the month.

Despite his failure to crush Rybalko's 3 GTA, von Manstein continued to conduct opportunistic counterattacks – at Radomschyl on December 6 and at Meleni on December 18–20. Cherniakhovsky's 60th Army was a particular problem, occupying a salient near Korosten, but it could not be eliminated. In fact, von Manstein's counterattacks failed to destroy any Soviet units and German losses were very heavy. The rainy, muddy weather hindered German operational mobility and the Luftwaffe was unable to provide any significant assistance. By the time that von Manstein called these futile operations off, Raus' PzAOK 4 had fewer than 200 operational tanks and very little infantry left. Raus was forced to employ Panzer divisions to hold sectors of the front – in complete violation of accepted German doctrine. Furthermore, the counteroffensive left Raus' army badly deployed, with most of its remaining armor on the left flank, near Korosten. While Vatutin was holding off von Manstein's counterattacks, the engineers of the 1st Ukrainian Front were assiduously building pontoon bridges across the Dnepr, which greatly improved Soviet

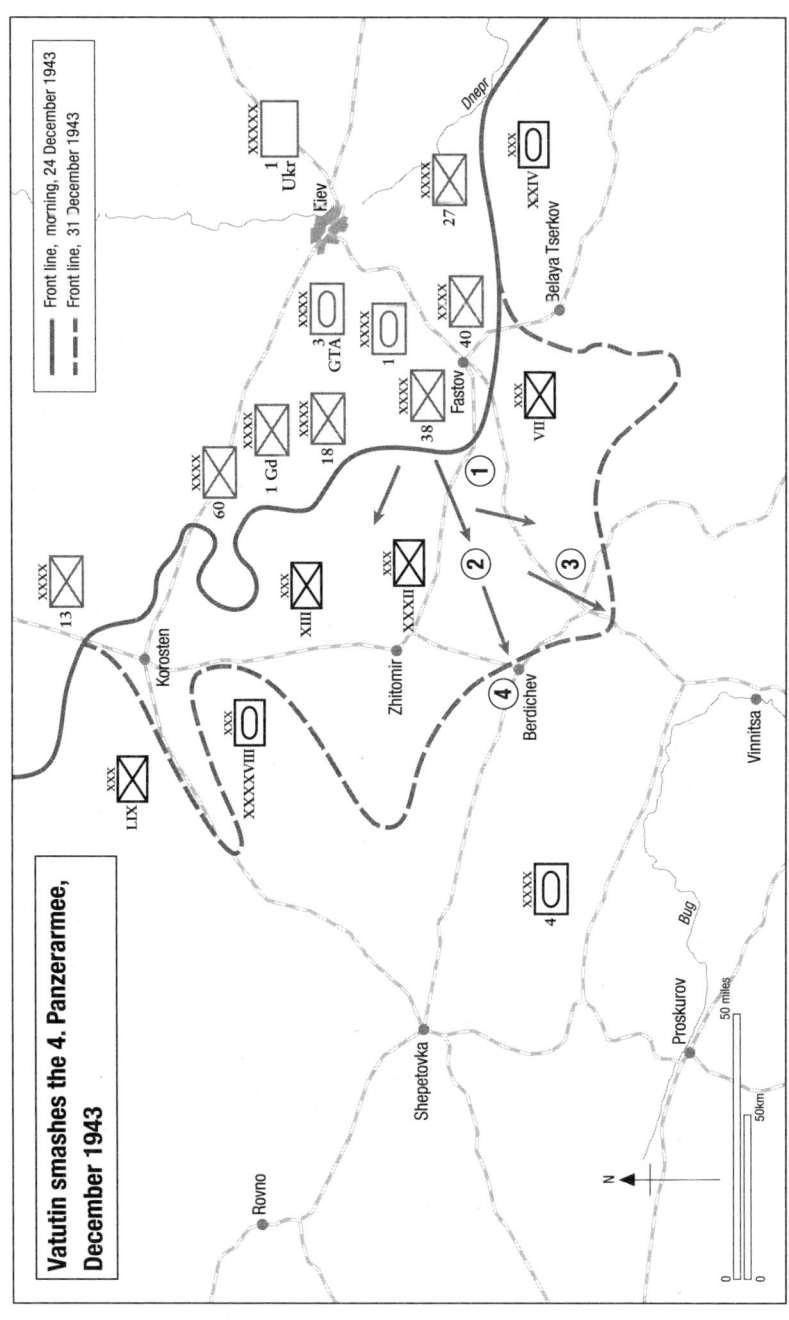

Vatutin smashes the 4. Panzerarmee, December 1943

Front line, morning, 24 December 1943
Front line, 31 December 1943

MAP KEY

1. Moskalenko's 38th Army starts the offensive, crushing the XXXXII Armeekorps.
2. Vatutin widens his breakthrough, tearing a larger hole in the German front.
3. Vatutin commits his two tank armies, pushing south.
4. The Germans manage to slow the Soviet advance with strongpoints at Berdichev and Belaya Tserkov.

---

logistic support on the western bank. In addition, the new bridges enabled replacement tanks to reach Rybalko's 3 GTA and for the Stavka to send Katukov's 1 TA across the Dnepr to reinforce Vatutin. Indeed, the Red Army's increased skill in tactical bridging operations played a key role in enabling Vatutin to continue his offensive. He now intended to follow up von Manstein's counteroffensive with a new offensive of his own, aimed at Raus' right flank against the XXXXII Armeekorps at Brusilov (east of Zhitomir). In this sector, Raus was holding a 40km-front with three depleted Panzer divisions (8, 19, 25), comprising 96 tanks and 5,000 troops. Vatutin intended to smash Raus' right flank then advance over 100km to the southwest, with Vinnitsa as the distant objective.[138]

On the morning of December 24, Moskalenko's 38th Army began a 60-minute artillery preparation against the XXXXII Armeekorps, followed with a ground assault by ten rifle divisions and 200 tanks. Von Manstein and Raus were shocked by the scale of Vatutin's offensive and Moskalenko achieved a tactical breakthrough within hours. Vatutin immediately committed Rybalko's 3 GTA and Katukov's 1 TA – a mass of 700 tanks – into the breach. By evening, the XXXXII Armeekorps' front was broken and both the 8. and 19. Panzer-Divisions were nearly surrounded. Raus responded quickly, shifting two Panzer divisions from his left flank to his right flank in order to hold Zhitomir. Although the XXXXII Armeekorps managed to conduct a fighting retreat, Vatutin's armor poured into the breach and on December 26 he began attacking the rest of Raus' crumbling line. Vatutin kept up the pressure and although Raus conducted a tenacious rearguard, the PzAOK 4 was broken into three pieces by December 30 and he was forced to evacuate Zhitomir.[139] As 1943 and the Dnepr campaign came to a close, Vatutin had achieved a major operational breakthrough and Raus' PzAOK 4 was in full retreat.

The Red Army won a great operational victory in the Dnepr campaign, which prevented the Ostheer from creating a new defensive line behind that river barrier. Instead, by aggressive maneuver warfare, three Soviet fronts were able to breach the Dnepr line before von Manstein's Heeresgruppe Süd was in a position to defend it. Hitler's Panther-Stellung evaporated on contact. Von Manstein's armies were badly bloodied in this disastrous campaign, which cost Heeresgruppe Süd 372,000 casualties (including 102,000 dead or missing). As a result, most of the German infantry divisions were so depleted that they were only capable of conducting defensive missions. Most of von Manstein's armor was also lost, leaving him with minimal mobile reserves. Due to Hitler's shift in priority to the west after the Allied invasion of Sicily, Heeresgruppe Süd received fewer than 200,000 replacements during the campaign and insufficient equipment to rebuild its shattered divisions. Unlike previous defeats, there would be no recovery for Heeresgruppe Süd this time. The price of victory was not cheap for the Red Army. During the Dnepr campaign, the four Soviet fronts involved suffered over 1 million casualties (including 290,000 dead or missing) and lost about 12,000 tanks. However, the recovery of most of the Ukraine enabled the immediate conscription of about 200,000 local replacements (most of indifferent quality) and Soviet industry was finally beginning to replace equipment losses in a timely fashion. Anglo-American Lend Lease was also beginning to tip the balance, by providing large amounts of motor transport to enhance the Red Army's operational mobility.

Hitler's poor decisions and interference with operational details was a contributing factor to German defeat in the Dnepr campaign, but the inability of German senior commanders (von Manstein, Hoth, Raus) to anticipate Soviet actions also played a major role. Having regarded the enemy as inferior for two years, these senior commanders now demonstrated real difficulty adjusting to the fact that the Red Army was evolving into a more capable and dangerous opponent that was able to conduct large-scale multifront offensives. Except for Hoth, who proved unable to properly prioritize his campaign objectives (crush the Bukrin bridgehead or defend Kiev), the other German commanders pursued distinct objectives. Only von Manstein was provided the reinforcements to employ mass, but he failed to use maneuver or surprise when he committed them to a counteroffensive, which ended up becoming a series of local, tactical actions. Hollidt proved the most successful German commander during the Dnepr campaign, achieving near miracles at Melitopol and in the Nikopol bridgehead. Overall, the German command performance during the Dnepr campaign was sub-par. Hoth was exhausted after years of continuous high-intensity campaigning and was beginning to make serious mistakes. Other commanders now doubted the *Endsieg* (Final Victory) – which caused Hitler to begin shuffling commanders around and insert officers regarded as more loyal to the regime. Hitler also lost faith in the professional military expertise of his senior commanders, once they proved unable to halt the inexorable Soviet advance westward.

On the Soviet side, Vatutin put in his best command performance of the war, demonstrating a keen ability to conduct aggressive maneuver warfare. During the Dnepr campaign, he caught von Manstein by surprise no less than three times. Konev demonstrated improved ability to employ the principles of war to shape his operations, but fumbled badly during the Myshurin Rog attack when he threw away operational success in order to pursue diverging objectives, then was pushed back by Schörner's counteroffensive. Malinovsky and Tolbukhin also put in fairly mediocre performances, simply attacking and attacking without achieving much success. Among the Soviet army commanders, all three tank army commanders (Rybalko, Rotmistrov and Katukov) and Moskalenko (38th Army) performed exceptionally well in conducting aggressive maneuver warfare. Many of the other field army commanders proved quite competent in accomplishing their missions. The Stavka rightly regarded the Dnepr campaign as a great success and the increased professionalism of the Red Army was becoming apparent.

Commander	Objective	Offensive	Mass	Maneuver	Surprise	Security	TALLY
Von Manstein	+	+	+	o	o	–	2
Von Kleist	+	o	o	o	o	+	2
Hoth	o	+	o	o	o	–	o
Raus	+	+	o	o	o	–	1
Hube Von Mackensen	+	o	o	o	o	+	2
Hollidt	+	+	o	o	o	+	3
Wöhler	+	o	+	o	o	o	2
Vatutin	+	+	+	+	+	+	6
Rokossovsky	+	+	o	+	+	o	4
Konev	o	+	–	+	+	o	2
Malinovsky	+	+	o	o	o	o	2
Tolbukhin	+	+	+	o	o	–	2

Rybalko Katukov Rotmistrov Moskalenko	+	+	+	+	+	o	5
Pukhov Shumilov Sharokhin Zhadov	+	+	o	+	+	o	4
Lelyushenko Chuikov Cherniakhovsky	+	+	o	o	o	+	3

Dnepr Campaign, 1943 Leadership Assessment

The Belorussian Offensive, November 10–30, 1943

Once Rokossovsky's Central Front (which was re-designated as the 1st Belorussian Front on October 20) reached the Dnepr River north of Kiev, the Stavka directed it to begin planning to push west into southern Belorussia. Rather ambitiously, the Stavka set Minsk and Bobruisk as distant operational objectives. On September 29, the Stavka shifted frontal boundaries, moving Rokossovsky's command further north; Pukhov's 13th Army and Cherniakhovsky's 60th Army were transferred to Vatutin's command. At the same time, Popov's Bryansk Front transferred Gorbatov's 3rd Army and Boldin's 50th Army to the Central Front. Popov's headquarters was then redesignated as the 2nd Baltic Front. Rokossovsky's front now comprised seven armies (3, 11, 48, 50, 61, 63, 65) with 485,000 troops, 493 tanks and 845 medium-caliber artillery pieces (122mm).[140]

Generalfeldmarschall Günther von Kluge had been badly injured in an accident on October 27 and was replaced as commander of Heeresgruppe Mitte by Generalfeldmarschall Ernst Busch (from AOK 16). Heeresgruppe Mitte now consisted of four armies: PzAOK 3 (Reinhardt), AOK 4 (Heinrici), AOK 9 (Model) and AOK 2 (Weiß). On October 15, Rokossovsky attacked Generaloberst Walter Weiß' AOK 2 in the Gomel sector, using Belov's 61st Army and Batov's 65th Army. Most of Weiß' combat strength was deployed further south, near Chernobyl, leaving his center rather thinly held. After two days' fighting, the Russian armies succeeded in gaining a small bridgehead across the Dnepr River at Loev, 54km south of Gomel.[141] Batov's 65th Army managed to carve out a larger lodgment across the Sozh River, an adjoining tributary of the Dnepr, which threatened the German position in Gomel. However, the Soviet offensive quickly ran out of steam and Weiß succeeded in holding onto Gomel by reinforcing it with the entire XXXV Armeekorps (four infantry divisions). After this initial phase culminated without accomplishing much, the Stavka directed Rokossovsky to regroup his forces and try again. As with the other Soviet fronts, Rokossovsky was plagued by logistic shortages and the autumn weather was beginning to reduce operational mobility. Furthermore, the marshy and heavily wooded terrain in the Gomel sector (which lay on the northeast corner of the Pripet Marshes) was poorly suited for maneuver warfare and heavily favored the defense.

Rokossovsky planned for a larger version of his initial offensive, using Belov's 61st Army, Batov's 65th Army and Romanenko's 48th Army as his main effort – which would attack northwest from the Loev bridgehead area. Belov's army was greatly reinforced, with more than double the strength of the other armies. Rokossovsky created two mobile groups to exploit the expected breakthrough, consisting of three cavalry corps and one tanks corps; the cavalry was often more useful in the marshy terrain than tanks. At the proper moment, Rokossovsky would launch a supporting attack against the left wing of AOK 2, using Fediuninskiy's 11th Army and Kolpakchi's 63rd Army. The new offensive commenced on November 10 and quickly overwhelmed the German XX Armeekorps. After two days of fighting, the three Soviet armies achieved a breakthrough and tore a large gap in Weiß' front line. Rokossovsky committed his mobile groups and they pushed into the breach, gaining considerable ground. Weiß' position was serious and the OKH transferred a Panzer division to his command to try to stem the incipient Soviet breakthrough. Although the German counterattack on November 18–20 failed, Hitler refused to consider any withdrawals. Yet when Rokossovsky committed his other armies into the offensive, particularly Fediuninskiy's 11th Army, it was apparent that Gomel could not be held. Rokossovsky also attacked the boundary between AOK 2 and AOK 9 with his 3rd and 50th Armies, further discomfiting Weiß. On November 26, the Germans were forced to evacuate Gomel. However, Rokossovsky's offensive gradually ground to a halt due to bad weather, fuel shortages and enemy resistance. Weiß was able to cobble together a new front along the line Mozyr-Zhlobin that blocked Rokossovsky's advance toward Bobruisk. A strongpoint at the town of Kalinkovichi proved to be a particularly annoying obstacle.

After a pause for a week, the Stavka urged Rokossovsky to resume his offensive in early December, although he only had the resources to attack with part of his forces. At the same time, the Stavka began taking units from the 1st Belorussian Front to reinforce Vatutin's command. Rather than waiting longer to replenish his forces, Rokossovsky decided to focus on eliminating the German strongpoint at Kalinkovichi, using Batov's 65th Army. Batov attacked on December 8–11 but gained little ground. The 65th Army now occupied a salient in the gap between AOK 2 and AOK 9, which forced Batov to spread his army out. Most of the rifle divisions in the 1st Belorussian Front were much reduced by this point and a good deal of the armor had been transferred south as well. Unknown to Rokossovsky, the OKH had decided to send the fresh 16. Panzer-Division to Model in order to seal the gap between the two German armies. The 16. Panzer-Division had just arrived from the Italian front and was equipped with 98 PzKpfw IV tanks and 42 StuG assault guns – a rather powerful unit. Model and Weiß planned to conduct a pincer attack against Batov's 65th Army; AOK 9 would attack south with two divisions (including the 16. Panzer-Division) while AOK 2 attacked northward with *Kampfgruppen* from the 4. and 12. Panzer-Divisions. The German counteroffensive began on the morning of December 20 and for once achieved operational surprise. Batov's vulnerable right flank was smashed in and the Germans managed to surround the bulk of the 95th Rifle Corps (four rifle divisions and a tank brigade).[142] Rokossovsky later criticized Batov for ignoring the threat to his flank, but he had not positioned his remaining mobile reserves to deal with this contingency. Once the gap in the front was sealed, the OKH decided to transfer the 16. Panzer-Division to PzAOK 4, which brought the German counteroffensive to a sudden end on December 26. Although most of the encircled Soviet troops escaped the *Kessel*, they lost the bulk of their equipment and Batov's army had been knocked back 25 kilometers. The well-timed German counterattack put a damper on Rokossovsky's plans and helped to stabilize Heeresgruppe Mitte's right flank by year's end.

During the Belorussian campaign, Rokossovsky could not use maneuver as much as he did in the race to the Dnepr due to terrain limitations, but he was able to mass his combat power to win set-piece battles. While he did not reach the distant objectives Stavka set out for his command, Rokossovsky inflicted nearly 26,000 casualties (including 7,300 dead or missing) on AOK 2 during October and November and pushed Weiß' line back nearly 100 kilometers. The losses of the 1st Belorussian Front in this campaign were also heavy, numbering well in excess of 100,000. The sudden German counteroffensive in December ended the campaign on a sour note for the Red Army. The campaign in Belorussia resulted in a Soviet partial victory but fell far short of the Stavka's expectations (which tended to ignore terrain, weather, logistics and the enemy). Most of Rokossovsky's field army commanders also performed fairly well and demonstrated an ability to organize and direct their forces over difficult terrain. Given the nature of the terrain in the region and the rainy weather conditions, the 1st Belorussian Front's autumn offensive was not able to fully employ tanks or aviation in support, which limited the operational tempo. On the German side, Weiß did the best he could in a crisis situation and managed to prevent an enemy operational-level breakthrough or the collapse of his army. When provided with adequate reinforcements, he and Model were able to launch a well-timed counteroffensive that knocked Rokossovsky back on his heels. Unlike other Ostheer commanders in late 1943, Weiß also maintained the confidence of his chain of command and was not removed for retreating.

Commander	Objective	Offensive	Mass	Maneuver	Surprise	Security	TALLY
Weiß	+	+	o	o	o	+	3
Rokossovsky Belov Romanenko Fediuninskiy Kolpakchi	+	+	+	o	o	o	3
Batov	+	+	+	o	o	–	2

Belorussian Offensive, 1943 Leadership Assessment

Over the course of 1943, the Red Army conducted 16 major operations (aggregating separate offensive pulses in the Kuban and along the Dnepr), of which nine were victories, two were partial victories and five were failures. As a result of these operations, the Red Army destroyed two Axis armies in 1943 (6. Armee and Hungarian 2nd Army) and crippled several others. In addition, the Red Army liberated eight important territorial objectives (Voronezh, Rostov, Krasnodar, Kharkov, Donetsk, Dnepropetrovsk, Smolensk and Kiev), which erased most of the German gains of the previous year. The Soviet rate of operational success had jumped considerably in 1943 and most of the defeats were in the first half of the year. By the end of 1943, the Red Army had the strategic initiative and was on a roll. During the same period, the Germans conducted seven major operations in the East, of which only two were successful (von Manstein's "Backhand Blow" and *Roland*), three were partial successes (Belorussia, Krivoi Rog and Zhitomir) and two were failures (*Neptun* and *Zitadelle*). Although the Ostheer succeeded in crushing isolated Soviet formations on a number of occasions in 1943, they did not destroy any armies and the Stavka was able to quickly rebuild its decimated units. Nor did the Ostheer capture or recapture any significant territorial objectives in 1943.

In strategic terms, the Ostheer suffered over 1.5 million casualties (including 587,000 dead or missing) in 1943 and lost 7,000 tanks and assault guns, whereas the Red Army suffered 7.85 million casualties (including 2.3 million dead or missing) and lost 22,400 tanks. Germany could no longer replace its manpower and material losses, which meant that each campaign further eroded the Ostheer. Nor were the Axis partners in any position to contribute much and were in fact beginning to look to exit the war. Consequently, the Ostheer was no longer capable of achieving major operational successes and could only wage an attrition-based struggle and hope that its superior equipment and training could help it to stop the Red Army's westward advance.

CHAPTER 6

Bagration: 1944 Operations

"We are standing on the threshold of the Fatherland. Every step back brings the war closer to Germany. Not a step back."
Generaloberst Georg Lindemann, April 1944

"We abandoned the template and began the operation in the evening."
Eremenko, July 10, 1944[1]

The Campaign in Western Ukraine,
January 1–April 16, 1944

At the start of 1944, Vatutin's winter offensive (later known as the Zhitomir-Berdichev operation) continued to pound on Raus' PzAOK 4, which had abandoned Zhitomir and Korosten. Vatutin hoped to smash PzAOK 4 and then push on to the Polish border. The most serious situation facing Raus lay between Zhitomir and Fastov, where Katukov's 1TA, Leselidze's 18th Army and Moskalenko's 38th Army had created a large breach in the German front line. Raus' center – the XIII, XXXXII Armeekorps and XXXXVIII Panzerkorps – was hard-pressed while his right wing (VII Armeekorps and XXIV Panzerkorps) had managed to briefly anchor a line around Belaya Tserkov. The only area where Raus was able to make a real stand was in the city of Berdichev, where Balck's XXXXVIII Panzerkorps (with 1. Panzer-Division and the *LSSAH*) managed to repulse the initial attacks by the 11th Guards Tank Corps (from 1 TA) and part of Rybalko's 3 GTA.[2] Although outnumbered 5-1, Balck's remaining armor succeeded in inflicting painful losses. Rybalko's 3 GTA was reduced to just one-third of its authorized tank strength.[3] According to German accounts, the Red Army lost over 100 tanks outside Berdichev, while according to Katukov's memoirs, he only lost a tank brigade. Despite stubborn resistance, Moskalenko's 38th Army and Rybalko's remaining armor succeeded in liberating Berdichev on January 5.[4] Katukov's primary operational objective was Vinnitsa, which was where von Manstein's Heeresgruppe Süd headquarters was located. Katukov's armored vanguard was less than 60 kilometers north of Vinnitsa. Von Manstein recognized that his top priority was to stop Katukov from reaching Vinnitsa and to seal the breach in Raus' front. Yet Hitler forbade von Manstein from making any large-scale transfers of units from Hube's PzAOK 1 to help Raus' PzAOK 4 because it would weaken the German position around Kirovograd. Nevertheless, von Manstein decided to conduct unauthorized transfers, so he ordered Hube to take command over Raus' two right wing corps and to develop the conditions for a counteroffensive to seal the breach. Hube quietly transferred most of Breith's III Panzerkorps toward his left flank to employ as a mobile blocking force.

On January 4, von Manstein met with Hitler at the *Wolfsschanze* in East Prussia. Von Manstein urgently requested permission to withdraw his forces from the Dnepr Bend and recommended that von Kleist's Heeresgruppe A should evacuate the Crimea and the Nikopol bridgehead. He also raised the idea of pulling back to shorter lines behind the Bug River, which would have meant abandoning most of western Ukraine. While von Manstein's recommendations were based on sound military judgment, Hitler regarded this line of reasoning as defeatist and he lost any remaining confidence in the commander of Heeresgruppe Süd. He refused to consider any major withdrawals and stated that Heeresgruppe Süd would receive no further major reinforcements until the expected Allied invasion in the west was defeated.[5]

By January 5, Hube had managed to insert Breith's III Panzerkorps (with 6. and 17. Panzer Divisions) into the gap north of Vinnitsa and partly closed the gap between PzAOK 4 and PzAOK 1. While Katukov's advance was slowed, Vatutin responded by increasing the pressure against

Raus' left flank (LIX Armeekorps), which fell back toward Rovno. As Raus later admitted, his LIX Armeekorps was crushed.[6] Vatutin also attacked the German strongpoint in Belaya Tserkov with Trofimenko's 27th Army and General-leytenant Filipp F. Zhmachenko's 40th Army, which evicted the VII Armeekorps from that position on January 6. The Stavka continued to provide Vatutin with more resources to keep his offensive going; the 1st Guards Army (1GA), now under Grechko, was transferred from Konev's command and other units were taken from Rokossovsky's command. On January 8/9, Katukov made his main play to take Vinnitsa by sending the 11 Guards Tank Corps and part of the 8th Guards Mechanized Corps in a long-end run to the southeast of the city. Katukov's tankers boldly bypassed Vinnitsa, then swung west to cross the Bug River at Gnivan, then pushed to the vital rail junction at Zhmerinka. Although Katukov's lead brigade managed to reach Zhmerinka, it unexpectedly found that the 16. Panzer-Division (which had a battalion of 40 Panther tanks) and 1. Infanterie-Division were just arriving there by rail.[7] Two other German infantry divisions (254. and 4. Gebirgs-Division) were also due to arrive soon in Vinnitsa, along with a battalion of Tiger tanks; these units were to be employed in a counteroffensive designated as *Winterreise*.[8] The OKH had decided to stop Vatutin's offensive at Vinnitsa and was sending enough reinforcements to make a difference.

At 0500 hours on January 9, Zhukov and Vatutin sent a joint proposal to the Stavka to continue the Vinnitsa-Berdichev operation for another 10–12 days. On the right flank of the 1st Ukrainian Front, Pukhov's 13th Army was pushing east toward Rovno against minimal opposition and Cherniakhovsky's 60th Army was near the rail junction at Shepetovka. In the center, four armies (1 GA, 18, 38, 3 GTA) were steadily, if slowly, pushing back Balck's embattled XXXXVIII Panzerkorps, while Katukov's 1 TA was on the outskirts of Vinnitsa. On Vatutin's left flank, the 27th and 40th Armies were pushing back the left flank of Hube's PzAOK 1. Overall, the Soviet situation seemed very favorable, despite the exhausted condition of front-line units and the shortage of fuel and ammunition. However, Soviet aerial reconnaissance failed to detect the arrival of the four fresh German divisions in Vinnitsa and preparations for a counteroffensive. From the German perspective, Raus and von Manstein were faced with very difficult choices; they had been provided just enough reinforcements to mount one significant counterattack – but where was the optimal point? The broken left flank of PzAOK 4 was flapping in the wind and urgently needed assistance. Balck's corps also badly needed help. The right flank of PzAOK 4 and its connection to Hube's PzAOK 1 was also in a state of flux, with Soviet forces approaching Uman. Von Manstein and Raus decided to accept risk in the other sectors and focus all their efforts in *Winterreise* to crush Katukov's 1 TA.[9] If the threat to Vinnitsa was relieved, the other threats would become more manageable.

On January 10, PzAOK 4 commenced its counteroffensive. The XXXXVI Panzerkorps was designated as the main effort and was given all four fresh divisions, including 16. Panzer-Division; its task was to smash Katukov's vulnerable right flank and encircle as much of his army as possible. The VIII Fliegerkorps was assigned to provide close air support. Katukov was caught off-balance, with very limited infantry or artillery support at hand, and the 11 GTC was badly mauled by the German counterattack. Two Soviet tank brigades were briefly surrounded, but they succeeded in escaping the trap, albeit without their vehicles. *Winterreise* was a brief affair, but it sufficed to force Katukov to pull back from Vinnitsa to save his overextended army. Stunned by the German counterattack, the Stavka allowed Vatutin to shift to the defense on January 14 in order to replenish his forces. The Stavka immediately sent 200 tanks from the RVGK to refit 1 TA and 3 GTA. Von Manstein gained a brief respite but he recognized that the Soviet threat to Vinnitsa and Uman was only deferred.

While von Manstein was fending off Vatutin's 1st Ukrainian Front, Konev was planning his own offensive with his 2nd Ukrainian Front. On December 29, the Stavka had directed Konev to attack and seize the key rail junction at Kirovograd in early January. When Konev recognized that part of Hube's PzAOK 1 had shifted laterally to the west, he accelerated preparations for an offensive against Wöhler's AOK 8. Up to this point in the war, Konev had proved to be a rather mediocre commander who often achieved less than what was expected of him. His long-serving chief of staff, General-polkovnik Matvei V. Zakharov, was experienced in leading a professional staff to produce quality operational plans. For the Kirovograd operation, Konev's staff prepared a sound plan for a set-piece offensive that would attempt a double pincer attack against the German front east of the city. The northern pincer would be comprised of Galanin's 53rd Army, Zhadov's 5 GA and two attached mechanized corps, while the southern pincer would consist of Shumilov's 7 GA and Rotmistrov's 5 GTA. Given that many of his previous losses had not yet been replaced (Vatutin's command had priority for replacements), Konev had no substantial superiority in armor, infantry or air support. Nevertheless, Wöhler's army was in even worse condition. General der Panzertruppe Nikolaus von Vormann's XXXXVII Panzerkorps was responsible for holding the Kirovograd sector and he was so short of infantry that he was forced to employ two Panzer divisions (11, 14) to hold his front line. German intelligence was aware of Konev's impending offensive and the 3. Panzer-Division was transferred to Kirovograd just as the blow was about to fall.

Konev's armies attacked on the morning of January 5, across a 70km frontage, after a 50-minute artillery barrage that fired 177,000 rounds at Vormann's troops. Zhadov's 5 GA was able to make a deep penetration on the first day, although enemy resistance was more tenacious in Shumilov's sector. Nevertheless, Konev fed Rotmistrov's 5 GTA into the battle on January 6 along with his remaining armored reserves, which gradually overwhelmed the German defense. Wöhler attempted to mount a limited pincer counterattack on January 6 with Generalmajor Fritz Bayerlein's 3. Panzer-Division and the 11. Panzer-Division (totaling about 40–50 tanks) against Zhadov's 5 GA, but this effort failed to achieve much. Instead, Zhadov sent his attached mechanized corps ahead to boldly outflank Kirovograd from the north. In the process, Soviet tanks overran the command post of Vormann's XXXXVII Panzerkorps and seriously disrupted German C2 at a crucial moment. Simultaneously, Rotmistrov's 5 GTA achieved a breakthrough and advanced into the outskirts of Kirovograd with a tank corps, which caused a panic-stricken evacuation by the support units in the city. By the morning of January 7, Wöhler discovered that four German divisions (3. and 11. Panzer-Division, 10. Panzergrenadier-Division and 376. Infanterie-Division) had been encircled in or near Kirovograd. Although only a division commander, Bayerlein had served in key staff positions under both Guderian and Rommel and had a wealth of experience in planning and conducting mobile operations in desperate conditions. Bayerlein took charge over all four encircled German divisions and quickly organized a breakout attack on January 7/8 which succeeded in escaping from the Soviet trap.[10] Although Konev planned a pincer attack to encircle German forces in Kirovograd he seemed not to have anticipated a breakout attempt, and Zhadov bears some measure of responsibility for allowing Bayerlein to escape his grasp. While the rapid capture of Kirovograd was a major success for Konev and his 2nd Ukrainian Front, the escape of the four encircled German divisions enabled Wöhler to rapidly form a new front line west of the city. Consequently, the Stavka ordered Konev to continue attacking for another week, but only minor gains were made southwest of Kirovograd.

Despite the territory gained by Vatutin and Konev in January, Heeresgruppe Süd still held a small section of frontage along the Dnepr River in the Korsun sector. The west side of the Korsun salient was held by the VII and XXXXII Armeekorps from Hube's PzAOK 1, while the eastern side was held by XI Armeekorps and XXXXVII Panzerkorps from Wöhler's AOK 8. Von Manstein recognized that the Korsun salient had no military value and required a minimum of six divisions to hold, so he pressed Hitler to evacuate the useless position and withdraw to a shorter, more defensible line. Hitler refused – the Korsun salient would be held. Unable to evacuate this vulnerable position, von Manstein assigned Breith's III Panzerkorps to respond to any Soviet attempt to cut off the salient. However, Katukov's 1 TA was soon revitalized and began to make another push toward Uman. Consequently, von Manstein was forced to organize another counteroffensive, dubbed Operation *Watutin*, to block Katukov's advance. Breith's III Panzerkorps and the XXXXVI Panzerkorps were committed to this operation (totaling four Panzer divisions), which began on January 24. As usual, the Germans attempted a pincer operation, with the two converging Panzer groups trying to cut off Katukov's spearhead. Operation *Watutin* achieved some success in encircling and destroying some Soviet units (mostly infantry) and halting Katukov's 1 TA. By the time that the operation concluded on January 30, von Manstein claimed that 13,500 enemy troops had been killed or captured and over 700 AFVs eliminated, but the number of tanks knocked out was likely one-third that number.[11] Katukov's spearhead units had been blunted (in his memoirs, Katukov made no mention of the German counteroffensive), but it came at the cost of committing virtually all of von Manstein's best mobile units to this one sector.

In Moscow, the Stavka also recognized the vulnerability of the Korsun salient and in mid-January 1944 Zhukov ordered Vatutin and Konev to prepare a coordinated pincer attack to isolate and destroy the German forces in this sector. Konev's forces were fairly depleted after the Kirovograd operation and were not given adequate time or resources to refit before embarking on their next offensive operation. Rotmistrov's 5 GTA had barely 200 operational tanks and assault guns – about one-third of its authorized strength.[12] Given the time constraints imposed by the Stavka, Konev had little time to redeploy any of his forces and opted for expedience by simply attacking with his *in situ* right wing – Galanin's 53rd Army, Zhadov's 5 GA, with Rotmistrov as the exploitation force. Vatutin would attack the west side of the salient with Trofimenko's 27th Army and Zhmachenko's 40th Army, with the newly established 6th Tank Army (210 tanks and assault guns) under General-leytenant Andrey G. Kravchenko as the exploitation force. However, Kravchenko's command was an improvised formation without an army-level staff and comprised only one tank and one mechanized corps.[13]

On January 25, 1944, Konev's 2nd Ukrainian Front struck the east side of the Korsun salient with Zhadov's 4th Guards Army (4 GA) and Galanin's 53rd Army; these two armies massed seven divisions against a single understrength German infantry division assigned to hold a 21km-wide front. Heavy fog covered the battlefield, which obscured visibility. The German 389. Infanterie-Division was quickly crushed and Konev committed Rotmistrov's 5 GTA to exploit the breakthrough.[14] Wöhler used his tactical reserves to try to plug the gap, but this only succeeded in limiting Rotmistrov to a 10km-deep penetration on the first day of the operation. The next day, Vatutin's 1st Ukrainian Front attacked the west side of the salient with Zhmachenko's 40th Army, supported by one mechanized corps from Kravchenko's 6th Tank Army (6 TA). Vatutin failed to mass sufficient combat power against the German VII Armeekorps, which limited Zhmachenko to minor gains. However, Trofimenko's 27th Army, mounting a supporting effort on Zhmachenko's left flank, succeeded in achieving a small penetration against the German XXXXII Armeekorps. Vatutin decided to commit a brigade-size mobile group into the breach effected by Trofimenko, and surprisingly this small force advanced rapidly into the German rear areas. At this point, both Hube and Vatutin were faced with important command decisions. For Hube, the question was whether to terminate Operation *Watutin* and transfer part of Breith's III Panzerkorps to support the VII Armeekorps against Kravchenko's armor, or to finish off the encircled Soviet units north of Uman; he opted to complete his *Kessel* battle. Hube also knew that Wöhler had succeeded in isolating part of Rotmistrov's spearheads, so the risk seemed acceptable. In operational-level warfare, commanders often face the dilemma of whether it is better to conduct operations in tandem (simultaneously) or sequentially (one after another); making the right choice, at the right time, is an essential element of battle command. For Vatutin, the question was what to do about the German counteroffensive against Katukov's forces – ignore it (and hope for the best) or divert forces to help Katukov. Whereas Hube accepted risk, Vatutin decided to play it safe: he diverted the 5th Mechanized Corps (about half of Kravchenko's armor) to support Katukov, thereby weakening his main effort against the Korsun salient. Nevertheless, through a certain amount of luck and fog of war, the converging Soviet armored spearheads from 5 GTA and 6 TA were able to link up at Zvenigorodka by noon on January 28, completing the encirclement of six divisions with nearly 59,000 German troops in the Korsun Pocket.[15] Inside the pocket, the 5. SS-Panzerdivision *Wiking* and five infantry divisions merged into Gruppe Stemmermann, which contracted in order to create a defensible perimeter around the small airfield near Korsun.

Von Manstein was determined not to repeat the mistakes made with the encircled 6. Armee at Stalingrad one year prior and he moved quickly to mount a rescue mission to save the troops in the Korsun pocket. He began by terminating Operation *Watutin* in order to shift Breith's III Panzerkorps east to attack into the flank of Kravchenko's 6 TA. Von Manstein also ordered Wöhler's 8. Armee to continue using the XXXXVII Panzerkorps against the flank of Rotmistrov's 5 GTA. Von Manstein's relief operation was designated Operation *Wanda* and he hoped that prompt action would enable his understrength and exhausted Panzer units to punch through to the Korsun pocket before the Soviets could crush Gruppe Stemmermann. Adverse weather conditions and poor logistics affected both sides during the Korsun operation. An early thaw created thick mud, which impaired operational mobility and also caused fog, which reduced visibility. Both sides were also desperately short of fuel and ammunition in the forward areas. Operating primarily from airfields around Uman, the Luftwaffe was tasked with flying in enough supplies – roughly 70 tons per day – to keep Stemmermann's troops combat-capable until the relief operation could reach them. Beginning on January 31, three *Gruppen* of Ju-52 transports were able to fly in 2,026 tons of supplies during the 17-day airlift operation and fly out about 2,400 wounded troops. Unlike Stalingrad, the German soldiers in the Korsun pocket were not starving, but morale was tenuous. While the distance between Uman and Korsun was only 106 kilometers, the Luftwaffe suffered heavy losses from enemy opposition and adverse weather conditions. Altogether, 32 Ju-52 transports were lost during the Kuban airlift operation and many of the remainder were damaged.[16] It is important to note that the Luftwaffe was simultaneously conducting a large-scale airlift to support the isolated Axis garrison in the Crimea – further stretching German theater logistic capabilities.

Von Manstein's basic concept for Operation *Wanda* was the usual armored pincer attack with von Vormann's XXXXVII Panzerkorps attacking from the east and Breith's III Panzerkorps attacking from the west. The rescue plan lacked unity of command, since von Vormann reported to Wöhler's AOK 8 while Breith reported to Hube's PzAOK 1. Nor would the two corps attack simultaneously due to fuel shortages and the time it would require Breith to shift his forces west over muddy roads. Thus, von Vormann attacked first, beginning *Wanda* on February 1. The XXXXVII Panzerkorps attacked with two Panzer divisions (11, 13) and initially made good progress through Konev's outer screening forces, which mostly consisted of Galanin's 53rd Army. Rotmistrov's 5 GTA was fairly dispersed after achieving its breakthrough and dash to Zvenigorodka, leaving it in a poor position to respond quickly to the German relief effort. However, von Vormann's Panzers were soon stopped at the Shpolka River when a bridge collapsed. German engineers managed to construct a pontoon bridge, but half of von Vormann's tanks were PzKpfw V Panthers, which were too heavy to cross (another example of how the late-war German heavy tanks were ill-suited to meet the requirements of their maneuver warfare doctrine). Meanwhile, Breith's III Panzerkorps struggled to reach its assembly areas due to the thick Ukrainian mud and thus could not join the relief operation until February 4. Breith's corps was fairly strong (16. and 17. Panzer-Divisions) with a total of 126 operational tanks and assault guns, and von Manstein promised two more Panzer divisions as reinforcements. As with von Vormann, Breith's corps was able to advance 19 kilometers on the first day of its attack but then became stalled at the Gniloi Tikich River due to mud, inadequate engineering support and limited fuel supplies. Vatutin quickly shifted Kravchenko's 6 TA into Breith's path, halting the German advance 36 kilometers short of the link-up with Gruppe Stemmermann.

Once the relief columns had been halted, Vatutin and Konev focused on reducing the pocket, but they decided to rely primarily upon artillery in order to conserve their limited amount of front-line infantry. Von Manstein reinforced Breith's depleted III Panzerkorps with the 1. Panzer-Division and a *Kampfgruppe* from LSSAH, increasing its armored strength to 155 tanks and assault guns (including 80 Panthers). On the morning of February 11, Breith resumed his attack; one *Kampfgruppe* succeeded in crossing the Gniloi Tikich River at Frankovka while another captured the town of Lisyanka. Von Vormann's XXXXVII Panzerkorps also attacked and made some progress toward a link-up before running out of steam. For a brief moment on February 13, it seemed that von Manstein's forces would relieve the Korsun Pocket. However, the dire shortage of fuel in the forward units immobilized the German tanks.

Although caught off-balance by the rapidly organized German relief operations, the Soviet commanders soon recovered and made countermoves. Zhukov provided Vatutin with four tank brigades from the 2nd Tank Army in the Stavka Reserves (RVGK), which were sent to block Breith's Panzers. The Stavka also committed several regiments of the new IS-1 heavy tanks to oppose Breith's Panthers and Tigers. Refueled by airdrop, Breith made one more short sprint on February 13, before being finally stopped 10 kilometers short of reaching Gruppe Stemmermann.

Von Manstein's relief operation could go no further. On the same day, Konev's forces overran the Korsun airfield, terminating the airlift to Gruppe Stemmermann.

Recognizing that the end of the airlift meant that the forces within the pocket would not remain combat-capable much longer, von Manstein ordered Stemmermann to attack south to reach Breith's III Panzerkorps.[17] On the night of February 16/17, Gruppe Stemmermann began its break-out attack. Although the German infantry were able to partly infiltrate through the Soviet perimeter, they were eventually detected and the result was a wild stampede in the dark by over 50,000 German troops. Stemmermann was killed and the breakout became a disaster when troops encountered the unfrozen 30m-wide Gniloi Tikich River. Eventually, over 36,000 German troops managed to reach Breith's III Panzerkorps at Lisyanka, but they lost virtually all of their equipment in escaping from the Korsun pocket.[18] Not only were six German divisions removed from von Manstein's order of battle, but many of the survivors had to be sent to the rear to recover. It would take nearly six months to rebuild the elite SS-Panzer-Division *Wiking*. Thus, while Vatutin and Konev were chagrined by the German escape, they still had succeeded in eliminating two corps, which von Manstein could not replace. Stalin, Zhukov and Konev papered over the German breakout and falsely claimed that almost all of the German troops in the Korsun pocket were captured or killed.[19] This falsehood would be perpetuated, even by Western historians, for decades after the war.[20]

Hube's 1. Panzerarmee suffered about 4,000 casualties during Operation *Wanda* and lost 156 tanks (most due to mechanical failure). By the end of the Korsun fighting, Breith's III Panzerkorps was reduced to just 66 operational tanks and assault guns.[21] Hube's best troops were left exhausted by weeks of extended winter combat, with no hope of relief in sight. Ironically, von Manstein had managed to save the lives of two-thirds of the troops in the Korsun pocket, but at the cost of seriously depleting his armored reserves. By early March 1944, von Manstein's Heeresgruppe Süd had suffered over 141,000 combat casualties in the past three months (including 50,000 dead or missing). German losses in equipment on the Eastern Front in this period had also been massive, with nearly 1,400 tanks lost – equivalent to 70 percent of total tank production. Since only half of German monthly tank production was going to the Eastern Front (the rest was going to build up armored reserves in Western Europe and the Italian front), it was unlikely that von Manstein would be able to replenish his armored reserve before the Soviets mounted another major offensive in the western Ukraine. Soviet losses during the Battle of the Korsun pocket had been heavy, with Vatutin's 1st Ukrainian Front suffering about 77,000 casualties and losing over 500 tanks, while Konev's 2nd Ukrainian Front suffered about 46,000 casualties. Nevertheless, the Stavka was in a far better position to replace its losses than the overextended Wehrmacht. Zhukov managed to secure the release of General-leytenant Vasily M. Badanov's 4th Tank Army (4 TA) from the RVGK and assigned to the 1st Ukrainian Front, as well as ensuring replacements to bring other depleted units up to strength.

Nor was Zhukov inclined to give von Manstein any kind of respite and he pushed for the Stavka to quickly begin planning the next round of offensives while Heeresgruppe Süd was still off-balance. The Stavka's foremost priority was to complete the eviction of all Axis forces from the western Ukraine and the Crimea, which was expected to precipitate the defection of Hungary and Romania. Despite the fact that the Soviet field armies were exhausted and operating on a logistical shoestring, the Stavka developed a rather grandiose operational concept that envisioned a coordinated offensive by no less than four fronts. Looking at the thinly-held enemy front line after the Battle of Korsun, Zhukov could see that von Manstein's left flank was extremely weak, because Raus' PzAOK 4 was holding a 240km-wide front with barely a dozen badly depleted divisions. While virtually all of von Manstein's Panzers had been focused on the Korsun situation, Vatutin had taken advantage of the enemy's distraction by sending his 13th and 60th Armies to attack the left wing of PzAOK 4. Raus did not have a continuous front in the Rovno-Lutsk sector and the 60th Army seized both cities by February 11, which put Vatutin's right flank across the pre-1939 border of Poland. Von Manstein hastily transferred two Panzer divisions to stabilize the Lutsk sector, but this weakened the center of the PzAOK 4 around Tarnopol. Hube's PzAOK 1 was also in a precarious position, barely connected to the German armies on either of its flanks. Zhukov, who was always looking for another opportunity to conduct a massive encirclement operation like Stalingrad, saw Hube's 1. Panzerarmee as his next target. If Hube's army could be isolated and destroyed, the entire German front in southwest Ukraine would collapse. Thus, the Soviet victory in the Battle of the Korsun pocket set the stage for an even more dramatic and large-scale battle of annihilation.

The Stavka directed that a new front, designated as the 2nd Belorussian Front under General-polkovnik Pavel A. Kurochkin, would be formed on February 17 from three of Vatutin's armies (47, 61, 70) in the Rovno-Lutsk sector and assigned the task of attacking due west toward Kovel – against

PzAOK 4's dangling left flank. Vatutin's 1st Ukrainian Front would attack in the Yampil-Shepetovka sector with the objective of slicing through Raus' right flank and then advancing to cross the Dniester River and seizing Chernovtsy. Konev's 2nd Ukrainian Front would advance from Zvenigorodka to smash the junction between PzAOK 1 and AOK 8, then advance to capture Uman and Jassy in Romania. The Stavka decided to ensure success by committing all six available tank armies to the Ukrainian operation; the 1st Ukrainian Front would get three tank armies (1 TA, 3 GTA and 4 TA) and 2nd Ukrainian Front would get the other three (2 TA, 5 GTA, 6 TA). On the left, the 3rd Ukrainian Front would advance due south to Odessa on the Black Sea. The grand Soviet offensive would begin on the right, in southern Belorussia, with each front attacking one day after its neighbor on the right. The Stavka expected this series of powerful hammer blows to shatter the Axis front in multiple places and demolish von Manstein's Heeresgruppe Süd. Any Axis fragments that survived the initial onslaught would be pushed back into Hungary or Romania, which were expected to opt out of the war at that point.

On February 18, the day after the German breakout from the Korsun pocket, the Stavka issued guidance for the next offensive to the 1st and 2nd Ukrainian Fronts (Stavka VGK Directive No. 22029). Five days later, Vatutin presented his operational plan for the offensive to the Stavka, which Stalin approved on February 25. However, Vatutin would not live to see the operation carried out, since he was shot and mortally wounded by Ukrainian partisans on February 29. Zhukov immediately stepped in and took command of the 1st Ukrainian Front in place of Vatutin.

The situation facing von Manstein was grim. All three of his armies were in poor condition and no longer able to maintain a continuous front. By shifting to a strongpoint-based defense with mobile reserves, Heeresgruppe Süd could create the appearance of a front line but it was increasingly porous. Hube's 1. Panzerarmee was unable to rest and refit after the Battle of the Korsun pocket; instead, it had to spend a great deal of effort trying to build a new front with its neighbors. In order to mend his weakened connections with Raus' PzAOK 4 on his left flank, Hube had to shift some Panzer units up to 250 kilometers westward. The intractable dilemma facing von Manstein's Heeresgruppe Süd in March 1944 was that there were no natural lines of defense in the remaining portion of Axis-held western Ukraine and Germany lacked the manpower, resources and time needed to rebuild his battered armies. Under these conditions, retreat to shorter, more defensible lines was the only credible military strategy, but Hitler rejected this line of thinking as defeatist. Anticipating that Zhukov would make his main effort in the Yampil sector, von Manstein began repositioning his meager armored reserves in late February to counter the expected enemy course of action. While these adjustments succeeded in reinforcing the sectors where Zhukov intended to make his main effort, they reduced the ability of Breith's III Panzerkorps to control its now dispersed armor and seriously weakened Hube's right flank boundary with the 8. Armee. Hitler optimistically hoped that adverse weather and supply difficulties might delay Zhukov's next offensive, but ordered von Manstein to hold his ground whenever the enemy attacked. Unsatisfied with von Manstein's preference for "mobile defense" to conserve his units, Hitler decided to further complicate Heeresgruppe Süd's already constricted options by mandating the use of hedgehog-style defenses known as Fortified Areas to slow enemy offensives. Von Manstein and his subordinate commanders tried to avoid the Fortified Area mandate as much as possible, but each subterfuge employed further increased Hitler's mistrust of his front-line commanders.

In early March 1944, Generaloberst Hans-Valentin Hube's PzAOK 1 consisted of 18 divisions with a total of roughly 220,000 troops and about 300 operational tanks/assault guns. Zhukov's 1st Ukrainian Front had three tank armies and four combined arms armies, totaling about 800,000 personnel and about 1,300 operational tanks/assault guns. Zhukov had a nearly unprecedented amount of armor available under his command for the upcoming offensive, consisting of no less than three tank armies (1 TA, 3 GTA, 4 TA); altogether these three tank armies comprised six tank corps, three mechanized corps, two independent tank brigades and five independent heavy tank regiments. However, logistic reserves were slim and Zhukov's tank armies started the offensive with just a two-day reserve of fuel (*boekomplekt*) in hand, which might be stretched to 4–5 days. Ammunition was also in relatively short supply, with three basic loads (*zapravki*) held by the tank armies.[22]

On March 4, Zhukov's 1st Ukrainian Front began its offensive in the Yampil-Shepetovka sector, with Cherniakhovsky's 60th Army attacking the LIX Armeekorps after a 90-minute artillery barrage. Grechko's 1 GA also launched a supporting attack against the LIX Armeekorps. After the Soviet infantry broke through the German front line, Zhukov committed Badanov's 4 TA and Rybalko's 3 GTA. German tactical reserves proved unable to stop the mass of Soviet armor advancing southward. By March 6, Rybalko's 3 GTA captured the town of Volochisk, which severed the main east-west German rail line of communications (LOC). Badanov's 4 TA nearly seized Tarnopol in a *coup de main* before the Germans hastily formed a garrison for the city. Despite a strong rearguard action by the LIX Armeekorps, Grechko's 1 GA captured Staro-Konstantinov on March 9. Meanwhile, Konev's 2nd Ukrainian Front attacked the boundary between the PzAOK 1 and AOK 8 on March 5. Trofimenko's 27th Army massed six rifle divisions against a single infantry division from the VII Armeekorps and crushed it, then Konev committed Kravchenko's 6 TA into the breach. The German VII Armeekorps was torn apart, with four divisions (34, 75, 82 and 198) retreating west toward Hube's PzAOK 1, while the other division (4. Gebirgs-Division) retreated east toward Wöhler's 8. Armee. In two days, Konev's forces advanced 20 kilometers and created an irreparable breach between PzAOK 1 and the AOK 8. Von Manstein had no significant reserves to commit and the Luftwaffe was powerless to stem multiple breakthroughs, leaving Hube's army in a near hopeless operational position. Yet unknown to the Germans, the Soviet armored steamroller was grinding to a halt due to fuel shortages after an advance of barely 70 kilometers. Zhukov was forced to put off the resumption of his main offensive on the Proskurov-Chernovtsy axis for nine days while supply columns struggled along muddy roads to restock the tank armies at the front.

Von Manstein tried to direct the limited reserves to where he thought they might do the most good. In particular, he ordered Balck's XXXXVIII Panzerkorps to move 50km west from Proskurov to try to intercept Badanov's 4th Tank Army before it drove a deeper wedge between the PzAOK 4 and PzAOK 1. Von Manstein trusted Balck to fight a clever mobile delaying action with even meager forces, as he had already demonstrated in the Battle of the Chir River in December 1942. Hube promptly ordered Balck's XXXXVIII Panzerkorps to mount a counterattack against Badanov's and Rybalko's spearheads near Volochisk on March 11.[23] The Luftwaffe even managed to contribute some close-air support sorties, which increased the power of the German counterattack. Breith's III Panzerkorps also joined the counteroffensive. Both sides sustained heavy losses in several days of fighting, but the Stavka was so alarmed by this sudden display of German Panzer strength that it ordered Zhukov to shift his entire front to the defensive and focus on replenishing his forward units before resuming his own offensive. Amazingly, Balck's small armored counterattacks not only temporarily halted Zhukov's main effort, but were even able to achieve the objective of re-establishing a common front between Raus' PzAOK 4 and Hube's PzAOK 1. Due to the efforts of Balck and Breith, Zhukov failed to take either of his two intermediate objectives – Tarnopol and Proskurov – in the first round of his offensive. Nor had Zhukov managed to encircle or destroy any German formations. Furthermore, Rybalko's 3 GTA had suffered significant losses and was no longer fully combat effective.[24] Zhukov decided he had to blame somebody for this setback and he selected Rodin, commander of the 10 GTC, as his scapegoat. Zhukov relieved Rodin of command and sent him off to obscurity in a training assignment.

Despite the temporary success achieved at Volochisk, Hube's situation was rapidly deteriorating. Due to the disruption of the main rail line from Tarnopol, beginning on March 7 the Luftwaffe began flying in a small amount of daily supplies to Hube's 1. Panzerarmee. On March 11, Luftflotte 4 began dropping supply cannisters directly to the III Panzerkorps and XXIV Panzerkorps, some loaded with tank ammunition, some with fuel. Nevertheless, the air resupply operation at this point was sporadic and amounted to barely 4 percent of daily requirements. On Hube's right flank, Konev's 2nd Ukrainian Front continued to widen the breach between PzAOK 1 and the left flank of Wöhler's AOK 8. Konev committed Bogdanov's 2 TA and Rotmistrov's 5 GTA, which smashed through any remaining resistance and headed straight for the Dniester River. By March 10, Konev's armor was in Uman and the battered remnants of Wöhler's 8. Armee were in full retreat to the southeast. Emboldened by Konev's success, Zhukov ordered his two left flank armies – General-leytenant Evgeniy P. Zhuravlev's 18th Army and Moskalenko's 38th Army – to step up their own attacks against Hube's right flank.

Von Manstein could see disaster looming and on March 11 – too late – he ordered Hube to pull his right flank formations back behind the Bug River. Konev's offensive was achieving spectacular results compared to Zhukov's semi-stalled offensive and Bogdanov's 2 TA spearhead crossed the Bug on March 13. By the afternoon of March 17, Bogdanov had reached Yampol on the Dniester River and two days later Kravchenko's 6 TA seized Mogilev Podolsky. As a result, not only was Hube's right flank completely exposed to envelopment, but PzAOK 1 was nearly isolated by these enemy advances. With the rail line to Tarnopol already severed by Zhukov's armor, Hube's only remaining line of communications lay southward through Kamenets-Podolsky and Chernovtsy into northern Romania. Hitler, distracted by political events in Hungary, refused to send additional reinforcements to sustain von Manstein's disintegrating army group. However, he did take the time to further meddle in personnel assignments. Hube's longstanding chief of staff, Generalmajor Walther Wenck, was transferred during this crisis and replaced by Generalmajor Walter Wagener. Wagener was an experienced General Staff officer, but switching out key staff members while PzAOK 1 was under full-scale assault added unnecessary friction into operational planning.

Konev continued to push back Hube's weakened right flank. In an effort to stabilize the situation, Hube ordered the XXXXVI Panzerkorps to fortify Vinnitsa and dig in with two infantry divisions. In previous Red Army offensives, hedgehog defenses had generally been effective at disrupting the Soviet operations tempo, but this was becoming less true. Moskalenko, in command of the 38th Army approaching Vinnitsa, was an experienced commander and he used his forces judiciously. Rather than a frontal attack, Moskalenko used maneuver to approach Vinnitsa from the south and captured the critical rail junction at Zhmerynka on March 18. He then conducted an assault crossing of the Bug River which outflanked most of the German defenses in Vinnitsa; it still required several days of heavy fighting to clear the city, but liberation was completed by the evening of March 20. After the loss of Vinnitsa and Zhmerynka, a gap of more than 100 kilometers existed between Hube's PzAOK 1 and Wöhler's routed 8. Armee. Conditions were now ripe for Zhukov's 1st Ukrainian Front to encircle and annihilate Hube's army with one more major offensive pulse. In order to reinforce his main effort, Zhukov decided to shift Katukov's 1st Tank Army from his left flank to his right flank. However, shifting Katukov's army nearly 200 kilometers would require several days, and in the meantime Pukhov's 13th Army was ordered to keep pushing against the German forces between Tarnopol and Dubno. On March 17, Dubno was captured, which put additional pressure on Raus' fragile army. Even as a few understrength units began to arrive to reinforce PzAOK 4, Raus was forced to commit them immediately into the line to plug various gaps. No tactical reserves of any kind were left.

On the morning of March 21, Cherniakhovsky's 60th Army opened a one-hour bombardment on the German positions between Tarnopol and Volochisk. Cherniakhovsky was short of both infantry and artillery ammunition, but the two German infantry divisions holding this sector were in much worse condition. After the bombardment, the two Soviet tank armies jumped off, with Katukov's 1 TA on the right and Badanov's 4 TA on the left; altogether these formations had perhaps 400 operational tanks, supported by five rifle divisions. The Soviet tank armies advanced on a 22km-wide front, overrunning the German infantry positions. By the end of the day, the two Soviet tank armies had advanced 25 kilometers and had ripped apart the tenuous connection between Raus' PzAOK 4 and Hube's PzAOK 1. German situational awareness deteriorated rapidly as the Soviet armored breakthrough accelerated and Balck was unable to properly deploy his remaining Panzers to stop the tidal wave. While Katukov's and Badanov's armor was flooding southward toward the Dniester, Zhukov ordered Grechko's 1 GA to keep pressure on Hube's center, which was anchored on the defense of Proskurov. By March 23 Soviet armor was on the outskirts of Tarnopol and by the next day, Katukov's spearhead units had crossed the Dniester River. At the same time, Kravchenko's 6 TA was crossing the Dniester at Mogilev-Podolsky. Hube's army was now isolated, although a potential escape route to the south still existed.

At this point in the campaign, on March 25, both sides were making crucial operational decisions. Confident that PzAOK 1 was trapped, Stalin personally ordered Konev to focus on pushing south into Romania, while Zhukov finished off Hube.[25] Rotmistrov's 5 GTA headed due south toward Kishinev while Bogdanov's 2 TA and Kravchenko's 6 TA headed for Jassy.[26] However, Zhukov assumed that Hube was going to retreat into Romania, so he directed Katukov to push deeper across the Dniester to seal off that route. Von Manstein flew to Berchtesgaden to meet with Hitler and requested permission for Hube to fight his way out to the west before it was too late. Grudgingly, Hitler was finally persuaded to accept this recommendation and he then agreed to transfer the II SS-Panzerkorps from France to provide a relief force. Von Manstein was satisfied and flew back to Lvov to begin planning the breakout operation. However, von Manstein had expended all his personal credit with Hitler, who was now determined to get rid of this argumentative *generalfeldmarschall*. While von Manstein was in Berchtesgaden, Grechko's 1 GA liberated Proskurov and a bold advance by part of Badanov's 4 TA surprised Hube by capturing his logistic base at Kamenets-Podolsky.[27]

Accepting that escape to the south was now blocked, Hube quickly began issuing orders to his army to prepare for a mobile breakout operation to the west. The first task – a daunting one – was to establish crossings over the Zbruch River. If successful, Hube's "wandering pocket" would then continue west another 67 kilometers until it linked up with a relief force from the 4. Panzerarmee on the Strypa River. Hube still had plenty of troops and about 140 operational tanks and 60 assault guns. The real question was whether he had enough ammunition and fuel to fight his way through two Soviet tank armies. On March 24, the 1. Panzerarmee's fuel reserves amounted to 665 tons of petrol and 66 tons of diesel, not including fuel already carried on front-line vehicles. Ammunition was adequate for limited fighting, but artillery support would be minimal. The situation with food was not as good, with only four days' rations on hand.[28] Luftflotte 4 was ordered to increase its airlift operations to support 1. Panzerarmee, but on March 26 only 47 tons of supplies were flown into Dunaivitsi airfield against a daily demand for 350 tons. In order to facilitate coordination between PzAOK 1 and Generalmajor Fritz Morzik's transport staff, a Luftwaffe signals detachment was flown in to Dunaivitsi. The Germans had learned a great deal about air-ground coordination at Stalingrad and Korsun, and now they intended to reap the benefits of that experience.

Hube was hard-pressed to pull together his scattered army and prepare it for a breakout to the west. Most of his forces were facing north or east, fending off the attacks of the Soviet 1st Guards Army, 18th and 38th Armies. On the western side of the army's perimeter, three divisions were already isolated from the rest of PzAOK 1. Hube quickly reorganized his army into two subordinate sub-commands: Korpsgruppe Chevallerie (consisting of the LIX Armeekorps and the XXIV Panzerkorps) and Korpsgruppe Breith (consisting of the III Panzerkorps and XXXXVI Panzerkorps). Hube's basic concept for the breakout was a two-pronged parallel advance, with Chevallerie in the north and Breith in the south. However, the PzAOK 1 would also have to conduct a tenacious rearguard operation in the east to prevent the Soviet 18th and 38th Armies from rolling up units as they began to withdraw. Given the urgency to break out before Zhukov could close in for the kill, Hube reckoned that he had just 48 hours to reorganize, redeploy and begin his operation, which meant there was no time for detailed planning. Due to the shortage of fuel on hand, Hube issued an order that priority would go to combat vehicles, and a large amount of the army's motor transport would have to be destroyed.

Although Zhukov appeared to be on the cusp of a major victory, circumstances were not as favorable as they might appear. Badanov's 4th Tank Army had managed to capture Kamenets-Podolsky, but it was reduced to fewer than 70 operational tanks, all of which were very low on ammunition and fuel. Furthermore, the Soviet armored units in Kamenets-Podolsky were themselves isolated and incapable of further offensive action until resupplied. Rybalko's 3 GTA was nearly fought out, reduced to just 60 operational tanks.[29] Katukov's 1 TA still had about 130 operational tanks but it was heavily engaged south of the Dniester; Zhukov had also given Katukov a diverging secondary mission to go after Kolomya, in the region where the Hungarian VII Army Corps was beginning to assemble. Consequently, Zhukov's armor was dispersed and he had no significant mobile reserve in hand just as the campaign was moving into its most critical phase. Yet Zhukov was still convinced that the 1. Panzerarmee would either stay put in order to receive aerial resupply or attempt a breakout to the south. Konev's forces had also begun to reorient to the southeast and Zhukov was satisfied that he did not need any further assistance from the 2nd Ukrainian Front beyond Zhmachenko's 40th Army (which continued to advance west along the southern side of the Dniester to cut off Hube's line of communications to Romania).

Hube's breakout operation began on March 27, but the Soviets did not immediately recognize it as such and Zhukov continued to assume that PzAOK 1 would try to escape into Romania. Indeed, Zhukov decided to pull Rybalko's 3 GTA back to refit, which actually reduced the Soviet forces deployed along Hube's real escape route. By the time that the Soviets did start to notice PzAOK 1 units shifting westward, Hube's vanguard had already secured two crossing sites across the Zbruch River. Overcast skies and frequent snow showers helped to partly conceal the German columns from Soviet aerial reconnaissance, which made it difficult for Zhukov to ascertain Hube's intentions. Meanwhile, with the fate of Hube's PzAOK 1 still hanging in the balance, Hitler decided to make sweeping command changes on March 30. Both von Manstein and von Kleist were ordered to Rastenburg, where they were peremptorily relieved of command. The northern portion of Heeresgruppe Süd (PzAOK 1, PzAOK 4 and the Hungarian 1st Army) was redesignated as Heeresgruppe Nordukraine and Generalfeldmarschall Model was assigned to command. Generaloberst Ferdinand Schörner was assigned to command Heeresgruppe Südukraine (AOK 6, AOK 8, AOK 17 and the Romanian 3rd Army). Von Manstein's removal was overdue since he had suffered one defeat after another for the past nine months and was openly critical of Hitler's decision-making. Von Kleist had been minimized since the 1942 Caucasus campaign and his command had been heavily micromanaged by Hitler. Yet these two commanders were responsible for many of the victories of 1940–42, whereas Schörner had been an obscure corps commander in the backwater Lapland theater just five months before. Hitler provided Schörner with Walther Wenck, Hube's chief of staff, to give him a veteran General Staff officer, but Schörner was not elevated to higher command due to his professional skills. With the war going poorly, Hitler had lost faith in the old-school officers and now pinned his hopes on the ability of ruthless commanders like Model and Schörner to stop the inexorable Soviet westward advance. Neither von Manstein nor von Kleist was ever assigned another command.

By April 1, Hube's vanguard was beginning to make good progress toward the west, despite constant Soviet attacks on the flanks and rear of the "wandering pocket." Luftwaffe aerial resupplies were crucial in delivering just enough fuel to keep the army moving, although a great deal of equipment was abandoned. Zhukov finally recognized that Hube's army was sliding west and he ordered five rifle divisions to move and establish blocking positions in their path – but this proved too late. Hube's vanguard units either bypassed or crushed Zhukov's "speed bumps" and continued west, gaining crossings over the Seret River. The only place where Zhukov checked Hube's progress was on the northern flank of the breakout corridor, at the city of Chortkov.[30] Zhukov now ordered Katukov to move part of his 1 TA north of the Dniester to try to block Hube, but German tactical skill prevailed in most of these meeting engagements. The Kamenets-Podolsky campaign provides an excellent example of how the OODA (Observe-Orient-Decide-Act) Loop can be exploited to gain an advantage over a numerically-superior opponent. Zhukov observed the German breakout, began to reorient his forces, made his decision where to disrupt the breakout and began to act by April 1–2. However, Hube's forces "got inside Zhukov's OODA loop" – in modern military parlance – by reacting more quickly than Zhukov did, which enabled the German forces to seize the initiative. Before Zhukov's blocking forces could reach their positions in strength, Hube's vanguard arrived there first. Zhukov also failed to ensure that the 2nd Air Army (2 VA) intercepted the Luftwaffe aerial resupply flights which kept Hube's army moving. Altogether, Luftflotte 4 flew about 8,000 sorties to support Hube's encircled army, delivering an estimated 3,500–4,000 tons of supplies.[31]

Meanwhile, the lead elements of the II SS-Panzerkorps were arriving from France, along with two fresh infantry divisions and a battalion of Tiger tanks. Raus took command over these reinforcements as they arrived, which amounted to a total of 230 tanks and assault guns. On paper, the II SS-Panzerkorps represented a powerful relief force, although Hitler stipulated that its losses should be kept to a minimum since he intended to transfer it back to the West as soon as possible.[32] Model, now in command of Heeresgruppe Nordukraine, also added his own conditions. The 4,000-man garrison in Tarnopol was under heavy attack by Cherniakhovsky's 60th Army and would be annihilated unless a rescue effort was mounted soon. In violation of the principles of mass and objective, Model decided that half the II SS-Panzerkorps should mount a relief operation to rescue the Tarnopol garrison while the other half went to link up with Hube's approaching army. Model was legitimately concerned that German front-line morale would suffer if nothing was done to help the Tarnopol garrison, but it would suffer even more if Hube's army was lost. Another factor to consider is that Model was deliberately cultivating a personal command style that emphasized trying to accomplish what others considered impossible – when it worked, which was fairly often in his case, it increased his prestige with Hitler, who rewarded him with more resources.

On April 6, Hube's vanguard established contact with the lead elements of the II SS-Panzerkorps near the town of Buchach on the Strypa River. Nevertheless, Hube's army was still at great risk and it took two weeks for all of PzAOK 1 to cross the Strypa River and rejoin the main German front. Hube's encircled army, with over 200,000 troops, had moved almost 100km through enemy-held territory under adverse weather conditions and with minimal supplies.

During the final phase of Hube's breakout, both Model and Zhukov allowed themselves to be distracted by the siege of Tarnopol, which was really little more than a sideshow. Model mounted a relief operation toward Tarnopol which failed, despite the help of II SS-Panzerkorps; then the 60th Army finally annihilated the encircled German garrison on April 16. Hube flew back to Berchtesgaden to meet with Hitler. Although normally averse to endorsing retreats, Hitler recognized the escape of the 1. Panzerarmee as a great feat of arms and was impressed with Hube's leadership. However, when flying back to the Eastern Front on April 21, Hube's aircraft crashed and he was killed, abruptly ending his military career.

Zhukov had achieved a major operational victory in the Proskurov-Chernovtsy operation, particularly in terms of territorial objectives, but he did not get the battle of annihilation which had been his primary campaign objective. Indeed, the escape of Hube's army from encirclement – coming so soon after the partly successful German breakout from the Korsun pocket – was embarrassing to Zhukov. In his post-war memoirs, Zhukov claimed that the 1. Panzerarmee lost more than half its personnel in the campaign (i.e. over 100,000 troops) and virtually all its equipment. Later Soviet historical studies claimed that the 1st Ukrainian Front captured 25,000 German soldiers, about 500 AFVs and 22,000 motor vehicles. While none of Hube's divisions were destroyed, all were decimated, with minimal heavy equipment and vehicles remaining. Six of the ten Panzer divisions (6, 11, 19, 25, SS-*Das Reich* and SS-*LSSAH*) that escaped from the *Kessel* had to be sent to the West to refit, and the four that remained on the *Ostfront* spent months rebuilding. In terms of casualties, German records, while incomplete for PzAOK 1 during the time it was encircled, suggest that Hube's army suffered a total of 21,300 casualties from March 10 to April 10, including an estimated 3,400 dead, 13,900 wounded and 4,000 missing. When casualties from the first week of Zhukov's offensive are included, Hube's losses rise to a total of about 22,000 or 10 percent of his starting strength. Hube's army had been badly battered, losing roughly

80 percent of its equipment, but nearly 90 percent of its troops had escaped to fight another day.

During the Proskurov-Chernovtsy operation, Zhukov's 1st Ukrainian Front suffered 220,000 casualties (including 60,000 dead or missing), or roughly 25 percent of its starting strength. According to one Russian source, Soviet armor losses in the operation amounted to 551 tanks and 134 self-propelled guns, or roughly 48 percent of the starting operational strength of AFVs.[33] In fact, all three of Zhukov's tank armies were so depleted at the conclusion of the operation that they would require at least two months to refit and replace their losses; both Rybalko's 3 GTA and Badanov's 4 TA were rendered combat ineffective. Badanov himself was wounded and would not return to any field commands. It is true that Zhukov had succeeded in removing a great deal of the Ostheer's armored strength from the battlefield, but it came at the cost of temporarily sidelining three of the six Soviet tank armies.

Hube managed to conduct a successful breakout attack, even with his depleted forces, primarily due to three reasons. First, Hube achieved operational-level surprise by advancing west instead of south; to be fair, the Western line of operations was von Manstein's idea, but it was up to Hube to pull it off. Second, Hube's breakout plan was simple and focused on a clear objective – reach the Strypa River. He also ensured that all subordinate commanders and subunits understood the commander's intent and were focused on that sole objective. Third, Hube employed his best remaining forces in order to achieve mass at the critical points on the battlefield. Hube's task organization ensured that he had maximum combat power at the tip of the spear and that these vanguard units did not run out of ammunition or fuel. Overall, the breakout of the 1. Panzerarmee was a *tour de force* in operational and tactical-level military leadership, demonstrating what unit cohesion and trained, motivated troops can achieve even when operating under the most adverse battlefield conditions.

In contrast, Zhukov underperformed throughout the campaign because he failed to realistically consider possible enemy courses of action and tried to conduct massive maneuver operations on a logistic shoestring. Due to his logistical shortfalls, Zhukov was forced to conduct his offensive in two distinct "pulses," with the first beginning on March 5 and the second on March 21. Both offensive pulses achieved impressive advances at first, but then quickly began to run out of steam after 4–5 days. Zhukov did not anticipate Balck's counteroffensive which halted his first offensive pulse, nor the German actions which got in the way of his second offensive pulse. Zhukov used maneuver to gain ground, but he failed to fully encircle isolated German units, thereby allowing them to escape. At the decisive moment in the campaign, Zhukov was caught off-guard because he was convinced that Hube would attempt to retreat to the south and did not immediately accept when his judgment proved incorrect. Rather than ensuring that his subordinate commanders were focused on cornering and annihilating Hube's army, Zhukov encouraged his subordinates to pursue competing priorities; Katukov was focused on crushing the Hungarian VII Army Corps while Cherniakhovsky was focused on crushing the German garrison in Tarnopol. Coordination between the other armies arrayed against 1. Panzerarmee became increasingly disjointed. The fact that Zhukov allowed his remaining armor to become so dispersed and opted not to maintain any significant operational-level reserves to deal with contingencies was a serious error. The escape of Hube's 1. Panzerarmee had far-reaching strategic consequences because it delayed a collapse of the German position on the Eastern Front by at least three months. To his credit, Zhukov would learn from his mistakes at Kamenets-Podolsky and his next round of offensives would prove far more decisive.

Looking at the opposing generalship during the campaigns in the western Ukraine from January to April 1944, it is evident that German senior commanders were often at a loss on how to counter the increased operational capabilities of the Red Army. In particular, von Manstein was drawn into a cycle of taking reserves from one sector to bolster another, akin to "robbing Peter to pay Paul." Von Manstein's "castling maneuver" had worked in 1942–43 against less skilled opponents, but it failed miserably in 1944. Indeed, von Manstein's expensive relief operations drained his limited armor reserves and created conditions which increased the chances for Soviet operational success. Obviously Hitler bore some blame in this outcome by refusing to abandon useless positions like the Korsun salient, but von Manstein was the commander on the spot who kept doubling his bets by adding more reinforcements to hopeless endeavors. In retrospect, von Manstein was not a very lucky commander; with better weather, the Korsun relief operation probably would have gone more smoothly. In terms of field commanders, Raus and Wöhler struggled to achieve their sole objective – which was to avoid having their armies encircled and annihilated. Neither of these commanders demonstrated any great skill and simply reacted to Soviet moves. Hube was the one exception in that he was able to seize the initiative and use maneuver to frustrate the enemy's campaign plans. Some commanders excel in a crisis – Hube was one of those men.

On the Soviet side, Konev turned in an excellent command performance, which relied upon well-planned offensive maneuvers to achieve its objectives. Konev and his staff were becoming adept at planning set-piece offensives. Vatutin's performance was good, but he could be inconsistent with objectives and still tended to allow his overextended forces to be smashed by unexpected enemy counterattacks. As mentioned, Zhukov's performance as a front commander was poor during the campaign, particularly in regard to maintaining focus on objectives and ensuring security. The six Soviet tank army commanders all performed quite well, using the mobility and shock effect of massed armor to achieve their operational objectives. As usual, Rybalko and Rotmistrov tended to suffer the heaviest casualties. Among the other Soviet army commanders, Moskalenko stands out in particular as one of the very best, although the general standard of competence was markedly higher than in previous campaigns. The Red Army of 1944 finally possessed the skill to execute the kind of operational warfare that had been envisioned in PU-36.

Commander	Objective	Offensive	Mass	Maneuver	Surprise	Security	TALLY
Von Manstein	o	+	o	o	o	o	1
Raus Wöhler	+	o	o	o	o	o	1
Hube	+	+	+	+	+	o	5
Vatutin	o	+	+	+	+	-	3
Zhukov	-	+	o	+	o	-	0
Konev	+	+	+	+	o	o	4
Rybalko Katukov Rotmistrov Kravchenko Badanov Bogdanov	+	+	+	+	o	o	4
Moskalenko	+	+	+	+	+	o	5
Cherniakhovsky Trofimenko Grechko Zhadov Pukhov Galanin Zhmachenko Shumilov	+	+	+	o	o	o	3

Western Ukraine Campaign, 1944 Leadership Assessment

The Defeat of Heeresgruppe A in Southern Ukraine, January 1–March 30, 1944

While the decisive operations were occurring in the western Ukraine, the Stavka also ordered Malinovsky's 3rd Ukrainian Front and Tolbukhin's 4th Ukrainian Front to defeat the German forces in the lower Dnepr region.* Yet unlike Vatutin and Konev, Malinovsky and Tolbukhin were not provided substantial reinforcements from the RVGK. At the start of 1944, Malinovsky had four armies (6, 46, 57, 8 GA) facing the right wing of Wöhler's AOK 8 (XXX Armeekorps and LVII Panzerkorps), which was holding the Krivoi Rog-Apostolovo sector. Malinovsky's front was weak in terms of armor and artillery, while Wöhler had created a fairly strong defense in the Krivoi Rog sector. Along the lower Dnepr, Tolbukhin's 4th Ukrainian Front had three armies (28, 3 GA, 5 Shock) facing Hollidt's AOK 6, which was anchored on the Nikopol bridgehead. Tolbukhin had a significant amount of armor and artillery, but as yet had been unable to budge Hollidt's army from its fortified positions. Tolbukhin also had one army (51), blocking the German-Romanian AOK 17 in the Crimea, which had been isolated since December 1943.

As part of the Stavka's planned winter counteroffensive, Malinovsky and Tolbukhin were ordered to seize Krivoi Rog and Nikopol, then push west to seize the southern Ukraine.[34] The 150,000 Axis troops in the Crimea, already isolated, would be dealt with later. Vasilevsky was sent by the Stavka to coordinate Malinovsky and Tolbukhin's fronts, but the initial attacks on January 10–12, 1944 failed. Frontal attacks in the Krivoi Rog sector, without any kind of numerical superiority, proved futile. Consequently, a revised plan was developed by Malinovsky, Tolbukhin and Vasilevsky and submitted to the Stavka on January 17. Under the revised plan, Malinovsky would shift his axis of advance to the east and attack with just two armies – Chuikov's 8 GA and General-leytenant Vasily V. Glagolev's 46th Army – on a relatively narrow front, then commit his mobile group to exploit toward Apostolovo and outflank the German Nikopol bridgehead. Tolbukhin would not attack with his armies until Malinovsky achieved a breakthrough. The Stavka provided Malinovsky some additional assets, including a mechanized corps (4 GMC) and more artillery, but not much ammunition. This time, Malinovsky and

---

*In January, von Manstein controlled Wöhler's AOK 8 and Hollidt's AOK 6, but on February 2, AOK 6 was assigned to von Kleist's Heeresgruppe A.

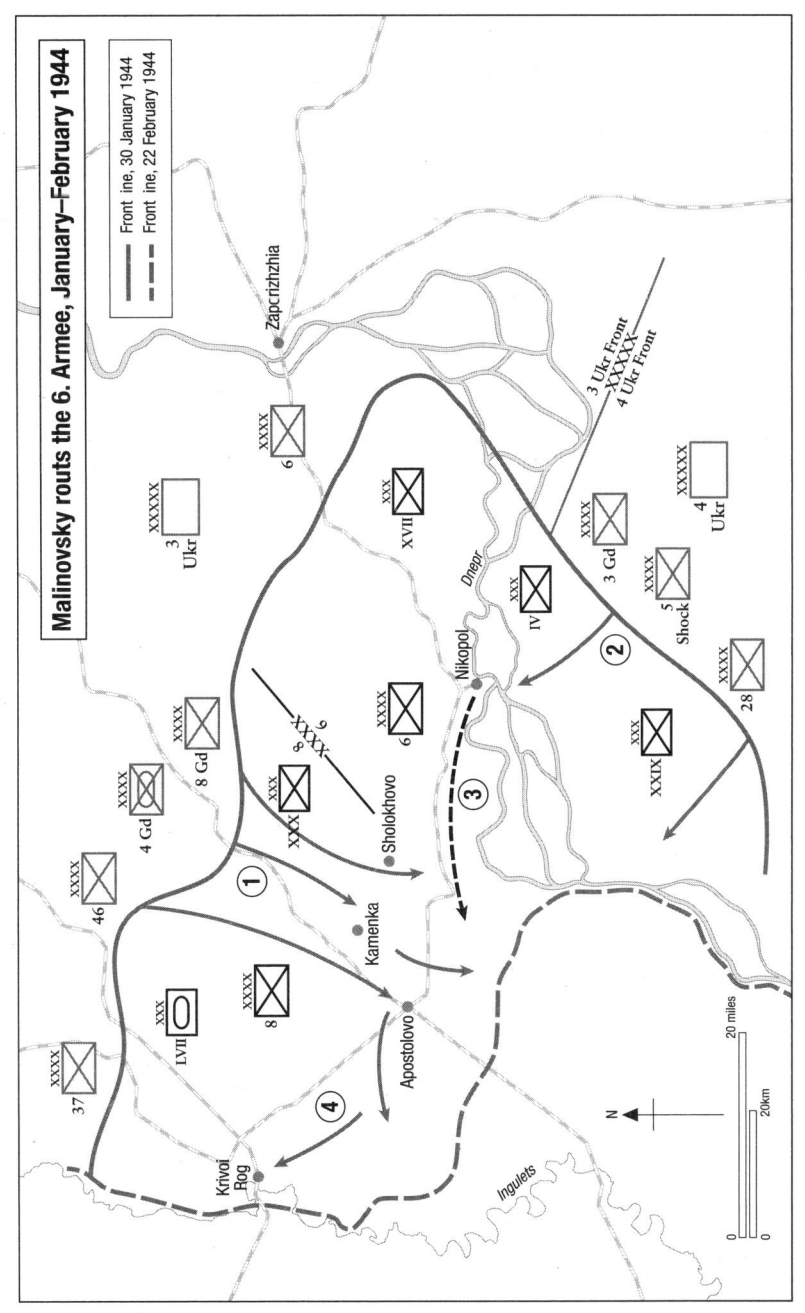

Malinovsky routs the 6. Armee, January–February 1944

Front line, 30 January 1944
Front line, 22 February 1944

Map key

1. The 8th Guards Army and 46th Army achieve a major breakthrough in the XXX Armeekorps sector. Malinovsky commits his mobile group to exploit to Apostolovo.
2. Tolbukhin's 4th Ukrainian Front launches attacks which gradually push 6. Armee out of the Nikopol bridgehead.
3. The 6. Armee withdraws west to avoid encirclement but suffers crippling losses.
4. Malinovsky pivots to seize Krivoi Rog. Heeresgruppe A establishes a flimsy line behind the Ingulets River.

---

his staff put a greater effort into *maskirovka* operations in an effort to convince Wöhler that the Soviet main blow would be directed against the LVII Panzerkorps at Krivoi Rog, instead of against the XXX Armeekorps near Apostolovo. However, Wöhler does not appear to have been deceived and he positioned his strongest tactical reserve – the 24. Panzer-Division (which had about 60 operational tanks and assault guns) – in an assembly area near Apostolovo. However, on the evening of January 28, von Manstein decided to shift the 24. Panzer-Division over 300 kilometers by rail to join the relief operation for the Korsun pocket.[35] It was an incredibly poor operational decision, aggravated by the fact that von Manstein failed to notify the OKH or Hitler about the transfer. Thus, the primary German mobile reserve backing up the XXX Armeekorps and the Nikopol bridgehead was transferred just before Malinovsky's offensive began.

On the morning of January 31, Malinovsky began his offensive. The German XXX Armeekorps was hit hard by Chuikov's 8 GA and Sharokhin's 37th Army and the infantry division holding this sector was smashed. Malinovsky immediately committed his mobile group (4 GMC) to push toward Apostolovo. Wöhler now had almost no tactical reserves left to stop the Soviet breakthrough, aside from two burnt-out Panzer divisions that had only a handful of tanks and infantry left. Despite an effort to form a hedgehog at Apostolovo, the town was taken by the 46th Army on February 4 and Hollidt was forced to begin evacuating the Nikopol bridgehead (which was held by eight infantry divisions) before it was isolated. Tolbukhin's front had also joined the offensive with Lelyushenko's 3 GA and General-polkovnik Viacheslav D. Tsvetaev's 5th Shock Army. Vasilevsky continued to coordinate the actions of the two fronts, which gradually squeezed the Germans out of Nikopol.

Hollidt's situation quickly became critical and the bulk of AOK 6 was threatened with encirclement and annihilation around Nikopol. Somehow Hitler and the OKH did not become aware of the transfer of the 24. Panzer-Division until February 8, when Nikopol was about to fall. When Hitler learned about the transfer, he ordered the Panzer-Division immediately returned to Hollidt's AOK 6, but it was too late. Nikopol fell, but Hollidt's army managed to escape by a hair's breadth thanks to rain and muddy roads, which slowed the Soviet pursuit. Malinovsky directed his 17 VA to concentrate its battlefield interdiction sorties against the narrow German escape corridor, and massed attacks by Il-2 Sturmoviks inflicted great slaughter. A German counterattack on February 10–11, which sacrificed an infantry division, succeeded in widening the corridor for the rest of the army. Nevertheless, Hollidt's hasty retreat cost him a large part of his army's vehicles and artillery, leaving AOK 6 in no condition to fend off large-scale attacks.[36] Logistic problems forced Malinovsky and Tolbukhin to briefly pause their operations, which enabled Hollidt to re-form his mauled army. Von Kleist formed a new convex front, over 200km in length, between Krivoi Rog and Kherson. Yet only the lower end of the line was still anchored behind the Dnepr River and the center of von Kleist's new front was deployed behind the Ingulets, a minor (50m-wide) water obstacle. The Romanian 3rd Army (six divisions) was deployed in the Kherson sector, primarily assigned to coastal security.

Malinovsky shifted his axes of attack from his left flank to his right flank and launched the 37th and 46th Armies against Krivoi Rog. By February 22, Sharokhin's 37th Army had liberated the city. Three days later, Chuikov's 8 GA gained a foothold across the Ingulets, which compromised the center of von Kleist's front. On February 28, the Stavka directed Malinovsky to complete the destruction of the German 6. Armee and clear southern Ukraine. Malinovsky formed a powerful cavalry-mechanized group (*konno-mekhanizirovannaya gruppa* or KMG, consisting of the 23 TC, 4 GMC, 4 GCC) under General-leytenant Issa A. Pliev, with which he intended to envelop 6. Armee, once Chuikov's 8 GA achieved a breakthrough. In spite of poor weather conditions (fog and mud created by the spring thaw), Malinovsky attacked on March 6. Hollidt had positioned some of his best units in the expected attack sector, including the 24. Panzer-Division, but Chuikov penetrated the German line by the end of the first day. Glagolev's 46th Army attacked on Chuikov's right flank, further widening the breach. Then Malinovsky committed Pliev's KMG, which sliced through the German front and advanced over 50 kilometers to Noviy Bug, where Hollidt's forward army command post was located.

After taking Noviy Bug early on March 8, Pliev pivoted to the south and advanced another 30km to Bashtanka; from this point, Pliev could either advance southeast to cut the main German rail line supplying AOK 6 or advance southwest to seize Nikolayev. He chose to do both, sending the 23 TC to the rail center at Snigirevka and the 4 GCC to Nikolayev. By March 10, five German divisions were isolated by Pliev's advance, while other divisions retreated westward to avoid encirclement. Hollidt's entire center was in a flux and there was nothing that von Kleist could do to stabilize the situation.

While Pliev's KMG continued to raise havoc against the German lines of communication, Malinovsky ordered his three other armies (37, 6, 5th Shock) to attack all along Hollidt's front. Tsvetaev's 5th Shock Army achieved particular success on March 10–12, pushing back Hollidt's right flank. Hollidt's primary concern at this point was to rescue his encircled divisions and slow Malinovsky's advance. He hoped to form a new line behind the Southern Bug River, with the help of the Romanian 3rd Army. Although Malinovsky had achieved a great breakthrough, most of his infantry armies were still tied up reducing German strongpoints or slowly pursuing, which left Pliev's KMG overstretched as it attempted to advance in two diverging directions and create a perimeter around encircled German divisions. By using bits and pieces of units that had escaped encirclement and some well-timed Luftwaffe close air support, Hollidt was able to strike at the overextended KMG. Eventually, the encircled divisions were able to escape westward to the Southern Bug, but lost most of their equipment in the process. The 24. Panzer-Division, fighting constant rearguard actions, lost most of its vehicles and heavy weaponry.[37] Schörner was forced to withdraw to the Southern Bug to save his army group, which enabled the 28th Army to liberate the port of Kherson on March 13. By March 18, Malinovsky's offensive culminated as his armies reached the Southern Bug and paused to prepare for the next round. Altogether, AOK 6 had suffered over 23,000 casualties in seven weeks (including about 9,000 dead or missing), but its material losses were far worse. Hitler reacted to the defeat by relieving Hollidt of command – he received no further assignments.

Malinovsky paused for a week on the Southern Bug in order to resupply and bring up his artillery. Given the weakness of AOK 6, von Kleist was forced to use the Romanian 3rd Army to hold his right flank, in the Nikolayev sector. Vasilevsky coordinated a joint operation by the 57th Army from Konev's front, in conjunction with 37th Army from Malinovsky's front, which became the main effort on March 26. The new offensive pulse started slowly, as the Soviets seized several bridgeheads across the Southern Bug and expanded them on March 27–28. In one of his last command actions, von Kleist managed to convince Hitler to allow AOK 6 and the Romanian 3rd Army to evacuate the Southern Bug and withdraw to a new line behind the Dniester River.[38] The Axis retreat began in a mix of rain and snow on the night of March 27/28. The Soviets were quick to note that the enemy was pulling back and Malinovsky immediately committed Pliev's KMG in Sharokhin's 37th Army sector. Once again, Pliev's mobile group moved rapidly and sought both to envelop the main enemy grouping while also sending spearhead units toward Tiraspol on the Dniester. Coordination between Pliev and the supporting infantry armies (Sharokhin) was somewhat improved in this operation, but some Soviet mechanized units still found themselves overextended and isolated. Malinovsky also ordered his other four armies (46, 8 GA, 6, 5th Shock) to attack along the rest of the Southern Bug to pin the Axis forces. Nikolayev was captured in a joint army-navy operation on March 28, with the Black Sea Fleet providing vital support.

By April 4, Pliev's KMG had captured Radzelnaya, severing AOK 6's rail line of communications. As a result, the bulk of AOK 6 and the Romanian 3rd Army were isolated. Schörner, who had just taken command of Heeresgruppe A, ordered a major breakout operation to the west. Once again, the KMG and the 37th Army proved unable to stop the Axis stampede to the west, so most of the enemy troops escaped, but abandoned their vehicles and heavy equipment. The Axis made no effort to defend Odessa, which was liberated on April 10. Malinovsky ordered the pursuit to continue for several days until Pliev's KMG captured Tiraspol. The remnants of AOK 6, reduced to shattered *Kampfgruppen*, huddled behind the Dniester, while the Romanians pulled most of their troops back behind the 1941 border.

Although Malinosky had not shown much flair or imagination in previous operations in 1942–43, he demonstrated an excellent use of the principles of war in the southern Ukraine campaign. In 2½ months, Malinovsky's 3rd Ukrainian Front had pushed Heeresgruppe A back over 300 kilometers, cleared out the southern Ukraine and liberated Odessa, and reached the Moldavan border. He did so with only minor assistance from Tolbukhin's 4th Ukrainian Front and at a reasonable cost in casualties (269,000 overall, with 55,000 dead or missing).[39] Malinovsky conducted the kind of Deep Operations envisioned in PU-36 and he did so without a tank army, but only an improvised cavalry-mechanized formation. In the process, the German 6. Armee was virtually destroyed again, suffering 57,000 casualties in this period (including 23,000 dead or missing).

Furthermore, both von Kleist and Hollidt were relieved of command due to their inability to stop Malinovsky – which was a significant loss to the German war effort. Tolbukhin played only a supporting role in the first offensive and thereafter shifted to focus on the upcoming Crimean operation. The army-level commanders in the 3rd Ukrainian Front performed capably, particularly Glagolev, Sharokhin and Tsvetaev. Chuikov was also capable, but Vasilevsky criticized his failure to prevent encircled German units from escaping through his sector – a valid point.

One has to have a certain amount of professional sympathy for von Kleist and Hollidt, since they were both highly competent officers who were handed a no-win situation by Hitler and von Manstein. Not only did von Manstein strip the army group of its best mobile units to support his rescue operations around Korsun, but the OKH failed to provide any significant reinforcements or replacements to help hold the southern Ukraine. Likewise, Romanian commitment to the defense of the southern Ukraine was ephemeral and of little value. Consequently, the onus of the campaign fell on Hollidt's 6. Armee, which was repeatedly enveloped and beaten into a pulp. Retreats were only authorized when the enemy had already isolated parts of AOK 6. Furthermore, Hitler's failure to evacuate the Crimea and use AOK 17 to bolster Heeresgruppe A's flimsy defense was a cardinal error. Under these conditions, the only objective for von Kleist and Hollidt was force survival, which they did accomplish. It is to their credit that no large units were surrounded and destroyed during this nerve-wracking campaign because of their prompt efforts in organizing breakout operations; they paid for this loyalty to their troops by seeing their military careers terminated (thus, I give each of them one additional point for moral courage). Schörner was put in charge of Heeresgruppe A because Hitler knew that he was ruthless and more likely to enforce die-in-place missions than his predecessors.

Commander	Objective	Offensive	Mass	Maneuver	Surprise	Security	TALLY
Von Kleist	++	o	o	o	o	o	2
Hollidt	++	o	o	+	o	–	2
Malinovsky	+	+	+	+	+	o	5
Tolbukhin	+	+	o	o	o	o	2
Chuikov	+	+	+	o	o	–	2
Glagolev Sharokhin Tsvetaev	+	+	+	–	o	o	2

Southern Ukraine Campaign, 1944 Leadership Assessment

The Crimean Campaign, April 8–May 12, 1944

On October 9, 1943, the Axis had completed Operation *Brunhild*, the naval evacuation of AOK 17 from the Kuban Peninsula. In just over three weeks, the Kriegsmarine successfully moved an entire army – 227,000 troops and all their equipment – by sea from the Kuban to the Crimea. Operation *Brunhild* was a remarkable joint operation by the Wehrmacht. Soviet efforts to disrupt the evacuation failed miserably. Once landed in the Crimea, General der Pionere Erwin Jaenecke's AOK 17 was primarily assigned to coast defense duties and training replacements. The OKH assessed that there was no immediate threat to the Crimea and began to pick AOK 17 apart, transferring the better German units to other commands, leaving Jaenecke with just three threadbare German infantry divisions and six Romanian divisions. For his part, Jaenecke also did not see any immediate threat to his command, so he took few measures to enhance his army's defensive posture. Jaenecke himself was an odd bird, being an engineer officer who had seen no front-line service in the first two years of the war. He was then given command of an infantry division at Stalingrad, where he was wounded and then flown out of the pocket at the last minute in January 1943. By late 1943, Jaenecke was unenthusiastic about his mission – bordering on defeatism – and not inclined to be a proactive leader, which made him the antithesis of what the Ostheer expected from a field commander. Up front, he violated the principles of objective (since he regarded evacuation as a better course of action than defense) and security (since he failed to take basic measures to protect his army from surprise). As a further complication, Axis C2 in the Crimea was in a muddle, split between the army, Luftwaffe, Kriegsmarine and Romanians.

In contrast to the OKH's assessment, the Stavka intended to liberate the Crimea as soon as possible, using forces from Tolbukhin's 4th Ukrainian Front and Petrov's North Caucasus Front. Two weeks after AOK 17 completed its withdrawal to the Crimea, Tolbukhin broke through Hollidt's front at Melitopol and forced AOK 6 to retreat. While pursuing Hollidt's army, Tolbukhin peeled off two armies – Kreizer's 51st Army and Grechkin's 28th Army – to try to take the Crimea on the bounce. At the same time, the Stavka directed Petrov to prepare an amphibious landing to seize a bridgehead across the Kerch Strait. There were four potential invasion routes into the Crimea: the narrow Perekop Isthmus, the shallow Sivash, the Chongar Narrows and the Kerch Strait. Jaenecke's AOK 17 was about to be hit from all four directions, nearly simultaneously. On October 30, the lead elements of Kreizer's 51st Army arrived at the Perekop Narrows, where Jaenecke had not even bothered to place any significant blocking force. It was only the actions of local German tactical commanders, using three battalions of replacements and some 8.8cm Flak guns, that delayed the Soviet armored vanguard until German reinforcements (Gruppe Konrad) could arrive. Similarly, Grechkin's 28th Army was also delayed by minor forces at the Chongar Narrows, just long enough for German infantry to be rushed to this sector. However, a Soviet rifle corps from the 51st Army waded across the shallow Sivash in broad daylight and established a large bridgehead before the Germans could react. Petrov landed a brigade-size force south of Kerch but this landing, at Eltigen, went awry.[40] A larger landing on November 4, northeast of Kerch, was more successful. The Axis forces in the Kerch sector were able to contain the Soviet landings and the Eltigen beachhead was finally destroyed after a month of fighting.

In his headquarters at Simferopol, Jaenecke could see the entire situation spinning out of control and he was looking to exit the Crimea, not defend it. Without authorization from the OKH, he ordered his staff to prepare a contingency evacuation plan known as *Michael*.[41] Instead, Hitler ordered that the Crimea was to be turned into a fortress and that he would send reinforcements. Jaenecke was forced to mount a defense and he repositioned his meager forces to contain the lodgments. While Hitler's refusal to evacuate the Crimea may seem pig-headed, his decision was based on the logic that one-third of AOK 17's troops were Romanians and the rest were mostly low-quality German units; in his mind, this second-rate formation was tying down three Soviet armies that would otherwise be added to the forces arrayed against Heeresgruppe Süd. Amazingly, the improvised German defenses held just long enough for Tolbukhin's offensive to run out of steam. On November 20, the North Caucasus Front was disbanded and Petrov took command over the Coastal Army, which primarily consisted of the forces in the Kerch beachhead. In order to try to break the stalemate on his front, Petrov attempted another amphibious landing in January 1944, but this turned into a disaster. Consequently, Stalin relieved Petrov of command and sent Eremenko to take over the Coastal Army. In March, Tolbukhin reorganized his forces arrayed against the Crimea: Zakharov's 2 GA took over the Perekop sector and Kreizer's 51st Army took over the Sivash sector. Ominously, Soviet engineers built two pontoon bridges across the Sivash, which allowed tanks and artillery to move into the bridgehead.

Although isolated, the Axis organized an effective air and sealift operation that not only kept AOK 17 supplied but enabled it to be reinforced.

During the winter, an assault gun battalion, two infantry *Kampfgruppen* and over 7,000 replacements were sent to the Crimea. Jaenecke was able to partially rebuild a few of his divisions. Given the narrowness of the Perekop Isthmus (only 9km in width), Gruppe Konrad was able to build a formidable triple line of defenses, complete with plenty of mines, trenches, barbed wire and bunkers The Luftwaffe also provided some high-quality units to the theater, which prevented the Soviet VVS from gaining air superiority over the Crimea. In Moscow, the Stavka met in March to plan the final offensive to liberate the Crimea. The plan was essentially the same as before, but better resourced. Zakharov's 2 GA would make the main assault to breach the German blocking position at the Perekop Isthmus while Kreizer's 51st Army would stage a breakout attack from its bridgehead across the Sivash. Eremenko's Coastal Army, which had been reinforced to eight rifle divisions and 80 tanks, would break out of its Kerch bridgehead when conditions were favorable. Compared to previous Soviet operations in the Crimea, the 1944 spring campaign was well-planned and the assault troops were properly prepared.

Tolbukhin knew that airpower would be the key element in this campaign and he intended to take the Luftwaffe out of the equation as rapidly as possible. Hoping for a knockout blow, Tolbukhin began his offensive on the morning of April 7 with a massive attack by the 8 VA against the Luftwaffe air bases in the Crimea and artillery positions near the Perekop Isthmus. The 8 VA committed an entire Ground Attack Aviation Corps (7 ShAK) with over 100 Il-2 Sturmoviks to the preemptive strike, which inflicted considerable damage.[42] The next morning, the artillery of both the 2 GA and the 51st Army delivered a punishing 2½-hour-long bombardment of the single German division defending the Perekop Isthmus, followed with more air attacks. Zakharov used novel tactics to breach the tough German defenses at the Perekop, relying upon combat multipliers instead of mass. He used a large amount of smoke to conceal his assault groups from defensive fire and flamethrower tanks to burn out the German positions. Rather surprisingly, Zakharov made a significant dent in Gruppe Konrad's defense, but did not achieve a breakthrough. Tolbukhin wisely held back his mobile group until the German defense was broken. Twenty kilometers to the east, Kreizer's 51st Army began its breakout attack and managed to penetrate a sector held by one of the Romanian divisions. The Germans committed their limited tactical reserves, but this could only delay the inevitable. By the second day of Tolbukhin's offensive, the German defenses at both Perekop and the Sivash were beginning to collapse. Tolbukhin's trump card was to send a tank corps with 220 tanks across the Sivash via the two pontoon bridges, which caught Jaenecke completely by surprise. Recognizing that the outer defenses had failed, Jaenecke ordered Gruppe Konrad and the Romanians to break contact and retreat south to the "Gneisenau-Stellung," a preplanned fallback line around Simferopol. Jaenecke also ordered the Axis forces in the eastern Crimea to abandon Kerch and retreat to Sevastopol; he issued these orders without authorization and without informing the OKH.

Eremenko attacked as soon as he recognized that the German V Armeekorps was pulling out of Kerch; his troops liberated the empty city on April 11. The Axis retreat from Kerch turned into a chaotic rout and Eremenko used his aviation to strike the German columns while his ground forces mounted an energetic pursuit that smashed the small enemy rearguards. The Germans deliberately sacrificed two Romanian battalions in the retreat, which caused considerable inter-allied friction within AOK 17. Jaenecke's entire army was in retreat, heading for the supposed safety of Sevastopol. Most of the horse-drawn artillery and heavy weapons were lost in the retreat, further reducing AOK 17's ability to resist. Unaware of the true state of affairs, Hitler ordered Jaenecke to pull back within the fortifications of Sevastopol – as the Soviets had done in 1941–42 – and prepare for a lengthy siege. However, the Soviet pursuit was simply too fast and Jaenecke's army was incapable of conducting a fighting retreat. Tolbukhin's armor liberated Simferopol on April 13, while Eremenko took the port of Feodosiya. When Gruppe Konrad reached the Gneisenau-Stellung, it found that Soviet armor was already there and they had to fight their way past to Sevastopol. Surprisingly, it was Romanian mountain infantry troops who repulsed the initial Soviet tank attacks on Sevastopol's outer defenses on April 15, not the German units, which were too disorganized. Indeed, the unexpected Romanian show of resistance was sufficient to convince Tolbukhin that he should wait for his artillery to arrive before mounting a major attack against the city. In fact, Jaenecke had fewer than 20,000 combat troops still effective and few heavy weapons. Most of the Luftwaffe units had already left the Crimea, leaving AOK 17 with inadequate air cover.

Hitler agreed to a limited evacuation of the Crimea on April 12, but only for excess rear-echelon personnel and wounded, in order to reduce the logistical requirements for AOK 17. The Kriegsmarine and Romanian Navy organized convoys to and from Sevastopol and succeeded in evacuating almost 72,000 personnel in two weeks. Despite frequent attacks by Soviet aircraft, patrol craft and submarines, the initial evacuation suffered less than 2 percent personnel losses. Jaenecke's army shrank by more than one-third in this period – including many unauthorized departures – so he issued a bombastic proclamation to AOK 17 on April 24 which stated that "We will stay here as long as the Führer orders us ... whoever will try to leave this mission, who will leave his post, those responsible for reducing the limited combat strength of our army, will be executed."[43] On April 16, the Stavka decided to transfer Eremenko to take over the 2nd Baltic Front. As a result, Eremenko handed over command of the Coastal Army to his deputy, General-leytenant Kondrat S. Mel'nik, who was now subordinated to Tolbukhin's 4th Ukrainian Front. While streamlining chains of command can improve operational efficiency, doing it in the middle of a pursuit operation is rather odd. Nevertheless, Mel'nik's Coastal Army had reached the German defensive position at Balaklava, east of Sevastopol, by April 19.

On paper, Jaenecke still had five German infantry divisions and three Romanian mountain divisions, but their combat effectiveness was marginal due to heavy losses in manpower and equipment. He deployed Gruppe Konrad (XXXXIX Gebirg-Korps) to defend the northern approaches to Sevastopol, while the V Armeekorps defended the eastern approaches. AOK 17 had no significant tactical or operational reserves left and it was about to be attacked by three Soviet armies. Morale was shaky. Despite his proclamation about holding the Crimea, Jaenecke was under no illusions about AOK 17's fate and he made the mistake of requesting "freedom of action" if Tolbukhin launched an all-out offensive against the Sevastopol perimeter. This kind of request was too much for Hitler and he ordered Jaenecke to report to him at Berchtesgaden on April 29. Once in Hitler's presence, Jaenecke argued that the rest of AOK 17 had to be withdrawn immediately or face destruction. Hitler was infuriated that a general would talk to him in this manner and began screaming at him. Jaenecke apparently took leave of his senses, turned and left the room, slamming the door. However, Jaenecke quickly found himself under arrest, pending a court martial.[44] Hitler put the V Armeekorps commander, General der Infanterie Karl Allmendinger, in charge of AOK 17. Like Jaenecke, Allmendinger's main objective was to escape Sevastopol and he did little to inspire a tenacious defense.

On the morning of May 5, Tolbukhin began his final offensive in the Crimea, with a massive two-hour artillery barrage against Gruppe Konrad. Soviet pressure rapidly built up all around Sevastopol's perimeter: Kreizer's 51st Army assaulted the Sapun Heights and Mel'nik's Coastal Army attacked at Balaklava. On the night of May 7/8, Allmendinger scraped up his last effective troops and a few assault guns to mount a counterattack against Kreizer's troops on the Sapun Heights – which failed. After that, Allmendinger reported to Schörner on the night of May 8 that Sevastopol could no longer be held. Hitler grudgingly authorized the evacuation of AOK 17 and the exodus began that night. On the morning of May 9, Tolbukhin committed his armor to the offensive, which put further pressure on the crumbling Axis defense. The Axis troops retreated pell-mell to the Chersonese Peninsula (where there were stockpiles of supplies), with Kreizer's 51st Army in hot pursuit. By late afternoon, Soviet troops entered the devastated ruins of Sevastopol. Tolbukhin assigned the mission of reducing the Axis troops on the Chersonese to Mel'nik. The last Luftwaffe airlift missions were flown that day, taking out 1,000 wounded, but the skies over the Crimea now belonged to the VVS.

The Axis naval evacuation of the Crimea was well-organized, but Soviet air attacks were far more intense now, since Luftwaffe air cover was gone. Five merchantmen were sunk in three days, with over 8,000 Axis troops lost. Consequently, the evacuation could only continue during hours of darkness. Meanwhile, Marshal Vasilevsky was eager to see the liberated city of Sevastopol but he was wounded when his staff car had the ill fortune to drive over an undetected German mine.[45] Tolbukhin kept up the pressure on the isolated Axis troops and during the night of May 11/12 the defense finally cracked, resulting in a mad scramble for the last evacuation boats. Almost 4,000 Axis troops succeeded in embarking before Soviet troops crushed all resistance in the Chersonese Peninsula on the morning of May 12. During the final days of the naval evacuation, the Kriegsmarine and Royal Romanian Navy managed to rescue 47,825 Axis personnel from the Crimea. Nevertheless, the troops that survived were little more than poorly equipped refugees, and five more German infantry divisions had been scratched from the Ostheer's order of battle. Overall Axis losses in the Crimea in April–May 1944 totaled about 35,000 Germans and 23,000 Romanians dead or missing. In contrast, Soviet losses in the Crimean campaign were 84,819 (including 17,754 dead or missing), which was a relatively cost-effective campaign by Red Army standards.[46] With the Crimea liberated, the 4th Ukrainian Front was disbanded and Tolbukhin was sent to take over the 3rd Ukrainian Front for the invasion of Romania (Malinovsky took over the 2nd Ukrainian Front from Konev, Konev took over the 1st Ukrainian Front from Zhukov, who returned to the Stavka).

As Napoleon once said, in war, the morale is to the material as three to one, which was quite evident in the 1944 Crimea campaign. Although the odds were heavily stacked against AOK 17, it did not run out of ammunition and food as the encircled 6. Armee did at Stalingrad. Nor were its soldiers dying from cold and frostbite. In addition, AOK 17 enjoyed more air support from the Luftwaffe and even received some replacements. However, the primary difference between AOK 17 and AOK 6 was that the former had an escape exit, which meant that it did not have to fight to the death. Many of the German and Romanian tactical leaders (at division, regiment and battalion) displayed immense courage and fortitude in the final weeks of the campaign, desperately fighting to stave off defeat. Yet at the corps and army level, the leadership was poisoned with the idea that defense was futile and escape the only course of action. Jaenecke's battle command in the Crimea was one of the worst of any German commander on the Eastern Front in 1941–44. While the long-term German situation in the Crimea was hopeless, he refused to see that dragging out the campaign would delay the redeployment of three Soviet armies to invade Romania. Other German commanders made impressive defensive stands under equally desperate conditions, but Jaenecke was simply the wrong man for the task of holding the Crimea as long as possible.

Soviet generalship in the Crimea was of a much higher caliber than displayed in the Kuban campaign. Tolbukhin finally had a chance to shine and he did, employing most of the principles of war in developing a sound and efficient campaign plan, then accomplishing it quickly and with reasonable losses. Unlike previous Soviet operations, Tolbukhin had plenty of time to prepare a set-piece operation and was not rushed into any ill-judged, hasty actions. Of note, Tolbukhin's decision to send a tank corps across the Sivash and use it to advance rapidly toward Sevastopol turned AOK 17's retreat into a rout and reduced enemy morale. Petrov's performance was adequate but he accepted high risks and suffered from ill-luck. To be fair, most of the Red Army's airborne and amphibious operations failed to meet expectations. Eremenko's performance was abbreviated but his pursuit was vigorous and effective. All three Soviet field army commanders in the Crimea conducted competent offensive operations, although they relied primarily on brute force to blast through enemy defenses. The Crimean campaign was one of the few chances for a Soviet front commander to integrate air and naval forces into his plans, although the Red Army's ability to conduct efficient joint operations was still rudimentary. With greater coordination and planning, the Soviets probably had the means to inflict far greater losses upon the Axis naval evacuation, but had not really planned for such an eventuality. While a large number of Axis troops escaped the *cul-de-sac*, the Crimean campaign was a major Soviet victory and demonstrated a new standard of competence in operational-level warfare.

Commander	Objective	Offensive	Mass	Maneuver	Surprise	Security	TALLY
Jaenecke	–	o	o	o	o	–	-2
Tolbukhin	+	+	+	+	+	o	5
Eremenko	+	o	+	+	o	o	3
Petrov	+	+	o	+	+	–	3
Zhakarov Kreizer Grechkin	+	+	+	o	o	o	3

Crimean Campaign, 1944 Leadership Assessment

Leningrad–Novgorod Offensive, January 14–March 1, 1944

At the start of 1944, the one place on the Eastern Front where the Ostheer had managed to hold its own was the Leningrad sector. Although the siege of Leningrad was broken in January 1943, von Küchler's Heeresgruppe Nord had lost remarkably little ground since then. However, the relative stability of the Leningrad sector encouraged the OKH to take resources away from von Küchler in order to assist other army groups which were losing ground. Consequently, the OKH transferred several of Heeresgruppe Nord's veteran infantry divisions to other commands, and in their place, von Küchler was provided low-quality Luftwaffe *Feld-Divisionen*. The OKH also took combat multipliers such as Tiger tanks and Luftwaffe air support away from von Küchler, which gradually transformed Heeresgruppe Nord into a static defense force. In early January 1944, Lindemann's AOK 18 had 20 divisions holding an extended front from the Oranienbaum bridgehead, to the southern outskirts of Leningrad and then down to Novgorod. Lindemann's tactical/operational reserves consisted of one infantry division and some assault gun battalions.

In September 1943, Hitler had authorized the creation of the Panther-Wotan Line as a potential fallback position and by the end of the year fortified positions at Narva and Pskov were nearly completed. Von Küchler and his staff developed a plan for a phased withdrawal to the Panther-Wotan Line, designated (rather unimaginatively) as Unternehmen *Blau*. Four intermediate strongpoints were also constructed, which Heeresgruppe Nord would occupy in succession as it pulled back. Von Küchler expected to begin the withdrawal to the Panther-Wotan Line in January 1944, but on December 22 Hitler put this contingency on hold. In part, Hitler was reluctant to give up so much ground before the Leningrad and Volkhov Fronts actually attacked; Heeresgruppe Nord was still confident that it could repulse any new offensives. Yet given the level of Soviet commitment to operations in the Ukraine, Hitler and the OKH were dubious that the Stavka had sufficient remaining resources to mount a large offensive at Leningrad as well. So the decision to begin the withdrawal was deferred until it became absolutely necessary.[47]

In early September 1943, the commanders and staff from the Leningrad and Volkhov Fronts went to Moscow to discuss plans with the Stavka for future offensives in the Leningrad sector. General Leonid A. Govorov, commander of the Leningrad Front, and his chief of staff General-leytenant Dmitry N. Gusev, wanted to try something different from the previous operations based simply upon frontal attacks. The Oranienbaum bridgehead, located on the coast 20km west of Leningrad, had been a quiet sector for over two years. Von Küchler recognized the potential threat posed by the bridgehead but was not provided sufficient forces by the OKH to crush it. Instead, in an economy of force measure, Heeresgruppe Nord was given low-quality Luftwaffe *Feld-Divisionen* to guard this sector. Govorov proposed moving a shock army into the Oranienbaum bridgehead, then using it to mount a surprise attack into the weak left flank of Lindemann's AOK 18. At the same time, the rest of the Leningrad Front and part of the Volkhov Front would attack the center of AOK 18. Ideally, AOK 18 would be overwhelmed by this surprise and either destroyed or pushed back toward Lake Ilmen. The Stavka was focused on other issues at this point and did not make an immediate decision on Govorov's proposals.

In early October 1943, Eremenko's Kalinin Front attacked the boundary between Heeresgruppe Nord and Heeresgruppe Mitte and achieved a breakthrough at Nevel. With the help of massive Luftwaffe air support – over 3,500 sorties in four days – the German ground forces were soon able to seal the breach.[48] Eremenko succeeded in creating a large salient in the AOK 16 sector, but he could not immediately exploit this success.[49] After the conclusion of the Nevel operation, the Kalinin Front was redesignated as the 1st Baltic Front and Bagramyan took over. The Bryansk Front became the 2nd Baltic Front under General Markian Popov. On the same day that Nevel was captured, the Stavka directed Govorov and Meretskov to begin planning their joint offensive. As part of the build-up for the offensive, General-leytenant Ivan I. Fediuninskiy's 2nd Shock Army was quietly moved into the Oranienbaum bridgehead in November. This transfer, conducted by the Red Banner Baltic Fleet, was a major undertaking and involved the transfer of 44,000 troops, 600 artillery pieces and about 150 AFVs.[50] German intelligence detected this transfer and Lindemann did what he could to reinforce this sector, sending additional infantry, assault guns and Flak guns.

The Leningrad Front's operational plan, developed by Gusev, was that Fediuninskiy's 2nd Shock Army would attack out of the Oranienbaum bridgehead, while General-polkovnik Ivan Maslennikov's 42nd Army attacked westward from Leningrad. The two pincers would meet at Ropsha, then diverge to push toward the west and south.[51] Once von Küchler shifted his limited reserves to deal with these attacks, Meretskov's Volkhov Front would attack with three armies (8, 54, 59) to smash AOK's right flank. Given the substantial Soviet superiority in artillery, tanks and air support, Govorov and Meretskov expected a fairly quick German collapse, followed by a pursuit to the Panther-Wotan Line. The ultimate operational objectives were Narva, Luga and Pskov. Govorov and Meretskov integrated *maskirovka* into their planning and tried to convince Heeresgruppe Nord that the main attacks would occur in the Mga sector; these efforts did induce von Küchler to reinforce that sector.[52] During the planning process, the Stavka decided to embellish the operation by adding General Markian Popov's 2nd Baltic Front, which would launch supporting attacks from the Nevel salient with the intent of preventing General der Artillerie Christian Hansen's AOK 16 from transferring troops to assist AOK 18. In the later stages of the campaign, Popov's front would converge with the other two fronts to destroy the enemy around Luga.

On the morning of January 14, 1944, Fediuninskiy's 2nd Shock Army began a 65-minute artillery bombardment against the two Luftwaffe *Feld-Divisionen* facing the east side of the Oranienbaum bridgehead. Two battleships from the Red Banner Baltic Fleet and heavy railroad artillery joined the barrage, which fired a total of 104,000 rounds at the hapless Luftwaffe troops. Then five rifle divisions and two tank brigades commenced a ground assault, but the prompt arrival of several battalions from the III SS-Panzerkorps limited Fediuninskiy to only a 3–4km advance by nightfall.[53] Fediuninskiy made the bold decision to commit additional armor to a night attack, which gained another 4km, but still fell short of a breakthrough. Further east, Maslennikov's 42nd Army attacked on the morning of January 15, supported by two artillery divisions. Govorov massed over 900 guns and mortars on a 15km-wide sector, which pulverized a single German division with 220,000 rounds.[54] Soviet firepower was overwhelming but the German defense did not break as quickly as Govorov expected.

Lindemann committed his only reserve to hold the town of Ropsha, which he expected was the immediate objective of both attacking Soviet armies. He also used his artillery and local counterattacks to hit the flanks of the attacking Soviet shock groups, in order to slow the advance of both armies. Nevertheless, the 2nd Shock Army and 42nd Army committed their mobile groups on January 17 and the German defense began to fall apart. By January 19, the Soviet armor had achieved a clear breakthrough and both armies linked up at Ropsha; some German forces were isolated by this double envelopment, but most escaped. While Govorov was defeating Lindemann's left wing, Meretskov attacked the right wing. General-leytenant Ivan Korovnikov's 59th Army launched a major attack against the German XXXVIII Armeekorps, which succeeded in capturing Novgorod on January 20. With both flanks caved in and no reserves left, Lindemann had no option but to retreat. On January 21, von Küchler requested permission to conduct tactical withdrawals to shorten his line, but Hitler refused.

Having accomplished the initial breakthrough, Govorov and Meretskov now moved to exploit their success. Fediuninskiy's 2nd Shock Army was ordered to push west towards Kingisepp and Narva, while Maslennikov's 42nd Army headed south. Korovnikov's 59th Army advanced slowly westward through marshy terrain toward Luga. Soviet partisans played a major part in disrupting German rail transport during this phase, which added further operational friction to Heeresgruppe Nord's response efforts. The OKH belatedly sent some Panzer reinforcements to Heeresgruppe Nord and Lindemann used these units to briefly check the advance of the 42nd Army at Krasnogvardeisk. Both sides suffered heavy losses in this action but the German rearguards were eventually overwhelmed. Von Küchler kept pressing Hitler for permission to withdraw to the Panther-Wotan Line, which was repeatedly denied. Under intense pressure, von Küchler appears to have settled into a funk, as Paulus did at Stalingrad. Consequently, his chief of staff, Generalleutnant Eberhard Kinzel, and the AOK 18 chief of staff, Generalmajor Friedrich Foertsch, decided to ignore Hitler's no-retreat orders and began quietly issuing oral orders that enabled withdrawals to occur on January 27–28.[55] On the Soviet side, Govorov and Meretskov were exasperated that their pursuit operations were failing to encircle and destroy German units; Sviridov's 67th Army, being in the vanguard, was particularly criticized for overly-cautious advances. Hitler eventually recognized that Heeresgruppe Nord was conducting unauthorized withdrawals and on January 30 Hitler relieved von Küchler of command and ordered Generaloberst Walter Model to take over Heeresgruppe Nord; von Küchler received no further assignments.[56] On the same day, the advance elements of the 2nd Shock Army and 42nd Army reached the Luga River.

Model arrived at the Heeresgruppe Nord headquarters in Pskov on the morning of January 31 and found a grim situation. Fediuninskiy's 2nd Shock Army had taken Kingisepp, crossed the Luga River and was threatening Narva, which was defended by remnants of the III SS-Panzerkorps.[57] Maslennikov's 42nd Army was also headed toward Narva. In the center, part of Sviridov's 67th Army was approaching the city of Luga, with two more Soviet armies (54, 59) not far behind. With the Germans in headlong retreat, Meretskov's armies were advancing up to 10–15km per day. On the right, Korovnikov's 59th Army was also pushing toward Luga and Popov's 2nd Baltic Front was slowly pushing back Hansen's AOK 16. Hitler insisted that Luga must be held, but AOK 18 barely had 17,000 combat troops left, spread across a 115km–wide front.[58] The OKH promised that two Panzer divisions would be sent to assist Heeresgruppe Nord, but for the time being, Model had very limited resources in hand. As a field commander, Model excelled at improvisation and possessed a high level of personal energy, which he demonstrated by immediately drafting infantry replacements from rear echelon personnel. He conducted limited withdrawals in order to gather enough forces to mount a serious counterattack, a tactic he dubbed *Schild und Schwert* (shield and sword), which restored some degree of fighting spirit in the army and slowed the Soviet pursuit.

Model also had a keen eye for terrain and he quickly deduced that holding Narva, not Luga, was the key to containing the Soviet advance. If Narva was lost, Govorov's armies would pour into Estonia and outflank the Panther-Wotan Line. General der Infanterie Otto Sponheimer was in charge at Narva and his command was designated as Armee-Abteilung Narwa. Although he had little to give, Model sent Sponheimer a detachment of Tiger tanks and promised one of the divisions that the OKH was transferring from Heeresgruppe Mitte. Although Fediuninskiy's 2nd Shock Army succeeded in gaining bridgeheads across the Narva River and virtually encircling the garrison, Sponheimer and his troops conducted an epic and fanatical defense that repulsed all Soviet attacks for the next six months.[59] By mid-February, Govorov had the bulk of three armies (2nd Shock, 8th Army, 42nd Army) committed at Narva, but he could not break the defense. Once his left flank was secure, Model turned to his center, where the enemy was massing for a major attack on the fortified city of Luga. By pulling together bits and pieces, Model was able to mount a small counteroffensive on February 9–10 that briefly slowed the enemy advance. Nevertheless, Sviridov's 67th Army entered Luga on February 12.[60] Model's willingness to attack, instead of just requesting retreat, actually made Hitler more amenable to the idea of withdrawals. Once it became clear that AOK 18 could not stop the Soviet armies at Luga and would soon be overwhelmed, Hitler agreed on February 17 to allow Model to pull back to the Panther-Wotan Line.

On the eastern flank, Hansen's AOK 16 was able to withdraw under somewhat less pressure, since the pursuit by Popov's 2nd Baltic Front was slowed by difficult terrain. Indeed, Popov did not notice that Hansen had evacuated Staraya Russa, which brought a special reprimand from the GKO.[61] General-leytenant Gennadiy P. Korotkov's 1st Shock Army made the best progress on Popov's Front, pushing back Hansen's left flank. By March 1, Soviet logistic problems and heavy losses in the vanguard units led to the culmination of the Leningrad-Novgorod operation. Model was able to stabilize Heeresgruppe Nord's front on the Panther-Wotan Line, although his left flank anchored on Narva was still under heavy pressure. A grateful Hitler promoted Model to *generalfeldmarschall*.

In just over six weeks, the Red Army advanced 300km and shattered the previously impregnable defenses of Heeresgruppe Nord. During the campaign, AOK 18 suffered over 71,000 casualties (including 23,000 dead or missing); two Luftwaffe *Feld-Divisionen* had been destroyed and eight other divisions were reduced to *Kampfgruppen*.[62] Altogether, the three Soviet fronts involved in the operation suffered over 313,000 casualties (including 76,686 dead or missing), plus the loss of 462 tanks.[63] Heeresgruppe Nord succeeded in retreating to the Panther-Wotan Line, but it lacked the strength to hold an extended front once the Soviet armies recovered and mounted another large-scale offensive. The Stavka disbanded the Volkhov Front and Meretskov was put in charge of the Karelian Front, which would mount a major offensive against the Finns in June.

The German command performance during the Leningrad-Novgorod campaign was generally below par, although much of this was due to unrealistic constraints imposed by Hitler and the OKH. While von Küchler had demonstrated sound command abilities in previous operations, he was essentially reduced to a cipher in January 1944 and could not identify whether his proper objective was to retreat and save his army or stand and fight it out as ordered; his abrogation of command responsibility to his chief of staff (as Paulus did at Stalingrad) was a career-ending mistake. Lindemann and Hansen were more inclined to ignore no-retreat orders and act to save their units, but they were essentially presiding over covert retreats. While it is true that Heeresgruppe Nord was in poor condition to stop the Soviet offensive as it gathered momentum, it is not necessarily true to say that it was impossible – as was demonstrated by Sponheimer's stand at Narva. To some extent, von Küchler, Lindemann and Hansen were psychologically defeated because this was the first time that Heeresgruppe Nord had suffered a defeat on this scale and they could not suddenly adapt to the kind of ruthless attitude required to make troops stand against such desperate odds. To them, withdrawal was the only logical option, although Heeresgruppe Nord actually suffered heavier losses in retreat than when it stood its ground. By 1944, the "fight or flight" reflex was becoming a serious factor in the Ostheer's response to Soviet offensives, with some commanders adopting a fanatical mindset and others opting for withdrawals, followed by more withdrawals. The Red Army had faced this situation in 1941–42 and survived, in part because Stalin forced commanders to stand and fight. The situation was even worse by the time that Model took over, but he had already experienced such desperate situations in the defense of the Rzhev and Orel salients. Unlike his predecessor, Model possessed the ruthless and aggressive mindset that was required to command in a full-blown crisis. Model was also an extremely lucky commander in that the Soviet offensive was slowing down by the time he arrived and OKH reinforcements were also available, which enabled him to counterattack and slow the enemy down a bit. Furthermore, Model had developed a savvy attitude in dealing with Hitler – unlike blockheads like Jaenecke or whiners like von Weichs – which enabled him to get more reinforcements and more freedom of action from the Führer. In modern parlance, Model knew how to work the system.

On the Soviet side, Govorov put in a superb command performance that incorporated all the principles of war into the planning and execution of the Leningrad-Novgorod operation. The use of the Oranienbaum bridgehead as a springboard for an attack against the weaker German left flank expertly combined mass, maneuver and surprise in order to achieve an overwhelming local advantage over the enemy. While Govorov did not succeed in capturing either of the two primary operational objectives (Narva and Pskov) or encircling and destroying AOK 16 as intended, the Leningrad Front did inflict a very heavy defeat on Heeresgruppe Nord. Meretskov's performance was good but relied more on firepower and mass than maneuver and surprise. Meretskov, like many senior Red Army commanders, had mastered the art of set-piece battles but struggled to convert battlefield success into wider operational success. Popov's poor performance was noted in Moscow and he was soon relieved of command and demoted. Fediuninskiy, a protégé of Zhukov, was the ablest of the Soviet field army commanders during the Leningrad-Novgorod operation and he would continue to command the 2nd Shock Army for the rest of the war. Maslennikov and Korovnikov also demonstrated competence in their operations. Sviridov was the one exception and was singled out as lethargic in the pursuit phase, but suffered no consequences. After three years of war, the Red Army had winnowed out most of its unsuccessful commanders and now had a stable of competent leaders who could plan and conduct operational-level warfare.

Commander	Objective	Offensive	Mass	Maneuver	Surprise	Security	TALLY
Von Küchler	-	o	o	o	o	-	-2
Lindemann	+	o	o	o	o	-	o
Hansen	+	o	o	o	o	o	1
Model	+	+	+	+	o	o	4
Govorov	+	+	+	+	+	+	6
Meretskov	+	+	+	o	o	o	3
Popov	+	-	+	-	o	o	o
Fediuninskiy	+	+	+	+	+	+	6
Maslennikov Korovnikov	+	+	+	+	o	o	4
Sviridov	+	+	+	-	o	o	2

Leningrad-Novgorod Campaign, 1944 Leadership Assessment

The Invasion of Romania (Jassy-Kishinev), April 8–June 6, 1944

By early April 1944, the Red Army had nearly completed the liberation of western Ukraine and Stalin was eager to continue the advance into Romania. Schörner's Heeresgruppe Südukraine appeared to be a broken reed, the Romanian army no longer a factor and the vital oil fields at Ploesti within tantalizing reach. Konev's 2nd Ukrainian Front was already across the Dniester River and there were few enemy forces blocking it. Consequently, on April 5 the Stavka ordered Konev's 2nd Ukrainian Front to advance deeper into northern Romania with Trofimenko's 27th Army and Zhmachenko's 40th Army, supported by Bogdanov's 2 TA;

the immediate objectives were the frontier cities of Jassy and Kishinev. The Stavka also ordered Malinovsky's 3rd Ukrainian Front to support Konev's advance, once the liberation of Odessa was completed.[64] Marshal Vasilevsky was assigned as Stavka representative to coordinate the Romanian operation. However, the Soviet front-line armies were much reduced after months of continuous fighting, short on supplies and in poor condition to mount another back-to-back offensive. Bogdanov's 2 TA was down to just 120 operational tanks. Furthermore, the Stavka pulled Rotmistrov's 5 GTA and Kravchenko's 6 TA back to refit, which left Konev with very little armor at the front. Military logic suggested that Konev's forces needed an operational pause, but Stalin was not interested in a prudent approach. Instead, he knew that the Anglo-Americans would be landing in France soon and he wanted to seize as much territory in Eastern Europe as possible before that event occurred. Thus, due to Stalin's geopolitical designs for post-war Central Europe, the Stavka pushed Konev and Malinovsky into the same kind of poorly-planned operations that had resulted in disaster in early 1943.

The Axis situation in Romania was critical, but the mountainous terrain and rainy weather favored the defense. The German supply situation also improved inside Romania due to the proximity of ammunition and fuel stockpiles. Nor were there any problems with annoying rear-area partisan attacks in Romania. As a result, Wöhler's battered AOK 8 was able to quickly reorganize itself once inside Romania. Even the Royal Romanian Army regained some of its composure once defending its own soil and it still had a few combat-effective units. Wöhler's command saw an unusually close integration of German and Romanian units that had heretofore been uncommon on the Eastern Front. Thanks to the influx of badly needed replacements from the OKH, Wöhler was able to mass five Panzer divisions at Kishinev and three more at Jassy. The most effective German unit was the elite Panzergrenadier-Division *Großdeutschland*, which still had 70 operational AFVs. However, Schörner and Wöhler did not intend to simply wait passively on the defense until the Soviets' armored spearheads arrived – they intended to do what the Ostheer did best, conduct a surprise counteroffensive once the enemy was overextended.

Trofimenko's 27th Army advanced fairly rapidly into northern Romania and captured the vital road junction at Targu Fromos (45km west of Jassy) on April 9. Wöhler reacted by ordering the *Großdeutschland* Division, in conjunction with the Romanian IV Corps, to retake the city. Led by the fiery Generalleutnant Hasso von Manteuffel, the *Großdeutschland* conducted a rapid 40km road march and caught Trofimenko completely by surprise.

Von Manteuffel attacked on the morning of April 10 and not only retook the city, but isolated one of Trofimenko's rifle corps.[65] Trofimenko succeeded in extracting his encircled troops but lost a good deal of equipment in the retreat. The Germans then settled down to fortify their positions around Targu Fromos, while conducting an active defense for the next several weeks to keep Konev's forces off-balance. Surprised by the repulse at Targu Fromos, Konev ordered Bogdanov's 2 TA to try to outflank the German strongpoint by moving further east toward Podu Iloaie, while Koroteev's 52nd Army followed in support. However, the German 24. Panzer-Division, with just 45 AFVs, was able to halt Bogdanov's armor on April 12–13 and block it from further advance. By mid-April, Konev recognized that he could not continue to advance into Romania with just three badly depleted armies (27, 52, 2 TA) and obtained permission for an operational pause in order to replenish and reorganize his armies.

The pause gave both sides an opportunity to reorganize their forces for the next round. Wöhler had two Romanian corps (I, V) defending the region west of Targu Fromos, General der Panzeruppen Friedrich Kirchner's LVII Panzerkorps anchoring his left flank at Targu Fromos, the mixed Gruppe Mieth holding the Jassy sector in the center and two corps (XXXX and XXXXVII Panzerkorps) holding his right flank near Dubossary/Orgeev. The Germans still possessed some strong Panzer units, but virtually all of their non-mechanized infantry support was Romanian. Konev was able to bring up Zhmachenko's 40th Army to strengthen his forces in the Targu Fromos sector. He also assigned three armies on his left flank (4 GA, 5 GA, 53) to push back Wöhler's right flank and two other armies (37, 57) to attack the left flank of the 6. Armee near Tiraspol. Galanin's 4 GA had already crossed the Dniester and captured Orgeev on April 6, but then became deadlocked in a battle of attrition with the XXXX Panzerkorps. Axis resistance had stiffened all along the new front line, affording few chances for Konev to make any progress.

Embarrassed by his setback at Targu Fromos, Konev brought up Shumilov's veteran 7 GA, Rotmistrov's 5 GTA (with about 350 tanks and assault guns) and three artillery divisions; he intended to use these forces to smash Wöhler's defenses east of that city. As a combat multiplier, the Stavka also provided Rotmistrov with JS-2 heavy tanks and some of the new T-34/85 medium tanks. Trofimenko's 27th Army, supported by Bogdanov's 2 TA (with 121 tanks and assault guns), would mount a supporting attack northeast of Targu Fromos. On the other side, Wöhler's forces had used their brief respite wisely by creating a strong defense in depth around Targu Fromos, complete with mines, and massing their available armor to create a strong mobile reserve.

Konev attacked on the morning of May 2, beginning his offensive with a powerful 60-minute artillery barrage that laid waste to some enemy front-line positions. Then Shumilov's 7 GA attacked with seven rifle divisions supported by a tank corps. Although hard-pressed, Kirchner's LVII Panzerkorps committed the *Großdeutschland* Division in a perfectly-timed counterattack that demolished the Soviet tank corps. Shumilov came close to overrunning some Romanian infantry before German counterattacks deprived him of most of his armor support. At the same time, Trofimenko's 27th Army did achieve some success in its attacks northeast of Targu Fromos before German Panzer counterattacks also routed his armor support.[66] Amazingly, Kirchner's LVII Panzerkorps ended up repulsing Konev's attacks and knocked out about one-third of his armor. Undeterred, Konev renewed his attacks on May 3–4 and was repulsed again and again. Both Bogdanov's 2 TA and Rotmistrov's 5 GTA were shattered on the solid German defenses and were no longer combat effective. Sensing the weakness of Konev's front-line forces, Kirchner's LVII Panzerkorps mounted counterattacks on May 7 which caught both Shumilov and Trofimenko by surprise. Remarkably, the Germans not only succeeded in inflicting losses on the enemy around Targu Fromos but pushing them back. Embarrassed by this setback, an angry Konev threatened Trofimenko that he might reintroduce military tribunals to punish senior officers who ceded ground to the enemy.[67] Further east, Konev's efforts to capture Kishinev also came up short. Galanin's 4 GA gained some ground but was burnt out in heavy fighting around Orgeev. Zhadov's 5 GA succeeded in capturing a bridgehead across the Dniester River at Tashlyk (40km east of Kishinev) on the night of April 12/13 and he demonstrated commendable energy in getting tanks and a complete guards rifle corps into the bridgehead in just two days. Yet when he attempted a breakout attack on April 16, the effort was ruined by a German counterattack that even had substantial air and artillery support.[68] Zhadov's 5 GA was stopped cold and two subsequent efforts to resume the breakout attempt were also shut down. Given these across-the-board failures and the sudden resurgence of German combat power, Konev was forced to shift to the defense.

Meanwhile Malinovsky's 3rd Ukrainian Front was also trying to cross the Dniester River but was blocked by the AOK 6 (now under General der Artillerie Maximilian de Angelis). The initial attempt by Glagolev's 46th Army to "bounce" the river on April 13/14 only gained a minor toehold which was of no real operational value. As a result, Malinovsky submitted a plan for a set-piece river-crossing operation involving coordinated attacks by five of his armies (5 SA, 6, 57, 37, 46) to Vasilevsky. While Malinovsky enjoyed a substantial numerical superiority over the 6. Armee in terms of manpower, artillery and tanks, his supply situation was poor and the rainy spring weather made river-crossing operations complicated. Instead of coordinated simultaneous attacks by all five armies, a variety of problems forced them to attack individually between April 19 and 25. The 6. Armee had recovered some of its former combat effectiveness and it was able to fend off each attacking Soviet army in turn. Malinovsky's set-piece operation had completely failed. Since he had no bridgeheads of his own Malinovsky requested that Konev's small Tashlyk bridgehead, held by Zhadov's 5 GA, should be transferred to his command so he could mount a new cross-river offensive. On April 28, the Stavka approved this request, but Zhadov's 5 GA would remain under Konev's command.[69] Consequently, Malinovsky decided to shift Chuikov's 8 GA northward to the Tashlyk bridgehead, which would take about a week to accomplish. Conducting an army-size relief in place operation is a very complicated – and potentially dangerous – affair.

Due to poor Soviet operational security, de Angelis, the new commander of AOK 6, noticed what Malinovsky was attempting to do and decided to conduct his own preemptive strike. De Angelis was an ardent Austrian Nazi but he was also an experienced front-line commander who had been well trained by the Austrian General Staff; before the war, he taught classes on operational-level warfare in Vienna. He now had a chance to put these theories into practice. Gruppe Knobelsdorff (XXXX Panzerkorps) was able to mass three Panzer divisions, two assault gun brigades and two infantry divisions and attacked the Soviet forces in the Tashlyk bridgehead on the morning of May 10. Chuikov's 8 GA was caught still moving into the bridgehead and lacked sufficient armor and antitank weapons to repel a surprise attack by over 100 German AFVs.[70] In three days of heavy fighting, Gruppe Knobelsdorff reduced the Soviet bridgehead and inflicted 30,000 casualties on Chuikov's 8 GA.[71] Malinovsky attempted to reduce the pressure on Chuikov by ordering Tsvetaev's 5th Shock Army to conduct an attack across the Dniester, but Gruppe Knobelsdorff repulsed this effort as well. With both Konev and Malinovsky having suffered stinging tactical defeats, the Stavka had no choice but to postpone a major advance into Romania until the summer months.

In late May, Wöhler decided to organize his own counteroffensive to push Konev's forces further back from Jassy. He and his staff developed a plan for a two-phased operation ("*Sonja*" and "*Katja*") that would first strike Koroteev's 52nd Army then Trofimenko's 27th Army. For the counteroffensive, Wöhler massed virtually all of AOK 8's available armor into a strike group that possessed about 100 operational AFVs. Just prior to the operation, AOK 8 received some replacement troops and AFVs, which helped to reinvigorate some of his combat units.[72] Operation *Sonja* began on May 30, using two Panzer divisions (23, 24) and one German infantry division; the two-day attack overran some of Koroteev's front-line infantry and accomplished its objectives.[73] The counterattack even received Luftwaffe close air support from Major Hans-Ulrich Rudel's elite III/SG 2, which knocked out roughly 30 enemy tanks north of Jassy.[74] The Luftwaffe also committed all of JG52 – its best fighter unit – to the Jassy area and this elite formation claimed 156 Soviet aircraft shot down in just two days (actual VVS losses may have been just 70).[75] Wöhler then shifted his Panzer group westward and began Operation *Katja* on June 2 against Trofimenko's army. By this point, Konev was reacting to the German counteroffensive and sent some of Bogdanov's remaining armor to support the 27th Army. Ultimately, Operation *Katja* achieved limited success and was terminated after four days of heavy fighting. Wöhler's counteroffensive further embarrassed Konev, but it did not change the operational situation in Romania.

Stalin's desire to overrun Romania as quickly as possible in spring 1944 led to unexpected defeats of the 2nd and 3rd Ukrainian Fronts. In attempting this feat, the Stavka repeated the kind of operational mistakes it made after Stalingrad in trying to advance too fast, too far, with depleted and exhausted forces, against an enemy who had not yet been beaten. The German powers of recovery astounded the Soviet leaders, who often ignored the human/psychological aspects of war. The German defensive success in Romania in April–June 1944 was not only one of their last real victories on the Eastern Front, but one of the very rare occasions where their tactical victories led to a major operational victory. Due to the stubborn defensive efforts and aggressive counterattacks, the Ostheer was able to prevent the Red Army from accomplishing any of its operational objectives in their spring offensive in Romania. According to David Glantz, the two Soviet fronts lost about 18 percent of their starting strength or about 150,000 casualties in these failed offensives. According to German claims, Soviet losses were even higher and included 12,000 prisoners and the loss of over 1,100 tanks.[76] It is clear that neither front was in a condition to resume offensive operations for some time. On the German side, Heeresgruppe Südukraine suffered roughly 43,000 casualties (including 14,000 dead or missing) in this period of April–May 1944. Despite Romanian participation in these operations, German commanders noted that their ally's will to continue the war was evaporating.

Schörner's contributions to the defense of Romania are difficult to gauge, since he was in command of Heeresgruppe Südukraine for less than four months and appears to have delegated much of the operational responsibilities to his two subordinate army commanders. Schörner was inexperienced in command at this level and also had to devote considerable time to managing increasingly reluctant Romanian commanders. Wöhler and de Angelis were the primary German operational commanders in Romania in April–June 1944 and they did a superb job rallying their battered armies and employing the principles of war to conduct successful defensive/offensive operations. Of note, the use of rapid maneuver, concentration of force at unexpected points and coordinated attacks repeatedly frustrated and embarrassed their Soviet opposite numbers. It is important to note, however, that German operational success in Romania was in large part due to the efforts of aggressive tactical commanders, particularly Kirchner, General Otto von Knobelsdorff and von Manteuffel.

The reputation of Soviet generalship, which had been on a successful roll since Kursk in July 1943, took a major hit in Romania. Konev and Malinovsky had mastered the art of planning set-piece operations, but they were pushed by the Stavka and Stalin to accelerate their plans for Romania and execute them immediately after clearing western Ukraine. The resulting operations reverted to the old formula of nonstop offensive action, with their edge in mass gradually ebbing due to attrition and exhaustion. The use of maneuver was noticeably absent in most of these operations, with the exception of Zhadov seizing the Tashlyk bridgehead before AOK 8 could react. Soviet operations in Romania were particularly undermined by the failure to anticipate or guard against enemy counter-responses; Trofimenko, Shumilov, Chuikov and others were caught by surprise and defeated by numerically inferior German forces. Chuikov, hero of Stalingrad, suffered humiliation when AOK 6 counterattacked at the most inopportune moment for him – such is war. Just as Hitler's interference repeatedly handicapped Heeresgruppe Süd's leadership in 1943–44, Stalin's interference in operations could also reduce even veteran Soviet commanders into mindlessly obedient automatons.

Commander	Objective	Offensive	Mass	Maneuver	Surprise	Security	TALLY
Schörner	+	+	o	o	o	o	2
Wöhler De Angelis	+	+	+	+	+	o	5
Konev Malinovsky	+	+	o	o	o	–	1
Zhadov	+	+	+	+	o	–	3
Rotmistrov Bogdanov	+	+	o	o	o	o	2
Trofimenko Shumilov	+	+	+	o	o	–	2
Zhmachenko Galanin Glagolev Tsvetaev Koroteev	+	+	o	o	o	o	2
Chuikov	+	o	o	o	o	–	o

Jassy-Kishinev Campaign, 1944 Leadership Assessment

Operation *Bagration*, June 22–July 8, 1944

Since retreating from Smolensk, Heeresgruppe Mitte (under Generalfeldmarschall Ernst Busch) had anchored its front on four fortified cities: Vitebsk, Orsha, Mogilev and Bobruisk. Busch's left flank extended just past the city of Polotsk on the Dvina River, while his right flank lay near the city of Kovel. The terrain in Belorussia, replete with marshes and forests, limited operational mobility and favored the defense. In particular, the Pripet Marshes on Busch's right flank were a serious obstacle to any kind of mechanized operations. In February–March, Bagramyan's Baltic Front and Sokolovsky's Western Front conducted a hastily-improvised offensive in an attempt to seize Vitebsk and Orsha. However, the offensive was a total failure, costing the two fronts 135,000 casualties (including 27,639 dead/missing) just to advance a few kilometers.[77] The German defense-in-depth in this sector remained intact and Sokolovsky was relieved of command for failure in the Vitebsk offensive (he was sent to become Konev's chief of staff in the 1st Ukrainian Front). Afterwards, Busch continued to improve his fixed defenses around the fortified cities, but he was hampered by the fact that most of the infantry divisions in Heeresgruppe Mitte had been reduced to the new six-battalion organization (instead of the normal nine-battalion structure) and were also seriously understrength. According to Wehrmacht doctrine, a full-strength infantry division could defend a 10km-wide sector, but Busch's depleted infantry divisions were expected to hold sectors that were 20–25km wide, which meant that the front line was inevitably quite porous in places. Furthermore, a number of Busch's veteran infantry divisions had been transferred to other commands and he received low-quality Luftwaffe *Feld-Divisionen* to replace them. Altogether, the three armies in Heeresgruppe Mitte that would bear the brunt of the enemy offensive had about 485,000 troops in 37 divisions (one Panzer, four Panzergrenadier, 25 infantry, two Luftwaffe and five security).

Heeresgruppe Mitte was also handicapped by its shortage of operational reserves and air support. Initially, Busch had the LVI Panzerkorps (with two Panzer divisions and a battalion of Tiger tanks) as his primary operational reserve, but Generalfeldmarschall Model requested reinforcements from the OKH because he expected Konev to launch the main Soviet summer offensive against Heeresgruppe Nordukraine. The OKH agreed and the LVI Panzerkorps was duly transferred to Model's command on May 29.[78] Busch was left with only a single Panzer division and one Panzergrenadier division as his mobile reserves, which possessed barely 100 operational tanks and assault guns. Altogether, Busch had about 600 AFVs in hand, but rather than concentrating his limited mobile reserves, he scattered them. Nor would Generaloberst Robert Ritter von Greim's Luftflotte 6 be of much help, since it had just 100 fighters and 100 ground attack aircraft on hand to support Heeresgruppe Mitte.[79] German weakness in the air also meant less aerial reconnaissance, which impaired intelligence collection capabilities and situational awareness.

For the most part, Busch handicapped his own operational decision-making by overly deferring to Hitler's dictates. He made an attempt, when he met with Hitler on May 20, to request permission for AOK 4 to conduct a 40km withdrawal behind the Dnepr River, even though this would only shorten the front line by about 30km. Busch also raised the idea of a larger 80–120km withdrawal behind the Berezina River, which would have meant abandoning three of the four fortified cities; this would have shorted AOK 4's front by about 20 percent. Not surprisingly, Hitler rejected the idea of abandoning so much territory when the enemy had not even attacked yet. Furthermore, the Soviets might detect a withdrawal while it was in progress and attack, catching the German troops out in the open; a fumbled withdrawal might lead to heavy losses of men and material. Busch's approach with Hitler was clumsy and he failed to gain any concessions for his command. Nor were Busch's four front-line army commanders willing to stick their necks out to challenge Hitler's increasingly unrealistic decisions. Generaloberst Georg-Hans Reinhardt (PzAOK 3) and Generaloberst Walter Weiß (AOK 2) were both veteran commanders but their performance during the defensive battles of 1942–43 was uninspired. Reinhardt's army had been stripped to the bone and assigned an overly wide sector that he could not properly defend, but he made only feeble complaints. Busch's other two armies had recently undergone changes in command. Generaloberst Gotthard Heinrici, commander of AOK 4, had protested openly and repeatedly requested permission to withdraw his army to shorter lines; Hitler relieved him of command on May 20 and replaced him with one of his corps commanders, General der Infanterie Kurt von Tippelskirch. In the AOK 9, Model secured the transfer of the veteran Generaloberst Josef Harpe to take over the 4. Panzerarmee; in his place, General der Infanterie Hans Jordan, another corps commander, was selected to take over AOK 9 one month prior to *Bagration*. Although only in command for a few weeks, Jordan complained bitterly about Busch's parroting of ridiculous OKH directives:

> The Commanding General [Busch] and Chief of Staff [Krebs] presented these thoughts to the army group in numerous conferences, but there, apparently, the courage was lacking to carry them higher up, for no counterarguments other than references to OKH orders were given. And that is the fundamental source of the anxiety with which the army views the future.[80]

In March 1944, the Soviet General Staff (GSHKA) and GKO began considering where and when the Red Army's summer offensives should occur. Essentially, there were four courses of action considered: northern axis (defeat Finland, clear out the Baltic States), Belorussia, Galicia/southern Poland and Romania. Stalin was persuaded that attempting all four courses of action simultaneously was not logistically feasible and could lead to failure or stalemate in some parts of the front.[81] Above all else, Stalin wanted to maintain the strategic initiative and finish the war before the Western Allies reached German soil. By April, the Stavka decided that liberation of Belorussia, which was the last major region of the USSR still occupied by the enemy, would be the top priority.[82] Zhukov was summoned to Moscow on April 22 to discuss planning for the Belorussian operation. The Stavka had studied the failure of the earlier Vitebsk operation and concluded the lack of operational-level surprise and inadequate logistic shortages were root causes of Sokolovsky's defeat, along with lackluster leadership. Based upon previous experience, there was great concern that the OKH might suddenly transfer reinforcements to Heeresgruppe Mitte and make it more difficult for the Red Army to achieve rapid or decisive success. The Stavka also knew that the Western Allies would land in northern France in early June, which was expected to tie down German mobile reserves in the West. Consequently, the Stavka decided that effective *maskirovka* was a *sine qua non* for a decisive operation and every possible artifice would be employed to convince the OKH that the Red Army's main summer offensive was not going to occur in Belorussia. Rather than move directly against Heeresgruppe Mitte, the Stavka decided that the Leningrad and Karelian Fronts would first conduct an offensive against Finland on June 10. Once the OKH was distracted and its reserves committed to other theaters, the Stavka would then commence the offensive to liberate Belorussia around mid-June, which was designated Operation *Bagration*.[83] After success was achieved in Belorussia, Konev's 1st Ukrainian Front would attack Heeresgruppe Nordukraine in mid-July in order to reach Lvov and the Vistula River. The 2nd and 3rd Ukrainian Fronts, now low on the priority list, would resume their Jassy-Kishinev offensive in Romania in July or August.

As part of the preparation for *Bagration*, the Western Front was dissolved on April 24 and its component armies assigned to two new formations: the 2nd and 3rd Belorussian Fronts. The Western Front had been rather too cumbersome to control (typically it had nine to ten armies) and the Stavka concluded that fronts with three to five armies were better suited for operational-level warfare. The Stavka also wanted new senior commanders on the Western axis to replace those who had failed to meet expectations. Amazingly, Vasilevsky and Zhukov recommended that Ivan D. Cherniakhovsky, commander of the 60th Army, should be promoted to take over the 3rd Belorussian Front – which was quickly approved.[84] At 35 years of age, Cherniakhovsky was three years younger than the next youngest Red Army front commander (Markian Popov) and most were in their mid-40s. In post-war Soviet historiography, Cherniakhovsky has enjoyed a lionized reputation, which is difficult to understand. It is claimed that he displayed "exceptional ability," although specifics are rather thin.* While he had been successful as commander of the 60th Army during the recent Dnepr campaign, other far more successful army commanders like Moskalenko, Lelyushenko and Fediuninskiy were never offered front command. Nor were any of the other senior tank officers (Katukov, Rybalko, Rotmistrov, Bogdanov) ever promoted to front command. Yet Cherniakhovsky enjoyed a meteoric career, being promoted five grades in just three years. The spotlight placed on Cherniakhovsky tends to demonstrate how the Red Army sometimes selected (or retained) commanders based more on political factors or the patronage of high-level officials rather than purely military qualifications. Markian Popov, another youthful commander, had been promoted five times in four years and constantly given front-line commands despite a record of failure and excessive drunkenness. My assessment, for what it is worth, is that Stalin was looking for ardent, youthful communists to lead the final offensives because he was wary of older, more experienced commanders gaining too much prestige in the waning days of the war. It is likely that Vasilevsky and Zhukov simply rubber-stamped Stalin's preferred candidate. Georgy F. Zakharov, another successful but unexceptional army commander, was promoted to lead the 2nd Belorussian Front.

The Stavka assigned four fronts to conduct Operation *Bagration*: Bagramyan's 1st Baltic Front, Rokossovsky's 1st Belorussian Front, Zakharov's 2nd Belorussian Front and Cherniakhovsky's 3rd Belorussian Front. Vasilevsky would coordinate the two northern fronts (1st Baltic and 3rd Belorussian Fronts) and Zhukov would coordinate the two southern fronts (2nd Belorussian and 1st Belorussian Fronts). Cherniakhovsky, a novice at front command, was picked to lead the main effort in the Red Army's most important offensive of 1944. Initially, the Stavka's basic plan for Operation *Bagration* was rather rudimentary and envisioned the main effort on the Vitebsk-Orsha axis, led by Cherniakhovsky's 3rd Belorussian Front and supported by Bagramyan's 1st Baltic Front. Cherniakhovsky was assigned Rotmistrov's 5 GTA as an exploitation force and plenty of additional artillery. Altogether, the four Soviet fronts were assigned a total

---

*Cherniakhovsky took over the 60th Army in July 1942, where his army accomplished little in the fighting around Voronezh. His first real success was the liberation of Kursk in February 1943. His army played no significant role in either the Battle of Kursk or Operation *Kutusov*. Pukhov's 13th Army gained the first crossings of the Dnepr but Cherniakhovsky's accomplishments during the Dnepr campaign received more attention. He did perform well in February 1944 capturing Rovno and Lutsk, but against minimal opposition.

of 2,715 tanks and 1,355 self-propelled guns, giving them a 6-1 numerical superiority in armor over the enemy. Likewise, the Soviets would enjoy a 3-1 superiority in manpower and 6-1 in artillery fire support. In terms of air support, five air armies (1, 3, 4, 6, 16VA) would provide an 8-1 numerical superiority over Luftflotte 6. Thus, the initial plans for Operation *Bagration* were based upon a brute-force approach to achieve a breakthrough via mass and firepower.

However, at a planning conference in Moscow on May 22–23, in which all the front commanders and staff participated (except Cherniakhovsky, who was supposedly "ill"), Rokossovsky objected to the minor role assigned to his 1st Belorussian Front and stated that an attack along a single axis was risky. The Germans might shift reserves to prevent a breakthrough on a single axis, which could lead to a costly battle of attrition like Operation *Suvorov*. Instead, Rokossovsky recommended employing two main axes of attack, with his front attacking along the Bobruisk axis in addition to Cherniakhovsky's advance. He also had the temerity to request a tank army for his front as well. In essence, Rokossovsky wanted to inject more emphasis on maneuver into the plan, rather than excessive reliance on mass to lead to a rapid conclusion. Stalin rejected these suggestions out of hand, but was surprised when Rokossovsky refused to simply acquiesce; this was not normal behavior for Soviet operational planning meetings in the Kremlin. Vasilevsky even took Rokossovsky aside and told him to watch his step. Eventually, Stalin agreed to let Rokossovsky mount a major push along the Bobruisk axis, but he would not get a tank army. By the end of May, the final version of *Bagration* was coming together and it now incorporated a double axis attack, although Cherniakhovsky's 3rd Belorussian Front was still designated as the main effort.[85]

Operation *Bagration* assigned the following objectives to the four fronts involved:

- Bagramyan's 1st Belorussian Front was assigned to attack the center and left flank of Reinhardt's PzAOK 3. General-major Pankrantiy V. Beloborodov's 43rd Army would envelop Vitebsk from the northwest and link up with Lyudnikov's 39th Army (3rd Belorussian Front) to isolate the city. At the same time, Chistiakov's 6 GA would attack the German IX Armeekorps west of Vitebsk and advance to seize crossings over the Western Dvina River.
- Cherniakhovsky's 3rd Belorussian Front was assigned three primary objectives. First, General-leytenant Ivan I. Lyudnikov's

39th Army and Krylov's 5th Army would advance to envelop and crush the German garrison in Vitebsk. Second, Galitsky's 11 GA and Glagolev's 31st Army would make a deliberate assault to break the left wing of AOK 4 and seize Orsha. Once Orsha was taken, Rotmistrov's 5 GTA would be committed to advance toward Senno and the Berezina River.

- Zakharov's 2nd Belorussian Front was assigned to smash in the center of AOK 4 and seize Mogilev with Kriuchenkin's 33rd Army, Grishin's 49th Army and Boldin's 50th Army. Following that, Zakharov would support the advance west toward Minsk.
- Rokossovsky's 1st Belorussian Front was assigned to defeat AOK 9 and seize Bobruisk. The front would attack with Gorbatov's 3rd Army and Romanenko's 48th Army east of the Berezina River and Belov's 65th Army and General-leytenant Aleksandr A. Luchinsky's 28th Army on the west side. Once AOK 9's front was broken, 1st Belorussian Front would commit Pliev's cavalry-mechanized group (KMG) to push west toward Baranovichi.

Altogether, Cherniakhovsky's 3rd Belorussian Front in the north and Rokossovsky's 1st Belorussian Front in the south were assigned 26 of the 41 rifle corps, six of the seven tank/mechanized corps, all four cavalry corps, both artillery corps and seven of the nine artillery divisions committed to *Bagration*. In contrast, Bagramyan's 1st Baltic Front had enough armor and artillery to support Cherniakhovsky's advance but was little more than a large flank guard. Zakharov's 2nd Belorussian Front, which was placed in the center, was the least capable formation and had no large armor or artillery units attached. The initial operational objective for *Bagration* was to capture the four German fortified cities, then push west to the Berezina River – an advance of about 150km – then to advance west to liberate Minsk. Operation *Bagration* was premised upon a high tempo as envisioned by the ideals of pre-war Deep Operations theory. In order to sustain this offensive, the assault armies on the main axes of attack in the 3rd Belorussian Front and 1st Belorussian Front were provided with 4.5 loads of ammunition (*zapravki*), 3 loads of fuel (*boekomplekti)* and enough rations/fodder for 10–15 days of operations.[86] In addition, the Soviet fronts involved in *Bagration* benefitted from a large infusion of Anglo-American motor transport provided by Lend Lease, which increased both operational mobility and logistic sustainability. The Red Army was beginning to move away from its reliance on horse-drawn transport, just as the Ostheer was heading in the opposite direction.

Operation *Bagration* also placed great emphasis on *maskirovka* (particularly communications security) to deceive and mislead the enemy. There is no doubt that the OKH's Foreign Armies East (Fremde Heere Ost, FHO) already had a poor track record of assessing Soviet operational intentions and capabilities, and it certainly failed to anticipate a major offensive in Belorussia in June 1944.[87] Yet some of the claims about the relative contribution of *maskirovka* to the success of Operation *Bagration* are contentious. According to Soviet post-war accounts, the Stavka wanted the OKH to think that the main Soviet offensive was going to be led by Konev's 1st Ukrainian Front into Galicia, but in fact the impending Lvov-Sandomierz operation was scheduled to begin just one month after *Bagration*.[88] Normally the point of deception operations is to convince the enemy that you are going to attack in a place where you do not intend to attack, such as the Allied effort to convince the OKW that the landing in France in June 1944 would occur in the Pas-de-Calais, not Normandy. It has also been suggested that the FHO was deceived because it used the location of the six Soviet tank armies as the primary indicator of where the Stavka intended to make its main effort and that the shift of Rotmistrov's 5 GTA to Cherniakhovsky's 3rd Belorussian Front caught them by surprise.[89] However, five of the six Soviet tank armies were in fact in the Ukraine (1 GTA, 3 GTA and 4 TA under Konev's 1st Ukrainian Front and 2 TA, 6 TA under Malinovsky's 2nd Ukrainian Front) and Rotmistrov's 5 GTA only completed its transfer to the 3rd Belorussian Front on June 22.[90] Claims that the FHO's failure to detect the movement of the 5 GTA to Belorussia was an "intelligence failure" are absurd, given the timeline of the transfer and that the bulk of Soviet armor remained in western Ukraine. It is true that Heeresgruppe Mitte did not expect a large-scale offensive in its area and that if one did occur, its fixed defenses were expected to hold until reinforcements could be shifted from other sectors.[91] Yet it is doubtful that better FHO intelligence assessments would have made much difference, given the limited amount of German mobile reserves remaining and the Luftwaffe's diminished ability to influence operations. In fact, the Germans were on the horns of a dilemma: if they reinforced Busch's Heeresgruppe Mitte, it came at the expense of weakening Model's Heeresgruppe Nordukraine, and vice versa.

Four days before Operation *Bagration* began, Soviet partisans began attacking German lines of communications in Belorussia. In 1943, the Stavka had established an office to coordinate partisan operations, led by General-leytenant Panteleimon K. Ponomarenko, a Communist Party leader. He hoped to coordinate the large number of partisan units scattered across Belorussia in an effort to isolate the battlefield, but the limited number of radios made this difficult. Furthermore, the partisan units were only lightly armed and Heeresgruppe Mitte conducted its own ruthless antipartisan operations. While the Belorussian partisans did inflict some serious disruptions on German rail traffic in RVD Minsk (the network supporting Heeresgruppe Mitte) and telephone lines, it was less than what was expected (or later claimed).[92] On the afternoon of June 20, Busch flew back to Germany on home leave (just as Rommel went on leave before the Allied landing in Normandy), with his chief of staff, General der Infanterie Hans Krebs, left in temporary command. On June 22, infantry from the 3rd Belorussian Front and 1st Belorussian Front began numerous small probing attacks all along the front line in an effort to begin peeling back the German security zones. As a result of these shaping efforts, Heeresgruppe Mitte's C3I and logistic functions were somewhat impaired, but all four army commanders were alerted to the fact that an enemy offensive was imminent.

The Soviet hammer was about to fall upon Reinhardt's PzAOK 3, which was particularly weak, both in terms of composition and dispositions. Since Hitler had mandated that Vitebsk must be held, Reinhardt was obliged to garrison the city and its environs with the entire LIII Armeekorps. However, two of the four divisions in this formation were low-quality Luftwaffe *Feld-Divisionen* and the city was in a vulnerable salient, with the enemy on three sides. On the morning of June 23, Operation *Bagration* began with massive artillery barrages that lasted two hours. Bagramyan, who had experience cracking German defensive lines from Operation *Kutusov*, massed 125 guns and mortars per kilometer of attack sector.[93] On the right, Chistiakov's 6 GA smashed through the flimsy German IX Armeekorps and achieved a major advance on the first day. Beloborodov's 43rd Army also helped to demolish the IX Armeekorps and began enveloping Vitebsk from the northwest. Cherniakhovsky's 3rd Belorussian Front used a full artillery corps to disrupt the German VI Armeekorps southeast of Vitebsk, then attacked with Lyudnikov's 39th Army and Krylov's 5th Army against the German VI Armeekorps. Both of these attacks made progress, but not as much as expected. Cherniakhovsky's left wing mounted a set-piece assault with the 11 GA and 31st Armies against the left flank of AOK 4, but here the German defenses were much stronger. The Germans had long expected an attack along the Minsk-Moscow highway and their defenses in this area were formidable. Thus on the northern axis, the 1st Baltic Front and 3rd Belorussian Front achieved some success on the first day, but no breakthroughs.

On the southern axis, Zakharov's 2nd Belorussian Front attacked with the 49th and 50th Armies, which succeeded in advancing a few kilometers through AOK 4's main defensive belt. Without authorization from Hitler or the OKH, von Tippelskirch began pulling his army back behind the Dnepr River in order to shorten his front.[94] Rokossovsky did not launch major attacks on June 23, but instead focused on mobility operations with his sappers (who were building numerous pontoon bridges), in anticipation of attacking the next day. In Germany, Busch was immediately informed by telephone about the offensive and managed to return to his headquarters in Minsk by afternoon. After conferring with Reinhardt, it was evident that the garrison in Vitebsk was in great danger and Busch requested reinforcements from the OKH – which were refused. From the OKH viewpoint, the Soviets had only achieved success against Reinhardt's PzAOK 3 and no large enemy armored formations had yet been identified – so tactical reserves might suffice to restore the front. If the offensive in Belorussia was a diversion – which the FHO believed – then shifting the LVI Panzerkorps back from Heeresgruppe Nordukraine might be exactly what the enemy was hoping to achieve. However, the "wait and see" approach also carried its own substantial risks.

On the second day of *Bagration*, Bagramyan's 1st Baltic Front achieved major success. After smashing Reinhardt's left flank, Bagramyan ordered Chistyakov's 6 GA to make a dash for the Western Dvina River (which was reached by midday), while a tank corps was sent west on the road to Polotsk. German situational awareness about these developments seems to have been poor, probably because units were being overrun or retreating without orders. Adding to Reinhardt's discomfiture, Beloborodov's 43rd Army severed the main line of communications into Vitebsk. When that occurred, Reinhardt requested permission from the OKH in the afternoon of June 24 to evacuate the four divisions of the LIII Armeekorps from Vitebsk – which was refused. Cherniakhovsky's 3rd Belorussian Front faced much stiffer resistance and only made slow progress against Reinhardt's right flank corps (VI) and the German defenses around Orsha. In particular, Galitsky's 11 GA was having difficulty getting through the enemy fortified lines, which were manned by some of the best units in AOK 4. Krylov's 5th Army was making the best progress, assisted by massive air support from the 1 VA. Elsewhere, Rokossovsky began his offensive in earnest on June 24 and achieved the most success on his left, with Luchinsky's 28th Army and Batov's 65th Army. Rokossovsky then committed the 1 GTC, which advanced 20km and threatened to envelop Bobruisk. The primary German operational reserve, the 20. Panzer-Division, was actually under

OKH control and Busch had to request permission to use it. The ensuing commitment of the 20. Panzer-Division by Jordan was badly fumbled and did nothing to mitigate any of the Soviet advances.

The third day of *Bagration*, June 25, proved critical for the outcome. Reinhardt's PzAOK 3 was rapidly disintegrating, with its left flank already broken and its right flank giving way. Vasilevsky directed Cherniakhovsky to shift Rotmistrov's 5 GTA into the breach created by Krylov's 5th Army, instead of waiting for Galitsky's 11 GA to achieve a breakthrough near Orsha. Consequently, Rotmistrov was forced to conduct a 60km road march with his army to shift to new attack positions, which consumed a significant amount of time and fuel.[95] When Rotmistrov's 5 GTA did attack, the German VI Armeekorps was quickly crushed and a 10km-wide gap was created.[96] At the same time, the 39th and 43rd Armies linked up, encircling the 30,000 troops of the LIII Armeekorps in Vitebsk. Belatedly, the OKH authorized the LIII Armeekorps to conduct a breakout attempt, but this effort on the night of June 26/27 failed.

By the morning of June 27, Vitebsk was liberated and four German divisions had been annihilated. Orsha was also liberated that day by Galitsky's 11 GA and Glagolev's 31st Army. With the connection between PzAOK 3 and AOK 4 severed and Soviet tanks pushing fast toward the Brezina River, von Tippelskirch began conducting unauthorized withdrawals to save as many of his troops as possible and simply did not report this to Busch or the OKH. Jordan's AOK 9 was also under heavy pressure, since Rokossovsky had four armies converging on Bobruisk while Pliev's KMG (1 GCC, 1 MC) was pushing west toward Slutsk. Thus, in the first five days of *Bagration*, the Soviet northern wing ripped apart PzAOK 3's front (Reinhardt was left with just two divisions) and had taken two important objectives. By the end of the day, it was obvious even to the OKH that the Red Army was mounting a serious offensive in Belorussia and Heeresgruppe Mitte needed immediate assistance. Model was ordered to transfer part of the LVI Panzerkorps (the 5. Panzer-Division and a Tiger tank battalion) back to Minsk by rail. Hitler ordered Lindemann's Heeresgruppe Nord to send the 12. Panzer-Division, an infantry division and two assault gun units to assist Busch, even though it was itself heavily engaged.[97] The Luftwaffe transferred a number of squadrons from France and Italy to reinforce Luftflotte 6, which had proved incapable of stemming the Soviet advance.

While this disaster was unfolding, Busch proved unable to do anything but continue to order his army commanders to stand fast, which was no longer possible. In desperation, Busch and Jordan (AOK 9) had flown to the *Wolfsschanze* on June 26 in a vain effort to request authorization for limited withdrawals. Not only did Hitler refuse, but he decided to relieve both Busch and Jordan of command.[98] The interesting thing about Busch was that despite his hyper-obsequious behavior in obeying orders, he was still relieved of command. Indeed, Busch's demise provides an enduring lesson in generalship during battlefield crisis, in that mindlessly obeying ill-judged orders tends to increase the impact of the crisis. Had Busch used his own professional judgment and ignored Hitler's no-retreat orders for even a day, he would still have been relieved, but at least salvaged something from his disintegrating army group. Instead, Busch chose the worst alternatives – in large part due to his lack of moral courage (noted by his subordinates), which completely sabotaged his ability to handle the crisis. Hitler decided to put Model in command of Heeresgruppe Mitte, but also allow him to retain command over Heeresgruppe Nordukraine.

Busch's orders to stand fast had already doomed both AOK 4 and AOK 9. While Busch was at *Wolfsschanze*, Rokossovsky's forces were closing in on Bobruisk from the east, south and west, but AOK 9 was not allowed to withdraw and its commander had just been relieved by Hitler. For once, the Red Army could use maneuver to outflank their opponents, while AOK 9 conducted a mindless static defense. Jordan did use his limited tactical reserves, including the 20. Panzer-Division, to try to slow the Soviet advance but rearguard skirmishing achieved very little. Over 50,000 German troops from two corps (XXXV Armeekorps and XXXXI Panzerkorps) were soon encircled in a large pocket around Bobruisk. Rokossovsky quickly moved to smash the pocket before the Germans could conduct a breakout operation and managed to split it into two pieces on June 27. The 12. Panzer-Division began arriving from Heeresgruppe Nord to assist a breakout, but Rokossovsky's 1st Belorussian Front used its artillery to reduce the pocket as his armies moved in for the kill. By June 28, the eastern pocket had surrendered and Soviet troops were already fighting their way into Bobruisk. The German forces west of the Berezina mounted a desperate breakout on the night of June 28/29, spearheaded by the remnants of the 20. Panzer-Division; this effort was a partial success that managed to save about 15,000 troops, but all German resistance around Bobruisk collapsed soon afterwards. The OKH sent General der Panzertruppe Nikolaus von Vormann to take command of AOK 9, but by the time he arrived only two divisions from the LV Armeekorps were still combat effective and the army headquarters had been bombed and its communications disrupted. Given the elimination of so much of AOK 9 at Bobruisk, the LV Armeekorps was soon transferred to Weiß' AOK 2, which left von Vormann without much to command.

Meanwhile, von Tippelskirch's AOK 4 continued to withdraw west toward the Berezina, pursued by three armies from Zakharov's 2nd Belorussian Front and two armies from Cherniakhovsky's 3rd Belorussian Front. Rotmistrov's 5 GTA advanced 75km and enveloped AOK 4 while pushing hard for Borisov. Von Tippelskirch could not sneak his entire army across the Berezina without being noticed by the OKH, so he decided to request permission from Heeresgruppe Mitte on the morning of June 27. The sarcastic tone of the request – "Army requests directive whether to fight its way west or let large elements be encircled" – guaranteed that it would be rejected.[99] Busch, still in command, ordered von Tippelskirch to hold his line on the Dnepr, anchored on Mogilev. However, Soviet troops were already across the Dnepr north of Mogilev and by that afternoon, Boldin's 50th Army was fighting its way into the city. Ignoring Busch, von Tippelskirch relocated his headquarters to Berezino on the Berezina River, where he intended to cross his army. On his last day in command, Busch finally authorized AOK 4 to withdraw behind the Berezina, but it was too late. The retreating German columns were repeatedly attacked by 4 VA air strikes, which inflicted enormous losses, including the elimination of two corps commanders (General der Infanterie Georg Pfeiffer and General der Artillie Robert Martinek).[100] Even before AOK 4 had begun to cross the Berezina, the Soviet spearheads were already closing around them. From the south, Pliev's KMG took Slutsk on June 29 and in the north, Rotmistrov's 5 GTA was approaching Borisov. Cherniakhovsky also sent the 2 GTC down the Smolensk-Minsk highway in pursuit. By June 30, the Soviets were across the Berezina River in several places and the remnants of AOK 4 and AOK 9 were falling back toward Minsk.

By the time that Model took command of Heeresgruppe Mitte, he had very little left to work with and the retreating fragments of the army group were too weak to hold anywhere. The Ostheer had never seen an avalanche like *Bagration* before and the rapidity with which its fixed defenses were rolled up. For most generals, taking command in the midst of such a disaster would have been a soul-crushing experience, but Model excelled in a crisis. While directing rear-echelon units to build a hedgehog defense in Minsk, he sent the 5. Panzer-Division and the Tiger tank battalion northeast of the city to delay Rotmistrov's 5 GTA. He sent part of the 12. Panzer-Division, arriving from Heeresgruppe Nord, to form a blocking force southeast of Minsk and link up with the survivors from the Bobruisk pocket. Cherniakhovsky ordered Rotmistrov to bypass the German blocking positions along the Minsk–Moscow highway and approach Minsk along secondary roads from the north, but the 5. Panzer-Division blocked this effort and fought a series of delaying actions which inflicted heavy losses on Rotmistrov's 5 GTA. Cherniakhovsky accused Rotmistrov of using faulty tactics and being too slow in his advance; the relationship between these two officers deteriorated.[101] Nevertheless, massive Soviet forces from the 3rd Belorussian Front and 1st Belorussian Front were converging on the city and Hitler finally agreed to authorize an evacuation. While 5. Panzer-Division was delaying Rotmistrov, a single Soviet tank corps (2 GTC) from Galitsky's 11 GA approached the city from the south along roads that were virtually undefended. On July 3, the 2 GTC fought its way into Minsk and German resistance quickly collapsed. Thereafter, the pincers of the 3rd Belorussian Front and 1st Belorussian Front closed around the disorganized remnants of the AOK 4 and AOK 9 that were still east of Minsk and slowly pounded them into submission. By July 8, the Minsk pocket had been completely crushed, with few German troops escaping. Heeresgruppe Mitte had suffered enormous losses in just two weeks, with roughly 300,000–350,000 troops dead, missing or captured out of an original force of more than 500,000 (over 60 percent losses).

Most of Heeresgruppe Mitte had been destroyed in just two weeks. The only relatively intact major formation left was Weiß' AOK 2 (which consisted of just a few low-quality infantry divisions and an assault gun brigade), which Model used to try to anchor a new line around Pinsk. The LV Armeekorps from AOK 9 had fallen back to Baranovichi and the IX Armeekorps from PzAOK 3 was near Molodechno, northwest of Minsk. The AOK 16 from Heeresgruppe Nord still held Polotsk, but there was a 170km-wide gap between the two army groups. West of Minsk, there was another 100km-wide gap, and the road to Vilnius and southern Lithuania was wide open. Heeresgruppe Mitte no longer had anything like a front line left, just pockets of resistance. Nor were there any mobile reserves left, since the two Panzer divisions (5, 12) employed in the fighting around Minsk escaped but lost most of their vehicles. The only way to quickly replace some of Heeresgruppe Mitte's losses was from the two neighboring army groups, but this was very dangerous because it further weakened these sectors as well. Nevertheless, Lindemann transferred several divisions from Narva and AOK 18 to help reinforce his open right flank. Hitler was not satisfied with defensive measures and ordered Lindemann to mount an offensive from Polotsk south with two infantry divisions to link up with the remnants of Reinhardt's PzAOK 3, which was a ridiculously unrealistic order. Both Lindemann and Model baulked at such foolishness, noting that AOK 16 could barely hold Polotsk, which was already under attack. Instead, on June 29 Lindemann requested "freedom of action" from the OKH in regard to dealing with the dangerous situation developing on his right flank – which was in effect requesting permission to evacuate Polotsk and fall back to more defensible lines. Hitler refused to abandon Polotsk or to cancel the counterattack, but to his credit, Lindemann canceled the counterattack on his own initiative and negated Polotsk's designation as a *Fester Platz* (fortress). Consequently, on the night of July 3/4, Hitler relieved Lindemann of command of Heeresgruppe Nord and replaced him with Generaloberst Johannes Frießner, who had distinguished himself as a corps commander at Narva.[102] Without authorization from Hitler, Model ordered the survivors of Heeresgruppe Mitte to fall back to the Polish border, although he couched this in terms of regrouping for local counterattacks.

The sudden collapse of Heeresgruppe Mitte enabled the Stavka to expand the objectives of Operation *Bagration*. Bagramyan's 1st Baltic Front boldly pushed west toward Polotsk with General-leytenant Pyotr F. Malyshev's 4th Shock Army and Chistiakov's 6 GA. Hansen's AOK 16 had two infantry divisions defending Polotsk, which was heavily fortified. Yet after four days of fighting, Malyshev's troops liberated Polotsk on July 4, and AOK 16 was forced to refuse its right flank as Chistiakov's 6 GA advanced past it to the northwest. Meanwhile, Cherniakhovsky's 3rd Belorussian Front headed west toward Vilnius against minimal opposition while Rokossovsky's 3rd Belorussian Front advanced from Slutsk toward Baranovichi. Pliev's KMG led the advance, supported by Luchinsky's 28th Army. On July 8, Pliev's group captured Baranovichi.

The rapid and decisive defeat of Heeresgruppe Mitte was the greatest catastrophe in German military history and, similarly, it was one of the greatest operational victories in Russian military history. In order to be effective, German operational-level defensive doctrine required: (a) steady front-line tactical defenses, (b) mobile reserves, (c) air support and (d) leaders capable of making timely decisions to anticipate or block enemy actions. Unlike previous German defensive successes, Heeresgruppe Mitte had none of these factors, which led to rapid defeat. Yet it is also important to note that the Red Army's operational capabilities had also changed and by June 1944 it was capable of conducting high-tempo maneuver warfare on the ground, augmented by an unprecedented level of air support. Soviet maneuver capabilities were significantly improved not only by more tanks and assault guns, but infantry units that could move faster due to the provision of Lend Lease motor transport and better communications. Even more important, the Red Army now had operational-level leaders who knew how to properly employ these capabilities and who were allowed greater flexibility in executing plans.

Due to Hitler's rigid insistence on a positional defense of Belorussia, the German operational-level leadership in Heeresgruppe Mitte turned in a very poor performance. Busch's execrable decision-making doomed his army group to defeat. As for the German army commanders, at least they understood that their real mission was to save as many of their troops as possible and that could only be accomplished by disobeying orders from Hitler and Busch. German commanders in the Ostheer had been selectively disobeying Hitler since December 1941, but the practice was becoming more widespread by mid-1944. Once the July 20 plot occurred, Hitler's trust in military leadership reached its nadir and willful disobedience by front-line commanders became more dangerous.

On the Soviet side, Operation *Bagration* was much less scripted than previous offensives and front and army-level commanders were afforded an opportunity to show more initiative. The offensive was also rare in that Soviet forces accomplished all their assigned objectives before supply shortages forced a premature culmination. Three of the front commanders conducted near-flawless operations and exceeded their operational objectives, while Zakharov's 2nd Belorussian Front lacked the resources to conduct the kind of free-wheeling operations that the other fronts could. Bagramyan and Rokossovsky both turned in stellar performances and they continued to aggressively develop the situation after the initial phase of *Bagration* had been accomplished. Cherniakhovsky did well in his first major front offensive, but it should be noted that Vasilevsky was constantly at his side, coaching him. Likewise, most of the Soviet army-level commanders performed quite well, particularly in terms of using mass and maneuver to overcome the enemy's fixed defenses. Rotmistrov's performance is more difficult to assess. While he accomplished his objectives (if not necessarily to the satisfaction of Vasilevsky), he suffered significant losses from a much smaller enemy blocking force and lost offensive momentum in the wooded terrain north of Minsk. While Rotmistrov had suffered mishaps in previous campaigns, such as Kursk, his army was still combat-effective after Minsk fell and he had inflicted heavy losses on the enemy. Yet Rotmistrov was at odds with his front commander, Cherniakhovsky, who was five years younger than he was, and it seems as though his actions were interpreted in a negative light.

Commander	Objective	Offensive	Mass	Maneuver	Surprise	Security	TALLY
Busch	–	o	o	–	o	–	-3
Reinhardt Jordan Tippelskirch Weiß	+	o	o	+	o	–	1
Bagramyan Cherniakhovsky Rokossovsky	+	+	+	+	+	o	5
Zakharov	+	+	+	o	o	o	3
Rotmistrov	+	+	+	+	o	–	3
Beloborodov Lyudnikov Chistiakov Krylov Galitsky Glagolev	+	+	+	+	o	o	4

Operation Bagration, *1944 Leadership Assessment*

The Baltic Gap, July 5–August 27, 1944

Frießner took over Heeresgruppe Nord the day that Polotsk fell. Although Heeresgruppe Nord still had a coherent front line – formed by AOK 16, AOK 18 and Armeeabteilung Narwa (formerly Gruppe Sponheimer) – its connection to Heeresgruppe Mitte had been severed. Aside from the open right flank, Heeresgruppe Nord's front was relatively quiet at the beginning of July, which had allowed Lindemann to transfer some divisions from the north and central parts of his front. In particular, the successful defense of Narva in March–April had exhausted both sides and the Leningrad Front had diverted significant resources to conduct the Vyborg operation against the Finns. While the Finns had taken a severe pounding and had fallen back in Karelia, they were still tying down over 400,000 Soviet troops. Reinhardt's PzAOK 3, effectively reduced to only a single infantry division, had been pushed back into Lithuania and was incapable of holding any ground. Nevertheless, Reinhardt orchestrated a series of successful delaying actions that bought time and preserved his very limited forces. He also managed to create more infantry by cannibalizing some of his army's superfluous support troops.

Due to the rapid collapse of Heeresgruppe Mitte, on July 4–5 the Stavka decided to continue the offensive of the two northern fronts (1st Baltic Front, 3rd Belorussian Front) to the west without any operational pause. While risky, this approach offered the potential to convert Operation *Bagration* into a strategic-level victory over the Ostheer. Cherniakhovsky's 3rd Belorussian Front was ordered to seize Vilnius, Kaunas and Suwalki, as well as crossings over the Nieman River. The 3rd Belorussian Front was expected to advance about 200 more kilometers to the west and reach the East Prussian border. At the same time, Bagramyan's 1st Baltic Front was ordered to seize Daugavpils (Dvinsk) and Siauliai, then pivot north to the Baltic Sea and cut off Heeresgruppe Nord, a distance of about 400 kilometers. In order to accomplish these tasks, Bagramyan received Kreiser's 51st Army and General-leytenant Porfiriy G. Chanchibadze's 2 GA, as reinforcements, but Cherniakhovsky had to make do with his existing forces. In order to assist the new offensive into the Baltic States, Eremenko's 2nd Belorussian Front and Maslennikov's 3rd Belorussian Front were ordered to attack to put additional pressure on Heeresgruppe Nord.

Model, Reinhardt and the OKH could clearly see that the Soviets were going to push into the large gap between AOK 16 and the remnants of PzAOK 3. Model recommended that Heeresgruppe Nord should pull back into Latvia in order to shorten its front, then transfer at least four infantry divisions to PzAOK 3 in order to give Reinhardt a chance to block the Soviet advance toward East Prussia and the Baltic. Hitler agreed to the transfer of three infantry divisions from Heeresgruppe Nord, but he would not accept large-scale withdrawals and he still wanted AOK 16 to mount an attack south to re-establish a connection with PzAOK 3.[103] These discussions went back and forth for a week and accomplished little, except demonstrating that German operational objectives were thoroughly muddled at this point.

The new Soviet offensive into the Baltic States got off to a slow start because many of Cherniakhovsky's formations were still involved in mopping-up operations around Minsk and Polotsk. Bagramyan needed time to reorganize his armies for an advance to the west. Consequently, the Germans were able to rush some reinforcements to Vilnius, which had been declared a *Fester Platz* (fortress). By the time that the lead elements of Rotmistrov's 5 GTA approached the outskirts of Vilnius on July 7, the Germans had about 12,000–15,000 troops under the command of Generalleutnant Rainer Stahel (Luftwaffe) in the city and more were arriving by air and rail. Complicating the situation, the Polish Home Army in Vilnius rose in rebellion when it appeared that the Germans were about to leave. Rotmistrov was reluctant to push into a defended urban area with just armored units, so he had to wait for Krylov's 5th Army to arrive – which caused further friction with Cherniakhovsky. In the interim, Rotmistrov used his tanks to encircle Vilnius and isolate the garrison. Krylov's troops began fighting their way into Vilnius on July 10, but German resistance under Stahel's direction was exceptionally fierce. Rotmistrov was ordered to commit some of his armor into city fighting, which proved costly.[104] Stahel was able to prolong resistance long enough that Reinhardt was able to organize a relief operation, using part of the 6. Panzer-Division and the *Großdeutschland* Panzergrenadier-Division. Amazingly, Reinhardt accompanied the German relief operation, which managed to open a tenuous corridor to the city just before Stahel's garrison was overwhelmed. At this point in the war, it was highly unusual for a German army commander to participate in a tactical operation, but Reinhardt's action probably helped to buck up morale among his hard-pressed troops. Although Krylov's 5th Army completed the liberation of Vilnius on July 13, somewhere between 3,000 and 5,000 members of the garrison (including Stahel) escaped.[105] Not only did Rotmistrov lose a brigade's worth of tanks fighting in the streets of Vilnius, but his 5 GTA required a pause in order to refit. Stahel's rearguard action at Vilnius had slowed the momentum of Cherniakhovsky's offensive.

Further south, Cherniakhovsky sent Galitsky's 11 GA and Glagolev's 31st Army to gain crossings over the Nieman River at Alytus and Grodno. The 11 GA captured Alytus on July 13 and gained a bridgehead over the Nieman. On the next day, the 31st Army reached the Nieman and gained a bridgehead near Grodno. Since Reinhardt no longer had a continuous front, Hitler's no-retreat orders were now meaningless and PzAOK 3 had the flexibility to conduct a mobile defense with whatever assets were available. Model also encouraged local counterattacks to slow the enemy avalanche marching toward East Prussia. The *SS-Totenkopf* Panzer-Division, transferred from the south via rail, arrived just in time to counterattack Glagolev's army. Reinhardt used *Kampfgruppen* from the 5. and 7. Panzer-Divisions to counterattack Galitsky's 11 GA at Alytus. While the German counterattacks did not eliminate the Soviet bridgeheads across the Nieman, they helped to buy time for additional German reinforcements to arrive. Indeed, the OKH was frantically transferring divisions from Italy, France and elsewhere to help restore Heeresgruppe Mitte. Yet despite the stand by the SS-*Totenkopf*, vanguard units from Glagolev's 31st Army reached the East Prussian border on July 18 before being halted by more German counterattacks.

Meanwhile, Eremenko's 2nd Baltic Front had been ordered by the Stavka to begin a major offensive against General der Infanterie Paul Laux's AOK 16 north of Polotsk on July 12. The plan was for the 2nd Baltic Front to attack with a northern group (Kazakov's 10 GA and General-leytenant V. A. Iushkevich's 3rd Shock Army) and a southern group (Korotkov's 22nd Army and Malyshev's 4 SA from 1st Baltic Front). The German defenses in the Opochka-Idritsa sector were part of the Panther-Stellung and were formidable, but AOK 16's main line had been weakened once Frießner began transferring divisions to support the open right flank. Reconnaissance units from the 2nd Belorussian Front detected some of these unit transfers and Eremenko suspected that AOK 16 might be preparing to conduct a withdrawal. Then a very strange thing occurred: Eremenko decided to attack early in order to achieve surprise and he made this decision independently, without informing the Stavka.[106] Since most Soviet offensives began in the morning, Eremenko also decided to launch his operation at dusk. At 1900 hours on July 10, the 2nd Baltic Front initiated a 30-minute artillery barrage, then attacked with the northern group of armies. The Germans were caught completely by surprise and their front-line defenses were quickly shattered. The next day, the southern group of armies joined the offensive, placing further stress on AOK 16. By July 12, Eremenko's 2nd Baltic Front had ripped an 80km-wide hole in AOK 16's front and Kazakov's 10 GA managed to advance 16km. Eremenko then committed his mobile reserve (5 TC) into the gap to exploit. Laux's AOK 16 was badly damaged and forced to fall back into central Latvia. By July 19, Eremenko had advanced over 100km and smashed Heeresgruppe Nord's right flank. On July 17, Maslennikov's 3rd Baltic Front also joined the offensive, with General-leytenant Nikanor D. Zakhvataev's 1 SA, Sviridov's 42nd Army and General-major Sergei V. Roginsky's 54th Army attacking General der Artillerie Herbert Loch's AOK 18 in the Ostrov-Pskov sector. Within three days, Zakhvataev's 1 SA managed to outflank the German defenses in Ostrov and AOK 18 evacuated the city the next day. At the same time Sviridov's 42nd Army captured Pskov on July 23. With most of Heeresgruppe Nord in retreat, the undefeated Arme-Abteilung Narwa was forced to evacuate Narva on July 25. On the same day, in a further round of musical chairs, Hitler had Frießner take command of Heeresgruppe Südukraine while Schörner took over Heeresgruppe Nord.

While Cherniakhovsky was advancing to the south and Eremenko to the north, Bagramyan's 1st Baltic Front offensive into the Baltic States had gotten off to a slow start due to a variety of battlefield frictions. The Stavka had ordered Bagramyan to transfer the 4th Shock Army to the 2nd Baltic Front and assigned him Kreiser's 51st Army and Chanchibadze's 2 GA from the RVGK to lead the next phase of his offensive, but both these formations were well to the rear. Likewise, the 1st Tank Corps, assigned to support 1st Baltic Front, was also still far back. Then Vasilevsky showed up and told Bagramyan that his priority was to support an advance southwest toward Kaunas, not west toward Daugavpils. Lyudnikov's 39th Army, just transferred from the 3rd Belorussian Front, was to support the push on Kaunas, while Chistiakov's 6 GA advanced to Daugavpils. Like Eremenko, Bagramyan decided on his own that he could not expect to split his front in order to pursue two operational objectives. After watching Chistiakov's 6 GA encountering stiff resistance from three German infantry divisions east of Daugavpils, Bagramyan decided that the direct path through Siauliai to Riga made more sense than pushing southwest toward Kaunas, which Cherniakhovsky's 3rd Belorussian Front could handle on its own. Unlike Eremenko, Bagramyan discussed this with Vasilevsky, who passed it up to Stalin. Eventually, the Stavka approved Bagramyan's recommendation to push along the Siauliai axis rather than on the Kaunas axis, and the 3 GMC was transferred to Bagramyan to spearhead his drive to the Baltic. It is evident from Bagramyan's memoirs that a considerable amount of muddle and indecision contributed to his delays; Chistiakov exaggerated the puny German attacks to try to link up with PzAOK 3 as a threat to his army, the Stavka held a different assessment of enemy intentions than Bagramyan and the supply situation seems to have been unusually chaotic.[107] When Kreiser's 51st Army and Chanchibadze's 2 GA reached the front, Bagramyan ordered them to bypass Daugavpils in the gap to the south and advance rapidly on the Siauliai axis, but the 3 GMC was not immediately available to support the advance. Reinhardt's PzAOK 3 was unable to stop this move and German opposition in Lithuania was sporadic, at best. Kreiser's 51st Army was able to advance 50 kilometers in two days and when the 3 GMC caught up, he was able to capture Siauliai by the night of July 27.[108] On the same day, Chistiakov finally captured Daugavpils, with help from Malyshev's 4th Shock Army (now part of Eremenko's front).

After taking Vilnius, Cherniakhovsky's 3rd Belorussian Front focused on the Kaunas axis, with Krylov's 5th Army in the lead followed by Rotmistrov's 5 GTA. By the end of July, Krylov was on the outskirts of Kaunas and once again, a hastily-deployed German garrison put up a tough fight for the city. Reinhardt had received a few infantry divisions from Heeresgruppe Nord and he judiciously placed them to hold key cities, which slowed the Soviet advance. When Rotmistrov's 5 GTA arrived, it was used in and around Kaunas, which further reduced its remaining combat power. Kaunas fell on August 1, then Krylov was ordered to push northwest to Raseiniai. Although Krylov occupied that place, Cherniakhovsky's spearhead was spent and he was forced to shift to the defense on August 10. Just before that, Rotmistrov was relieved of command and he was replaced by General-leytenant Vasily T. Volsky, a staff officer with limited command experience. Cherniakhovsky had clashed with Rotmistrov repeatedly and it came to a head during the Vilnius operation.[109] While Rotmistrov's handling of his tank army was sub-par at times, it should be noted that he was often ordered to attack into urban areas and marshy terrain that was unsuitable for armored operations. When he tried to bypass cities, Rotmistrov was criticized for not supporting the Soviet infantry armies. At any rate, his career as a tank army commander was over.

Once Siauliai was secure, Bagramyan ordered Kreiser to reorient toward the north and send his mobile group, the 3 GMC, north to the Baltic Sea to cut off Heeresgruppe Nord. On July 30, a mechanized brigade from the 3 GMC reached the town of Tukums, 60km west of Riga, and severed Heeresgruppe Nord's line of communications.[110] For the first time, the Red Army used maneuver operations to isolate an entire enemy army group, comprised of more than 600,000 troops. Without regular daily supply trains, Heeresgruppe Nord quickly found itself short of ammunition and fuel, although supply by sea through the port of Riga was possible. On July 31, the 3 GMC captured the city of Jelgava (Mitau), southwest of Riga, and created a major blocking position. Bagramyan ordered the bulk of Kreiser's 51st Army to occupy positions south of Riga, while Beloborodov's 43rd Army was also moved up in support, but the Soviet perimeter – particularly the western flank - was very thin. Heeresgruppe Nord still held Riga and Schörner was able to assemble a strike group from AOK 16 that attacked part of Beloborodov's 43rd Army on August 1. One Soviet rifle division was encircled and mauled, but Heeresgruppe Nord lacked the logistics to conduct anything more than local counterattacks. Despite the critical situation on so many other fronts, the OKH was able to assemble a fairly large Panzer force in Lithuania by mid-August to launch a serious counteroffensive. On August 15, Reinhardt moved up to take command of Heeresgruppe Mitte, while Raus was brought in to take over PzAOK 3. Model was sent to the Western Front to deal with the disaster unfolding in France.

Upon arrival, Raus was immediately handed the task of executing Unternehmen *Doppelkopf*, which had the twin objectives of re-establishing ground communications with Heeresgruppe Nord and eliminating the Soviet threat to Riga. Due to an infusion of reinforcements, PzAOK 3 was able to commit the XXXIX Panzerkorps and XXXX Panzerkorps, with a total of five Panzer divisions (4, 5, 7, 12, 14), one Panzer brigade and the *Großdeutschland* Panzergrenadier-Division; altogether about 280 AFVs, including many Panther heavy tanks. Raus did not like the fact that the operational plan had been developed by Oberst Otto Heikaemper (Chief of Staff) and Oberstleutnant Hans-Joachim Ludendorff (Ia, operations) from the PzAOK 3 staff without any input from himself. With some exaggeration, he complained in his memoirs that *Doppelkopf* lacked a true *Schwerpunkt* and instead spread its spearheads across a 100km front.[111] In fact, the bulk of the German armor was committed on just a 67km-wide frontage, with the XXXX Panzerkorps attacking Chanchibadze's 2 GA in the Siauliai sector and the XXXIX Panzerkorps attacking into the flank of Kreiser's 51st Army. Generalmajor Hyazinth Graf von Strachwitz led a special *Panzerkampfgruppe* that was assigned to smash through the 3 GMC at Tukkums and re-establish ground communications with Heeresgruppe Nord. Nevertheless, Raus had a point that the Ostheer's skill at planning offensive operations had seriously deteriorated over the past year and hasty improvisation was becoming more common. As a result, the principles of war were often given short shrift, particularly massing combat power to achieve a single objective. The counteroffensive began on August 16 and was assisted by naval gunfire support from the Kriegsmarine. *Doppelkopf* achieved partial success in that von Strachwitz did reopen a ground connection to Heeresgruppe Nord and that corridor was gradually widened.[112] However the bulk of the German Panzer forces committed to the operation only pushed back the Soviet forces 10–15km and Kreiser's 51st Army remained within 40km of Riga. Despite the evident threat to the narrow corridor, Hitler refused to consider evacuating Heeresgruppe Nord from Estonia, which further reduced the value of an operation which cost 15,000 German casualties and the loss of 80 AFVs. After 11 days of fighting, the German counteroffensive was terminated and a brief lull settled over the sector.[113]

When *Doppelkopf* began, the Stavka transferred the 5 GTA to Bagramyan's command, but the formation was in no condition to play much of a role in stopping the German counteroffensive. Had the 5 GTA been used on the Siauliai axis, as Bagramyan requested, the 1st Baltic Front might have achieved a tighter stranglehold around Heeresgruppe Nord instead of pursuing secondary objectives. The misuse of the 5 GTA was a mistake made by Vasilevsky and the Stavka, which tried to pursue too many objectives at once. Yet the Red Army's thrust into Lithuania was a major operational success that capitalized on the accomplishments of *Bagration* and left the Ostheer in a terrible position. Heeresgruppe Nord remained in semi-isolation, which would deprive the Wehrmacht of troops and material to defend East Prussia and Poland. The obvious course of action was to use the brief lull to evacuate Estonia and have Heeresgruppe Nord shift into East Prussia to reinforce the Reich's eastern defenses. However, Hitler was unwilling to abandon the Baltic States for arcane political reasons (he thought it would discourage the Finns, even though they were getting close to signing an armistice with the Soviets), which condemned Heeresgruppe Nord to a pointless demise.

Soviet operational art was on full display in the advance into the Baltic States: *maskirovka* was used to produce surprise, followed by relentless offensive maneuver actions to seize critical objectives and keep the enemy on the run. Although the offensive began to run out of steam as it approached Riga, the Soviet operational commanders did not allow themselves to get so overextended that they could be defeated in detail. In previous campaigns, a German counteroffensive on the scale of *Doppelkopf* would likely have wreaked significant damage on the Soviet vanguard armies, but in this case, the Red Army fought the Panzers to a standstill. Eremenko and Bagramyan planned and conducted superb operations that fully accomplished their objectives. Cherniakhovsky's operations were also successful, although he spread his armies out too much, trying to simultaneously accomplish multiple objectives. Bagramyan's 1st Baltic Front should have become the main effort after Siauliai was captured, but Vasilevsky allowed Cherniakhovsky's 3rd Belorussian Front to keep Rotmistrov's 5 GTA and keep pushing toward Kaunas and the East Prussian border, even though this was less imperative than isolating Heeresgruppe Nord. The Soviet army-level commanders in the operation performed well, particularly Kreiser (51st Army). Rotmistrov and Chistiakov under-performed. Part of the problem was that the Red Army still tended to waste too much time and effort reducing encircled city garrisons rather than simply bypassing them and assigning second-echelon forces to deal with them. In operational-level warfare, when dealing with enemy-occupied cities, attempting a *coup de main* is reasonable, but if that fails, reinforcing failure and accepting urban combat is done at the cost of losing offensive momentum. The Red Army had still not fully learned that lesson in July 1944. Another part of the problem is that a number of Soviet commanders were still rigidly following orders to advance along a given axis, irrespective of terrain restrictions or enemy resistance. The bolder, more experienced commanders, like Eremenko and Bagramyan, were adapting to a more flexible, freewheeling style and were willing to deviate from the plan if they could accomplish their objectives more quickly. Rotmistrov did as told and led his tanks into marshland, dense forests and urban areas rather than seek alternatives. Chistiakov put his head down and tried to brute force his way through the right flank of AOK 16, which he lacked the strength to accomplish on his own. Daugavpils eventually fell because Malyshev's 4th Shock Army bypassed the city, not because Chistiakov achieved a breakthrough. Veteran Soviet commanders looked for the enemy flanks, but others were still comfortable with a frontal attack mindset.

German generalship in the Baltics, as with Belorussia, was hindered by rigid no-retreat orders from Hitler. Lindemann, Frießner and Schörner had few options – they had to hold too much terrain with too few troops and minimal mobile reserves. After the loss of Polotsk, Heeresgruppe Nord had no good options except withdrawal and they were not allowed to do that. Reinhardt's situation with PzAOK 3 was somewhat easier – he had few troops but also was not tied to holding a fixed line. Reinhardt conducted a fairly effective rearguard campaign, delaying the enemy advance as much as possible until reinforcements arrived. Model also favored withdrawal but couched it in terms of regrouping for counterattacks. The Germans did not quite stop the Soviet advance into the Baltic States but contributed enough operational friction that the Red Army's inherently weak logistic system did the rest. Heeresgruppe Nord and PzAOK 3 avoided being decisively defeated before the Soviet offensive culminated, but only by a very narrow margin.

Commander	Objective	Offensive	Mass	Maneuver	Surprise	Security	TALLY
Lindemann Frießner Schörner	+	o	o	o	o	o	1
Model Reinhardt	+	+	o	+	o	o	3
Raus	+	+	+	o	o	o	3
Eremenko	+	+	+	+	+	o	5

Bagramyan Cherniakhovsky	+	+	+	+	o	o	4
Kreiser	+	+	+	+	o	o	4
Galitsky Glagolev	+	+	o	+	o	o	3
Rotmistrov	o	+	o	+	o	o	2
Chistiakov	+	+	o	o	o	o	2

Baltic Gap, 1944 Leadership Assessment

Lvov-Sandomierz, July 13–August 29, 1944

While Operation *Bagration* was smashing Heeresgruppe Mitte, Konev's 1st Ukrainian Front had been preparing to launch its own grand offensive against Heeresgruppe Nordukraine in Galicia. The 1st Ukrainian Front had replaced its losses from the spring campaigns and by early July it could employ three tank armies (1 GTA, 3 GTA, 4 TA) and five combined-arms armies, totaling roughly 1 million troops and 2,000 AFVs. In contrast, Heeresgruppe Nordukraine (now under the command of Generaloberst Josef Harpe), was stretched thin, with PzAOK 1 and PzAOK 4 defending a 330km-wide front from north of Kovel down to the Dniester River with 32 German divisions.[114] Amazingly, the Germans had been able to partly rebuild both armies and create a fairly stable front line, although the terrain did not particularly favor the defense. The area south of the Dniester, also under Harpe's command, was defended by the Hungarian 1st Army with eight Hungarian and three German divisions. While Konev enjoyed an overall numerical superiority of at least a 2-1 in manpower and armor and 3-1 in airpower, it was not an overwhelming superiority. The Ostheer was learning to adapt to the new Soviet operational methods and was still capable of making effective countermoves.

The Stavka had hoped to secure the key rail junction at Kovel prior to the summer offensives in Belorussia and Galicia, but this plan went awry in mid-March. At that time, the short-lived 2nd Belorussian Front under General-polkovnik Kurochkin had mounted a direct assault against Kovel with the 47th Army which managed to encircle the city. However, the PzAOK 4 was able to quickly assemble an effective strike group, spearheaded by part of the rebuilt SS-*Wiking* Division, which managed to lift the siege and restore the front line. Afterwards, PzAOK 4 reinforced the Kovel salient with the bulk of the LVI Panzerkorps.

Rokossovsky was assigned by Zhukov to support Konev's Lvov-Sandomierz operation when it began, using armies from his left flank. Yet when Model began pulling units from the Kovel sector to reinforce Heeresgruppe Mitte in a vain effort to hold Minsk, Rokossovsky decided to accelerate his own plans. In fact, Model had already decided to evacuate Kovel. On July 6, General-leytenant Nikolai I. Gusev's 47th Army attacked as the Germans were beginning to pull out of Kovel. By that evening, Gusev's troops had secured the city and were in pursuit of two retreating German infantry divisions. On July 7/8, Rokossovsky assigned the 11th Tank Corps (which was equipped with the new T-34/85 medium tanks) to Gusev to use as a mobile group and push on to the Bug River. However, Gusev's pursuit went awry when the 11 TC was ambushed by the SS-*Wiking Kampfgruppe* southwest of Kovel on the morning of July 8 and lost 84 of its tanks in four hours of fighting.[115] Gusev's advance was abruptly halted.

Konev's initial operational objective in the Lvov-Sandomierz campaign was to encircle and destroy enemy forces in Lvov, then advance to the Vistula River. The basic concept for the Lvov-Sandomierz operation was a double pincer attack, with three armies (1 GTA, 3 GTA, 13 Army) attacking north of Lvov toward Rava Russka and then swinging around behind the city, while three other armies (4 TA, 38, 60) attacked from the south. Two separate cavalry-mechanized groups (KMG) would assist in the pursuit and 5 GA was assigned as a second-echelon formation. In addition, the 3 GA would make a direct drive for the Vistula River, assisted by two of Rokossovsky's armies (69, 8 GA). Zhukov was supposed to coordinate the operations of the 1st Belorussian Front and 1st Ukrainian Front, but he was heavily committed to the other ongoing operations and left most details to Konev and Rokossovsky. Having provided Konev with three tank armies, the Stavka insisted that these formations would not be committed until the infantry armies had achieved significant breakthroughs. In addition to providing Konev with the Red Army's best ground combat formations, the Stavka ensured that the 2 VA would be able to deliver an unprecedented amount of air support for the Lvov-Sandomierz operation. The 2 VA was increased to over 3,200 aircraft, including 1,400 fighters, 1,000 Sturmoviks and 670 bombers.[116]

Unlike Operation *Bagration*, the Germans expected a major Soviet offensive in the Lvov sector, so Konev could only hope to deceive the enemy about the timing of his attack. According to Hermann Balck, commander of the XXXXVIII Panzerkorps in the Lvov sector, the Germans only knew that an offensive in Galicia was pending, but could not determine where or when.[117] According to von Mellenthin, Balck's chief of staff, "Wireless intercept and interrogation of prisoners produced most contradictory reports. At one moment attack was believed to be imminent, and at another it seemed improbable."[118] Although Model enforced a continuous front upon Heeresgruppe Nordukraine, after he left to take charge of Heeresgruppe Mitte Harpe allowed local commanders greater flexibility to thin out their front-line infantry in order to reduce casualties from enemy air and artillery bombardments. Raus, now commander of PzAOK 1, referred to this as "Zone Defense Tactics," with the emphasis on reducing front-line casualties.[119] Furthermore, Harpe had some significant tactical reserves, with two Panzer divisions assigned to support General der Panzertruppe Walther Nehring's PzAOK 4 and two more to support Raus' PzAOK 1. Altogether, these four Panzer divisions had over 200 operational tanks and 90 assault guns/tank destroyers, plus there was a separate Tiger tank battalion. The VIII Fliegerkorps was also expected to play a major role in stopping any Soviet offensive, since it still had about 930 combat aircraft (including 185 fighters, 358 ground attack and 388 bombers).[120]

On July 10, Luftwaffe aerial reconnaissance detected enemy attack preparations east of Sokal, so Nehring decided to thin out the front lines of the XXXXII Armeekorps on the night of July 12/13. The 1st Ukrainian Front noticed this German evacuation and Konev decided to move his offensive forward by 48 hours. On the morning of July 13, Gordov's 3 GA advanced without an artillery preparation and occupied a large stretch of the evacuated German security zone. At the same time Pukhov's 13th Army attacked the left flank of PzAOK 1 north of Brody, which was held by the XIII Armeekorps. Initially, the two northern attacking armies made only limited progress and struggled to fight their way through the German defense lines. Harpe held off on committing his reserves since the scale of the Soviet offensive was not yet certain. On July 14, the two northern Soviet armies continued chewing through the tactical defenses on the boundary of PzAOK 1 and PzAOK 4. Southeast of Lvov, Moskalenko's 38th Army and Kurochkin's 60th Army attacked the XXXXVIII Panzerkorps at 0820 hours, beginning with a one-hour artillery barrage. The Soviet ground attacks were preceded by massive air strikes by 2 VA, which pulverized the German 349. Infanterie-Division, enabling the 60th Army to achieve a small penetration in PzAOK 1's front line. On the evening of July 14, Harpe authorized Raus to commit the two Panzer divisions (1, 8) from Breith's III Panzerkorps to stop the Soviets from expanding their penetration. He also released two Panzer divisions (16, 17) to Nehring to use to seal any penetrations in his sector, as well.

Previously, the timely commitment of German Panzer reserves had usually brought Soviet offensives to a sudden halt, but not on this occasion. First, the Panzer divisions no longer had the offensive punch they had back in mid-1943. The strongest formation, the 16. Panzer-Division, had 85 tanks and 19 assault guns, but the 17. Panzer-Division only had 53 AFVs while the 8. Panzer-Division had 33 AFVs. While the Panther and Tiger tanks had exceptional firepower, they had poor mobility, which severely limited their ability to contribute to operational-level maneuver warfare. Heavy losses of veteran small-unit leaders had also begun to reduce the German advantage in tactical maneuver warfare, which meant that the Panzer units were becoming blunt instruments, rather than rapiers as German doctrine intended. In contrast, Soviet tank brigades equipped with the new T-34/85 medium tank had the mobility to outmaneuver the increasingly ponderous Panzer units. The Red Army also had plenty of veteran armor leaders now, who knew how to properly employ their units. Second, Soviet tactical aviation was now a factor to be reckoned with and Panzer divisions could no longer operate with impunity in daylight hours. When Breith's Panzers were committed, the 1. Panzer-Division managed to push Moskalenko's 38th Army back a bit, but the 8. Panzer-Division was caught in the open and pounded by relentless 2 VA air strikes. In a first for the VVS, General-major Ivan S. Polbin, commander of the 2nd Guards Bomber Aviation Corps, circled overhead in a Pe-2 fighter-bomber equipped as a command aircraft and coordinated air strikes against the Panzers via radio.[121] Von Mellenthin stated that the Soviet air strikes devastated the 8. Panzer-Division, noting that "long columns of tanks and lorries went up in flames and all hope of a counterattack disappeared."[122] Likewise, the German Panzer counterattack north of Lvov briefly held the Soviets, but ultimately could not restore the broken front. In the air, the VIII Fliegerkorps counterattacked and inflicted heavy losses on the 2 VA, but Luftwaffe losses were also heavy. In desperation, the Luftwaffe even committed its level bombers *en masse* to try to stop the Soviet advance. By the end of July 15, the battle of attrition was beginning to turn against the Germans and they had committed all available reserves, while Konev had not yet committed his mass of armor.

Kurochkin's 60th Army had created a small penetration on the right flank of the XIII Armeekorps sector near the village of Koltov, 27km south of Brody, but was stopped by the second German defensive line. The Stavka had ordered Konev not to commit his tank armies until he had achieved a clean breakthrough – in order to avoid costly mishaps like in the past – but after three days of heavy fighting, Konev decided to take a risk. On the morning of July 16, he committed Rybalko's 3 GTA into the narrow Koltov corridor, which was only 3 kilometers wide. It was also raining heavily, the corridor was in low-lying marshland that was flooded and German artillery was lobbing shells onto the narrow dirt road. Typically, a mobility corridor for a tank army should be at least 10km in width and could be up to 50km in open terrain, but a 3km-wide corridor along a single dirt road is likely to lead to a massive traffic jam. Rybalko cautiously pushed just two of his brigades up the muddy trail to support the 60th Army's attacks. In response, German infantry and artillery blocked the Koltov corridor, briefly isolating Rybalko's spearhead. What followed was not elegant, but Rybalko's 3 GTA fought desperately along the muddy trail to widen the corridor and by July 17, a breakthrough had been achieved.[123] Amazingly, right after the rest of Rybalko's 3 GTA went through the Koltov corridor, Konev sent all of Lelyushenko's 4 TA through as well. Struck by a mass of Soviet armor, the German XIII Armeekorps' front was broken. Raus ordered the XIII Armeekorps to evacuate Brody and withdraw to the west before it was outflanked and cut off.

The situation was even worse north of Brody, where Pukhov's 13th Army had made a 12km-wide gap in the XXXXVI Panzerkorps sector. On the morning of July 16, Konev committed General-leytenant Viktor K. Baranov's KMG (1 GCC, 25 TC) into the gap, which advanced rapidly toward Rava Russka. The next morning, Konev sent Katukov's 1 GTA after Baranov, easily brushing aside the 17. Panzer-Division. Katukov then advanced rapidly and seized a bridgehead across the Western Bug River 8km south of Sokal. By the end of July 18, Baranov's KMG had linked up with the vanguard of Rybalko's 3 GTA, completing the encirclement of about 50,000 German troops from the XIII Armeekorps in the so-called "Brody Pocket." Konev then ordered Kurochkin's 60th Army to focus on the annihilation of the Brody Pocket, which it accomplished in four days of heavy fighting. Raus ordered the XIII Armeekorps to abandon its equipment and attempt a breakout when collapse seemed imminent.[124] About 6,000 Germans managed to escape after the breakout attempt on the night of July 21/22, but 17,000 were captured and over 25,000 dead or missing. Another five divisions were removed from the Ostheer's dwindling order of battle.[125]

On the morning of July 18, Rokossovsky's 1st Belorussian Front resumed its offensive west of Kovel, beginning the so-called Lublin-Brest operation. Gusev's 47th Army and Chuikov's 8th Guards Army were the main effort, striking the left wing of PzAOK 4. In two days of heavy fighting, the two Soviet armies defeated the LVI Panzerkorps and advanced to seize crossings over the Western Bug River. Having achieved a breakthrough, Rokossovsky committed Bogdanov's 2 TA on July 21. Bogdanov was ordered to move west to seize Lublin, then pivot to the northwest and head for Warsaw – an advance of over 300km. On the morning of July 22, Bogdanov's 2 TA conducted a forward passage-of-lines through Chuikov's 8 GA and reached the outskirts of Lublin by the evening of July 23. Bogdanov hoped to seize the city by *coup de main* and tried to lead a spearhead unit into Lublin, but was badly wounded in an ambush. General-major Aleksei I. Radzievskiy, Bogdanov's chief of staff, took command of the 2 TA.[126] Radzievskiy was a 32-year-old General Staff-trained officer with no previous command experience and was now in command of a tank army assigned to conduct the deepest operation the Red Army had ever attempted. After some heavy fighting, Lublin was taken on July 24 and Radzievskiy was given 15 hours to plan the next phase of the advance along the Vistula to Warsaw. On July 25, the lead elements of 2 TA and Chuikov's 8 GA reached the Vistula River and two days later, Chuikov seized a bridgehead over the river at Magnuszew. Meanwhile, three of Rokossovsky's other armies (28, 61, 70) were also pushing Weiß' AOK 2 back toward Brest, which was captured on July 28. As a result of Rokossovsky's advance, the remnants of Heeresgruppe Mitte had no opportunity to form a new line in eastern Poland.

Having eliminated the Brody Pocket, Konev tried to move directly against Lvov, but Heeresgruppe Nordukraine was still capable of putting up a serious defense. Consequently, Konev decided to continue frontal attacks with the 38th and 60th Armies while sending Rybalko's 3 GTA and Lelyushenko's 4 TA to encircle the city. Raus requested permission to evacuate the city and fall back toward the Carpathian Mountains, which Hitler refused. However, Hitler finally relented on July 26 and PzAOK 1 immediately began evacuating Lvov. On July 27, Konev's forces surged forward, securing Lvov and pushing on to seize Przemysl, 90km further west. Raus refused his left flank and began a delaying action that traded space for time. Nehring's PzAOK 4 was also fighting a rearguard action, falling back toward the Vistula River. On July 25, the OKH sent the 17. Armee staff to assume command of the area between PzAOK 1 and PzAOK 4, west of the San River. General der Infanterie Friedrich Schulz was assigned to command the new AOK 17, which initially consisted of just the LIX Armeekorps (formerly part of the right flank of PzAOK 1). Nevertheless, Heeresgruppe Nordukraine had no time to establish a defense along the Vistula River because the Soviet armor was advancing so rapidly. Katukov's 1 GTA seized a bridgehead across the river at Sandomierz on July 29. Thus, both Rokossovsky and Konev were able to gain bridgeheads over the Vistula in the first phase of their offensives; the next phase was to exploit this success.

Harpe's Heeresgruppe Nordukraine fought a tenacious series of delaying operations but it was unable to stop the mass of Soviet armor and its four Panzer divisions lost over 180 tanks/AFVs and 3,100 personnel in less than two weeks. Luftwaffe losses in Galicia were also heavy in July, amounting to more than 300 aircraft. In a little over two weeks, Heeresgruppe Nordukraine had been badly defeated, losing about half its combat strength and being pushed back up to 200km. South of the Dniester River, the 1st Hungarian Army had also been defeated by a combination of attacks from Grechko's 1 GA and General-leytenant Yevgeny Zhuravlev's 18th Army. Despite the presence of a few German divisions south of the river, the Hungarian units were too lightly equipped to stand up to a full-scale assault, and they abandoned Stanislav on July 27 and fell back in disorder to the relative safety of the Carpathian Mountains. Raus shifted Hermann Balck's XXXXVIII Panzerkorps eastward to cover the Hungarian retreat and Balck managed to ambush and maul a pursuing Soviet rifle division at Dolyna, which helped stabilize the sector.[127]

The second phase of the twin operations (Lvov-Sandomierz and Lublin-Brest) began with Radzievskiy's 2 TA's rapid advance to the outskirts of Warsaw. On July 31, the vanguard reached the Praga district, on the eastern bank of the Vistula. Altogether, 2 TA still had about 500 operational tanks and assault guns, but it had limited infantry and artillery. At this point, Soviet operational intentions become murky due to political factors. Based upon the Stavka orders on July 27, it is clear that there was no intent to have 2 TA mount a direct attack into a major urban area on its own. Gusev's 47th Army was the closest support formation, but Rokossovsky was averse to a major city battle. The German garrison in Warsaw was large enough (16,000 troops) that it would take considerable effort to dislodge them. Instead, the intent seems to have been for the 2 TA to secure a bridgehead at Pultusk, north of Warsaw, which would have enabled a double envelopment of the city in conjunction with Chuikov's 8 GA from the Magnuszew bridgehead. Yet Soviet radio broadcasts made it sound like the Red Army was about to enter Warsaw at any moment and enjoined the Polish Home Army (AK) to rise up and take control of their capital. Consequently, the AK leadership decided to begin their armed uprising at 1700 hours on August 1. What neither the Stavka nor the AK knew was that the Germans had no intention of evacuating Warsaw and strong reinforcements were just beginning to arrive near the city. Generaloberst Kurt Zeitzler, chief of the OKH, had suffered a complete meltdown after the destruction of Heeresgruppe Mitte and resigned; Hitler decided to replace him with Generaloberst Heinz Guderian. Due to the failed July 20 Assasination Plot against Hitler, the OKH was in virtual freefall in late July, with numerous senior officers either being arrested, dismissed or committing suicide. Guderian himself was heavily involved in Hitler's purge of the OKH, which left him little time for directing operations on the Eastern Front. Nevertheless, Guderian and General der Panzertruppe Nikolaus von Vormann, commander of the rump AOK 9, quickly pulled together a plan to use the incoming reinforcements to launch a major counteroffensive against the 2 TA east of Warsaw.

By dawn on August 1, the Germans had assembled a small strike force east of the Vistula consisting of the XXXIX Panzerkorps (4., 19. Panzer-Division) and the IV SS–Panzerkorps (*Totenkopf, Wiking*), with the *Hermann Göring* (HG) Panzer-Division en route. Altogether, the Germans would have about 174 tanks and assault guns for the counterattack. However, the chain of command and operational planning were muddled; the XXXIX Panzerkorps reported to PzAOK 3 and the IV SS Panzerkorps reported to AOK 9. The initial attacks began on the morning of August 1 but resulted in little more than skirmishing. Eleven hours later, the Polish Home Army began the Warsaw rebellion and took control over part of the city, which meant that AOK 9 had to simultaneously deal with enemies both in front and in back. Once it became clear that the Germans were mounting a major Panzer counterattack east of Warsaw, Rokossovsky ordered Radzievskiy to shift to the defense and wait for Gusev's infantry to arrive. The German counteroffensive evolved awkwardly and did not really escalate until August 3. In two days of fighting, the five German Panzer divisions managed to maul one of Radzievskiy's tank corps and push it away from Warsaw, but that was it. Guderian called off the operation when it became evident that it could not achieve a significant victory. In military terms, the German counteroffensive at Warsaw was badly bungled and achieved very little. Yet Stalin was not disposed to assist the Polish Home Army and he used the German counteroffensive as an excuse to pull the 2 TA back from Warsaw. For over two weeks, Rokossovsky's forces sat immobile on the opposite side of the Vistula while the Germans methodically crushed the Warsaw rebellion.

Further German reinforcements continued to reach the Eastern Front in early August, including over 500 tanks and a dozen of the new *Volksgrenadier* (VG) divisions. In a remarkably short time, the Germans began to form a new line behind the Vistula. While much of their armor was used to conduct counterattacks near Riga and Warsaw, the OKH also decided to mount a major effort to eliminate the Magnuszew bridgehead held by Chuikov's 8 GA. Von Vormann's AOK 9 assigned the XXXXVI Panzerkorps to contain Chuikov, and the nearly full-strength 19. Panzer-Division and part of the *Hermann Göring* (HG) Panzer-Division to launch a counterattack on August 5. By August 8, the Germans had four divisions surrounding the Magnuszew bridgehead and heavy fighting was underway. For political reasons, the Stavka decided to commit the 1st Polish Army, formed from POWs and led by the traitor General-leytenant Zygmunt Berling, into the Magnuszew bridgehead in early August. Nehring's PzAOK 4 made a similar effort to reduce the Baranov-Sandomierz bridgeheads using its remaining armor. The OKH even sent a battalion of the new King Tiger heavy tanks to support the counterattack at Baranov on August 11, but it failed nonetheless. Konev soon had elements of four armies (Pukhov's 13th, Zhadov's 5 GA, Katukov's 1 GTA and Rybalko's 3 GTA) in the Sandomierz bridgehead and was able to greatly expand it, but he could not yet break through the German cordon. The bridgehead battles at Magnuszew and Sandomierz continued until the end of August, but devolved into costly battles of attrition. Nehring fell ill during the fighting at the Sandomierz bridgehead and Hermann Balck stepped up to command the PzAOK 4. When Raus was transferred to take over PzAOK 3 in Lithuania, Generaloberst Gotthard Heinrici took over PzAOK 1.

Although significant fighting continued along the Vistula for some time, the central front had once again become relatively static, while the northern and southern parts of the Eastern Front became more volatile. Part of the reason for this was political: Stalin wanted to accelerate military operations that would bring about the defection of Finland and Romania from the Axis cause. Nor did Stalin want the Red Army to seize Warsaw before the Polish Home Army was defeated, which was taking longer than expected. Another reason for the shift in priority was also logistics-driven, since both the 1st Belorussian Front and 1st Ukrainian Front had outrun their supplies lines and needed to replenish supplies before continuing large-scale operations. The Lvov-Sandomierz and Lublin-Brest operations were major successes for Konev and Rokossovsky. The Ostheer had not only been evicted from western Ukraine, but it had been driven back to the Vistula and the Red Army was now poised to continue the advance west into Germany. Altogether, Heeresgruppe Nordukraine had suffered about 144,000 casualties (including 74,000 dead or missing) in six weeks. Konev's 1st Ukrainian Front had accomplished all its operational objectives at a cost of 289,000 casualties (including 65,000 dead or missing), plus the loss of 1,269 tanks.[128] Although individual German units had fought tenaciously in rearguard actions and along the Vistula, it was now evident that the Ostheer was in an irrevocable state of decline.

The German commanders involved in trying to stop the Lvov-Sandomierz and Lublin-Brest operations conducted competent but ultimately unsuccessful operations because they lacked the flexibility or resources to accomplish their missions. Each German commander opted to use their limited mobile reserves to try to halt the enemy advances, but none achieved any significant success. If Harpe had massed all four Panzer divisions he might have been able to stop one of the Soviet tank armies, but then would have had nothing left to counter the others. Once the front was broken, Nehring and Raus managed to conduct rearguard operations and avoid losing any other major formations besides the encircled XIII Armeekorps. However, German commanders were running out of options and no longer able to conduct operations in accordance with their own doctrine.

The Red Army commanders involved in the twin offensives focused on conducting aggressive maneuver warfare to achieve clear objectives and achieved more than the original objectives assigned by the Stavka. The lack of serious interference or micromanagement from above enabled front and army-level commanders to conduct professional operations that came close to the idealized Deep Operations espoused by PU-36. In addition, the close integration of maneuver and fire support assets, particularly massed tactical aviation, indicated that the Red Army had reached a new level of operational competence. Likewise, C2 of complex maneuver operations involving multiple armies demonstrated vast improvement. The only area where the Red Army still struggled was in regard to operational logistics. Although the VVS was beginning to experiment with supplying armored spearheads via air delivery with ammunition and fuel as the Germans once had, Soviet offensives still tended to culminate after a few weeks due to supply shortages in the forward units. More than anything else, it was the Red Army's logistic problems which enabled the Germans to survive catastrophic defeats in Belorussia and Galicia.

Commander	Objective	Offensive	Mass	Maneuver	Surprise	Security	TALLY
Harpe	+	+	o	+	o	o	3
Raus Nehring Von Vormann	+	+	o	+	o	o	3
Konev Rokossovsky	+	+	+	+	o	o	4
Katukov Rybalko Lelyushenko Chuikov	+	+	+	+	o	o	4
Bogdanov Radzievskiy Gusev	+	+	+	+	o	–	3
Gordov Pukhov Moskalenko Kurochkin	+	+	+	o	o	o	3

Lvov-Sandomierz Operation, 1944 Leadership Assessment

The Balkans, July 20–October 29, 1944

On July 25, Generaloberst Johannes Frießner took over Heeresgruppe Südukraine, which was still defending Moldavia and northern Romania. Frießner took command over an organization that was an odd mixture of German and Romanian units, jumbled together. Altogether, Heeresgruppe Südukraine had about 800,000 troops in four armies (Frette-Pico's AOK 6, Wöhler's AOK 8 and the Romanian 3rd and 4th Armies), which totaled 46 divisions (21 of which were Romanian). The Romanians held about 40 percent of the 625km-wide front of Heeresgruppe Südukraine. Although the Axis troops had created a strong double line of defense between Jassy and the Black Sea, the army group was one-third weaker than it had been when it successfully repulsed the Soviet offensive in March and April due to unit transfers. Virtually all of the armored reserves had been sent to other fronts, leaving Frießner with just two depleted Panzer divisions (13, 20). In addition, Luftflotte 4 had suffered heavy losses from American air raids over Romania, which left Frießner with very little air support. Yet Frießner's most serious concern was the Romanian will to continue the war, which seemed to be rapidly ebbing. Most Romanians now expected Germany to lose the war and wanted to quit the Axis before the Red Army moved into central Romania. Schörner had warned him that the Romanians were no longer reliable and Frießner passed his own doubts on to the OKH, which were ignored.

On the Soviet side, the Stavka had been steadily replenishing Malinovsky's 2nd Ukrainian Front and Tolbukhin's 3rd Ukrainian Front in anticipation of mounting another offensive in Romania. Malinovsky had seven armies (27, 40, 52, 53, 4 GA, 7 GA, 6 TA) totaling 771,000 troops, while Tolbukhin had four armies (37, 46, 57, 5 Shock) with 523,000 troops. Malinovsky had Kravchenko's 6 TA as his primary mobile force, with about 350 tanks. The 2nd Ukrainian Front and 3rd Ukrainian Front would also enjoy substantial air support from the 5 VA and 17 VA, which had over 1,700 aircraft available. On July 15, just after the Lvov-Sandomierz operation had begun, the Stavka notified Malinovsky and Tolbukhin to begin planning a new offensive into Romania. The basic concept developed by the two front commanders and their staffs was a two-pronged offensive, with the 2nd Ukrainian Front making the main effort against the Romanian 4th Army in the Jassy sector, while the 3rd Ukrainian Front broke out of its bridgeheads over the Dniester and overwhelmed the Romanian 3rd Army. The Black Sea Fleet would support the operation with amphibious landings behind the Romanian 3rd Army. Ideally, the German AOK 6 would be encircled around Chisinau and AOK 8 pushed back into Hungary. The Stavka approved the plan on July 31 and Marshal Timoshenko (who had been cooling his heels in Moscow for over a year) was assigned to coordinate the two fronts.

Although Heeresgruppe Südukraine detected the Soviet build-up, there was little that could be done about it. Frießner knew that all available German reserves were committed to other sectors and that no substantial aid would be forthcoming. Frießner was in a difficult position, taking command just five days after the attempt on Hitler's life and Hitler had already criticized his failure to hold the line with Heeresgruppe Nord. He did try to request permission to conduct withdrawals to shorten his front line, but Hitler refused to authorize any voluntary surrender of terrain. Frießner's position was similar to Busch's predicament with Heeresgruppe Mitte in June. Left without any real options, Heeresgruppe Südukraine could only wait for the hammer to fall. On August 19, both Malinovsky's 2nd Ukrainian Front and Tolbukhin's 3rd Ukrainian Front began aggressive probing against the Axis forces in the sectors they intended to attack. The main Soviet offensive began the next morning, with a two-hour artillery barrage on a 25km front between Targu Frumos and Jassy, followed by ground attacks by Trofimenko's 27th Army, Shumilov's 7 GA and Koroteev's 52nd Army. Soviet air and artillery firepower was overwhelming and one Romanian front-line division was quickly crushed. Other Romanian troops put up little or no resistance.[129] Axis counterattacks were limited and feeble. By the afternoon of July 20, Koroteev's troops had already taken Jassy and the Axis troops were falling back to their secondary line of defense. Malinovsky decided to commit Kravchenko's 6 TA to put further pressure on the crumbling Axis defenses.[130] At the same time, Tolbukhin's 3rd Ukrainian Front began attacking the Romanian 3rd Army from the Chitcani bridgehead, using General-leytenant Ivan Shlemin's 46th Army to drive a wedge between AOK 6 and the Romanians. Sharokhin's 37th Army widened the breach. Then Tolbukhin committed two mechanized corps (4 GMC, 7 MC) against the crumbling Romanian 3rd Army.

Initially, Frießner did not appear to recognize the scale of the developing Soviet offensive and seemed to think that tactical reserves could restore the front. Fretter-Pico's AOK 6 was holding firm against General-leytenant Nikolai A. Gagen's 57th Army. However, as reports of Romanian units falling apart or retreating began to reach his headquarters, he became less certain. Marshal Ion Antonescu, the military dictator of Romania, urged an immediate withdrawal from Bessarabia and Moldavia, but the German chain of command assured them that help was on the way and that the best policy was to dig in and hold on until the Soviet offensive ran out of steam. Yet by the second day of the Soviet offensive, Romanian units were collapsing in both sectors and even German divisions were beginning to retreat without orders. By the time that Hitler grudgingly agreed to a limited withdrawal, Tolbukhin's mechanized units were already advancing rapidly to the south. At the same time, Timoshenko urged Malinovsky and Tolbukhin to punch through the remaining Romanian forces in their sector and then advance to encircle Fretter-Pico's AOK 6. Cooperation between German and Romanian staffs virtually ceased, as both sides only focused on their own narrow interests. Even worse, the Romanian king and some of his generals were planning a coup to depose Antonescu and then switch sides. German situational awareness about both battlefield conditions and the changing political landscape was poor, which made operational decision-making increasingly faulty.

By August 22, Antonescu ordered the Romanian armies to begin falling back whether or not the Germans approved. Frießner tried to reverse these decisions, but events were rapidly spinning beyond his power to control. The next day, Antonescu was overthrown by the coup in Bucharest and the retreating Romanian armies fell apart. Shortly after this the new Romanian regime broke off diplomatic relations with Germany and ordered all Wehrmacht forces to leave the country. By evening on August 23, Frießner learned that Romania had left the Axis and his lines of communication were effectively severed. During the night, the Luftwaffe tried to organize an *ad hoc* operation to suppress the coup and Hitler ordered air strikes against the capital on the morning of August 24. The Germans made a clumsy effort to try to secure Bucharest by force, which quickly failed. At the front, Romanian resistance evaporated and Soviet mechanized spearheads raced toward the virtually unguarded Prut River and the "Focsani Gap." Fretter-Pico made a desperate effort to disengage his AOK 6, but his army had limited mobility and Soviet armor moved too quickly. By the time that AOK 6 reached the Prut River crossings, Soviet tanks were already there; the spearheads from Malinovsky's and Tolbukhin's fronts had closed around them. Virtually all of AOK 6, ten divisions, was surrounded in the woods south of Kishinev. In one of the weird quirks of fate in the Second World War, the 6. Armee once again found itself surrounded because the Romanian armies on both of its flanks suddenly collapsed.

On August 25, Romania declared war on Germany and the Wehrmacht garrison at Ploesti was surrounded. Once Fretter-Pico's AOK 6 was isolated southeast of Jassy, Trofimenko's 27th Army headed for Ploesti and Kravchenko's 6 TA advanced toward Bucharest. By August 29, Soviet forces had reached both objectives. The remnants of Fretter-Pico's encircled army continued to resist around Kishinev and they received a lucky break when General-leytenant Ivan V. Galanin's 4 GA failed to cover a gap in the perimeter along the Prut River. A German breakout attempt on August 28 succeeded in forcing a passage for thousands of troops through the gap before Galanin realized his mistake. It is unclear how many troops from AOK 6 escaped the Kishinev pocket; the Soviets later admitted 25,000, but the actual number was probably higher. Fretter-Pico was one of those who did escape.[131] In any case, the rest of AOK 6 remained trapped and finally surrendered on September 5. Altogether, the 6. Armee lost 158,000 dead or missing. The Ostheer lost another ten German infantry divisions destroyed and six more crippled.

Once Romania defected, Heeresgruppe Südukraine's position became untenable. Wöhler's AOK 8, reduced to just four German divisions, was the only significant formation to survive the catastrophe and it did so by immediately retreating into the Carpathian Mountains in eastern Hungary. Some of AOK 6's rear-echelon units avoided encirclement and escaped into Hungary with about 5,000 motor vehicles.[132] Frießner was assigned the Hungarian 2nd Army to supplement Wöhler's diminutive army. Frießner was concerned about the mountain passes leading into Transylvania, so he decided to mount a local attack on September 5–8 to seize this key terrain before Soviet troops arrived, but the effort failed. Nevertheless, Frießner gained a brief reprieve as Soviet armies poured into the Balkans, forcing Bulgaria to defect as well. The loss of the Ploesti oilfields was a major strategic defeat for the Wehrmacht, since fuel shortages would soon seriously impair German operational mobility and air support. Soviet losses in the Jassy-Kishinev operation were remarkably light, totaling 67,000 (with only 13,000 dead or missing) casualties, 75 tanks and 111 aircraft.[133]

After the defection of Romania and Bulgaria, Heeresgruppe E in Greece was obliged to begin evacuating the region and retreat north to Serbia. Von Weichs' Heeresgruppe F, headquartered in Belgrade, was responsible for the defense of Yugoslavia. In theory, von Weichs had over 300,000 troops under his command, but they were highly dispersed and most were second- or third-rate units, totaling just 15 German divisions plus a potpourri of Croatian, Bosnian and other SS auxiliaries. Although von Weichs had very little armor or artillery, he did have a few first-rate mountain divisions, which were well-suited for operations in the Balkan region. Yet virtually all the units in Heeresgruppe F, concentrated in the 2. Panzerarmee, were optimized for counterinsurgency missions, not conventional defense. The remnants of Heeresgruppe Südukraine were responsible for the defense of Hungary; over the next month, the army group was redesignated as Heeresgruppe Mitte. The German forces in the Balkans spent most of September retreating and regrouping, trying to assemble sufficient mass to defend key points like Belgrade.

On the Soviet side, the Stavka ordered Tolbukhin's 3rd Ukrainian Front to push into Serbia and head for Belgrade. Two Bulgarian armies would assist in the operation. Tolbukhin was also ordered to link up with Tito's partisan army (the National Liberation Army) and cooperate in the liberation of Yugoslavia; joint operations with non-Soviet forces was one area that Red Army doctrine had ignored and the Belgrade campaign would be a novel experiment. Due to overstretched supply lines, the Belgrade operation would be conducted with limited forces, consisting of less than half of Tolbukhin's 2nd Ukrainian Front. The primary maneuver elements would be Gagen's 57th Army and the 4 GMC, supplemented by Yugoslav and Bulgarian forces. Malinovsky's 3rd Ukrainian Front was ordered to advance into Hungary with its entire strength with the ultimate objective of taking Budapest. The Stavka decided to recreate the 4th Ukrainian Front under Petrov to conduct operations in the Carpathian Mountains. Although the Soviet forces had strong numerical superiority and even better equipment in most cases, the distances involved were significant and the transportation networks in the region were inadequate to support large-scale mobile operations. The mountainous terrain and numerous rivers also favored the defense. Nevertheless, the Stavka initiated a series of follow-on operations in the Balkans, hoping to conquer as much territory as possible while the Axis were disorganized and before the Western Allies arrived in the region (Britain was already beginning a small-scale military intervention in Greece in mid-September).

As German military power ebbed in the Balkans, local forces moved quickly into the vacuum. Tito had about 400,000 partisans in Yugoslavia, of which about 100,000 could support Tolbukhin's forces. Meanwhile, in Slovakia, local forces began a national uprising on August 29 and quickly secured a large portion of the country. Somehow, the Germans managed to scrape up enough security troops to invade Slovakia in September and begin a protracted counterinsurgency campaign. Unlike the situation with the Polish Home Army in Warsaw, the Stavka decided to help the Slovak uprising. On September 8, the Red Army began the East Carpathian operation; Konev's 1st Ukrainian Front contributed Moskalenko's 38th Army and Baranov's KMG (1 GCC, 25 TC), while Petrov's 4th Ukrainian Front committed Grechko's 1 GA and Zhuravlev's 18th Army. The PzAOK 1, now under Generaloberst Gotthard Heinrici, was defending the Carpathian sector with a handful of German and Hungarian infantry divisions but benefited from the fortifications of the "Arpad Line." Typically the Ostheer had to rely upon improvised field fortifications, but the Hungarian Army had been building the "Arpad Line" for several years and by late 1944 it had hundreds of concrete bunkers, underground structures and antitank obstacles. In addition, the "Arpad Line" was established on mountainous terrain that heavily favored the defense.

Moskalenko's 38th Army was assigned to reach the Dukla Pass, about 30km from its start line. Moskalenko was able to seize the town of Krosno and push back the German XVII Armeekorps, but only advanced 15km in a week. To the southeast, Grechko's 1 GA made even less progress. Heinrici was provided just enough reinforcements to maintain a front line and get in an occasional counterattack. On September 15, the two Soviet fronts escalated their attacks and overran a larger area, but progress was still fairly slow even though Konev provided additional forces. The main fighting began at the heavily fortified Dukla Pass in late September. Eventually, Moskalenko's 38th Army was able to secure the pass by October 6; however, the rainy season was beginning and the Germans had crushed the Slovak Uprising, so the Red Army failed to achieve its operational objectives. Unlike the decisive Jassy-Kishinev operation, the East Carpathian offensive was indecisive and costly, with Soviet casualties amounting to 126,000 (including 26,000 dead or missing), plus 478 tanks/AFVs lost. Without the rationale of linking up with the Slovak rebels, the Stavka decided to terminate this fruitless operation and concentrate on more productive endeavors.

It took several weeks for Tolbukhin to reorganize his forces in Romania and prepare for the offensive into Serbia. On September 28, Gagen's 57th Army crossed the Danube River south of Turnu Severin and easily defeated von Weichs' small screening forces. Tolbukhin's advance, led by the 4 GMC, covered 200km in the next two weeks, brushing aside sporadic resistance. At the same time, Tito's partisan army approached Belgrade from the southwest. Gagen's army reached the outskirts of Belgrade on October 4 but was not in a position to mount an immediate assault into a major urban area. While this was occurring, Heeresgruppe F was still in the process of withdrawing from Greece through Macedonia and Albania. Oddly, the Stavka gave the primary responsibility of cutting off Heeresgruppe E's escape to the Romanian and Bulgarian armies, which failed. While Tolbukhin was taking Belgrade, Malinovsky's 2nd Ukrainian Front began advancing into southern Hungary but encountered stiff resistance and was forced to pause its offensive. Von Weichs lacked the forces to mount a prolonged defense of Belgrade and he was forced to evacuate the city on October 19. After that, the Stavka redirected Tolbukhin to assist Malinovsky in Hungary, rather than finish off either Heeresgruppe E or Heeresgruppe F. Consequently, von Weichs was able to re-form a new line in central Bosnia for the winter. The Belgrade operation was another cheap victory for the Red Army and cost fewer than 20,000 casualties.

Frießner met with Hitler at the *Wolfsschanze* on September 12 to discuss the situation in Hungary. Hitler promised reinforcements (as usual) but demanded that Frießner use them in a counterattack against Kravchenko's 6 TA (which became 6 GTA on September 12).[134] Hitler also expressed his concern that Hungary might attempt to defect as well. Thus Frießner, who was merely seeking reinforcements to create a viable defensive line, was instead directed to counterattack a numerically-superior foe while keeping any reserves he might gather focused on rear-area threats. By October 5, Frießner's Heeresgruppe Mitte had established a new front line, roughly 450km in width, from Mohacs to the Dukla Pass. The 3rd Hungarian Army held the right flank anchored at Arad, Fretter-Pico's reformed AOK 6 and Wöhler's AOK 8 held the center, then the newly-formed Hungarian 1st Army with Heinrici's PzAOK 1 was on the left flank.

Altogether, Frießner had a mixed force of 15 German and Hungarian divisions holding the center of his front, although he had weighted his defense in the Debrecen sector. Frießner gave Fretter-Pico virtually all of the available armored reinforcements, which were concentrated in General der Panzertruppe Dietrich von Saucken's III Panzerkorps (1. and 23. Panzer-Division, with 109 tanks and 25 assault guns).

On October 6, Malinovsky's 2nd Ukrainian Front resumed its offensive into southern Hungary, spearheaded by Pliev's KMG (4 GCC, 6 GCC, 7 MC), Gorshkov's KMG (5 GCC, 23 TC) and Kravchenko's 6 GTA (9 GMC, 5 GTC). Soviet armored strength was much reduced at this point – mostly due to mechanical defects rather than combat losses – and Malinovsky's primary mobile formations could only muster a total of about 600 tanks and 200 assault guns at the start of the offensive. The Stavka developed the operational plan – not Malinovsky's staff – and it called for three major lines of advance. On the left, Shlemin's 46th Army, Managarov's 53rd Army and Pliev's KMG would advance from Arad to Budapest, a distance of 225km. In the center, Kravchenko's 6 TA would advance from Oradea to Debrecen. On the right, Trofimenko's 27th Army, Gorshkov's KMG and a Romanian army would advance from Cluj to Debrecen. By spreading out its forces across multiple sectors, the Soviet plan paid little heed to the principles of objective and mass, but this kind of insouciance can occur when armies feel like they are on a roll. When the offensive began, Managarov's 53rd Army and Pliev's KMG easily punched through the Hungarian 3rd Army in the Arad sector and achieved a major breakthrough. However, Kravchenko's 6 GTA encountered unexpectedly stiff resistance from von Saucken's III Panzerkorps near Oradea. Malinovsky decided to switch Pliev's KMG to assist Kravchenko and together they were able to push on toward Debrecen. Von Saucken's III Panzerkorps, threatened from two directions, pulled back.

By the time that Pliev's KMG and Kravchenko's tankers reached the outskirts of Debrecen, the III Panzerkorps was concentrated in the vicinity and more German reinforcements were on the way. A major armored meeting engagement developed around Debrecen on October 11–12 and both sides suffered heavy losses. At the same time, Wöhler's AOK 8 mounted a determined defense of Nyiregyhaza, 48km north of Debrecen. Yet while Malinovsky was briefly stalled in the center, Petrov's 4th Ukrainian Front was pushing back Frießner's left flank and AOK 8 was threatened with envelopment. On Frießner's right flank, the Hungarian 3rd Army collapsed, enabling Managarov's 53rd Army to advance 80km in three days. Having failed to take Debrecen on the first attempt, Malinovsky decided to briefly pause, regroup and try again. On October 19, Pliev's KMG resumed its advance and after heavy fighting, occupied Debrecen. Malinovsky then ordered Pliev and Kravchenko to continue north to Nyiregyhaza. Ideally, a large part of Wöhler's AOK 8 would be caught between the jaws of Kravchenko's 6 TA and Grechko's 1 GA, approaching from the north. Further adding to German difficulties, the Hungarian leadership attempted to implement an armistice with the Soviets on October 15, but this effort was suppressed by a German countercoup in Budapest; the event added further uncertainty about the reliability of the remaining Hungarian units embedded in AOK 6 and AOK 8.

Although Wöhler urgently wanted to retreat, Frießner and his staff had developed a plan for a counteroffensive, dubbed Unternehmen *Zigeuner Baron* (Operation *Gypsy Baron*). Pliev's KMG had created a vulnerable salient and Fretter-Pico was ordered to attack into its left flank with the III Panzerkorps. If possible, AOK 8 would attack into Pliev's right flank with some mountain divisions. Four mechanized divisions and several infantry divisions would be committed to the operation. Compared to previous German operational-level counteroffensives, *Zigeuner Baron* was rather unimaginative. The counteroffensive began on October 23 and by the next day, Pliev's KMG was isolated. Heavy fighting continued for five days, but the Germans lacked the strength to crush Pliev's encircled command; instead, they had to settle for mauling it. Furthermore, Wöhler's AOK 8 was still in a very difficult position and only narrowly escaped encirclement itself. After *Zigeuner Baron*, Wöhler abandoned Nyiregyhaza and retreated behind the Bodrog River, while Fretter-Pico formed an adjoining line behind the Tisza River. By October 29, Malinovsky had succeeded in occupying a large chunk of southern Hungary, despite unexpectedly tenacious enemy resistance. German propaganda claimed that Pliev's KMG had been destroyed – which was not true – but striking back at the enemy did help to bolster front-line morale. Malinovsky did lose about 300 tanks/AFVs in the fighting in October and Kravchenko's 6 GTA had to be pulled out of the line to refit.[135] The German counteroffensive actually achieved little beyond a slight delay in Soviet plans. The Stavka ordered Malinovsky to resume his offensive and seize Budapest as soon as possible, with the forces he had available.

In just three months, Malinovsky's 2nd Ukrainian Front and Tolbukhin's 3rd Ukrainian Front (with some help from 1st Ukrainian Front and 4th Ukrainian Front) had conducted four back-to-back operations which knocked two Axis countries out of the war, destroyed one German field army, liberated an allied capital (Belgrade) and severed the Wehrmacht's primary source of crude oil. At a cost of about 250,000 casualties, the Red Army had advanced over 600km in three months, which was one of its most spectacular successes of the war. During the Balkan campaigns, the Red Army was also forced to operate in a manner that had not been foreseen by pre-war doctrine, particularly in terms of operating with non-Soviet allies and operating in mountainous terrain. The Red Army also had to deal with a plethora of administrative/political details in terms of establishing lines of communication over infrastructure they did not fully control and negotiating with local partisan units. Nevertheless, the Red Army proved highly adaptable and was able to achieve most of its operational objectives. Logistics continued to handicap Soviet operations, despite the increased availability of motor transport provided by Lend Lease. German operations in the Balkans were badly handicapped by unrealistic no-retreat orders issued by Hitler and the volatile loyalty of the local Axis armies. The sudden defection of Romania was a catastrophe for Heeresgruppe Südukraine and opened the floodgates to Soviet invasion. German armies were forced to conduct lengthy retreats over mountainous terrain, with pursuing enemies on one side and uncertain political situations in their rear areas. In spite of these huge difficulties, the German units were able to keep re-forming new lines and occasionally strike back while maintaining their fighting spirit.

In terms of battlefield command, Malinovsky and Tolbukhin both planned and conducted professional operations that allowed them to achieve most of their campaign objectives. Malinovsky tended to rely more upon mass, whereas Tolbukhin was better at using surprise to gain an advantage. Kravchenko's performance as commander of the 6 TA/6 GTA was mediocre at best and he was openly criticized by Stalin and other senior leaders. Nevertheless, he would retain command of the 6 GTA until the end of the war. Most of the Soviet field army commanders in the Balkan campaign also conducted sound operations, relying heavily upon offensive and mass to reach their objectives. Galanin, as commander of the 4 GA, seriously failed in allowing part of AOK 6 to escape, but he was not removed from command for another three months. As final victory became closer, the Red Army (and the Communist Party leadership) was becoming more tolerant of battlefield mistakes, with fewer commanders being relieved – which in itself increased the willingness of leaders to take more chances than they had in 1941–42. By late 1944, Red Army commanders were demonstrating greater flexibility and initiative, which heretofore had been a distinct advantage for German commanders. The German commanders in the Balkans had very limited options. Frießner failed to conduct a professional campaign and instead merely reacted to enemy initiatives; his primary objective seems to have been merely to follow orders from the OKH. Fretter-Pico deserves credit for being dealt an extremely bad hand but still managing to keep returning to fight again another day. Von Weichs, Wöhler and Fretter-Pico intuitively understood that they had to trade space for time and that their primary objective was to salvage as many of their troops as possible – in this, they were generally successful. Yet it is significant that when adequate reinforcements became available to conduct one large-scale counteroffensive against Malinovsky's spearhead units, the operation was not based upon using maneuver to gain an advantage over the enemy.

Commander	Objective	Offensive	Mass	Maneuver	Surprise	Security	TALLY
Frießner	o	o	o	o	o	–	–1
Fretter-Pico Wöhler Weichs	+	o	o	o	o	o	1
Malinovsky	+	+	+	+	o	o	4
Tolbukhin	+	+	o	+	+	o	4
Kravchenko	+	+	o	+	o	–	2
Trofimenko Shumilov Koroteev Gagen Grechko Moskalenko Managaro Berzarin	+	+	+	o	o	o	3
Galanin	+	+	+	o	o	–	2

Balkan Campaigns, 1944 Leadership Assessment

Baltic/Courland, September 14–December 31, 1944

Schörner's Heeresgruppe Nord retained a precarious position in the Baltic States at the start of September 1944. Hitler refused to evacuate Estonia because he regarded control of this region as necessary to convince Finland to remain in the war, but Finland was already seeking an exit by this point. For two months, Govorov's Leningrad Front and Meretskov's Karelian Front had been conducting a major offensive against the Finns, which devolved into a costly battle of attrition that the Finns could not win. By September 4, the Finns agreed to a ceasefire and negotiations were underway for an armistice. With Finland out of the way, the Stavka turned to complete the destruction of Heeresgruppe Nord and occupying the remainder of the Baltic States. At the start of September, Hitler decided to replace the commanders of the two main field armies in Heeresgruppe Nord: General der Infanterie Carl Hilpert took over AOK 16 and General der Infanterie Ehrenfried Boege took over AOK 18.

Heeresgruppe Nord had created strong defenses in all the critical sectors, particularly around Riga, but the Stavka was able to coordinate a multifront offensive involving about 900,000 troops, which began on September 14. The operational concept behind the Baltic offensive was for Bagramyan's 1st Baltic Front to begin by driving on Riga and isolating AOK 18 and the German forces in Estonia. In order to complete this task, Bagramyan was given almost half the available armor. Bagramyan attacked first, behind a massive artillery barrage, with Beloborodov's 43rd Army trying to breach the German defenses south of Riga; these attacks made some progress, but German resistance was tenacious.[136] Simultaneously, Eremenko's 2nd Baltic Front attacked east of Riga with two armies (22, 3 SA) while Maslennikov's 3 PF attacked into southern Estonia with the 1st Shock Army. At first, the German defenses held, in part because the terrain favored the defense and in part because the Soviets were forced to mount frontal attacks into well-prepared defenses. Boege's AOK 18 put up a particularly strong defense against Eremenko's three armies and even managed a partly successful local counterattack with the 14. Panzer-Division. Schörner used all his operational reserves to check Bagramyan's advance on Riga, but it was not enough.

The OKH decided to place Raus' PzAOK 3 – which was not under serious attack itself – temporarily under Schörner's command.[137] Raus had been carefully husbanding his armor in von Saucken's XXXIX Panzerkorps, and Schörner seized this mobile reserve to conduct a counteroffensive into Bagramyan's left flank, using five mechanized divisions (4, 5, 7, 12 Panzer, *Großdeutschland*). The counteroffensive, designated Unternehmen *Cäsar* (Operation *Caesar*), began on September 16. Despite massing nearly 400 AFVs in one sector, southwest of Jelgava (Mitau), Raus was only able to gain a few kilometers and inflicted only limited losses (the Germans claimed the destruction of about 90 enemy AFVs but lost 145 of their own) on Bagramyan's forces. After two days, *Cäsar* was terminated.[138] Having committed his operational reserves and failed to halt the enemy's progress, Schörner requested permission to evacuate Estonia before Boege's AOK 18 gave way. He even took the bold step of flying to the *Wolfsschanze* to put the request directly to Hitler; very grudgingly, Hitler acquiesced to a withdrawal, sort of, if it could be delayed by a few days. The evacuation of Estonia was designated Unternehmen *Aster*. As usual in a crisis, Hitler hoped for some kind of miracle to retrieve the situation, rather than face military facts.

Returning to the front, Schörner did an amazing job of improvisation, scraping up replacements from rear-echelon troops. He also took the prudent precaution of ordering his engineer units to begin constructing a new fortified line across the base of the Courland Peninsula, so his army group would have a refuge to retreat to if needed.[139] By September 17, both AOK 16 and AOK 18 were beginning to give ground after being hit repeatedly by strong enemy attacks. The tipping point came when Govorov's Leningrad Front joined the offensive, attacking with two armies (8, 2 SA) against Armee-Abteilung Narwa north of Lake Peipus. On the first day, Fediuninskiy's 2nd Shock Army sliced through the German defenses and achieved a 16km-deep penetration. Maslennikov's 3rd Baltic Front also stepped up its attacks south of Lake Peipus, with Romanovskiy's 67th Army pushing toward Tartu against a modest German blocking force. Schörner had already quietly begun Unternehmen *Aster*, the evacuation of Estonia, so now there were no tactical reserves on hand to stop Govorov or Romanovskiy. On September 18, Schörner officially implemented *Aster* and ordered Armee-Abteilung Narwa, under General der Infanterie Anton Grasser, to evacuate Estonia as quickly as possible. The III SS-Panzerkorps was assigned to conduct the rearguard.[140] On the same day, Tartu fell to the 67th Army.

As Armeeabteilung Narwa evacuated Estonia, AOK 18 began retreating into the prepared fortified lines on the eastern approaches to Riga. The Kriegsmarine played a major role in evacuating German troops from Estonia before the port of Tallinn was taken by Govorov's armies on September 22. Two days later, the last rearguards from III SS-Panzerkorps crossed into Latvia. With Bagramyan's offensive stalled south of Riga, Stalin agreed to a brief operational pause while the main armies resupplied and Govorov conducted mop-up operations in Estonia. The initial phase of the Soviet Baltic offensive had succeeded in driving the Germans out of Estonia, but it had not succeeded in destroying or encircling any large formations from Heeresgruppe Nord. Indeed, Heeresgruppe Nord had actually been rid of its Estonian liability and could now use the forces released to build a stronger front between Riga and the East Prussian border. If Hitler agreed to abandon Riga and reconcentrate Heeresgruppe Nord's veteran units in East Prussia, this would actually improve the German situation on the Eastern Front. Yet Hitler was unwilling to consider giving up Riga, which essentially nailed Heeresgruppe Nord to the ground and deprived Schörner of any freedom of action.

As it was replenishing the three Baltic Fronts, the Stavka considered the next phase of its Baltic offensive. One option was simply to reinforce Bagramyan with additional artillery and armor and then make further attempts to bash his way to the Baltic, which was about 40 kilometers away. However, a brute-force attack of this sort would be costly and by no means certain of success. Schörner had concentrated the bulk of the combat power of two armies around Riga, and the fortified lines were very strong. Another option, recommended by Bagramyan, was to opt for operational surprise by attacking in a sector that the enemy did not expect, such as due west toward Memel. Raus' PzAOK 3 held the Memel sector with a thin screen of *Volksgrenadier* divisions, backed up by just the 7. Panzer-Division; it was an inviting target. On September 24, Stalin personally approved the Memel operation and ordered all attacks on Riga's defenses to cease for the moment. In order to conduct this operation, Bagramyan had to shift his entire front's line of operations (LOO) 90° and transfer a large portion of his forces from his right flank to his left flank, up to 150km – without being detected by the Germans. Thus, operational surprise, achieved through effective use of *maskirovka*, was a critical component of the Memel operation.[141] Bagramyan successfully completed this regrouping in six days. At the last moment, the Germans detected the regrouping and Schörner began transferring a Panzer division and other units to reinforce Raus, but it was too late.

At 1110 hours on October 5, Bagramyan's 1st Baltic Front opened its offensive against Raus' PzAOK 3; the attack began somewhat prematurely due to the weather and the initial artillery bombardment was ineffectual due to fog and rain. At his forward command post, Bagramyan described visibility as "miserable." Nevertheless, Chistiakov's 6 GA, Beloborodov's 43rd Army and Chanchibadze's 2 GA struck the center of Raus' front and crushed the front-line *Volksgrenadier* divisions. Raus committed his limited armored reserves, plus some of the reinforcements sent by Schörner, which briefly hindered the Soviet advance. Nevertheless, when Bagramyan committed Volsky's 5 GTA on October 6, the PzAOK 3 quickly fell apart and the survivors fled toward Memel or the East Prussian border. Raus' command post was overrun in the chaos, disrupting German operational C2 in this crucial sector. By the evening of October 8, Volsky's 5 GTA was on the outskirts of Memel, but the city was fortified and could not be taken by *coup de main*. The Kriegsmarine was also on hand to provide naval gunfire support from the cruisers *Lutzow* and *Prinz Eugen*. Furthermore, due to poor supply arrangements, Volsky's spearheads had run out of fuel at a critical moment.[142] Bagramyan had kept Kreiser's 51st Army in second echelon and did not commit it until the enemy front was broken, but then its fresh divisions were able to vault forward and reach the Baltic Sea at Palanga, north of Memel, on October 10. Cherniakhovsky's 3rd Belorussian Front also contributed its 39th Army to the Memel operation, which assisted the 2 GA advance to the Nieman River. Although Raus still held Memel with three divisions in the XXVIII Armeekorps (including the elite *Großdeutschland* Division and 7. Panzer-Division), it was isolated and the rest of the East Prussian border was only lightly defended. Worst of all, Bagramyan's advance to the coast had isolated virtually all of Schörner's Heeresgruppe Nord – two armies (16, 18) totaling 32 divisions.

As soon as PzAOK 3 had been defeated, the 1st, 2nd and 3rd Baltic Fronts began launching powerful concentric attacks on the German defenses around Riga. Fighting was very heavy, and at first the Germans managed to repulse the Soviet attacks. Yet after just three days of intense combat, Soviet troops began fighting their way into Riga, and Schörner – ignoring Hitler's order to stand fast – ordered his armies to withdraw into the fortified Courland Peninsula.[143] On October 13, Riga fell to Maslennikov's 3rd Baltic Front; immediately afterwards his front was disbanded and Maslennikov was put out to pasture in the Caucasus. Altogether, roughly 500,000 Wehrmacht personnel were isolated in Courland, but their supply situation was not immediately critical since the Kriegsmarine was able to escort convoys into the ports of Libau and Windau. Hitler ordered Schörner to use his three Panzer divisions to launch a counteroffensive south to reach Memel and then re-establish a link with PzAOK 3; this half-baked scheme was designated Unternehmen *Geier*. However, before Schörner could attempt this operation, the Stavka ordered Bagramyan's 1st Baltic Front and Eremenko's 2nd Baltic Front to immediately mount attacks into the Courland Peninsula with the objective of crushing Heeresgruppe Nord. The initial attacks on October 16–19 encountered fierce enemy resistance and failed completely, but they did force Schörner to abandon planning for *Geier*.[144] Both sides now became locked into a protracted, pointless struggle over the Courland Pocket. Hitler declared the peninsula to be a "Festung" and Schörner was ordered to hold it, even though Guderian (chief of the OKH) recommended evacuating the army group by sea to reinforce East Prussia. For his part, Stalin became obsessed with occupying this remote corner of Latvia and kept ten Soviet armies tied up in a futile battle of attrition. Neither side would employ economy of force in Courland

and essentially decided to discard the principles of war in this large-scale sideshow operation that would drag on to the end of the war.

In the remainder of 1944, the Soviets mounted three set-piece offensives against Heeresgruppe Nord. Schörner deployed AOK 18 on the west side of the peninsula and AOK 16 on the east side. Given that he had 32 divisions to defend an approximately 170km-wide front, in wooded terrain, Schörner could build a strong front line with III SS-Panzerkorps as his operational reserve. On October 27, Bagramyan's 1st Baltic Front and Eremenko's 2nd Baltic Front began their first major set-piece offensive against the Courland pocket, with their main effort directed against the center of the German line, on the boundary between AOK 16 and AOK 18. After five days of heavy fighting, the German front was still intact and the Soviet offensive had ground to a halt due to heavy casualties and ammunition shortages. Eremenko achieved the most success, advancing up to 25km. Heavy rains further inhibited mobility and a brief lull ensued. Although Schörner preferred to evacuate his army group to aid in the defense of East Prussia, he did an excellent job preparing it for a protracted defense of Courland. He disbanded and amalgamated burnt-out units to replenish his front-line infantry divisions and formed a powerful mobile reserve with his three Panzer divisions (4, 12, 14). Engineer units improved forward defensive positions, laid minefields, fortified key points and built a new rail line from the two ports to support the front line. Schörner evacuated thousands of rear-echelon personnel in order to reduce the supply burden and reshaped his command into a combat-heavy force that could be sustained for months. In this regard, he was totally successful.[145]

On November 19, the Soviets began their second major Courland offensive, which was mostly limited to the right wing of Bagramyan's 1st Baltic Front. After gaining some more ground in the center, this offensive also ran out of steam. Heavy rains and fierce German resistance quickly sapped Soviet offensive strength. Combat losses on both sides were enormous; in November Heeresgruppe Nord suffered over 33,000 casualties and Soviet losses were heavier. In the past two months, the four Soviet fronts in the Baltic campaign had suffered 249,000 casualties (including 56,000 dead). Even though the VVS had nearly complete air superiority over Courland, the Stavka was slow to appreciate that severing the enemy's sea lines of communications would quickly bring Heeresgruppe Nord to its knees. It was not until mid-December that the VVS began conducting large-scale attacks on the port of Libau, by which point the Luftwaffe was organized enough to inflict heavy losses on the raids. Likewise, Soviet submarines were not able to seriously interdict Heeresgruppe Nord's sea lines of communication. Bagramyan and Eremenko mounted a third major offensive on December 21–31, which gained additional small slivers of terrain, at considerable cost.

In mid-January 1945, Heeresgruppe Nord was renamed Heeresgruppe Kurland and Hitler finally agreed to transfer some of its most combat-capable formations by sea to reinforce the defense of East Prussia. In February, the III SS-Panzerkorps, the 4. Panzer-Division and three infantry divisions were successfully transferred, despite efforts by Soviet air and naval forces to interdict this movement.[146] Nevertheless, 20 German divisions with over 200,000 troops would remain in Courland until the final surrender in May 1945. After a fourth Soviet offensive failed in January, the Stavka finally decided to make some changes. Bagramyan and his 1st Baltic Front were redirected toward East Prussia, leaving only the 2nd Baltic Front, but Eremenko was sent to take command of the 4th Ukrainian Front in the Carpathians. Marshal Govórov took over the 2nd Baltic Front, which still had six armies in April 1945. Despite six attempts, the Soviets never broke into the Courland position or took either of the two ports that kept Heeresgruppe Kurland alive, but the extended campaign cost them well over 300,000 casualties.

In September and October, the Red Army put in a superb performance driving the enemy out of Estonia, smashing Raus' PzAOK 3, then isolating Heeresgruppe Nord and capturing Riga. These were all major accomplishments, but there was an incompleteness to them since most of the operational objectives were not achieved. The Stavka compounded this partial victory by committing large forces to containing an enemy force that no longer had any ability to influence the war's outcome. Bagramyan employed the principles of war to great advantage in this campaign, while the other three front commanders were forced to conduct rather pedestrian-style operations, lacking in surprise or operational-level maneuver. Among the Soviet army commanders, Kreiser and Fediuninskiy stand out for their aggressive operational styles, but most of their peers conducted professional operations. The only real failure was Volsky, whose performance at the head of the 5 GTA was markedly poor; he was the only senior Soviet commander to fail to take any of his assigned objectives in the campaign. Furthermore, Volsky's army lost well over 100 percent of its assigned tank strength during the Memel operation and the initial attacks on the Courland Peninsula, leaving it virtually toothless. Bagramyan noted in his memoirs that Volsky was evasive about reporting problems, which normally would have resulted in his relief, but he remained in command until March 1945.

On the German side, it is obvious that Heeresgruppe Nord suffered a major defeat in being isolated in the Courland Peninsula, yet its combat power was sufficient to repeatedly fend off attacks by numerically superior enemy forces. Despite his innate limitations as a senior commander, Schörner demonstrated considerable ability in holding his army group together under a situation of constant crisis. Unlike Paulus at Stalingrad, Schörner remained mission-focused and made sound decisions that preserved the bulk of his forces. Schörner did show a certain lack of timing in his ability to integrate intelligence and operations in order to commit his mobile reserves at the time and place where they could do the most damage to the enemy; instead, he tended to hurl his Panzer reserves at the enemy and hope for the best. Hilpert and Boege, although new to army-level command, proved competent and able to lead tough defensive operations, then break contact and withdraw into prepared positions in Courland. The only real failure on the German side in this campaign was Raus, who failed to provide adequate security measures to safeguard his fragile *Volksgrenadier* divisions from surprise attack. When Raus' PzAOK 3 was struck, it literally crumbled in a matter of 48 hours and he did little to stop the rout. If the 5 GTA had been commanded by a more aggressive commander than Volsky, Raus' army would probably have been slaughtered and Memel overrun.

Commander	Objective	Offensive	Mass	Maneuver	Surprise	Security	TALLY
Schörner	+	+	+	o	o	+	4
Raus	+	o	o	o	o	–	0
Hilpert Boege	+	+	o	o	o	o	2
Bagramyan	+	+	+	+	+	o	5
Eremenko Maslennikov Govorov	+	+	+	o	o	o	3
Kreiser Fediuninskiy	+	+	+	+	o	o	4
Chistiakov Beloborodov Chanchibadze	+	+	+	o	o	o	3
Volsky	o	o	o	o	o	o	0

Baltic/Courland, 1944 Leadership Assessment

East Prussia, October 16–31, 1944

As the Baltic campaign was developing, the Stavka decided that it could mount a concurrent offensive into East Prussia, spearheaded by Cherniakhovsky's 3rd Belorussian Front. Once Raus' PzAOK 3 was defeated around Memel, Cherniakhovsky was ordered to advance west through the "Insterburg Gap" and seize the port of Königsberg, 180km away. General-polkovnik Aleksandr P. Pokrovsky, 3rd Belorussian Front chief of staff, was the principal architect of the operational plan.[147] The concept for the East Prussian operation was extremely simplistic: a single front would conduct a "two-up-one-back" style frontal attack, with Krylov's 5th Army and Galitsky's 11th Guards Army in first echelon and Luchinsky's 28th Army in second echelon.* The initial objective was Gumbinnen. Furthermore, a large portion of the 3rd Belorussian Front's strength, Glagolev's 31st Army and Lyudnikov's 39th Army, would conduct supporting attacks on either flank of the main assault force – which tended to violate the principle of applying mass in the critical sector. Cherniakhovsky had no large armored formations to support this one-front operation, he had limited artillery and his troops were exhausted after three months of continuous combat, but the Stavka apparently expected their fair-haired boy to march to an easy victory.

On the German side, Reinhardt's Heeresgruppe Mitte had deployed General der Infanterie Friedrich Hoßbach's AOK 4 to defend the East Prussia border. Hoßbach was primarily a staff officer and relatively new to senior field command; he was also anti-Nazi, although not involved with the July 20 Plot. He had 15 divisions, half of which were *Volksgrenadier* or security troops, to defend a 350km-wide front. Hoßbach had a few good infantry divisions but very limited mobile reserves – one battalion equipped with Panther tanks and about two dozen assault guns. The terrain on the East Prussian border was mixed – lakes, forests and some open areas – and only a limited amount of field works had been completed by mid-October. Nor was the Luftwaffe capable of providing much air support at this point.

At dawn on October 16, the 3rd Belorussian Front commenced a one-hour artillery preparation, then began its ground assault at 0600 hours. In the attack sector of Galitsky's 11 GA, the Soviet artillery massed 196 guns per kilometer. On the right, Shafronov's 5th Army

---

*Krylov fell ill just before the offensive began and General-leytenant Pyotr G. Shafronov took over.

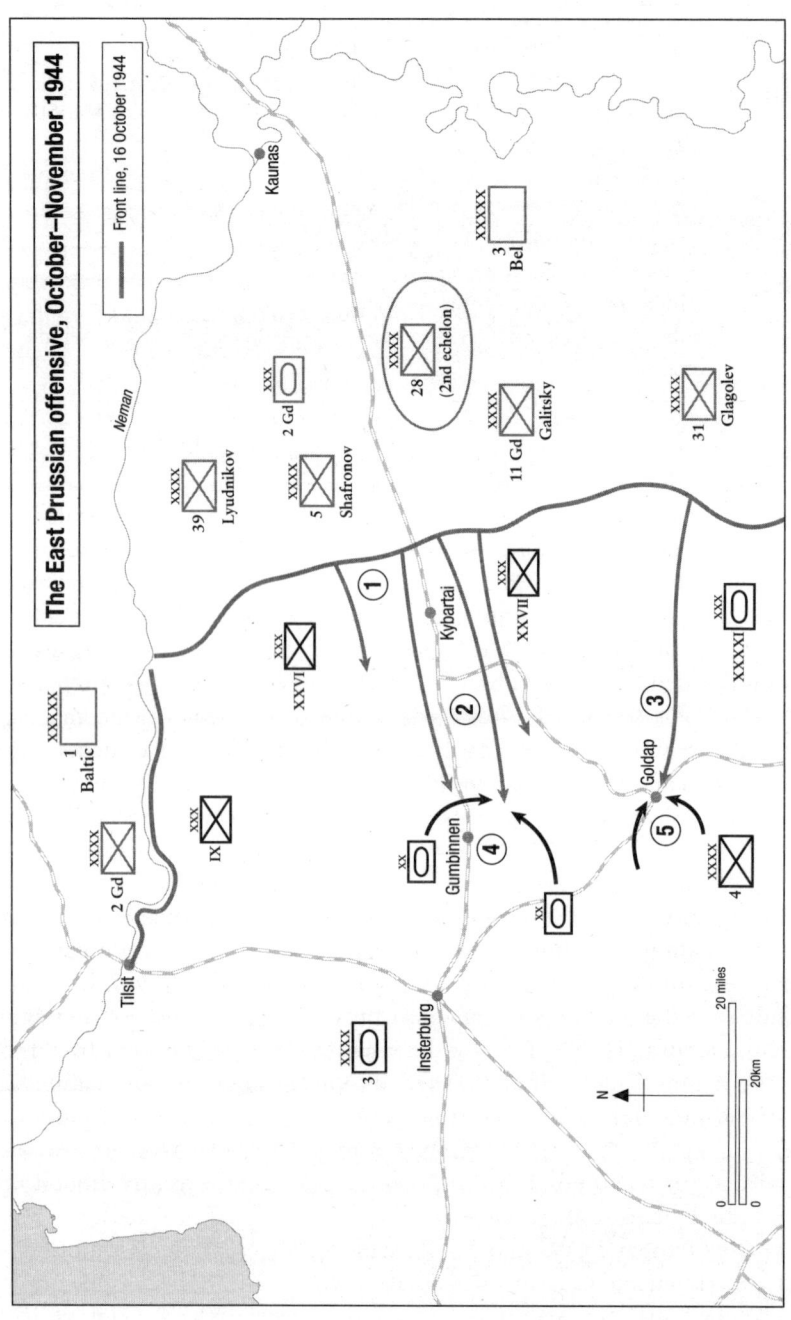

The East Prussian offensive, October–November 1944

MAP KEY

1. The 3rd Belorussian Front launches its main effort with the 5th and 11th Guards Army, but German resistance slows the advance.
2. Cherniakhovsky commits his armored exploitation force, which pushes toward Gumbinnen, the initial objective.
3. Glagolev's supporting 31st Army reaches Goldap.
4. Hoßbach conducts an armored counterattack near Gumbinnen which mauls the main Soviet spearhead.
5. Subsequently, Hoßbach conducts a second counterattack which retakes Goldap.

---

attacked the German XXVI Armeekorps, while on the left, Galitsky's 11 GA attacked the XXVII Armeekorps. Galitsky's 11 GA was reinforced with 193 tanks and 105 self-propelled guns, which were distributed in its three corps-size shock groups.[148] Despite a major advantage in firepower and troops, neither Shafronov nor Galitsky gained much ground on the first day of the offensive. On the second day, Shafronov's 5th Army was stymied by strong German resistance and his attacks were repulsed; in fact, this sector was defended by one of the few veteran infantry divisions, supported by assault guns. Galitsky had more success; the 11 GA managed to maul one of the *Volksgrenadier* divisions and create a gap. Galitsky showed flexibility in bypassing the strong resistance to his front and veering off to the south, then advancing 15km, which caught the Germans by surprise. Over the next two days, Galitsky continued to push westward while skirting around the German strongpoints on the direct path to Gumbinnen, but as he advanced his penetration corridor became more and more narrow. The *Volksgrenadier* divisions could not stop the 11 GA, but they also proved difficult to crush and kept slipping away to occupy new defensive positions, supported by a few assault guns. Cherniakhovsky seemed to have difficulty coordinating his five armies and soon only Galitsky's 11 GA was making real progress. For his part, Hoßbach massed his limited combat power to slow the advance of Shafronov's 5th Army to a crawl, while urgently requesting reinforcements from Reinhardt.

On October 20, Galitsky finally achieved a breakthrough southeast of Gumbinnen and Cherniakhovsky decided to commit his mobile group (2 GTC) into this sector to exploit the success. The 2 GTC rushed forward, and by the next day its mechanized spearhead was just south of Gumbinnen. However, Hoßbach had delayed the Soviet breakthrough for four critical days and now German reinforcements were arriving near Gumbinnen. Just as the 2 GTC approached Gumbinnen, the 5. Panzer-Division and *Hermann Göring* Panzer-Division arrived from the north, while the Führer Grenadier Brigade (FGB) was arriving from the south. The arrival of these reinforcements initiated a large-scale meeting engagement which halted Galitsky's 11 GA. Apparently Cherniakhovsky was not fully aware that Galitsky was running into difficulty and was sufficiently satisfied with progress on the Gumbinnen axis to consider other options. He had been holding Luchinsky's 28th Army in second echelon and this fresh formation should have been used to reinforce his main effort – either the 5th Army or the 11 GA. Instead, on the evening of October 20, Cherniakhovsky decided to send one corps from Luchinsky's army to support Shafronov's 5th Army, and then later committed another corps to reinforce Glagolev's 31st Army, which was slowly pushing toward Goldap. Consequently, Goldap was occupied by the 31st Army on the evening of October 22, but Galitsky's 11 GA was left unsupported against a large-scale German counterattack.[149]

The German armored counterattack on October 21–23 was a pincer operation that succeeded in cutting off the entire 2 GTC and one rifle corps. Altogether, the Germans were able to mass fewer than 200 AFVs in the attack sector, but they did receive some Luftwaffe close air support. While Hoßbach lacked the strength to crush the isolated enemy forces, Galitsky's spearhead was badly mauled and his army was obliged to retreat from the outskirts of Gumbinnen. Over the next few days, Cherniakhovsky tried to revitalize Shafronov's 5th Army and Luchinsky's 28th Army to advance and support Galitsky, but their efforts bogged down. Shafronov managed to take the town of Stalluponen on October 25, but that was his high-water mark. Amazingly, the veteran 1. Infanterie-Division was able to fight a delaying operation that inflicted 35 percent casualties on Shafronov's army. By October 30, Cherniakhovsky was forced to admit that his armies could no longer advance and the Stavka authorized him to shift to the defense. Hoßbach decided to take advantage of the apparent confusion in the 3rd Belorussian Front and use his armor to mount a counterattack to retake Goldap as well. On the night of November 2, the 5. Panzer-Division and FGB began a pincer attack across the snowy landscape and succeeded in encircling the Soviet garrison in Goldap. By November 5, Goldap was back in German hands and Hoßbach had achieved two small-scale but important victories which saved East Prussia for the moment.

Cherniakhovsky's East Prussian operation was a bungled effort that failed to achieve any of its objectives and suffered heavy casualties. In two weeks, the 3rd Belorussian Front suffered nearly 80,000 casualties (including 16,800 dead or missing) and lost most of its armor (about 350 tanks destroyed and another 300+ damaged), which left the front incapable of further offensive action for two months. Hoßbach's AOK 4 suffered about 16,000 casualties (one-third dead or missing) but it had accomplished its defensive mission and defeated the enemy incursions into East Prussia – not bad for an army that was heavily comprised of *Volksgrenadier.* The Stavka erred in committing the 3rd Belorussian Front into a single-front operation where enemy resistance could expect to be fierce.

Given his extremely poor performance in the East Prussian operation, it is difficult to see how post-war Soviet historians have regarded Cherniakhovsky as such a brilliant commander. In his memoirs, Galitsky was critical of Cherniakhovsky and implied that his decisions were often impulsive rather than well-considered. During this two-week operation, neither Cherniakhovsky's planning nor execution demonstrated any real commitment to the principles of war. He flip-flopped on objectives (Gumbinnen, Stalluponen or Goldap?), failed to mass his second echelon where it could reinforce success, failed to use maneuver to achieve an advantage, failed to use surprise as a combat multiplier and then allowed his own forces to be surprised by enemy countermoves. Unlike Operation *Bagration*, where he had Marshal Vasilevsky perched on his shoulder and coaching him with advice, Cherniakhovsky was essentially unsupervised in East Prussia and he made one costly mistake after another. Galitsky's command performance was by far the best for the Soviets in the campaign, but he could not defeat AOK 4 on his own; by virtue of his tactical success, he found himself at the end of a long, thin salient with no support within range. The other Soviet army commanders turned in mediocre performances and none achieved their objectives. Despite his limited senior command experience, Hoßbach demonstrated a firm grasp of principles of war and conducted a classic hold-win operation that smashed the initial Soviet invasion of East Prussia. Given the humiliation of this campaign, it is not surprising that it became one of the "forgotten battles" of the Eastern Front.

Commander	Objective	Offensive	Mass	Maneuver	Surprise	Security	TALLY
Hoßbach	+	+	+	+	+	o	5
Cherniakhovsky	o	+	o	o	o	–	o
Galitsky	+	+	+	+	+	–	4
Shafronov Luchinsky Glagolev Lyudnikov	+	+	o	o	o	o	2

East Prussia, 1944 Leadership Assessment

Budapest, October 29–December 31, 1944

Even though a lull had fallen across most of the Eastern Front by November 1944, the Stavka still wanted to take Budapest before the end of the year. The strategic rationale was weak, since Hungary could no longer contribute much to the German war effort and rapid advances were unlikely in the face of adverse terrain conditions and the onset of winter weather. Nevertheless, in late October, Malinovsky was ordered to continue his push across Hungary to seize Budapest. Most of Frießner's Heeresgruppe Süd was holding a line east of Budapest out to the Slovak border. The actual capital region was held by a mixed force of fewer than a dozen German and Hungarian divisions. Malinovsky decided to use his left wing – primarily Shumilov's 7 GA, Shlemin's 46th Army and two mechanized corps – to make a direct push toward Budapest. Malinovsky's troops were exhausted after months of fighting, units were worn down and supplies were low, which meant that only part of the 2nd Ukrainian Front could play an active role in the operation.

Malinovsky's offensive began on October 29, initially relying primarily on Shlemin's 46th Army. He hoped to take Budapest on the run with his mechanized corps before the Germans could transfer any reinforcements to the area. Shlemin succeeded in breaking through the Hungarian 3rd Army without much trouble, but Frießner used the LVII Panzerkorps to mount several stinging counterattacks into Shlemin's right flank. After four days of fighting, the Soviet 4 GMC advanced over 100km and reached the southern approaches of Budapest before running out of steam. The Hungarians had built a strong defensive line southeast of Budapest, known as the Atilla Line, which would require a deliberate assault to breach. Furthermore, Frießner transferred five German divisions to the Budapest sector, which prevented Shlemin from making an immediate assault on the city. By November 3, the front line had coalesced on the outskirts of Budapest and it was clear that Malinovsky would need to conduct a deliberate operation to breach the city's outer defenses. While this was occurring, Shumilov's 7 GA attacked Fretter-Pico's AOK 6 and gained some ground, but did not stay abreast of Shlemin's 46th Army.

After a week-long pause, Malinovsky resumed his offensive against Budapest but made very little progress. On November 7, Tolbukhin's 3rd Ukrainian Front joined the offensive, with the 4 GA and 57th Army trying to get across the Danube between Apatin and Mohacs; this effort took nearly three weeks. Shlemin made repeated efforts to cross the Danube in an effort to bypass the Atilla Line, but was continually repulsed. Everywhere the Soviet offensive into Hungary was moving at a sluggish pace. Malinovsky decided to commit Kravchenko's 6 GTA to support Shumilov's 7 GA on November 14 and ordered these two armies to approach Budapest from the northeast. Kravchenko's armor made steady progress despite the presence of some German Panzer units in this sector, and by November 26 his vanguard was in Hatvan, 46km northeast of the capital. By this point, it was evident that the Soviets would soon be threatening to encircle Budapest. Already, on November 23, Hitler had declared Budapest to be a *Festung* and ordered Frießner to hold it at all costs. So far the Axis defenses in the city had repulsed all direct assaults, but Frießner lacked the forces to defend the vulnerable flanks.

On December 5, Malinovsky mounted another offensive, with Shumilov's 7 GA and Kravchenko's 6 GTA striking the northeast corner of the Atilla Line. For two weeks, the Axis fought tenaciously and gave up little ground, but Malinovsky's forces were gradually enveloping the city to the east. When Tolbukhin's vanguard appeared on the western side of the Danube in mid-December, the jig was up. On December 20, Malinovsky and Tolbukhin mounted a joint offensive which broke through on both flanks and raced to link up and encircle the city. When the Axis line broke, Hitler relieved Frießner of command and replaced him with Wöhler, who was certainly no miracle worker. By December 26, the Axis garrison in Budapest was encircled. About 80,000 Axis troops were trapped in the Budapest pocket, including the 13. Panzer-Division and the Panzergrenadier-Division *Feldherrnhalle*. Malinovsky wasted no time and immediately began attacking into the eastern outskirts of the city, but progress was slow. He opted to commit a large portion of his front to protracted urban combat rather than simply besiege the city and conserve his forces. As the year ended, the siege of Budapest was well underway and would continue for another six weeks. By the time that the city fell in February 1945, the two Soviet fronts had suffered 320,000 casualties (including 80,000 dead or missing) in the campaign and lost no fewer than 1,766 tanks.[150] Malinovsky's 2nd Ukrainian Front suffered nearly 50 percent casualties, which were extravagant losses merely to expedite the exit of Hungary from the war and a corps-size German garrison.

The quality of battlefield command during the Budapest operation was pretty mediocre on both sides. Frießner did the best he could with the resources available and was able to commit his armored reserves at the proper moment – but the reserves were too depleted to accomplish more than delay. Simply put, the Ostheer no longer had the ability to conduct effective operational-level offensive operations, even when it could assemble several depleted Panzer divisions on the battlefield. Instead, German operations by this point could only produce occasional tactical successes. On the Soviet side, the Stavka's willingness to order offensive operations under unfavorable conditions (terrain, weather, enemy resistance) led to unsatisfactory outcomes and unnecessarily heavy losses. Malinovsky's operations around Budapest were unimaginative and lacked any element of surprise, so the result was brutal slug-fests. Shlemin was assigned far too difficult a mission for a single army to accomplish and ended up conducting paint-by-numbers operations, simply doing as ordered. Shumilov and Kravchenko, both seasoned commanders, demonstrated a bit more flexibility and initiative and their actions managed to transform a potential stalemated campaign into an eventual Soviet victory. The Budapest campaign, like the East Prussian offensive, were disappointments after the brilliant victories in Belorussia, Galicia, Romania and the Baltic States, and were caused by a certain amount of hubris in Moscow.

Commander	Objective	Offensive	Mass	Maneuver	Surprise	Security	TALLY
Frießner	+	+	o	o	o	o	2
Malinovsky	+	+	o	o	–	o	1
Shlemin	+	+	o	o	o	o	2
Shumilov Kravchenko	+	+	o	+	o	o	3

Budapest, 1944 Leadership Assessment

During the course of 1944, the Red Army conducted 20 major operations (not counting branches), of which 12 resulted in victories and four achieved only partial victories; this was a very high level of success. Only four Soviet operations resulted in defeat (Vitebsk, 1st Jassy-Kishinev, East Carpathian and East Prussia) and none of these failures led to serious negative consequences. Three of the unsuccessful operations occurred late in the year, when the Stavka was attempting to accomplish too much with depleted forces under adverse conditions – this was the same kind of faulty methodology that had resulted in previous failures, such as Operation *Zvezda* (Star) in 1943. The Red Army paid for these successes with 6.8 million casualties in 1944, including 1.76 million dead or missing. In material terms, the Red Army lost 40 percent of its armor in 1944, including 16,900 tanks and 6,800 self-propelled guns. However, the Red Army lost no major formations in 1944 and by the end of the year it had about 6.7 million troops at the front. The Red Army had developed a war-winning operational-level doctrine, based on the combination of theory from PU-36 and hard-won experience on the battlefield – and now many of its commanders had become proficient in its use. Stalin relieved a few senior commanders in 1944, such as Rotmistrov, but mistakes were more likely to be tolerated now that final victory was within sight.

In contrast, the Ostheer conducted 12 operations in 1944 and only three – the breakout of Hube's PzAOK 1, elimination of the Tashlyk bridgehead and Gumbinnen/Goldap – were successes with significant operational impact. Seven German operations achieved partial success, either in disrupting ongoing Soviet offensives or evacuating isolated German forces. Two operations, the counterattack against the Magnuszew bridgehead and *Cäsar*, were abject failures. The German doctrine of *Bewegungskrieg* was becoming irrelevant because the Ostheer no longer had the ground troops or air support to conduct the kind of freewheeling operations it had conducted in 1941–43. By mid-1944, most German counteroffensives were stumbling, poorly-coordinated affairs that were only capable of simple, short-duration jabs at the enemy. Even when Soviet formations were encircled, they could no longer be crushed as in the *Kesselschlacht* of 1941–42. During 1944, the Ostheer suffered 2.8 million casualties, including 1.5 million dead or missing. Three German armies – AOK 4, AOK 6 and AOK 9 – had been demolished (and then partly rebuilt) and two more were isolated (AOK 16, AOK 18). The loss of so many veteran commanders and troops led to a sharp reduction in the quality of the Ostheer's combat capabilities. Increasingly, large portions of the line were being held by *Volksgrenadier* or foreign SS-auxiliaries, who lacked the training to conduct difficult missions. Nevertheless, the fact that after absorbing such damage the Ostheer was still able to form a nearly continuous front from Hungary to the Baltic Sea demonstrates an amazing resiliency. Fuel shortages were becoming endemic, but German industry was still producing enough tanks and antitank weapons to enable the Ostheer to continue inflicting heavy losses upon the enemy right to the end of the war. Yet it was not as easy to produce competent senior commanders and the Ostheer was rapidly running out of that commodity. Hitler created a great deal of command turbulence by relieving a dozen senior Ostheer commanders in 1944, including six army group commanders (Busch, Frießner, Kleist, Küchler, Lindemann and Manstein) and six army commanders. He also transferred many of the other commanders around willy-nilly, which was highly disruptive without commensurate operational gain. Meanwhile, competent commanders like Manstein, Kleist and Hollidt were out of favor and sitting out the rest of the war at home.

CHAPTER 7

The Final Campaigns: 1945 Operations

"I understood completely that after our Ardennes Offensive failed the war was lost. Now came the most difficult of all leadership challenges in war — ending it without bigger catastrophes."

Hermann Balck[1]

"As usual, we stuck to the book and by now the Germans know our methods. They pulled back their troops a good eight kilometers. Our artillery fire hit everything but the enemy."

General-polkovnik Vasily I. Kuznetsov[2]

The Soviet Steamroller, January 12–31, 1945

In November 1944, the Stavka began planning the final phase of the War on the Eastern Front, which would be initiated by a series of winter offensives. On November 18, Zhukov took over command of the 1st Belorussian Front, which would be the main effort in the forthcoming offensive. Konev's 1st Ukrainian Front, Rokossovsky's 2nd Belorussian Front and Cherniakhovsky's 3rd Belorussian Front would all mount their own offensives at nearly the same time. Zhukov had been away from front-level command for nearly six months, but when he arrived at the 1st Belorussian Front headquarters in Poland, he inherited a veteran staff from Rokossovsky: General-polkovnik Mikhail S. Malinin as chief of staff, General-leytenant Ivan I. Boykov as head of operations and General-leytenant Nikolai A. Antipenko (an NKVD officer) in charge of logistics.[3] He also had some excellent veteran field commanders: Simoniak (3rd Shock Army), Katukov (1 GTA) and Chuikov (8 GA). Although Zhukov had to present the plan for his upcoming offensive to the Stavka for approval, he did not have a senior representative looking over his shoulder. Unlike previous Soviet offensives (or the ongoing operations in Courland and Hungary), Zhukov was afforded plenty of time to plan the Vistula–Oder operation and received priority for replacements and supplies. The Stavka approved the basic plan at the end of November 1944, but Zhukov and his staff were given six weeks before the operation was to begin in mid-January 1945. Indeed, the logistic effort that went into preparing for the Vistula-Oder offensive was unprecedented by Soviet standards and, for once, there would be plenty of ammunition and fuel.

Zhukov intended to use *maskirovka* to gain operational surprise, then mass and maneuver to overwhelm Heeresgruppe A's defenses in central Poland. He intended to begin the offensive with major breakout attacks from the 3rd Belorussian Front's bridgeheads over the Vistula at Magnuzew and Pulawy to unhinge Heeresgruppe A's right flank, then use his two tank armies to roll up the German center and exploit westward. The overall objective was to reach the Oder River, 450km away, in just 15 days – a highly ambitious plan. The concurrent offensives by Rokossovsky and Konev would push back the enemy's flanks and create a breakthrough corridor for Zhukov to quickly reach the Oder. In Zhukov's opinion, which he conveyed to Stalin, the Germans would be caught flat-footed and unable to build a new front on the Oder before Zhukov's vanguard was across, optimistically hinting that Berlin might be within reach.

Facing Zhukov's 3rd Belorussian Front, central Poland was defended by Heeresgruppe A (headquarters in Krakow), under the command of Generaloberst Josef Harpe. Generalleutnant Walther Wenck was chief of staff of Heeresgruppe A. The main force holding the Vistula front was AOK 9, under General der Panzertruppe Smilo Freiherr von Lüttwitz. The perimeter around the Magnuszew bridgehead was defended by three *Volksgrenadier* divisions, backed up by two understrength Panzer divisions (19, 25), while the Pulawy sector was held by two infantry divisions. German intelligence regarded Konev's 1st Ukrainian Front as the most severe threat, so Harpe reinforced his right flank with his two best Panzer divisions. He expected his tactical reserves to hold the Vistula front, but there were no appreciable operational reserves. Even if Harpe had possessed more armor, fuel shortages were now seriously limiting German operational mobility; by default, the principle of maneuver was now less relevant for the Ostheer. Likewise, the fuel-starved Luftwaffe was only capable of conducting limited ground support operations and was badly outnumbered by the more confident VVS.

Konev's 1st Ukrainian Front attacked Harpe's right flank first, on the morning of January 12, achieving major success in the first few days. On the morning of January 14, Zhukov began his offensive with a crushing artillery bombardment that severely disrupted the German front-line infantry holding the perimeter around the two bridgeheads. At the Magnuszew bridgehead, Berzarin's 5 SA and Chuikov's 8 GA broke through the *Volksgrenadier* units, which led to the collapse of the VIII Armeekorps. Tsvetaev's 33rd Army, attacking from the Pulawy bridgehead, also smashed through the thin German infantry line. Zhukov ensured that the army-level shock groups had plenty of engineer support, which helped them to quickly clear the enemy obstacle belts. Four hours after the offensive began, von Lüttwitz committed his tactical reserves, but he violated the principle of mass by splitting it up, sending one Panzer division to each of the bridgehead battles. Zhukov easily fended off these feeble counterattacks and his troops were able to advance over 30km on the first day of the offensive. On the second day, Zhukov committed both Katukov's 1 GTA and Bogdanov's 2 GTA into the fluid center of von Lüttwitz' AOK 9. Once his front was broken and his tactical reserves were committed, von Lüttwitz had no further cards to play and Harpe was also busy trying to counter Konev's offensive, as well. In addition to his main breakout attacks from the bridgeheads, Zhukov also sent General-leytenant Frants I. Perkhorovich's 47th Army to cross the Vistula north of Warsaw. By January 16, Warsaw was being enveloped on both sides. Harpe decided to evacuate the destroyed city the next day. By January 17, Zhukov had achieved a complete breakthrough and the battered remnants of AOK 9 were in full retreat, pursued by Bogdanov's 2 GTA.

Hitler reacted to this sudden defeat by relieving both Harpe and von Lüttwitz of command; both officers received other commands in the last weeks of the war. Heeresgruppe A was briefly redesignated as part of Heeresgruppe Mitte and Schörner was assigned to take command. General der Infanterie Theodor Busse, one of von Manstein's former staff officers, was assigned to take command of the retreating AOK 9.

Then on January 24, Hitler decided to create Heeresgruppe Weichsel to control AOK 2 and AOK 9; instead of putting a senior officer in charge, as Guderian recommended, Hitler decided to give the command to Reichsführer-SS Heinrich Himmler. As chief of staff, Himmler selected one of his SS cronies, Generalmajor Heinz Lammerding. Himmler had no military experience and Lammerding's experience was limited to seven months as commander of the SS-*Das Reich* Panzer-Division; these two amateurs had no ability to deal with a military catastrophe and proved incapable of exercising leadership or direction.

While this was occurring, Zhukov's armor roared across the flat Polish plains. The only place where Busse was able to organize a defense was Poznan (Posen), on the main route to Berlin, where 45,000 troops were collected. However, Katukov's 1 GTA isolated the city on January 25 and Zhukov committed most of Chuikov's 8 GA to reduce this *Festung*-city. On January 31, the vanguard of Berzarin's 5 SA reached the frozen Oder River at Kienitz, only 70km from Berlin, and seized a bridgehead. The river was mostly frozen, but the ice was only capable of supporting tanks and heavy equipment in some places. By February 1, Berzarin had a division across the Oder, Kolpakchi's 69th Army seized a bridgehead further south near Küstrin and Tsvetaev's 33rd Army created a bridgehead near Frankfurt an der Oder. Initially, there were no significant German forces in the immediate vicinity of any of these bridgeheads and Zhukov considered making an attempt to seize Berlin by *coup de main*. At this point, the weather turned against Zhukov – a sudden thaw prevented armor and artillery from crossing the Oder. Furthermore, Zhukov had outrun his air support and now the Luftwaffe mercilessly attacked his bridgeheads, inflicting heavy losses. While Zhukov was delayed, the OKH managed to transfer some reinforcements to the Oder sector and garrison Küstrin, which ended any hope for an immediate push to Berlin. Nevertheless, Zhukov had led one of the best-executed Soviet offensives of the entire war, smashing Heeresgruppe A and advancing over 300km in two weeks.

Konev's role in the Vistula-Oder operation was to break out of the Sandomierz bridgehead, defeat General der Panzertruppe Fritz Gräser's PzAOK 4, then advance to the Oder River on Zhukov's left flank. As a follow-on objective, Konev was expected to occupy Silesia. Konev's 1st Ukrainian Front was built up to an immense size, with eight combined-arms armies and two tank armies (3 GTA, 4 TA). The Sandomierz bridgehead, which had expanded to a width of 75km along the Vistula, was crammed with troops, tanks and artillery. Konev's rear-echelon troops used the last months of 1944 to build additional bridges over the Vistula and to repair the nearby rail lines, which greatly aided the logistic build-up for the offensive. Gräser had seven infantry divisions, supported by 70 assault guns, deployed around the Sandomierz bridgehead. The primary German reserve force in this sector was Nehring's XXIV Panzerkorps (16., 17. Panzer-Division, 20. Panzergrenadier-Division and a Tiger tank battalion), deployed south of Kielce, which on paper was a powerful force with 214 tanks, 67 assault guns and 30 tank destroyers. However, Nehring's XXIV Panzerkorps was under army group control, not PzAOK 4. Furthermore, Nehring's armor was deployed too close to the front and directly in the path of Konev's main effort.

On the morning of January 12, Konev began his offensive with a brief but intense artillery preparation, employing 230 guns per km of attack frontage. Then the breakout attack was led by Gordov's 3 GA, Pukhov's 13th Army, General-polkovnik Konstantin K. Koroteev's 52nd Army and Zhadov's 5 GA. The German front line was broken in a matter of hours under this avalanche of massed firepower and manpower. By 1400 hours, Konev decided to commit Rybalko's 3 GTA and Lelyushenko's 4 TA to exploit the gap that was opening in the German front and this onrush of armor caught PzAOK 4 by surprise.[4] German C2 quickly collapsed and Nehring's corps received no orders until the afternoon. By the time that the German Panzer reserve started to react, Lelyushenko's 4 TA was already arriving in its assembly areas and Nehring finally received some garbled orders to move to Kielce.[5] The powerful Tiger tank battalion received no orders to move at all.[6] Nehring was unable to launch any kind of counterattack and instead quickly found his command isolated by Lelyushenko's spearheads and forced to conduct a fighting retreat to the west. The 2 VA conducted over 400 strike sorties against Nehring's Panzers, caught in the open near Kielce; many AFVs and motor vehicles were damaged.[7] Konev had three armies in second echelon (21, 59, 60) which he committed, adding further impetus to the battering ram striking the crumbling PzAOK 4. By the fourth day of the offensive Kielce was taken and by January 19, Krakow had been taken. PzAOK 4 was a broken reed, although Nehring succeeded in extracting the survivors of XXIV Panzerkorps, after losing most of their equipment. At this point, the obvious objective was to continue pushing on to the Oder River, but Stalin wanted the 1st Ukrainian Front to simultaneously seize industrial facilities in Silesia, so Konev was forced to split his efforts. Five armies (4 TA, 3 GA, 5 GA, 13th Army, 52nd Army) continued west toward the Oder, but four armies (3 GTA, 21, 59, 60) turned south to push into Silesia.

By January 22, the 5 GA had seized a bridgehead over the Oder at Ohlau and by the next day both 4 TA and 13th Army also had troops across the Oder. Konev's offensive was a model operation that owed its success to effective utilization of mass and maneuver, although Stalin interfered with the principle of objective by forcing Konev to split his attention during the exploit phase. In their pursuit operations, the Red Army demonstrated an excellent integration of mechanized forces and tactical aviation.

Konev's advance was also assisted by the concurrent offensive into southern Poland and northern Slovakia by Petrov's 4th Ukrainian Front and part of Malinovsky's 2nd Ukrainian Front. Petrov attacked with three armies (18, 38, 1 GA) and Malinovsky with three armies (27, 53, 40). The terrain in this region was rough (mountains and forests), but Schulz' AOK 17 and Armeegruppe Heinrici (PzAOK 1) had only a dozen infantry and *Volksgrenadier* divisions to defend a lengthy front. Petrov started his offensive with just Moskalenko's 38th Army on his right, then six days later committed Grechko's 1 GA. Together, these two armies cleared out southern Poland and assisted Konev's advance to Krakow and the Silesian border. Schulz' AOK 17 lost no major units in its retreat and managed to form a new line in Silesia by the end of January. Malinovsky succeeded in pushing back Heinrici, but the German-Hungarian line in the Carpathians remained intact.

While Zhukov and Konev were racing through Poland, Cherniakhovsky and Rokossovsky were engaged in a tougher fight in East Prussia. The Stavka had learned its lesson from the unsuccessful first East Prussian campaign and now intended to use three fronts to wrest this province from the Third Reich. Cherniakhovsky's 3rd Belorussian Front would begin the operation, pushing west through the Insterburg Gap to seize Königsberg, while Rokossovsky's 2nd Belorussian Front punched through Weiß' AOK 2 and then pivoted northwest to the Baltic coast. Bagramyan's 1st Baltic Front was expected to finish off the German garrison in Memel, then cross the Narew River to assist Cherniakhovsky's 3rd Belorussian Front. In early January, Reinhardt's Heeresgruppe Mitte had two infantry divisions holding Memel (which was supplied by sea), while Raus' PzAOK 3 and Hoßbach's AOK 4 defended the borders of East Prussia. Weiß' AOK 2 defended the right flank of the army group in northern Poland. Reinhardt had created some strongpoints to anchor his defense and he had some first-class mobile units (*Großdeutschland* and the *Hermann Göring* Fallschirm-Panzerkorps) in reserve, but he was tasked with holding too much territory. Furthermore, Hitler transferred the IV SS-Panzerkorps to Hungary in early January, depriving Reinhardt of vital mobile reserves.

Cherniakhovsky began his offensive on January 13, attacking with just General-leytenant Ivan I. Lyudnikov's 39th Army, Krylov's 5th Army and Luchinsky's 28th Army against Raus' PzAOK 3 in the Tilsit-Gumbinnen sector. Progress was minimal in three days of fighting, particularly once Raus committed his tactical reserve (5. Panzer-Division). Cherniakhovsky did not mass his combat power in one particular sector but spread it out across a wide frontage, so consequently he did not achieve a rapid breakthrough as had the other front commanders. Bagramyan sent Beloborodov's 43rd Army across the Nieman, but this did not immediately help Cherniakhovsky's efforts. Rokossovsky's 2nd Belorussian Front began attacking Weiß' AOK 2 north of Warsaw on January 14 and initially fighting was also heavy. Reinhardt committed Panzerkorps *Großdeutschland* to stop Rokossovsky's advance, which temporarily succeeded. However, Rokossovsky carefully gauged the situation, allowing the enemy to commit their limited reserves while he held his main strike group back. On January 16, he committed his main effort, Gusev's 48th Army, Batov's 65th Army and Fediuninskiy's 2nd Shock Army, against the boundary between AOK 2 and AOK 4 near Mlawa. Soviet tactical aviation pounded the enemy, with 4 VA flying about 2,500 sorties in a single day. Rokossovsky's shock groups achieved a major breakthrough and he immediately sent Volsky's 5 GTA into the gap. Rokossovsky's maneuver was akin to the 1914 "Schlieffen plan," with an arc swinging to the northwest, slicing through German infantry units in its path. In just a few days, Reinhardt's right wing fell apart, with AOK 2 retreating to the west while AOK 4 refused its right flank. Cherniakhovsky escalated his attacks once Heeresgruppe Mitte was off balance, enabling the 3rd Belorussian Front to slowly start pushing PzAOK 3 back in the Gumbinnen sector.

The East Prussian campaign swung sharply in the Soviets' favor on January 20, when Rokossovsky's main effort pivoted northward toward the Baltic Sea. Weiß' AOK 2 fought desperately to block Rokossovsky's advance but was roughly shoved to the west, creating a 30km gap between it and the right flank of AOK 4. For his part, Hoßbach could see what was developing and began trying to shift his main effort toward his right, which of course meant weakening his left. Eight of AOK 4's division were holding a large salient west of the Masurian Lakes, essentially spectators as the bulk of Rokossovsky's front moved to outflank them. Hitler issued his usual no-retreat orders to Reinhardt, permitting only minor tactical withdrawals. On January 22, the 5 GTA took Allenstein, which had been the anchor of Hoßbach's right flank, while Luchinsky's 28th Army (3rd Belorussian Front) took Insterburg, which unhinged PzAOK 3's front.

Without authorization, Hoßbach began disengaging his AOK 4 the next day and accelerated his shift to the west, which included abandoning the fortress town of Lötzen. Reinhardt was aware of these withdrawals and quietly concurred. Nevertheless, Volsky's 5 GTA reached the outskirts of Elbing on January 24 and by nightfall, one of its brigades had reached the Vistula Lagoon (Frisches Haff), thereby cutting off the PzAOK 3 and AOK 4 in East Prussia. Once again, another large German force – totaling over 400,000 troops and 26 divisions – was isolated by a surprise Red Army offensive. Hitler's reaction – once he learned of this development – was to relieve both Reinhardt and Hoßbach of command because they had conducted unauthorized withdrawals.[8]

By January 27, Cherniakhovsky's armies were beginning to close in upon Königsberg, isolating five German divisions in the city. The garrison in Memel was evacuated by sea, which allowed Bagramyan to occupy it without costly urban combat. Reinhardt, in his final days in command, tried to organize a link-up operation near Elbing, since 5 GTA's blocking force on the coast was fairly small; during this effort, Reinhardt was seriously wounded by shrapnel. Hoßbach used *Kampfgruppen* from five divisions and began attacking westward, while Weiß' AOK 2 tried to attack eastward with 7. Panzer-Division. Although the attempt to open an escape corridor briefly came close to achieving success, Rokossovsky rushed troops from Gusev's 48th Army to reinforce this critical sector. The breakout attempt failed and AOK 4 was gradually compressed into the Heiligenbeil pocket. General Friedrich-Wilhelm Müller was assigned to take over the encircled AOK 4, which Hitler now ordered to hold its ground, rather than trying any further breakout attempts. Amazingly, AOK 4 would survive for another two months, supplied by sea, but its fate was sealed.

While Soviet armies were rampaging across Poland in their race to the Oder River, a considerable portion of Hitler's attention was focused on Hungary, as well as Operation *Nordwind*, a counteroffensive in Alsace. The siege of Budapest was a relative sideshow, but Hitler placed a great deal of effort into organizing a relief operation by the rebuilt AOK 6. In early January, he sent Guderian, as head of the OKH, to discuss plans for a major operation in Hungary. Hermann Balck was hurriedly brought back from the Western Front and sent to Hungary to take command of AOK 6 and lead the counteroffensive. In addition to the badly depleted III Panzerkorps, Balck was given the IV SS-Panzerkorps (which had 285 tanks and assault guns), which had just been transferred from the Vistula front. Balck's mission was to mount a direct assault to open a corridor to Budapest, although Hitler stipulated that the city would not be evacuated even if the operation was successful. Knowing that Tolbukhin's 3rd Ukrainian Front forces in the perimeter around Budapest were numerically superior to his own, Balck selected a course of action that emphasized surprise and maneuver – he would attack in a sector that the enemy least expected. Amazingly for 1945, Balck's initial attack, known as *Konrad I*, began with an infantry division conducting an assault crossing of the Danube River to seize a crucial road for the Panzers to advance upon. As a further effort to gain surprise, Balck ordered III Panzerkorps to conduct feint attacks in another sector to distract Tolbukhin. The attack commenced on January 6 and the sudden advance of the IV SS-Panzerkorps caught Shlemin's 46th Army by surprise; but this effort was stopped just 20km short of the city.[9] The Stavka reacted by ordering Malinovsky to commit Kravchenko's 6 GTA north of the Danube in an effort to outflank the German armored thrust. Kravchenko's 6 GTA had been refitting behind the lines and was not completely ready for combat, but it attacked the German LVII Panzerkorps north of the Danube, which put pressure on Balck to halt his operation.[10] Kravchenko's 6 GTA, having suffered heavy losses in its *ad hoc* attacks, was pulled out of the line. After some regrouping, Balck made another attempt on the northern axis, known as *Konrad II*, but Malinovsky reinforced this sector with a mechanized corps.

Despite the lack of success, Hitler would not give up on Budapest and ordered Heeresgruppe Süd (Wöhler) to try again. Balck again opted for surprise by shifting his line of operations (LOO) 60km to the south, which meant moving the IV SS-Panzerkorps to an assembly area near Lake Balaton. Altogether, Balck would attack with four Panzer divisions (1, 3, SS-*Wiking*, SS-*Totenkopf*) against Zakharov's 4 GA. When *Konrad III* began on January 18, Zakharov was caught completely by surprise and the German Panzer spearheads advanced over 60km on the first day. Luftflotte 4 even managed to provide some air support, which assisted the advance. By the second day of the offensive, German armor reached the Danube and managed to isolate two of Zakharov's rifle corps. However, the German window of opportunity was narrow and by January 27 Tolbukhin was counterattacking and Balck was stopped cold. *Konrad III* was an asinine misallocation of the Wehrmacht's dwindling armor reserves, which should have been used to prevent Zhukov and Rokossovsky from gaining bridgeheads over the Oder instead of reinforcing failure at Budapest. Guderian continually argued this point with Hitler and always lost.

In less than three weeks, concurrent offensives by six Soviet fronts brought the Wehrmacht to the brink of total defeat. More than half the

Ostheer was now isolated in Courland and East Prussia, sidelined from the defense of the German homeland. A large portion of the remaining German armor was engaged in a sideshow operation in Hungary, with even more on the way. All six Soviet front-level offensives were successful, although enemy garrisons at Königsberg, Thorn and Budapest would require further siege combat to reduce them. In contrast, Heeresgruppe Süd under Wöhler was the only German army group with some degree of freedom of maneuver left. At the end of January, Heeresgruppe Weichsel was little more than a string of minor blocking positions behind the Oder, while Heeresgruppe Mitte's remaining combat power was mostly clumped around Breslau.

For the most part, the German commanders trying to stop the Soviet offensives in January 1945 lacked the freedom to employ the principles of war due to the increasingly unhinged no-retreat orders coming from Hitler. On the defense, Heinrici did slightly better because he was in mountainous terrain that favored the defense and was not being overrun by Soviet tank armies. Balck was the only senior Ostheer commander to conduct offensive operations in January 1945 and, although there was little chance for real success, he conducted them in accordance with the principles of war. On the Soviet side, Zhukov, Konev and Rokossovsky conducted extremely well-planned set-piece offensives in accordance with all the major principles of war and were rewarded with great success. Petrov's offensive was also well handled, but did not benefit from surprise. Cherniakhovsky's performance was noticeably disappointing, particularly in failing to designate a main effort, lack of maneuver and lack of surprise. Instead, the 3rd Belorussian Front conducted a rather unimaginative broad front advance that gradually pushed PzAOK 3 back into the Königsberg fortress. Malinovsky and Tolbukhin were conducting a positional campaign in January 1945 and one of the greatest sins of a besieging army is to be caught by surprise by an unexpected relief attempt; both were caught off guard when Balck mounted his winter offensive and struggled for nearly three weeks to contain it. It should also be remembered that Malinovsky was concurrently conducting a rather clumsy siege of Budapest, which dragged on for much longer than necessary. Overall, in the January 1945 offensives, the Red Army demonstrated its level of operational maturity, which enabled it to now rip apart German front-line infantry positions like cardboard. Aside from the perennial problems with operational-level logistics, Red Army leaders were still prone to getting bogged down in trying to reduce German fortified cities and towns.

Commander	Objective	Offensive	Mass	Maneuver	Surprise	Security	TALLY
Harpe	+	o	o	o	o	o	1
Reinhardt	+	+	o	o	o	-	1
Heinrici	+	o	o	o	o	+	2
Von Luttwitz	o	o	-	o	o	o	-1
Balck	+	+	+	+	+	o	5
Zhukov Konev Rokossovsky	+	+	+	+	+	o	5
Petrov	+	+	+	+	o	o	4
Cherniakhovsky	+	+	-	o	o	o	1
Malinovsky Tolbukhin	+	+	o	o	o	-	1

Vistula-Oder operations, 1945 Leadership Assessment

February Campaigns, February 1–28, 1945

At the beginning of February 1945, the Ostheer had four army groups (Nord, Weichsel, Mitte, Süd) comprised of 11 armies, four of which were isolated. The Ostheer was still relatively strong on both flanks, with considerable combat power in East Prussia and Hungary, but it was extremely weak in the center. Both the Oder front and Silesia were protected only by bits and pieces. Fortified cities such as Breslau and Küstrin would slow the Soviet advance, but there really was very little to stop a direct advance to Berlin. At the same time, the Red Army had nine active fronts, two of which were tied down in Courland, one in East Prussia and two in Hungary, but four fronts (2nd Belorussian Front, 1st Belorussian Front, 1st Ukrainian Front and 4th Ukrainian Front) were well-positioned to continue the advance into the heart of Germany. Yet after three weeks of bold advances in January, the Stavka suddenly became more cautious in February. Rather than push on to Berlin, the Stavka recommended finishing off the encircled German armies in East Prussia and Budapest, while completing the conquest of Silesia and Slovakia. Senior Soviet leaders were wary about unexpected German counteroffensives, given the Ardennes operation in the West and Operation *Konrad* in Hungary. The Red Army was no longer operating on friendly soil and it was apparent that Hitler was throwing all available manpower reserves into the fight and encouraging fanatical resistance. Stalin wanted an assured victory and did not want it delayed because the

Red Army became overextended and made operational mistakes, as had occurred in the past. Thus the entire month of February essentially ended up becoming a series of large-scale Soviet mop-up operations, while the Germans conducted numerous spoiling attacks to gain time to build a defense along the Oder. Much of the combat occurred at the tactical level, rather than at the operational level.

In the northern theater, Bagramyan's 2nd Baltic Front was ordered to launch another offensive against Heeresgruppe Kurland in the Courland pocket. Generaloberst Heinrich von Vietinghoff was now in command of the forces in Courland. The fifth offensive began on February 12 and continued for two weeks, without accomplishing any significant results; losses on both sides were heavy. The primary Soviet objective in Courland was now to fix Heeresgruppe Nord in place and prevent it from transferring divisions by sea to reinforce Heeresgruppe Weichsel – this effort failed. In February, the Kriegsmarine was able to continue to keep a path open for convoys to transfer troops and equipment to the west and Heeresgruppe Kurland never ran out of ammunition or food.

In East Prussia, Cherniakhovsky's 3rd Belorussian Front focused on reducing the isolated AOK 4 in the Heiligenbeil pocket, the large German garrison in Königsberg and the nearby Samland Peninsula. German resistance was fierce and neither formation was entirely cut off, since they had access to supply by sea. On February 18 Cherniakhovsky was mortally wounded by an enemy antitank gun near the town of Melzak, 57km southwest of Königsberg. Cherniakhovsky had just been promoted to marshal and was riding in a staff car within one kilometer of the front and on a road known to be under enemy fire. Earlier, during the first East Prussian campaign, General Galitsky had noted an incident where Cherniakhovsky recklessly exposed himself to enemy fire and was nearly killed. In any case, his luck ran out and Marshal Vasilevsky took over the 3rd Belorussian Front for the remaining two months of the war. By the end of February, the Germans still retained both positions and siege warfare continued.

In Pomerania, Weiß' AOK 2 desperately tried to hold the line of the northern Vistula from Danzig down to Kulm (Chelmno) against the onslaught of Rokossovsky's 2nd Belorussian Front, but the line was already outflanked. On February 10, Rokossovsky attacked west of the Vistula with three armies (49, 65, 70), slowly clawing his way north toward Danzig across muddy terrain. By February 19, Rokossovsky halted his offensive, 70km southwest of Danzig. Zhukov's 1st Belorussian Front was essentially halted on the Oder and he focused considerable attention on the city of Küstrin and the fight to expand the nearby Soviet bridgeheads. Küstrin lay on the direct path to Berlin, but it had not been initially specified as an objective for either Chuikov's 8 GA or Berzarin's 5 SA until the Vistula-Oder operation was underway. By the time that Berzarin's 5 SA and some of Katukov's 1 GTA approached Küstrin, the Germans had just managed to slip a Panzergrenadier division into the city. It was soon obvious that the 1st Belorussian Front needed Küstrin in order to push on to Berlin, but efforts to storm the city failed. Consequently, Zhukov was left in a quandary. Efforts by Berzarin and Chuikov to encircle the city were frustrated by the arrival of a German Panzer division and a sudden thaw made it difficult to get Soviet armor and artillery across the Oder. Instead, two of Zhukov's armies spent much of February struggling to establish a siege around Küstrin; when the month ended, the city was still not fully encircled.

Zhukov also made an effort with his right wing to push into Pomerania using Bogdanov's 2 GTA and Belov's 61st Army in order to protect his flank. At the start of February, Pomerania was defended by a hodgepodge of German units, nominally reporting to Himmler's Heeresgruppe Weichsel. Himmler appointed General der Waffen-SS Felix Steiner to command the 11. Armee in Pomerania on January 26 and soon thereafter it was redesignated as the 11. SS-Panzerarmee (SS-PzAOK 11). Even though the Third Reich was on the verge of total defeat, Himmler used the apocalyptic situation to escalate the role of his Waffen-SS over the Heer. Hitler, no longer trusting the regular army, accommodated Himmler's agenda, which led to a vast expansion of the SS "franchise" in the last few months of the war. Previously, Waffen-SS commanders had only served at the tactical level and had no real experience or training for higher command, but now they were suddenly put in charge of major operations. Zhukov's thrust into Pomerania threatened to isolate AOK 2, so it was clear to the OKH that something had to be done to prevent this outcome. Panzer reserves, including some units withdrawn from Courland by sea, were hastily assembled near Stettin and Guderian recommended using them to conduct a counteroffensive against Zhukov's forces in Pomerania. Hitler was instead preoccupied with his own idea of mounting a counteroffensive in Hungary, using Generaloberst Sepp Dietrich's 6. SS-Panzerarmee, which was being transferred from the west. After much heated argument, Guderian finally convinced Hitler on February 13 to authorize a counterattack against Zhukov's forces in Pomerania, but Himmler wanted to lead it, which was ridiculous. Guderian insisted that his deputy, General der Panzertruppe Walther Wenck, would be attached to Himmler's staff to plan the operation, which was designated Unternehmen *Sonnenwende* (Operation *Solstice*).[11] Altogether, the OKH was able to gather nine divisions (six of which were Waffen-SS formations) for the offensive, including seven mechanized divisions. On paper, the three corps-size assault groups seemed impressive, but in reality these units totaled only 319 AFVs and were desperately short of fuel. Wenck was given just a few days to plan and organize the operation, which was complicated by poor communications and the fact that many of the units involved had not yet arrived in the assembly area.

Nevertheless, the German offensive began on February 15, with part of the III SS-Panzerkorps striking Belov's 61st Army. Initially Belov was caught by surprise and when more formations from the SS-PzAOK 11 joined the offensive on February 16, the Germans had some tactical success. However, Bogdanov's 2 GTA was soon on hand, initiating an armored battle of attrition near Stargard that sapped German strength. Steiner and his small SS staff were ineffective and could not decide on operational objectives, so the offensive devolved into uncoordinated tactical actions.[12] When Wenck was injured in a non-combat accident on February 17, the driving force behind the operation was gone. Once Zhukov reinforced this sector with Simoniak's 3 SA, the jig was up and Himmler terminated the operation. The only benefit from Unternehmen *Sonnenwende* was that it convinced Zhukov and the Stavka that the German forces in Pomerania should be crushed before moving on to Berlin. Thus, the Wehrmacht was afforded an extra month to strengthen its defenses along the Oder. Just as *Sonnenwende* was ending, Raus and the headquarters of PzAOK 3 arrived in Stettin and took over this sector. Raus reported to Himmler, but PzAOK 3 took command over most of Steiner's units, leaving SS-PzAOK 11 as little more than a rump command (which was soon grandiloquently redesignated as Armeegruppe Steiner). In just four months, Steiner went from being a corps commander to an army group commander, despite the lack of any formal officer training. Raus was left with ten weakened divisions and 70 tanks to hold a 240km-wide front in Pomerania.[13]

The momentum of Zhukov's advance to the Oder was sapped by the siege of Küstrin, the German counteroffensive in Pomerania and the need to deal with a number of bypassed German garrisons in Poland, such as Poznan (Posen) and Thorn. In addition, the adverse winter weather (including a sudden thaw with heavy rains) reduced Soviet operational mobility at a key moment. Supplying forces across the Oder proved nearly impossible until the weather improved and more pontoon bridges could be installed. Zhukov's theater-level logistics were also overstretched, since the railroad bridges over the Vistula had not yet been repaired. Despite all these problems, Zhukov's 1st Belorussian Front had suffered just 77,000 casualties during the Vistula-Oder offensive, leaving him with a level of operational reserves that the Germans lacked. Given the chaotic situation along the Oder River in early February, this might have been an opportune moment to use the Red Army's airborne brigades to seize key terrain across the river, but Zhukov was no longer sanguine about airborne operations as he once had been. A greater level of operational risk taking might have exploited gaps in the thin German line on the Oder, but Zhukov decided to play it safe. After the war, Chuikov argued that Zhukov could have made a push toward Berlin in February while the Germans were disorganized, but Zhukov disputed this.[14] Among historians, camps are divided – just as they are about the German decision not to push on to Moscow in September 1941 – about whether Zhukov might have taken Berlin sooner. Left unstated is the fact that Zhukov expected the Germans to mass their best units around Berlin for a fanatical, last-ditch defense – as he had done at Moscow in 1941.

In contrast to Zhukov's caution, Konev's 1st Ukranian Front continued its offensive after reaching the Oder River and plunged into Silesia. Schörner's Heeresgruppe Mitte lacked the strength to hold a continuous front and relied upon fanatical resistance at fortified positions to slow the enemy. When fanatical resistance was lacking, Schörner used draconian measures to try to instill it – namely by routinely executing soldiers accused of desertion or shirking their duties, which earned him the nickname of "the Hangman (der Henker)."[15] Schörner's personal motto was "Strength through Fear," which worked against the teamwork ethos in the Wehrmacht.[16] Gottlob Bidermann, a junior infantry officer who served under Schörner, stated that "every visit to the front [by Schörner] would be accompanied by threats."[17] Hitler liked this kind of commander, but Schörner's methods caused more harm than good and for all his chest-thumping, he proved to be a poor field commander. For his main effort, Konev massed three combined arms armies (3 GA, 13, 52) and two tank armies (3 GTA, 4 TA) which attacked from the Steinau bridgehead on February 8 and ran roughshod over Gräser's PzAOK 4. By the end of February, Konev had advanced to the Neisse River and was well positioned to support Zhukov's advance on Berlin. Konev assigned Gluzdovsky's 6th Army to deal with the German fortified city of Breslau, which was defended by a garrison of about 25,000. Gluzdovsky was able to surround Breslau by February 13, but an attempt to seize the city on

February 22 failed. Consequently, the siege of Breslau would continue until the end of the war.

The front in Slovakia was static in February 1945, with Petrov's 4th Ukrainian Front accomplishing nothing of note. Malinovsky's 2nd Ukrainian Front remained focused on the siege of Budapest, which was finally drawing to a close. On the night of February 11/12, the German garrison in Budapest attempted a breakout operation, even though Hitler had forbidden it. Of the 16,000 troops involved in the breakout, only 785 reached German lines – the rest were killed or captured.[18] Altogether, the Budapest operation cost Malinovsky's 2nd Ukrainian Front and Tolbukhin's 3rd Ukrainian Front a total of 320,000 casualties (including 80,000 dead or missing) and the loss of 1,766 tanks/SP guns.[19] Interestingly, the Soviets lost a great deal of artillery in the Budapest operation, totaling 4,127 guns and mortars – this was more than the Red Army lost at either Stalingrad or Kursk. The capture of Budapest was a costly Soviet victory, which was almost immediately followed up by a surprise German counteroffensive. At Heeresgruppe Süd, Wöhler had begun planning on February 10 for a counteroffensive against the Soviet Hron River bridgehead, which was expected to be the springboard for a Soviet offensive toward Vienna. The 6. SS-Panzerarmee was en route from the west, but Wöhler wanted to eliminate the bridgehead as a shaping operation to assist the anticipated larger offensive. The operation was designated Unternehmen *Südwind* (Operation *Southwind*).

The operation was planned by AOK 8, now under the leadership of General der Gebirgstruppe Hans Kreysing; he was a veteran commander who had demonstrated great ability as a division commander in the dark days after Stalingrad and again at the Nikopol bridgehead. Kreyser had virtually no staff experience and had spent the majority of his career in mid-level command assignments, but he had apparently learned a great deal after three years on the Eastern Front. AOK 8 was provided with the 1. SS-Panzerkorps with two SS-Panzer divisions (1 SS, 12 SS), which possessed a total of about 280 AFVs, plus several infantry divisions to conduct the operation. The bridgehead was defended by two rifle corps from Shumilov's 7 GA and a mechanized corps in tactical reserve. Kreysing's forces attacked on the morning of February 17; the weather was favorable and Shumilov's divisions in the bridgehead were caught by surprise. Kreysing massed his two SS-Panzer divisions into a *Schwerpunkt* and sliced through the Soviet front. In a week of heavy fighting, the Germans smashed the Soviet forces in the bridgehead and eliminated it – this was the last German operational victory on the Eastern Front.

A lot of things went right for the Germans in *Südwind*; Kreysing proved to be a competent operational-level commander who was able to mass effective combat power to achieve a clear objective through offensive maneuver, assisted by the use of surprise. Shumilov's infantry was up against some of the best remaining units in the Wehrmacht, and insufficient Soviet armor and airpower was made available to support the embattled 7 GA. As a result, Shumilov's 7 GA was defeated, although Kreysing's victory did not really change the situation in Hungary. Following this victory, Wöhler wanted to use all of the 6. SS-Panzerarmee (SS-PzAOK 6) to conduct an even larger offensive in Hungary, to be designated as Unternehmen *Frühlingserwachen* (Operation *Spring Awakening*); he submitted the operational outline to Hitler on February 22.[20] Hitler authorized the offensive to begin in early March.

March Campaigns, March 1–31, 1945

Amazingly both the Stavka and the OKH wanted to conduct major offensive operations in March 1945. The Stavka intended to defeat the German forces in both Pomerania/East Prussia and Hungary in order to set up the decisive final advances to Berlin and Vienna. In contrast, the OKH was preparing a major counteroffensive in Hungary, although it lacked the resources to be decisive and even its objectives were ambiguous. Harsh winter weather conditions had a major impact on these operations, as snow, rain and mud hindered mobility and air support at inopportune moments.

At the beginning of March, Heeresgruppe Nord (now under Lothar Rendulic) still had AOK 4 (General der Infanterie Friedrich-Wilhelm Müller) holding out at Königsberg and in the adjoining Samland and Heiligenbeil pockets. Bagramyan's 1st Baltic Front was responsible for taking Königsberg, while the 3rd Belorussian Front, now under Marshal Vasilevsky, was responsible for crushing the Heiligenbeil pocket. Bagramyan had four armies (39, 43, 50, 11 GA) while Vasilevsky had six armies (3, 28, 31, 48, 2 GA, 5 GTA). Vasilevsky recognized that the Germans had built a very strong defense around Königsberg, so he focused on crushing the Heiligenbeil pocket first. The 3rd Belorussian Front began its offensive against the pocket on March 13 and German resistance was desperate and fierce. Müller had 15 divisions in the pocket, including elite units like the *Großdeutschland* Panzergrenadier-Division. To reduce the pocket, Vasilevsky relied heavily upon artillery and aerial bombing.

After two weeks of fighting, the pocket finally collapsed, leading to the utter destruction of AOK 4 by March 28. Vasilevsky's operation was brutal and efficient. Some German survivors escaped by sea, but these refugees would contribute little in the few remaining weeks of the war. With the Heiligenbeil pocket out of the way, Bagramyan and Vasilevsky could focus all their attention on reducing the Königsberg garrison next.

In Pomerania, Heeresgruppe Weichsel had Weiß' AOK 2 defending the Danzig-Gdynia area in the east and Raus' PzAOK 3 holding the Stargard sector in the west. Rokossovsky's 2nd Belorussian Front, which had five armies (19, 49, 65, 70, 2 SA), was arrayed against Weiß' AOK 2, while Zhukov's 1st Belorussian Front had six armies (1 GTA, 2 GTA, 3 SA, 47, 61, 1st Polish) arrayed against Raus' army. Altogether, Zhukov and Rokossovsky had nearly 1 million troops and had plenty of air, artillery and armor support. The basic concept of the Soviet Pomeranian offensive was for both fronts to push north toward the Baltic Sea, then for Rokossovsky to pivot northeast to seize Danzig while Zhukov pivoted northwest to seize Stettin and gain additional crossings over the Oder. By late February the Soviets had already created a salient around Neustettin, lodged in the junction between the two German armies. The offensive began on March 1 and immediately put heavy pressure on Raus' thin line. By the second day, the German front was breaking apart and one German corps was encircled. By the fourth day, Katukov's 1 GTA had reached the Baltic near Kolberg, while Bogdanov's 2 GTA and Kreiser's 51st Army were approaching Stettin. Rokossovsky's 2nd Belorussian Front joined the offensive on March 5, pushing north from Neustettin and took the town of Köslin, just 6km from the coast, on the first day. The loss of Köslin severed communications between PzAOK 3 and AOK 2.

Himmler was stupefied by these rapid events and proved incapable of directing a defense of Pomerania; instead, he claimed an angina attack and retreated to a hospital bed to recover while his subordinate armies were fighting for their existence. After losing part of his army to encirclement and overrunning by rampaging Soviet armor, Raus fell back to the Oder to try to establish a new line. Raus grabbed all Wehrmacht personnel available, including many Kriegsmarine sailors, and equipped them with Panzerfaust antitank rockets for a final stand on the Oder. At the same time, Weiß' AOK 2 began falling back toward Danzig-Gdynia. Hitler was incensed by the rapid loss of Pomerania and relieved Raus of command on March 9; General der Panzertruppe Hasso von Manteuffel took over PzAOK 3 in its final days.[21] Much of the rest of the month was spent with the Soviets trying to seize the ports of Stettin and Danzig. Himmler was quietly relieved on March 20 and replaced by Generaloberst Gotthard Heinrici, although it made little difference at this point. The remnants of PzAOK 3 were crushed in desperate rearguard operations near Stettin, while AOK 2 was ground into dust at Danzig. By the end of March, Heeresgruppe Weichsel had effectively been obliterated, although mop-up operations continued. On March 28, Guderian was dismissed by Hitler as head of the OKH; at least there would be no further arguments about operational priorities.

Meanwhile, the rest of Zhukov's 1st Belorussian Front was focused on trying to expand its bridgeheads over the Oder and encircle the German garrison in the fortress of Küstrin. The city blocked the direct path to Berlin and was sited on terrain that heavily favored the defense, nestled between the Oder and Warta rivers. Much of the terrain around the fortress was flooded at this time, which made direct assaults almost suicidal. General der Infanterie Theodor Busse had been appointed head of AOK 9 in late January and charged with holding the Oder front. Busse had been von Manstein's senior staff officer for over three years and was a thoroughly professional officer – the sort that was becoming increasingly rare in the Wehrmacht of 1945. Guderian told Busse that "no matter what happens elsewhere, the Russians must be stopped on the Oder. It's our only hope."[22] Thanks to Zhukov's slow build-up along the Oder, Guderian was able to provide Busse with enough reinforcements to create a line of sorts on the Oder, but even by early March AOK 9 consisted of just six divisions. Even still, Busse succeeded in keeping a narrow corridor to the 10,000-man Küstrin garrison open for six weeks, despite repeated Soviet efforts to close it, with just a single mechanized division. In case Küstrin was lost, Busse also began constructing a main line of resistance further west, on the Seelow Heights. The Luftwaffe also concentrated its limited remaining strength to conduct air strikes (including some using guided missiles) on Zhukov's bridges over the Oder and did achieve limited success.[23]

Zhukov lost some of his focus on the Oder front in late February/early March due to the fluid situation in Pomerania and a trip he made back to Moscow to consult with Stalin. Returning to the front, on March 13 Zhukov ordered a new effort to eliminate the troublesome Küstrin position. On March 18, the Soviets began a massive air and artillery bombardment of the German defenses at Küstrin, which went on for four days. Then Zhukov launched a pincer operation, with Berzarin's 5 SA attacking from the north and Chuikov's 8 GA attacking from the south. Each Soviet army used only two reinforced rifle divisions in this effort. By the afternoon of March 22, the pincers had linked up and Küstrin was fully encircled.

Busse wanted to use his small tactical reserve to help the encircled Küstrin garrison effect a breakout, but Hitler would not allow the position to be evacuated. Heinrici, having just taken over Heeresgruppe Weichsel, managed to convince Hitler to authorize a major counterattack to reopen the corridor to Küstrin, which was acceptable. Busse was given some additional reinforcements, enabling him to concentrate four divisions and a Tiger tank battalion in the XXXIX Panzerkorps for the operation. On the morning of March 27, the Germans attacked with four divisions on line across a 6km-wide front; they were opposed primarily by Chuikov's 8 GA. Despite heavy fighting, the XXXIX Panzerkorps could not break through to Küstrin and Busse's relief operation faltered after one day. Chuikov's forces were now closing in on the encircled fortress, reducing one position after another. In the final actions, Chuikov employed three batteries of 203mm howitzers to use direct fire against the fortress, inflicting heavy damage. With no hope of relief and their ammunition nearly exhausted, the Küstrin garrison conducted a fairly successful breakout operation, with about 1,000 troops managing to reach German lines.[24] Once Küstrin was occupied and any threats from Pomerania removed, Zhukov could now begin planning his final advance to Berlin. The bridgehead at Küstrin would be the springboard for that advance.

Further south, Konev continued to overrun the rest of Silesia. Gräser's PzAOK 4 was able to organize a line in the Oder-Neisse triangle to block the southern approaches to Berlin, but Rybalko's 3 GTA was threatening to outflank the line. Rybalko's immediate objective was the town of Gorlitz and his army had recently captured the town of Lauban, 22km to the east, which sat astride a key rail line of communications for Schörner's Heeresgruppe Mitte. Rybalko's capture of Lauban initiated an unexpectedly potent German response. Gräser's PzAOK 4 had just received significant reinforcements, which he intended to use in a counterattack to retake Lauban and remove the threat to Gorlitz. Nehring was put in charge of the operation (Unternehmen *Gemse*), involving the XXXIX Panzerkorps and LVII Panzerkorps. The concept, as usual, was to conduct a pincer attack against two of Rybalko's corps near Lauban. Altogether, Nehring was able to mass three Panzer divisions (8, 16, 17) and four other divisions, with a total of about 200 AFVs. The operation began on March 1, amidst snow showers, and caught Rybalko's army completely by surprise.[25] The 3 GTA was down to only about one-third of its authorized strength in AFVs and it was dispersed, which made it highly vulnerable to a sudden flank attack. Nehring's Panzers succeeded in encircling and mauling the Soviet 7 GTC near Lauban, forcing Rybalko to request permission from

Konev to abandon the town. Although most of the encircled Soviet troops were able to escape, they had to abandon much of their equipment. *In toto*, the 3 GTC lost at least 80 tanks and 30 assault guns, while Nehring's forces lost about 40 AFVs.[26] Amazingly, the counterattack at Lauban was not only a tactical victory for PzAOK 4, but Rybalko's 3 GTA was so battered that it had to be pulled out of the line to refit. Afterwards, Konev was critical of Rybalko, accusing him of becoming overextended and underestimating the enemy.[27]

Flushed by this success, Schörner decided to shift some of Nehring's armor eastward to attempt an operation to relieve the siege of Breslau. A smaller pincer attack with two divisions was mounted against Zhadov's 5 GA near Striegau on March 9–14, but the results were unimpressive and Schörner called off the relief attack. The Soviet ring around Breslau was now impenetrable. Despite the setback suffered by Rybalko's 3 GTA, Konev continued with his preparations to clear the southern portion of Silesia. For the Upper Silesian operation, Konev planned a double pincer offensive, with the northern group consisting of Gusev's 21st Army and Lelyushenko's 4 TA and a southern group consisting of Korovnikov's 59th Army and Kurochkin's 60th Army. The objective of the converging pincers was the town of Neustadt, 95km southeast of Breslau. Konev opened his offensive on March 15. Schulz' AOK 17 put up stiff resistance along the Oder and inflicted heavy losses on Lelyushenko's armor, but within four days the Soviet spearheads reached Neustadt and trapped over 40,000 German troops from Korpsgruppe Schlesien (four divisions) in a pocket near Oppeln. Schulz used the XXIV Panzerkorps to assist a breakout effort, but this was brushed aside. In just two days, the pocket was crushed, with 14,000 prisoners taken.[28] AOK 17 took a beating from Konev's forces and Schulz was wounded in an air raid. The left flank of PzAOK 1 was also forced back, creating a gap between it and AOK 17. By the end of March, virtually all of Silesia was under Konev's control, except for the encircled garrisons in Breslau and Glogau, which would not last much longer.

Konev's victory in Silesia was not cheap, costing the 1st Ukrainian Front about 166,000 casualties (including 39,000 dead or missing), as well as a large amount of armor. Rybalko's 3 GTA lost two corps commanders and most of its tanks and Lelyushenko's 4 TA (upgraded to 4 GTA in March) also suffered heavy losses. Even though the Ostheer had few tanks and antitank guns left, the mass production of the expendable Panzerfaust antitank rocket was beginning to have an unexpected operational impact on Soviet armored operations. Konev noted in his memoirs that "in analyzing the causes of increased vulnerability of our tank units we must not forget that in Upper Silesia we had come up against such mass use of Panzerfausts for the first time during the war, and that we did not yet know how to fight them properly."[29] Soviet armor commanders had adopted an insouciant attitude toward German infantry – particularly *Volksgrenadier* – who had been easy to overrun before the advent of the Panzerfaust. Yet even the resource-starved Third Reich was able to produce the Panzerfaust in large numbers, greatly amplifying the antitank firepower of its infantry in the final weeks of the war. Israeli commanders would encounter a similar problem with missile-armed Egyptian infantry at the outset of the Yom Kippur War in October 1973.

While Konev was overrunning Silesia, Petrov's 4th Ukrainian Front was stumbling in its efforts to advance into Moravia. On February 13, the Stavka assigned Petrov the mission to seize the industrial city of Ostrava, then develop the situation for a follow-on advance to Prague. Rather unrealistically, the Stavka expected the 4th Ukrainian Front to advance 350km in 40–45 days.[30] Petrov had always been a "paint-by-numbers" kind of commander, but he displayed an elevated level of obtuseness during the planning phase of the so-called Moravian-Ostrava operation. Due to a lack of *maskirovka*, Armeegruppe Heinrici (PzAOK 1) was alerted to Soviet preparations for an offensive and even learned the location and timing of the attack, so any hope of surprise was lost. Then Petrov failed to mass adequate combat power to achieve his objective, assigning only part of Moskalenko's 38th Army and Grechko's 1 GA to the operation. His left wing, General-leytenant Anton I. Gastilovich's 18th Army, was merely assigned to conduct a reconnaissance in force. Heinrici's forces were limited to just the LIX Armeekorps in the Ostrava sector, but the mountainous terrain heavily favored the defense and the Germans had created four lines of field works, which incorporated some pre-war Czech fortifications. Moskalenko was a veteran commander and his 38th Army was reinforced with an artillery division and two Guards tank brigades for the offensive. However, when the morning for the start date arrived on March 10, a heavy snowstorm reduced visibility to near zero. Moskalenko urged Petrov to request a delay from the Stavka, as did Grechko. Petrov replied that "the dates have been approved by Headquarters, they are final. I will not ask for a postponement of the offensive time."[31]

As a result, the 4th Ukrainian Front offensive proceeded on schedule, without surprise, mass or effective artillery support. Consequently, the attacks by Moskalenko's 38th Army and Grechko's 1 GA failed to achieve a breakthrough and suffered heavy casualties. After a week of bloody and indecisive combat, the offensive was terminated. The Stavka was extremely annoyed with Petrov for this failure, and he was soon relieved of command and given a senior staff position in Konev's headquarters; Eremenko was selected to take his place but would not arrive until March 26. In the interim, Moskalenko took the lead in reworking the operational plan for the offensive in an effort to improve the odds for success. When Eremenko arrived, the offensive was resumed and was beginning to achieve some success by the end of March. Nevertheless, it is fair to say that Heinrici achieved a defensive success in the first phase of the operation by preventing the 4th Ukrainian Front from making any progress toward its objectives.

In Hungary, the final stages of the war in the East took an unexpected turn in March. Hitler insisted on committing the bulk of his remaining armor – ten Panzer divisions with a total of about 770 operational AFVs – to a major counteroffensive at Lake Balaton. The overall objective of Unternehmen *Frühlingserwachen* (Operation *Spring Awakening*) was to eliminate all Soviet forces west of the Danube, which consisted of four of Tolbukhin's armies (4 GA, 26, 27, 57). Several versions of the operational plan were developed, but the variant chosen was compiled by Generalmajor Helmuth von Grolman, chief of staff of Heeresgruppe Süd. The plan was unduly complicated because it involved units from four different armies, each of which was assigned its own operational objectives. The main effort would be made by Dietrich's SS-PzAOK 6 with five Panzer divisions (totaling 309 AFVs), which would smash through the front held by Gagen's 26th Army and, then push on to the Danube. Balck's AOK 6 would make a supporting attack on Dietrich's left flank with two Panzer divisions (109 AFV) against Zakhvataev's 4 GA to clear the area east of Lake Velencei. In addition, the PzAOK 2 would make a supporting attack with four divisions south of Lake Balaton and Heeresgruppe E would cross the Drava River with four infantry divisions. The basic scheme of maneuver was a strong frontal attack, but fairly weak supporting attacks on the flanks. Balck also decided to keep the IV SS-Panzerkorps and 6. Panzer-Division (totaling 170 AFVs) in reserve. In terms of operational art, *Frühlingserwachen* was rather crudely put together and its weaknesses were exacerbated by the failure to fully consider terrain, weather and enemy resistance. Furthermore, the Soviets detected the impending German offensive and Tolbukhin quickly moved to reinforce the antitank defenses in the likely attack sectors. Both the 26th Army and 4 GA were given a tank corps and a brigade of tank destroyers (Su-100) and Trofimenko's 27th Army was deployed nearby in second echelon.

On March 6, *Frühlingserwachen* began and Dietrich's main effort quickly found that the Red Army had perfected the integration of mines and antitank guns in its deliberate defense tactics. However unlike *Zitadelle*, the German Panzer spearheads no longer had engineers to clear the mines, artillery to suppress the enemy Pak fronts and Luftwaffe close air support to knock out enemy armored reserves. German mobility was also seriously hindered by thick mud and waterlogged terrain. In three days of fighting, Dietrich did manage to advance about 30km, but his armored spearheads were unable to make any real progress over the Sarviz Canal. Tolbukhin committed Trofimenko's 27th Army to stiffen the defenses in front of SS-PzAOK 6 and also requested Kravchenko's 6 GTA and Glagolev's 9 GA. The German attacks on the flanks achieved even less success and made only minor advances. By March 12, it was apparent that *Frühlingserwachen* had ground to a halt everywhere and that Tolbukhin's forces were simply too strong. Wöhler decided to allow the operation to continue for several more days, but finally terminated it on March 15. The German Panzer assault groups were left holding an exposed salient, with insufficient infantry to hold the line. Not only had the counteroffensive failed to achieve any of its operational objectives, but it was an extravagant diversion of the Wehrmacht's dwindling armored reserves in a secondary theater. Had Dietrich's SS-PzAOK 6 been sent to the Oder front – as Guderian wanted – it might have served a more useful purpose. German material losses during the counteroffensive were not crippling, perhaps 10 percent of the committed AFVs deployed were destroyed and another 20 percent damaged, but fuel reserves and spare parts were virtually exhausted.

Once it was clear that the German counteroffensive had been halted, Tolbukhin immediately shifted gears and began his own offensive, designated as the Vienna operation. On March 16, Tolbukhin committed the 4 GA and 9 GA against Balck's AOK 6, holding the sector north of Lake Velencei. Although the IV SS Panzerkorps enabled Balck to withstand the initial Soviet attacks, the Hungarian 3rd Army soon disintegrated. Tolbukhin also committed the 26th and 27th Armies to launch concentric attacks against the salient held by SS-PzAOK 6, in an effort to pin Dietrich's best divisions. This was the moment to commit Kravchenko's 6 GTA (which had just been transferred from Malinovsky's 2nd Ukrainian Front) to exploit the Hungarian collapse and envelop the main German assault force, but the situation on the ground changed too rapidly. By the time that Kravchenko's 6 GTA began its forward passage of lines through the 9 GA on the morning of March 19, Dietrich was already pulling back out of the salient – without authorization from Wöhler.[32] Balck's AOK 6 put up an intense rearguard action against 6 GTA on March 20–21, which enabled the SS-PzAOK 6 to slip out of the potential trap. Balck had more difficulty disengaging and lost one of his infantry divisions, which he blamed on the Waffen-SS. Indeed, Balck pointedly referred to "false reporting" and disobedience by Waffen-SS commanders; the poor state of relations between AOK 6 and SS-PzAOK 6 certainly helped to undermine any remaining hope for the defense of western Hungary.[33]

It is clear that Balck was left holding the bag as SS-PzAOK 6 retreated to save itself. Wöhler proved fairly helpless and Hitler was enraged when he learned that Waffen-SS divisions were retreating without permission. On March 22, a combined assault by the 9 GA, 4 GA and 6 GTA in the region between Lake Balaton and Lake Velencei blasted a huge hole in Balck's front, which could not be repaired. By the next day, most of Heeresgruppe Süd was withdrawing – without authorization – into Austria. On March 25, Malinovsky's 2nd Ukrainian Front joined the offensive by attacking Kreysing's AOK 8, which began falling back into western Slovakia. Wöhler lost control over the retreating fragments of Heeresgruppe Süd and his relief was imminent. Dietrich's SS-PzAOK 6 did not even bother conducting a fighting retreat but retreated as fast as it could to Austria, which left Balck's flank exposed. Indeed, even veteran Waffen-SS units like the *LSSAH* began to disintegrate into small *Kampfgruppen* that were incapable of resisting Tolbukhin's advance. On March 30, Kravchenko's 6 GTA crossed the Austrian border and it was apparent that Vienna would soon fall. Tolbukhin had achieved a double operational success: first in stopping the German counteroffensive, then in launching his own offensive which shattered Heeresgruppe Süd and opened the path to Vienna.

Both sides struggled with battlefield command during February and March 1945 due to a variety of factors. The Ostheer was a wounded animal, shorn of many of its veteran leaders and increasingly led by amateurs and constrained by near suicidal no-retreat directives from Berlin. The Red Army was approaching its peak capabilities, but it was overextended and its leaders were trying to avoid making any mistakes that could delay the final victory. On the German side, none of the army group commanders were able to make much of a difference at this point and were increasingly managers of dwindling resources. Among the army-level commanders, Kreysing and Nehring stand out for demonstrating that the Wehrmacht still had the ability to pull off an operational success, under the right conditions. Busse demonstrated considerable ability in frustrating Zhukov's efforts to encircle Küstrin for six weeks – a significant accomplishment. Weiß and Raus were in charge of doomed armies and could do little but try to inflict the maximum damage on the enemy while holding key terrain as long as possible. The two senior Waffen-SS commanders demonstrated no skill at operational-level warfare and the equipment lavished on their formations would likely have been better used by veteran Ostheer commanders.

On the Soviet side, Tolbukhin's performance in Hungary was outstanding, employing all the principles of war, and resulted in a rare double operational victory. Zhukov and Rokossovsky also conducted excellent campaigns in Pomerania, although Zhukov's performance along the Oder was sub-par. Konev and Vasilevsky also performed well as front commanders and both achieved major successes in this period as well. Petrov was the only front commander who failed in this period. He had always been a mediocre field commander, but Petrov's real problem was that the commissar for the 4th Ukrainian Front was Lev Mekhlis, a malignant figure who had been tongue-lashing Petrov since the Crimean campaign in 1942. Simply put, Petrov was intimidated by Mekhlis and rather than request a delay in his offensive and invite censure, he allowed it to go forward and fail. In many respects, Petrov's discomfiture was a legacy of the purges, with some Red Army commanders more focused on personal repercussions than on sound military decision-making. Among the tank army commanders, who now led the Red Army's great advances, most continued to perform well. The one exception was Rybalko, who continued to suffer unnecessary losses and was caught off guard, leading to a significant reverse. The Red Army now had its winning team, with few changes among senior cadre in the final months of the war.

Commander	Objective	Offensive	Mass	Maneuver	Surprise	Security	TALLY
Wöhler	+	+	+	o	-	o	2
Schörner	+	+	o	o	o	o	2
Kreysing Nehring	+	+	+	+	+	o	5
Busse	+	o	o	o	o	+	2
Balck	+	+	o	o	o	o	2
Weiß Raus	+	o	o	o	o	o	1
Steiner	o	+	o	o	o	o	1
Dietrich	+	+	+	-	-	o	1
Tolbukhin	+	+	+	+	+	+	6
Zhukov Rokossovsky	+	+	+	+	+	o	5

Konev Vasilevsky	+	+	+	+	o	o	4
Petrov	+	+	o	o	–	–	o
Katukov Bogdanov Kravchenko	+	+	+	+	o	o	4
Rybalko	+	+	o	+	o	–	2

February–March operations, 1945 Leadership Assessment

The Final Campaigns, April 1–May 2, 1945

Soviet planning for the final offensive against Berlin had begun in late 1944 and was heavily influenced by Stalin's preferences. In early 1945, Stalin stipulated that he wanted Zhukov's 1st Belorussian Front to take Berlin, but he also told the Stavka that he wanted at least two fronts to be assigned to this objective. However, Marshal Konev's 1st Ukrainian Front was initially prevented from participating in operational planning because the front demarcation lines stipulated that his command would operate south of Berlin. Unwilling to point this contradiction out to Stalin, the Stavka let it slide until late March.[34] It was not until a planning conference on April 1 that the demarcation line issue was resolved – sort of – by Stalin; Konev would be allowed to use part of his front to swing north toward Berlin, but the rest had to push on into Saxony, toward Dresden and the Elbe River. On April 2, Stalin, through the Stavka, approved the operational concept for the final offensive in Germany.

In short, Zhukov's 1st Belorussian Front was designated as the main effort. He would attack west from Küstrin with six armies (8 GA, 3 SA, 5 SA, 47, 1 GTA, 2 GTA) in first echelon and one in second echelon (3) to seize Berlin. Konev's 1st Ukrainian Front would conduct a support effort, clearing enemy forces from around Cottbus, then sending two or more armies toward Berlin and the rest toward Dresden. Based on Stalin's guidance, whoever (Zhukov or Konev) achieved a breakthrough first could mount a direct attack on Berlin, which was unusually open-ended for Soviet operational planning. North of Berlin, Rokossovsky's 2nd Belorussian Front would continue to eliminate the German forces along the Baltic coast.[35] Detailed planning at the front level was fairly rushed for the Berlin operation because Stalin wanted to take the city before the

Western Allies reached the Elbe River; Zhukov and Konev and their staffs were given just two weeks to complete their work.

The 1st Belorussian Front immediately began building up its forces in the Küstrin bridgehead, including constructing more pontoon bridges and moving artillery and supplies into the crowded area. Zhukov could not conceal the build-up and the Luftwaffe used its limited remaining aircraft to repeatedly attack the bridges. At the same time, the Soviet 16 VA flew 2,600 reconnaissance sorties over the region, photographing the German defenses in great detail.[36] The 1st Belorussian Front's rear services moved over 1 million artillery rounds to the forward assembly areas. By mid-April, the Küstrin bridgehead was jam-packed with 41 rifle divisions, over 10,000 artillery pieces and 2,600 tanks. Zhukov knew that Busse's AOK 9 had placed its main line of resistance on the Seelow Heights, but he expected to blast through this position in a day or so, then release his two tank armies to exploit westward. Bogdanov's 2 GTA would approach Berlin from the northeast while Katukov's 1 GTA would swing around the city to the south. Stalin expected the operation to begin in mid-April and be completed in two weeks. Zhukov's operational concept, developed by his chief of staff General-polkovnik Mikhail S. Malinin, relied upon mass and aggressive offensive action, with some maneuver, to achieve a clear objective. However, Zhukov's plan was not based on a good understanding of the terrain and enemy resistance that the 1st Belorussian Front would need to overcome to reach that objective.

Heinrici, now in command of Heeresgruppe Weichsel, faced an extremely poor situation at the beginning of April. Busse's AOK 9 stood between Berlin and Zhukov's coiled masses with just 15 divisions, most of which were hastily created ersatz formations, supplemented by drafts of Luftwaffe and Kriegsmarine personnel, plus numerous *Volkssturm* (militia) detachments. Busse had a total of about 200,000 troops with 2,600 artillery pieces and 500 AFVs to hold the Oder front, but ammunition and fuel shortages would severely constrain operations. Heinrici's only operational reserve available was Steiner's III SS-Panzerkorps (three divisions) deployed north of Berlin on the Oder front, in the PzAOK 3 sector. If Heinrici moved Steiner's corps south to support Busse, then von Manteuffel's PzAOK 3 would be left in the lurch. As it was, the PzAOK 3 was only holding onto Stettin with difficulty against Rokossovsky's 2nd Belorussian Front and was near the breaking point. South of Berlin, Schörner's Heeresgruppe Mitte was holding off Konev's 1st Ukrainian Front with Gräser's PzAOK 4 in the Cottbus sector; this once-proud Panzerarmee was reduced to just a single Panzer division and four infantry divisions.

Southwest of Berlin, a new German army – the AOK 12 – was stood up on April 10 to defend the Elbe line near Magdeburg. Wenck, recovered from his injuries, was put in charge of AOK 12, which consisted of nine "instant" divisions formed from new conscripts, labor personnel, cadres from military schools and garrison soldiers from Norway. Aside from the original Panzer divisions – most of which were in Hungary – the Ostheer had very few veteran troops left at the front. The Luftwaffe was also at a low ebb – it had plenty of aircraft but very little fuel. A new command, known as Luftwaffenkommando Nordost, was formed on April 12 to support Heinrici's army group; this formation had 1,433 aircraft. Although the Ju-87 Stukas and level bombers could no longer effectively operate in airspace dominated by enemy fighters, the German Fw-190 fighter bombers still had the ability to conduct low-level attack sorties.

Prior to the Second World War, the Wehrmacht had never put much effort into developing defensive doctrine, but four years of combat on the Eastern Front had changed that mindset. For the final defense of the Oder, Heinrici put all the lessons that the Ostheer had learned about stopping Soviet offensives into play. He created a defense in depth extending back 40km from the forward edge of the battle area (FEBA); the first zone was 8–10km in width and intended to slow the enemy, the second zone extended another 10km back, then a third zone of fortified villages was created to block any Soviet armored breakthrough units. The Seelow Heights, 17km southwest of the Küstrin bridgehead, had natural defensive benefits since the ridgeline overlooked a flat plain crisscrossed by irrigation ditches. Due to the spring thaw, the surrounding ground was waterlogged and virtually a bog. Heinrici's troops established minefields and antitank ditches on all the approaches, which were covered by interlocking fire from multiple positions. By mid-April, the Seelow Heights were a formidable position, with a lethal kill zone prepared, even when defended by inexperienced second-rate troops. However, in order for Heinrici's defensive system to have a chance of success, he needed to have mobile reserves to crush any enemy breakthrough, but these reserves were lacking. For tactical reserves, Busse only had the brigade-size *Müncheberg* Panzer-Division (51 AFV), the *Kurmark* Panzergrenadier-Division (62 AFV) and a battalion of Tiger tanks. When Heinrici asked Hitler for more reserves, he was rebuffed.[37]

Although Zhukov could not hope to gain operational surprise (the Germans could easily see the build-up in the Küstrin bridgehead) he hoped to gain tactical surprise by attacking two hours before sunrise. He intended to use 143 searchlights to provide illumination. Buoyed by the rapid success in the Vistula-Oder operation, Zhukov expected another rapid breakthrough and occupation of the Seelow Heights by the end of the first day. He expected to be on the outskirts of Berlin by the fourth day of the operation. Zhukov placed great faith in his artillery and massed an unprecedented amount of firepower to support his advance – over 16,000 guns, mortars and MRLs. The highest density would be achieved in Chuikov's 8 GA sector, with 326 artillery pieces per kilometer of front.[38] General-polkovnik Vasily I. Kazakov, the front artillery commander, would direct the barrage. Zhukov started an aggressive counter-reconnaissance battle on April 14, with each of the assault armies committing 6–12 reinforced rifle battalions to probe the enemy defenses to their front. During this two-day effort, Soviet engineers began clearing paths through the German minefields, but the Soviet probing actions failed to identify many of the German front-line positions and suffered fairly heavy losses. Furthermore, the scale of the counter-reconnaissance effort alerted Busse and Heinrici that a large-scale enemy offensive was imminent, so on the evening of April 15 they requested permission from Hitler to thin out the number of troops in the first defensive zone. Amazingly, he agreed to the request.

Before dawn on April 16, Zhukov went to Chuikov's forward command post to observe the opening of the offensive. At 0400 hours (local), the massive Soviet artillery preparation began; it was one of the greatest concentrations of firepower in the history of warfare. Soon, over 700 Soviet bombers joined in, dropping 884 tons of bombs on the German forward positions (which were now only lightly manned). Along most of the Oder front, the armies of the 1st Belorussian Front succeeded in breaking through AOK 9's first defensive zone. On the right, the 1st Polish Army (LWP) managed to cross the Oder River. Next in line, Perkhorovich's 47th Army advanced 9km on the first day, Kuznetsov's 3 SA advanced 8km and Berzarin's 5 SA advanced 10km. However, in the center, at the Küstrin bridgehead, Chuikov's 8 GA was barely able to advance 1,500 meters during the morning and suffered very heavy casualties. Zhukov's use of searchlights proved worse than useless by enabling the German artillery to better see the advancing Soviet shock groups. When Chuikov informed Zhukov about his lack of progress, the latter snapped back, "What the hell do you mean – your troops are pinned down?"[39] In response, Zhukov did an incredible thing – at 1100 hours he decided to commit Katukov's 1 GTA into the battle, even though the enemy defense on the Seelow Heights was still intact. The result was massive congestion on the battlefield, which the German artillery pounded. The Luftwaffe also arrived in force, flying over 800 sorties against ground targets and destroying both railway bridges at

Küstrin. By the end of the first day, Zhukov's armies had seriously dented the German defense on the right, but the center was intact. From the German point of view, the AOK 9 had done better than expected on the first day and achieved a limited defensive success; forcing an enemy to prematurely commit his armor reserve was a bonus. Yet Busse had needed all his tactical reserves to hold the line on the first day and these small units would not last long.

On April 17, the offensive became a battle of attrition, with the 1st Belorussian Front gradually grinding forward against fierce German resistance. Some German infantry units were beginning to crumble and ammunition was running short. Heinrici requested the release of the III SS-Panzerkorps to reinforce Busse's AOK 9; Hitler spent much of the day considering this action, but finally approved it. Consequently, the SS-*Nordland* Division and other units would arrive in the AOK 9 sector by April 18. After two days of heavy fighting, Zhukov had not achieved a breakthrough. On April 18, the same battle of attrition continued, but Busse's left flank was beginning to give way. The German center was also beginning to crumble under the constant pounding, but Busse committed his best units to this sector and managed to hold Chuikov back for another day. However, by the fourth day, the battle swung in Zhukov's favor when AOK 9's depleted units began to fold up. Much of the success was due to the northern wing of 1st Belorussian Front – Perkhorovich's 47th Army and the 1st Polish Army. By the evening of April 19, AOK 9's defense was broken, but it had been achieved at the cost to 1st Belorussian Front of 33,000 dead and 743 AFVs destroyed.[40] Many of the German defenders slipped away to join the Berlin garrison.

Zhukov's management of the seizure of the Seelow Heights was grotesque, with decision-making made without regard to terrain, casualties or enemy resistance. Zhukov's battle plan made a fetish of mass and firepower, but eschewed maneuver and surprise. Even though his flank armies were achieving more success than Chuikov's 8 GA – which attacked straight into the enemy buzzsaw – Zhukov apparently never considered shifting his main effort to his right. Instead, he adopted tunnel vision and just keep seeking a breakthrough in the center, which allowed Busse to mass his best units there to frustrate him for four days of intense combat. Once AOK 9 was broken, Zhukov sent Chuikov's 8 GA and Katukov's 1 GTA on a direct path to Berlin, while the 3 SA and 5 SA would head for the northern suburbs of Berlin.

While Zhukov was hung up on the Seelow Heights, Konev's 1st Ukrainian Front was enjoying great success against Gräser's PzAOK 4.

Konev began his offensive at 0615 hours on April 16, with a 40-minute artillery preparation followed by an assault crossing of the Neisse River. The 1st Ukrainian Front made its main effort with three armies attacking on line (Gordov's 3 GA, Pukhov's 13th Army, Zhadov's 5 GA), with each army crossing the Neisse in two places. In a clever move, Konev used extensive smoke screens to conceal his river crossing from German artillery fire, which undoubtedly helped to keep his casualties down.[41] The PzAOK 4 only had five divisions in the Cottbus sector and it was unable to prevent all three Soviet armies from gaining large bridgeheads; Pukhov had the most success and was able to advance over 10km. Gräser launched a counterattack with the 21. Panzer-Division but this was too puny to have any significant effect. By nightfall, Soviet engineers had built pontoon bridges over the Neisse and both the 3 GTA and 4 GTA had begun crossing to the west bank. On April 17, Konev attacked in full force and smashed the center of PzAOK 4, then the two tank armies were committed to exploit this success. Konev requested that he be allowed to pivot his right wing to the north to envelop Berlin and Stalin agreed, since Zhukov had yet to achieve a breakthrough. By the third day of his offensive, Konev was advancing rapidly as the remnants of PzAOK 4 retreated.

Despite the collapse of the Oder front, Hitler ordered Busse to hold his positions, which was a death warrant for AOK 9. In the second phase of the Berlin offensive, Zhukov's 1st Belorussian Front converged on the capital from the east and northeast, while Konev's 1st Ukrainian Front moved in from the south. By April 25, Zhukov and Konev had surrounded Berlin and began reducing the garrison. On the same day, some of Konev's forces reached the Elbe River and met US Army units at Torgau. Rokossovsky's 2nd Belorussian Front joined the operation on April 20 and it took one week of heavy fighting to push PzAOK 3 back from the Oder River and achieve a breakthrough. The final phase of the Berlin operation consisted of two distinct types of operations: mop-up of encircled German garrisons in Berlin and other cities, and pursuit/exploitation operations. All of the fighting in Berlin, which lasted one week, was at the tactical level. About 150,000 troops from Busse's AOK 9 were isolated southeast of Berlin, and on April 28 Heinrici tried to save them from destruction by Konev's forces by ordering them to break out to the west. Upon hearing this, Hitler relieved Heinrici of command. Nevertheless, AOK 9 was able to conduct a fighting withdrawal to the west, through Konev's forces. The army was virtually destroyed in the process, but perhaps 20–25,000 survivors reached Wenck's AOK 12, which was itself withdrawing to the Elbe to surrender to the Americans.[42] Inside Berlin, the remnants of the garrison surrendered on May 2. The Berlin operation was an expensive victory given the disparity of forces, costing the three Soviet fronts (1st Belorussian Front, 2nd Belorussian Front, 2nd Ukrainian Front) a total of 352,000 casualties (including 78,000 dead or missing) and the loss of nearly 2,000 AFVs in just over two weeks of fighting.[43]

Elsewhere, Vasilevsky completed the East Prussian operation by launching a massive assault against Königsberg on April 6, which brought about the capitulation of the garrison three days later. A follow-on operation was conducted to eliminate the trapped German forces in Samland and capture Pillau, but resistance continued until April 27. Between January and April 1945, the Red Army formations (3rd Belorussian Front, 2nd Belorussian Front, 1st Baltic Front) involved in the East Prussian campaign suffered a grand total of 584,000 casualties (including 126,000 dead or missing) and the loss of 3,525 AFVs; this was one of the most costly Soviet victories in the Second World War.

Further south, Tolbukhin's 2nd Ukrainian Front was advancing rapidly toward Vienna with three armies (6 GTA, 9 GA, 46) and there was nothing that Wöhler's Heeresgruppe Süd could do to stop them. It was not so much a matter of equipment – Wöhler had the best-equipped divisions left in the Wehrmacht – but as Balck reported to Berlin, morale was low and the fighting spirit was gone. Kravchenko's 6 GTA was not a particularly strong force since it had suffered heavy losses in March that had not yet been replaced, but its veteran troops quickly swooped in on Vienna from the south while two other armies approached from the east. Hitler demanded that Wöhler launch counterattacks to stop them, but when these failed to materialize he was relieved of command and replaced by Rendulic on April 7. Rendulic ordered the III SS-Panzerkorps to establish a defense of sorts on the outskirts of Vienna and Hitler sent two divisions to reinforce them. Normally, the SS-*Das Reich* and SS-*Totenkopf* Divisions could be expected to conduct fanatical resistance, but not in this case. After less than a week of fighting, when Vienna was not yet surrounded, the Waffen-SS units disengaged and evacuated the city so they could head west and surrender to the Western Allies. Tolbukhin's troops marched into Vienna on April 13, effectively bringing that operation to a close. At the same time, Malinovsky's 2nd Ukrainian Front occupied Bratislava on April 4 and cleared southwestern Czechoslovakia. Eremenko's 4th Ukrainian Front, after a tough fight that lasted two weeks, finally occupied the town of Ostrava on April 30.[44] Although enemy resistance was inconsistent in these final weeks of the war, Tolbukhin and Malinovsky still suffered over 50,000 dead in these final operations.

The last Soviet offensive in Europe in the Second World War was the Prague operation, which involved three fronts (1st Ukrainian Front, 2nd Ukrainian Front, 4th Ukrainian Front). In the closing stages of the Battle of Berlin, Stalin turned to the next objective and ordered Konev to begin preparing part of his front to move against Prague. In addition to the fact that the remnants of Heeresgruppe Mitte were trying to re-form around Prague, Stalin wanted to occupy the Czech capital before local nationalists could launch an uprising, as the Poles had in Warsaw. It should be noted that in addition to operations in Berlin, Konev also still had two of his armies besieging *Festung* Breslau (which would hold out until May 6). Konev and his staff demonstrated a great deal of flexibility in juggling current operations while simultaneously regrouping their armies and preparing for another operation in an opposite direction. The hastily planned operation, put together in just three days, envisioned a broad front advance by the 1st Ukrainian Front into northern Bohemia by no fewer than ten armies; the main effort would be made on the Dresden-Prague axis by Lelyushenko's 4 GTA, Rybalko's 3 GTA, Pukhov's 13th Army and Gordov's 3 GA. Malinovsky's 2nd Ukrainian Front and Eremenko's 4th Ukrainian Front would support Konev's operation by continuing to advance west through Moravia. The operation was expected to begin on May 6.

However, before Konev could act, Czech insurgents staged a national uprising on May 5 and seized a good portion of Prague. At this point, Schörner's Heeresgruppe Mitte held Bohemia with the remnants of Gräser's PzAOK 4 and AOK 17 (now under General der Infanterie Wilhelm Hasse), while AOK 8 and PzAOK 1 were trying to make a stand in Moravia. Schörner promptly committed some of his Waffen-SS units to suppress the uprising, rather than keep them as a reserve against the impending Soviet offensive. On the morning of May 6, Konev began his offensive and had little difficulty overwhelming PzAOK 4's thin front line. Within three days, Rybalko's 3 GTA and Zhadov's 5 GA had captured Dresden and Lelyushenko's 4 GTA was closing in on Prague. Despite learning about the impending capitulation, Schörner ordered his subordinates to continue resisting the Soviet advance, although some troops were already trying to slip westward to surrender to the US Army, which had entered western Bohemia. Most German forces evacuated Prague on the night of May 8/9 and Konev's armored spearheads entered the city on the morning of May 9. Schörner abandoned his army and flew westward to Bavaria, where he was captured in civilian clothes by the Americans, who then handed him over to the Red Army.[45] Although some German units succeeded in reaching American lines, the bulk of Heeresgruppe Mitte's personnel in Czechoslovakia were captured by Konev's 1st Ukrainian Front by the time the operation was terminated on May 11. Despite minimal German resistance in this final week of the war in Europe, the Prague operation still cost the Red Army 49,000 casualties (including 11,000 dead or missing) and 373 AFVs.

In the final month of the war in Europe, German operational commanders could do very little to influence the course of events due to the unrealistic guidance received from Hitler. Heinrici did the best of the senior German commanders in maintaining his front on the Oder for as long as possible and inflicting maximum casualties upon Zhukov's forces. He was singlemindedly focused on his objective (unlike Hitler, who kept shifting priorities to anywhere but the Oder front) of blocking access to Berlin and he was fairly successful in adopting security measures to prevent Zhukov from gaining operational surprise against AOK 9. Schörner's conduct in Czechoslovakia was less successful and showed his limitations as a senior commander and his lack of moral integrity (e.g. shooting deserters then deserting himself). Indeed, Heeresgruppe Mitte was virtually leaderless and coasting on inertia for the last few weeks of the war. The army group objective was either to create a national redoubt in Bohemia or to escape west to surrender to the Americans, but conducting a deliberate defense of the region seems to have been a low priority.

On the Soviet side, Zhukov's performance at the Seelow Heights was heavily criticized by his contemporaries, particularly by General-polkovnik Vasily I. Kuznetsov (3 SA) and Chuikov (8 GA).[46] Zhukov (and his staff) built their final battle plan around the principles of mass, offensive and objective, but failed to utilize maneuver or surprise. Indeed, by cramming so many units into the German kill zone in front of the Seelow Heights, Zhukov's use of maneuver put his own forces at a grave disadvantage. As a result, approximately 33,000 of Zhukov's troops died in a four-day fight for a minor terrain feature that was defended by an enemy that was outnumbered 10-1.[47] Compounding his errors during the breakout battle, Zhukov was left short of infantry for the final push into Berlin and forced to use tank armies and Polish (LWP) rifle units for the final phase of urban combat. Consequently, Zhukov's poor performance on the Oder is in stark contrast to his excellent planning for the Vistula-Oder operation. In large part, Zhukov's sub-par generalship during the Berlin operation appears based upon his underestimation of the fanatical nature of last-ditch enemy resistance; he was flabbergasted that the Germans could stop Chuikov's 8 GA and hold their ground for four days. He was also mesmerized by mass – as Russian commanders have often been – and failed to appreciate the moral dimension of warfare. The morale in Wehrmacht units in Hungary was dissipating, but not on the Oder front, where the troops were fighting to defend their native soil against a hated enemy; Zhukov could not comprehend that kind of non-empirical data. Russian commanders had made this mistake in Finland in 1939 and they would make similar mistakes in underestimating their enemies in Afghanistan in the 1980s, Chechnya in the 1990s and Ukraine in 2022.

The rest of the Soviet front-level commanders did quite well in the final campaigns. Konev's performance was superb and he demonstrated great flexibility, first by executing a "be prepared" mission to support the push into Berlin, then quickly reorienting his line of operations (LOO) 180° degrees to advance to Prague (hence the extra + here, for maneuver). Rokossovsky and Tolbukhin also properly used offensive, mass and maneuver to achieve all their operational objectives along the Baltic coast and in Austria. Malinovsky and Eremenko, in charge of what were essentially supporting operations, still achieved all their objectives despite adverse terrain and enemy resistance.

Commander	Objective	Offensive	Mass	Maneuver	Surprise	Security	TALLY
Heinrici	+	o	o	o	o	+	2
Schörner	o	o	o	o	o	o	o
Zhukov	+	+	+	–	–	o	1
Konev	+	+	+	++	o	o	5
Rokossovsky Tolbukhin	+	+	+	+	o	o	4
Malinovsky Eremenko	+	+	+	o	o	o	3

The Final Battles, 1945 Leadership Assessment

Between January and May 1945, the Red Army conducted ten major operations (not counting branches), of which eight resulted in victories and one was a partial victory (Moravia). Only one Soviet operation failed to achieve its objectives before the end of the war, which was the reduction of the Courland Pocket, but this had no serious consequences. Even though the Red Army enjoyed a large numerical superiority over the Ostheer in the final months of the war, it still suffered 3 million casualties (including 800,000 dead) and lost 13,700 tanks and self-propelled guns. The Red Army lost one front commander killed (Cherniakhovsky) and another relieved of command (Petrov), but otherwise the senior command cadre was fairly stable for the last six months of the war. By early 1945, most of the Soviet senior operational commanders were capable of planning and executing combined arms operations that incorporated the principles of war. At the soldier level, the Red Army rank and file could see that victory was imminent and that the way home lay through Berlin.

The Ostheer was in a much reduced status in 1945 and it only had the resources to conduct five major operations; two were successful (elimination of the Hron River bridgehead and the Lauban operation), but the other three were failures. In addition, the protracted defense of the Courland Peninsula and the heavy losses inflicted on multiple Soviet offensives in that theater should be regarded as a defensive success of sorts. Up until March, the Ostheer was still capable of conducting large-scale armored counterattacks, despite the shortage of fuel and ammunition. However, these counterattacks were only capable of achieving localized tactical successes at best. The OKH would assemble a small Panzer reserve, but then it would hastily be thrown into battle without realistic objectives and the men and material would end up being squandered. Even when Heeresgruppe Mitte managed to maul part of the 3 GTA at Lauban, there was very limited operational gain from this success. By 1945, almost all of the Ostheer's senior commanders from the salad days of 1941–42 were gone and the men left to defend the borders of the Reich were often hastily promoted and shifted around to new sectors, where they were strangers to their staffs and subordinate commanders. Nor were the Waffen-SS a significant factor in operational planning until 1945, when they were suddenly put in charge of armies. Most of all, the troops in the Ostheer of 1945 lacked the cohesiveness of earlier armies; instead of trained veterans who had been through campaigns together, the hastily assembled late-war divisions were a motley crew of half-trained recruits and personnel scraped up from other Wehrmacht branches. Consequently, the team spirit that had made the Ostheer so formidable in 1941–42 was noticeably absent in the operations of 1945.

CHAPTER 8

A Performance Assessment

Evaluating the performance of operational commanders is an inexact science, involving some quantitative and qualitative metrics, but also some subjectivity as well. This study has used the principles of war, as understood by both sides in 1941, as the essential framework, in large part because they are still in widespread use today, 80 years later. Each campaign synopsis has tried to evaluate how the principles were used by the leaders of both sides to plan and conduct their operations. Now it is the task of this work to try to circle the square in order to render some conclusions.

The Most Effective German Generals on the Eastern Front

The first factor in evaluating operational performance is to determine which commanders were the most significant by dint of longevity in command. In Table IV, the top 15 senior German commanders are listed, with one point assigned per month of army-level command and three points for each month of army group command, then totaled. The point of this exercise is to highlight those commanders who commanded large numbers of troops on the Eastern Front for extended periods of time. Noticeably, officers like Guderian and von Rundstedt are missing for the simple reason that they only commanded troops on the Eastern Front for 5–6 months in 1941, then held no further commands in this theater. This method of ranking disproportionately favors army group commanders, particularly those in Heeresgruppe Nord and Heeresgruppe Mitte, where officers held the same billets for extended periods.

Table IV: Top 15 German Commanders (by Length of Command)

Name	Army Command (months)	Army Group Command (months)	Impact
Von Küchler	6	24	78
Von Klüge	6	22	72
Von Kleist	17	16	65
Von Manstein	14	16	62
Busch	28	8	52
Reinhardt	34	5	49
Model	24	7	45
Von Reichenau	6	12	42
Schörner	1	13	40
Von Bock	0	12	36
Lindemann	26	3	35
Heinrici	31	1	34
Von Weichs	11	7	32
Weiß	25	1	28
Hoth	28	0	28

The next factors to examine are demonstrated skill level (the employment of the principles of war during operations) and operational successes (Table V). The skill level was arrived at simply by adding up all the subtables compiled during each campaign synopsis, then dividing by the total number of campaigns in which the particular commander was an active participant. A number of 3.0 or higher indicates that this commander was routinely using at least half the principles of war. The impact is then multiplied by the skill level to produce an overall score, which is necessary to start sorting commanders with high longevity but low skill (like von Küchler) from those with lower longevity but greater skill (like von Bock). Finally, a tally of operational victories is used to further sort commanders with high degrees of operational success from those who do not have much success. Thus, both Schörner and von Weichs drop from the ranks of the top 15 Ostheer commanders because they had virtually no operational successes.

Four of the top German commanders in the Ostheer – von Bock, von Manstein, von Kleist and Hoth – rode roughshod over the Red Army in 1941–42, inflicting numerous defeats. Von Bock consistently demonstrated a high level of professional skill in planning and conducting his operations; in fact, he was only defeated once – in front of Moscow in 1941 – and no large formations under his command were ever encircled or destroyed by the enemy. Von Manstein was also a very highly skilled commander, but his inability to recognize that the Red Army was improving their operational methods in 1943 proved to be his Achilles heel. Hoth and von Kleist were two of the best senior armor commanders in the Second World War, but they had difficulty adapting to static, positional warfare in 1943–44. Despite the high level of skill and success demonstrated by these four veteran commanders, Hitler relieved all of them by March 1944 and they saw no further service in the war. Von Reichenau would likely have followed the same career path had he not died prematurely in early 1942; there is no doubt that he was sorely missed at Stalingrad. Almost all the other German commanders on this list made their names primarily as specialists in defensive operations, not through offensive action – which is interesting, considering the emphasis of German doctrine upon *Bewegungskrieg*. Of note, only one of these 15 top Ostheer commanders was still in charge of troops in the last few weeks of the war – the Austrian, de Angelis. In April 1945, Weiß, Heinrici and Wöhler were relieved and three others were dead (Reichenau, Kluge and Model).

The supposed superiority of German operational methods in the Second World War is taken as a given by most historians, despite plenty of contradictory evidence. In fact, the Ostheer was actually quite amateurish in its use of operational art, as demonstrated by the development of overly broad plans designed to accomplish vague and ever-changing campaign objectives. German officers cherished the principles of offensive, maneuver and mass but neglected factors such as intelligence and logistics, particularly when they got in the way of "perfect" maneuver plans. Dangerous planning assumptions were left unresolved. *Barbarossa*, *Blau* and *Zitadelle* – the three main German summer offensives in the Soviet Union – were all hastily planned and their operational objectives were borderline non-achievable from the start. All three plans were developed with very thin margins for error and virtually ignored terrain, weather, enemy resistance and the distances involved. In short, the three main German operational plans that the Ostheer developed to win the war in the East could only work under the most ideal circumstances, as if

Table V: Top 15 German Commanders (Impact × Skill Score)

Name	Impact	Skill	Impact × Skill	Operational Victories
Von Bock	36	4.6	165	19
Von Manstein	62	2.5	155	21
Von Kleist	65	4.0	260	10
Model	45	3.5	157	9
Hoth	28	3.4	95	14
Von Klüge	72	1.6	115	5
Von Küchler	78	1.8	140	4
Busch	52	1.8	93	8
Von Reichenau	42	2.3	96	4
Heinrici	38	2.5	95	2
de Angelis	13	5.0	65	3
Lindemann	35	1.8	63	3
Wöhler	25	2.2	55	2
Weiß	28	1.75	49	4
Reinhardt	49	1.75	85	1

they were map exercises conducted in the OKH headquarters complex in Zossen. While Hitler chose the strategic objectives, in each case the faulty plans were developed by General Staff-trained professional officers. How did such well-trained staff officers produce such second-rate operational plans? The likely answer (i.e. Occam's Razor) points to a combination of hubris and contempt for the enemy as the likely proximate cause. After relatively easy victories in the campaigns of 1939–40, the Wehrmacht was beginning to see itself as an invincible force and the Russians (particularly after the Russo-Finnish War and the purges) were regarded as third-rate opponents. The disaster at Stalingrad began to change this mindset, but it still influenced the decision to attack at Kursk in mid-1943. By the time that the Ostheer's leadership recognized the changes occurring in the Red Army, it was too late and the war in the East was spiraling out of control.

As a result of their training, which emphasized von Moltke's aphorism that "no plan survives contact with the enemy," most German senior officers were conditioned to regard war as a series of *ad hoc* decisions rather than as a linear process which could be directed toward the accomplishment of worthwhile objectives. German generals actually proved to be one-trick ponies, with their default method being double-pincer offensives in order to produce a *Kesselschlacht*. When they could not use this method – such as during *Wintergewitter* and *Wanda* – their offensives quickly sputtered out. Even with the *Spring Awakening* and *Sonnenwende* operations in 1945, the Ostheer tried to pull off double pincer attacks, yet these methods no longer made any sense. Furthermore, the actual selection of campaign objectives tended to be rather arbitrary, marked by a continuous tug-of-war between Hitler and the OKH Großer Generalstab mindset. Hitler wanted to destroy enemy military forces and seize economic resources in order to wage a protracted war, whereas the OKH assessed victory mostly in terms of territorial objectives. Both Hitler and the OKH leadership also allowed themselves to be continuously distracted by secondary concerns, rather than focusing on achieving realistic operational goals. At the operational level, German senior officers proved unable to master coalition warfare with their Axis partners, deriving very little benefit from over 500,000 troops provided by these countries.

Rather than operational superiority, the Wehrmacht's main advantage on the Eastern Front lay at the tactical level, particularly in terms of its training, junior leadership and doctrine. Even when German operational plans proved unworkable, tactical leaders were often able to achieve impressive local successes (at least temporarily) that inflicted brutal losses and humiliation upon the Red Army. Yet tactical actions do not win wars. The most serious problem that hindered the Ostheer from the beginning was the lack of appreciable operational reserves. Aside from the brief period after the fall of Sevastopol where von Manstein's 11. Armee was refitting, the Ostheer never had more than a handful of divisions in operational reserve. Whenever a real crisis developed on the Eastern Front, the OKH was forced to transfer some divisions from the West, but this expedient method was little more than a stopgap. Exacerbating the lack of operational reserves, Hitler's insistence on leaving large formations to hold useless positions such as the Kuban, the Crimea and the Courland Peninsula deprived the Ostheer of vital forces to hold its main lines of resistance.

Hitler's role in the defeat of the Ostheer was significant, but initially he gave his generals a relatively free hand when the war was going well. The Kiev diversion in 1941 has certainly attracted a great deal of controversy, but Hitler's decision to divert Panzergruppe Guderian south to envelop Kirponos' Southwest Front was based on sound military logic. Indeed, there was sound military logic in going for either Kiev or Moscow and Hitler chose the option he thought aligned best with his campaign objectives. Both options had potential negative consequences. In the 1942 campaigns, Hitler also gave his generals considerable leeway – particularly von Manstein – but became annoyed at what he regarded as the leisurely pace of his commanders securing key objectives in the Caucasus and at Stalingrad. What Hitler failed to appreciate was that *Fall Blau* was conducted on a logistical shoestring and his field commanders were unable to pursue their objectives with the same kind of speed employed in 1941. It was Hitler who short-changed his main effort of resources by endorsing simultaneous offensives in secondary areas such as Heeresgruppe Mitte (*Wirbelwind*) and even tertiary areas (North Africa). Once the war in the East began to turn against Germany, Hitler increasingly tried to direct events at the front, which usually resulted in poor operational decisions.

Yet while Hitler's micromanagement increasingly hobbled the Ostheer's ability to conduct efficient operational-level warfare, historical interpretations that emphasize this one factor tend to risk ignoring a host of other weaknesses that contributed to Germany's defeat in Russia. Despite the embrace of technology (tanks, aircraft, radio) most German commanders in the Second World War did not think in modern military terms (considering economic or political factors, understanding the needs of coalition warfare) but rather looked backward toward an ideal, pure form of warfare as envisioned by 19th-century military pundits. Until Stalingrad, most German commanders on the Eastern Front did not even consider the need to expedite training new recruits in the homeland and increasing the anemic production of armaments, as if this was not their concern. Professional myopia and narrow-mindedness was embedded so deeply within the German military education system that it was not even recognized. Looking at German post-war memoirs, many German generals seem to regard the Soviet use of numerical superiority against them as some kind of underhanded trick, which ignores the fact that Soviet leaders prepared for a war of attrition and they did not. German commanders sought to demonstrate their professional perfection through synchronized operations that often proved incapable of accomplishment due to unanticipated complications from terrain, weather and a desperate enemy that was fighting for its existence. The Wehrmacht was not built for a protracted crusade in the East but when assigned this task by Hitler, its leaders enthusiastically marched forward to catastrophic failure.

The Most Effective Soviet Generals on the Eastern Front

Many readers would assume that Zhukov would be at the top of any list of Red Army senior commanders in the Second World War, but the fact is that he never commanded at army level and there were eight officers who had more experience in front-level command than he did. Indeed, he did not command any large formations in 1943. Konev was a front-level commander for almost the entire war and by far the most experienced senior Soviet commander, with more than double Zhukov's level of experience. Furthermore, Konev achieved 11 operational victories while suffering four defeats, while Zhukov achieved only five operational victories and suffered four defeats. Rokossovsky and Eremenko were also critical players throughout the war, both in the bitter days of defeat in 1941–42, then the days of victory in 1943–45. Vatutin, with Operations *Uranus*, *Little Saturn* and *Rumyantsev* to his credit, was also a very significant commander in the crucial period of 1942–43. Indeed, had Vatutin not been mortally wounded in March 1944, it is likely that Zhukov would not have had another field command until the final months of the war. Similarly, Govorov, Malinovsky, Meretskov, Tolbukhin and Kurochkin are not household names in the West, but they played a larger role than many post-war histories might suggest. Both during and after the war, Zhukov did his best to hog the limelight, elevating his own contributions (particularly in regard to Stalingrad) while ignoring those of other commanders.

Table VI: Top 15 Soviet Commanders (by Length of Command)

Name	Army Command (months)	Front Command (months)	Overall Impact
Konev	2	41	125
Govorov	6	36	114
Malinovsky	8	34	110
Rokossovsky	10	32	106
Meretskov	3	32	99
Tolbukhin	7	25	82
Kurochkin	18	19	75
Eremenko	1	22	67
Bagramyan	16	17	67
Vatutin	0	19	57
Petrov	13	14	55
Zhukov	0	18	54
Popov, M.	13	13	52
Cherniakhovsky	20	9	47
Berzarin	43	0	43

Table VII: Top 15 Soviet Commanders (Impact × Skill Score)

Name	Impact	Skill	Impact × Skill	Operational Victories
Konev	125	2.6	325	29
Vatutin	57	3.3	188	24
Rokossovsky	106	2.9	307	20
Tolbukhin	82	3.2	262	19
Eremenko	67	3.1	207	14
Malinovsky	110	2.3	253	11
Zhukov	54	1.8	97	12
Bagramyan	67	4.0	268	7
Golikov	28	2.0	56	7
Cherniakhovsky	47	2.9	136	6
Katukov	27	4.0	108	6
Govorov	114	3.4	387	4
Petrov	55	2.1	115	4
Meretskov	99	2.3	227	2
Maslennikov	40	2.75	110	4

Once relative skill levels and battlefield victories are included, the list of top Soviet generals changes, with ne'er do-wells like Popov dropping off and mediocre commanders like Petrov, Meretskov and Govorov moving downward. Konev, Vatutin, Rokossovsky, Tolbukhin and Eremenko all displayed considerable skill in their operational methods and achieved significant numbers of victories. Bagramyan demonstrated a very high level of skill, but also was involved with more than his share of operational mishaps. As for Zhukov, despite an impressive performance against the Japanese at Khalkin Gol in 1939, his performance against the Ostheer in 1941–43 resulted in several embarrassing defeats which he later sought to whitewash from the pages of history (particularly his defeats at Vyazma and Rzhev in 1942). Zhukov had one perfect victory against the Ostheer – the Oder-Vistula offensive – although his follow-through, or lack of, was highly controversial. While the Berlin operation was a success, it was marked by brutal expediency, which led to excessive casualties – not that Zhukov bothered himself with the human cost of his victories. Of the top 15 Soviet field commanders, ten were still in command billets at the end of the war; two were dead (Vatutin, Cherniakhovsky) and three others (Petrov, Maslennikov, Golikov) had been put out to pasture. Of all the army commanders, Katukov was one of the few who consistently accomplished his assigned missions, and his tank army was one of the primary spearheads that led the Red Army to victory.

At the start of the war, Stalin kept his generals on a tight leash, which led to one disaster after another. His imposition of the dual command structure allowed Communist Party commissars (who often lacked any military training) to veto the decisions of military professionals. Even worse, the use of front- and army-level "military councils" led to the military decision-making process being run by committee. On top of these constraints, the Red Army entered the Second World War with no commonly-understood doctrine, since PU-36 was in abeyance. Unable to make timely, militarily-sound decisions or use the carefully-developed pre-war doctrine, Red Army generals were often forced into no-win situations. Military defeats in 1941–42 often led to imprisonment, execution or removal from command, which prevented Red Army field commanders from learning from their mistakes. It was only in desperation, when the fall of Stalingrad seemed imminent, that Stalin began to listen to his military professionals and accept some of their recommendations – which led to a sea-change in how the Red Army fought. As the war began to turn in the Soviet favor in 1943, Stalin loosened the reins a bit, allowing his field commanders some latitude in the timing of operations. Given how the Red Army performed in 1944–45, the claim could be made that the Red Army won the war in spite of Stalin and the Communist Party (CPSU).

By mid-1944, Red Army field commanders had become experts in planning and conducting multifront operations that used combined-arms warfare to achieve important objectives. In particular, the Red Army excelled in the integration of armor, massed artillery and tactical air support to blast through German fortified lines. Attacking in two echelons also proved to be the key to overwhelming even the best German defenses. Nevertheless, Soviet commanders continued to prematurely deploy their mobile reserves and to try to direct them into unsuitable terrain, such as major cities. The lack of mechanized infantry – not rectified until the development of the BTR wheeled armored personnel carriers in the 1950s – also had a serious impact on the ability of Soviet infantry to support fast-moving armored spearheads. Unlike the German air-ground tactics, Soviet ground commanders failed to appreciate how the use of aerial battlefield interdiction operations could break up enemy counterattacks before they occurred. Consequently, until almost the end of the war,

German Panzer reserves were able to assemble behind the front, even in broad daylight. In terms of logistics, the Red Army started the war unable to support large-scale mechanized operations, but once Anglo-American Lend Lease aid arrived in bulk, Soviet theater logistic capabilities showed marked improvement. Nevertheless, logistics remained as a serious operational constraint until the end of the war and even afterwards.

In terms of operational-level warfare, the real Soviet ace in the hole was the Stavka's RVGK reserves, which were used to rebuild shattered fronts and sustain new offensives. Throughout the critical phase of the war in the East, from 1942 to 1943, the RVGK typically had around six armies with 30–40 divisions and 500–1,000 AFV in reserve. Furthermore, the Stavka excelled at restocking the RVGK after major operations, and was able to quickly refit burnt-out formations and return them to the front. As a result, the Red Army was well positioned to win a war of attrition and appeared inexhaustible to the Germans. In contrast, the OKH had not prepared for protracted warfare and its method of refitting burnt-out units in Western Europe usually kept them sidelined for six months or more. Some units, like the 8. and 19. Panzer-Divisions, were never sent west to refit, which left them in a debilitated condition for most of the war.

The Red Army did have two intrinsic weaknesses that caused it operational problems throughout the war, even when it had veteran commanders and plenty of men and material available. The first problem was training. The Red Army simply did not train its troops or junior officers to anywhere near the same standard as the Wehrmacht, so units were sent into combat inadequately prepared to achieve their operational goals. In 1941–42, Soviet armies could suddenly fall apart under combat pressure. Gradually, the Red Army accumulated some veteran troops and these formations were redesignated as guards units, but even these units were not particularly well trained. Nor was this problem resolved after the war. Indeed, even with the current Russo-Ukrainian War in the 21st century, the Russian Army still demonstrates a willingness to send poorly trained troops onto the battlefield, leading to ridiculous casualty levels. The second structural problem that undermined the Red Army's capabilities is the lack of fighting spirit (*Kampfgeist* in German). While Hitler caused many problems for the Wehrmacht, he should be given credit for areas where the regime improved the fighting ability of its troops. Through the Third Reich's propaganda efforts, the Nazis strove to create an atmosphere of teamwork or *Kameradschaft* (comradeship) and this proved to be a resounding success for the Wehrmacht. The sense of teamwork, combined with a cogent rationale for the war in the East (destruction of the Bolshevik threat to European stability), helped to create a strong fighting spirit that remained intact in the Ostheer up to the last month of the war. In contrast, the Red Army had nothing like this sense of teamwork or fighting spirit, and many troops from the Ukraine or Caucasus had good reason to despise Stalin's regime. Indeed, the Communist system had conditioned troops (and leaders) to testify against other soldiers for the slightest criticism of the regime.[1] Consequently, tens of thousands of Soviet troops defected to join the Wehrmacht rather than fight as cannon fodder for Stalin. By mid-1942, hundreds of thousands of Russian auxiliaries (*Hiwis*) were serving, mostly in support roles, in the Wehrmacht – which had a definite impact on operations. Again, this lack of teamwork and fighting spirit is still evident in the modern Russian Army, leading to low morale and poor combat performance. From the point of view of Stalin and the Stavka, Soviet industry had provided the Red Army with quality weapons and in quantity, so the human aspects of warfare were regarded as irrelevant (if not dangerously bourgeois). Instead, the whole issue of troop morale was handed over to unit political commissars, who berated the troops with lectures on Communist Party ideology in order to motivate them and threatened them with execution if they retreated. Consequently, Russian generals focused on mastering operational maneuver warfare while remaining relatively indifferent to the morale and welfare of their front-line soldiers (*frontoviki*).

The Red Army's inherent problems in the Second World were never resolved and continue to undermine the Russian ability to wage operational-level warfare up to the present day. Soviet combat performance in Afghanistan, against a third-rate enemy, was pathetic and ended in defeat. Likewise, the Russian Army's poor performance in Ukraine in 2022–25 can be attributed to the usual reasons: inadequately-trained troops, low morale, poor logistics and a failure by commanders and staff to properly evaluate the terrain and enemy. Indeed, the Russo-Ukrainian War offers stark reminders why the application of the principles of war into operational planning is a necessary ingredient for success. In particular, the poor Russian performance in the ground war was caused by a failure to synchronize maneuver and mass to achieve realistic objectives before Ukrainian resistance could solidify. Typically, invaders (Korea 1950, Falklands 1982, Kuwait 1990) at least benefit from operational surprise, but in Ukraine the Russian invasion did not even enjoy that advantage. After failing to seize their initial objectives, the Russian invasion force quickly lost momentum, which allowed the Ukrainians to seize the initiative. In 2024, the failure to ensure the security of the Russian border allowed the Ukrainians to mount an embarrassing counteroffensive into the Kursk-Sumy region. It seems incredible that modern Russian generals would conduct operations that employ none of the principles of war and expect any outcome other than a costly defeat. The principles of war are immutable and a failure to employ them in the planning and conduct of operational-level warfare is akin to military malpractice. Likewise, in order for the principles of war to become practicable on the battlefield, an army needs well-trained, motivated soldiers, a coherent operational doctrine and adequate reserves to prevent premature culmination of protracted campaigns.

Final Observations

It is important to note that even the most skilled and successful generals on the Eastern Front suffered their share of defeats, as well as victories. Manstein, Zhukov, von Kleist and Konev are known for their victories, but each also had their failures – demonstrating that there are no guarantees in warfare. Consistency is important in generalship, if for no other reason than the staff can make provisions to deal with a vacillating or capricious commander. All the top commanders knew their trade – there is no doubt of that – but often could only perform at their peak under favorable circumstances. Fatigue, exhaustion, illness and wounds are significant factors that begin piling up the longer a campaign goes on. Zhukov spent most of his time in the rear areas and was never wounded, but Eremenko was wounded multiple times. Even mediocre leaders like Paulus, commander of the 6. Armee, had moments where he demonstrated the ability to command an army with some skill. Hubris – created by easy successes – can also act as a corrosive agent upon good generalship by undermining prudence. It is also evident that some commanders were better suited to offensive operations, while others were best in defensive roles. Professional armies need both kinds of commanders and to recognize where they are best suited to achieve mission success.

Readers may note the inclusion of some rather obscure commanders such as de Angelis or Berzarin in the list; these commanders represent the "old warhorse" leaders who had some skill and operational success, although not enough to cast them into the historical limelight. The armies of both sides relied heavily upon such veteran commanders. Nikolai Pukhov commanded the 13th Army from January 1942 to the end of the war (39 months), through multiple major campaigns. On the German side, Busch commanded AOK 16 for 27 months, Lindemann AOK 18 for 26 months and Weiß AOK 2 for 25 months; these officers made their reputations fending off increasingly powerful Soviet offensives for over two years. Neither army had a particularly good system for selecting senior command cadre, resulting in a trial-and-error approach – this remains a problem even for armies in the 21st century.

Afterwards

Although the German generals lost the war in the East, some of them managed to achieve significant victories in the post-war historiography of the conflict. Of course, initially the German field commanders were handicapped by being prisoners of war. Von Bock had the misfortune of being killed by a British fighter in the final week of the war, but all of his former surviving comrades were soon scooped up either by the Anglo-Americans or the Soviets. Ernst Busch died a broken man in British captivity, just two months after the end of the war. A few senior officers – Heinrici, Lindemann, Raus and Weiß – were not indicted for any war crimes and were released by the Anglo-Americans in 1947–48. Hoth, Reinhardt and Wöhler were convicted of war crimes at Nürnberg and received prison sentences; all three men were released between 1951 and 1954. Von Manstein dodged judgment at Nürnberg but was convicted of war crimes by a British military tribunal in 1949 and spent four years in prison. Of these senior officers, the memoirs written by Erich von Manstein (*Verlorene Siege* [Lost Victories], 1955), Erhard Raus and Hermann Hoth had become staples of Eastern Front literature by the early 1960s. All three men directed virtually all of their opprobrium for the Wehrmacht's defeat in Russia toward Hitler's decision-making and refused to acknowledge their own operational mistakes or admit criminal actions by the formations under their command. Instead, the memoirs of these officers – and others, such as those by Balck, Guderian and von Mellenthin – endeavored to create a mythologized version of German military operations in the Soviet Union. Unfortunately, this version of events was long accepted as ground truth by many in the West.

Von Kleist, von Küchler, de Angelis and Schörner all spent at least a decade in Soviet prison camps after the war. Kleist was the only German *generalfeldmarschall* to die in Soviet captivity, while the others were released by 1955. Returning to Germany, Schörner was convicted of illegal executions by a German court and spent four more years in prison. None of the senior leaders imprisoned in the Soviet Union published memoirs. Despite his cooperation, Paulus remained in Soviet custody until 1953, when he was allowed to live out his life in East Germany. Although granted a nominal position in military research, the Soviets did not allow Paulus to write his memoirs either.

Although the Red Army's senior commanders were not prisoners of war after 1945, they were still under the thumb of Stalin, Beria's NKVD and the Communist Party (CPSU). Stalin wasted no time in launching a new purge of the Red Army, beginning with Zhukov. After being allowed a brief moment to bask in the afterglow of victory in Berlin, Zhukov was recalled to Moscow in June 1946 and was accused of being politically unreliable and involved in a conspiracy against Stalin. He was then stripped of his title as Commander-in-Chief of Soviet Ground Forces. Both Rokossovsky and Konev joined the denunciation of Zhukov as "an enemy of the central committee."[2] Since Zhukov was too high profile to imprison, he was put out to pasture in backwater commands in Odessa, then the Ural Military District (MD). Similar fates befell seven of the other senior wartime commanders: Tolbukhin was sent to the Transcaucasus MD (where he died in 1949), Eremenko was sent to Siberia, Malinovsky to the Far East, Petrov to Turkestan, Meretskov to the far north, Maslennikov also went to the Transcaucasus and Bagramyan to the Baltic States. In return for their loyalty to Stalin, Konev was given Zhukov's position as commander of Soviet ground forces and Rokossovsky was sent to take command of the Polish military. Katukov also did well, remaining as an armor specialist and given good post-war command billets in East Germany. Surprisingly, Govorov also did well, serving as deputy minister of defense for nearly a decade. Yet for the most part, Stalin treated his victorious cadre of generals with a mixture of contempt and indifference – they had served their purpose and now had little value in his eyes. None of the wartime commanders were allowed to write memoirs while Stalin was alive and thus, there was no general examination of the Red Army's operational performance in the war.

After the death of Stalin, the situation began to change. Once Khruschev was in power, he initiated rehabilitation of some of the individuals that had been victimized by Stalin. Konev and Rokossovsky remained in top leadership billets, but Zhukov was made deputy minister of defense. Khruschev also selected Zhukov to be in charge of the Soviet Union's first major nuclear weapons test in September 1954, known as Exercise *Snezhok* (Snowball). Upon completion of the nuclear test, Zhukov proudly reported its results to Khruschev, but *Snezhok* proved to be one of the worst environmental disasters in post-war Soviet history. Following this dubious success, Zhukov was promoted to minister of defense, but it proved to be his swansong because he had little understanding of Cold War strategy, guided missiles or nuclear weapons. In 1957, Khruschev forced Zhukov into retirement, but would not allow him to write his memoirs. It was not until Brezhnev seized power in the 1960s that Zhukov was finally allowed to write his memoirs and even then, the book that was finally published in 1969 was highly adulterated. Zhukov's memoirs had to be re-edited in subsequent editions until it was finally satisfactory to his political masters. Yet of all the Soviet post-war memoirs, Zhukov's remains the best known in the West.

Many of the other senior Soviet commanders published their memoirs in the period 1969–77, including Konev, Rokossovsky, Eremenko, Bagramyan and Katukov. However, Tolbukhin, Maslennikov, Govorov and Petrov died prior to this relaxed period and published no memoirs. The official Soviet history of the war – the six-volume *History of the Great Patriotic War* – was published in 1960 and all subsequent memoirs had to comply with this party-sanctioned version of events for the next 30 years. Under this rubric, failed Soviet military operations either were minimized or omitted altogether. Red Army decision-making was presented in a sanitized manner, with mistakes glossed over and all-knowing commissars assisting rather than hindering the process. Stalin's colossal mistakes in the lead-up to war were acknowledged, but the party's role in the purges and undermining the pre-war Red Army were not given much weight. Not surprisingly, memoirs built on this framework of falsehoods did not do well with Western readers, who had already been exposed to the German version of the war for a decade. Later, as some of the truth began to emerge during the *Glasnost* period, Soviet wartime memoirs were afforded even less weight. It is only in the post-Soviet period, as a new generation of Russian military historians has appeared, that greater balance in the historiography of the Eastern Front has begun to appear.

The basic problem in the historiography of the Eastern Front, as presented by both sets of combatants, is a lack of objective reflection. The German generals failed to explain why they lost the war in operational terms because they spent most of their efforts on projecting blame onto Hitler. Von Manstein claimed that "victory was lost" or thrown away due to Hitler's faulty decisions, but at no point in his post-war ruminations did he spell out how he could have won the war in the East if given greater latitude. Certainly the Ostheer could have won some more campaigns in 1942–43, but such successes would not have altered the fact that Germany lacked the resources to fight a protracted struggle against a global coalition. The same objective facts had shaped the outcome of the First World War, which was well known among Wehrmacht leaders. As for the Soviet generals, their post-war memoirs failed to adequately explain why they won the war, because this would have involved awkward discussions about doctrine, the purges and the catastrophic defeats of 1941–42. Consequently, most Soviet memoirs tread lightly on the first half of the war and focused heavily on the final year of the war, so the transitional period is covered almost in passing. For both sides, the fact that senior field commanders were chained to supporting brutal, authoritarian regimes that had much to hide rendered any attempt at honest historical inquiry impossible. Indeed, the generals in this study were not just working for brutal regimes, but actively involved in trying to spread the authority of these criminals across a wider swath of humanity.

Despite this lack of objective reflection, the analysis of generalship on the Eastern Front still has important lessons for modern operational-level warfare because it was the most protracted, intense peer vs. peer large-formation combat in all of military history. For over 46 months, the Ostheer and Red Army engaged in a death struggle that involved millions and killed millions. A number of observations about Eastern Front operations remain germane for modern operational warfare:

- Commanders must see the battlefield in objective – not emotional or ideological – terms, which means paying close attention to intelligence and logistics. Sound operational planning requires effective input from these functional areas.
- Campaign planning should be directed against enemy Centers of Gravity (COG) in order to produce decisive results. In Russia, the Wehrmacht could only really target the Red Army's COG by means of attrition-based operations, since it lacked the means to neutralize key armaments factories in the Urals. Likewise, the Red Army had to rely upon attrition methods to gradually reduce the efficiency of the German air-ground strike forces. When both sides opt for attrition-based methods, campaigns will be costly in terms of casualties and material losses.
- One of a field commander's most important operational decisions is when and where to commit his mobile reserves, either in the defense or offense; this decision-making process must be assisted by intelligence analysis which properly identifies enemy actions and responses.

- Operational reserves can be created by employing the principle of economy of force in secondary/tertiary sectors.
- Patience is a virtue in decision-making in operational-level warfare, particularly if the enemy is using deception operations to mask their true intent.
- Operational doctrine and pre-war training must encompass the needs of coalition warfare. Neither the Ostheer nor the Red Army proved adept at cooperating with allied armies.
- Combined-arms warfare is a must in order to achieve success. Particular emphasis needs to be placed on air-ground cooperation and incorporating engineer mobility/countermobility capabilities. Naval capabilities should also be considered, if campaigns occur in coastal regions.
- Realistic large-scale training is what enables units to translate doctrine into reality on the modern battlefield. Doctrine needs to be continuously validated in command-post and field-training exercises.
- Tactical operations can be conducted in *ad hoc* fashion and still be successful, but in operational-level warfare there are too many moving pieces. Campaigns need to be carefully planned out in advance with clear-cut objectives, not driven by improvisation (as in *Fall Blau*, 1942).
- Breakthrough battles need to be amply resourced in case a decision is not quickly reached.
- Major combat operations in urban and mountainous areas should be avoided unless (a) specialist formations are available (e.g. combat engineers, light infantry) and (b) there is an overarching reason to seize or move through this terrain.
- Deception planning is critical in gaining surprise and forcing errors on the enemy commander.
- In peer vs. peer warfare, expect heavy casualties in major operations and plan on refitting units forward in order to keep them mission-capable. Commanders must carefully gauge how close their formations are to reaching their culmination point and ensure they have the resources to accomplish their missions. Plans to refit worn-out units must be in place, along with methods to push replacement troops and equipment forward.
- River-crossing operations need to be preplanned, with adequate engineer and artillery resources allocated. Huge armies can still be stymied by remarkably narrow bodies of water.

- Ground commanders should expect supporting aviation units to conduct four key missions to support their campaign objectives: long-range reconnaissance, air superiority, close air support and battlefield interdiction.
- Theater logistics and real-time secure communications are the key enablers for operational-level warfare; without adequate support and C2, operations will quickly break down
- Human factors matter even in operational-level warfare. Commanders must be aware of the health and morale of their front-line troops and do what they can to preserve this.
- Terrain and weather should be known factors; if major surprises occur, the military decision-making process has gone off the rails.

Appendices

APPENDIX 1: THE PRINCIPLES OF WAR

The principles defined here (with a nod to the US Army's FM 100-5, Operations) are the ones that best align with German doctrine espoused in *Truppenführung* (1933/34) and the Soviet PU-36 (1936). It does not include all principles of war that appear in contemporary US Army and British Army doctrinal-related field regulations.

- **Objective:** an operational plan must have a clearly defined, decisive and attainable objective. At the operational level of war, it is permissible to have more than one final objective, or sequential objectives (e.g. intermediate and final objectives). The objectives could either be territorial (e.g. seize a city or region) or one that seriously degrades the enemy's ability to continue the war (e.g. eliminate their mobile reserves or destroy their logistic infrastructure).
- **Offensive:** operations should seek to gain/retain the initiative in order to achieve decisive results and impose our side's will upon the enemy. Although defense is often necessary, it rarely can win wars unless the enemy is unusually incompetent.
- **Mass:** concentrating overwhelming combat power at the decisive time and place is the best way to achieve rapid success in the offense. While a 3-1 force ratio is generally considered adequate for success in an open field campaign, higher ratios tip the balance even more heavily in favor of the attacker.
- **Maneuver:** operational-level movements are used to place the enemy at a disadvantage, typically through an envelopment or by the breach of a front line followed up with a breakthrough and pursuit. Maneuver is used to threaten an enemy's lines of communications (LOC) to put their supplies at risk, to divide their forces so they can be defeated in detail or to strike at vulnerable allied forces.

- **Surprise:** to strike at a time and place – or manner – which the enemy did not expect and is unprepared to counter. This is the most enduring principle of war, going back to ancient warfare. Achieving operational-level surprise can enable a smaller force to defeat a numerically stronger force and serves as a potent short-term combat multiplier.
- **Security:** avoiding unexpected surprises by an enemy is the essence of operational security, which seeks to prevent the enemy from gaining advance warning of friendly dispositions and maneuvers. By use of stringent security measures, a friendly force increases the probability of achieving success in its planned operations. *Example: in 1944 the Anglo-Americans undertook numerous security measures to prevent the Germans from learning that the D-Day landings were to occur in Normandy; if the Allies had failed in this regard, the Germans would have reinforced the landing areas and thereby jeopardized Operation* Overlord.
- **Economy of force:** only the minimum necessary combat forces should be allocated to secondary or tertiary missions. Both the Wehrmacht and the Red Army paid lip service to the principle, but often ignored it in practice – often due to pressure from above. *For example, in 1942 the Germans chose to commit five divisions to hold the vulnerable Demyansk salient, even though this position had no military value and was quickly encircled by the Red Army's winter counteroffensive. Likewise, in 1943 the Red Army committed 400,000 troops to reducing the German position in the Kuban, a secondary mission, rather than on the decisive Kharkov axis.*

APPENDIX 2: OPERATIONAL ART FUNDAMENTALS

In military theory, stretching from von Clausewitz to modern military manuals, there have been a number of fundamental concepts, in addition to the principles of war, which are essential in campaign planning. This section will summarize the most important ones and put them in the context of the Eastern Front of 1941–45.

Center of Gravity (COG) is usually defined as a moral or material factor upon which an armed force's ability to successfully conduct its primary missions rests. COGs can exist at both the strategic and operational level, but not the tactical level. A COG enables or produces Critical Capabilities to be used against an opponent, but is dependent upon Critical Requirements to exercise it. Critical Vulnerabilities are factors which put the COG at risk of failure.

The German operational center of gravity on the Eastern Front was the combination of their Panzer groups and Luftwaffe close air support, which produced a Critical Capability – powerful, synchronized combined-arms offensives. German doctrine and C2 structures were designed to harness this COG and direct it to annihilate enemy ground/air combat power and then seize critical territorial objectives.

- The Critical Requirements for the German operational COG were (1) a dependence upon rail lines to move ammunition and fuel to the front, and (2) encrypted field communications networks to enable near real-time coordination in mobile campaigns.
- The Critical Vulnerabilities were (1) enemy attacks upon primary rail lines of communication (LOC) and logistic depots by enemy partisans, long-range bombing and airborne operations or weather/mechanical factors that negatively impact rail line operations and (2) jamming attacks or code-breaking against encrypted C2 networks.

The Red Army's operational center of gravity was its RVGK (Reserve of the Supreme Command), particularly the large tank formations (armies, corps) and heavy artillery support in the reserve, which produced the Critical Capability to mount large-scale offensives in depth in accordance with the pre-war theory espoused in PU-36. In 1941, the Red Army had entire armies in the RVGK, which helped it to slow the German advance, but these quickly-raised armies lacked the equipment or training necessary to conduct more than rudimentary offensive operations. However, once stocked with better quality formations in 1942–43, the RVGK reserves became a real game-changer. The Red Army's COG had the following parameters:

- The Critical Requirement was a dependence upon (1) theater logistics to build up front-level stockpiles of equipment, ammunition and fuel and (2) professional Stavka and front-level staff planning to activate the COG.
- The Critical Vulnerabilities were enemy air attacks on key rail facilities, rail bridges and army/front command posts to hinder deployment of operational reserves.

Lines of Operation (LOO) can be defined in several ways. In the most basic form, a LOO is essentially an axis of advance (or retreat), which serves to link a combat formation with its base of operations and its objective. For example, the German Heeresgruppe Mitte in 1941 operated on the Minsk-Smolensk-Moscow LOO. Another way of looking at LOO is in terms of interior/exterior lines. A force operating in defense of a single central point, such as Moscow, is operating on interior lines. Armies that are converging upon that single point are operating on exterior lines of operation. Generally, in operational-level warfare, the force employing interior lines is regarded as having an advantage, particularly in terms of logistics and mass.

Culmination Point is the moment in an offensive when the attacker's combat power is reduced to the point that it no longer exceeds that of the defender.

Typically, if the attacker's offensive culminates prior to reaching their operational objective, the operation has failed. As FM 100-5 states, "the art of the attack ... is to secure the objective before reaching culmination."

Operational Phases are complex military operations that are usually subdivided into phases in which certain activity is expected to occur and/or interim objectives are to be taken. Operation *Barbarossa* was designed with three distinct phases, expected to occur over a period of 6–10 weeks. A branch is a contingency plan that is built into the basic plan; in Operation *Barbarossa*, the OKH envisioned possible branches after Heeresgruppe Mitte took Smolensk, with Panzer groups possibly sent to support the advances by one or both of the other army groups. A sequel is a subsequent operation added to the basic plan, such as Operation *Typhoon* in 1941.

APPENDIX 3: GERMAN SENIOR COMMANDERS ON THE EASTERN FRONT, 1941–45

Name	Age[1]	Comm.[2]	Original Branch[3]	Army Command[4]	Heeresgruppe Command[5]	Overall Impact[6]
KÜCHLER	60	1901	Artillery	6	24	78
KLÜGE	58	1901	Artillery	6	22	72
KLEIST	59	1901	Artillery (Cavalry)	17	16	65
MANSTEIN	53	1906	Infantry	14	16	62
BUSCH	55	1904	Infantry	28	8	52
REINHARDT	54	1908	Infantry	34	5	49
MODEL	50	1910	Infantry	24	7	45
REICHENAU	56	1904	Artillery	6	12	42
SCHÖRNER	49	1914	Infantry	1	13	40
BOCK	60	1898	Infantry	0	12	36
LINDEMANN	57	1904	Cavalry	26	3	35
HEINRICI	54	1906	Infantry	35	1	38
WEICHS	59	1902	Cavalry	11	7	32
WEIß	50	1909	Infantry	25	1	28
HOTH	56	1905	Infantry	28	0	28
RENDULIC	53	1910	Infantry	17	3	26
WÖHLER	46	1914	Infantry	16	3	25
HARPE	53	1911	Infantry	7	5	22
LEEB	64	1897	Artillery	0	7	21

Name	Age[1]	Comm.[2]	Original Branch[3]	Army Command[4]	Heeresgruppe Command[5]	Overall Impact[6]
SCHMIDT	55	1908	Infantry (Signal)	16	0	16
RUOFF	57	1904	Infantry	16	0	16
RUNDSTEDT	65	1893	Infantry	0	5	15
RAUS	52	1910	Infantry	14	0	14
de ANGELIS	52	1908	Artillery	13	0	13
PAULUS	50	1911	Infantry	13	0	13
HOLLIDT	50	1910	Infantry	13	0	13
MACKENSEN	51	1910	Cavalry	11	0	11
FRIEßNER	59	1912	Infantry	1	3	10
HILPERT	52	1909	Infantry	6	1	9
SALMUTH	52	1909	Infantry	9	0	9
JAENECKE	51	1912	Pioniere	9	0	9
HANSEN	56	1904	Artillery	8	0	8
BOEGE	52	1914	Infantry	8	0	8
SCHULZ	43	1916	Infantry	8	0	8
STRAUß	61	1901	Infantry	7	0	7
GRÄSER	52	1906	Infantry	7	0	7
LIST	61	1900	Infantry	0	2	6
GUDERIAN	53	1908	Infantry (Signal)	6	0	6
HUBE	50	1910	Infantry	6	0	6
HÖPNER	54	1906	Cavalry	6	0	6
HOSSBACH	46	1914	Infantry	6	0	6
FRETTER-PICO	49	1912	Artillery	5	0	5
BALCK	48	1914	Infantry	5	0	5
LOCH	54	1908	Artillery	5	0	5
LÜTTWITZ	45	1915	Infantry	4	0	4
KREYSING	50	1910	Infantry	4	0	4
BUSSE	43	1917	Infantry	3	0	3
STÜLPNAGEL	55	1906	Infantry	3	0	3
NEHRING	48	1913	Infantry	2	0	2
VORMANN	45	1915	Infantry	2	0	2
LAUX	53	1908	Infantry	2	0	2
ALLMENDINGER	50	1913	Infantry	2	0	2

Name	Age[1]	Comm.[2]	Original Branch[3]	Army Command[4]	Heeresgruppe Command[5]	Overall Impact[6]
SCHOBERT	58	1904	Infantry	2	0	2
STEINER	45	1914	Infantry	2	0	2
DIETRICH	49	1928	SS	2	0	2

Notes:
1. Age on June 22, 1941.
2. Year commissioned as an officer.
3. Original branch of commissioning. If they switched to another branch early in their career, this one is listed in parentheses.
4. Months in Army-level command on the Eastern Front.
5. Months in Heeresgruppe/Front-level command on the Eastern Front.
6. Total of months in senior command (1 point for each month at Army level, 3 points for each month of Heeresgruppe/Front level).

Ostheer Senior Commander Composition (55 total)
- Branch: Infantry 38 (69 percent), Artillery nine (16 percent), Cavalry five (9 percent), Signal 2, Pioniere 1
- Ethnicity: three Austrian, 52 German
- General Staff training: 33 of 55 had GS training (60 percent)
- Political Loyalty: Pro-regime 18 (32 percent), Neutral 3, Anti-regime 12 (22 percent, including two active members of resistance), Unknown 22
- Paramilitary experience: Freikorps 7, SA 1
- Average age in 1941: 52 years

APPENDIX 4: SOVIET SENIOR COMMANDERS ON THE EASTERN FRONT, 1941–45

Name	Age 1941	Comm	Original Branch	Army Command	Front Command	Overall Impact
KONEV	43	1919	Artillery	2	41	125
GOVOROV	44	1920	Artillery	6	36	114
MALINOVSKY	42	1920	Infantry	8	34	110
ROKOSSOVSKY	44	1920	Cavalry	10	32	106
MERETSKOV	44	1919	Infantry	3	32	99
TOLBUKHIN	47	1918	Infantry	7	25	82
KUROCHKIN	40	1920	Cavalry	18	19	75
EREMENKO	48	1920	Cavalry	1	22	67

Name	Age 1941	Comm	Original Branch	Army Command	Front Command	Overall Impact
BAGRAMYAN	43	1920	Infantry	16	17	67
VATUTIN	39	1920	Infantry	0	19	57
PETROV	44	1918	Infantry	13	14	55
ZHUKOV	44	1920	Cavalry	0	18	54
POPOV, M.	38	1920	Infantry	13	13	52
CHERNIAKHOVSKY	34	1924	Artillery	20	9	47
BERZARIN	37	1919	Infantry	43	0	43
SVIRIDOV	43	1919	Artillery	41	0	41
ROMANENKO	44	1919	Cavalry	39	0	39
BOLDIN	48	1920	Infantry	39	0	39
PUKHOV	46	1918	Infantry	39	0	39
TROFIMENKO	41	1919	Infantry	39	0	39
SOKOLOVSKY	43	1919	Infantry	0	13	39
MASLENNIKOV	40	1919	Cavalry	13	8	37
POPOV, V.	46	1919	Cavalry	37	0	37
TIMOSHENKO	46	1918	Cavalry	–	12	36
GORDOV	44	1919	Infantry	36	0	36
STARIKOV	44	1920	Infantry	36	0	36
KOROVNIKOV	39	1919	Artillery	36	0	36
MOSKALENKO	39	1922	Artillery	35	0	35
CHEREPANOV	45	1918	Infantry	54	0	34
PURKAEV	46	1918	Infantry	9	8	33
BELOV	44	1920	Cavalry	33	0	33
ZAKHAROV	44	1919	Infantry	18	5	38
RYBALKO	46	1919	Cavalry	32	0	32
GOLUBEV	45	1918	Infantry	32	0	32
LELYUSHENKO	39	1919	Cavalry	32	0	32
FEDIUNINSKIY	40	1924	Infantry	32	0	32
SHUMILOV	44	1918	Infantry	32	0	32
BATOV	44	1920	Infantry	32	0	32
GRECHKO	37	1919	Cavalry	32	0	32
IUSHKEVICH	44	1919	Infantry	31	0	31
GUSEV	43	1919	Cavalry	31	0	31
GALITSKY	43	1919	Infantry	31	0	31

Name	Age 1941	Comm	Original Branch	Army Command	Front Command	Overall Impact
CHUIKOV	41	1919	Infantry	30	0	30
GALANIN	40	1919	Infantry	30	0	30
ROMANOVSKIY	44	1919	Infantry	30	0	30
KOROTEEV	40	1919	Infantry	30	0	30
CHISTIAKOV	40	1920	Infantry	30	0	30
ZHADOV	40	1919	Cavalry	30	0	30
GOLIKOV	40	1919	Infantry	4	8	28
NIKOLAEV	51	1918	Infantry	28	0	28
KOROTKOV	42	1919	Infantry	28	0	28
KOLPAKCHI	41	1919	Cavalry	27	0	27
REITER	54	1919	Infantry	6	7	27
KATUKOV	40	1922	Infantry	27	0	27
KREIZER	35	1923	Infantry	26	0	26
DANILOV	44	1919	Infantry	26	0	26
KUZNETSOV, V.	47	1920	Infantry	25	0	25
KOZLOV	44	1918	Infantry	1	8	25
GLAGOLEV	45	1918	Artillery	25	0	25
ZHURAVLEV	44	1919	Cavalry	24	0	24
TSVETAEV	48	1918	Infantry	24	0	24
POLENOV	40	1920	NKVD	23	0	23
CHEREVICHENKO	46	1919	Cavalry	8	5	23
GRISHIN	40	1920	Infantry	23	0	23
MANAGAROV	43	1923	Cavalry	23	0	23
ZAKHARKIN	52	1918	Infantry	22	0	22
MOROZOV	44	1918	Infantry	22	0	22
GORBATOV	50	1919	Cavalry	22	0	22
GLUZDOVSKY	38	1919	Infantry	22	0	22
ZHMACHENKO	45	1919	Infantry	22	0	22
ROGINSKY	40	1921	Engineer	22	0	22
TYULENEV	49	1918	Cavalry	0	7	21
KHOZIN	43	1918	Infantry	6	5	21
GAGEN	46	1919	Infantry	20	0	20
IAKOVLEV	46	1918	Infantry	19	0	19
CHIBISOV	48	1918	Infantry	19	0	19

Name	Age 1941	Comm	Original Branch	Army Command	Front Command	Overall Impact
SHAROKHIN	42	1919	Cavalry	19	0	19
SHVETSOV	43	1920	Infantry	18	0	18
KUZNETSOV, F.	42	1918	Infantry	15	1	18
BUDYONNY	58	1918	Cavalry	0	6	18
KHARITONOV	42	1919	Infantry	18	0	18
KRYLOV	38	1919	Infantry	18	0	18
KOSTENKO	44	1918	Cavalry	2	5	17
ROTMISTROV	39	1921	Infantry	17	0	17
KHOMENKO	42	1920	NKVD	16	0	16
LESELIDZE	37	1922	Artillery	16	0	16
KAZAKOV	39	1920	Cavalry	16	0	16
MALYSHEV	42	1919	Infantry	16	0	16
KRIUCHENKIN	47	1919	Cavalry	16	0	16
GERASIMENKO	40	1920	Infantry	15	0	15
BOGDANOV	46	1918	Infantry	15	0	15
KRAVCHENKO	40	1920	Infantry	15	0	15
LOPATIN	44	1918	Cavalry	14	0	14
ZYGIN	45	1918	Infantry	14	0	14
DUKHANOV	44	1918	Engineer	14	0	14
SUKHOMLIN	40	1918	Infantry	13	0	13
KLYKOV	52	1918	Infantry	12	0	12
KURASOV	43	1921	Infantry	12	0	12
MELNIK	41	1920	Cavalry	12	0	12
GUSEV	46	1918	Infantry	12	0	12
RIABYSHEV	47	1918	Cavalry	8	1	11
KOZLOV	47	1918	Infantry	11	0	11
BELOBORODOV	38	1926	Infantry	11	0	11
LYUDNIKOV	38	1925	Infantry	11	0	11
CHANCHIBADZE	39	1922	Infantry	11	0	11
TARASOV	35	1927	NKVD	10	0	10
KAMKOV	43	1919	Cavalry	10	0	10
KIRPONOS	49	1918	Infantry	0	3	9
GORODNIANSKIY	45	1918	Infantry	9	0	9
ZAKHVATAEV	42	1918	Infantry	9	0	9

Name	Age 1941	Comm	Original Branch	Army Command	Front Command	Overall Impact
TSYGANOV	44	1918	Cavalry	9	0	9
LUCHINSKY	41	1919	Cavalry	9	0	9
RADZIEVSKIY	29	1931	Cavalry	9	0	9
PODLAS	47	1919	Infantry	8	0	8
SHLEMIN	43	1920	Infantry	8	0	8
VOLSKY	44	1918	Cavalry	8	0	8
SOBENNIKOV	46	1918	Cavalry	4	1	7
CHERNIAK	41	1918	Infantry	7	0	7
ERMAKOV	41	1920	Infantry	6	0	6
SIMONIAK	40	1919	Cavalry	6	0	6
RODIN	39	1922	Cavalry	6	0	6
SHAFRONOV	40	1923	Artillery	6	0	6
GRECHKIN	48	1918	Infantry	6	0	6
VASILEVSKY	45	1919	Infantry	0	2	6
KULIK	50	1918	Artillery	5	0	5
EFREMOV	44	1918	Artillery	5	0	5
VOSTRUKHOV	46	1919	Infantry	5	0	5
PERKHOROVICH	47	1918	Infantry	5	0	5
KHETAGUROV	38	1922	Artillery	5	0	5
GASTILOVICH	38	1924	Infantry	5	0	5
LVOV	44	1918	Infantry	4	0	4
TRUFANOV	41	1919	Infantry	4	0	4
KIRIUKHIN	44	1919	Infantry	3	0	3
POTAPOV	38	1920	Infantry	3	0	3
VLASOV	40	1919	Infantry	3	0	3
SMIRNOV	45	1918	Infantry	3	0	3
KOTOV	38	1921	Infantry	3	0	3
RAZUVAEV	41	1921	Infantry	3	0	3
TRUBNIKOV	52	1918	Infantry	3	0	3
ANTONIUK	45	1918	Infantry	1	0	1

Red Army Senior Commander Composition (140 total)
- Branch: Infantry 88 (62 percent), Artillery 12 (8 percent), Cavalry 35 (25 percent), Engineer 2, NKVD/OGPU 3

- Ethnicity: Russian 90 (64 percent), Ukrainian 21 (15 percent), Belarusian 6, Latvian 1, Georgian 2, Armenian 1, Ossetian 1, other/unknown 18
- General Staff training: 26 (18 percent)
- Political Loyalty: CPSU members 88 (62 percent), Purge victims 17 (12 percent)
- Average age in 1941: 43 years

APPENDIX 5: COMPARATIVE OFFICER RANKS

German Army (Heer) Rank	Waffen-SS Rank	Soviet Rank	US Army Rank
Generalfeldmarschall	N/A	Marshal of the Soviet Union	General of the Army
Generaloberst	SS-Oberstgruppenführer	General Army	General
General der (Infanterie)	SS-Obergruppenführer	General Polkovnik	Lieutenant General
Generalleutnant	SS-Gruppenführer	General Leytenant	Major General
Generalmajor	SS-Brigadeführer	General Major	Brigadier General
Oberst	SS-Standartenführer	Polkovnik	Colonel
Oberstleutnant	SS-Obersturmbannführer	Podpolkovnik	Lieutenant Colonel
Major	SS-Sturmbannführer	Major	Major
Hauptmann	SS-Hauptsturmführer	Kapetan	Captain
Oberleutnant	SS-Obersturmführer	Starshiy Leytenant	First Lieutenant
Leutnant	SS-Untersturmführer	Mladshiy Leytenant	Second Lieutenant

Acronyms

Generic

AFV	Armored Fighting Vehicle
C2	Command & Control
CP	Command Post
km	Kilometers
LOO	Line of Operations
MRL	Multiple Rocket Launcher

Soviet

CPSU	Communist Party of the Soviet Union
DP-41	State Defensive Plan 1941
GCC	Guards Cavalry Corps
GKO	State Defense Committee (*Gosudarstvennyy komitet oborony*)
GMC	Guards Mechanized Corps (*Gvardeyskiye mekhanizirovannyye korpusa*)
GRU	Main Intelligence Directorate (*Glavnoye razvedyvatel'noye upravleniye*)
GSHKA	Red Army General Staff (*General'nyy shtab Sovetskoy Armii*)
GTA	Guards Tank Army (*Gvardeyskiye tankovyye armii*)
KMG	Cavalry-mechanized Group (*konno-mekhanizirovannaya gruppa*)
KOVO	Kiev Special Military District (*Kiyevskogo osobogo voyennogo okrug*)

LVO	Leningrad Military District (*Leningradskiy voyennyy okrug*)
MC	Mechanized Corps (*Mekhanizirovannyye korpusa*)
NKO	People's Commissariat of Defense (*Narodnyy komissariat oborony*)
NKVD	People's Commissariat for Internal Affairs (*Narodný komissariat vnutrennih del*)
OdVO	Odessa Military District (*Odesskiy voyennyy okrug*)
PribOVO	Baltic Military District (*Pribaltiyskiy voyennyy okrug*)
PU-36	*Provisional Field Regulations for the Red Army (1936)*
RKKA	Red Army (*Raboche-krest'yanskaya Krasnaya armiya*)
RVGK	Reserve of the Supreme Command (*Rezerv Verkhovnogo Glavnokomandovaniya*)
SOR	Sevastopol Defense Region (*Sevastopol'skiy oboronitel'nyy rayon*)
Stavka/SVGK	Headquarters of the Supreme High Command (*Stavku verkhovnogo glavnokomandovaniya*)
TA	Tank Army (*Tankovyye armii*)
TC	Tank Corps (*Tankovyye korpusa*)
UMD	Unified Military Doctrine
VA	Air Army (*vozdushnaya armiya*)
VVS	Soviet Air Force (*Voenno-Vozdushnye Sily*)
ZapOVO	Western Special Military District (*Zapadnyy osobyy voyennyy okrug*)

German

AOK	Army [command] (*Armeeoberkommando*)
FHO	Foreign Armies East (*Fremde Heere Ost*)
FHQ	Führer Headquarters (*Führerhauptquartier*)*
GFM	Field Marshal (*Generalfeldmarschall*)
HArko	Higher Artillery Command (*Höheres Artillerie-Kommando*)
OKH	Army High Command (*Oberkommando des Heeres*)
OKW	Armed Forces High Command (*Oberkommando der Wehrmacht*)
PzAOK	Tank Army (*Panzerarmee*)
PzKpfw	Tank (*Panzerkampfwagen*)

*Initially located near Rastenburg, East Prussia in a camp known as the "Wolf's Lair" (*Wolfsschanze*). A forward headquarters known as "*Werwolf*" was activated near Vinnitsa on July 16, 1942.

Notes

Introduction

1. Antoine Henri de Jomini, *The Art of War* (Westport: Greenwood Press Publishers, 1961), p. 15.
2. Ferdinand Foch, *Des principes de la guerre* (Paris: Berger-Levrault, 1918).
3. Correlli Barnett (ed.), *Hitler's Generals* (New York: Grove Weidenfeld, 1989).
4. Harold Shukman (ed.), *Stalin's Generals* (London: Phoenix Press, 1993).
5. John I. Alger, *The Quest for Victory: The History of the Principles of War* (Westport: Praeger, 1982), pp. 138–139.
6. Alger, *Quest for Victory*, pp. 17–23.
7. Ibid., pp. 219–220.
8. Alaric Searle, "Inter-service Debate and the Origins of Strategic Culture: The Principles of War in the British Armed Forces, 1919–1939," *War in History*, vol. 21, no. 1 (January 2014), p. 10.
9. Captain Edson L. M. Burns, "The Principles of War: A Criticism of Colonel J. F. C. Fuller's Book 'The Foundations of the Science of War,'" *Canadian Defence Quarterly* 4, no. 2 (January 1927), pp. 168–175.
10. *FM 100-5, Tentative Field Service Regulations, Operations* (Washington, DC: US War Department, 1 October 1939).
11. Iyeronim P. Uborevich, "Principles of Waging Battle," [1922] in Harriet F. Scott (ed.), *The Soviet Art of War: Doctrine, Strategy and Tactics* (Boulder: Westview Press, 1982), pp. 53–55.

Chapter 1

1. Siegfried Knappe, *Soldat: Reflections of a German Soldier, 1936–1949* (New York: Dell Publishing, 1992), p. 121.
2. Martin van Creveld, *The Training of Officers* (New York: The Free Press, 1990), p. 28.

3. Barry Leach, *German General Staff* (New York: Ballantine Books, 1973), pp. 48–49.

4. Albert C. Wedemeyer, G-2 Report on the German General Staff School (US War Dept, General Staff, Military intel file, August 3, 1938) G-2, maintained in the US Army Military History Institute (MHI).

5. Robert M. Citino, *The German Way of War* (Lawrence: University Press of Kansas, 2005), pp. xiv–xv.

6. James S. Corum, *The Roots of Blitzkrieg: Hans von Seeckt and German Military Reform* (Lawerence, KS: University Press of Kansas, 1992), pp. 132–134.

7. Gerhard P. Gross, *The Myth and Reality of German Warfare: Operational Thinking from Moltke the Elder to Heusinger* (Lexington, KY: The University Press of Kentucky, 2016), pp. 142–145.

8. Robert M. Citino, *The Path to Blitzkrieg: Doctrine and Training in the German Army, 1920–39* (Mechanicsburg, PA: Stackpole Books, 1999), pp. 173–176.

9. Bruce Condell and David T. Zabecki (eds.), *On the German Art of War: Truppenführung* (Mechanicsburg, PA: Stackpole Books, 2009), p. 7.

10. Georgy K. Zhukov, *The Memoirs of Marshall Zhukov* (New York: Delacorte Press, 1969), p. 62.

11. Mikhail V. Frunze, *"Edinaia Voennaia Doktrina I Krasnaia Armiia"* (*Unified Military Doctrine and the Red Army*) in *Izbrannye Proizvedeniia* (Moscow: Voenizdat, 1977).

12. Zhukov, *Memoirs*, pp. 99–103.

13. Andrei I. Eremenko, *V nachale voyny* [At the Beginning of the War] (Moscow: Nauka, 1965), p. 512.

14. Charles C. Sharp, *Red Sabers: Soviet Cavalry Corps, Divisions, and Brigades, 1941 to 1945*, Soviet Order of Battle World War II, Vol. 5 (George F. Nafziger, 1995), pp. 2–4.

15. Petro Grigorenko, *Grigorenko Memoirs* (New York: W. W. Norton & Co., 1982), pp. 88–91.

16. David M. Glantz, *Stumbling Colossus: The Red Army on the Eve of World War* (Lawrence, KS: University of Kansas Press, 1998), pp. 30–31.

17. David M. Glantz, *When Titans Clashed: How The Red Army Stopped Hitler* (Lawrence, KS: University Press of Kansas, 1995), p. 39.

18. Aleksandr M. Vasilevsky, *Delo vsey zhizni* [The Work of a Lifetime] (Moscow: Politizdat, 1978), Chapter 10.

19. Glantz, *Stumbling Colossus*, p. 92, Glantz, *When Titans Clashed*, p. 39 and Vasilevsky, *Delo vsey zhizni*.

20. Glantz, *Stumbling Colossus*, pp. 90–96.

21. Barton S. Whaley, *Codeword Barbarossa* (Cambridge: MIT Press, 1974), pp. 24–129.

22. Pavel N. Bobylev, "Repetitsiya katastrofy" [*Rehearsal of a disaster*], *Voyenno-istoricheskiy zhurnal* [Military Historical Journal] 1993, No. 7–8.

23. Glantz, *Stumbling Colossus*, p. 103.

24. Richard W. Harrison, *The Russian Way of War: Operational Art, 1904–1940* (Lawrence, KS: University Press of Kansas, 2001), p. 229.

25. Aleksandr N. Lapchinsky, 'The Fundamentals of Air Forces Employment' [1932], in Harriet F. Scott (ed.), *The Soviet Art of War: Doctrine, Strategy and Tactics* (Boulder, CO: Westview Press, 1982), pp. 60–65.

26. Ian Kershaw, *Hitler: 1936–1945 Nemesis* (New York: W. W. Norton & Co., 2000), p. 305.

27. George E. Blau, *The German Campaign in Russia: Planning and Operations, 1940–1942*, Department of the Army Pamphlet No. 20–261a (Washington, DC: Department of the Army, 1955), pp. 1–3.

28. Charles Burdick and Hans-Adolf Jacobsen (ed.), *The Halder War Diary 1939–1942* (Novato, CA: Presidio Press, 1988), pp. 244–245.

29. Rolf-Dieter Müller, *Enemy in the East: Hitler's Secret Plans to Invade the Soviet Union* (London: I. B. Tauris & Co. Ltd., 2015), p. 207.

30. E. R. Hooten, *War over the Steppes: The Air Campaigns on the Eastern Front 1941–45* (Oxford: Osprey Publishing, 2016), pp. 40–41. Also, David Kahn, *Hitler's Spies: German Military Intelligence in World War II* (Boston, MA: Da Capo Press, 1978), pp. 449–450.

31. *The Halder War Diary*, p. 255.

32. Ibid., pp. 293–294.

33. *Die wichtigsten Panzerkampfwagen der Union der Sozialistischen Sovietrepubliken* (USSR), June 1, 1941, Panzerarmee 3, Ic Anlagen Band A, Teil I z. Tatigkeitsbericht Nr. 2, NAM (National Archives Microfilm), series T-313, Roll 222.

34. Hermann Hoth, *Panzer Operations: Germany's Panzer Group 3 During the Invasion of Russia, 1941* (Philadelphia: Casemate Publishers, 2017), p. 65.

35. H. G. W. Davie, "The Influence of Railways on Military Operations in the Russo-German War 1941–1945," *The Journal of Slavic Military Studies*, Vol. 30, No. 2 (2017), pp. 321–346.

Chapter 2

1. Kahn, *Hitler's Spies*, pp. 122–129.

2. Hermann Balck, *Order in Chaos: The Memoirs of General of Panzer Troops Hermann Balck* (Lexington, KY: University Press of Kentucky, 2017), p. 333.

3. Kahn, *Hitler's Spies*, pp. 199–207.

4. Erhard Raus, *Panzer Operations* (Cambridge, MA: Da Capo Press, 2003), p. 280.

Chapter 3

1. Zhukov, *Memoirs*, p. 230.

2. N. F. Kovalevsky, "Combat composition of the Red Army and the USSR Navy on June 22, 1941," *Voyenno-istoricheskiy zhurnal* [Military-history journal], No. 6 (2009), pp. 3–8.

3. Charles C. Sharp, *The Deadly Beginning: Soviet Tank, Mechanized, Motorized Divisions and Tank Brigades, 1940–1942*, Soviet Order of Battle World War II, Vol. 1 (George F. Nafziger, 1995), pp. 38–41, 60.

4. *Direktiva № 1 voyennym sovetam Pribaltiyskogo, Zapadnogo, Kiyevskogo Osobykh, Leningradskogo i Odesskogo voyennykh okrugov,* June 21, 1941, TsAMO. F. 208. Op. 2513. D. 71. L. 69.

5. Werner Haupt, *Army Group North: The Wehrmacht in Russia, 1941–1945* (Atglen, PA: Schiffer Military History, 1997), p. 2.

6. Condell and Zabecki, *Truppenführung,* sections 554–556, p. 148.

7. Christer Bergstrom and Andrey Mikhailov, *Black Cross and Red Star: The Air War over the Eastern Front,* Volume 1 (Pacifica, CA: Pacifica Military History, 2000), pp. 75, 79.

8. Haupt, *Army Group North,* p. 39.

9. Aleksandr M. Vasilevsky, *Delo vsey zhizni* [The Work of a Lifetime] (Moscow: Politizdat, 1978).

10. Ia, Anlagenband A II 1-2 z. KTB Nr. 5, Befehle nach unten, 1 June–17 September 1941, Panzerarmee 4, NAM (National Archives Microfilm), series T-313, Roll 331.

11. Erich von Manstein, *Lost Victories* (Novato, CA: Presidio Press, 1985), pp. 186–187.

12. *The Halder War Diary,* pp. 445–446. See also Haupt, *Army Group North,* p. 58.

13. David M. Glantz, *The Battle for Leningrad 1941–1944* (Lawrence, KS: University Press of Kansas, 2002), p. 39.

14. Glantz, *The Battle for Leningrad,* p. 40.

15. Werner Haupt, *Die 8. Panzer-Division im 2. Weltkrieg* (Eggolsheim: Podzun-Pallas Verlag, 1987), pp. 158–160.

16. Hugh Trevor-Roper, *Hitler's War Directives 1939–1945* (Edinburgh: Birlinn, 2004), pp. 145–146.

17. Bergstrom and Mikhailov, *Black Cross and Red Star,* Vol. 1, pp. 136–137.

18. Ibid., pp. 187–190.

19. Glantz, *The Battle for Leningrad,* p. 81.

20. G. F. Krivoshein, *Soviet Casualties and Combat Losses in the Twentieth Century* (Mechanicsburg, PA: Stackpole Books, 1993), pp. 111, 115.

21. Neil Short, *The Stalin and Molotov Lines: Soviet Western Defences 1928–1941* (Oxford: Osprey Publishing, 2008), pp. 14–15, 46–47.

22. David M. Glantz, *Colossus Reborn: The Red Army at War 1941–1943* (Lawrence, KS: University Press of Kansas, 2005), p. 201.

23. Bergstrom and Mikhailov, *Black Cross and Red Star,* Vol. 1, p. 32.

24. David M. Glantz, "The Border Battles in the Bialystok-Minsk Axis: 22–28 June 1941," in David M. Glantz (ed.), *The Initial Period of War on the Eastern Front, 22 June–August 1941* (Portland, OR: Frank Cass, 1997), pp. 196–200.

25. NKO Directive No. 3 to the military councils of the Northwestern, Western, Southwestern and Southern fronts. No. 52, June 22, 1941 // TsAMO. F. 48a. Op. 1554. D. 90. L. 260–262.

26. Ivan V. Boldin, *Stranitsy zhizni* [Pages of Life] (Moscow: Voenizdat, 1961), Chapter 4.

27. Glantz, "The Border Battles in the Bialystok-Minsk Axis: 22–28 June 1941," p. 210.

28. Klaus Gerbet (ed.), *Generalfeldmarschall Fedor von Bock: The War Diary, 1939–1945* (Atglen, PA: Schiffer Military History, 1996), pp. 225–229.

29. Heinz Guderian, *Panzer Leader* (New York: Ballantine Books, 1968), p. 131.

30. German prisoner figures from Gerbet (ed.), *Von Bock War Diary*, p. 243. Soviet casualty figures from Krivoshein, pp. 111–112.

31. Bergstrom and Mikhailov, *Black Cross and Red Star*, Vol. 1, p. 62.

32. Gerbet (ed.), *Von Bock War Diary*, p. 231.

33. David M. Glantz, *Barbarossa Derailed: The Battle for Smolensk, 10 July–10 September 1941,* Volume 2 (Solihull: Helion & Co. Ltd., 2012), p. 864.

34. B. Bytkov, *"Kontaudar 5-go mekhanizirivannogo korpusa na lepel'skom napravlenii (6–11 iiulia 1941 goda)"* [The Counterstroke of the 5th Mechanized Corps along the Lepel axis (6–11 July 1941)], *Voennoistoricheskii zhurnal*, No. 9 (September 1971), p. 60.

35. Glantz, *Barbarossa Derailed*, pp. 71–74.

36. Alexey V. Isaev, *Neizvestnyy 1941. Ostanovlennyy blitskrig* [Unknown 1941. The Stopped Blitzkrieg] (Moscow: Eksmo, 2010).

37. Bergstrom and Mikhailov, *Black Cross and Red Star*, Vol. 1, p. 87.

38. Guderian, *Panzer Leader*, p. 139.

39. Gerbet (ed.), *Von Bock War Diary*, p. 244.

40. H. G. W. Davie, "The Influence of Railways on Military Operations in the Russo-German War 1941–1945," *The Journal of Slavic Military Studies*, Vol. 30, No. 2 (2017), pp. 321–346.

41. Guderian, *Panzer Leader*, pp. 142–149.

42. Hoth, *Panzer Operations*, p. 113.

43. Gerbet (ed.), *Von Bock War Diary*, p. 255.

44. *The Halder War Diary*, p. 469.

45. Trevor-Roper, *Hitler's War Directives*, p. 143.

46. Gerbet (ed.), *Von Bock War Diary*, p. 274.

47. Zhukov, *Memoirs*, pp. 289–291.

48. Gerbet (ed.), *Von Bock War Diary*, pp. 287, 305.

49. Glantz, *Barbarossa Derailed*, p. 585.

50. Gerbet (ed.), *Von Bock War Diary*, p. 263.

51. Ibid., pp. 298, 304.

52. Hoth, *Panzer Operations*, p. 111.

53. O. Qu., Anlagenband 2 z. KTB, May 4, 1941–April 28, 1942, Panzerarmee 4, NAM (National Archives Microfilm), series T-313, Roll 335, Frame 8617204.

54. Victor J. Kamenir, *The Bloody Triangle: The Defeat of Soviet Armor in the Ukraine, June 1941* (Minneapolis, MN: Zenith Press, 2008), p. 68.

55. Ibid., pp. 77–82.

56. Kamenir, *Bloody Triangle*, pp. 88–89.

57. John Erickson, "The Soviet Response to Surprise Attack: Three Directives, 22 June 1941," *Soviet Studies*, Vol. 23, No. 4 (April 1972), pp. 519–553.

58. Kamenir, *Bloody Triangle*, pp. 101–102.
59. Bergstrom and Mikhailov, *Black Cross and Red Star*, Vol. 1, p. 70.
60. Dmitry Ryabyshev, *Pervyy god voyny* [The First Year of the War] (Moscow: Voenizdat, 1990), pp. 25–27.
61. Glantz, *The Initial Period of War on the Eastern Front*, p. 282.
62. Klaus Jurgen Muller, "Witzleben, Stülpnagel and Speidel," in Correlli Barnett (ed.), *Hitler's Generals* (New York: Grove Weidenfeld, 1989), pp. 50–54.
63. Walter Gorlitz, "Reichenau," in Barnett (ed.), *Hitler's Generals*, p. 216.
64. Cornel I. Scafes et al., *Armata romana 1941–1945* (Bucharest: Editura RAI, 1996).
65. Zhukov, *Memoirs*, pp. 288–289.
66. Bradley Martin et al., *Russian Logistics and Sustainment Failures in the Ukraine Conflict*, RAND Corporation, RR-A2033-1 (2023).
67. Trevor-Roper, *Hitler's War Directives*, p. 147.
68. Guderian, *Panzer Leader*, pp. 158–162.
69. Guderian, *Panzer Leader*, p. 164.
70. E. R. Hooton, *War over the Steppes: The Air Campaigns on the Eastern Front 1941–45* (Oxford: Osprey Publishing, 2016).
71. David M. Glantz, *Forgotten Battles of the German-Soviet War 1941–1945*, Volume 1 (self-published, 1999), pp. 91–98.
72. John Erickson, *The Road to Stalingrad: Stalin's War with Germany*, Volume I (New Haven, NJ: Yale University Press, 1999), pp. 207–208.
73. David Stahel, *Kiev 1941: Hitler's Battle for Supremacy in the East* (New York: Cambridge University Press, 2012), p. 247.
74. David M. Glantz, *Barbarossa: Hitler's Invasion of Russia 1941* (Charleston: Tempus Publishing Inc., 2001), p. 132.
75. Krivoshein, *Soviet Casualties*, p. 114.
76. Gerbet (ed.), *Von Bock War Diary*, pp. 303–304 and *The Halder War Diary*, p. 523.
77. Trevor-Roper, *Hitler's War Directives*, pp. 152–155.
78. *The Halder War Diary*, p. 519.
79. Thomas L. Jentz, *Panzertruppen: The Complete Guide to the Creation and Combat Employment of Germany's Tank Force, 1933–1942*, Vol. I (Atglen, PA: Schiffer Military History, 1996), p. 206.
80. Martin van Creveld, *Supplying War: Logistics from Wallenstein to Patton* (London: Cambridge University Press, 1977), p. 170.
81. Niklas Zetterling and Anders Frankson, *The Drive on Moscow 1941: Operation Taifun and Germany's First Great Crisis in World War II* (Philadelphia, PA: Casemate Publishers, 2012), p. 253.
82. Gerbet (ed.), *Von Bock War Diary*, p. 315.
83. Werner Haupt, *Assault on Moscow 1941* (Atglen, PA: Schiffer Military History, 1996), pp. 76–77.
84. Gerbet (ed.), *Von Bock War Diary*, p. 306.
85. Charles C. Sharp, *Red Tides: Soviet Rifle Divisions formed from June to December 1941*, Soviet Order of Battle World War II, Vol. 9 (George F. Nafziger, 1995), pp. 2–3.

86. Zetterling and Frankson, *The Drive on Moscow 1941*, pp. 65, 77.

87. Erickson, *The Road to Stalingrad,* p. 215.

88. Ibid., pp. 216–217.

89. Report of the commander of the Bryansk Front to the Chief of the General Staff of the Red Army on the military operations of the armies of the Bryansk Front for the period from October 1 to October 26, 1941, TsAMO. F. 202, op. 5, d. 38, l. 1–30.

90. Konstantin K. Rokossovsky, *A Soldier's Duty* (Moscow: Progress Publishers, 1970), pp. 51–53.

91. Zetterling and Frankson, *The Drive on Moscow 1941*, p. 106.

92. Report of the commander of the Bryansk Front to the Chief of the General Staff of the Red Army on the military operations of the armies of the Bryansk Front for the period from October 1 to October 26, 1941 // F. 202, op. 5, d. 38, l. 1–30.

93. Gerbet (ed.), *Von Bock War Diary*, pp. 336 and Zetterling and Frankson, *The Drive on Moscow 1941*, pp. 249–251.

94. Ia, Anlagenband A 1 z. KTB Nr. 6, 29 September–14 October 1941, Panzerarmee 4, NAM (National Archives Microfilm), series T-313, Roll 340.

95. Van Creveld, *Supplying War*, p. 174.

96. Zetterling and Frankson, *The Drive on Moscow 1941*, pp. 195–197.

97. Bergstrom and Mikhailov, *Black Cross and Red Star*, Vol. 1, pp. 232–235.

98. O.Qu., Anlagenband 5 z. KTB, Verschiedene Tagesmeldungen, Panzerarmee 4, 22 June 1941–28 April 1942, NAM (National Archives Microfilm), series T-313, Roll 338.

99. Vasilevsky, *Delo vsey zhizni,* chapter 12.

100. Gerbet (ed.), *Von Bock War Diary*, p. 396.

101. Timothy A. Wray, *Standing Fast: German Defensive Doctrine on the Russian Front During World War II, Prewar to March 1943* (Fort Leavenworth, KS: US Army Combat Studies Institute, Research Survey No. 5, 1986), p. 62.

102. Wray, *Standing Fast*, pp. 75–76.

103. Trevor-Roper, *Hitler's War Directives*, p. 154.

104. Glantz, *The Battle for Leningrad*, p. 94.

105. Gerald R. Kleinfeld, *Hitler's Spanish Legion: The Blue Division in Russia* (St Petersburg, FL: Hailer Publishing, 2005), pp. 43–59.

106. R. Michael Berry, *American Foreign Policy and the Finnish Exception: Ideological Preferences and Wartime Realities* (Helsinki: Societas Historica Finlandiae, 1987), pp. 192–206.

107. Trevor-Roper, *Hitler's War Directives*, pp. 152–153.

108. Ibid., p. 167.

109. Erickson, *The Road to Stalingrad,* pp. 289–291.

110. Robert Forczyk, *Where the Iron Crosses Grow: The Crimea 1941–1944* (Oxford: Osprey Publishing, 2014), p. 102.

111. Sharp, *Red Tides,* pp. 2–3.

112. VVS losses noted in Bergstrom and Mikhailov, *Black Cross and Red Star*, Vol. 1, p. 252. All other Soviet material losses are based on numbers provided in Krivoshein, *Soviet Casualties,* pp. 250–258.

113. Bundesarchiv, MA RW 6/556, 6/558.

114. James F. Dunnigan et al., *War in the East: The Russo-German Conflict, 1941–45* (New York: Simulations Publications, Inc., 1977), p. 4.

115. Robert Forczyk, *Tank Warfare on the Eastern Front 1941–1942, Schwerpunkt* (Barnsley, UK: Pen & Sword Books, 2013), pp. 160–161.

116. H. Pottgiesser, *Die Reichsbahn im Ostfeldzug 1939–1944. Die Wehrmacht im Kampf Band 26 [The Imperial Railway in the Eastern Campaign 1939–1944]* (Vowinckel Verlag, 1961).

117. R. L. DiNardo and Austin Bay. "Horse-Drawn Transport in the German Army," *Journal of Contemporary History*, vol. 23, no. 1 (1988), pp. 129–142.

118. Bergstrom and Mikhailov, *Black Cross and Red Star,* Vol. 1, pp. 254–255.

119. Gerbet (ed.), *Von Bock War Diary*, pp. 396–401.

120. Glantz, *Colossus Reborn,* p. 504.

Chapter 4

1. Wilhelm Adam and Otto Rühle, *With Paulus at Stalingrad* (Philadelphia: Penn & Sword Books, 2018), p. 5.

2. Hans Pottgiesser, *Die Deutsche Reichsbahn im Ostfeldzug 1939–1944* (Neckargemund: Kurt Vowinckel Verlag, 1975), p. 35

3. *Kirill A. Meretskov, Na sluzhbe narodu* [In the service of the people] (Moscow: Politizdat, 1968), pp. 265–266.

4. Catherine Andreyev, "Andrei Andreyevich Vlasov," in Harold Shukman (ed.), *Stalin's Generals* (London: Phoenix Press, 1997), pp. 306–311.

5. Glantz, *The Battle for Leningrad*, pp. 207–208.

6. Erickson, *The Road to Stalingrad*, pp. 305.

7. Ibid., pp. 306.

8. Franz Kurowski, *Deadlock Before Moscow: Armee Group Center, 1942/1943* (West Chester, PA: Schiffer Military History, 1992), p. 37.

9. Kurowski, *Deadlock Before Moscow*, pp. 49–64.

10. O. Qu., 16. Armee, 22 December 1941–31 March 1942, NAM (National Archives Microfilm), T312, Roll 552 and O. Qu., II. Armeekorps, T314, Roll 116.

11. Fritz Morzik, *German Air Force Airlift Operations* (Honolulu, HI: University Press of the Pacific, 2002), p. 172.

12. Walter Görlitz, *Strategie der Defensive Model* (Wiesbaden: Limes Verlag, 1982), p. 116.

13. Erickson, *The Road to Stalingrad*, p. 314.

14. David M. Glantz, *The Soviet Airborne Experience* (Fort Leavenworth, KS: US Army Combat Studies Institute, Research Survey No. 4, 1984), pp. 44–67.

15. Paul Carell, *Hitler Moves East 1941–1943* (Winnipeg: J. J. Fedorowicz Publishing, 1991), pp. 363–365.

16. David M. Glantz, *Forgotten Battles of the German-Soviet War 1941–1945*, Vol. II, *The Winter Campaign, 5 December 1941 – April 1942* (Self-published, 1999), pp. 21–46.

17. Von Manstein, *Lost Victories*, p. 228.

18. Glantz, *Forgotten Battles of the German-Soviet War 1941–1945*, Vol. II, *The Winter Campaign*, pp. 128–129.

19. Aleksandr B, Shirokorad, *Bitva za Krym* [Battle of the Crimea] (Moscow: AST, 2005).

20. Simon Sebag Montefiore, *Stalin: The Court of the Red Tsar* (New York: Vintage Books, 2003), p. 413.

21. *The Halder War Diary*, p. 614.

22. Trevor-Roper, *Hitler's War Directives*, pp. 178–179.

23. David M. Glantz, *Kharkov 1942* (Chatham, UK: Ian Allen, 1998), p. 78.

24. Korpsbefehl, LI. Armeekorps, Abt. Ia, Nr. 1704/42 geheim, 12 May 1942, found in XVII Armeekorps KTB 7, 1 April–12 August 1942, NAM (National Archives Microfilm), series T-314, Roll 582.

25. Gerbet (ed.), *Von Bock War Diary*, p. 490.

26. David M. Glantz, *To the Gates of Stalingrad: Soviet-German Operational Combat Operations, April–August 1942, The Stalingrad Trilogy*, Volume I (Lawrence, KS: University Press of Kansas, 2009), p. 98.

27. *The Halder War Diary*, pp. 611–613.

28. Dietrich Eichholtz, *War for Oil: The Nazi Quest for an oil Empire* (Washington, DC: Potomac Books, 2012), pp. 62–63, 66–68, 76–80.

29. Dr Peter W. Becker, "The Role of Synthetic Fuel in World War II Germany," *Air University Review*, vol. XXXII, no. 5 (July-August 1981), pp. 54–53.

30. Trevor-Roper, *Hitler's War Directives*, pp. 178–181.

31. David M. Glantz, *Companion to Colossus Reborn: Key Documents and Statistics* (Lawrence, KS: University Press of Kansas, 2005), p. 195.

32. *The German Campaign in Russia: Planning and Operations, 1940–1942*, Historical Study, No. 20-251a (Washington, DC: Department of the Army, 1955), pp. 127–128.

33. David M. Glantz, *To the Gates of Stalingrad*, Volume I, pp. 102–104. Also, Erickson, *The Road to Stalingrad*, p. 354.

34. Gerbet (ed.), *Von Bock War Diary*, pp. 504–505.

35. Erickson, *The Road to Stalingrad*, pp. 358–359.

36. *The Halder War Diary*, p. 634.

37. Gerbet (ed.), *Von Bock War Diary*, pp. 525–527.

38. Ibid., pp. 504–505.

39. *The Halder War Diary*, p. 649.

40. Igor Sdvizhkov, *Confronting Case Blue: Briansk Front's attempt to derail the German drive to the Caucasus, July 1942* (Solihull, UK: Helion & Company Ltd., 2017), pp. 21–22, 280, 409–411.

41. Ia, Anlagenband 3 z. KTB 5e, VII. Armeekorps, June–September 1942, NAM (National Archives Microfilm), series T-314, Roll 353.

42. Alexander Hill, *The Red Army and the Second World War* (Cambridge: Cambridge University Press, 2017), pp. 353–354.

43. David R. Higgins, *Behind Soviet Lines: Hitler's Brandenburgers capture the Maikop oilfields 1942* (Oxford: Osprey Publishing, 2014), pp. 25–26.

44. Geoffrey Jukes, *Hitler's Stalingrad Decisions* (Berkeley, CA: University of California Press, 1985), pp. 46–47.

45. Wilhelm Tieke, *The Caucasus and the Oil: The German Soviet War in the Caucasus 1942/43* (Winnipeg: J. J. Fedorowicz Publishing, 1995), pp. 59–61, 84–85.

46. Tieke, *The Caucasus and the Oil*, 149–159.

47. David M. Glantz, *Forgotten Battles of the German-Soviet War 1941–1945*, Volume III (12 May–18 November 1942) (Self-published, 1999), p. 103.

48. Konstantin K. Rokossovsky, *A Soldier's Duty* (Moscow: Progress Publishers, 1970), chapter 9.

49. *The Halder War Diary*, p. 660.

50. Walter Gorlitz, *Strategie der Defensive Model* (Munich: Limes Verlag, 1982), p. 121.

51. Earl F. Ziemke and Magna E. Bauer, *Moscow to Stalingrad: Decision in the East* (Washington, DC: Center of Military History, US Army, 1987), p. 252.

52. Ia, KTB, 6. Armee, 29 October 1942, NAM (National Archives Microfilm), series T-312, Roll 1458.

53. David M. Glantz, *Endgame at Stalingrad, Book 1: November 1942* (Lawrence, KS: University Press of Kansas, 2014), pp. 21–23.

54. David Kahn, *Hitler's Spies: German Military Intelligence in World War II* (Boston, MA: Da Capo Press, 1978), pp. 437–439.

55. Sergei M. Shtemenko, *The Soviet General Staff at War 1941–1945* (Honolulu, HI: University Press of the Pacific, 1970), pp. 123–126.

56. Glantz, *Endgame at Stalingrad, Book 1*, pp. 78–79.

57. Adam, *With Paulus at Stalingrad* pp. 93–96.

58. Glantz, *Endgame at Stalingrad, Book 1*, p. *258*.

59. Jason D. Mark, *Panzer Krieg: German Armoured Operations at Stalingrad*, Vol. 1 (Sydney: Leaping Horseman Books, 2017), pp. 300–309.

60. See the OKH, Lage Ost for both November 19, 1942 (no 5 TA depicted) and November 20, 1942 (5 TA depicted). Gehlen's FHO was responsible for updating the daily enemy situation on Lage Ost maps.

61. Ia, Anlagenband 2 u. 3 z. KTB, Heeresgruppe Don, 27 November–14 December 1942, item 39694/3b, 4, NAM (National Archives Microfilm), series T-311, Roll 268.

62. O. Qu., KTB, 6. Armee, 11 November 1942, NAM (National Archives Microfilm), series T-312, Roll 1458.

63. Antony Beevor, *Stalingrad: The Fateful Siege, 1942–1943* (New York: Viking Penguin, 1998), p. 267.

64. Beevor, *Stalingrad*, p. 272.

65. Adam, *With Paulus at Stalingrad*, pp. 102–105.

66. Ia, Anlagenband 5 z. KTB, Heeresgruppenbefehl fuer Neugliederung der Befehlsverhaeltnisse, Heeresgruppe Don, 24 December 1942–3 January 1943, item 39694/6, NAM (National Archives Microfilm), series T-311, Roll 270.

67. Glantz, *Endgame at Stalingrad, Book 1*, pp. 387–388.

68. Ibid., p. 391.

69. Adam, *With Paulus at Stalingrad*, pp. 125–126.

70. Robert Forsyth, *To Save an Army: The Stalingrad Airlift* (Oxford: Osprey Publishing, 2022), pp. 106–113.

71. Joel S. A. Hayward, *Stopped at Stalingrad: The Luftwaffe and Hitler's Defeat in the East, 1942–1943* (Lawrence, KS: University Press of Kansas, 1998), p. 243.

72. Jukes, *Hitler's Stalingrad Decisions*, p. 107

73. Forsyth, *To Save an Army*, p. 114.

74. Von Manstein, *Lost Victories*, pp. 321–322.

75. Friedrich W. von Mellenthin, *Panzer Battles: A Study of the Employment of Armour in the Second World War* (New York: Ballantine Books, 1971), pp. 211–218.

76. Von Manstein, *Lost Victories*, p. 326.

77. John Erickson, *The Road to Berlin* (London: Cassell, 2003), p. 12.

78. Beevor, *Stalingrad*, p. 298.

79. Raus, *Panzer Operations* pp. 172–176.

80. Order from Heeresgruppe Don to 6.Armee (Geheim), 1800 hours, December 19, 1942, listed in Appendix IV, Von Manstein, *Lost Victories*, pp. 562–563.

81. Dana V. Sadarananda, *Beyond Stalingrad: Manstein and the Operations of Army Group Don* (Mechanicsburg: Stackpole Books, 2009), pp. 53–54.

82. David M. Glantz, *Endgame at Stalingrad, Book 2: December 1942–February 1943* (Lawrence, KS: University Press of Kansas, 2014), p. 327.

83. Glantz, *Endgame at Stalingrad, Book 2*, pp. 227–233.

84. Hope Hamilton, *Sacrifice on the Steppe: The Italian Alpine Corps in the Stalingrad Campaign, 1942–1943* (Philadelphia, PA: Casemate Publishers, 2011), pp. 73–75.

85. Ia, Anlagenband 4 z. KTB, Heeresgruppe Don, 15–23 December 1942, item 39694/5, NAM (National Archives Microfilm), series T-311, Roll 269.

86. Vasily M. Badanov, *Glubokii tankovyi reid* [Deep Tank Raid] in A. M. Samsonov (ed.), *Stalingradskaya epopeya* (Moscow: Nauka Publishers, 1968), pp. 625–640.

87. David M. Glantz, *From the Don to the Dnepr: Soviet Offensive Operations December 1942–August 1943* (London: Frank Cass Publishers, 1991), p. 74.

88. Erickson, *The Road to Stalingrad*, p. 470.

89. Glantz, *Companion to Colossus Reborn*, pp. 15–16.

90. David M. Glantz, *Zhukov's Greatest Defeat: The Red Army's Epic Disaster in Operation Mars, 1942* (Lawrence, KS: University Press of Kansas, 1999), pp. 87–88.

91. Thomas L. Jentz, *Panzertruppen: The Complete Guide to the Creation and Combat Employment of Germany's Tank Force, 1943–1945*, Vol. II (Atglen, PA: Schiffer Military History, 1996), p. 24.

92. Glantz, *Zhukov's Greatest Defeat*, p. 224.

93. Ibid., p. 249.

Chapter 5

1. From *Kursk* by Steven Newton copyright © 2002. Reprinted by permission of Grand Central Publishing, an imprint of Hachette Book Group, Inc., p. 357.
2. Jukes, *Hitler's Stalingrad Decisions,* pp. 126–127.
3. Dana V. Sadarananda, *Beyond Stalingrad: Manstein and the Operations of Army Group Don* (Mechanicsburg: Stackpole Books, 2009), pp. 55–55.
4. Andrei Grechko, *Battle for the Caucasus* (Honolulu, HI: University Press of the Pacific, 2001), pp. 220–221.
5. Jukes, p. 155 and Wilhelm Tieke, *The Caucasus and the Oil: The German Soviet War in the Caucasus 1942/43* (Winnipeg: J. J. Fedorowicz Publishing, 1995), pp. 313–314.
6. Von Manstein, *Lost Victories*, pp. 396–398.
7. Grechko, pp. 285–286.
8. Aleksei Isaev, *Stalingrad: Za Volgoi dlia nas zemli net* [Stalingrad: There is no land for us behind the Volga] (Moscow: Eksmo, 2008), pp. 398–402.
9. John Erickson, *The Road to Berlin: Stalin's War with Germany*, Vol. 2 (London: Cassell, 2003), pp. 25–27.
10. Glantz, *Endgame at Stalingrad, Book 2,* pp. 400–403.
11. Ibid., p. 425.
12. Ibid., p. 582.
13. Glantz, *The Battle for Leningrad*, pp. 264–271.
14. Werner Haupt, *Army Group North: The Wehrmacht in Russia, 1941–1945* (Atglen, PA: Schiffer Military History, 1997), p. 152.
15. Glantz, *The Battle for Leningrad*, pp. 268–269.
16. Harrison E. Salisbury, *The 900 Days: The Siege of Leningrad* (Cambridge, MA: Da Capo Press, 2003), p. 548.
17. Glantz, *The Battle for Leningrad*, p. 285.
18. Zhukov, *Memoirs*, p. 426.
19. Richard N. Armstrong, *Red Army Tank Commanders* (Atglen, PA: Schiffer Publishing, 1994), pp. 163–164.
20. Erickson, *The Road to Berlin*, p. 33.
21. Peter Mujzer, *Hungarian Armored Forces in World War II* (Lublin: Kagero Publishing, 2017), pp. 40–43.
22. Hope Hamilton, *Sacrifice on the Steppe: The Italian Alpine Corps in the Stalingrad Campaign, 1942–1943* (Philadelphia, PA: Casemate Publishers, 2011), p. 183.
23. Sadarananda, *Beyond Stalingrad,* p. 74.
24. Kirill S. Moskalenko, *Na Yugo-Zapadnom napravlenii: Vospominaniya komandarma* [*On South-Western direction: Memoirs of an Army Commander 1943–1945*] (Moscow: Nauka, 1972), pp. 403–411.
25. Erickson, *The Road to Berlin*, pp. 34–35
26. Sergei M. Shtemenko, *The Soviet General Staff at War 1941–1945* (Honolulu, HI: University Press of the Pacific, 1970), p. 99.

27. Shtemenko, *The Soviet General Staff*, p. 104.
28. David M. Glantz, *After Stalingrad: The Red Army's Winter Offensive 1942–1943* (Solihull: Helion & Company Ltd., 2008), pp. 113–117.
29. David M. Glantz, *From The Don to the Dnepr: Soviet Offensive Operations, December 1942–August 1943* (London: Frank Cass Publishers, 1991), p. 86.
30. George M. Nipe, Jr, *Last Victory in Russia: The SS-Panzerkorps and Manstein's Counteroffensive* (Atglen, PA. Schiffer Military History, 2000), p. 52.
31. Shtemenko, *The Soviet General Staff*, p. 101.
32. Glantz, *From The Don to the Dnepr*, p. 87.
33. Ia, KTB Generalkommando z.b.v. Cramer, NAM (National Archives Microfilm), series T-314, Roll 489.
34. Eberhard Schwarz, *Die Stabilisierung in Süden der Ostfront nach der Katastophe von Stalingrad und dem Rückzug aus dem Kaukasus* (Köln: University of Köln, 1981), pp. 376–378.
35. Manstein, *Lost Victories*, p. 402.
36. Shtemenko, *The Soviet General Staff*, p. 101.
37. Manstein, *Lost Victories*, p. 413.
38. Ibid., pp. 424–428.
39. Ibid., pp. 425–428.
40. Nipe, *Last Victory in Russia*, p. 232.
41. Hooton, *War over the Steppes*, pp. 161–162.
42. Glantz, *From the Don to the Dnepr*, p. 141.
43. Ibid., pp. 193–194.
44. Shtemenko, *The Soviet General Staff*, pp. 112–113.
45. Glantz, *After Stalingrad*, pp. 203, 210.
46. Wolfgang Schneider, *Tigers in Combat*, Volume I (Mechanicsburg, PA: Stackpole Books, 2004), p. 124.
47. Reports on combat operations, 4th Guards Mechanized Corps, 02/23/1943, TsAMO, Fund: 303, Inventory: 4005, Case: 71.
48. Gerhard P. Gross, *The Myth and Reality of German Warfare: Operational Thinking from Moltke the Elder to Heusinger* (Lexington, KY: The University Press of Kentucky, 2016), pp. 230–231.
49. Shtemenko, *The Soviet General Staff*, p. 115.
50. Zhukov, *Memoirs*, p. 430.
51. Hooton, *War over the Steppes*, p. 162.
52. Glantz, *After Stalingrad*, p. 307.
53. Ibid., p. 325.
54. Hans Schäufler, *Knights Cross Panzers: The German 35th Panzer Regiment in WWII* (Mechanicsburg, PA: Stackpole Books, 2010), pp. 219–220.
55. Glantz, *After Stalingrad*, pp. 398–399.
56. Zhukov, *Memoirs*, p. 428.
57. Glantz, *After Stalingrad*, p. 328.
58. Krivoshein, *Soviet Casualties*, p. 104.

59. Edwin Bacon, "Soviet Military Losses in World War II," *Journal of Slavic Military Studies*, Vol. 6, no. 4 (December 1993), p. 623.

60. Grechko, *Battle for the Caucasus*, p. 286.

61. Shtemenko, *The Soviet General Staff at War*, pp. 88–89.

62. Von Hardesty and Ilya Grinberg, *Red Phoenix Rising: The Soviet Air Force in World War II* (Lawrence, KS: University Press of Kansas, 2012), p. 170.

63. Von Manstein, *Lost Victories*, pp. 446–447.

64. Christopher A. Lawrence, *Kursk: The Battle of Prokhorovka* (Sheridan, CO: Aberdeen Books, 2015), pp. 88–89.

65. Zhukov, *Memoirs*, pp. 445–446.

66. David M. Glantz (ed.), *The Battle for Kursk 1943: The Soviet General Staff Study* (London: Frank Cass Publishers, 1999), p. 10.

67. Lukas Friedli, *Repairing the Panzers: German Tank Maintenance in World War II, Volume I* (Monroe, NY: Panzerwrecks, 2010), pp. 152–156.

68. Niklas Zetterling and Anders Frankson, *Kursk 1943: A Statistical Analysis* (London: Frank Cass Publishers, 2000), pp. 34–35, 43. Also see Lawrence, *Kursk: The Battle of Prokhorovka*, pp. 199–202.

69. Zhukov, *Memoirs*, p. 451.

70. Steven H. Newton (ed.), *Kursk: The German View* (Cambridge, MA: Da Capo Press, 2002), pp. 71–72.

71. Christer Bergstrom, *Kursk: The Air Battle, July 1943* (Hersham: Ian Allen Printing Ltd., 2007), pp. 18–24.

72. David M. Glantz and Jonathan M. House, *The Battle of Kursk* (Lawrence, KS: University Press of Kansas, 1999), p. 84.

73. Lawrence, *Kursk: The Battle of Prokhorovka*, p. 189.

74. Mikhail E. Katukov, *Na ostrie glavnogo udara* [*On the Point of the Main Attack*] (Moscow: Military Publishing House, 1974), p. 216.

75. Didier Lodieu, *III. Pz. Korps at Kursk* (Paris: Histoire & Collections, 2007), pp. 10, 26.

76. Katukov, *Na ostrie glavnogo udara*, p. 220.

77. Glantz and House, *The Battle of Kursk*, p. 102.

78. George M. Nipe, *Blood, Steel and Myth: The II. SS-Panzerkorps and the Road to Prokhorovka, July 1943* (Stamford, CT: RZM Publishing, 2011), p. 121.

79. Pavel Rotmistrov, *Stal'naya gvardiya* [*Steel Guards*] (Moscow: Voenizdat, 1984), p. 177.

80. Valeriy Zamulin, *Demolishing the Myth: The Tank Battle at Prokhorovka, Kursk, July 1943, An Operational Narrative* (Solihull, UK: Helion & Company, Ltd., 2011), p. 167.

81. Lodieu, *III. Pz. Korps at Kursk*, pp. 102–103.

82. Zamulin, *Demolishing the Myth*, pp. 270–280.

83. Rotmistrov, *Stal'naya gvardiya*, p. 183.

84. Nipe, *Blood, Steel and Myth*, pp. 318–319.

85. Zamulin, *Demolishing the Myth*, pp. 336–337, 440–441.

86. Rotmistrov, *Stal'naya gvardiya*, p. 197.
87. Zetterling and Frankson, *Kursk 1943*, Appendix 6, pp. 185–190.
88. Lawrence, *Kursk: The Battle of Prokhorovka*, pp. 817–818.
89. Rotmistrov, *Stal'naya gvardiya*, pp. 204–205.
90. Glantz and House, *The Battle of Kursk*, p. 230.
91. Glantz and House, *The Battle of Kursk*, pp. 232–233.
92. Ivan K. Bagramyan, *Tak shli my k pobede* [Thus we went on to victory] (Moscow: Voenizdat, 1988), p. 199.
93. Vasilevsky, *Delo vsey zhizni*, p. 374.
94. Aleksandr V. Gorbatov, *Gody i voiny* [Years and Wars] (Moscow: Voenizdat, 1980), pp. 217–218.
95. Glantz and House, *The Battle of Kursk*, p. 232.
96. Ia, Anlagen zum KTB 2, 262. Infanterie-Division, 1 July–31 August 1943, NAM (National Archives Microfilm), T315, Roll 1834.
97. Bagramyan, *Tak shli my k pobede*, p. 203.
98. Bagramyan, *Tak shli my k pobede*, p. 204.
99. Bergstrom, *Kursk: The Air Battle*, pp. 86–87.
100. Ic, Tätigkeitsberichte, XXXV Armeekorps, June 1–August 31, 1943, NAM (National Archives Microfilm), T314, Roll 868.
101. Bergstrom, *Kursk: The Air Battle*, p. 90.
102. Glantz and House, *The Battle of Kursk*, p. 236.
103. Ibid., p. 240.
104. Krivoshein, *Soviet Casualties and Combat Losses*, pp. 133, 262.
105. Vitaliy Gorbach, *Aviatsiia v Kurskoi bitve* [Aviation in the Battle of Kursk] (Moscow: Eksmo, 2008), pp. 475, 486.
106. Vasily I. Chuikov, *Ot Stalingrada do Berlina* [From Stalingrad to Berlin] (Moscow: Voenizdat, 1980), p. 357.
107. Von Manstein, *Lost Victories*, p. 452.
108. Zetterling and Frankson, *Kursk 1943*, pp. 138–139.
109. Martin Francke, "Sixth Army Defends the Mius River Line" in Steven H. Newton (ed.), *Kursk: The German View* (Boston, MA: Da Capo Press, 2002), p. 307.
110. Francke, "Sixth Army Defends the Mius River Line," p. 321.
111. George M. Nipe, *Decision in the Ukraine: Summer 1943, II. SS and III. Panzerkorps* (Winnipeg: J. J. Fedorowicz Publishing, Inc. 1996), pp. 99–102.
112. Francke, "Sixth Army Defends the Mius River Line," p. 327.
113. Nipe, *Decision in the Ukraine: Summer 1943*, p. 252.
114. Francke, "Sixth Army Defends the Mius River Line," pp. 348–349.
115. Nipe, *Decision in the Ukraine: Summer 1943*, p. 261.
116. Glantz, *From the Don to the Dnepr*, p. 292.
117. Glantz and House, *The Battle of Kursk*, p. 245.
118. Glantz, *From the Don to the Dnepr*, p. 247.
119. Nipe, *Decision in the Ukraine: Summer 1943*, pp. 268–271.

120. Von Manstein, *Lost Victories*, p. 456.

121. Raus, *Panzer Operations*, pp. 242–245.

122. Krivoshein, *Soviet Casualties and Combat Losses*, pp. 134, 262.

123. Erickson, *The Road to Berlin*, pp. 129–130.

124. Vasily P. Istomin, *Smolenskaya nastupatel'naya operatsiya 1943* [*Smolensk Offensive Operation 1943*] (Moscow: Military Publishing House, 1975).

125. 4.Armee (Ia, Ic, O. Qu.), January–June 1943, NAM (National Archives Microfilm), T312, Rolls 216–219.

126. Krivoshein, *Soviet Casualties and Combat Losses*, pp. 135, 262.

127. Von Manstein, *Lost Victories*, p. 467.

128. Zhukov, *Memoirs*, pp. 479–482.

129. David M. Glantz, *The Soviet Airborne Experience* (Fort Leavenworth, KS: US Army Command and Staff College, 1984), pp. 93–99.

130. Rolf Hinze, *Crucible of Combat: Germany's Defensive Battles in the Ukraine, 1943–1944* (Solihull, UK: Helion & Company, Ltd., 2009), p. 39.

131. David M. Glantz, *Forgotten Battles of the German–Soviet War 1941–1945*, Volume V, Part 2 (Self-published, 2000), p. 674.

132. Vasilevsky, *Delo vsey zhizni*, p. 307.

133. Kirill S. Moskalenko, *Na Yugo-Zapadnom napravlenii: Vospominaniya komandarma* [*On South-Western direction: Memoirs of an Army Commander 1943–1945*] (Moscow: Nauka, 1972), pp. 162–163.

134. Von Manstein, *Lost Victories*, pp. 489–490.

135. Hermann Balck, *Order in Chaos: The Memoirs of General of Panzer Troops Hermann Balck* (Lexington, KY: University Press of Kentucky, 2017), pp. 312–314.

136. Glantz, *Forgotten Battles of the German–Soviet War 1941–1945*, p. 697.

137. Hinze, *Crucible of Combat*, pp. 105–112.

138. Stephen Barratt, *Zhitomir-Berdichev: German Operations west of Kiev, 24 December 1943–31 January 1944* (Solihull, UK: Helion & Company, Ltd., 2012), pp. 22, 71.

139. Barratt, *Zhitomir-Berdichev*, p. 163.

140. Glantz, *Forgotten Battles of the German–Soviet War 1941–1945*, pp. 411–413.

141. David M. Glantz, *Battle for Belorussia: The Red Army's Forgotten Campaign of October 1943–April 1944* (Lawrence, KS: University Press of Kansas, 2016), pp. 90–91.

142. Glantz, *Forgotten Battles of the German–Soviet War 1941–1945*, pp. 545–554.

Chapter 6

1. Andrei I. Eremenko, *Pamyat' Gody vozmezdiya* [Years of Retribution, 1943–1945] (Moscow: Nauka, 1969), pp. 210–211.

2. Friedrich W. von Mellenthin, *Panzer Battles: A Study of the Employment of Armour in the Second World War* (New York: Ballantine Books, 1971), pp. 323–324.

3. Aleksandr M. Zvartsev, *3-ya gvardeyskaya tankovaya Boyevoy put' 3-y gvardeyskoy tankovoy armii* [*The Combat Path of the 3rd Guards Tank Army*] (Moscow: Voenizdat, 1982), p. 149.

4. Mikhail E. Katukov, *Na Ostrie glavnogo udara* [*At the Point of the Main Attack*] (Moscow: Voenizdat, 1974), p. 284.

5. Von Manstein, *Lost Victories*, pp. 501–503.

6. Raus, *Panzer Operations*, p. 266.

7. Barratt, *Zhitomir-Berdichev*, pp. 277–278.

8. Ia, KTB, Bände I–II, PzAOK 4, 1 January–31 March 1944, 229/44, 9 January 1944. NAM (National Archives Microfilm), series T-313, Roll 387.

9. Von Manstein, *Lost Victories*, p. 507.

10. Veterans of the 3rd Panzer Division, *Armored Bears: The German 3rd Panzer Division in World War II*, Volume II (Mechanicsburg, PA: Stackpole Books, 2013), pp. 208–211.

11. Hinze, *Crucible of Combat*, pp. 172–174.

12. David M. Glantz (ed), *The Battle for the Ukraine: The Red Army's Korsun'-Shevchenkovskii Offensive, 1944* (Abingdon, UK: Routledge, 2007), p. 115.

13. Armstrong, *Red Army Tank Commanders*, p. 417.

14. Niklas Zetterling and Anders Frankson, *The Korsun Pocket: The Encirclement and Breakout of a German Army in the East, 1944* (Philadelphia: Casemate, 2008), pp. 55–57.

15. O. Qu., Anlagenband z. KTB, AOK 8 (11 February 1944) 1–29 February 1944, NAM (National Archives Microfilm), series T-312, Roll 63, Frame 7581371.

16. Fritz Morzik, *German Air Force Airlift Operations* (Honolulu, HI: University Press of the Pacific, 2002), pp. 219–225.

17. Von Manstein, *Lost Victories*, p. 516.

18. Douglas E. Nash, *Hell's Gate: The Battle of the Cherkassy Pocket, January–February 1944* (Stamford, CT: RZM Publishing, 2005), p. 366.

19. Zhukov, *Memoirs*, p. 509.

20. Glantz, *When Titans Clashed*, p. 188. See also Gerhard L. Weinberg, *A World At Arms: A Global History of World War II* (New York: Cambridge University Press, 1994), p. 669.

21. Zetterling and Frankson, *The Korsun Pocket,* pp. 286–287.

22. H. G. W. Davie, "Logistics of the Tank Army: The Uman–Botoşani Operation, 1944," *Journal of Slavic Military Studies*, Volume 33, Issue 3 (December 2020), pp. 420–441.

23. Balck, *Order in Chaos*, pp. 338–340.

24. Journal of military operations 3rd Guards Tank Army (Журнал боевых действий 3 гв. ТА), 1–31 March 1944, TsAMO, Fund: 315, Inventory: 4440, File: 334.

25. Erickson, *The Road to Berlin*, p. 185.

26. David M. Glantz, *Red Storm over the Balkans: The Failed Soviet Invasion of Romania, Spring 1944* (Lawrence, KS: University Press of Kansas, 2007), pp. 6–7.

27. Evgeni Bessonov, *Tank Rider: Into the Reich with the Red Army* (Philadelphia: Casemate, 2005), pp. 69–74.

28. KTB Nr. 13, 1a, 1. Panzerarmee, 25–31 March 1944 and 1–10 April 1944, National Archives and Research Administration (NARA), T313, Roll 71.

29. Journal of military operations 3rd Guards Tank Army (Журнал боевых действий 3 гв. ТА), 1–31 March 1944, TsAMO, Fund: 315, Inventory: 4440, File: 334.

30. Hinze, *Crucible of Combat*, pp. 393–395.

31. Morzik, *German Air Force Airlift Operations*, pp. 256–257.

32. Michael Reynolds, *Sons of the Reich: II. SS-Panzerkorps* (Barnsley: Pen & Sword Books, 2002), pp. 4–5.

33. Aleksei Isaev, *"Kotol" Khube. Proskurovsko-Chernovitskaya Operatsiya 1944 goda* [Hube's "cauldron". Proskurov-Chernivtsi Operation in 1944] (Moscow: Yauza, 2017).

34. Erickson, *The Road to Berlin*, p. 165.

35. Nash, *Hell's Gate*, p. 128 and von Manstein, *Lost Victories*, p. 515.

36. Hinze, *Crucible of Combat*, pp. 206–207.

37. Ibid., p. 213.

38. Ibid., p. 221.

39. Krivoshein, *Soviet Casualties*, pp. 140–141.

40. Andrei Kuznetsov, *Bolshoi desant Kerchensko Eltigenskaya operatsiya* [*Large Landing Operation at Kerch-Eltigen*] (Moscow: VECHE, 2011).

41. Ia, Anlagenband 2 z. KTB Nr. 8, Unternehmen "Michael" mit Sondervorgang, AOK 17, October 19–31, 1943, NAM (National Archives Microfilm), Series T-312, Roll 738.

42. Christer Bergstrom, *Bagration to Berlin: The Final Air Battles in the East, 1944–1945* (Hersham, UK: Ian Allan Publishing, 2008), p. 46.

43. Robert A. Forczyk, *Where the Iron Crosses Grow: The Crimea, 1941–44* (Oxford: Osprey Publishing, 2014), pp. 283–284. This proclamation was listed in the KTB for AOK 17 on April 24, 1944.

44. Neitzel Soenke, *Tapping Hitler's Generals: Transcripts of Secret Conversations, 1942–1945* (St Paul, MN: MBI Publishing, 2007), p. 259.

45. Vasilevsky, *Delo vsey zhizni*, p. 395.

46. Krivoshein, *Soviet Casualties*, p. 143.

47. Glantz, *The Battle for Leningrad*, p. 322.

48. Bergstrom, *Bagration to Berlin*, p. 31.

49. Steven H. Newton, *Retreat from Leningrad: Army Group North, 1944/1945* (Atglen, PA: Schiffer Military Publishing, 1995), p. 21.

50. Erickson, *The Road to Berlin*, p. 170.

51. Ibid., p. 168.

52. Glantz, *The Battle for Leningrad*, p. 336.

53. Wilhelm Tieke, *Tragedy of the Faithful: A History of the III. (germanisches) SS-Panzer-Korps* (Winnipeg: J. J. Fedorowicz Publishing Inc., 2001), pp. 32–35.

54. Werner Haupt, *Army Group North: The Wehrmacht in Russia, 1941–1945* (Atglen, PA: Schiffer Military Publishing, 1997), p. 201.

55. Ia, KTB, Heeresgruppe Nord, Nr. 24/44, an Chef GenStdH, 29 January 1944, NAM (National Archives Microfilm), series T-311, Roll 58, Item H 22/226.

56. Earl F. Ziemke, *Stalingrad to Berlin: The German Defeat in the East* (Washington, DC: Center of Military History, US Army, 1987), p. 257.

57. Tieke *The Tragedy of the Faithful*, p. 74.

58. Ia, KTB, Heeresgruppe Nord, 1–31 January 1944 (29 January 1944), NAM (National Archives Microfilm), series T-311, Roll 58, Item 75128/33.

59. Newton, *Retreat from Leningrad: Army Group North, 1944/1945*, pp. 130–135.

60. Haupt, *Army Group North*, p. 208.

61. Erickson, *The Road to Berlin*, p. 175.

62. Wolfgang Schumann, Olaf Gröhler, *Deutschland im zweiten Weltkrieg, V* (Berlin: Akademie Verlag, 1981), p. 70.

63. Krivoshein, *Soviet Casualties*, pp. 142, 262.

64. Glantz, *Red Storm over the Balkans*, p. 24.

65. Ibid., pp. 66–69.

66. Ibid., p. 249.

67. Ibid., p. 268.

68. Ibid., p. 96.

69. Ibid., p. 162.

70. Ia, Abwehrkämpfe der 6. Armee am Dnjestr und Reut, AOK 6, 20 April–31 May 1944, NAM (National Archives Microfilm), series T-312, Roll 1469, Item 51542/3.

71. Glantz, *Red Storm over the Balkans*, pp. 317.

72. Ernst Rebentisch, *The Combat History of the 23rd Panzer Division in World War II* (Mechanicsburg, PA: Stackpole Books, 2012), pp. 355–357.

73. Ia, Anlage z. KTB Nr. 3, Chefsache "Sonja," AOK 8, May 1944, NAM (National Archives Microfilm), series T-312, Roll 65, Item 58298/16.

74. Hans Ulrich Rudel, *Stuka Pilot* (New York: Bantam Books, 1984), pp. 153–155.

75. Bergstrom, *Bagration to Berlin*, p. 55.

76. Glantz, *Red Storm over the Balkans*, pp. 379–380.

77. Anatoliy A. Krivorot, *Nastupatel'nyye deystviya Krasnoy Armii na Vitebskom napravlenii zimoy 1944 g.* ["Offensive actions of the Red Army in the Vitebsk direction in the winter 1944"], *Journal of Russian and East European Historical Research,* No. 1 (12) (2018), pp. 92–106.

78. Ziemke, *Stalingrad to Berlin*, p. 314.

79. Bergstrom, *Bagration to Berlin*, p. 58.

80. Kriegstagebuch Nr. 10, *Führungsabteilung*, AOK 9, 22 June 1944, NAM (National Archives Microfilm), series T-312, Roll 336 59691/16 file.

81. Glantz, *When Titans Clashed*, pp. 195–196.

82. Shtemenko, *The Soviet General Staff at War*, p. 224.

83. Zhukov, *Memoirs*, pp. 515–519.

84. Erickson, *The Road to Berlin*, p. 197.

85. Ibid., pp. 201–204.

86. David M. Glantz and Harold S. Orenstein (ed.), *Belorussia 1944: The Soviet General Staff Study* (New York: Frank Cass Publishers, 2001), pp. 63–64.

87. OKH, FHO Nr. 1794/44, *Auszug aus kurze Beurteilung der Feindlage der Heeresgruppe Mitte vom 2 June 1944 – 3 June 1944,* H 3/185 file.

88. Erickson, *The Road to Berlin*, p. 198.
89. Shtemenko, *The Soviet General Staff at War*, pp. 230–231.
90. Armstrong, *Red Army Tank Commanders*, p. 370.
91. Hill, *The Red Army*, p. 504.
92. Erickson, *The Road to Berlin*, p. 215.
93. Glantz and Orenstein, *Belorussia 1944:The Soviet General Staff Study,* p. 38.
94. Erickson, *The Road to Berlin*, p. 220.
95. Armstrong, *Red Army Tank Commanders*, pp. 371–372.
96. Walter S. Dunn, Jr, *Soviet Blitzkrieg:The Battle for White Russia, 1944* (Mechanicsburg, PA: Stackpole Books, 2008), p. 149.
97. Samuel W. Mitcham, Jr, *The German Defeat in the East 1944–45* (Mechanicsburg, PA: Stackpole Books, 2007), p. 121.
98. Mitcham, *The German Defeat in the East 1944–45*, p. 48.
99. Ziemke, *Stalingrad to Berlin*, p. 322.
100. Bergstrom, *Bagration to Berlin*, p. 63.
101. Armstrong, *Red Army Tank Commanders*, p. 374.
102. Newton, *Retreat from Leningrad:Army Group North, 1944/1945*, pp. 190–196.
103. Ibid., pp. 202–207.
104. Petr Ia. Egorov, *Dorogami pobed: boeboi 5-i gvardeiskoi tankovoi armii* [5th Guards Tank Army combat history] (Moscow:Voenizdat, 1969), pp. 248–250.
105. Hans-Joachim Jung, *The History of Panzerregiment Großdeutschland* (Winnipeg: J.J. Fedorowicz Publishing, 2000), pp. 284–285.
106. Andrei I. Eremenko, *Pamya" Gody vozmezdiya* [Years of Retribution, 1943–1945] (Moscow: Nauka, 1969), pp. 210–211.
107. Ivan K. Bagramyan, *Tak shli my k pobede* [Thus we went on to victory] (Moscow: Voenizdat, 1977), pp. 352–359.
108. Semen M. Sarkisyan, *51-ia armiia* [51st Army] (Yerevan: Hayastan, 1988), p. 233.
109. Egorov, *Dorogami pobed*, pp. 262–263.
110. Bagramyan, *Tak shli my k pobede*, p. 383.
111. Raus, *Panzer Operations*, pp. 295–296.
112. Newton, *Retreat from Leningrad:Army Group North, 1944/1945*, pp. 242–245.
113. Gerd Niepold, *Panzeroperationen "Doppelkopf" und "Cäsar": Kurland – Sommer '44* (Herford: E.S. Mittler, 1987).
114. Mitcham, *The German Defeat in the East 1944–45*, pp. 66–67.
115. Rolf Hinze, *To The Bitter End: The Final Battles of Army Groups North Ukraine, A, and Center – Eastern Front, 1944–45* (Philadelphia: Casemate, 2010), pp. 19–21.
116. Bergström, *Bagration to Berlin*, p. 67.
117. Balck, *Order in Chaos*, pp. 352–354.
118. Von Mellenthin, *Panzer Battles*, p. 338.
119. Raus, *Panzer Operations*, pp. 275–276.
120. Bergstrom, *Bagration to Berlin*, pp. 67–68.
121. Bergstrom, *Bagration to Berlin*, p. 70.

122. Von Mellenthin, *Panzer Battles*, p. 341.

123. Armstrong, *Red Army Tank Commanders*, pp. 213–214.

124. Raus, *Panzer Operations*, p. 288.

125. Alex Buchner, *Ostfront 1944: The German Defensive Battles on the Russian Front 1944* (Atglen, PA: Schiffer Publishing, 1997), pp. 235–236.

126. Armstrong, *Red Army Tank Commanders*, pp. 135–138.

127. Balck, *Order in Chaos*, pp. 364–365.

128. *Zhurnal boyevykh deystviy voysk 1 Ukrainskogo fronta za avgust mesyats 1944* [Journal of combat operations of the troops of the 1st Ukrainian Front for the month of August 1944], TsAMO, Fund: 236, Inventory: 2673, Case: 1070. Also Krivoshein, *Soviet Casualties*, pp. 146, 263.

129. Ziemke, *Stalingrad to Berlin*, p. 350.

130. Erickson, *The Road to Berlin*, p. 356.

131. Ibid., pp. 363–364.

132. Ziemke, *Stalingrad to Berlin*, p. 355.

133. Krivoshein, *Soviet Casualties*, p. 147.

134. Ziemke, *Stalingrad to Berlin*, p. 359.

135. Armstrong, *Red Army Tank Commanders*, pp. 431–432.

136. Erickson, *The Road to Berlin*, pp. 412–413.

137. Raus, *Panzer Operations*, p. 297.

138. Werner Haupt, *Army Group Center: The Wehrmacht in Russia, 1941–1945* (Atglen, PA: Schiffer Publishing Ltd, 1997), p. 218.

139. Mitcham, *The German Defeat in the East 1944–45*, pp. 148–149.

140. Tieke, *The Tragedy of the Faithful*, pp. 158–159.

141. Bagramyan, *Tak shli my k pobede*, pp. 434–435.

142. Ibid., p. 465.

143. Haupt, *Army Group North*, p. 278.

144. Ibid., pp. 328–329.

145. Ibid., p. 336.

146. Jak P. Mallmann Showell (ed.), *Fuehrer Conferences on Naval Affairs, 1939–45* (London: Greenhill Books, 2006), p. 441.

147. Kuzma N. Galitsky, *V boyakh za Vostochnuyu Prussiyu: Zapiski komanduyushchego 11-y gvardeyskoy armiyey* [In the battles for East Prussia: Notes of the commander of the 11th Guards Army] (Moscow: Nauka, 1970), pp. 22–23.

148. Galitsky, *V boyakh za Vostochnuyu Prussiyu*, pp. 45–48.

149. Ibid., pp. 134–136.

150. Krivoshein, *Soviet Casualties*, pp. 152, 263.

Chapter 7

1. Balck, *Order in Chaos*, p. 407.

2. Cornelius Ryan, *The Last Battle* (New York: Simon & Schuster, Inc. 1966), p. 345.

3. Zhukov, *Memoirs*, p. 558.

4. Ivan S. Konev, *Year of Victory* (Honolulu, HI: University Press of the Pacific, 2005), p. 21.
5. Christopher Duffy, *Red Storm on the Reich: The Soviet March on Germany, 1945* (New York: Da Capo Press, 1993), p. 70.
6. Russ Schneider, *Gotterdammerung 1945: Germany's Last Stand in the East* (Philomont, VA: Eastern Front Warfield Books, 1998), p. 46.
7. Bergstrom, *Bagration to Berlin*, p. 94.
8. Guderian, *Panzer Leader*, pp. 328–329.
9. Balck, *Order in Chaos*, pp. 408–410.
10. Armstrong, *Red Army Tank Commanders*, pp. 437–438.
11. Guderian, *Panzer Leader*, pp. 342–343.
12. Ziemke, *Stalingrad to Berlin*, p. 447.
13. Raus, *Panzer Operations*, pp. 324–326.
14. Otto Preston Chaney, *Zhukov* (Norman, OK: University of Oklahoma Press, 1971), p. 302.
15. Duffy, *Red Storm on the Reich*, p. 128.
16. Schneider, *Gotterdammerung 1945*, p. 133.
17. Gottlob Herbert Bidermann, *In Deadly Combat: A German Soldier's Memoir of the Eastern Front* (Lawrence, KS: University Press of Kansas, 2000), p. 255.
18. Balazs Mihalyi, *Siege of Budapest 1944–45* (Oxford: Osprey Publishing, 2022), pp. 82–89.
19. Krivoshein, *Soviet Casualties*, pp. 151–152, 263.
20. Ia, Kriegstagebuch, Heeresgruppe Süd, 25–27 February 1945, NAM (National Archives Microfilm), series T-311, Roll 299, 75126/55 file.
21. Raus, *Panzer Operations*, p. 340.
22. Ryan, *The Last Battle*, p. 72.
23. Bergstrom, *Bagration to Berlin*, p. 109.
24. Tony Le Tisier, *Marshal Zhukov at the Oder: The Decisive Battle for Berlin* (Gosport: Sutton Publishing, 2008), pp. 85–98.
25. Hinze, *To The Bitter End*, pp. 179–180.
26. Schneider, *Gotterdammerung 1945*, pp. 163–166.
27. Konev, *Year of Victory*, p. 64.
28. Duffy, *Red Storm on the Reich*, p. 146. Erickson, *The Road to Berlin*, pp. 525–526.
29. Konev, *Year of Victory*, p. 73.
30. Kirill S. Moskalenko, *Na Yugo-Zapadnom napravlenii: Vospominaniya komandarma* [*On South-Western direction: Memoirs of an Army Commander 1943–1945*] (Moscow: Nauka, 1972), pp. 556–557.
31. Moskalenko, *Na Yugo-Zapadnom napravlenii*, pp. 562–563.
32. Armstrong, *Red Army Tank Commanders*, pp. 439–440.
33. Balck, *Order in Chaos*, p. 421.
34. Shtemenko, *The Soviet General Staff at War*, pp. 308, 317.
35. Ibid., pp. 320–321.
36. Bergstrom, *Bagration to Berlin*, p. 117.

37. Le Tisier, *Marshal Zhukov at the Oder*, pp. 122–125.

38. Ibid., p. 142.

39. Ryan, *The Last Battle,* pp. 344–345.

40. Le Tisier, *Marshal Zhukov at the Oder*, p. 240.

41. Konev, *Year of Victory*, pp. 91–92.

42. Tony Le Tisier, *Slaughter at Halbe: The Destruction of Hitler's 9th Army* (Thrupp: Sutton Publishing, 2005), pp. 85, 228.

43. Krivoshein, *Soviet Casualties*, p. 158.

44. Erickson, *The Road to Berlin*, p. 624.

45. Bidermann, *In Deadly Combat*, p. 255.

46. Vasily I. Chuikov, "*Konets Tretego Reykha*" [The End of the Third Reich], *Sovetskiy voin* (April 1965), p. 145.

47. Le Tisier, *Marshal Zhukov at the Oder*, p. 267.

Chapter 8

1. Catherine Merdale, *Ivan's War: Life and Death in the Red Army, 1939–1945* (New York: Metropolitan Books, 2006), p. 136.

2. Chaney, *Zhukov,* pp. 372–373.

Bibliography

Memoirs

Wilhelm Adam, *With Paulus at Stalingrad* (Barnsley, UK: Penn & Sword Books, 2018).

Vasily M. Badanov, *Glubokii tankovyi reid* [Deep Tank Raid] in A. M. Samsonov (ed.) *Stalingradskaya epopeya* (Moscow: Nauka Publishers, 1968), pp. 625-640.

Ivan K. Bagramyan, *Tak nachalas' voina* [This is how the war began] (Moscow: Voenizdat, 1971). http://militera.lib.ru/memo/russian/bagramyan1/index.html

Ivan K. Bagramyan, *Tak shli my k pobede* [Thus we went on to victory] (Moscow: Voenizdat, 1977). http://militera.lib.ru/memo/russian/bagramyan2/index.html

Hermann Balck, *Order in Chaos: The Memoirs of General of Panzer Troops Hermann Balck* (Lexington, KY: University Press of Kentucky, 2017).

Ivan V. Boldin, *Stranitsy zhizni* [Pages of life] (Moscow: Voenizdat, 1961).

Charles Burdick and Hans-Adolf Jacobsen (ed.), *The Halder War Diary 1939–1942* (Novato, CA: Presidio Press, 1988).

Ivan M. Chistiakov, *Sluzhim Otchizne* [In the Service of the Fatherland] (Moscow: Military Publishing House, 1975).

Vasily I. Chuikov, *Ot Stalingrada do Berlina* [From Stalingrad to Berlin] (Moscow: Voenizdat, 1980). http://militera.lib.ru/memo/russian/chuykov_vi4/index.html

Andrei I. Eremenko, *V nachale voyny* [The Arduous Beginning] (Moscow: Nauka, 1965).

Andrei I. Eremenko, *Pamyat' Gody vozmezdiya* [Years of Retribution, 1943–1945] (Moscow: Nauka, 1969). http://militera.lib.ru/memo/russian/eremenko_ai3/index.html

Kuzma N. Galitsky, *V boyakh za Vostochnuyu Prussiyu: Zapiski komanduyushchego 11-y gvardeyskoy armiyey* [In the battles for East Prussia: Notes of the commander of the 11th Guards Army] (Moscow: Nauka, 1970).

Klaus Gerbet (ed.)., *Generalfeldmarschall Fedor von Bock: The War Diary, 1939–1945* (Atglen, PA: Schiffer Military History, 1996).

Aleksandr V. Gorbatov, *Gody i voiny* [Years and Wars] (Moscow: Voenizdat, 1980).

Andrei Grechko, *Battle for the Caucasus* (Honolulu, HI: University Press of the Pacific, 2001).

Heinz Guderian, *Panzer Leader* (New York. Ballantine Books, 1968).

Hermann Hoth, *Panzer Operations: Germany's Panzer Group 3 During the Invasion of Russia, 1941* (Philadelphia, PA: Casemate Publishers, 2017).

Mikhail E. Katukov, *Na Ostrie glavnogo udara* [*At the Point of the Main Attack*] (Moscow: Voenizdat, 1974).

Ivan S. Konev, *Year of Victory* (Honolulu, HI: University Press of the Pacific, 2005).

Erich von Manstein, *Lost Victories* (Novato, CA: Presidio Press, 1985).

Friedrich W. von Mellenthin, *Panzer Battles: A Study of the Employment of Armour in the Second World War* (New York: Ballantine Books, 1971).

Kirill S. Moskalenko, *Na Yugo-Zapadnom napravlenii: Vospominaniya komandarma* [*On South-Western direction: Memoirs of an Army Commander 1943–1945*] (Moscow: Nauka, 1972). http://militera.lib.ru/memo/russian/moskalenko-1/index.html

Erhard Raus, *Panzer Operations* (Cambridge, MA: Da Capo Press, 2003).

Lothar Rendulic, *Gekämpft, Gesiegt, Geschlagen* [Fought, victorious, vanquished] (Heidelberg: Verlag Welsermühl Wels, 1952).

Konstantin K. Rokossovsky, *A Soldier's Duty* (Moscow: Progress Publishers, 1970).

Pavel Rotmistrov, *Stal'naya gvardiya* [*Steel Guards*] (Moscow: Voenizdat, 1984). http://militera.lib.ru/memo/russian/rotmistrov2/index.html

Sergei M. Shtemenko, *The Soviet General Staff at War 1941–1945* (Honolulu, HI: University Press of the Pacific, 1970).

Aleksandr M. Vasilevsky, *Delo vsey zhizni* [A lifelong Cause] (Moscow: Politizdat, 1978). http://militera.lib.ru/memo/russian/vasilevsky/index.html

Georgy K. Zhukov, *The Memoirs of Marshal Zhukov* (London: Jonathan Cape Ltd., 1971).

Secondary Sources

John I. Alger, *The Quest for Victory: The History of the Principles of War* (Westport, CT: Praeger, 1982).

Correlli Barnett (ed.), *Hitler's Generals* (New York: Grove Weidenfeld, 1989).

Stephen Barratt, *Zhitomir-Berdichev: German Operations west of Kiev, 24 December 1943–31 January 1944* (Solihull, UK: Helion & Company, Ltd., 2012).

George E. Blau, *The German Campaign in Russia: Planning and Operations,*
1940–1942, Department of the Army Pamphlet No. 20-261a (Washington:
Department of the Army, 1955).

Robert M. Citino, *The Path to Blitzkrieg: Doctrine and Training in the German Army,*
1920–39 (Mechanicsburg: Stackpole Books, 1999).

Otto Preston Chaney, *Zhukov,* revised edition (Norman, OK: University of
Oklahoma Press, 1996).

Bruce Condell and David T. Zabecki (eds.), *On the German Art of War:*
Truppenführung (Mechanicsburg, PA: Stackpole Books, 2009).

Christopher Duffy, *Red Storm on the Reich: The Soviet March on Germany, 1945*
(New York: Da Capo Press, 1993).

John Erickson, *The Road to Stalingrad: Stalin's War with Germany,* Volume I
(New Haven: Yale University Press, 1999).

John Erickson, *The Road to Berlin: Stalin's War with Germany,* Volume II
(London: Cassell, 1983).

David M. Glantz, *After Stalingrad: The Red Army's Winter Offensive 1942–1943*
(Solihull: Helion & Company Ltd., 2008).

David M. Glantz, *Barbarossa Derailed: The Battle for Smolensk, 10 July–10 September*
1941, Volume 1 (Solihull, UK: Helion & Co. Ltd., 2010).

David M. Glantz, *Barbarossa: Hitler's Invasion of Russia 1941* (Charleston: Tempus
Publishing, Inc., 2001).

David M. Glantz, *The Battle for Leningrad 1941–1944* (Lawrence, KS: University
Press of Kansas, 2002).

David M. Glantz, *Colossus Reborn: The Red Army at War 1941–1943* (Lawrence,
KS: University Press of Kansas, 2005).

David M. Glantz, *Endgame at Stalingrad, Book 1: November 1942* (Lawrence, KS:
University Press of Kansas, 2014).

David M. Glantz, *From the Don to the Dnepr* (London: Frank Cass, 1991).

David M. Glantz (ed)., *The Initial Period of War on the Eastern Front,*
22 June–August 1941 (Portland, OR: Frank Cass, 1997).

David M. Glantz and Jonathan M. House, *The Battle of Kursk* (Lawrence, KS:
University Press of Kansas, 1999).

David M. Glantz, *Stumbling Colossus: The Red Army on the Eve of World War*
(Lawrence, KS: University Press of Kansas, 1998).

David M. Glantz, *To the Gates of Stalingrad: Soviet-German Operational Combat*
Operations, April–August 1942, The Stalingrad Trilogy, Volume I (Lawrence, KS:
University Press of Kansas, 2009).

Gerhard P. Gross, *The Myth and Reality of German Warfare: Operational Thinking*
from Moltke the Elder to Heusinger (Lexington, KY: The University Press of
Kentucky, 2016).

Mary R. Habeck, *Storm of Steel: The Development of Armor Doctrine in Germany and*
the Soviet Union, 1919–1939 (Ithaca: Cornell University Press, 2014).

Richard W. Harrison, *The Russian Way of War: Operational Art, 1904–1940*
(Lawrence, KS: University Press of Kansas, 2001).

Russell A. Hart, *Guderian: Panzer Pioneer or Myth Maker?* (Sterling: Potomac Books, 2006).

Alexander Hill, *The Red Army and the Second World War* (Cambridge: Cambridge University Press, 2017).

Johannes Hürter, *Hitlers Heerführer: Die Deutschen Oberbefehlshaber Im Krieg Gegen Die Sowjetunion 1941/42* (Oldenbourg: Walter de Gruyter, 2007).

Geoffrey Jukes, *Hitler's Stalingrad Decisions* (Berkeley: University of California Press, 1985).

Jacob W. Kipp, *Mass, Mobility, and the Red Army's Road to Operational Art, 1918–1936* (Fort Leavenworth, KS: Soviet Army Studies Office, 1990).

Christopher A. Lawrence, *Kursk: The Battle of Prokhorovka* (Sheridan, CO: Aberdeen Books, 2015).

Barry Leach, *German General Staff* (New York: Ballantine Books, 1973).

Samuel W. Mitcham, Jr, *The Men of Barbarossa: Commanders of the German Invasion of Russia, 1941* (Philadelphia: Casemate Publishers, 2009).

Steven H. Newton, *Hitler's Commander: Field Marshal Walther Model–Hitler's Favorite General* (Boston: Da Capo Press, 2006).

Richard Overy, *Russia's War: A History of the Soviet War Effort, 1941–1945* (New York: Penguin Books, 1997).

Geoffrey Roberts, *Stalin's General: The Life of Georgy Zhukov* (New York: Random House, 2012).

Dana V. Sadarananda, *Beyond Stalingrad: Manstein and the Operations of Army Group Don* (Mechanicsburg, PA: Stackpole Books, 2009).

Harriet F. Scott (ed.), *The Soviet Art of War: Doctrine, Strategy and Tactics* (Boulder, CO: Westview Press, 1982).

Amnon Sella, "Red Army Doctrine and Training on the Eve of the Second World War," *Soviet Studies,* vol. 27, no. 2 (1975), pp. 245–264.

Harold Shukman (ed.), *Stalin's Generals* (London: Phoenix Press, 1997).

Boris Sokolov, *Marshal K. K. Rokossovsky: The Red Army's Gentleman Commander* (Warwick: Helion & Company, 2015).

William J. Spahr, *Zhukov: The Rise and Fall of a Great Captain* (Novato, CA: Presidio Press, 1993).

Timothy A. Wray, *Standing Fast: German Defensive Doctrine on the Russian Front During World War II, Prewar to March 1943* (Fort Leavenworth, KS: US Army Combat Studies Institute, Research Survey No. 5, 1986).

Valeriy Zamulin, *Demolishing the Myth: The Tank Battle at Prokhorovka, Kursk, July 1943, An Operational Narrative* (Solihull, UK: Helion & Company, Ltd., 2011).

Niklas Zetterling and Anders Frankson, *The Drive on Moscow 1941: Operation Taifun and Germany's First Great Crisis in World War II* (Philadelphia, PA: Casemate Publishers, 2012).

Niklas Zetterling and Anders Frankson, *Kursk 1943: A Statistical Analysis* (London: Frank Cass Publishers, 2000).

Index